A WORLD HISTORY OF RAILWAY CULTURES, 1830–1930

A WORLD HISTORY OF RAILWAY CULTURES, 1830–1930

Edited by
Matthew Esposito

Volume IV
The Americas

LONDON AND NEW YORK

First published 2020
by Routledge
2 Park Square, Milton Park, Abingdon, Oxon OX14 4RN

and by Routledge
52 Vanderbilt Avenue, New York, NY 10017

Routledge is an imprint of the Taylor & Francis Group, an informa business

© 2020 selection and editorial matter, Matthew Esposito; individual owners retain copyright in their own material.

The right of Matthew Esposito to be identified as the author of the editorial material, and of the authors for their individual chapters, has been asserted in accordance with sections 77 and 78 of the Copyright, Designs and Patents Act 1988.

All rights reserved. No part of this book may be reprinted or reproduced or utilised in any form or by any electronic, mechanical, or other means, now known or hereafter invented, including photocopying and recording, or in any information storage or retrieval system, without permission in writing from the publishers.

Trademark notice: Product or corporate names may be trademarks or registered trademarks, and are used only for identification and explanation without intent to infringe.

British Library Cataloguing-in-Publication Data
A catalogue record for this book is available from the British Library

Library of Congress Cataloging-in-Publication Data
A catalog record for this book has been requested

ISBN: 978-0-8153-7722-1 (set)
eISBN: 978-1-351-21184-0 (set)
ISBN: 978-0-8153-7755-9 (Volume IV)
eISBN: 978-1-351-21162-8 (Volume IV)

Typeset in Times New Roman
by Apex CoVantage, LLC

Publisher's Note
References within each chapter are as they appear in the original complete work

CONTENTS

VOLUME IV   The Americas   1

   Transcontinental dreams and subcontinental nightmares:
   railroad prosperity and peril in the Americas   3

PART 1
**America the perilous: cultures of speed, equality,
and freedom in the United States**   53

1 Edward Hungerford, 'Getting the Traffic Through',
    Harper's Magazine 119, 1909, 876–887   55

2 *Letters from David Henshaw to the Boston Morning Post,
    on the Western Rail-Road, and the Greatly Beneficial
    Effects of Internal Improvements* (Boston: Beals and
    Greene, 1839), pp. 3–8   66

3 Henry David Thoreau, *Walden: A Story of Life in
    the Woods* (New York: A. L. Burt, 1902 [originally
    published in 1854]), pp. 56–59   70

4 Isabella Bird (Mrs. Bishop), *The Englishwoman in
    America* (London: John Murray, 1856), pp. 90–115   72

5 Charles Weld, *A Vacation Tour in the United States*
    (London: Longman, Brown, Green, and Longmans, 1859),
    pp. 192–197, 245–253   84

6 Walt Whitman, 'To a Locomotive in Winter', in *Leaves
    of Grass* (London: D. Bogue, 1881), pp. 358–359   90

7 Emily Pfeiffer, *Flying Leaves from East to West*
    (London: Field and Tuer, 1885), pp. 118–120   91

CONTENTS

PART 2
Rivers of iron: cultures of railway construction and management   93

8 Henry L. Abbot and R. S. Williamson, 'Narrative and Itinerary-Pit River Valley', *Report of Lieut. Henry L. Abbot upon Explorations for a Railroad Route from the Sacramento Valley to the Columbia River* (Washington D.C., 1857), pp. 56–75   95

9 'Railway Engineering in the United States', *The Atlantic Monthly* 2, 13 (Nov. 1858), 644–645   116

10 Charles De Lano Hine, *Letters from an Old Railway Official to His Son, and Division Superintendant* (Chicago: The Railway Age, 1904), pp. 1–17   119

PART 3
From Eastern excursions to transcontinental tourism   125

11 Isabella Bird (Mrs. Bishop), *The Englishwoman in America* (London: John Murray, 1856), pp. 125–126, 133–152   127

12 'New York's Elevated Train', *Frank Leslie's Illustrated Newspaper* (May 25, 1878), p. 203   138

13 'The East Side Elevated Railway', *Frank Leslie's Illustrated Newspaper* (September 7, 1878), p. 12   140

14 Isabella Bird (Mrs. Bishop), *The Englishwoman in America* (London: John Murray, 1856), pp. 153–158, 344–345, 439–441   142

15 William H. Rideing, 'Scenery of the Pacific Railway', *Art Journal*, New Series, III (1877), pp. 105–108, 137–140   147

16 W. G. Marshall, *Through America: or, Nine Months in the United States* (London: S. Low, Marston, Searle & Rivington, 1881), pp. 239–241   154

17 Robert S. Minot, *Railway Travel in Europe and America* (Boston: A. Williams, 1882), pp. 9–12   156

18 J. L. Dow, *The Australian in America* (Melbourne: The "Leader" Office, 1884), pp. xi–xii, 19–21   159

CONTENTS

19 George Edward Wright, 'The Chicago Limited Express', *A Visit to the States*, 2 vols. (London: G.E. Wright, 1887–88), pp. 362–372 — 164

20 Lilian Leland, *Traveling Alone. A Woman's Journey around the World* (New York: American News Company, 1890), pp. 302–313 — 170

21 Lady Howard, *Journal of a Tour in the United States, Canada, and Mexico* (London: S. Low, Marston, 1897), pp. 76–80 — 179

22 John Foster Fraser, *America at Work* (London: Cassell, 1903), pp. 124–132 — 182

23 Isabella Bird, *A Lady's Life in the Rocky Mountains* (London: John Murray, 1910), pp. 25–39 — 187

PART 4
Railroad problems and public health in the U.S.   195

24 Sidney Andrews, *The South Since the War* (Boston: Ticknor and Fields, 1866), pp. 11, 28–32, 107–109, 201 — 197

25 Figure 2, 'The Discomforts of Travel-Weary Passengers', *Frank Leslie's Illustrated Newspaper* (February 9, 1878), p. 389 — 202

26 David Christie Murray, *The Cockney Columbus* (London: Downey & Co., 1898), pp. 9, 98–106 — 203

27 William A. Pinkerton, *Train Robberies, Train Robbers, and the "Holdup" Men* (1907), pp. 8–11, 16, 18, 20, 22, 24, 56, 58 — 207

28 Jno. C. King and M. D. Banning, 'Tuberculosis among Railroad Employees', *California State Journal of Medicine* 11, 2 (Feb. 1913), pp. 70–71 — 212

29 '100 Killed, 100 Hurt in Train Wreck', *The New York Times*, July 10, 1918, p. 10 — 214

30 'Scores Killed or Maimed in Brighton Beach Tunnel Wreck', *The New York Times*, November 2, 1918, pp. 1, 6 — 216

PART 5
Extreme encounters and the octopus — 221

31 Rose G. Kingsley, *South by West; or, Winter in the Rocky Mountains and Spring in Mexico* (London: W. Isbister, 1874), pp. 160–162 — 223

32 Sir Richard Tangye, *Reminiscences of Travel in Australia, America, and Egypt* (Birmingham: Printed at the Herald Press, 1883), pp. 151–157 — 225

33 Theodore Roosevelt, 'The Rough Riders', *Scribner's Magazine* 25, 2 (Feb. 1899), pp. 136–146 — 229

34 Frank Norris, *The Octopus: A Story of California* (New York: Doubleday, 1907), pp. 247–262 — 236

PART 6
The best in the world: the dominion of the Canadian Pacific Railway — 247

35 J. T. Breeze, *The Dominion of Canada. The Great Institution of Our Country. A Poem on the Grand Trunk Railway* (Montreal: n.p., 1867), pp. 6–8 — 249

36 Charles Westly Busk, *Notes of a Journey from Toronto to British Columbia via the Northern Pacific Railway, June to July 1884, Being Letters to his Sister and Mother* (London: Taylor and Francis, 1884), pp. 3–6 — 252

37 George Edward Wright, *A Canadian Tour: A Report of Letters from the Special Correspondent of the Times* (London: George Edward Wright, 1886), pp. 17–21 — 255

38 W. S. Caine, *A Trip Round the World in 1887–8* (London: G. Routledge & Sons, 1888), pp. 92–118 — 266

39 James Francis Hogan, *The Sister Dominions: Through Canada to Australia by the New Imperial Highway* (London: Ward and Downey, 1896), pp. 91–96 — 273

40 George Edward Wright, *A Canadian Tour: A Report of Letters from the Special Correspondent of the* Times (London: George Edward Wright, 1886), pp. 22–29 — 276

CONTENTS

41 David Christie Murray, *The Cockney Columbus* (London: Downey & Co., 1898), pp. 109, 150–156   291

42 John Foster Fraser, *Canada As It Is* (London: Cassell, 1905), pp. 153–160   294

PART 7
Corridos and *calaveras*: ballads of Mexican railroads   **299**

43 'The Railways from Vera Cruz to Jalapa and Mexico', in *Ferguson's Anecdotical Guide to Mexico, with a Map of the Railways* (Philadelphia: Claxton, Remsen, & Haffelfinger, 1876), pp. 25–38   301

44 'The Corrido of the Electric Trains', in 'Corridos from the Porfiriato (the Early 1900s)' in Nora E. Jaffary, Edward W. Osowski and Susie S. Porter (eds.), *Mexican History: A Primary Source Reader* (Westview Press: 2010), pp. 288–291. Translation by the editors from original publication in Higinio Vazquez Santa Anna, Canciones, cantares y corridos mexicanos (Mexico: Segundo Tomo, León Sánchez, 1925–1931), pp. 244–245, 247–249   312

45 John Stealey III (ed.), *Porte Crayon's Mexico: David Hunter Strother's Diaries in the Early Porfirian Era, 1879–1885* (Kent, Ohio: The Kent State University Press, 2006), pp. 741–743, 745–746   316

46 Fig. 3. *Shooting on a Trolley*, Fig. 4. *Gran Calavera Eléctrica*, Fig. 5. *Collision of an Electric Streetcar with a Hearse*, from José Guadalupe Posada's Mexican Prints, Roberto Berdecio and Stanley Applebaum (eds.), *Posada's Popular Mexican Prints* (New York: Dover Publications, 1972)   321

47 John L. Stoddard, *Lectures*, 10 vols. (Boston: Balch, 1899), vol. VII: Mexico, pp. 89–90, 93–94, 97–98, 101–102, 105   323

48 *Mexico's Great Isthmus Route: A Souvenir of the Visit of President Porfirio Díaz to Tehuantepec to Inspect the Isthmus Railway and the Port Works at Coatzacoalcos and Salina Cruz* (n.p., 1905), pp. 1–5   326

49	Johnson Sherrick, *Letters of Travel* (n.p., 1905), pp. 191–198	330
50	John Kenneth Turner, *Barbarous Mexico* (Chicago: C. H. Kerr, 1910), pp. 49–69	334
51	Robert Welles Ritchie, 'The Passing of a Dictator', *Harper's Magazine* 124 (1911–1912), pp. 782–789	346
52	John Reed, *Insurgent Mexico* (New York: D. Appleton, 1914), pp. 175–187, 191–204	356

PART 8
Sugar, coffee, and bananas: railroads in Cuba, Central America, and British Jamaica — 369

53	David Turnbull, *Travels in the West: Cuba, with Notices of Porto Rico, and the Slave Trade* (London: Longman, Orme, Green, and Longmans, 1840), pp. 194–197	371
54	W. T. Brigham, 'An Uncommercial Republic', *Scribner's Magazine* 1 (Jan.–June 1887), pp. 711–716	373
55	Nevin O. Winter, *Guatemala and Her People of To-day* (Boston: L. C. Page and Company, 1909), pp. 24–29	377
56	Henry R. Blaney, *The Golden Caribbean: A Winter Visit to the Republics of Colombia, Spanish Honduras, Belize, and the Spanish Main via Boston and New Orleans* (Boston: Lee and Shepard, 1900), pp. 73–85	379
57	Henry R. Blaney, *The Golden Caribbean: A Winter Visit to the Republics of Colombia, Spanish Honduras, Belize, and the Spanish Main via Boston and New Orleans* (Boston: Lee and Shepard, 1900), pp. 87–93	385
58	Edgar M. Bacon and Eugene Murray-Aaron, *The New Jamaica* (New York and Kingston: A. W. Gardener, 1890), pp. 73–82	388

CONTENTS

PART 9
Railroads as the Amazon in tropical Brazil   **393**

59 Franz Keller, *The Amazon and Madeira Rivers. Sketches and Description from the Notebook of an Explorer* (Philadelphia: J. B. Lippincott, 1875), pp. 140, 157–158   395

60 Neville B. Craig, *Recollections of an Ill-Fated Expedition to the Headwaters of the Madeira River* (Philadelphia: J. B. Lippincott, 1907), pp. 367–369, 380–383   397

61 Frank Vincent, *Around and About South America: Twenty Months of Quest and Query* (New York: D. Appleton and Co., 1890), pp. 249–250, 260–261, 265–266, 303   400

62 Nevin O. Winter, *Brazil and Her People of To-day* (Boston: L. C. Page and Company, 1910), pp. 91–95, 127–133, 254–256   403

PART 10
Conquering *América del Sur*: railroad cultures in the River Plate, Chile, and Caribbean South America   **409**

63 Central Argentine Railway Company, *Letters Concerning the Country of the Argentine Republic (South America), Being Suitable for Emigrants and Capitalists to Settle In* (London: Waterlow and Sons, 1869), pp. 1–16, 32–33   411

64 John Foster Fraser, *The Amazing Argentina. A New Land of Enterprise* (London: Cassell, 1910), pp. 134–138   425

65 Carlos María de Pena, *The Oriental Republic of Uruguay at the World's Columbian Exhibition, Chicago, 1893* (Montevideo: n.p., 1893), pp. 24, 36–38   428

66 W. H. Koebel, *Paraguay* (London: T. F. Unwin, 1917), pp. 231–239   431

CONTENTS

67 Mrs. George B. Merwin, *Three Years in Chili* (New York: Follett, Foster, 1863), pp. 1–9, 121–123 ... 436

68 Francis E. Clark, *The Continent of Opportunity*, Second ed. (New York: Young People's Missionary Movement of the United States and Canada, 1907), pp. 181–189 ... 441

69 Johnson Sherrick, *Around the World and South America* (Canton, Ohio: The Repository Press, 1912), pp. 235–243 ... 446

70 Adolfo de Clairmont, *Guide to Modern Peru: Its Great Advantages and Vast Opportunities* (Toledo, Ohio: Barkdull, 1907), pp. 50–60 ... 450

71 Marie Robinson Wright, *The Old and the New Peru* (Philadelphia: G. Barrie & Sons, 1908), pp. 367–374, 377–386 ... 457

72 Edward Whymper, *Travels amongst the Great Andes of the Equator* (New York: C. Scribner's Sons, 1892), pp. 385–391 ... 467

73 Marie Robinson Wright, *Bolivia: The Central Highway of South America* (Philadelphia: G. Barrie & Sons, 1907), pp. 203–218 ... 470

74 Santiago Pérez Triana, *Down the Orinoco in a Canoe* (New York: Crowell, 1902), pp. 240–248 ... 482

75 Henry R. Blaney, *The Golden Caribbean: A Winter Visit to the Republics of Colombia, Spanish Honduras, Belize, and the Spanish Main via Boston and New Orleans* (Boston: Lee and Shepard, 1900), pp. 4–12 ... 486

76 Hamilton Mercer Wright, *A Traveler in Northern Colombia* (Washington, D. C.: Government Printing Office, 1918), pp. 6, 8, 10, 12, 14 ... 490

77 Fassenden N. Otis, *Illustrated History of the Panama Railroad* (New York: Harper & Brothers, 1862), pp. 46, 49, 72, 75–82, 85–86, 89–92, 95–98, 103–104, 110, 115–116, 121, 127 ... 495

Volume IV

THE AMERICAS

TRANSCONTINENTAL DREAMS AND SUBCONTINENTAL NIGHTMARES

Railroad prosperity and peril in the Americas

> The rails go Westward through the night. . . . Brother, have you seen starlight on the rails? Have you heard the thunder of the great express?
> – Walt Whitman

Railroad historians in the United States have upheld the longstanding thesis that popular support for affordable locomotive travel and freight service overwhelmed the occasional upstart protest. The title of David Haward Bain's magisterial *Empire Express* encapsulated the "providential progress" of American transcontinental railroads, and no cry from the wilderness ever justified slowing their inevitable march.[1] Bain described one Asa Whitney, evoking God's providence as his guide to filling American landscapes with twin ribbons of iron.[2] Leo Marx found the same theme interwoven through triumphal narratives by American literary figures and artists in his highly original work *The Machine in the Garden*.[3] Reading nineteenth-century accounts of American travel, one is struck how often travel writers from both sides of the Atlantic, as well as their fellow passengers, referred to the U.S. as "God's country." Like the panoramic American paintings of the nineteenth century, travel narratives expressed America's divine appointment as civilizer of the west.[4] In addition, American trains were depicted as havens of white male social equality. When British travelers on U.S. trains found themselves defending the first-, second-, and third-class carriage system of the UK, Americans responded with some version of the statement: "Why, in God's country we're all equal, and we have just one class."[5] It appears that the railway, like equality, was considered an American birthright, which, along with every other natural right of nineteenth-century U.S. citizens, ultimately descended from the Almighty.

From 1830 to 1930, U.S. railroad development proceeded at a speed of decadal progress that was only appreciable and depreciable in hindsight. America was the second nation to open a railroad line just months after the L&M inauguration, but few questioned how the technology might affect the Baltimore and Ohio economies. In the 1830s, the decade of the Panic of 1837, the Baltimore and Ohio Railroad (B&O) and Pennsylvania Railroad (PR) opened up the Ohio River Valley and Western New York. Railroad fever broke out, linking other east coast cities, but few questioned if new settlements might compete with the old. In the 1840s, when the track mileage of American railroads surpassed that of all Europe,[6] only a few mossbacks questioned whether the building of that many route miles made sense for a nation with a population only three million larger than England's. John Louis O'Sullivan's statement in 1845 represented the baldest of expansionist propaganda except on the subject of exploding demographics: "Our manifest destiny is to overspread the continent allotted by Providence for the free development of our yearly multiplying millions."[7] The nation grew from seventeen million to twenty-three million, a 35 percent increase in just ten years (1840–1850). In the 1850s, America crossed the Missouri into the "Great American Desert," but few wondered if new lines to the west would bypass older towns. In the 1860s, trains were envisioned as a means of communication with the Pacific, but few objected to such lofty objectives in the midst of the Civil War. In the 1870s and 1880s, transcontinentals threatened the bison herds that stabilized the Plains Indians' way of life, but few objected to the arguments of expansionists that both Native Americans and buffalo impeded western settlement.[8] Few noticed the second wave of exported Baldwin locomotives that arrived in Latin America for use on U.S.-built tracks. In the 1890s, financial panic set in, but the golden age of railroads tamped down any worry that railroads might be overbuilt. In the 1900s, fewer still questioned whether the U.S. should have more track miles than the rest of the world combined. U.S. firms had built the lion's share of railroads in Mexico, Central America, Cuba, Peru, and the rest of Latin America, but few questioned if "God's country" should conquer the Mexican Sierras, the Sonoran Desert, the Andes, and the Amazon. Only after 1900, with the myriad publications of the tireless yellow journalist Ambrose Bierce and the rhetorical muckraker Frank Norris (*The Octopus*), did anyone seriously challenge the railroad establishment. In 1915, public health reports described U.S. railroads as "disabling mills." U.S. railroads employed over two million men and women, 197,000 of whom were injured, 63,000 crippled, and more than 10,000 killed.[9] The Great Depression forever disposed of the idea that Americans lived in an invulnerable egalitarian society. An attendant casualty of the 1930s was the notion that railroads represented providential equality. Empire Express is a superior metonym not only for American railroads but also for the United States of America. Historian Richard White's indictment of the overbuilt transcontinentals introduced new metonymy from good old-fashioned Gilded Age corruption in his book *Railroaded* (2011). The problem of empowering unregulated industrial monopolies to conduct national tasks at "locomotive speed" was that they escaped thoughtful scrutiny until costly, inhumane, and irreversible mistakes were made. As White surmised, "[Railroads] created modernity as much by their failure as their success."[10]

U.S., Canadian, and Mexican railroads were nevertheless more than "pioneer railways." They carried out all the scientific duties of imperial geographers, surveyors, cartographers, engineers, and settlers. American success in building more than 263,000 miles of railroads is owed in part to the accident of its geography. As Jared Diamond explained, the Americas are two continents with north-south axes, which affected the spread of crop domestication, food production, and technology.[11] Africa appears to share this characteristic, but latitude and longitude can be deceiving.[12] In North America, the north-south axis not only affected human and animal migratory patterns along mountain barriers that run north to south, such as the Canadian Rockies, the Colorado Rockies, and the Sierra Madres of Mexico, but it also influenced the geological development of huge navigable rivers such as the Mississippi and Missouri. These rivers also course from north to south and are complemented by the Great Lakes region, with their distant outlet through the St. Lawrence in the Atlantic. The tundra and boreal forests of Canada where few humans live are oriented east and west, but the temperate forests of Canada and the U.S., grasslands of the American Midwest, deserts of the U.S. and Mexican border, and tropical forests of Mexico all have north-south orientations. Dense settlements on America's eastern seaboard relied heavily on water-borne transportation along the Potomac, Hudson, and James Rivers. During the Early Republic and Jacksonian Era, steamboats powered up the Mississippi and Missouri as private companies and petty merchants continued to develop canals on the north-south axis. Private regional railway companies defied that orientation, essentially arguing that rivers of iron must run from east to west and compete with the Erie Canal. Before western expansionism, the outcome of the U.S.-Mexican War, and the birth of the misnamed transcontinentals (they started at the Missouri),[13] Baltimore, New York, and Philadelphia served as the capitals of financial investment in regional railroads. After mid-century, Chicago became the center of national railway expansion. Due to its proximity to the major rivers, the Great Lakes, the agricultural heartland of the Midwest, and eastern markets, Chicago was the continental American equivalent of London on the Thames, Calcutta on the Ganges, Moscow on the Moskva (a tributary of the Volga), and Shanghai on the Yangtze. Montreal on the St. Lawrence River put Canada on the world railway map in the 1840s. Canadian railways radiated from Montreal much like they did from Paris or London, but trade activity concentrated on the Grand Trunk Railway and its connections to Ottawa, Toronto, and New England. Railroads soon extended west to the Pacific. As White argued, the Canadian Pacific and the 130-mile railroad across the Isthmus of Tehuantepec in Mexico were the only nineteenth-century transcontinentals.[14] The first was the best railroad ever built, and the second an unmitigated disaster.

In contrast to its North American neighbors, Mexico lacks navigable rivers flowing in any direction and is instead an internally draining basin that once held enough water to constitute a Great Lakes region of its own at Texcoco. The only other major geographical features lie in the northern Sierra Madres – Mexico's Rockies – and the southern Lacandón jungle that impeded overland travel from Chiapas to Yucatán. Mexican railroads succumbed to the forces of historical geography when a British company built its first national railway from the Caribbean port city of Veracruz west to Mexico City. In 1872, British tourists Rose and Charles Kingsley in Mexico made use of their "old enemy" – the stagecoach – over the tough roads of rural Mexico. Reaching the suburb of La Garita outside of Mexico City, Rose exclaimed:

> Oh wonder and delight! – the shriek of a locomotive, and coming to an open railway-crossing, jolted once more over real iron rails. I never thought I should have rejoiced so to see a railroad: but the ugly American engine, with its wide smoke-stack seemed to us, after two months of bad roads and stage-coaches, like a harbinger of law, order, and civilisation; and we all indulged in frantic congratulations to each other on the joyful sight.[15]

World railway history must also account for the transcontinental dreams and subcontinental nightmares of railroads through Panama, the Amazon, the Peruvian Andes, Argentine Pampas, and Chilean deserts. Even before the opening of the Suez Canal (1869) and Panama Canal (1914), capitalists in Europe and the Americas dreamed of a trans-isthmian railway to move freight overland from the Atlantic coast of Central America in the Caribbean Sea and Gulf of Mexico to the Pacific Ocean side of Latin America – a distance of forty miles in some areas. Ships bound for San Francisco, Lima, Guayaquil, Valparaiso, and even Manila and Tokyo might then exchange commercial goods with peoples throughout the Pacific Rim. In the sixteenth century, conquistador Francisco Pizarro had already proven that the Panamanian isthmus was crossable at the gulf port of Darién when he twice contracted thousands of Indian porters to carry ship parts and provisions for his military expeditions to Peru. In the 1850s, the government of Great Britain, British colonists in Nicaragua, and American filibusters such as William Walker all embarked on a number of Central American misadventures that historian Robert Naylor called "penny ante imperialism."[16] E. G. Squier negotiated with the Honduran and Nicaraguan governments for railroads. Capitalists never stopped to consider what indigenous groups along the Mosquito Coast thought as they devised grand schemes to export mahogany, rubber, and bananas. The French engineer Ferdinand de Lesseps completed the Panamanian Railway in 1855. The U.S. Civil War and the completion of the Union Pacific, linking Chicago and San Francisco, diminished American interest in trans-isthmian projects. Meanwhile, Nicaraguan tappers relied on rivers to supply 3.5 million pounds of rubber to the world market in 1878, until depleting forest lands. In the 1890s, the American-owned Bluefields Banana Company employed Jamaican laborers to cultivate, harvest, and haul over a million bunches of bananas per year by private railroads to Gulf ports, where dock workers loaded the fruit on ships bound for U.S. markets.[17] The rich harvests of tropical fruit, minerals, rubber, and oil covers over the calamities of accidents and epidemic disease like so much guano over the coastal islands of Peru.

Inception

Wolfgang Schivelbusch's oft-quoted distinction between English and American railroads can be reinforced with important demographic factors. In 1977, he asserted that the principal lines in England were built as straight as possible because labor was cheap and land expensive. In America, where the opposites were the case, railroads "did not proceed in a straight line through natural obstacles, but ran around them like a river."[18] The greater obstacles were the people of England, rich estate owners and poor farmers, who formed dense settlements of towns and villages with growing populations at the confluence of rivers where railway expansion coincided. In 1830–1831, the populations of Great Britain and the U.S., including slaves but excluding Native Americans, were uncannily similar at 12.1 million and 12.9 million, respectively. The relatively high population density of England did not exist in any part of the U.S., including New York and Philadelphia, and once clear of the Ohio River Valley and West Virginia, railroads proceeded due west into empty space without consideration of settlements in general. Since English railway companies were to disturb populated areas in whatever direction they surveyed, they may as well have chosen the shortest distance between two points. In America, travel writers rode the rails to the west and shed light on what may be called "America the void."

The Englishwoman Isabella Bird and several other Victorian women writers viewed America both east and west of the Rockies as a vast, unpopulated empty space ready for settlement and exploitation. In the 1870s, it took six days for the Transcontinental Railway to complete the journey from Chicago to San Francisco because there were 250 stations along the way, many representing the only material evidence of white settlement in the void.[19] Bird overcame serious physical illnesses to travel and report on her experiences in the UK, the U.S., Asia, the Middle East, and Hawaii. Her travelogues *The Englishwoman in America* (1856) and *A Lady's Life in the Rocky Mountains* (1879) revealed her to be a refined but tough-minded woman willing to brave railroad journeys through the northeastern U.S. and the wilds of Colorado and Wyoming. She admitted her biases against the "smoking, spitting, gouging" Americans and their affinity for bowie knives, monster hotels, steamboat explosions, railway collisions, and repudiated debts. But she also felt that touring the U.S. was an English birthright.[20] As the author of nine exceptional travel books, Bird is very well represented throughout this collection, but her two most important works described her time on American railroads.

In Karen Morin's *Frontiers of Femininity*, Bird serves as the *enfant terrible* who commented candidly on America's use of railroads as tools of territorial expansion and settlement. Bird's many biographers and the scholars who have studied travel narratives as a genre commented on her status as affluent debutante and the first woman elected to London's Royal Geographical Society.[21] The events she related in *The Englishwoman in America* changed her outlook. By the time she published *A Lady's Life in the Rocky Mountains* in the journal *Leisure Hour* (1878), her life experiences mastering the imperial geography of the U.S. rail system transformed her gender identity. More than any other travel writer of her time, she evolved from an elite Victorian woman whose written words validated her social position, national superiority, and British imperialism to a fiercely honest narrator who resisted identification with all three. Classist and bigoted statements in her early writings decline in *A Lady's Life*. She compensated for ongoing gender marginalization through the acquisition of knowledge about places.[22] Although Bird reformulated her gender identity through writing that contested masculine prescriptions for proper Victorian womanhood, her writings belong to that corpus of travel accounts that criticize the interiors of train compartments for lacking feminine comforts, describe virgin landscapes as ripe for (male) plucking, and detail botanical splendors with appropriate attention to gardening aesthetics, all of which reconstituted masculinist hegemonic ideologies about domesticity and femininity.[23] Other travel writers who Morin examined, including Thérèse Longworth (1872), Rose Kingsley (1874), and Rose Pender (1888), underwent similar transformations, but the works they churned out clearly reproduced existing hegemonic relations and processes.

Still, there is much we can learn about U.S. railroads from Bird, her contemporaries, and literary scholar Karen Morin. Bird escaped Victorian domesticity by taking to the road, but she used her feminine voice to comment on the accommodations of modern railroad carriages and the conduct of railway staff and passengers. Like other women writers, she augmented her voice in complaints about the filthy, uncomfortable, and tight confines of American trains. The railway companies often deserved criticism, but Morin also identified the "princess and the pea" trope as a writing device attributable to Victorian expectations of women as morally responsible for upholding social standards. It was feminine to register such complaints and masculine to look past them. As paying customers, women asserted their rights to a clean and comfortable train.[24] Feminized discourse extended to women's descriptions of garden-like landscapes filled with sagebrush, wildflowers, sunflowers, trees, and the occasional prairie dog colonies and bison herds. Such botanical references depicted a garden sanctuary that reinforced the domesticity of women while away from the home. Women also described the grasslands of the Midwest in the same way travelers described Russian Siberia, as dreary, desolate, and monotonous. The only other geographical feature of comparable boredom was the ocean during a dull voyage.[25]

This brings us to western railway expansion as historical simulacra of the thirteen colonies' foundation myths, including the Pilgrim's Crossing of the Atlantic. Late-nineteenth-century travel writers on railroads often likened the unvarying scenes of prairies and plains to oceans, and equated the boundless rivers and Great Lakes with seas.[26] In letters to his sister and mother, Canadian Charles Westly Busk took the Northern Pacific Railway in the U.S. to British Columbia. Along the way, the boundless prairies of the Dakotas reminded him of a heavy Atlantic swell: "You have a view right clear to the horizon in every direction.... [An inhabited house] looks like a piece of wreck halfway up the side of a long sweeping wave."[27] Even mountains were compared to oceans, not as geographical features but as barriers to overland trade. Behind the logic of such analogies lay the insidious notion that aboriginal peoples populated lands, but oceans belonged only to those with the technology to cross them. Oceans harbored no people to dispossess. To no one's surprise, Busk filled his letters with stories of whites dispossessing Indians of their hunting grounds.[28]

Western expansion came at a price, mostly to America's indigenous populations and neighbors. The 250 railroad depots from Chicago to San Francisco may as well have been islands armed with soldiers. Since Lewis and Clark's 1804–1805 expedition, which dovetailed with the Louisiana Purchase, the oceanic distance that was the North American continent belonged to U.S. pioneers. Journalist Ambrose Bierce once wrote that "War is God's way of teaching Americans geography." Americans received a huge geography lesson in the Mexican War (1846–1848). The Treaty of Guadalupe Hidalgo (1848) ceded one-half of Mexico's territory to the U.S. for the sum of $18.25 million. This imperialist land grab included what became the U.S. Southwestern states of California, Nevada, Arizona, Utah, New Mexico, Texas, most of Colorado, and southern portions of Kansas and Wyoming. In the Gadsden Purchase (1853), Mexican president Antonio López de Santa Anna added insult to injury by selling Arizona's Mesilla Valley to the U.S. for an additional $10 million, which allowed the Southern Pacific Railroad to engineer an easier route to California. The "vast, trackless, and treeless" grasslands of the Midwest[29] now had a mirror reflection in the huge, undefined, and sparse deserts of the Southwest. Shortly after the ballasting began, Indian removal became an afterthought of America's ocean-sized land claims. Western traveler Emily Faithful was more concerned about the railway "ogre" disrupting the "serenity of the eagles, hawks, and coyotes" in the Colorado Rockies than Native American settlements.[30] The California gold rush all but sealed their doom. For Native American tribes, the late nineteenth century represented the most deplorable phase in history. Travelers who encountered them on trains or at depots generally denigrated them. Significantly, travelogues often credited frontier expansion to railway companies, not the U.S. government. Great Britain brought civilization to India, Egypt, Australia, and South Africa, but the Atchison, Topeka, and Santa Fe Railroad (ATSF) and the Union Pacific-Central Pacific Railroad (UP&CP) brought prosperity, peace, and order to the American continent.[31]

Reception

The Canadian Pacific Railroad (CPR) has been regularly exalted as the greatest line ever built, and this study of the railway cultures it created confirms the honorific title by a large margin. No railroad was perfect, but most suffer immediate disqualification because they were built 1) too soon, 2) undercapitalized, 3) with faulty surveys, 4) shoddily, 5) too expensively and elaborately, 6) by unskilled and unfree laborers who died in droves, 7) without local economies in mind, 8) by the government or army, 9) by foreign companies, and/or 10) only to be swallowed up by amalgamation and rendered the product of any combination of 1–9. In contrast, railroad executive

William C. Van Horne completed the CPR five years ahead of schedule and avoided most pitfalls, except a brief slowdown due to undercapitalization, poor treatment of Chinese coolies out of British Columbia, and the second Manitoba Rebellion (1886). The railroad interlinked Quebec, Montreal, Ottawa, and Ontario, then from Port Arthur it carved an ideal path along the northern shores of the Great Lakes. Through untamed wilderness it conquered the Canadian Rockies and reached British Columbia, which joined the union on the condition that a railroad linked east with west.[32] The CPR combined several of the positive metonyms of the previous volumes. Foremost among its successes was the creation of 800 new settlements through the Prairie Provinces of Manitoba, Saskatchewan, and Alberta, as well as the North-West Territory and British Columbia. Its original eastern and western termini of Montreal and Vancouver served as the gateways to unlimited potential for human settlement and economic prosperity. In the lead article of *The Times* (London) on October 25, 1886, the editors correctly assessed that the railroad "create[d] a demand to which no assignable future limits can be conjectured." Settlements started as small towns such as Stephen, Donald, Dunmore, and Revelstoke, but soon blossomed into major metropolitan cities like Calgary and Vancouver. Since just 220,000 folks lived west of Manitoba in 1886, the Canadian government offered 160 acres of free land to prospective settlers. The "godlike animator" peopled the town of Mirror (Alberta) in eleven hours, at least on paper, when markets opened and 577 lots sold at a rate of one per minute. As Nicholas Faith wrote, "Before the town was a month old, it had two banks, five stores, three lumberyards, a hotel, three restaurants, two pool rooms, a sash and door factory, and a newspaper."[33]

"The advance is gradual but it is sure," remarked the prophetic *Times* editors:

> Pass a few years and the whole face of the country will be changed. Towns will have near neighbours, pressing up to them; the wilderness will have become a fruitful field, pouring forth its richness and abundance, and drawing to itself new settlers from the thronging populations of the East and the Old World. It has been the Canadian Pacific Railway that has made this progress possible, or has so accelerated its pace as to crowd the work of centuries into the span of a single life.[34]

After 1886, CPR directors bridged the St. Lawrence to grant access to the Maritime Provinces and New England, achieving status as a true transcontinental. Each year brought a new grain elevator with the capacity of 600,000 bushels. Hundreds of tons of rolling stock were built in its massive workshops along the St. Lawrence. Notions of east and west expanded quickly from the loci of Montreal to Cartier, Calgary, Regina, and Vancouver, and finally to Canada's new accessibility to the Pacific Rim of the U.S., Russia, Japan, China, and Australasia. Promotional advertisements encouraged emigration but also tourism, boasting that the CPR offered the cheapest and most direct route to the west without facing the inconvenience of customs when crossing the U.S. border. The *Times* editors contrasted the fertile prairies of Canada with the "American Desert and bad lands" of its neighbor to the south.[35]

Incursion

In Mexico, a latecomer in railroad advances, peasants and indigenous groups remained isolated from trunk lines and any technology at all. José Maria Velasco's famous nineteenth-century landscapes *El Puente de Metlac* (1881) and *El Citlaltépetl* (1892) depict locomotives traversing the vast, unsettled expanse of Mexican territory. Although peasants draw attention in his other sweeping masterpiece, *Valley of Mexico* (1875), which shows the twin peaks of the volcano Popocatépetl and adjoining mountain ridge Itzaccihuátl, the artist never incorporated people in paintings that showcased locomotives. Instead, these emphasized man's material conquest of an unspoiled natural environment unpopulated by humans. Indeed, technology either escaped the casual observer in the Mexican countryside or never existed there in the first place. Exploring the "unwritten almanac of Maya folk knowledge," historian Terry Rugeley commented on how little nineteenth-century Maya folk tales referred to technology at all. Advances in agriculture, industry, and medicine, known elsewhere, seemed not to have alleviated the miseries and hardships of Mexican daily life, much less captured the imaginations of folktellers. The countryside lacked precise coordinates, maps, or modern reference points in that sublime indeterminacy that characterized Yucatán.[36]

In central and southern Mexico, there was a dearth of heavy machinery or anything mechanical until 1900 – few mills, vehicles, wheeled carts, or even watches. Plows, whether attached to oxen or not, resembled those used in Ancient Egypt. Only foreigners used shovels instead of the digging stick. Freight traveled on the backs of mules and men. Animal-drawn carts were a creaking conspicuous luxury. Mexican *campesinos* (peasants) who used imported wheelbarrows filled them and carried them on top of their heads. When a village priest first saw a thresher, he declared that it was possessed by the devil and forbade parishioners from approaching it. The machine was shipped out of the region to prevent the fate of the lone threshing machine in Silao, Guanajuato: field-hands wrecked it.[37] Even when heavy machines began to litter the countryside after 1900, peasants identified them as tools of their enslavement and violently destroyed them.[38] Nor were railroads eagerly received. Newspapers published accounts of Mexicans throwing ties and rails into the nearest lakes or ravines. Once railroads were firmly implanted, rural Catholics acknowledged their danger during Holy Week. People strapped effigies of Judas to the front of the locomotive engines like the proverbial damsel in distress and poked, prodded, and burned the betrayer of Christ, hurling any number of objects at him as the train steamed ahead.[39]

Conditions were no different in Central America. In 1826, John Hale, an Englishman who tried to recruit 100 families from the U.S. and England to establish a colony in Costa Rica, remarked that local inhabitants owned no wheelbarrows, casks, barrels, or machines for cotton planting and coffee cleaning. They also lacked paint, turpentine, oil, iron shovels, hoes, and garden rakes. Hale wrote: "Agriculture and horticulture are more than a century behind that of Europe or the United States. Almost all tools are made of wood." He also claimed that woodsmen and carpenters were lucky if they yielded a single beam from each felled tree and that a saw mill would yield a profit of 1,000 percent.[40] A century later, only floods and landslides slowed the Costa Rican railroads from carrying passengers and heavy freight from Cartago and Limon to San José. Coffee, tobacco, and banana growers exported tons of their products via railroads unless mudslides disrupted traffic. The United Fruit Company alone owned eighty-three miles of railroads on thirty-six plantations (25,000 acres) worth $5.35 million. The Northern Railway of Costa Rica from Port Limon to the interior was just one of several that the company controlled in Central America. All told, United Fruit owned twenty-one locomotives, 473 freight cars, and 173 miles of track.[41] After 1914, whenever tourists on the United Fruit Company's cruises in the Gulf ports were stranded in San José, the company arranged for their departure through the Pacific town of Punta Arenas and on to the Panama Canal, where they caught steamers to New York.[42] Technology transfer from the U.S. and Europe to Latin America played a secondary role in the development of the region.

Rural agrarian reactions to the "creative destruction" of intrusive modernizing technologies in Latin America might have been mitigated if the English Reform Bills of 1832 and 1867 that accommodated some of the needs of the lower classes in Great Britain applied in all colonial and neocolonial settings. Instead, peasants without such rights or protections deployed strategies of resistance against the strange vehicles and their operators with a high degree of redundancy worldwide. Cultivators challenged land grabs in court, objected to land surveyors, mapmakers, and telegraph builders trespassing on their lands, and made off with surveying equipment and building materials. They tore up track and obstructed lines with the very sleepers and rails that the companies delivered to yards. Landslides could not always be blamed on nature nor could the sudden appearance of boulders and tree trunks on rails, especially at junctions. During rebellions, insurgents destroyed water towers and pumps, sabotaged bridges, broke switches, and stole locks from switch boxes. To protest against new routes or cash in on the compensation policies of railway companies, farmers tethered sick livestock between rails. Railway workers and operators fell under deadly attack from ambushes and snipers. Rebel armies even burned railway stations to destabilize centralizing regimes. In Cuba and Mexico, like Russia, revolutionaries even reversed the formula of railroad invasion and "pacification" – that euphemism for genocide – by capturing locomotives in the periphery and launching coordinated attacks against counter-revolutionary government forces.[43] Insurgent forces advanced along the railroads in the reverse direction. Where revolutionaries controlled the railroads, they soon controlled the state.[44]

Since the 1850s, nationalist movements also targeted foreign-owned railroad sectors without resorting to war. Prior to 1914, Argentina had the largest railroad network in Latin America. The British-owned railroads, highly touted as "harbingers of civilization," opened up thousands of acres for colonization, united remote parts of the fledgling nation, and transformed Argentina from an isolated backwater into a modern food producer.[45] Railroads, however, also destroyed regional markets to the interior and ended the livelihood of merchants who traversed the pampas in bullock carts. Farms and industries in the hinterlands became dependent on Buenos Aires and Rosario monopolies as railway lines bypassed regional and local markets in favor of exporting to international ones. The ambitious British-financed *Transandino Argentino*, for example, linked Buenos Aires with Valparaíso, Chile through the western Argentine province of Mendoza in 1910. Exports from the pampas-based agricultural sector to the coasts far outstripped local manufacturing and industrial development, and instead profited Great Britain.[46] During global recessions, the first businesses to go bankrupt when the world no longer bought were those in the interior, whereas the companies in the port cities that were capitalized differently, had diversified interests, and benefited from forward and backward linkages withstood market fluctuations. Nationalist groups criticized the British for showing little concern for Argentine interests and accused them of lording over public utilities monopolies that strangled national development. As late as the 1930s, British companies still controlled 66 percent of Argentina's railroads.[47] Ecuadorians were similarly disaffected with their American-built railroad, which they called "the Yanqui octopus."[48] Even in Colombia, the state-owned Antioquia Railroad transported 50,000 bags of coffee per year from the interior highlands to Puerto Berrío on the Magdalena River. Port workers loaded the coffee on steamships destined for markets in the Caribbean rim. The export volumes of this single commodity could never match the heavy imports of foreign goods transported in reverse from the U.S. and Europe to the main cities and towns of Colombia. In this neocolonial relationship, the nation failed to develop an industrial base.[49] There were worse fates. Under the dictator Francisco Solano López, Paraguay had no railway system or industrial plant to aid the country in the event of war. Years after Paraguay's military defeat by Argentina, Brazil, and Uruguay, Scottish poet R. B. Cunninghame Graham toured the Cruz Alta to the capital of Asunción. Admiring the gorgeous panorama, the Scotsman remarked, "Seldom in any country have I seen a railway so fall into the landscape as did the line at the little terminus of this the only railway in all Paraguay." His rich account is almost devoid of older men. The Paraguayan army had suffered 70 percent casualties in the war. Absent of a generation of males, women were left to work the fields and smoke cigars on the train. The poet later met a drunk British emigre who complained that his "several wives" were all Catholics.[50]

For every successful railroad that European and American companies built in Latin America, another was built to nowhere. Lands characterized by labor scarcity, low agricultural productivity, mile-high elevations, and other geographical obstacles did not matter. After all, capitalists were contracted to build working railroads, not profitable ones. Peru's regional railroads were intended to parlay guano exports into railway development into the highlands, where minerals and agricultural products could be transported to Pacific ports.[51] The *Ferrocarril Central de Peru* was Henry Meiggs' great achievement in standard-gauge railroad construction, with sixty-one bridges, sixty-five tunnels, twenty-one switchbacks, and five compound switchbacks, but the highland market of Huancayo through which the line ran still operated by the ancient rules of inter-zonal barter.[52] The railroad reached an altitude of 15,692 feet at Ticlio. Peruvian president Manuel Pardo declared: "All the primary schools of Peru would not teach our native population in a century what the locomotive would teach in ten years."[53] The 30,000 residents of Huancayo disproved Pardo's prophecy by using the railways to promote their subsistence economy. All the presidents of a century did not learn that railroads reflected the communities for which they were built. Beyond Sao Paolo and Rio de Janeiro, Brazilian railroads expanded directionless for decades, a fact proven later by the isolated peasants who rose against the Brazilian government in the Canudos Rebellion (1896–1897) and Contestado Rebellion (1912–1916).[54] The only functioning railroads in Brazil were those short lines like the Little Mauá (1854), which led from Rio de Janeiro to the Serra, a distance of eleven miles. The Dom Pedro II line and four other Brazilian railroads totaled less than 400 miles through 1867. About that time, the Sao Paolo Railroad still relied on stationary engines and steel cable traction. The Bahia and Pernambuco railroads and the Cantagallo in Rio remained unprofitable due to a lack of passenger traffic. In the 1870s, German explorer Franz Keller could not find a single regular carriage road, much less a railroad, 100 miles from Brazil's coast. *Tropeiros* (mule drivers) drove goods through knee-high mud in rainy seasons at ten to twelve miles per day. Any agricultural product more than 300 miles to the interior was the equivalent of melting ice, losing its value due to transportation costs and dead loss by the time it reached ports.[55] Any product harvested within 100 miles of the coast had to be processed by hand or machinery before being transported to the coast; coffee was hulled, sorted, polished, bagged, and weighed before packed on donkeys or "iron mules."[56] *The Sea and the Jungle* by H. M. Tomlinson recounted the initiatives of Colonel George Church and Phillip and Thomas Collins of Philadelphia to bring railroads to Brazil's interior. Brazil's torturous river systems and "nineteen dangerous cataracts" were mirror images of the African Congo. Somewhat reminiscent of Joseph Conrad's *Heart of Darkness*, Tomlinson's account describes a nightmarish descent into "the charnel house" of hell. The Mad Mary, the nickname for the Madeira-Mamoré Railroad, came to signify mankind's vain attempt to subdue with one railroad an Amazon that was millennia in the making. Sadly, the remains of railroad workers, rolling stock, and track became a permanent part of the Amazon.[57] In the quaint highlands of Ecuador, the narrow-gauge rails to Quito replaced footpaths so thin, indistinct, and covered with jungle canopy that Andean peasants referred to them as *caminos para pájaros* (roads for birds).[58] Hundreds of miles of railway line built in 1876 were covered with jungle foliage or buried in landslides by 1885. To redeem itself for the lost track, Ecuador hired English engineer Marcus Kelly, who in turn hired the Paris firm of Eiffel to construct an iron bridge over the Chimbo River. This monument to progress was overshadowed by Eiffel's Tower, but the bridge was practically the only railway structure to survive a single rainy season. When Kelly's project failed and a two-million-franc investment by French count Thadée d'Oksza never materialized, Ecuadorian President Antonio Flores quit on railroads and devoted his attention to rehabilitating the old mule trail and wagon roads from Babahoyo to Guaranda.[59] Like lines in Libya, China, Cochinchina, and Tonkin, Indochina (Vietnam), many railroads in Latin America never found local utility. They fell into disrepair, were torn up, or otherwise abandoned.[60]

One South American fiasco involved Ecuador's Guayaquil and Quito Railroad built by U.S. railway entrepreneur Archer Harman from 1897 to 1908. Harman was contracted during the 1890s cocoa boom when exports helped him renegotiate Ecuador's national debt and access British loans. The amount secured, $17.5 million, was seven times the annual customs revenue of Ecuador and five times its annual national budget. Anthropologist A. Kim Clark's objective summation of the project was a challenging exercise in self-restraint:

> In 1900 the work done to date by Harman was indeed destroyed by landslides in the rainy season (as had occurred in 1888 and would again in 1925). As a result, the original route to ascend the highlands through the Chimbo Valley was modified in favor of construction in the valley of the Chanchán River. The Chanchán was crossed twenty-six times by the rail line, which ascends 3,050 meters in 80 kilometers, around the double-switchback built on the mountain face known as the *Nariz del Diablo*, the Devil's Nose. The Guayaquil-Quito Railway turned out to be one of the most expensive railroads in the world. In fact, it only operated at a profit for a few years in the 1920s and again in the 1940s.[61]

Since landslides and overgrowth rendered this national marvel unusable for years at a time, peasants began using the tracks as guides to drive their donkeys, making it the most expensive footpath ever built. Ecuadorians occasionally had no other choice but to use railroad tracks as regular roads because the railroad company's construction methods rendered existing wagon roads inaccessible.[62]

The worst cases of labor exploitation in the Americas were owed not to the lengths of track laid, but the geographical hurdles, environmental conditions, and epidemic diseases that inexperienced crews faced. In the 1880s and 1890s, capitalists employed mobile and cost-effective labor pools that returned workers to conditions of debt servitude and slavery. These were not the fabled navvies, but slaves, convicts, political prisoners, conscripted soldiers, and contract workers (coolies or *enganchados*, literally "hooked" or "snared" workers) of mostly Chinese, Indian (South Asian), Amerindian (*peones acasillados*), Irish, African American, Afro-Caribbean (Jamaican and Barbadian), and African descent. Unfree labor prevailed in Cuba as slaves and indentured Chinese did the hardest construction work in the 1880s. Cuba became the first colony in Latin America to have railroads (1837), even before its mother country Spain. After Cubans won their independence, Chinese, Spanish, Cuban, and black freed slaves sold their manpower to the highest bidding sugar mill, plantation, or railway at no more than two pesos per month to start, with the potential to earn twenty to thirty pesos as a switchman, thirty-four to thirty-five pesos as a fireman, and sixty-eight to one hundred pesos as a machinist. Substitute workers were paid one-fifth the normal wage during the first month and one-quarter for the second month.[63] In Ecuador, Andean Indians from the highlands migrated to the Guayaquil coast to earn higher pay as cocoa planters (*sembradores*), but they generally refused to work on railroads. Labor recruiters called *enganchadores* offered advanced wages and free transportation to the coast, but indigenous peasants refused outright during harvest seasons, signed on with a recruiter and deserted, or paid fines for refusing obligatory labor mandated by the Liberal government. When foreign engineers recommended hiring Chinese contract workers instead, Ecuadorians staunchly refused and passed a law prohibiting Chinese immigrant labor in 1889. The Guayaquil and Quito Railway Company imported 4,000 Jamaicans from Kingston to construct the miserable embankment work up the western cordillera of the Andes. The Jamaicans had earned their reputation for completing the Panama railway under dreadful conditions. They now faced the Andean mountain section, where previous railway projects went to die, along with hundreds of native laborers. Malaria, smallpox, snake bites, and accidents had killed 500 railroad workers in the late 1880s. A mysterious insect claimed enough lives to justify a mass burial at Kilometer 106 in 1900.[64] For a while it appeared that the Jamaicans faced new lows in contracting tropical diseases, enduring harsh working conditions (cutting through rock), and withstanding heinous managerial abuse. In 1902, approximately 40 to 50 percent of the contracted laborers were so ill they performed no work at all, and many deserted the railway camps to work on cocoa plantations in Guayaquil. The British Colonial Office in Kingston had to intervene and secure promises of better safety and treatment from the railway company before the Jamaican workers returned.[65] Cheap indentured labor was also the secret to success in Colombia, where railway entrepreneur Francisco Javier Cisneros completed the Barranquilla line in 1900.[66]

Other groups of railway workers were highly paid, but their wages compensated them for both grueling work and the high incidence of disease and accidental death in dangerous environments. Although railway-related fatalities are difficult to compile, at least 620,000 workers died during the construction and operation of the 620,000 miles of track that crisscrossed the planet by 1914. By this conservative estimate, every mile of track cost one human life. The catalog of engineering marvels that characterizes railroad historiography prior to WWI is only now being matched with studies chronicling these manmade railroad disasters. Russia's infamous "Road of Bones" (Kolyma Highway), named after the bodily remains of gulag laborers who died and were buried under the highway during the Stalin Era, had four predecessors in railroads. The most excruciating historical experiences were the Indian, Trans-Panamanian, Brazilian, and Trans-Siberian Railroads, with a minimum of 50,000 fatalities each during construction. Outbreaks of epidemic disease culled railroad work crews in the Indian Ghats, Ganges, Deccan, and Punjab; the jungles of Panama; the Urals, Irkutsk, the Baikal, and Eastern Siberia; and the Brazilian Amazon and its tributaries. These railroads consumed the lives of 2,000–10,000 sick workers at a time and included the mass suicide of Chinese laborers in Panama. Although many of these catastrophes have been well documented, journalist and popular railroad historian Christian Wolmar has garnered a conscientious international audience by examining them in detail.[67]

Crowd diseases spread during the mass mobilization of workers who moved into railway camps already infected with lice, fleas, parasites, bacteria, and other microorganisms that spread disease. The camps were filthy with unsanitary living conditions. The spread of cholera, influenza, and tuberculosis by other humans, typhoid fever by flies, typhus by lice, and yellow fever and malaria by mosquitos was a foregone conclusion along the permanent way, in railway housing, in stations, and on trains. The saying "a death a sleeper" applied to the thousands of workers who died while building the biggest railway projects. But the iron horse also brought unwelcome guests in the form of deadly microbes to towns and villages. Locomotives were also transporters of livestock diseases like rinderpest. Death rode the rails during the notorious Spanish influenza epidemic of WWI. Tuberculosis, common among station employees and telegraphers, killed more Americans in the 1920s than bullets and shrapnel did in WWI. Tropical diseases (malaria and yellow fever) had always threatened the peoples of Latin America, which is why they avoided the coasts in the first place. But Europeans, Americans, and non-white construction crews all fell victim while building tropical railways. Africa remained the "White Man's grave." The word "terminus" for Lord Cowdry's Tehuantepec Railway at the Pacific town of Salina Cruz carried special meaning as the gravesite of one-quarter of the railway's workforce.[68] Tens of thousands of Maya and Yaqui perished of communicable diseases after the transportation revolution in the Yucatán peninsula.

By the 1880s, the steam shovel put navvies out of business in the UK, but their counterparts abroad had just begun to offend people. Foreign immigrant laborers recruited by the railway gangers of U.S. and European companies were largely perceived as undesirables by bigots the world over. Whether coolie laborers or small business owners, the Chinese were rarely welcomed with open arms. In the U.S., the Chinese Exclusion Act of 1882 – timed perfectly with the completion of the U.S. transcontinentals – forced thousands of Chinese to return to their home provinces or work for U.S. railway companies somewhere else in the Americas. In underpopulated states like Sonora, Mexico, the Chinese began as day laborers but eventually started up small businesses in boom towns. Many set up shop as grocers, launderers, shoe manufacturers, and tailors. Successful entrepreneurs, such as Juan Lung Tain, established stores in several Sonoran cities. His firm relied on the railroads to export shoes and clothing items in exchange for imported goods from the U.S. and even Hamburg, Germany.[69] By 1910, no fewer than 4,486 of the 13,203 Chinese in Mexico lived in Sonora.[70] Because of their success as *petit bourgeoisie*, the Chinese were targets of racist anti-foreign sentiment, especially during economic crises. The competition that Chinese merchants represented motivated anti-Chinese laws and policies in Ecuador as well.[71] Coolies died building railroads in the Americas, but Chinese merchants could not have thrived in business without railroads.

Invasion

The construction and operation of the Mexican railway system provides an ideal case to which historical processes of resistance can be compared worldwide. During the Porfirian Era (1876–1911) and Mexican Revolution (1910–1920), railroad building and operation took on regional variations according to their geographical, political, and economic integration into the world market. More than 15,000 miles of track were laid in Mexico from 1874–1910. For comparative purposes, this section examines how peasants, indigenous groups, and landowners reacted to railroads. It divides Mexico into three regions – the Central-South, the North, and the Yucatán peninsula – to examine peasant and rebel activity in the "Many Mexicos" of the Porfirian and Revolutionary era. The study also draws comparisons to other nations in Central and South America, as well as colonies and regions elsewhere. Persistent resistance to railroads reveals a significant global backlash against these symbols of imperial expansion and national modernization. Referring to the *invasión pacífica*, or "peaceful invasion" of Mexico, historian Ramón Ruiz dubbed the Mexican railroads the "Trojan horses of U.S. imperialism."[72]

After 1870, national legislatures in each of the three countries of North America passed significant land acts. The Homestead Acts (1870s) and Dawes Act (1887) in the U.S., the Dominion Acts (1870s) in Canada, and two Colonization Laws (1883 and 1894), a Mining Code (1884), and a Commercial Code (1884) in Mexico all opened the continent to settlement and economic development. The laws in Mexico privatized "vacant public lands" (*terrenos baldíos* in Mexico), divided Indian holdings, encouraged white settlement, and granted subsoil mineral rights to international investors. The Mexican government privatized ninety-six million acres of untitled land.[73] Nearly sixty-eight million acres of this land – about 14 percent of the total land area of the country – transferred into the hands of foreign land survey companies from 1881 to 1889. When one-fifth of the nation was converted into private property, peasants who could not produce titles faced the legal possibility of losing their lands. The ensuing land grab over the next two decades stimulated unprecedented investment in railroads, mining, and agriculture. Territorial disputes broke out with Indians who defended their territories from the St. Lawrence River in Canada to Yucatán, Mexico. Since railroads, banks, and speculators controlled markets in the U.S., Indian lands and the frontier properties of yeoman farmers and military colonists came under attack from the 1860s through the 1890s. Travel accounts from that time period described tribal war parties retaliating against railroads, stagecoaches, and telegraphs. Indian leaders protested that wagon and railway routes ran through their hunting grounds. Railroads contributed to the disappearance of bison herds and the overgrazing of prairie lands by livestock introduced by settlers. The Dawes Act signified the ultimate marginalization of the American Indian through law rather than force. Frank Norris inveighed against the railroads' detrimental impact on the American West in his muckraking book *The Octopus* (1901). His character Presley walks through the pleasant San Joaquin Valley of California only to be interrupted by the "enormous eye, cyclopean, red" of a train. Cyclops was an apt metaphor as the soulless train plowed into a herd of sheep.[74] The politically charged rhetoric and imagery of the machine's menace and destruction contradicted the views of Daniel Webster and Ralph Waldo Emerson in the first half of the nineteenth century. Between 1880 and 1900, railroad companies had built an additional 100,000 miles of track, bringing the U.S. national total to 263,000 miles.[75]

Economic historian John Coatsworth argued that railroads in Latin America produced a massive new concentration of land ownership in once-isolated regions populated by indigenous groups and peasants. Attempts to commercialize agriculture spurred violence in the more densely populated areas of North America, which happened to be provinces in central and southern Mexico and in the Andean highlands of Peru. Rural unrest followed in the footsteps of land survey companies, encroaching commercial estates, and railway gangs, resulting in conflict from the 1870s to 1910s. In some parts of Latin America, petty producers along trunk, branch, and spur lines were divested of lands and disallowed access to forests, pastures, ranges, and river waters that had been historically available to them. Indebted peasants who lost their plots or communal landholdings were converted to wage laborers for mines and large estates producing cash crops for export markets. The proletarianization of the countryside did not materialize as completely in Latin America as it did in industrialized nations. Ironically, the process of modernizing the land tenure system through privatization of untitled lands reinforced preexisting conditions of debt servitude. Crippling grain shortages increased the prices of basic staples and forced landless low-wage laborers into multigenerational debt.[76]

In the Central-South of Mexico, where the planter class, the federal government, and foreign investors combined their resources to build railroads, peasants felt their usual mistreatment intensify in scale from 1874–1910. The principal culprits were landowners who used federal and state laws to disentail peasant lands. *Hacendados* (landed estate owners) denounced Indian land claims and forced individuals and communities to produce titles to prove legal ownership. *Ejidos*, communal village lands, also fell under attack and were subjected to privatization and division. As Alan Knight has argued, four-fifths of Mexican agrarian communities were located within hacienda boundaries and subject to the socio-political control of *hacienda* labor.[77] Indigenous peasants and smallholders defended against the division of their lands by *hacendados* and land speculators, who anticipated increases in real estate values accompanying railway development.[78] Since the construction of the Mexican National Railway in 1874, Indian communities contended with the classic sequence of railroad planning, land seizures, commercial land development, and an end to Indian planting of crops, pasturage, and water rights. From 1877 to 1884, the fifty-five violent uprisings in the hotbeds of *agrarismo* (agrarianism, Hidalgo, Mexico, Morelos, Veracruz, Puebla, Guerrero, Michoacán, San Luis Potosí) followed the roadbeds of locomotives. Fully 60 percent of these *motines* (rebellions) erupted within twelve miles of railroads or projected routes.[79] The ruling class assault on Indian free villages and small property owners spread nationwide as the heights of modernization brought with it the depths of living standards for landless Mexicans.[80] Railway companies and government officials collaborated to cut labor costs and mete out harsh and sometimes inhumane punishments (e.g., the death penalty) to armed protestors, angry saboteurs, and railway robbers.[81]

Whether in England, France, Japan, Ecuador, or Mexico, irritated peasants, poor farmers, and even *petit bourgeoisie* did not mind trains swiftly passing by; they balked when the trains stopped to unload strangers in their towns and villages.[82] The arrival of makeshift camps of foreign railway workers, military personnel, and immigrant settlers alarmed locals, disrupted daily routines, and introduced rural townsfolk and native groups to the previously unknown world of modern vice. Japanese farmers and Meiji officials alike warned of the new foreign presence that railroads would bring.[83] In Ecuador, railway camps drew in ambulant vendors, musicians, prostitutes, and bums who lived off the wages of railway workers and stole railroad property.[84] Historian William French found that the *gente decente* of Chihuahua, Mexico perceived the "floating population" that accompanied the railroads as the source of criminal vice and moral turpitude. A growing army of beggars, drifters, and unemployed workers poured into the state capital and major cities with every new train. "Our jail is already full of people from Zacatecas," claimed one alarmed newspaper editor.[85] In contrast, official newspapers in 1880s Sonora hailed the railroad companies for clearing city streets of vagrants and drunkards by providing them with gainful employment. Conditions in the temporary camps, however, deteriorated on paydays, which brought high incidences of public drunkenness, theft, and murder. One safety-minded American engineer recalled sleeping in a well-secured storm cellar to escape the debauchery. To preserve the peace, the Sonoran governor appointed special railroad police and prohibited the sale of alcohol to line workers.[86] Begging, thievery, prostitution, gambling, card-sharking, fraud, and the growing trade in cheap thrills also boomed along U.S. railroads. Travelers noted signs that cautioned against uncouth tricksters: "Passengers are hereby warned against playing games of chance with strangers, or betting on three cards, monte, strap, or other games. You will surely be robbed if you do." American conductors literally threw transgressors off trains, even through a double-paned plate-glass window in one incident on the Northern Pacific Railway.[87] Locals also loathed the 1890s arrival of special law enforcement officials, such as the Pinkertons, Texas and Arizona Rangers, and the Mexican *Rurales*, as well as federal soldiers. These vice cops and counter-insurgents were placed in the lawless territories where trains needed protection, but locals felt they needed protection from the corruption of these representatives of law and order.

Overcoming their initial fears of surveyors and foreign peoples, peasants quickly began to view the new railroad construction yards as stores of free merchandise.[88] Foraging for food and supplies was a standard survival practice of peasant households worldwide. Petty larceny was the favored reaction to the sudden arrival of artificial building materials in railway yards, camps, and canvas towns. After lines were built, rural dwellers hardly deserved punishment for scavenging the piles of iron rail, lumber, wooden crossties, gravel, firewood, and coal that littered rural landscapes. Much of these materials were left behind by contractors who were disinterested in cleaning up after themselves. Isolated incidences of theft probably had nothing to do with power relations, but endemic pilfering became a weapon of the weak as peasants and native groups construed theft of railway property as just redistribution of the extravagant wealth of railway companies. Peasants everywhere rummaged alongside half-built tracks that may never have been completed due to companies failing. Ecuadorian indigenous peasants, carpenters, and landowners absconded with wooden ties, iron spikes, metal pins, and dynamite. Some of the more spectacular thefts were community affairs such as the overnight disappearance of Bridge No. 66 in Riobamba, Chimborazo (Ecuador) in 1903. In a separate incident a year later, a local carpenter from Alausí in the same central highlands province faced trial for possessing wood that belonged to the railway. A court trial revealed that he received the lumber from five different sellers, including a parish priest. The carpenter alleged that a railway policeman delivered the ties at night to every home in town. Even political bosses got caught with rolls of telegraph wire.[89]

In the 1890s, it was common everyday Indians – peasant freeholders and *ejidatarios* (communal landholders) – who felt new pressures that irrevocably threatened their survival during the construction of branch lines that ran through their lands.[90] Some historians believe railroads contributed to the partial proletarianization of the rural workforce by forcing subsistence farmers into propertyless wage laborers and instilling capitalist discipline on a peasantry once described by elites as "feckless, idle, unreliable, indolent, and vice-ridden."[91] This simply meant that Indians now joined the ranks of thousands of Mexican peasants in debt servitude. It happened to Tarascan Indians in Naranja near Pátzcuaro, Michoacán, in which communal landholders transitioned to sharecroppers and wage-earners earning 37 *centavos* per day. It occurred in Huixtla and Soconusco, Chiapas, as the Pan-American Railroad and land companies gobbled up Indian lands, reduced corn production by 70 percent in favor of coffee produced by imported temporary workers, and then offered to sell back lands to local villagers who were suffering through food shortages at inflated prices.[92] Social savings was passed on, but not to the poor. The railway reduced freight costs by 50 percent and increased coffee production 100 percent from 1908–1910.[93] Central and southern plantations of cash crops such as cacao, chicle, coffee, cotton, henequen, rubber, sugar, and tobacco emerged near Indian population centers and pending railway lines. As two historians of provincial Mexico wrote: "For most Mexicans, progress meant poverty."[94] The pattern of usurpation of Indian lands in Mexico differed in the U.S., where the railroads rewarded family farmers for their courage and hard work."[95] America never had a traditional peasantry, and U.S. railroads simply were not needed to effect Indian removal.

The unholy trinity of agricultural commercialization, land seizures, and division of ejidal lands to enable railway right-of-way privileges also spurred property disputes and peasant uprisings in Papantla (Veracruz), San Luís Potosí, and Morelos. In the Tamazunchale rebellion (SLP) led by Father Mauricio Zavala and Chief Juan Santiago, peasants reacted to bogus railway land claims by seizing hacienda lands, forging documents found in the national archives to assert ownership, and killing the district governor.[96] Their anti-modern slogan "Death to those who wear trousers!" waged class warfare on their oppressors. In Morelos, thirty Indian communities disappeared from 1876–1885.[97] Between 1884 and 1905, eighteen villages in Morelos vanished during their conversion to haciendas that produced sugar for the world market. Zapatista rebels later repaid the sugar plantocracy by downing telegraphs and destroying railway track along plantations. During the Mexican Revolution, Zapatistas hanged federal soldiers and their sympathizers from the telegraph poles that ran alongside railway tracks in plain sight of train passengers.[98]

In contrast to Europe, the U.S., and Japan, railroads in Latin America did little to stimulate industrial production. Mexican capitalists turned ten cash crops into commodities – sugar, henequen, cotton, coffee, cacao, chicle, rubber, vanilla, livestock, and timber. Each left the country by rail to be processed or refined in the U.S. and Europe. Extracted mineral resources such as gold, silver, copper, zinc, lead, and petroleum fed the U.S. industrial economy via railway to ten Mexican ports (and by ship to New Orleans, New York, Los Angeles, and San Francisco) and four railway stations on the U.S.-Mexican border. By 1910, 56 percent of the gross revenues of all Mexican railroads left the country in the form of stockholder dividends, interest on loans, additional parts and equipment for the railroads, and consumer goods purchases for foreigners employed by the railroad companies. The remaining 44 percent went mostly to employee salaries, the highest of which were paid to Yankee engineers, machinists, and managers.[99] "Indispensible" railroads rewarded foreign capitalists with growth but without commercial and industrial development. Nevertheless, railroads saved the regime of Porfirio Díaz (1876–1911) from probable failure and played a decisive role in integrating Mexico into the world market and international division of labor.[100]

In peripheral Northern Mexico, intrusive railroads angered significant segments of every social class, including landowners, merchants, agricultural laborers, and indigenous groups. To Sonorans, Chihuahuans, and Coahuilans, as well as citizens in the Huasteca and southern Tamaulipas, the railroads symbolized the undesirable encroachment of three external forces: foreign capitalists, the federal government in Porfirian Mexico City, and local rivals with connections to the former two. Social alliances had formed between landowners and indigenous communities who provided work for haciendas and ranches. The Maytorenas, Alvarados, Méndezes, Obregóns, and de la Huertas of Sonora, for example, depended heavily on Indian labor on their ranches but generally left the lands of Yaqui Indians alone. The Mayo Indians in Coahuila also sold their labor to local ranchers. In the 1880s, new modernizing cliques in state government with ties to the railroads challenged local *hacendados* and indigenous communities for access to lands and Indian labor. Precious minerals and commercial agriculture attracted foreign capitalists to these previously isolated regions. Privatization facilitated the division and seizure of Indian lands and the conversion of rural cultivators to wage laborers.[101] Governor of Sonora Luis Torres predicted that the new land laws and commercial codes would force Indian communities to provide the cheap labor necessary to construct railroads to the interior.

The railroad boom that Torres predicted reached Chihuahua in 1898. That year companies began installing east-west track through the presidios and villages of the former military colonies that provided frontier defense against marauding Apaches. They were now under attack by aggressive landowners with the law and railroads on their side. Land values soared along the projected route of the Mexican Central Railroad (north-south) and the Chihuahua Pacific (east-west).[102] Between 1881 and 1898, 96 percent of the Galeana district of Chihuahua (nearly ten million acres) was transferred to private hands just in time for the appearance of the Rio Grande, Sierra Madre, and Pacific Railroad (1897). Land speculators, lawyers, and estate owners went to court but soon brandished new land titles as a result of the Municipal Land Law (1905), which bilked smallholders and towns out of their lands. Governor Enrique Creel's timing could not have been worse, as the landmark legislation pushed the discontented masses of *medieros*, poor farmhands and wage laborers, toward *magonismo*.[103] The poor radicalized and joined the Magón brothers, and Chihuahua became another crucible of revolutionary activity.[104]

On balance, any gains earned by the export-oriented economy were negated by the Porfirian regime's Indian policy, which was enforced by militarizing the railroads against indigenous groups that rebelled. In Chihuahua (1892), Tomochic rebels took up arms against the encroachment of land developers, lumberjacks, and the Northwestern Railroad when Canadian magnate F. S. Pearson received 3.5 million acres for the railroad's construction. Peasants belonging to a millenarian movement that followed Santa Teresa de Cabora defeated the Federal Army in March.[105] Indian rebellions also broke out against the *yori* (whites) and *trocoyori* (Indians allied with white) in Sonora to defend Indian land and labor rights.[106] The resulting Yaqui Wars brought the tribe to the brink of extinction and signified one of the most deplorable episodes in Mexican history.

The emergence of global markets wrought havoc on indigenous Americans. For the southern and northern Mexican peripheries, the ethnocidal Yaqui campaigns (1874–1910) and Caste War of Yucatán (1847–1901) were major catastrophes. The Federal Army's military victories over the *indios rebeldes* of the northwest and the *sublevados* of the unconquered southeast were inconceivable without steamships and railroads. To no one's surprise, Indian rebels and recalcitrant peasants directed their strategic guerrilla attacks against the railroads. Federal armies and state officials retaliated by working Yaquis to death on henequen plantations in Yucatán and shipping Maya insurgents to sugar and tobacco plantations in Cuba. The Mexican state rationalized the forced labor as alternatives to death sentences, but in both cases exile was the equivalent of death. Deportation of Yaquis, Huastecs from the Gulf Coast, and petty criminals from Mexico City to Yucatán or the *Valle Nacional* of Oaxaca was justified on the basis of replacing the convict labor of hundreds of Maya rebels exported to Cuba. Scholars generally agree that the labor conditions on henequen plantations constituted *de facto* slavery.[107]

The railroad's role in integrating the mines and cash crops of the Mexican north into the world economy resembled late nineteenth-century processes elsewhere. Indian communities such as the Yaqui brought their claims to court, tore up railway tracks, and attacked railway stations throughout the 1880s and 1890s. Like the Maori kings, Yaqui Chief José María Leyva Cajeme adopted the strategy of non-sale of native lands in 1885. When an attempt on his life failed, Cajeme launched an offensive against haciendas, ranches, and railway stations. Rebels loyal to him set fire to twenty-one ships at El Médano and burned the port of Agiabampo. Cajeme's fortification at Añil easily withstood sieges by state militias bearing rifles. But the completion of the Sonoran Railroad in 1886, which linked the Pacific coast port of Guaymas with the town of Nogales on the Arizona border, brought federal troops, heavy artillery, and Gatling guns. President Díaz sent Generals Angel Martínez and Marcos Carrillo to destroy Cajeme's Yaquis. A yellow fever epidemic struck Yaqui camps and rendered their "impregnable" fortification of Buatachive defenseless. Cajeme fled into the Sierra de Bacatete but was captured in April 1887 and sent to the firing squad. Cajeme drew his last breath after a long campaign defending Yaqui autonomy against the Mexican government.[108]

As popular railway historian Christian Wolmar observed, nations often used locomotives to deploy troops against their own dissenting people. The more railroads the British built in Ireland, Egypt, and India, the fewer garrisons were needed to rule the Emerald Isle, the gateway to Africa, and the Raj.[109] The Yaqui people had transitioned to the capitalist market before the violence began. The construction of secondary railroads and spur lines in Sonora set off a second round of land expropriations and Yaqui uprisings from 1900–1910.[110] No Mexican actually served on the Sonoran Railroad Company's board of directors, and nearly all of the capital, building materials, and rolling stock came from the U.S. Almost 1,500 Mexicans and Yaquis, as well as 200 African Americans, built the railway.[111] Once installed, it crossed the Yaqui and Mayo rivers, prompting the Porfirian government to award the Sonora and Sinaloa Irrigation Company 547,000 acres of the Yaqui Valley, three-fourths of which was to be irrigated by water from canals built by the company.[112] In 1875, government land sales in Sonora stood at 2,126 hectares (1 hectare = 2.471 acres). Upon the completion of the railway in 1886, claims multiplied over 100 times to 245,782 hectares of prime real estate.[113] By 1902, U.S. investments in haciendas, ranches, and farms exceeded $3.7 million, ranking second among all Mexican states.[114] On the tail end of railway development, an "Indian Republic" that survived three centuries of subjugation faced unimaginable hardships, including the Mazocoba Massacre of 400 Yaquis (January 18, 1900) by the Mexican army. Juan Maldonado, who carried on Cajeme's fight and was known to history by his Yaqui name Tetabiate, was killed at a second attack on Mazocoba in 1901. In ensuing years, state authorities and federal soldiers arbitrarily rounded up and imprisoned several hundred suspected Indian rebels, which included false arrests of peaceful Yaquis, Pimas, Opatas, Papagos, Mayos, and even Mexican mestizos. All indigenous people of Sonora fell under state surveillance and terror. Yaqui children were taken from their mothers and either farmed out to prominent Sonoran families or left to die in the squalor of prisons. The Yaqui answered with guerrilla attacks on railway construction sites and raids on haciendas, ranches, and mines. State governors Rafael Izábal and Luis Torres escalated the Yaqui Wars by carrying out mass deportations of several thousand Yaqui men, women, and children to forced labor camps in Yucatán.[115] Federal troops placed the Yaquis in chains and sent them by train to Guaymas port. Steamships took them to Progreso or they left Guaymas by train to Oaxaca's Valle Nacional. They may as well have been shipped to Siberia, for every Yaqui died. Railroad companies prohibited Yaquis from working on the railroads for fear of sabotage.[116]

John Kenneth Turner blew the whistle on this ethnocide in his book *Barbarous Mexico* (1910).[117] Whether or not one agrees with the socialist muckraker's casualty figures, historian Evelyn Hu-DeHart proved that Sonoran state governors colluded with dictator Porfirio Díaz and Yucatán Governor Olegario Molina (1902–1906) to punish Yaqui rebels with enslavement on plantations that Molina owned outside of Mérida. Deportation resulted in the deaths of thousands. As the former governor of Yucatán, Molina had already compiled a deplorable record of deporting Maya guerrillas to Cuban plantations. Now he sold Yaquis to forced labor camps. Rather than deny the practice, Mexican politicians took credit for it in the annual reports of their achievements. Governor Izábal reported that from 1903–1907, around 2,000 Yaquis were deported. The number probably fell between 8,000 and 15,000, constituting between one-fourth and one-half of the Yaqui population, since the rural police force and army began raiding all large-scale operations that employed Indian laborers.[118] Rosalio Moisés, a Yaqui survivor, remembered the 1900s:

> Governor Izábal was called the second god by the Yaquis. He liked to preside at the Sunday morning sessions sitting on the portal out in the middle of the *cuartel* [jail], Yaqui men were sorted into three lines. Men in one line were to be killed; men in the second line were to be deported; men in the third line were released to work another week.[119]

In June 1908, Governor Torres threatened Yaqui leader Luis Bule: "you are the cause for the death of your tribe [and] . . . the government . . . is disposed to exterminate all of you if you continue to rebel."[120] The effects on family life were abominable on both peripheries, as sugar and henequen planters in Yucatán forced Yaqui women to marry Maya or Chinese men to produce children to work in henequen fields.[121] The Porfirian regime's record of dehumanizing the Yaqui and atomizing their kinship units forever blights its historical legacy.

Thus did Yaqui resistance to railroads predate the storied attacks on locomotives by Pascual Orozco, Pancho Villa, and Alvaro Obregón during the Mexican Revolution. Yaqui resistance to the Díaz regime merged with revolutionary forces in 1910, preventing the construction of the El Paso to Guaymas railway.[122] *Norteño* support for Mexican revolutionary Francisco I. Madero coalesced around the desire to restore local control over regional markets, redress labor conditions, and oust the dictator Díaz. When Díaz was sent into exile in 1911, *Maderistas* took over positions in the Sonoran government. After Madero's assassination, Yaqui leaders Luis Bule, Lino Morales, and Francisco Urbalejo joined the ranks of General Salvador Alvarado and later combined with Obregón's Army of the Northwest. In spring 1915, more than 2,000 Yaquis and Mayos under Chief Felipe Bachomo formed the strongest force in Pancho Villa's army. Yaqui officers were the only indigenous leaders to command their own battalions. The Yaqui people waited a century for vindication. On January 10, 1997, President Ernesto Zedillo of the Partido Revolucionario Institucional (PRI) awarded 32,000 Yaquis in Sonora control over 1.14 million acres of land in the Yaqui River Valley and surrounding territories.[123]

Meanwhile in Yucatán, railway construction stalled as long as the Caste War between the Mexican government and the Maya raged on. Yucatán boasted the most extensive railway system in the republic due to a combination of 500 miles of main lines, 370 miles of privately owned track, and 620 miles of moveable train tracks, all of which fed cash crops to the port at Progreso.[124] Railway developers laid only thirty miles of track and steered clear of territory controlled by the recalcitrant Cruzob Maya. In the annual reports of the Mérida to Peto Railroad (1886 and 1887), Coatsworth found railway officials predicting "the Caste War of Yucatán will end without doubt when this railroad arrives at its last station," and secondly, that its completion will open up a vast expanse of alienable lands.[125] Nelson Reed's *The Caste War of Yucatán* and Moisés González Navarro's *Raza y Tierra* documents the Indian resistance in the states of Yucatán, Campeche, and Quintana Roo, including the violent uprising at Maxcanu in September 1891. The rebellion caused hundreds of Maya elders, women, and children to flee over the border to Campeche. *Ejidatarios* in Calkiní (Campeche) and Peto (Yucatán) also took up arms when the Mérida to Peto line split communal lands in 1892.[126] Some of the worst offenders against railroads were not peasants at all but hacendados, who fought off railway companies with every means at their disposal: entering lengthy litigation, placing boulders on track, and refusing *jornaleros* (day laborers) access to roads (*sahcabs*). One insuppressible landowner, Manuel Lara, challenged the Mérida to Peto line's right-of-way privileges on his lands near Oxkutzcab by derailing trains in 1894 and repeatedly placing the same blind mule on the track to disrupt schedules. As Allen Wells explained, "a southbound train accidentally hit the forlorn animal, causing still another derailment and putting the mule out of its misery."[127] Four hundred Maya rose up against the railroads because the family of Yucatán state governor Francisco Cantón controlled the Mérida to Peto Railroad.[128] Villagers trampled the hacienda fields, downed telephone lines, discharged their rifles in the air, and used their machetes to hack at the front doors of property owners. In Mérida, Governor Daniel Traconis mobilized 400 policemen and National Guardsmen, as well as 100 soldiers of the 22nd Battalion of the Federal Army, to put down the uprising. Troops rode the train three hours south, disembarked, and set up defensive positions in the central plaza. Federal soldiers kept the peace into 1892, when a deadly smallpox epidemic raged through the peninsula.[129] The Southeastern Railway Company tried to privatize communal lands in the late 1890s, but Maya peasants confronted surveyors, downed markers, and may have been responsible for the disappearance of a railroad surveyor.[130]

Scholars have different opinions about the primary causes of the national tragedy known as *La Guerra de Castas* (Caste War), a race war pitting Maya rebels (*macehualob*) who shouted "Kill the Whites!" against white Yucatecan landowners, foreign nationals, and the state and federal government (*dzulob*). A confluence of several factors, including agricultural commercialization and land usurpation, division of ejidal lands, encroachment on water rights, the undermining of local and regional autonomy, increased taxation, coerced labor and debt peonage, broken legal promises, political distrust, and the introduction of life-threatening diseases all provoked a prolonged Maya social rebellion.[131] The Maya had remembered their servitude on plantations as the "time of slavery," when they were "forced to learn the scientific and complete utilization of labor as defined by their masters."[132] Underlying the Caste War was the Maya's multigenerational distrust of foreigners since the Spanish conquest. The culture developed an historical awareness of white motives as impure, demonstrated persistent hostility toward outsiders, and embraced violence as a means to forge communal solidarity during rebellions. The Mexican government systematically retaliated by exporting rebellious Maya Indians to Spanish Cuba. The conflict rapidly escalated into an armed religious crusade. A cult of nominally Christian Maya warriors followed the prophecies of a series of "Talking Crosses" that inspired Indian rebels and guided their military decisions. The Maya took advantage of a territorial dispute between Mexico and Great Britain to trade with gun runners from bordering British Honduras (Belize). Wielding serviceable rifles, they raided and killed with impunity, capturing more than 250 towns and villages in the peninsula. The ongoing violence helped ensure Maya autonomy but at tremendous cost in human lives on both sides. Smallpox, cholera, whooping cough, and other diseases claimed the lives of thousands of Maya. The inhabitants of peaceful villages migrated to safer zones. From 1855–1900, the population of the headquarters of the Maya rebellion, Chan Santa Cruz, decreased from 40,000 to 10,000.[133] The remainder of the eastern Maya headquartered at the "Village of the Holy Cross" were not subdued until the arrival of the Federal Army in 1901.

Economic deprivation had fueled the religious war. The self-nominated *Casta Divina*, or Divine Caste, of henequen planters in the Yucatán Northwest controlled all state commerce through the strategic construction of railroads from their estates directly to the Gulf port of Progreso. Planters then stopped purchasing grain and foodstuffs from small proprietors in the southeastern region of the state. Instead, rich *henequeneros* imported cheaper corn, beans, and sugar from Central Mexico and foreign nations, which weakened smallholder producers in the southeast. The south soon depended on the northwestern henequen zone for imported food. Southeastern villagers had no choice but to abandon their *milpas* (small plots) and sell their labor to king henequen. The ultimate outcome was the expansion of the henequen zone into the southeast, along with new railroads such as the Mérida to Peto line. Railroad entrepreneurs then leveraged the institution of debt peonage against their own labor force. *Ferrocarrileros* (railroad workers) accumulated substantial debts from 1899–1908.[134]

Scholars have remarked on the compliant labor force of the great sugar and henequen estates of Yucatán. General Francisco Canton took two decades to finish the Mérida to Valladolid line.[135] Whereas the first spikes for the Mérida to Peto railroad were driven in 1879, the line did not reach Oxkutzcab and Tekax until 1891 and 1893, respectively. Although the railroad approached within twenty miles of Peto in 1898, the final segment was not completed until 1900.[136] The line from Mérida to Campeche was similarly delayed for decades. The unintended consequence of the slow pace of railroad development was Maya peasants who gradually adapted to the changes in market conditions resulting from the henequen oligarchy's incremental privatization of lands. This pattern of delayed completion also worked in Colombia, where the Bogotá-Giradot railway took fifteen years to complete in the 1880s and 1890s. The Nationalist party was duly criticized for building a road to the Sabana de Bogotá for the sole purpose of hauling imported railway equipment by ox-cart and building a second line backwards from the city to the Magdalena River. After the small network proved its worth during the War of a Thousand Days against the Liberals, Rafael Reyes courted foreign capitalists to complete several new lines.[137]

As Mexican historian Alfonso Villa Rojas explained, the military campaign to subjugate the Maya was both extensive and costly. The Mexican government negotiated a treaty with the British recognizing territorial boundaries with British Honduras (Belize) in exchange for their cooperation in preventing arms from reaching Maya rebels. The army built a customs station at the mouth of the Río Hondo. In October 1899, Maya rebels spoke clearly about their objections to encroachment from Mérida and Peto: "What do the Mexicans want our territory for? We are content with our small houses and our forest. They have their fine homes and cities. Why do they . . . trouble us?"[138] In 1901, President Díaz sent General Ignacio Bravo to Yucatán to defeat the Maya and end the fifty-year Caste War. Bravo arrived by railroad and steamship from Mexico City and rode the train from Progreso to Mérida to Peto. He later wrote to President Díaz:

> [The Cruzob] are a race that for humanity's sake must be extinguished, because they will never amount to anything good. . . . I am convinced that the only way to guarantee the interests of the zone in general is to finish off the race, if that would be possible.[139]

Rail lines originally constructed to transport sugar, henequen, lumber, and cotton to ports for export now transported troops to the front. Prisoners of war, convicts, Afro-Caribbeans, Mexicans, Indians, and even Koreans and Chinese rapidly extended the rail lines into Maya-controlled territory in the new state of Quintana Roo. Reaching Ichmul and Balche with four federal battalions, Bravo advanced past the end of the railway lines in Peto by makeshift road toward the Maya capital of Chan Santa Cruz. The general established headquarters at Peto and guard posts along the road at intervals of ten kilometers. Maya rebels attacked road-building crews and chopped down telephone and telegraphs poles. Low on ammunition, the Cruzob used cut pieces of telegraph wire as shot in their muzzle-loading rifles.[140] Skirmishing along the way, the general deployed Mausers, mountain guns, quick-fire artillery cannon, and machine guns, none of which could have been remotely available without the railroads and steamships. Bravo deployed patrol dogs in advance of his forces to search and detect any human presence.[141]

An extremely contagious measles epidemic, likely transmitted by released Maya prisoners, ravaged the rebel camps long enough for the Mexican army to advance. Bravo captured Santa Cruz with little opposition. Estimates of the remaining Cruzob forces varied from 500 to 2,200 men. Rebels and refugees fled across the borders of British Honduras and Guatemala. Bravo then prepared ground for a new railway to the sea and also dug a canal for metal barges to ply the waters of Chetumal and Chaak Bay, where the Mexican Army engineered a forward base to quarter thousands of men and fortify the region.[142] The Caste War was a nineteenth-century campaign reminiscent of the sixteenth-century conquest. Instead of the horses, cannon, steel, and smallpox of the early sixteenth century, the conquerors deployed the Iron Horse, artillery, repeating rifles, and measles three centuries later. As Moisés González Navarro explained, one no longer heard the war cries of Maya warriors but the whistles of the locomotives.[143]

Bravo's victory was short-lived, and over the next decade the Cruzob proved that their motivation to attack railroads was not based on some misplaced antiquarianism so much as military strategy. In Bravo's mop-up campaign, the July rains rendered the new transportation system inoperable. The Mexican army had to rely upon 300 mules sent by Governor Cantón.[144] Mule teams never came under fire, but rebels continued to destroy track. Bravo ordered Colonel Aurelio Blanquete to build a new horse-drawn railway that connected Santa Cruz with a new port fifty-six kilometers (thirty-six miles) away at Vigia Chico. Political prisoners labored under horrific conditions constructing this short line through the mangrove swamps of Quintana Roo, a *de facto* penal colony. Workers fell under fire from Cruzob snipers or died of tropical diseases. When they attempted to escape, they were caught and executed by the Mexican Army. The railway line was called the *callejón de la muerte*, or "passageway of death," because each short stretch of rail cost five lives. As disease and ambush killed Maya rebels and federal troops destroyed villages, crops, and seed, natives retaliated by dynamiting stretches of railroad track and telegraph poles. Maya also ambushed the occasional military column.[145] The Porfirian government spent thirty million pesos on the ports, wharfs, warehouses, electric lights, telegraphs, and railway to Santa Cruz.[146] This was a high price to pay for territory that federal forces never fully controlled.

The vicious cycle of armed conflict and conciliation repeated itself when the Porfirian regime fell in May 1911 and revolutionary forces entered Yucatán. The installation of a new governor, the socialist Salvador Alvarado, curbed neither violence nor the attacks on railroads. Alvarado moved the capital south to Chetumal, granted autonomy to the Indians of northern Quintana Roo, and ordered federal forces to vacate Santa Cruz. In his book *The Caste War of Yucatán*, Nelson Reed described the end of the Cruzob Maya's half-century struggle and their return home to Chan Santa Cruz in 1915:

> The Maya homecoming was not happy. The dzul [white men] were gone but their evil winds remained. The jungle fighters stared for a time at the transformations – the wooden houses and other "improvements" – and then they set to work with the purifying torch, ax, and dynamite. They burned the locomotives, coaches, and railroad platform cars; tore up the railroad tracks in several places and threw them into the jungle; and cut the telegraph lines; they dynamited the new market, the pump, and the reservoir and burned the former school buildings that had served as barracks. There is some argument about the destruction; some claimed later that the departing garrison carried off all it could, then vandalized the rest, but there was no doubt about Maya intentions. They wanted the place isolated and put in such a condition that the dzul would have no reason to come back.[147]

The destruction of trains and other symbols of the foreign invasion highlighted the efforts of Cruzob leaders to restore Chan Santa Cruz to its original state and reestablish its religious sanctity as the site of the original Speaking Cross. In subsequent years, Maya leaders such as Juan Bautista Vega and Francisco May withstood smallpox epidemics and negotiated greater autonomy with new regimes. In a remarkable reversal of fortune in 1917, President Venustiano Carranza met with Francisco May in Mexico City and gave him the rank of General in the Mexican Army. General May agreed to negotiate peace with the Cruzob, rebuild the Santa Cruz to Vigia Chico line with Maya labor, and operate a generous railway concession. In addition, May received 20,000 hectares of land and a monopoly on *aguardiente* sales in the region.[148]

By the time the Mexican Revolution arrived in tidal wave force, Mexican peasants and Indians already knew how to derail locomotives and with it the Porfirian state. Mexican historian Hector Aguilar Camín wrote:

> It is surely significant that it was this Northern region . . . which in 1910 dispatched its troops to the South, on the very railroads which had united it to the rest of the nation, in order to dominate the country both politically and militarily for the next quarter century.[149]

The railway workers brought trains to a standstill with work stoppages and strikes, protesting against unequal pay between American managers and Mexican machinists. When attacking the railroads amounted to assaults on the Díaz regime, the federal government proved decrepit in its defense of railway and communication lines. In November 1910, Tlaxcalan rebels in support of Aquiles Serdán in Puebla destroyed a bridge on the Mexican Railway near Santa Cruz to delay federal troops. Trains became targets of gunfire in Puebla, track was sabotaged daily, and rebel dynamite brought down several bridges along the Interoceanic near Morelos. Attacks came so frequently after January 1911 that the *Mexicano del Sur* suspended service, and railway employees refused to operate the trains without armed protection. Cautious civilian passengers avoided locomotives carrying federal soldiers for fear of losing their lives.[150] In no part of rebel territory could the Porfirian army defend the railroads much less deploy them strategically. In the spring, the forces of Orozco and Villa seized the Northwestern Railroad and the Mexican Central, and the American consul in Chihuahua complained that "not a mile of railroad is being operated." Villa's exploits with trains at Torreón and Ciudad Juárez soon became legendary.[151] Since Villa commandeered the railroads, trains have come to represent the rebels and Indians of *La Revolución* instead of the "Peaceful Invasion" of U.S.-backed dictator Porfirio Díaz.

Insurgents worldwide used local knowledge to disrupt railway lines with devastating effect, but in some cases railroad managers and workmen identified with the colonial state. When the Cuban Independence wars erupted in the mid-1890s, the railroad companies became willing allies of the Spanish counter-insurgency. Just as the price of sugar plunged on the world market in 1894, rebels further destabilized the colonial government's primary source of income by destroying sugar mills and plantations. Revolutionary Mambí forces under Generals Máximo Gómez and Antonio Maceo then turned on the railroads. Instead of commandeering the railroads, the forces deployed inexpensive tactics to immobilize them. They bombed or removed sections of track to derail trains, awaited repairs, then attacked the same weak points again. The *Ferrocarril de Matanzas* reported five boxcars burned at the Diana switch, "a locomotive number 46 was sent off along the Atrevido branch with its valve open heading downhill toward Navajas with two boxcars and a flatbed car," all overturned and sustained considerable damage.[152] In 1895–1896, Cuban rebels burned out twelve railway stations, including the United Railroads of Havana installations at Madan, Tosca, Coliseo, and Sumidero. The quartermaster-general of the Spanish army had to consolidate the boxcars and tracks of four different railroad companies just to move his troops east and west. The companies supported the Spanish war effort by constructing fortifications at stations and bridges, turning freight warehouses into military barracks, and outfitting trains with armor. Rebels struck each facility in turn, rendered the main lines impassable, and bankrupted the railway companies. With U.S. intervention, Spanish joint-stock companies yielded to a British takeover after 1900. The Cuban Independence movement and Spanish-American War accelerated the denationalization of the Cuban railroad industry.[153]

By 1900, Americans on both continents needed little convincing that they belonged to progressive Republics and participated in new democratic experiments matching technology to the natural landscape. Leo Marx examined this theme over fifty-five years ago: "The soft veil of nostalgia that hangs over our urbanized landscape is largely a vestige of the once dominant image of an undefiled, green republic, a quiet land of forests, villages, and farms dedicated to the pursuit of happiness."[154] His assertion that America realized Virgil's Arcadia as a symbolic landscape blending myth and reality[155] applied to the quasi-fictional pastoral foundations of other nations, not just the American republics. This argument internationalizes his research, but however much we apply it to other nations, the history of U.S. railroads still occupies the very extreme position of the spectrum. The great majority of Americans ultimately accepted railroads because they agreed with Guillaume Poussin's claim that "the railroad, animated by its powerful locomotive, appears to be the personification of the American."[156] Daniel Webster argued that railroads held three American promises: national unity, social equality (by equalizing the condition of men), and property ownership, as in the farmer's exclamation, "Our railroad!"[157] This triad of oaths was transgenerational. When American schoolboys were granted free time to sketch, they drew trains and steamboats. Women of all ages conducted themselves with respectability and rode the rails to visit relatives and maintain family networks.[158] *The Lackawanna Valley* (1855), a panoramic landscape painting by George Inness in which a train appears miniaturized in its surroundings as livestock animals grazed undisturbed, united the railway and its passengers to the natural landscape in America. More than this, nineteenth-century writers set aside the majestic views from U.S. trains and compared the unspoiled environmental surroundings of the American railroad system to magnificent Alpine scenery, vast oceans, and plains.[159] The railroads in India may have been the largest colonial project in modern times, but the Empire Express sextupled the staggering output of the Raj and then expanded the machine ensembles south of the border.

The period from 1830 to 1930 brought an ordered world to the fore and set the stage for what Eric Hobsbawm dubbed the Age of Extremes.[160] The cultural insensitivity to rural folk in the developing world, where proxy wars over lands, markets, and resources escalated into the mutual destruction of European dynastic states, ended European hegemony. Twenty-first-century attitudes toward time- and space-saving technology, Amazon.com, and the military deployment of drones and other stealth weapons will never reverse the West's decline in world leadership. As global citizens, educating ourselves about the "extraordinary bundle of relations" of an engineered world is the only solution to the seemingly intractable problems created by nation-states, hyper-capitalism, and rigid class systems. Marx for one had faith in knowledge as the prescription for society's ills when he wrote: "the problem itself arises only when the material conditions necessary for its solution already exist or are at least in the process of formation."[161] U.S. President John F. Kennedy expressed the same sentiment succinctly: "No problem of human destiny is beyond human beings."

Part 1: America the perilous: cultures of speed, equality, and freedom in the United States

The opening essay by correspondent Edward Hungerford identified the railway as a dynamic source of economic opportunity, a major theme in American railroad history. Despite the overwhelming popularity of U.S. railroads, that opportunity came at a cost. Through precise anecdote and thoughtful reflection, Hungerford related his journey from the quiet station of anytown USA to the bustling docks and freight elevators of an Atlantic port. His trip to the Midwest aboard the PK-5 freight train quickly indoctrinated him in the relentless demands and dangers of industrialized transport. He interacted with a handful of technical specialists of an unnamed railroad company that had 11,000 employees in 1908. Hungerford described freight operations that required train schedules to adjust to business cycles rather than vice versa. The way-bills for $250,000 worth of merchandise snowed the men under in clerical work. In the "Titanic" scale of sorting at transfer houses, LCLs (less than carloads lots) waited until the freight car was judged full. Hungerford toured the cabin-like caboose for brakemen. The air-shock after brake release nearly pitched him out of the window. At the center stood a mountain of old lockers piled high to serve as a ladder to the roof. With the train in motion, he scaled the scrap heap to the roof and walked along the carriage roofs, redefining the passenger's mobility. The brakeman leading the tour spots a "telltale" and slaps Hungerford across the face, a signal to drop to his belly before the train slips into a tunnel or under a bridge. Inside the tunnel, smoke filled his eyes and nostrils, and he later learned of the danger of icicles hanging from the tunnel bore. Exiting the tunnel, he then turned into a gymnast and jumped the gaps between carriage roofs. He learned that brakemen go to all fours when roofs grow slippery in winter. At the coal tender he was told that firemen shoveled ten tons in nearly six hours. Guard chains save them from lurching into the abyss when fatigue set in. Hungerford was intimidated by the headlight of a train passing in the opposite direction, as its coal cinders spray the roof of his train. The colors of signals and flags confused him, especially when the driver said that red meant slow down because only a fool willfully brought a freight train to a dead stop. A whole different culture of perpetual motion governed the switch-engine and pole car operators who ran the "hump" or gravity yards. Military metaphors abound. Hungerford reported on the guerrilla war between railroad men and tramps. Collins the engineer and "superman" Sam Jones conducted the ground operations. Yardmaster Randall served as field marshal. The despatcher barked orders like a cabinet minister or general. The Superintendent ruled the kingdom. Climate and natural disasters took casualties during Hungerford's ride. Landslides derailed a night-flyer Limited, costing the lives of two men. In a 24-hour period, a traffic of 199 freight trains pulling 6,800 cars arrived and departed the station. A train left for Pittsburgh, Cleveland, Chicago, the Transcontinentals, and points north and south every 7 ½ minutes. The freight got through. All the moving parts of the Empire Express – metonym for America and its railroads – were reset for the next day.

Railroads were natural adjuncts to the American way, according to editorialist David Henshaw and poet Walt Whitman. In contrast, transcendentalist Henry David Thoreau considered railroads as unnecessary, and Englishwoman Isabella Bird regarded them as perilous when left to Americans. Henshaw's letters to the *Boston Morning Post* revealed the mix of transport options for western sojourners in the 1830s. He left Baltimore in Admiral Reeside's coach line in November 1838 and reached the western Alleghenies practically on foot, where he reported on the state of the Cumberland "national road" before reaching Frederick, Maryland and the Baltimore and Ohio Railroad (B&O). Less than a decade after the introduction of the iron horse, Henshaw asserted that no other form of overland travel competed with their "convenience, comfort, and speed." He also noted the B&O's ideal proximity to canals, coal mines, and railroads out of Pennsylvania and Virginia. After catching a steamer south from Wheeling, Virginia to Cincinnati, Ohio, he projected that railroads between major cities would within a few years unite Illinois, Indiana, Ohio, western New York, and New England. In 1854, philosopher Henry David Thoreau questioned the economic and environmental rationale of railroads that conflicted with leading a simple life. Walt Whitman's tangible optimism for railroads left generations of Americans pondering if technology can indeed be so beautiful. Excitement filled Isabella Bird's famous travelogues. Her characterizations of well-established cities on the East Coast in the 1850s read like railway adventures in the Wild West. Despite her preconceptions about American life, she learned to appreciate the warm generosity of lower-class Americans with whom she interacted. By the time she reached the Rockies on a separate trip years later in the 1870s, she possessed the characteristics that allowed her to blend in with the "rugged and uncouth" Americans. Charles Weld, a fellow countryman from England, commented on the Underground Railroad to Chicago and the outbound train. He joined the chorus of complainants whose misfortunes on U.S. railroads saw print in the 1850s and 1860s. Emily Pfeiffer coped with screaming children she dubbed "vampires" and contemplated the connection between railroads and American democracy.

Part 2: rivers of iron: cultures of railway construction and management

Just fifty years after Lewis and Clark's pioneering expedition, Lieutenant R. S. Williamson and his first assistant Lieutenant Henry L. Abbot surveyed the Sacramento Valley north to the Columbia River Valley for a railway. Their arduous trek in summer 1855 contrasted greatly with travel conditions in Colorado and other scenic regions that Americans called "Palace-Car States." Railroads eventually removed the veil of unconquered nature by surmounting previously impassable barriers to transcontinental travel but, as the Richardson expedition proved, California and Oregon were still rough country occupied by Indians variously designated as Putos, Diggers, Pit River, and Klamath. Abbot's journal is an excellent source for California's immigration history as the surveyors encounter the remnants of Spanish colonization, hostile and peaceful indigenous villages, and regional flora and fauna that included malaria-carrying anopheline mosquitos that transmitted "intermittent fever." Well before germ theory proved the mosquito carrier, Williamson's survey party blamed their illness on miasmas. Following the Mexican War (1846–1848) and the gold discoveries (1849), California territorial governors in Sacramento and the city fathers of San Francisco were anxious to tame the wild with a railway from Sacramento Valley to the Columbia River. The topographical engineer Williamson headed a twenty-five-man expedition that included Abbot, a civilian geologist and botanist, a physician and naturalist, a draughtsman, an assistant engineer, and eighteen workmen under the supervision of packmaster Charles Coleman. The campaign began in July 1855 and required every person to guide the wagon of a pack train carrying delicate survey instruments through rough territory. They passed through Benícia, Vacaville, Frémont, Marysville, Hamilton, Red Bluffs, Fort Reading, McCumber's Flat, and Noble's Pass. The party found the old Oregon Trail, the Upper Klamath Lake and River, and the Des Chutes River. Both Williamson and Abbot kept separate diaries, and their experiences of July and August are presented here.

An article in *The Atlantic Monthly* (1857) cited by Wolfgang Schivelbusch in *The Railway Journey* illustrates a basic difference between American and British railway engineering. Once built, U.S. railroads required armies of workers. Generations of railway families settled near and worked on the iron rails that girdled the planet. Previous volumes concentrated on railway construction workforces, but this section addresses railway operations. Charles De Lano Hine was a West Point graduate, U.S. Army Major, and General Manager of the Southern Pacific and Arizona Eastern. His letters to his son, who later rose to division superintendent and railway manager, represent a unique example of turn-of-the-century Americana. The fatherly warmth and pride, coupled with an experienced railway official's wisdom and advice that was found in his first book (1904), yielded to more technical and managerial details in the second set of letters serialized in the *Railway Age Gazette* (1911) and collected and published the following year.

Part 3: from Eastern excursions to transcontinental tourism

Travelers in the U.S. wrote of such contradictions induced by the speed with which the U.S. altered its urban infrastructure to accommodate rapid transit systems. Pages from *Frank Leslie's Illustrated Newspaper* (1878) about "New York's Elevated Train" provided ample evidence of this theme. The Pennsylvania Railroad's (PR) ferry over the Hudson left a great impression on *Times* (London) correspondent George Edward Wright. He learned that Jersey City, once named Paulus Hook with a population of thirteen, was a product of thirty years of railroad expansion. Eighty-ton locomotives pulled dozens of PR passenger and freight cars over a masterfully engineered New York Division. In John Foster Fraser's largely disagreeable account of American railroad travel in the late 1890s, the author compared train service in the U.S. and UK at the turn of the twentieth century. He contrasted everything from costs and classes, conveniences and comforts, bag-checking procedures and train speeds, to the quality of sleeping berths and dining cars. Passengers aboard Pullmans had access to a barber, a library, and a typist, which might have explained how quickly the well-groomed and prolific author published his popular works. But the only aspect of American railroad conveyance he favored over British railroads was the baggage check system. He stated plainly that English corridor coaches were "rabbit hutches" compared to American cars, but the intermittent invasions of the cars by obnoxious newsboys at every U.S. station negated spatial advantages. His lengthy descriptions of the American children who hawk sundries and newspapers and the characteristics of U.S. managers on the Pennsylvania Railroad draw particular attention.

In Isabella Bird's *The Englishwoman in America*, among the best nineteenth-century travelogues, America branched out before her like the dozens of railroads simultaneously under construction. Her inimitable descriptions of Cincinnati as the City of Pigs or Porkopolis and similar characterizations of other large cities earned her huge readerships on both sides of the Atlantic. Often mistaken as a New Englander, Bird gradually grew more comfortable interacting with American passengers. She traveled through free and slave states. U.S. writer Lilian Leland traveled over 60,000 miles around the world in the mid-1880s, after which she lauded the pioneering travel writer Ida Pfeiffer and expressed gratitude for the reliable transportation of her home country. Instead of continuing directly west to San Francisco, Leland rode the Denver and Rio Grande Railroad south through the Rockies, along the Arkansas River, past the Grand Canyon, and on to Utah's Wahsatch Mountains and Salt Lake City. She furnished rich and insightful characterizations of fellow passengers, from consumptive conductor to presumptive women. She commented on polygamy and compared the "crushed and broken womanhood" of Mormons to demoralizing slavery. She found Indian families at stations on the Central Pacific both dignified and pleasant. In another travel account, Lady Howard overcame her fears to hike among sequoias and cross trestles between San Jose and Santa Cruz, California. Isabella Bird wrote another ballad of the American West with her phenomenal travelogue *A Lady's Life in the Rocky Mountains*. The letter extracted from this account detailed her travels through "God forsaken, and God forgotten" Cheyenne, and a few towns in Colorado.

American tourists rode the transcontinentals expecting to see what they heard from word-of-mouth or read in travel magazines. English-born writer and Chicagoan William H. Rideing (his real name, not a pen name) published a four-part series on "Scenery of the Pacific Railway" for the *Art Journal*. This text combined promotional artwork in the style of the early engravers of England with the detailed descriptions of exotic peoples and places along the railroads in high Victorian-era travel accounts. Rideing later participated on the Wheeler Survey expedition of Colorado and other western states. Selections from W. G. Marshall, Robert S. Minot, and J. L. Dow provide glimpses of passing travelers that in combination relate to the important themes of tourist travel in the western U.S. Arriving at Ogden, Utah, Marshall detrained to the clanging, banging, and booming of gongs announcing dinner was ready at four competing restaurants near the station. The station served the Utah Central and Central Pacific, and its clocks posted three times: local, Laramie, and San Francisco (1 hour and 16 minutes behind Ogden). Minot remarked on the benefits of expedited, *democratic* travel and impressive locomotives in the U.S. We turn to J. L. Dow for an evaluation of San Francisco's Cable Cars in the summer months of 1883. Dow was a special correspondent for the *Leader*, a newspaper in Melbourne, Australia. He traveled 10,000 miles by train from San Francisco to New York and back in just three months, summarizing the American railway system as "absolute perfection."

Part 4: railroad problems and public health in the U.S.

Shortly after the U.S. Civil War, railroads encountered a series of increasingly complex problems related to postwar reconstruction, safety, and public health that required decades of reform to resolve. Sidney Andrews' *The South since the War* (1866) introduced the prospect of repairing destroyed railroad networks in South Carolina and North Carolina in the first year of Reconstruction. Andrews toured Charleston and Columbia, where he noted complete destruction of several lines of railroad tracks within thirty- to forty-mile radii encircling the cities. The author described the first segregated train, a box freight-car with seats for Negroes and a passenger coach for whites. He also observed freed blacks ("late slaves") engaged in the recovery of their city. "If it were not for the tramcar, the pavements and the elevated railway, New York would be one of the noblest cities in the world." So said David Christie Murray before he really bit into the Big Apple's abysmal rapid transit system. *Frank Leslie's Illustrated Newspaper* showed the growing dissatisfaction with railroad travel in 1878. Other period sources focused on health issues. Public health officials faced new challenges of containing the spread of communicable microorganisms on railroads. The close quarters, lack of ventilation, and unsanitary lavatories facilitated the transmission of crowd diseases. Doctors and mainstream Americans both blamed immigrant populations. Health inspections and, if necessary, quarantines and fumigation were mandated by public health officers along the U.S.-Mexico border. To control the spread of mosquito-borne diseases such as malaria, health inspectors and railway employees tested water stops and eradicated larvae. Medical doctors also fought "consumption," tuberculosis, on California railroads, implicating Pullman conductors and Mexican peons as the primary infected carriers. William Pinkerton's semi-autobiographical account of his law enforcement activities on the western railroads captivated readers for it illustrated how emboldened stagecoach robbers grew upon the arrival of trains. *The New York Times* reported on a spate of tragic train wrecks in 1918, the year WWI ended.

Part 5: extreme encounters and the octopus

The final section on American trains as imperial geographers follows travelers Rose G. Kingsley and Richard Tangye through the harsh winters, sheer precipices, and extreme peaks of Utah, Nevada, and Alaska. Rose G. Kingsley's *South by West; or, Winter in the Rocky Mountains and Spring in Mexico* (1874) exemplified two recurring themes: Anglo and American racial contempt for Native Americans and abiding respect for the western railroad engineers who conquered the Sierra Nevada summit of 7,000 feet. Kingsley counted herself among the hopelessly unoriginal narrators to use the trope of "Indian ugliness" to elevate her own racial status in the eyes of her readers. Where other writers saw picturesque beauty in Indian women and their children wrapped in papooses, Kingsley depicted the Shoshonee at Elko Station in Utah as ugly, starving mongrels:

> Nothing has ever given me an idea of more thorough degradation than the way those Indian women clawed bits of bone and skin, and either gnawed them like wild beasts, or thrust them into their pouches, to feast on at their leisure.

Although more charitable toward the Chinese men in the same setting, Kingsley found the two races "rivalling each other in ugliness." Sir Richard Tangye utilized every derogatory racial epithet he could muster in his *Reminiscences of Travel in Australia, America, and Egypt* (1883). His account is notable for recording the subservience, alienation, and destitution of America's permanent underclasses, but he also reported on an attempted arson at one of the viaducts between Chicago and Omaha. The railroad engineer shuttled the train over the viaduct one car at a time, and it collapsed shortly thereafter. Tangye also counted over twenty cow carcasses along the Central Pacific Railroad: "on one occasion, while sitting on the steps of the Pullman car, I felt a sudden check, and immediately after the body of a cow flew past." Tangye saw the remains of a goods train that had been derailed by a bull. The section concludes with the role that trains played in the Spanish-American War. After training the First United States Volunteer Cavalry in San Antonio, Texas, Colonel Leonard Wood and Colonel Roosevelt entrained the Rough Riders and left for Tampa eager to fight in Cuba. Roosevelt related the rest of the story in his article "The Rough Riders" for *Scribner's Magazine* in 1899. The muckraking author Frank Norris wrote *The Octopus: A Story of California* to expose the negative impact that railroads had on the American West.

Part 6: the best in the world: the dominion of the Canadian Pacific Railway

Canada's Grand Trunk Railway generated interest in establishing a counterpart to the west, the Canadian Pacific Railway. The Canadian section of the collection starts with J. T. Breeze's laudatory railway poem of the GTR, which exemplified the new genre that emerged in North America. The extract from Charles Westly Busk's *Notes of a Journey from Toronto to British Columbia via the Northern Pacific Railway* (1884) showed that Canadians still relied on the U.S. railroad system to reach the Canadian Northwest. Once again, an insightful correspondent of the *Times* furnished the best reports on the CPR in the fateful year of 1886, when the last Manitoba Rebellion took place. The data-rich letters of George Edward Wright appear intermittently in this section as he traveled from east to west through the provinces of Manitoba, Alberta, the Northwest Territory, and British Columbia. Outside Port Arthur, Wright commented on the confusing switch to Central Standard Time. He balanced his account of Manitoba with a historical background of the Hudson Bay Company and detailed descriptions of the unforgiving terrain of the Laurentian and Huronian ridges. He saw countless waterways, an Ojibway (Chippewa) family starting a fire on the shores of the Savanne River, lumberjacks busily working along log-jammed rivers, and the many "mushroom frontier settlements" outside of Winnipeg. Two Manitoba Rebellions (1869–1870, 1886) did not prevent the CPR from building spur lines in six directions out of Winnipeg and other large towns. Wright's eye for detail never failed him in letters about Winnipeg, Binscarth, towns in the Northwest Territory, and Calgary.

Narratives of crossing the Canadian Selkirks resembled accounts of travelers traversing the Rocky Mountains. W. S. Caine provided snapshots of a bear hunt, sightseeing at the Selkirk range, the Stony Creek Bridge, and the snow sheds that protected the tracks, all from the comforts of the train. In *The Sister Dominions* (1896), James Francis Hogan took the train from Regina, Saskatchewan to Calgary, a distance of 500 miles. To ascend to high elevations in the Canadian Rockies, an extra engine had to be attached to his train. The scenery both inspired and intimidated him: "rushing rivers, foamy cataracts, snow, ice, and colossal rocks." In his praise for the CPR, David Christie Murray attested that there was "no better appointed carriages on any line." He called the settlers he saw west of Quebec "children of the CPR" and described a forest fire that was visible from his train. Consistent with his other travel narratives, John Foster Fraser provided counter-evidence for the CPR's sterling track record of promoting successful settlements. Beyond the small capital city of Regina (population 2000) in Saskatchewan, Fraser found railway station settlements consisting of "two rude cabins and a tent."

Part 7: *corridos* and *calaveras*: ballads of the Mexican railroads

The Mexican people accepted railroads with mixed feelings, much like traditional landowners and peasantries in other world regions. Initially, *campesinos* (peasants) and Indians understood locomotives to be useful for pilgrimages, market day, and *jornadas*, or journeys for extended periods of work. By the end of the Porfirian Era, however, railroads symbolized foreign control of the Mexican economy and the nation's dependence on foreign capital, especially from the U.S. Mexican *corridos*, or ballads, described the impact of trains during the Porfiriato and Mexican Revolution. Higinio Vazquez Santa Anna published the lyrics of renowned songs from the early 1900s. Recently, scholars Nora E. Jaffary, Edward W. Osowski, and Susie S. Porter restored memory of "The Corrido of the Electric Trains" in their outstanding collection *Mexican History: A Primary Source Reader* (2010). Susie S. Porter's elegant translation facilitates understanding among English readers of the threats that electric trollies represented in turn-of-the-century Mexico. One of the most colorful travel guides of the nineteenth century contained station-by-station descriptions of Mexico's first railway just two years after its inauguration in 1874. *Ferguson's Anecdotical Guide to Mexico* (1876) came with a map of the British-built Mexican National Railway. The U.S. Consul in Mexico City, David Hunter Strother, a celebrated American writer under the pen name Porte Crayon, kept a diary of his travels along the Mexican Central Railroad in the 1880s. The consul visited San Juan del Rio, Querétaro, Silao, Lagos, and Zacatecas, Fresnillo, Chihuahua City, and El Paso del Norte. Editor John Stealey preserved the original character of Porte Crayon's notes, which brings us into the train carriages with him to meet important Mexican figures of the time. This section also features several of the *calaveras* (playful skeletons) of the celebrated Mexican engraver José Guadalupe Posada. His broadsheets *Gran Calavera Eléctrica* and *Collision of an Electric Streetcar with a Hearse* appeared in the penny press, published newspapers, and commemorative prints at the turn of the twentieth century. This section also includes John L. Stoddard's account of the train ride from Veracruz in his *Lectures*. The government-subsidized illustrated magazine *México Moderno* published a souvenir edition of President Porfirio Díaz's visit to Coatzacoalcos and Salina Cruz on the Isthmus of Tehuantepec. Díaz and his cabinet inspected the ambitious project of Sir Weetman Pearson, the British industrialist and engineer, to construct a trans-isthmian railway to rival Ferdinand de Lesseps' Panamanian Railway. Johnson Sherrick's letters described tourist sites in Mexico City before returning by railroad to coastal Veracruz. John Kenneth Turner's heart-wrenching reports of Yaqui deportation and extermination campaigns in *Barbarous Mexico* forever blighted the record of the Díaz regime. In Robert Welles Ritchie's "The Passing of a Dictator," Díaz went into exile by fighting his way through to Veracruz port, where a steamship awaits him. Journalist John Reed provided an early participant account of the Mexican Revolution in *Insurgent Mexico*.

Part 8: sugar, coffee, and bananas: railroads in Cuba, Central America, and British Jamaica

Railroads in the Caribbean rim from the islands of Cuba and Jamaica to the Central American isthmus primarily served export-oriented economies and therefore highlighted race relations between white plantation owners and Indian and black agricultural laborers. Englishman David Turnbull mentioned the discovery of coal just outside of Havana in quantities that might replace wood-burning locomotives.

His *Travels in the West: Cuba, with Notices of Porto Rico, and the Slave Trade* has a section on the Cuban railroads. W. T. Brigham's "An Uncommercial Republic," written for *Scribner's Magazine*, dourly condemned Guatemala's trade policies and lack of infrastructural development. Nevin O. Winter's crowded Guatemalan train took fourteen hours to cover a distance of 150 miles. He vividly described the harvesting of cochineal insects for dyes, the picturesque ox-carts on dirt roads, and women food sellers at railway stations between the coast and Guatemala City. Henry R. Blaney was more optimistic about Central America's commercial future. In Costa Rica, he rode private railroads through plantations that were the property of the United Fruit Company, which hired what Blaney perceived to be "Jamaicans" from Costa Rica's Caribbean coast. Despite all the bustling activity of this foreign enclave, Blaney had no contact whatsoever with government officials. Edgar Bacon and Eugene Murray-Aaron traveled through Jamaica, where "polite colored men in military uniform" were surrounded by crowds of diverse races and skin colors. After the emancipation of black slaves, Chinese and Indian coolies migrated to Jamaica to work on sugar plantations that were largely vacated. A second generation of Asians, whites in greater numbers, and blacks of mixed complexion began appearing on railroads. Again, the writer emphasized a single export, this time logwood, which was gathered and loaded in bundles on trains.

Part 9: railroads as the Amazon in tropical Brazil

The German engineer and explorer Franz Keller embarked on a journey by steamer along the Amazon and Madeira Rivers in June 1867. Keller was commissioned by the Brazilian government to project a railway along the Madeira River, a tributary of the Amazon that took seven days of steamer travel to reach from the Atlantic coast. In 1872, just before Keller published his account, Brazil emancipated the children of slaves and opened up the Amazon to foreign steam navigation companies willing to explore, settle, and identify products for export such as cacao, timber, dye woods, resins, and most importantly rubber. European colonization and tourism, seemingly out of the question due to the recent arrival of yellow fever and cholera, were also long-term goals of the companies and of the Brazilian monarchy. Settlers began trickling into the town of San Antonio (Porto Velho) near the first impassable cataracts of the Madeira. Railway contractors and crews followed in succession. In the first selection, Keller compared white settler encroachment in Brazil and the United States. Keller was fully informed by America's remorseless frontier policy of removal, whereby railroad stations replaced Native American wigwams. In Brazil, Keller reported that settlers and railway employees similarly fell victim to the attacks of hostile groups like the Arára and Parentintin, but he urged the Brazilian government to intervene with paternalistic protection of peaceful tribes. He recommended government-built jungle stations that simulated the successes of two centuries of Jesuit missions. He also felt that selfless German settlers could carve out a living in Amazonia. Neville B. Craig participated in a later expedition down Brazil's Madeira River to San Antonio to build one of the infamous railroads of death – the "Mad Mary." American engineers and superintendents originally christened it the Mad Mary as a diminutive of the Madeira-Mamoré Railroad. But Brazilians, West Indians, and others soon called it the Devil's Railroad for the thousands of workers who died building it.

As we learned in Volume 2, Frank Vincent capably turned his travel observations into insightful anecdotes about nineteenth-century railroads in Africa. *Around and About South America: Twenty Months of Quest and Query* (1890) chronicled Vincent's journey into the Brazilian tropics. Vincent steamed and rode his way through Rio de Janeiro, Mauá, Petropolis, Sao Paulo, and Campinas, describing his adventures on the mixed-rail and cog-rail system that combined a Philadelphia locomotive, English cars, and Brazilian seats made of straw. Vincent rarely shortchanged his readers with superficial glosses of familiar-looking places; he had a trained eye for difference. In Sao Paulo, rows upon rows of coffee along the railroad lines were only interrupted by a few fields of manioc and corn. Huge manor houses occupied the centers of plantations, or *fazendas*. His writings strongly affirm neocolonial dependence on coffee exports to the U.S. Nevin O. Winter wrote about the railroad ascent to Petropolis and Minas Gerais. He corroborated much of Vincent's observations and provided new vignettes about agrarian life along the Leopoldina, Central, and Mogyana railroad lines. Colonel Francisco Schmidt reminded Winter of a feudal lord from bygone days.

Part 10: conquering *América del Sur*: railroad cultures in the river plate, Chile, and Caribbean South America

Along with the U.S. and Canada, Argentina tried to attract European immigrants in the latter half of the nineteenth century. The British-owned Central Argentine Railway Company played a role in promotion by publishing letters from English immigrants who were already making a steady living along fully operational railroads. The compilation of *Letters Concerning the Country of the Argentine Republic (South America), Being Suitable for Emigrants and Capitalists to Settle In* (1869) is one example of this promotional literature. It stands as a useful resource for demonstrating the pros and cons of Argentine commercial farming and ranching. Argentina left an indelibly positive impression on the otherwise ornery travel writer John Foster Fraser. At the height of his career, Fraser produced a travel narrative every few years. In 1910, *The Amazing Argentina* brought his experiences to readers on five continents. He devoted one chapter alone to the 20,000 miles of railways built by British companies at a cost of £20 million. The first two decades of the twentieth century ushered in the internationalization of the Latin American republics that had avoided revolutions such as the one in Mexico. The finance minister of Uruguay, Carlos María de Pena, prepared a promotional booklet, *The Oriental Republic of Uruguay at the World's Columbian Exhibition, Chicago, 1893*, to attract foreign investment from the U.S. and Europe. The term "Oriental" has a strategic double meaning in the context of a geographical and statistical compendium of places and resources in Uruguay. Exhibition organizers wanted consumers to know that Uruguay was in Eastern South America (along with the rich countries of Brazil and Argentina) as well as endowed with the commercial riches of the orient (China and India). W. H. Koebel furnished some detail about the impact of the Paraguayan War and the opening of a steam ferry across the Alto Paraná in his country study *Paraguay* (1917).

Visitors to Chile, mostly traveling in different decades, reported on the rapid development of railroads around Santiago and Valparaiso. Sometime between 1855 and 1857, Mrs. George B. Merwin (Loretta L. Wood) left New York City and arrived five weeks later in Valparaiso, Chile. Along the way, her steamship stopped at Port Royal, Jamaica to load more coals before they steamed to the Panama Railroad that conveyed them across the isthmus. The travelers then hugged the western coast of South America until reaching the Chilean port. Francis E. Clark's travel guide, the *Continent of Opportunity* (1907), narrated his ascent up the Andes to the Chilean terminus at Juncal. There, the Christ the King statue marked the transition between Chile and Argentina. Clark and eighty other passengers loaded twenty horse-drawn coaches to descend the Andes' eastern slopes. They reached Mendoza and switched to a sleeper train that traveled 650 miles in twenty-three hours to reach Buenos Aires. Johnson Sherrick of Canton, Ohio traveled in the opposite direction from Buenos Aires to Santiago. He traversed 1,000 miles of pampas, passing herds of sheep, cattle, horses, and ostriches on a "curveless railroad as level as the sea." A narrow-gauge mountain railroad aided the ascent up the eastern slope of the Andes. On the Chilean side, Johnson ran into two American acquaintances, the second of whom was the engineer John Shertzer who helped build railroads and extract nitrates in Peru before he was captured in the Pacific War.

The nations of the Andes and Caribbean South America faced challenging geographical obstacles to maritime and overland transportation. The Peruvian government completed contracts with intrepid engineers like the "American Pizarro" Henry Meiggs as a means to access highland mines and agriculture. Adolfo de Clairmont served as one of Peru's consuls in the U.S. His publication *Guide to Modern Peru: Its Great Advantages and Vast Opportunities* (1907) is reminiscent of American, Russian, and Canadian promotional literature to attract immigrants and foreign capital to the U.S. West, Siberia, and Manitoba. Marie Robinson Wright produced two important and superbly illustrated early-twentieth-century accounts of Peru and Bolivia. Edward Whymper's *Travels amongst the Great Andes of the Equator* related his tour through Ecuador. Santiago Pérez Triana was one of many young Latin Americans who embarked on a "Ride of Passage" to explore the continent, its regions, and peoples as a means to discover his own identity. Ernesto "Che" Guevara and his closest friend Alberto Granado rode a motorcycle from Buenos Aires across the Andes to the heart of the continent in the film *Motorcycle Diaries*. *Down the Orinoco in a Canoe* gave Pérez Triana a platform to express his views about the future of Venezuelan transportation. Henry Blaney visited *fin de siècle* Colombia and rode the Baranquilla Railroad and Cartagena-Magdalena Railroad. Hamilton Mercer Wright added to this journey the Santa Marta Railway to Magdalena. Fassenden Otis appropriately closes the section, volume, and collection on railway cultures with detailed observations of new communities along the Panama Railroad (1855–1914).

Notes

1 David Haward Bain, *Empire Express: Building the First Transcontinental Railroad* (New York: Penguin, 1999).
2 *Ibid.*, 3–7.
3 Leo Marx, *The Machine in the Garden: Technology and the Pastoral Ideal in America* (New York: Oxford University Press, 1964; 2nd ed., with new Afterword, 2000).
4 Michael Adas, *Dominance by Design: Technological Imperatives and America's Civilizing Mission* (Cambridge: The Belknap Press of Harvard University Press, 2006), 84.
5 John Foster Fraser, *America at Work* (London: Cassell, 1903), 125.
6 Adas, 80; Bain, 19.
7 *United States Magazine and Democratic Review* (August 1845).
8 Adas, 98–99.
9 *Public Health Reports* 1, 1472–1473.
10 Richard White, *Railroaded: The Transcontinentals and the Making of Modern America* (New York: W.W. Norton, 2011), xxi.
11 *Guns, Germs, and Steel: The Fates of Human Societies* (New York: W.W. Norton, 1997), 176–191.
12 The African continent is centered at the equator. An argument can be made that the Sahara and Sahel divide the continent into two subcontinental regions with east-west orientations. The first runs east and west from the Nile River Valley in Egypt to the desert steppes of the Maghreb in North Africa, and the second sub-Saharan plateau is traversed by several rivers running from both central coasts. Swaths of tropical woodlands, rainforests, and savannahs run east and west, a product of their equatorial orientation.
13 White, xxi.
14 *Ibid.*, xxi–xxii.
15 Rose G. Kingsley, *South by West; or, Winter in the Rocky Mountains and Spring in Mexico* (London: W. Isbister, 1874), 284.
16 Robert A. Naylor, *Penny Ante Imperialism: The Mosquito Shore and the Bay of Honduras, 1600–1914: A Case Study in British Informal Empire* (London and Toronto: Associated University Presses, 1989), 199–200, 280 fn35; Charles Stansifer, "E. George Squier and the Honduras Interoceanic Railroad Project," *Hispanic American Historical Review* 46 (1966): 1–27.
17 *Ibid.*, 201.
18 Wolfgang Schivelbusch, *The Railway Journey* (Berkeley: University of California Press, 1986), 95–96.
19 Robert G. Athearn, *Westward the Briton* (Lincoln: University of Nebraska Press, 1962), 17.
20 Isabella Bird Bishop, *The Englishwoman in America* (London: John Murray, 1856), 3.
21 Karen Morin, *Frontiers of Femininity: A New Historical Geography of the Nineteenth-Century American West* (Syracuse, NY: Syracuse University Press, 2008), 1–2, 29–30. The literature on nineteenth-century women travel writers in America is impressive. See Dea Birkett, *Spinsters Abroad: Victorian Lady Explorers* (Oxford: Basil Blackwell, 1989); Pat Barr, *A Curious Life for a Lady: The Story of Isabella Bird* (London: Macmillan, 1970); David Boorstin, "Introduction," in Isabella Bird, *A*

Lady's Life in the Rocky Mountains (Norman: University of Oklahoma Press, 1969); Dorothy Middleton, *Victorian Lady Travellers* (Chicago: Chicago Academy, 1965); Sara Mills, *Discourses of Difference: An Analysis of Women's Travel Writing and Colonialism* (London: Routledge, 1991), Alison Blunt and Gillian Rose, eds. *Writing Women and Space: Colonial and Postcolonial Geographies* (New York: Guilford Press, 1994), Susan Morgan, *Place Matters: Gendered Geography in Victorian Women's Travel Books about Southeast Asia* (New Brunswick: Rutgers University Press, 1996); and Marjorie Morgan, *National Identities and Travel in Victorian Britain* (London: Palgrave, 2001). See also Anne McClintock, *Imperial Leather: Race, Gender, and Sexuality in the Colonial Contest* (New York: Routledge, 1995); Edward Said, *Orientalism* (London: Routledge and Kegan Paul, 1978); Said, *Culture and Imperialism* (New York: Alfred A. Knopf, 1993); Brigitte Georgi-Findlay, *The Frontiers of Women's Writing: Women's Narratives and the Rhetoric of Western Expansion* (Tucson: University of Arizona Press, 1996); Shirley Foster, *Across New Worlds: Nineteenth-Century Women Travellers and Their Writings* (New York: Harvester Wheatsheaf, 1990); Krista Comer, *Landscapes of the New West: Gender and Geography in Contemporary Women's Writing* (Chapel Hill: University of North Carolina Press, 1999). Morin argued against the tide that Bird tried to distance herself from the "crass, commodified, mass tourism of the day, as well as the period's emergent 'New Woman' image." Her gender identity was produced "in place," or rather in many places of nineteenth-century America.
22. Morin, 2–3, 6.
23. *Ibid.*, 52.
24. *Ibid.*, 31.
25. *Ibid.*, 33, 38, 40.
26. David Christie Murray, *The Cockney Columbus* (London: Downey & Co., 1898), 150–156; Martha M. Allen, *Traveling West: Nineteenth Century Women on the Overland Routes* (El Paso: Texas Western Press, 1987), 7; Morin, 38.
27. *Notes of a Journey from Toronto to British Columbia via the Northern Pacific Railway, June to July 1884, Being Letters to his Sister and Mother* (London: Taylor and Francis, 1884), 14–15. See also Murray, 150–156.
28. *Ibid.*, 7–11, 25–26.
29. Morin, 38.
30. *Three Visits to America* (Edinburgh: David Douglas, 1884), 145–146. Quoted in Morin, 46.
31. Cited in Morin, 47.
32. George Edward Wright, *A Canadian Tour: A Report of Letters from the Special Correspondent of the Times* (London: George Edward Wright, 1886), 5.
33. *The World the Railways Made* (New York: Carroll & Graf, 1991), 139.
34. George Edward Wright, 57.
35. *Ibid.*, 5, front advertising section, n. p., 57–58.
36. Terry Rugeley, *Of Wonder and Wise Men* (Austin: University of Texas Press, 2001), 6–7, 25–26.
37. William H. Beezley, *Judas at the Jockey Club and Other Episodes of Porfirian Mexico* (Second ed., Lincoln: University of Nebraska Press, 2004), 71–74; "The Railroad Invasion," *Harper's Magazine* LXV, no. 389 (1882), 745.
38. Allen Wells and Gilbert M. Joseph, *Summer of Discontent, Season of Upheaval: Elite Politics and Rural Uprising in Yucatán, 1876–1915* (Stanford: Stanford University Press, 1996), 175.
39. See illustration in Beezley, 89.
40. John Hale, "Seis Meses de Residencia y Viajes en Centro América, Etc.," in Ricardo Fernández Guardia, *Costa Rica en el Siglo XIX* (San José: 1929), 27, Trans. and

quoted by Delmer G. Ross, "The Construction of the Interoceanic Railroad of Guatemala," *The Americas* 33: 3 (Jan. 1977), 430.
41 United Fruit Company (Pamphlet), Boston: n. p., 1902.
42 *New York Times*, 27 December 1927, 32.
43 Wells and Joseph, 45.
44 Adolfo Gilly, *The Mexican Revolution* (London: Verso, 1983), 31; Oscar Zanetti and Alejandro García, *Sugar and Railroads: A Cuban History, 1837–1959*, Trans. Franklin W. Knight and Mary Todd (Chapel Hill: The University of North Carolina Press, 1998).
45 Winthrop R. Wright, *British-Owned Railways in Argentina: Their Effect on the Growth of Economic Nationalism, 1854–1948* (Austin: University of Texas Press, 1974), 4–5.
46 William J. Fleming, "Profits and Visions: British Capital and Railway Construction in Argentina, 1854–1886," in Davis and Wilburn, Jr., eds., *Railway Imperialism*, 72–84.
47 Winthrop R. Wright, 5–9.
48 A. Kim Clark, *The Redemptive Work: Railways and Nation in Ecuador, 1895–1930* (Wilmington. Del.: Scholarly Resources, 1998), 196.
49 Charles W. Bergquist, *Coffee and Conflict in Colombia, 1886–1910* (Durham: Duke University Press, 1986), 26.
50 R. B. Cunninghame Graham, *Thirteen Stories* (London: Heinemann, 1901), 76–79.
51 Paul Gootenberg, *Imagining Development: Economic Ideas in Peru's "fictitious prosperity" of Guano*, 1840–1880 (Berkeley: University of California Press, 1993; *Between Silver and Guano: Commercial Policy and the State in Postindependence Peru* (Princeton: Princeton University Press, 1989).
52 C. Langdon White, "Huancayo and its Famous Indian Market in the Peruvian Andes," *The Journal of Geography* 50: 1 (Jan. 1951), 1–14.
53 Quoted in Chase S. Osborn, *The Andean Land* (South America), 2 vols. (Chicago: A. C. McClurg, 1909, I: 19–20.
54 See Todd A. Diacon, *Millenarian Vision, Capitalist Reality: Brazil's Contestado Rebellion, 1912–1916* (Durham: Duke University Press, 1991).
55 *The Amazon and Madeira Rivers. Sketches and Description from the Notebook of an Explorer*. New Edition. Philadelphia: J. B. Lippincott, 1875), 17–18.
56 Nicholas Faith, *The World the Railways Made* (New York: Carroll & Graf, 1991), 139.
57 H. M. Tomlinson, *The Sea and the Jungle* (London: Duckworth, 1913), 160–163.
58 Dawn Wiles, "Land Transportation within Ecuador, 1822–1954," (Ph.D. dissertation, Louisiana State University and Agricultural and Mechanical College, 1971), 1. Cited in Clark, 17.
59 Clark, 34–35.
60 David Wilson Del Testa, "Paint the Trains Red: Labor, Nationalism, and the Railroads in French Colonial Indochina, 1898–1945," (Ph.D. dissertation, University of California, Davis, 2001), 32.
61 Clark, 37.
62 *Ibid.*, 191.
63 *Ibid.*, 157, 159–160
64 *Ibid.*, 83–84.
65 *Ibid.*, 75, 83–92.
66 Hernán Horna, "Francisco Javier Cisneros: A Pioneer in Transportation and Economic Development in Colombia," (Ph.D. Thesis, Vanderbilt University, 1970).
67 Wolmar, *Blood, Iron, and Gold: How the Railroads Transformed the World* (New York: Public Affairs, 2010), 59. Wolmar claimed that railways cost millions of lives. See Wolmar, *The Great Railway Disaster* (Shepperton: Ian Allen, 1996); *Broken Rails: How Privatisation Wrecked Britain's Railways* (London: Aurum Press, 2001);

On the Wrong Line: How Ideology and Incompetence Wrecked Britain's Railways (London: Aurum, 2005); *Fire and Steam: How the Railways Transformed Britain* (London: Atlantic Books, 2008); and *Engines of War: How Wars Were Won and Lost on the Railways* (New York: Public Affairs, 2010).

68 Knight, *The Mexican Revolution*, I: 14.
69 Evelyn Hu-DeHart, *Yaqui Resistance and Survival: The Struggle for Land and Autonomy, 1821–1910* (Madison: University of Wisconsin Press, 1984), 196–198.
70 Census figures cited in Hu-DeHart, 195.
71 Clark, 89–90.
72 Ramón Ruiz, *Triumphs and Tragedy: A History of the Mexican People* (New York: W. W. Norton, 1992); *The People of Sonora and Yankee Capitalism* (Tucson: University of Arizona Press), 1988).
73 Moisés González Navarro, *El Porfiriato: La vida social*, in Daniel Cosío Villegas, ed., *Historia moderna de México*, IV: 188, 196; Alan Knight, *The Mexican Revolution*, 2 vols. (Cambridge: Cambridge University Press, 1986), I: 95. Conversion from 39 million hectares to 96.37 million acres.
74 Frank Norris, *The Octopus: A Story of California* (New York: Doubleday, Page, and Co., 1901), 49–50; See Leo Marx, 343–344.
75 Adas, *Dominance by Design*, 96–98, 103, 107, 112; Patricia Nelson Limerick, *The Legacy of Conquest: The Unbroken Past of the American West* (New York: Norton, 1987), 78–87, 124–133.
76 John Coatsworth, "Structures, Endowments, and Institutions in the Economic History of Latin America," *Latin American Research Review* 40: 3 (October 2005), 130–131, 143; Coatsworth, "Measuring Influence: The United States and the Mexican Peasantry," in *Rural Revolt in Mexico: U.S. Intervention and the Domain of Subaltern Politics*, edited by Daniel Nugent (Durham: Duke University Press, 1998), 68; Alan Knight, "The United States and the Mexican Peasants circa 1880–1940," in *Ibid.*, 41–43; John Mason Hart, "Social Unrest, Nationalism, and American Capital in the Mexican Countryside, 1876–1920," in *Ibid.*, 72–73.
77 Knight, *The Mexican Revolution*, I: 96.
78 This is a recurrent theme in the historical literature of the Mexican Revolution and provincial Mexico. See Alan Knight, *The Mexican Revolution*, 94–95, and the collections of Benjamin and McNellie, eds., *Other Mexicos*; Thomas Benjamin and Mark Wasserman, eds., *Provinces of the Revolution: Essays on Regional Mexican History, 1910–1929* (Albuquerque: University of New Mexico Press, 1990); Thomas Benjamin, *A Rich Land, A Poor People: Politics and Society in Modern Chiapas* (Albuquerque: University of New Mexico Press, 1989); and Dudley Ankerson, *Agrarian Warlord: Saturnino Cedillo and the Mexican Revolution in San Luís Potosí* (DeKalb: Northern Illinois University Press, 1984)
79 John Coatsworth, "Railroads, Landholding, and Agrarian Protest in the Early Porfiriato," *Hispanic American Historical Review* 54 (February 1974), 48–71. Conversion of 20 km to 12 miles.
80 Cited in Benjamin and McNellie, eds., *Other Mexicos*, 12.
81 David Pletcher, *Rails, Mines, and Progress: Seven American Promoters in Mexico, 1867–1911* (Port Washington, NY: Kennikat Press, 1972), 216.
82 Weber, *Peasants into Frenchmen*; Noguchi, "The 'One Railroad Family'", 41.
83 Paul H. Noguchi, "The 'One Railroad Family' of the Japanese National Railways: A Cultural Analysis of Japanese Industrial Familialism" (Ph.D. diss., University of Pittsburgh, 1977), 21.
84 Clark, 100, n44.
85 William E. French, "In the Path of Progress: Railroads and Moral Reform in Porfirian Mexico," in Clarence B. Davis and Kenneth E. Wilburn, Jr., eds. with Ronald Robinson, *Railway Imperialism* (New York: Greenwood Press, 1991), 93–94.

86 David M. Pletcher, "American Capital and Technology in Northwest Mexico, 1876–1911" (Ph.D. dissertation, University of Chicago, 1946), 68; Miguel Tinker Salas, *In the Shadow of the Eagle: Sonora and the Transformation of the Border during the Porfiriato* (Berkeley: University of California Press, 1997), 136–137.
87 See Chapter "Western Travel Facilities" in Athearn, especially 20–21.
88 Anton Rosenthal, comment at session entitled "It's Not Laissez-Faire: Peasant and Worker Resistance in Latin America and the World," Rocky Mountain Council on Latin American Studies Meeting in Santa Fe, New Mexico, April 8, 2011.
89 Clark, *The Redemptive Work*, 187–190.
90 Friedrich Katz and Jane Dale Lloyd, "Introducción," in *Porfirio Díaz frente al descontento popular regional* (1891–1893) (México: Universidad Iberoamericana, 1986), 14–15.
91 Knight, "The United States and the Mexican Peasantry," 59.
92 See Paul Friedrich, *Agrarian Revolt in a Mexican Village* (Englewood Cliffs, N.J.: Prentice-Hall, 1970), 43–44; Daniela Spenser, "Soconusco: The Formation of a Coffee Economy in Chiapas," in Benjamin and McNellie, eds., *Other Mexicos*, 138, 143fn63. In 1895, Soconusco's population of 30,333 produced 185,000 hectoliters of maize; by 1909, with a population of 36,631, maize production fell to only 48,223 hectoliters. According to Spenser, this shortfall forced residents to purchase expensive imported corn when the cost of living soared and wages remained static; John H. Coatsworth, *Growth Against Development: The Economic Impact of Railroads in Porfirian Mexico* (DeKalb: Northern Illinois University Press, 1981), 173–174, *passim*.
93 Mark Wasserman, *Everyday Life in Nineteenth Century Mexico* (Albuquerque: University of New Mexico Press), 179.
94 Benjamin and McNellie, eds., *Other Mexicos*, 12.
95 Coatsworth borrows this from Albert Fishlow, *American Railroads and the Transformation of the Antebellum Economy* (Cambridge: Harvard University Press, 1965), Chapter 4; Coatsworth, *Growth Against Development*, 174.
96 Ankerson, *Agrarian Warlord*, 10, 15–16; Knight, *The Mexican Revolution*, I: 118.
97 Coatsworth, "Railroads, Landholding, and Agrarian Protest in the Early Porfiriato," 62–63; Knight, *The Mexican Revolution*, I: 106.
98 David LaFrance, "Many Causes, Movements, Failures, 1910–1913: The Regional Nature of Maderismo," in Benjamin and Wasserman, eds., *Provinces of the Revolution*, 20, 24, 34.
99 Wasserman, *Everyday Life in Nineteenth Century Mexico*, 174.
100 Coatsworth, "Structures, Endowments, and Institutions" 143; "Measuring Influence," 68–69. See also John H. Coatsworth, *Growth Against Development;* "Railroads, Landholding, and Agrarian Protest in the Early Porfiriato," 48–71; "Indispensable Railroads in a Backward Economy: The Case of Mexico," *Journal of Economic History* 39: 4 (December 1979): 939–960; "Patterns of Rural Rebellion in Latin America: Mexico in Comparative Perspective," in *Riot, Rebellion, and Revolution: Rural Social Conflict in Mexico*, ed. Friedrich Katz (Princeton: Princeton University Press, 1988), 21–62; *Latin America and the World Economy Since 1800* (Cambridge: Harvard University Press, 1998).
101 Coatsworth, "Railroads, Landholding, and Agrarian Protest," 59.
102 Friedrich Katz, "Pancho Villa, Peasant Movements, and Agrarian Reform in Northern Mexico," in Caudillo and Peasant in the Mexican Revolution, Ed. by D. A. Brading (Cambridge: Cambridge University Press, 1980), 61.
103 Jane-Dale Lloyd, "Rancheros and Rebellion: The Case of Northwestern Chihuahua, 1905–1909," in *Rural Revolt in Mexico: U.S. Intervention and the Domain of Subaltern Politics*, edited by Daniel Nugent (Durham: Duke University Press, 1998), 107–110.

104 Mark Wasserman, "Chihuahua: Family, Power, Foreign Enterprise, and National Control, in Benjamin and McNellie, ed., *Other Mexicos*, 48.
105 Paul J. Vanderwood, *The Power of God against the Guns of Government: Religious Upheaval in Mexico at the Turn of the Nineteenth Century* (Stanford: Stanford University Press, 1998); Alan Knight, *The Mexican Revolution*, I: 119; John Mason Hart, *Revolutionary Mexico: The Coming and Process of the Mexican Revolution* (Berkeley: University of California, 1987), 44, 131.
106 Hu-DeHart, Yaqui Resistance and Survival, 11, 204–205; Knight, "The United States and the Mexican Peasants," 45.
107 Moisés González Navarro, *Raza y Tierra*, 205–206; Gilbert M. Joseph, *Revolution from Without: Yucatán, Mexico, and the United States, 1880–1924* (Cambridge: Cambridge University Press, 1982), 75.
108 Hu-DeHart, Yaqui Resistance and Survival, 105–115.
109 Wolmar, *Engines of War*, 13, 90, 93.
110 Robert H. Holden, *Mexico and the Survey of Public Lands: The Management of Modernization* (DeKalb: Northern Illinois University Press, 1994); Wasserman, *Everyday Life in Nineteenth Century Mexico*, 170, 187; Hu-DeHart, *Yaqui Resistance and Survival*, 100, 159.
111 Tinker Salas, *In the Shadow of the Eagle*, 127–128, 133–134.
112 Evelyn Hu-DeHart, "Sonora: Indians and Immigrants on a Developing Frontier," 182.
113 *Memoria of the Secretaría de Fomento*, 1877–82 3: 553–55, 374–77, cited in Coatsworth, *Growth against Development*, 170–171.
114 Hu-DeHart, "Sonora: Indians and Immigrants on a Developing Frontier," 182.
115 Hu-DeHart, "Development and Rural Rebellion," 80–83; *Yaqui Resistance and Survival*, 113–123, 143, 147, 167.
116 Hu-DeHart, "Sonora: Indians and Immigrants on a Developing Frontier," 181–189; "Development and Rural Rebellion," 86.
117 John Kenneth Turner, *Barbarous Mexico* (Chicago: C. H. Kerr, 1910).
118 Hu-DeHart, *Yaqui Resistance and Survival*, 171, 188.
119 Hu-DeHart, "Development and Rural Rebellion," 81–84, quote is on 83–84. See also *Yaqui Resistance and Survival*, 167.
120 Cited in Hu-DeHart, "Development and Rural Rebellion," 88, fn61.
121 *Ibid.*, 91; Hu-DeHart, *Yaqui Resistance and Survival*, 182.
122 Hart, *Empire and Revolution*, 122
123 *Ibid.*, 45, 326–327, quote on 491.
124 Joseph, *Revolution from Without*, 34. Track mileage converted from km.
125 Cited in Coatsworth, *Growth Against Development*, 171; See also Coatsworth, "Railroads, Landholding, and Agrarian Protest," 68.
126 Daniel Traconis to Díaz, September 18, 1891, *Colección Porfirio Díaz* (hereafter cited as CPD followed by legajo, caja, and document numbers, Universidad Iberoamericana) 16: 23: 011358; Coatsworth, "Railroads, Landholding, and Agrarian Protest," 69; Wells, "All in the Family," 172; Dumond, *The Machete and the Cross*, 387–388.
127 Allen Wells, "All in the Family: Railroads and Henequen Monoculture in Porfirian Yucatán," *Hispanic American Historical Review* 72, no. 2 (May 1992), 159–209.
128 Nelson Reed, *The Caste War of Yucatán* (Stanford: Stanford University Press, 1964), 7–8, 235; Moisés González Navarro, *Raza y tierra: La guerra de castas y el hénequen* (México: El Colegio de México, 1970), 192; Coatsworth, *Growth Against Development*, 171–172, fn74.
129 Report of José Arjona (copy of the hacendados' version) CPD 16: 21: 010206; Manuel Vega to Porfirio Díaz, September 15, 1891, CPD 16: 24: 011679; Daniel Traconis to

Díaz, September 18, 1891, CPD 16: 23: 011358; Traconis to Díaz, September 24, 1891, 16: caja not identified: 013075. All documents reproduced in Friedrich Katz and Jane Dale Lloyd, eds., *Porfirio Díaz frente al descontento popular regional (1891–1893): antología documental* (Mexico: Universidad Iberoamericana, 1986), 206–214; Allen Wells, "All in the Family," 172. Wells relied on letters between the governors of Campeche and Yucatán, Machado and Cantón found in the Yucatán state archives as well as *El Eco del Comercio*, September 15 and 26, 1891. Moisés González Navarro, *Raza y Tierra*, 192; Alfonso Villa Rojas, *The Maya of East Central Quintana Roo* (Washington D.C.: Carnegie Institute of Washington, 1945), 26. See also Wells, *Yucatán's Gilded Age*, 103–4, n. 27.

130 Wells and Joseph, *Summer of Discontent, Seasons of Upheaval*, 179.
131 The historical literature on the Caste War is rich and vast, with several authoritative works readily available in both English and Spanish. See the works of Allen Wells and Gilbert M. Joseph, as well as Villa Rojas; Reed, *The Caste War*; Moises González Navarro, *Raza y tierra: La Guerra de Castas y el henequén* (México: El Colegio de México, 1970); Terry Rugeley, *Yucatán's Maya Peasantry and the Origins of the Caste War* (Austin: University of Texas Press, 1996), *Rebellion Now and Forever: Mayas, Hispanics, and Caste War Violence in Yucatán, 1800–1880* (Stanford: Stanford University Press, 2009); Don E. Dumond, *The Machete and the Cross*; Victoria Reifler Bricker, *The Indian Christ, the Indian King: the Historical Substrate of Maya Myth and Ritual* (Austin: University of Texas Press, 1981), 87–117.
132 Reed, 283–306. Quote is on p. 283.
133 Villa Rojas, 20; D. E. Dumond, "Competition, Cooperation, and the Folk Society," *Southwestern Journal of Anthropology* 46, no.3 (Autumn 1970), 271; González Navarro, *Raza y Tierra*, 216.
134 Gilbert Joseph, *Rediscovering the Past at Mexico's Periphery: Essays on the History of Modern Yucatán* (Tuscaloosa: University of Alabama Press, 1986), 51–52; Gilbert M. Joseph and Allen Wells, "Yucatán: Elite Politics and Rural Insurgency," in Benjamin and Wasserman, eds., *Provinces of the Revolution*, 112; Allen Wells, *Yucatán's Gilded Age*, 157, n.17.
135 Wells and Joseph, *Summer of Discontent, Seasons of Upheaval*, 51.
136 Dumond, *The Machete and the Cross*, 384–386.
137 Bergquist, 26, fn.4, 67, 133, 138.
138 Dumond, *The Machete and the Cross*, 389, 528 fn.4. Dumond found this testimony among British Colonial Office documents in the Public Record Office, London and Kew. It was found in a confidential dispatch from the commissioner of the northern district of British Honduras Robert W. Pickwood, who met with rebel leaders in October.
139 Cited in Allen Wells and Gilbert M. Joseph, *Summer of Discontent, Seasons of Upheaval*, 46.
140 Dumond, *The Machete and the Cross*, 393. Reported in the *Revista de Mérida*, February 23, 1900, 2.
141 Dumond, *The Machete and the Cross*, 394.
142 *Ibid.*
143 González Navarro, *Raza y Tierra*, 219.
144 Dumond, *The Machete and the Cross*, 397.
145 Oscar A. Forero and Michael R. Redclift, "The Role of the Mexican State in the Development of Chicle Extraction in Yucatán, and the Continuing Importance of Coyotaje," *Journal of Latin American Studies* 38, no. 1 (February 2006), 72; Alfonso Villa Rojas, 30.
146 Villa Rojas, 29–30.
147 Reed, 307.

148 Forero and Redclift, "The Role of the Mexican State in the Development of Chicle Extraction in Yucatán," 73.
149 Hector Aguilar Camin, "The Relevant Tradition: Sonoran Leaders in the Revolution," in D.A. Brading, ed., *Caudillo and Peasant*, 93.
150 David G. LaFrance, *The Mexican Revolution in Puebla, 1908–1913: The Maderista Movement and the Failure of Liberal Reform* (Wilmington: SR Books, 1984), 47, 63, 72, 79–80, 187.
151 Louis A. Perez, Jr., "Some Military Aspects of the Mexican Revolution, 1910–1911," *Military Affairs* 43, no. 4 (December 1979), 192–193.
152 Zanetti, 163–165, 168–179.
153 *Ibid.*, 166, 179–193.
154 *The Machine in the Garden*, 6.
155 *Ibid.*, 19.
156 *Ibid.*, 208.
157 *Ibid.*, 210.
158 Amy G. Richter, *Home on the Rails: Women, the Railroad, and the Rise of Public Domesticity* (Chapel Hill: University of North Carolina Press, 2005), 36.
159 Leo Marx, 195.
160 *The Age of Extremes: A History of the World, 1914–1991* (New York: Pantheon Books, 1994).
161 Karl Marx, *A Contribution to the Critique of Political Economy*, Trans. N. I. Stone (Chicago: Charles H Kerr, 1904), 13.

Part 1

AMERICA THE PERILOUS
Cultures of speed, equality,
and freedom in the United States

1

EDWARD HUNGERFORD, 'GETTING THE TRAFFIC THROUGH', *HARPER'S MAGAZINE* 119, 1909, 876–887

THE railroad is a monster – his feet are dipped into the navigable seas and his many arms reach into the uplands. His fingers clutch the treasures of the hills—coal, iron, timber—all the wealth of Mother Earth. His busy hands touch the broad prairies—corn, wheat, fruits—the yearly produce of the land. With ceaseless activity he brings the raw products that they may be made into the finished. He centralizes industry. He fills the ships that sail the seas. He brings the remote town in quick touch with the busy city. He stimulates life. He makes life.

His arms stretch through the towns and over the land. His steel muscles reach across great rivers and deep valleys, his tireless hands have long since burrowed their way through God's eternal hills. He is here, there, everywhere. His great life is part and parcel of the great life of the nation.

He reaches an arm into an unknown country and it is known! Great tracts of land that were untraversed become farms, hillsides yield up their mineral treasure, a busy town springs into life where there was no habitation of man a little time before, the town becomes the city, Commerce is born. The railroad bids death and stagnation begone. It creates. It reaches forth with its life, and life is born.

The railroad is life itself!

My train departed from no gay terminal. Instead I found my way to a railroad yard that stretched its length along the waterside of the city. It was three o'clock in the morning, and the city was as quiet as ever a big city becomes. The clocks in its towers were solemnly speaking the triple hour, and the only noise that came from its streets was the occasional rumble of carriage-folk returning from an evening's gayety, or the many wagons bringing the city's food and drink for the morrow. The electric lights blinked brightly in long vistas. The houses, the hotels, and the apartments were mere black bulks. Only here and there a single lighted window showed that a great city never sleeps.

My train had no fanfare to precede its departure. There was no lighted bulletin to denote it, no important and liveried functionary to demand my right to board, none of the delightfully human business of farewells about its entrances. Instead a huge hulk of a locomotive, a hundred tons in weight upon the rail, sidled up to a string of freight cars, hidden between other and almost entirely similar strings of freight cars, there were shouted orders, waving of distant lanterns, and we were off—off with mighty creakings and jerkings. We were no longer a mere string of cars in the waterside yard, we were PK-5, if you please, a preference freight bound across the continent, and a train entitled to more than an ordinary measure of respect.

Collins, the conductor for the first part of PK-5's run, looked at me suspiciously, at my orders wonderingly. He had a natural suspicion of strangers. Passengers are not wanted on freight trains. When they come they receive no cordial welcome. The railroad hires detectives to ferret them out from under trucks and the like, and the men along the line regard them as their natural enemies. They told of one man over on the Middle Division who had a record for throwing tramps off coal trains so that they would strike against telegraph poles every time—quite a feat, coming down a mountainside at forty miles an hour. In justice to the brakeman it might be added that the probabilities are that if he had not been quick in his way, the tramps would have done the throwing in most cases. The whole record of the freight service is a record of unending guerrilla warfare between the railroad men and the tramps.

But my credentials were unimpeachable. I could see that from Collins' face as he held his lantern over them—he would not even let me into his caboose until his own mind was set. After that there was barely time to jump. The jerkings had begun, and PK-5 had been thrilled by her great engine into animation.

"You won't find our hack any fancy place," said he. "We've had it nine years now, and it seems kind of homelike to us after all that time."

The "we" consisted of Collins and his rear brakeman. The forward brakeman, who was held responsible for the front half of the train, had his headquarters in the cab of the locomotive. The brakemen were supposed to be out upon the tops of the cars when we passed stations, and also on the steep mountain grades, where entire reliance is not placed upon the air-brakes. This is jolly business in summer, but there are times in winter when it is something less—when wind and sleet and cold combine to make the life a difficult thing.

At such times it was comfort for the rear man to get back into the "hack." It *was* a home-like place, snugly warmed by a red-hot stove fixed in the corner, and lined with bunks made into beds. Pullman fashion; only never was there a Pullman that gave you less sense of the impressive and a greater sense of a snug cabin. Squarely placed in its centre was a sort of wooden pyramid or mountain, and the steps up this led to the lookout where by day the long snaky train and the sweep of the surrounding country were to be seen.

Collins offered an apology for his mountain. "Kind of old-fashioned, that," he stammered out. "The las' time I had the cabin in to the shops for overhaulin' they offered to take it out and put in the ladders, but I says 'no,' and this is why":

One by one he lifted its steps. It was a mountain built of a set of lockers, a regular treasure-house of railroad necessities. There were all sorts of ropes and jacks and wrenches, extra parts, against every emergency. There was a foodcloset and another locker filled with neat stacks of stationery.

"They give us more forms to fill out now than the Superintendent's office used to get twenty years ago," he growled. "I spend more than half my time at that desk."

The clerical work on PK-5 was considerable. Collins had to keep all the way-bills of his train—sixty cars, more than a quarter of a million dollars in merchandise—and if he made a serious error it was apt to cost him his job, despite a good long term of service. He wrote a neat hand—he was a quiet, thoughtful man, after the way of railroad men—and his records, like his caboose, were kept in shipshape fashion. Like every other one of his kind, he was a careful student of the ethics and practices of railroad management and operation. He had his own ideas on each of these, and when you got to them they were good ideas. Of such as he railroad executives are made in America every year.

It took a long time before we were clear of the terminal yard, apparently an endless thing; a shadowy tangle of rails and switches underneath, overhead an ever-changing kaleidoscope of colored signal lamps. Off at the left were the docks and the elevators where the railroad giant really came into close touch with the wanderers of the sea, and where under gleaming, hissing arcs the transfer of freight from cars to ships went forward day and night. At the right the city rose above the din and confusion of the railroad yard. A squat roundhouse, like a giant cruller, sent its smoke and gases up under the windows of many-storied apartments. The railroad hung tenaciously to every inch of its water-front yard. The town crowded hard against it.

When we were clear of the city as I had known it, there were still more yards, and the point where we were to be admitted to the main line. We halted for a moment, a procedure of endless bumps and reports, the rumbling of the car-couplings coming along the train like gun-echoes repeating in a deep cañon. I heard those rumblings, should have heard the cautionary whistlings of our locomotive, did not, and was nearly pitched through the lookout window when the air-shock reached the caboose. That struck Collins' sense of the ridiculous.

"You want to keep yerself braced," was his tardy advice. He was showing me a badly bruised eye that all the time I had accredited to some unruly train-hand. "I went all the way through that window las' week. They ain't got the preference freights runnin' as slick as the limited yet."

A passenger train, her sleeping-cars black and only showing dim lights in monitors and at vestibules, swept proudly past us. When its red lights at the rear of the last sleeper grew faint, friendly signals were shown us, our engineer tooted his acknowledgment quite gayly, and we were off up the main line. My watch showed me that we had lost some twenty-five minutes there at the outer gate of the city. A little later I found that we were due to lose time all the way up the run. There seemed to be no end of things that might halt PK-5, and I asked Collins how they ever stuck to the schedule. He laughed again. It seemed to be tonic to him to have a passenger in his tidy caboose.

"Schedule?" he repeated. "It's a joke. They give us a time to get out on, an' then one of them bright office-boys gets a figure out of his head an' puts it down for an arrivin' time. He never hits on it, never expects to. So more an' more they're gettin' to move this freight on special orders. They can regulate it better then, accordin' to volume. Mos' of the men carries the schedule of the fas' freights in their domes. The coarse tonnage stuff don't even get special orders. When there is enough of it to make a train, they get an engine out o' the roundhouse, give the train the engine number, and start off. In big times they may do that every fifteen minutes; slack times, they may be lucky if they do it twice in twenty-four hours. Railroad traffic, along the freight end, follows business conditions mighty close."

That was a long speech for Collins, and he silently set to work making supper, or breakfast—call it what you will—on the stove in the corner of the caboose.

It was broad daylight when we halted at a junction across a frozen river from a city. The city was set upon a steep hillside, and its houses rose from the river in even terraces. At the top a great domed structure, the State House, crowned it. It was a still, winter's morning, and the smoke from all the chimney-pots extended straight heavenward. We waited patiently upon a long siding until everything else had been moved—through fast expresses, heavily laden with opulent-looking Pullmans, jerky little suburban trains, long "draughts" of empty coaches being drawn by consequential passenger switch-engines in and out of the train-shed of the passenger station. Finally a certain semaphore blade dropped, and we began pulling around a sharp curve across the river, clear of the station with its confusion of business, through and almost past the city to still another yard. That was our first resting-place, the ending-point of the initial division of the trip. Before PK-5 should resume its trip, the train would be torn apart and set together anew, there would be a new engine and crew to haul it, another caboose and conductor swung on behind.

Collins introduced me to Sam Jones, the yard-master there.

"If you want types, size up Jones," said he. "He's a type of railroad man; the type that are getting frozen out now, thank God!"

Jones was the autocrat of that busy yard. In dull times it was busy and he without a moment to spare. When the factory wheels were turning all night and the traffic flowing through that floodgate of railroad activity Jones was super-man. Night, day—day, night, Jones was the autocrat. The dust grew thick upon his books, his desk lid was not raised for a week at a time, but he was out in his domain, urging, cursing, shoving, keeping the switching crews hard at it, taking a hand himself in clearing the yard—Jones was something of a railroad executive and very little human.

Just now the yard was running at low tide, there were plenty of men handy, and engines "white-leaded" and standing in the roundhouse waiting for good times once more, and Jones was half human. He began telling me something of the work that was done within his domain.

"Ef it was only changin' engines an' crews it wouldn't be so bad a trick," he told me, "but, say—that transfer house!"

Now here was a phase of railroad energy. I found my way to a gaunt freight house, to whose doors no truck had ever backed, and which was hemmed in by many rows of sidings and of sheds. In this structure one of the busiest functions of the whole transportation business went forth by day and by night.

You ship a box—sixty pounds to a hundred pounds—from Wilkesharre, Pennsylvania, to Berlin, Wisconsin. Here comes another box from Watertown, New York, to Norfolk, Virginia. A third is bound from Easthampton, Massachusetts, to Chillicothe, Ohio; a fourth from Terra Haute, Indiana, to Plainfield, New Jersey, and so on, *ad infinitum*. You can readily see how in such cases the railroads have a problem in freight that closely approximates that of the government mail service. Ten thousand currents and cross-currents of merchandise rising here and there and everywhere, and crossing and recrossing on their way to destination, make a puzzle that does not cease when the rate-sheet experts have finished their difficult work.

If all this freight might be expressed in even multiples of cars the problem would not be quite so appalling. But your box is a hundred pounds weight—less, perhaps. From its destination it goes with other boxes in a car to the nearest transfer point. It is known to the traffic men as "LCL," which is readily translated "less than car-load lot." At the transfer house the car in which it is placed is drilled quickly into an infreight track, seals are broken, doors opened, and reassorting begins. The transfer house is roomy and systematic. If it were anything less it would resemble chaos.

But the chief freight points of that particular system and its connecting points have regular stands, upon which nightly are placed cars bound for these points. Each city—in the case of a large city each freight house—each transfer point, has a number, and its through car stands opposite that number. When the in-freight arrives and is unloaded piece by piece, a checker, who is nothing less than an animated guide-book, gives each its proper number, and it is promptly trucked off to the waiting car. It is mail-sorting on a Titanic scale.

Nor is this an absolute order. Certain towns demand an occasional through car from time to time, and a car must be assigned number and place at the transfer house against such emergencies. Sometimes there is enough freight to more than fill the car allotted to any given point, and then one of Jones' switching crews must drill that out and find another empty to replace it. Beyond that, Jones' superiors are all the time demanding that he show judgment in picking the cars to be filled.

When a freight car gets off the system to which it belongs it collects forfeits from the other lines over which it passes if they do not expedite its passage, and this the railroaders know as "per diem." The great trick in operation is to keep "per diem" down, and so the "foreign" cars, so called, must be promptly returned to their home roads.

"We load out of the transfer house a through car over the Northwestern from Chicago every day," Jones explains. "It's up to me to have a Northwestern empty for that when I can. When I can't I do the best I can." He scratched his head. "Perhaps I'll use a Canadian Pacific, and so get her started along toward home. If not, something from the Sault, just as I am going to start that New Haven car over toward Connecticut to-night. If I was to send that New Haven out beyond

Chicago there'd be trouble, and I've got to dig out something empty from the Boston and Maine to take that stuff over to Lowell. Mos' generally, though, when we've got a turn of Western stuff, I've got my 'empty' tracks stuffed full o' them New England cars."

I mentioned something about the transfer house being a mighty good thing. Jones corrected me.

"It's a necessary evil," he said, "an' lots of times I wish that we didn't have it here."

He took a fresh chew of tobacco and started to explain. "See here. We got near a car-load of that fancy porcelain brick through from Haverstraw las' week, and that young whelp of a college boy that's hangin' round here learnin' the railroad business gets it into his noodle that it's somethin' awful, awful for that stuff to be goin' through to middle Ohio in a Maine Central box, an 'LCL' at that. So out he dumps it into a system car right here an' now, and saves the road about one dollar and fifty cents per diem. Of course we pays about one hundred and thirty-five dollars for damages to that brick in the transferrin'. But the boy's all right in the transfer house. If he was out on the engine he might blow up the b'iler."

Jones was telling how judgment counts, how judgment is the thing in railroading. A few hours later a veteran engineer was complaining that he had no opportunity under the operating scheme of the railroad to use anything that even approached judgment.

There came over me, as I sat in the caboose that evening, a wild desire to ride with the engineer in the cab. Planning to slip ahead along the half-mile or so of train at the first stop, I made known my desire to our conductor over that part of the run.

"They'll be glad to see you," he told me. "You won't have any trouble gettin' there. It's a mild evening'." He swung open the window of the lookout and called to his rear brakeman, "Jimmie, run along with this here party." Jimmie pulled me through the window of the lookout before I clearly realized the entire plan.

It was a slippery path over the roofs of sixty cars to the big engine that was pulling us, and the wind that swept in from the shores of the ice-bound lake, along which the tracks ran for many miles, snapped sharply over those car roofs. Jimmie hung on to his lantern with one hand, to his convoy with the other. Long miles over those slippery car roofs had taught him to regard it as no very serious business.

"This ain't nothin'," was his assurance. "It sometimes gets nasty when we get down to zero an' a blizzard comes a-rippin' from off over the lake. Sometimes you have to get down an' crawl on all-fours. It wouldn't be much fun to be swept off the tops of those cars."

There was no disputing that; nor that the three lengthwise planks at the gable of the car roofs were not wide promenades. You jump from one to another to cross from car to car, and a man has got to have something of a gymnastic training, and some circus as well as railroad blood in his veins, to do it many times without dropping into one of the hideous dark abysses between them.

A hand out of the dark slapped me in the face. "Drop," said Jimmie, and fearing possibly that I might not obey, he pulled me flat down upon the car roof.

"That was a 'telltale'!" he explained, and before I could ask further we were in a short reach of tunnel, and I understood. We were whirled through that tunnel like a package in a tube, and if we had raised our arms we could have touched the flying roof of the bore. The smoke lay heavy in the place; it filled our eyes and nostrils.

"Not real nice," said Jimmie, cheerily. "But no danger in the holes, save now and then an icicle gets a crack at your nut. You see there ain't much use in arguin' the matter after that 'telltale' strikes you."

After that I came to have more respect for the "telltales," those long gallows-like strips of heavy fringe that warn "low bridge" to the forgetful trainman on top of the cars.

The engine was not clean and gayly trimmed like a passenger-hauler. She was big and she was overpoweringly dirty, but the fireman said that he did not care about that.

"They keep on jumpin' up the size of the fire-box on us," was his plaint, "an' I'm busy enough feedin' her old stummick 'thout cuttin' any other didoes roun' the machine."

"That's the trouble with him," laughed his cabmate. "He's out of the division shops an' afraid of hard work. He's the last one for me. I'd rather break in the little farm-boys to fire for me. I like to take hold of them when they come in here with the barnyard mud on their boots."

To this the fireman said nothing, but pulled the chain out of his fire-box door and spread a shovelful of coal upon the raging blaze within. When we started from the terminal we held ten tons of soft coal in our rangy tender. At the far end of the division there would be less than a ton remaining. If you think it is an easy task to handle nine tons of coal, steadily, shovelful upon shovelful, five hours and a half, you are entitled to the experiment. Add to that the finding of a foothold upon a careening engine floor, and you have still more of an experiment. When we rocked a little more than usual round about one sharp curve, the shovelful of coal went flying out into the night between tender and caboose. That was a mighty joke. I asked the fireman if there was no danger that he might go with the coal.

"I always catch the guard-chain," he grinned at me.

There was less talking from the man with his hand at the throttle. He could not shout more than a mere word at a time across the tumult of the craft, and so we were all silent for many and many a cross-country mile, snarling sullenly through bridge spans and tunnels, clattering briskly along the sides of long rows of standing cars, every now and then an eye of fire poking out of the darkness just ahead, flaming into a glare of headlight, then the rush and swish of the opposite train past us, followed by the pelting of cinders upon the cab roof—for long hours at a time we kept our speed up. We did not pause for water; we would only slacken ever and ever so little at the pumping-stations while the fireman dropped the tender scoop of the thirsty engine into the reach of track tank. For sixty seconds there would be a mighty splashing round the tender, and then the fireman would look at his water-gauge and say that it was all right.

After that, glance into the night once again. Ahead is a long stretch of straight track and the monotonous reach of signal lights, protecting the blocks into which the line is divided for safe operation. Each should spell yellow and safety before the train passes it, and the engineer reads the signal for repetition to his fireman as a safety precaution. But when the lamp reads red at a single block he does not stop, only slackens the speed of his train.

"A man would be a fool if he came to a dead stop on a straight line," he complains to you afterward, "when he can see with his own eyes his track clear ahead to the next block and that reading safety."

"A red light a red light always," you may return to him.

"They don't allow you no leeway for judgment," he continues. "They seem to think that you must follow that rule-book blindly, and that a man is going to ditch his train a-purpose. Moreover, if you're running passenger—any one of the high-class trains—and follow the rule-book to a 'T,' not using any judgment, you're not a-goin' to make your schedule, and after a while the boss will be askin' you the why of it. Then you've got to make your schedule or you'll find yourself changed from your swell run. They won't say the real why, but the boss has been using judgment. You get that point?"

It is not an agreeable topic for any railroader, and he quickly changes it. He evidences real pride in "the road."

"If all the rolling-stock on this system were piled up end to end on one track it would stretch from New York to Milwaukee and a little beyond. There's a heap of power on this road."

"Where did you get that?" you ask him. He is insulted.

"I worked it out from the annual report," he tells you.

You have not done credit enough to the intelligence of the American railroad engineer. If you were to ask him about the theory and the practices of English and Continental railroading, he would probably give you intelligent answers. The railroad employs no poor grade of labor in its operation.

Here is another great railroad yard—this almost filling a mighty crevice between God's eternal hills. This is within the mountain country, and the gossip that you get around the roundhouse is all of grades—you hear how Smith and the 2999 pulled seven Pullmans around the Saddleback without a pusher; how some of the big preference freights take four engines to mount the summit; the tales of daring are tales of pushers and of trains breaking apart on the fearful climbing stretches.

Randall is yard-master, and you could put Sam Jones' yard in one corner of this preserve of Randall's. Randall is the antithesis of Jones. He is everything that Jones is not, and a capital railroader besides. He does not swear; he does not get excited; his system of administration is so perfectly devised that even in a stress he never has to turn to work with his own hands. With him railroading is a fine, practical science. He will tell you of the methods at Collinwood, at Altoona, at Buffalo—wherein they differ. He is cool, calculating, clever, the measure of a fine man.

You speak of his yard as being something overwhelmingly big. He answers in his deliberate way: "We've more than two hundred miles of track in this yard; something more than a thousand switches to operate it."

Then he takes you down from his elevated office in an abandoned tower looking down over his domains. He explains with great care that, his yard being a main-line division point and not a point with many intersecting branches or "foreign" roads, its transfer house is inconsequential. The same process of classification that goes forward with the package freight in the transfer house Randall carries on in the outside yard with the cars. These operations are separated for east-bound and west-bound freight, and each is given an entirely separate yard, easily reached from the roundhouse that holds the freight motive power of the system. Randall's, being an unusually big yard further divides these activities into separate yards for loaded and empty cars bound in each direction over the main line.

I followed him to the nearest operating point—the west-bound classification yard for loaded cars. In the old days this was a broad flat reach of a score of parallel tracks, terminating at either end in an approach of lead track. Upon each set of three or four tracks a switch-engine was busy drilling cars in the eternal classification process. In these more modern days the "hump," or gravity yard, has come into its own. Half of the work of the switch-engines is done by gravity, and this new type of yard has an artificial hill, just above the termination of the tracks, where they cluster together, and upon this "hump" one switch-engine with an especially trained crew does the work of six engines and crews in the old-type yard.

Another preference freight, of similar claim as that PK-5 which brought me into the Middle West, rolls in to the receiving yard for the west-bound classification. Its engine uncouples and steams off for a well-earned rest in the smoky roundhouse. A switch-engine uncouples the caboose that has been tacked on behind over the division, and it is shunted off on to the near-by caboose track, where its crew will have close oversight over it—perhaps sleep in it—until it is ready to convoy some east-bound freight a few hours hence.

Blue flags—blue lights at night—are fastened at each end of the dismantled cars, and the inspectors have a quarter of an hour to make sure if the equipment is in good order. If a car is found with broken running-gear it is marked and soon after drilled out from its fellows, sent to the transfer house to have its contents removed, to the shops for repairs, or the "cripple" track for junk, if its case be well-nigh hopeless.

With the "O. K." of the car inspectors finally pronounced, the train that was comes up to the hump, and the expert crew that operates there makes short work of sorting out the cars—this track for "stuff" southwest of Pittsburg, this next for Cleveland and Chicago, the third for transcontinental, and so it goes. Two lines of cars are drilled at the same time, for just ahead of the switch-engine is an open-platform car, known as the "pole-car," and by means of heavy timbers the "pole-man" guides two rows of heavy cars down the slight grades to their resting-places.

The cars do not rest long upon the classification-yard tracks. From the far end of each of these they are being gathered in solid trains, one for Pittsburg, another for Cleveland and Chicago, the third transcontinental, and so on. Engines of the next division are being hitched to them, pet "hacks" brought from the caboose tracks, and the long strings of loaded box-cars are off toward the West in incredibly short time.

Of course there are some trains that never go upon the "classification" at Randall's yard. There are solid coal trains bound in and out of New York, of Philadelphia, and of Boston, that pass him empty and filled, and only change engines and cabooses at his command. There are through freights, bound from one seaboard to the other, from far East to far West, that do likewise. But the majority of the freight movement has the "sorting out" within his domain, his four "humps" are busy day and night with an ordinary run of traffic, and you shudder to think what must be the condition when business begins to run at high tide.

"We get it a-humming every once in a while," he finally confesses. "We had one day, a little time ago, when we received one hundred and twenty-one eastbound trains in twenty-four hours, more than thirty-two hundred cars all told. That meant, on an average, a train every eleven minutes and a half. That same day we got seventy-eight west-bound freights, with more than thirty-six hundred cars. That meant nearly seven thousand cars handled on the in-freight in twenty-four hours, or a train coming in to me every seven minutes and a half during day and night. They don't do much better than that on some of the subway and elevated railroads in the big cities, and I haven't said a word about the trains and cars we despatched—just about as much again, of course."

Randall's figures were startling. I called him "king of the situation." He corrected me.

"I'm only a field-marshal," he laughed. "I'll take you to the king. He is up at the other end of the yard."

That sounded simple and was in reality a good five miles. Over that five miles we pounded our way until we came to the dull and grimy general offices of the division. Through a long hall, up one flight of stairs, and at its head a door stood open, commanding a view of a line of shirt-sleeved men sitting before telegraph instruments at a long table, a still farther room where another shirt-sleeved man— their chief—sat alone.

"The despatcher," explained Randall. "He plays with trains as we play with cars. Now, *there's* a man that's got to show real head-work. He moves all this traffic, freight and passenger, and if something turns up wrong and goes helter-skelter, he's the man they light upon."

"He's the king of the railroad?" I asked.

"Not so quick," cautioned Randall. "He's only a high minister in the cabinet. I'll take you to the real king."

There were brass railings to guard him, and long rows of desks, at each of which sat a pale-faced, tired-looking clerk. A haughty negro messenger held open a swing door of green baize and bade us enter.

"You may find the boss a little nervous this morning," Randall whispered, as we went into the inner office. "His pet train, the night-flying Limited, went into the ditch forty miles below here this morning. Landslide—it's bad railroad to operate up through these mountains, and the fog and all to tangle us in the early mornings."

But the Superintendent did not seem nervous. He was a veteran railroader, if you please, and he wore the medals of long service in the fine, kindly lines of his face. His was a big desk, and faced a bay-window, which in turn commanded, through the vista of an open park, the passenger station. A long train lay in the shed at that moment. Its passengers were getting lunch in the station restaurant, a fine old place whose reputation for the good things of real American cookery had spanned a continent, and Randall said that "thirty-two was mighty late."

"Did you get through all right?" the Superintendent asked me. "We had a nasty time of it last night west of here, sleet and blow and ice. There's forty miles of poles down through Indiana. I'm sending as far East as Burlington, Vermont, for linemen."

Randall told me something of this man's kingdom as the Superintendent ran through his mail—a miniature mountain of letters.

"We've got three hundred miles through here of the realest railroad in the land," said he, proudly. "We've got a ton mileage on this division that's equal to the entire ton mileage of one of those big roads that reach from Chicago to the Pacific. The boss here has eleven thousand men under him, and when we get hard times it keeps him guessing as to how to hold them on the pay-roll. It worries him to think of folks in this little city going without coal and bread and butter 'cause the traffic is slacking off."

Here was a kingdom. Freight traffic, passenger traffic, shops, maintenance of line, men, thousands upon thousands of living men, of keen intellects and diverse minds, a thousand operations a day—this cool-headed veteran was a real king. His was a kingly proposition—getting the traffic through in good times and in poor. To it he brought the resources of energy, more than energy—ability, more than ability—genius, sheer genius.

We hurried out. There was a delegation from some one of the many brotherhoods waiting to see the Superintendent. The vexed questions of pay, promotion, discipline, were to be threshed out still again. The king would have every use for each of his wits.

"Too bad about your accident this morning," I said to him at leaving.

"Two of the finest fellows that we ever put in a cab gone," he said, quietly. "I never get to sleep nights without hoping that that hair-raising Limited of ours has passed all the mountain turns in safety."

2

LETTERS FROM DAVID HENSHAW TO THE BOSTON MORNING POST, ON THE WESTERN RAIL-ROAD, AND THE GREATLY BENEFICIAL EFFECTS OF INTERNAL IMPROVEMENTS (BOSTON: BEALS AND GREENE, 1839), PP. 3–8

WHEELING, Nov. 20, 1838.

Here I am, fairly on the western side of the Alleghanies. I left Baltimore on Saturday morning, in our old friend Admiral Reeside's fast line, so *called*. We were promised to be brought here in fifty-two hours, and accomplished the journey in three days and three nights. Twenty-four hours of the time we had a severe snow storm on the mountains. The load was so heavy the night before last that on the steep acclivities of the Cumberland, or national, road, the passengers were obliged to walk, and in one case to put the shoulder to the wheel to aid the horses. We had a hearty laugh yesterday morning on changing coaches at Uniontown, to find the carriage that we had been pushing along up the hills, and walking up the mountains ourselves to relieve, was pretty heavily loaded with *freight boxes of fresh oysters* for Wheeling. We concluded that Admiral Reeside had improved upon the tactics of the Ohio stage proprietors, where, it is said, they oblige the passengers to walk and carry a rail with which to pry the stage out of the mud. After this discovery we declined walking.

We came to Frederick, in Maryland, on the Baltimore and Ohio Rail Road—distance by this way sixty-one miles from Baltimore, and by the old road forty-eight. Parr's Ridge, some sixteen miles from Frederick, is surmounted by inclined plains, by horse power; the highest inclination, or grade, of these plains is about 370 feet per mile. The rail-road company are, however, now constructing a new road, of about six miles, around this ridge, which is to be finished in a few weeks. They find a route, the highest inclination being eighty-three feet to the mile, that enables them to surmount the elevation with locomotive engines. They are also in two other places cutting off curves by new pieces of road. They are likewise laying, in place of the old plate rail, new edge rails of the T pattern, weighing 55 lbs. to the yard. They intend to put the line from the present terminus of the road to Cumberland, under contract next year. It would be a great relief to travellers, crossing this formidable chain of mountains, to be able to do it by rail road. The national road from Cumberland to this place, is a good road of the kind, but it is not in all cases well located, and no common road can ever come in competition, for convenience, comfort and speed, with rail roads.

Maryland appreciates her position, and is wisely expending large sums for internal improvements to avail herself of her natural advantages.

The country around Frederick is very good, the farmers appear in a thriving condition, and large quantities of land are in cultivation for wheat. The wheat appears green and luxuriant, and if not winter killed, the crop in that quarter will be great the next year.

Cumberland is a thriving town, of some three thousand people, surrounded by lofty mountains. The mountain scenery in the vicinity is on a magnificent scale, and of the wildest and most romantic character. I regretted that I could make no stay here. Cumberland is about 150 miles from Baltimore, and near to the lines of Pennsylvania and Virginia. It is on a small stream that empties into the Potomac. The place suffered a few years since heavily from fire, and in fact has not yet fully recovered from that calamity. It is situate in the coal region, and must be greatly benefitted by the extension of the Baltimore and Ohio Railroad and the Chesapeake and Ohio Canal, which will both reach her neighborhood within a few years.

A few miles this side of Cumberland we passed over the famed battle ground of Braddock's defeat in the old French war of 1755. It was here that General Washington first shew that military sagacity and tact, which in after times so much exalted his fame, and that, on the occasion of this disaster, saved the remainder of Braddock's army. There is a monument a short distance from the road, on an eminence, that marks the place where Braddock fell.

Ten miles this side of Cumberland we reach Frostburg, a region famous for its bituminous coal. A Boston company own inexhaustible mines here, of coal of the finest quality, and when the railroad and canal shall have been brought to the vicinity, these mines must yield a never-failing profit. Coal, equal to the best Orrel coal in your market, is delivered at the houses in Frostburg at four cents per bushel.

At some two hundred and twenty miles from Baltimore, in the midst of the mountains on the western side of the Alleghany range, we reached Brownsville. It is on the Alleghany river, and built upon the site of the old frontier fort, Redstone. It is a village of about three thousand people—noted in this section for its iron works and ship building. A new steamboat, of 300 tons, built at this place, left a few hours before we arrived, for Pittsburg, by the river 55 miles distant—she was then to descend the Ohio for Louisville. The Alleghany is navigable for steamers sixty miles above Brownsville.

I noticed a beautiful iron bridge, of a single arch, some thirty feet high, supported by stone abutments, over a stream that empties into the Alleghany, at Brownsville, made by the iron masters and artists of Brownsville. The work would be considered a wonder in any part of the country.

We took our supper at Washington, Pa., a good town of two thousand people. It is in the midst of an excellent farming country—wheat commands very readily

$1 12½ per bushel, which is called there a high price. Though my ride over the mountains has been a tiresome one, I have been much pleased with it, and it has given me the desire to try the route again more leisurely at a more favorable season of the year.

Wheeling, on the Virginia bank of the Ohio, has grown much of late years, and now counts a population of nearly or quite, ten thousand. It is surrounded by a good farming country. Its population is a busy and thriving community. There are four iron factories, two steam flouring mills, and some ship building, carried on here. The handicraft trades employ, advantageously, many of its citizens. It is a thriving, but not a handsome, place.

LOUISVILLE, Nov. 29th, 1838.

I descended the Ohio, from Wheeling, on the 20th, in the steamer Brownsville, owned and built at Brownsville, formerly Redstone. The boat was crowded with passengers, and almost sinking with freight; wet, dirty, and uncomfortable. It was the best of the two that were in port. The weather was inclement, and the season quite unpropitious for enjoyment. The Ohio is a beautiful river, not averaging, I think, more than eighty rods wide above Cincinnati. The shores are generally settled, and every four miles, on either, side, a village is seen, decorating the river's bank, many of them handsome, and most of them flourishing. Some of the more important points we passed in the night, including Marietta, Guyandotte, and Ports-mouth. Maysville, on the Kentucky shore, some sixty or seventy miles above Cincinnati, numbers about 3000 people, is surrounded by a fertile, farming country, and is a place of business and note. While our boat was discharging freight, and landing her passengers for this place, I had time to walk up in town, and to examine, as the greatest lion in the place, a "Pork House"; in other words, a slaughter-house for hogs There are two in this place, at which are killed and dressed about twenty thousand hogs during the pork season. Sixty men were employed in the one I visited, and the whole operation of killing, (knocking the hogs in the head,) scalding, cleaning, dressing, cutting up, assorting, packing, trying and straining the lard, pressing the scraps, cleaning the sausage skins, was going on actively, under the eye of a fat jolly superintendent. There were about 250 pigs strung up to drain and cool, that had been killed and dressed that morning. The pork is small, the pigs not averaging, I think, 200 lbs. and cost 3½ to 4 cents per lb. The salt is procured from the Virginia Springs, on this side the mountains, which, since they have commenced making it by solar evaporation, is very good.

The shores of the Ohio give ample proof of the wonderful industry of its inhabitants. It is but about sixty years since the first attempts were made to settle its banks,—it now smiles, with farms, habitations, villages, and cities. There is a marked difference, however, in the improvement of the two shores. In passing from the United States to Canada, one would suppose that he had entered a new region, differing widely in soil and climate from the one he had left a few rods behind him; something of the like kind, though not to the same extent, is observed on the two shores of the Ohio. In both cases the scenes bear testimony to the value of *free* institutions in elevating and improving the moral and physical condition of man.

Cincinnati is a beautiful city, truly "the Queen of the West." It has now nearly 45,000 people. It is laid out in regular squares—ascending somewhat abruptly from the river. There is much wealth, great activity, and an extensive business there. Many of the private dwellings rival in elegance and cost your Beacon street, Summer street, and Tremont street, residences—and are furnished as sumptuously as the best houses in the Atlantic cities. In fact, I think the general style of furnishing is more costly than with you.

They are displaying a good deal of taste, and incurring great expense, on some of their public edifices. The country around Cincinnati is rich, and in high cultivation. A canal is made to Dayton and Piqua, some 80 miles, and is to unite at Defiance with the Wabash and Erie Canal, and will thus open a communication with Lake Erie by the Maumee Valley. This artificial tributary pours the vast amount of produce from the bordering country into Cincinnati. It is also in contemplation to run a railroad from Cincinnati to Lake Erie—when this is completed, they can reach the lake in about twelve hours, Buffalo by steam in thirty hours from the lake end of the road, and, when your great Western Railroad is done to Albany, they will go from Buffalo to Boston in thirty hours, at the rate of twenty miles per hour, making seventy-two hours from Cincinnati to Boston. The time is not far distant, if Massachusetts does her duty to herself, when she will come in for a large share of the trade of these vast regions, by the way of the lakes.

A road is commenced from Madison, Indiana, about fifty miles above this place, to Indianapolis, ninety mile distant. Twenty miles and upwards are already completed, and the residue is to be done next year. The road was formally opened on Monday last. The Benj. Franklin, steamer, that I came in from Cincinnati, took on board a goodly number of young people of both sexes at Nevay, and left them at Madison to join in the celebration, and the ball that was to follow in the evening. They were anticipating great doings and much pleasure. Indiana will, it is said, soon have a road from Indianapolis to the lake. Madison is a thriving village of nearly 3000 inhabitants; many of them Yankees, possessing intelligence, enterprise, and industry. It will become a large place. New England habits, spirit and industry, are visible in many of the towns along the Ohio river. In fact, where the Yankees settle in any numbers in the west, the place is sure to thrive.

The weather is pleasant, but dry and cold. Ice is making in the river to day, but none to impede navigation.

The low stage of the Ohio for months past put an effectual embargo on all business. Merchandise, manufactures, produce, all remained on the hands of their owners. A good deal of pecuniary embarrassment has been the consequence; business, however, is very brisk.

3

HENRY DAVID THOREAU, *WALDEN: A STORY OF LIFE IN THE WOODS* (NEW YORK: A. L. BURT, 1902 [ORIGINALLY PUBLISHED IN 1854]), PP. 56–59

Which would have advanced the most at the end of a month, – the boy who had made his own jackknife from the ore which he had dug and smelted, reading as much as would be necessary for this,—or the boy who had attended the lectures on metallurgy at the Institute in the mean while, and had received a Rogers' penknife from his father? Which would be most likely to cut his fingers? . . . To my astonishment I was in formed on leaving college that I had studied navigation!—why, if I had taken one turn down the harbor I should have known more about it. Even the *poor* student studies and is taught only *political* economy, while that economy of living which is synonymous with philosophy is not even sincerely professed in our colleges. The consequence is, that while he is reading Adam Smith, Ricardo, and Say, he runs his father in debt irretrievably.

As with our colleges, so with a hundred "modern improvements;" there is an illusion about them; there is not always a positive advance. The devil goes on exacting compound interest to the last for his early share and numerous succeeding investments in them. Our inventions are wont to be pretty toys, which distract our attention from serious things. They are but improved means to an unimproved end, an end which it was already but too easy to arrive at; as railroads lead to Boston or New York. We are in great haste to construct a magnetic telegraph from Maine to Texas; but Maine and Texas, it may be, have nothing important to communicate. Either is in such a predicament as the man who was earnest to be introduced to a distinguished deaf woman, but when he was presented, and one end of her ear trumpet was put into his hand, had nothing to say. As if the main objects were to talk fast and not to talk sensibly. We are eager to tunnel under the Atlantic and bring the old world some weeks nearer to the new; but perchance the first news that will leak through into the broad, flapping American ear will be that the Princess Adelaide has the whooping cough. After all, the man whose horse trots a mile in a minute does not carry the most important messages; he is not an evangelist, nor does he come round eating locusts and wild honey. I doubt if Flying Childers ever carried a peck of corn to mill.

One says to me, "I wonder that you do not lay up money; you love to travel; you might take the cars and go to Fitchburg to-day and see the country." But I am wiser than that. I have learned that the swiftest traveller is he that goes afoot. I say to my friend, Suppose we try who will get there first. The distance is thirty miles; the fare ninety cents. That is almost a day's wages. I remember when wages were sixty cents a day for laborers on this very road. Well, I start now on foot, and get there before night; I have travelled at that rate by the week together. You will in the mean while have earned your fare, and arrive there some time to-morrow, or possibly this evening, if you are lucky enough to get a job in season. Instead of going to Fitchburg, you will be working here the greater part of the day. And so, if the railroad reached round the world, I think that I should keep ahead of you; and as for seeing the country and getting experience of that kind, I should have to cut your acquaintance altogether.

Such is the universal law, which no man can ever outwit, and with regard to the railroad even we may say it is as broad as it is long. To make a railroad round the world available to all mankind is equivalent to grading the whole surface of the planet. Men have an indistinct notion that if they keep up this activity of joint stocks and spades long enough all will at length ride somewhere, in next to no time, and for nothing; but though a crowd rushes to the depot, and the conductor shouts "All aboard!" when the smoke is blown away and the vapor condensed, it will be perceived that a few are riding, but the rest are run over,—and it will be called, and will be, "A melancholy accident." No doubt they can ride at last who shall have earned their fare, that is, if they survive so long, but they will probably have lost their elasticity and desire to travel by that time. This spending of the best part of one's life earning money in order to enjoy a questionable liberty during the least valuable part of it, reminds me of the Englishman who went to India to make a fortune first, in order that he might return to England and live the life of a poet. He should have gone up garret at once. "What!" exclaim a million Irishmen starting up from all the shanties in the land, "is not this railroad which we have built a good thing?" Yes, I answer, *comparatively* good, that is, you might have done worse; but I wish, as you are brothers of mine, that you could have spent your time better than digging in this dirt.

4

ISABELLA BIRD (MRS. BISHOP), *THE ENGLISHWOMAN IN AMERICA* (LONDON: JOHN MURRAY, 1856), PP. 90–115

THE city of Portland, with its busy streets, and crowded wharfs, and handsome buildings, and railway *depôts*, rising as it does on the barren coast of the sterile State of Maine, fully bears out the first part of an assertion which I had already heard made by Americans, "We're a great people, the greatest nation on the face of the earth." A polite custom-house officer asked me if I had anything contraband in my trunks, and on my reply in the negative they were permitted to pass without even the formality of being uncorded. "Enlightened citizens" they are truly, I thought, and, with the pleasant consciousness of being in a perfectly free country, where every one can do as he pleases, I entered an hotel near the water and sat down in the ladies' parlour. I had not tasted food for twenty-five hours, my clothes were cold and wet, a severe cut was on my temple, and I felt thoroughly exhausted. These circumstances, I thought, justified me in ringing the bell and asking for a glass of wine. Visions of the agreeable refreshment which would be produced by the juice of the grape appeared simultaneously with the waiter. I made the request, and he brusquely replied.

"You can't have it, *it's contrary to law*" In my half-drowned and feint condition the refusal appeared tantamount to positive cruelty, and I remembered that I had come in contact with the celebrated "*Maine Law*" That the inhabitants of the State of Maine are not "*free*" was thus placed practically before me at once. Whether they are "*enlightened*" I doubted at the time, but leave the question of the prohibition of fermented liquors to be decided by abler social economists than myself.

I was hereafter informed that to those who go down stairs, and ask to see the "*striped pig,*" wine and spirits are produced; that a request to speak with "*Dusty Ben*" has a like effect, and that, on asking for "*sarsaparilla*" at certain stores in the town, the desired stimulant can be obtained. Indeed it is said that the consumption of this drug is greater in Maine than in all the other States put together. But in justice to this highly respectable State, I must add that the drunkenness which forced this stringent measure upon the legislature was among the thousands of English and Irish emigrants who annually land at Portland. My only companion here was a rosycheeked, simple country girl, who was going to Kennebunk, and, never having been from home before, had not the slightest idea what to do. Presuming on my antiquated appearance, she asked me "to take care of her, to get her ticket for her, for she dare'nt ask those men for it, and to let her sit by me in the car." She said she was so frightened with something she'd seen that she didn't know how she should go in the cars. I asked her what it was. "Oh," she said, "it was a great thing, bright red, with I don't know how many wheels, and a large black top, and bright shining things moving about all over it, and smoke and steam coming out of it, and it made such an awful noise it seemed to shake the earth."

At half-past three we entered the cars in a long shed, where there were no officials in uniform as in England, and we found our way in as we could. "All aboard!" is the signal for taking places, but on this occasion a loud shout of "Tumble in for your lives!" greeted my amused ears, succeeded by "Go a-head!" and off we went, the engineer tolling a heavy bell to notify our approach to the passengers in *the streets along which we passed*. America has certainly flourished under her motto "Go a-head!" but the cautious "All right!" of an English guard, who waits to start till he is sure of his ground being clear, gives one more confidence. I never experienced the same amount of fear which is expressed by *Bunn* and other writers, for, on comparing the number of accidents with the number of miles of railway open in America, I did not find the disadvantage in point of safety on her side. The cars are a complete novelty to an English eye. They are twenty-five feet long, and hold about sixty persons; they have twelve windows on either side, and two and a door at each end; a passage runs down the middle, with chairs to hold two each on either side. There is a small saloon for ladies with babies at one end, and a filter containing a constant supply of iced water. There are rings along the roof for a rope which passes through each car to the engine, so that anything wrong can be communicated instantly to the engineer. Every car has eight solid wheels, four being placed close together at each end, all of which can be locked by two powerful breaks. At each end of every car is a platform, and passengers are "prohibited from standing upon it at their peril," as also from passing from car to car while the train is in motion; but as no penalty attaches to this law, it is incessantly and continuously violated, "free and enlightened citizens" being at perfect liberty to imperil their own necks; and "poor, ignorant, benighted Britishers" soon learn to follow their example. Persons are for ever passing backwards and forwards, exclusive of the conductor whose business it is, and water-carriers, book, bonbon, and peach venders. No person connected with these railways wears a distinguishing dress, and the stations, or "depôts" as they are called, are generally of the meanest description, mere wooden sheds, with a ticket-office very difficult to discover. If you are so fortunate as to find a man standing at the door of the baggage-car, he attaches copper plates to your trunks, with a number and the name of the place you are going to upon them, giving you labels with corresponding numbers. By this excellent arrangement, in going a very long journey, in which you are obliged to change cars several times, and cross rivers and lakes in steamers, you are relieved of all responsibility, and only require at the end to give your checks to the hotel-porter, who regains your baggage without any trouble on your part.

This plan would be worthily imitated at our termini in England, where I have frequently seen "unprotected females" in the last stage of frenzy at being pushed out of the way, while some persons unknown are running off with their possessions.

When you reach a *depôt*, as there are no railway porters, numerous men clamour to take your effects to an hotel, but, as many of these are thieves, it is necessary to be very careful in only selecting those who have hotel-badges on their hats.

An emigrant-car is attached to each train, but there is only one class: thus it may happen that you have on one side the President of the Great Republic, and on the other the *gentleman* who blacked your shoes in the morning. The Americans, however, have too much respect for themselves and their companions to travel except in good clothes, and this mingling of all ranks is far from being disagreeable, particularly to a stranger like myself, one of whose objects was to see things in their everyday dress. We must be well aware that in many parts of England it would be difficult for a lady to travel unattended in a second-class, impossible in a third-class carriage; yet I travelled several thousand miles in America, frequently alone, from the house of one friend to another's, and never met with anything approaching to incivility; and I have often heard it stated that a lady, no matter what her youth or attractions might be, could travel alone through every State in the Union, and never meet with anything but attention and respect.

I have had considerable experience of the cars, having travelled from the Atlantic to the Mississippi, and from the Mississippi to the St Lawrence, and found the company so agreeable in its way, and the cars themselves so easy, well ventilated, and comfortable, that, were it not for the disgusting practice of spitting upon the floors in which the lower classes of Americans indulge, I should greatly prefer them to our own exclusive carriages, denominated in the States "*'coon sentry-boxes.*" Well, we are seated in the cars; a man shouts "Go a-head!" and we are off, the engine ringing its heavy bell, and thus begin my experiences of American travel.

I found myself in company with eleven gentlemen and a lady from Prince Edward Island, whom a strange gregarious instinct had thus drawn together. The engine gave a hollow groan, very unlike our cheerful whistle, and, soon moving through the town, we reached the open country.

Fair was the country that we passed through in the States of Maine, New Hampshire, and Massachusetts. Oh very fair! smiling, cultivated, and green, like England, but far happier.; for slavery which disgraces the New World, and poverty which desolates the Old, are nowhere to be seen.

There were many farmhouses surrounded by the nearly finished harvest, with verandahs covered with vines and roses; and patriarchal-looking family groups seated under them, engaged in different employments, and enjoying the sunset, for here it was gorgeous summer. And there were smaller houses of wood painted white, with bright green jalousies, in gardens of pumpkins, and surrounded by orchards. Apples seemed almost to grow wild; there were as many orchards as corn-fields, and apple and pear trees grew in the very hedgerows.

And such apples! not like our small, sour, flavourless *things*, but like some southern fruit; huge balls, red and yellow, such as are caricatured in wood, weighing down the fine large trees. There were heaps of apples on the ground, and horses and cows were eating them in the fields, and rows of freight-cars at all the stations were laden with them, and little boys were selling them in the cars; in short, where were they not? There were smiling fields with verdant hedgerows between them, unlike the untidy snake-fences of the colonies, and meadows like parks, dotted over with trees, and woods filled with sumach and scarlet maple, and rapid streams hurrying over white pebbles, and villages of green-jalousied houses, with churches and spires, for here all places of worship have spires; and the mellow light of a declining sun streamed over this varied scene of happiness, prosperity, and comfort; and for a moment I thought—O traitorous thought!—that the New England was fairer than the Old.

Nor were the more material evidences of prosperity wanting, for we passed through several large towns near the coast—Newbury Port, Salem, and Portsmouth—with populations varying from 30,000 to 50,000 souls. They seemed bustling, thriving places, with handsome stores, which we had an opportunity of observing, as in the States the cars run right into the streets along the carriageway, traffic being merely diverted from the track while the cars are upon it.

Most of the railways in the States have only one track or line of rails, with occasional sidings at the stations for the cars to pass each other. A fence is by no means a matter of necessity, and two or three animals are destroyed every day from straying on the line. The engines, which are nearly twice the size of ours, with a covered enclosure for the engineer and stoker, carry large *fenders* or guards in front, to lift incumbrances from the track. At eight o'clock we found ourselves passing over water, and between long rows of gas-lights, and shortly afterwards the cars stopped at Boston, the Athens of America. Giving our baggage-checks to the porter of the American House, we drove to that immense hotel, where I remained for one night. It was crammed from the very basement to the most undesirable locality nearest the moon; I believe it had seven hundred inmates. I had arranged to travel to Cincinnati, and from thence to Toronto, with Mr. and Mrs. Walrence, but on reaching Boston I found that they feared fever and cholera, and, leaving me to travel alone from Albany, would meet me at Chicago. Under these circumstances I remained with my island friends for one night at this establishment, a stranger in a land where I had few acquaintances, though I was well armed with letters of introduction. One of these was to Mr. Amy, a highly respected merchant of Boston, who had previously informed me by letter of the best route to the States, and I immediately despatched a note to him, but he was absent at his country-house, and I was left to analyse the feeling of isolation inseparable from being alone in a crowd. Having received the key of my room, I took my supper in an immense hall, calculated for dining 400 persons. I next went into the ladies' parlour, and felt rather out of place among so many richly dressed females; for as I was proceeding to write a letter, a porter came in and told me that writing was not allowed in that saloon. "Freedom again," thought I. On looking round I did feel that my antiquated goose-quill and rusty-looking inkstand were rather out of place. The carpet of the room was of richly flowered Victoria pile, rendering the heaviest footstep noiseless; the tables were marble on gilded pedestals, the couches covered with gold brocade. At a piano of rich workmanship an elegantly dressed lady was seated, singing "And will you love me always?"—a question apparently satisfactorily answered by the speaking eyes of a bearded Southerner, who was turning over the pages for her. A fountain of antique workmanship threw up a *jet d'eau* of iced water, scented with *eau de Cologne;* and the whole was lighted by four splendid chandeliers interminably reflected, for the walls were mirrors divided by marble pillars. The room seemed appropriate to the purposes to which it was devoted—music, needlework, conversation, and flirting. With the single exception of the rule against writing in the ladies' saloon, a visitor at these immense establishments is at perfect liberty to do as he pleases, provided he pays the moderate charge of two dollars, or 8*s*. a day. This includes, even at the best hotels, a splendid *table d'hôte,* a comfortable bedroom, lights, attendance, and society in abundance. From the servants one meets, with great attention, not combined with deference of manner, still less with that obsequiousness which informs you by a suggestive bow, at the end of your visit, that it has been meted out with reference to the probable amount of half-sovereigns, shillings, and sixpences at your disposal.

It will not be out of place here to give a sketch of the peculiarities of the American hotel system, which constitutes such a distinctive feature of life in the States, and is a requirement arising out of the enormous extent of their territory, and the nomade life led by vast numbers of the most restless and energetic people under the sun.

"People will turn hastily over the pages when they come to this" was the remark of a lively critic on reading this announcement; but while I promise my readers that hotels shall only be described once, I could not reconcile it to myself not to give them information on "Things as they are in America," when I had an opportunity of acquiring it.

The American House at Boston, which is a fair specimen of the best class of hotels in the States, though more frequented by mercantile men than by tourists, is built of grey granite, with a frontage to the street of 100 feet. The ground floor to the front is occupied by retail stores, in the centre of which a lofty double doorway denotes the entrance, marked in a more characteristic manner by groups of gentlemen smoking before it. This opens into a lofty and very spacious hall, with a chequered floor of black and white marble; there are lounges against the wall, covered over with buffalo-skins; and, except at meal-times, this capacious apartment is a scene of endless busy life, from two to three hundred gentlemen constantly thronging it, smoking at the door, lounging on the settees, reading the newspapers, standing in animated groups discussing commercial matters, arriving, or departing. Piles of luggage, in which one sees with dismay one's light travelling valise crushed under a gigantic trunk, occupy the centre; porters seated on a form wait for orders; peripatetic individuals walk to and fro; a confused Babel of voices is ever ascending to the galleries above; and at the door, hacks, like the "*eilwagon*" of Germany, are ever depositing fresh arrivals. There is besides this a private entrance for ladies. Opposite the entrance is a counter, where four or five clerks constantly attend, under the superintendence of a cashier, to whom all applications for rooms are personally made. I went up to this functionary, wrote my name in a book, he placed a number against it, and, giving me a key with a corresponding number attached, I followed a porter down a long corridor, and up to a small clean room on the third story, where to all intents and purposes my identity was lost—merged in a mere numeral. At another side of the hall is the bar, a handsomely decorated apartment, where lovers of such beverages can procure "toddy," "nightcaps," "mint julep," "gin sling," &c. On the door of my very neat and comfortable bed-room was a printed statement of the rules, times of meals, and charge per diem. I believe there are nearly 300 rooms in this house, some of them being bed-rooms as large and commodious as in a private mansion in England.

On the level of the entrance is a magnificent eating saloon, principally devoted to male guests, and which is 80 feet long. Upstairs is a large room furnished with a rare combination of splendour and taste, called "The Ladies' Ordinary," where families, ladies, and their invited guests take their meals. Breakfast is at the early hour of seven, and remains on the table till nine; dinner is at one, and tea at six. At these meals "every delicacy of the season" is served in profusion; the daily bill of fare would do credit to a banquet at the Mansion House; the *chef de cuisine* is generally French, and an epicure would find ample scope for the gratification of his palate. If people persist in taking their meals in a separate apartment, they are obliged to pay dearly for the indulgence of their exclusiveness. There are more than 100 waiters, and the ladies at table are always served first, and to the best pieces.

Though it is not part of the hotel system, I cannot forbear mentioning the rapidity with which the Americans despatch their meals. My next neighbour has frequently risen from his seat after a substantial and varied dinner while I was sending away my soup-plate. The effect of this at a *table-d'hôte,* where 400 or 600 sit down to dine, is unpleasant, for the swing-door is incessantly in motion. Indeed, the utter absence of repose is almost the first thing which strikes a stranger. The incessant sound of bells and gongs, the rolling of hacks to and from the door, the arrivals and departures every minute, the trampling of innumerable feet, the flirting and talking in every corridor, make these immense hotels more like a human beehive than anything else.

The drawing-rooms are always kept very hot by huge fires of anthracite coal, and the doors are left open to neutralise the effect. The temperance at table filled me with surprise. I very seldom saw any beverage but pure iced-water. There are conveniences of all descriptions for the use of the guests. The wires of the electric telegraph, constantly attended by a clerk, run into the hotel; porters are ever ready to take your messages into the town; pens, paper, and ink await you in recesses in the lobbies; a man is ever at hand to clean and brush soiled boots—in short, there is every contrivance for abridging your labour in mounting up stairs. But the method of avoiding the confusion and din of two or three hundred bells must not be omitted. All the wires from the different rooms centre at one bell, which is located in a case in the lobby, with the mechanism seen on one side through a sheet of plate-glass. The other side of the case is covered with numbers in rows. By each number is a small straight piece of brass, which drops and hangs down when the bell is sounded, displaying the number to the attention of the clerk, who sends a waiter to the apartment, and places the piece of brass in its former position.

Steam laundries are connected with all the large hotels. At American House the laundry is under the management of a clerk, who records all the minor details. The linen is cleansed in a churn-like machine moved by steam, and wrung by a novel application of the principle of centrifugal force; after which the articles are dried by being passed through currents of hot air, so that they are washed and ironed in the space of a few minutes. The charge varies from six to ten shillings a dozen. There are also suites of hot and cold baths, and barbers' shops.

Before I understood the mysteries of these hotels, I used to be surprised to see gentlemen travelling without even carpet-bags, but it soon appeared that razors and hair-brushes were superfluous, and that the possessor of one shirt might always pass as the owner of half a dozen, for, while taking a bath, the magic laundry would reproduce the article in its pristine glories of whiteness and starch. Every attention to the comfort and luxury of the guest is paid at American House, and its spirited proprietor, Mr. Rice, deserves the patronage which the travelling public so liberally bestow upon him. On ringing my bell it was answered by a garcon, and it is rather curious seldom or never to see a chambermaid.

I ROSE the morning after my arrival at five, hoping to leave Boston for Cincinnati by the *Lightning Express*, which left at eight. But on summoning the cashier (or rather *requesting* his attendance, for one never *summons* any one in the States), and showing him my bill of exchange drawn on Barclay and Company of London, he looked at *me*, then at *it*, suspiciously, as if doubting whether the possessor of such a little wayworn portmanteau could be the *bonâ fide* owner of such a sum as the figures represented. "There's so much bad paper going about, we can't possibly accommodate you," was the discouraging reply; so I was compelled patiently to submit to the detention.

I breakfasted at seven in the ladies' ordinary, without exchanging a syllable with any one, and soon after my kind friend, Mr. Amy, called upon me. He proved himself a friend indeed, and his kindness gave me at once a favourable impression of the Americans. First impressions are not always correct, but I am happy to say they were fully borne out in this instance by the uniform kindness and hospitality which I experienced during my whole tour. Mr. Amy soon procured me the money for my bill, all in five-dollar notes, and I was glad to find the exchange greatly in favour of England. He gave me much information about my route, and various cautions which I found very useful, and then drove me in a light "waggon" round the antiquated streets of Boston, crowded with the material evidences of prosperity, to his pretty villa three miles distant, in one of those villages of ornamental dwelling-houses which render the appearance of the environs of Boston peculiarly attractive. I saw a good deal of the town in my drive, but, as I returned to it before leaving the States, I shall defer my description of it, and request my readers to dash away at once with me to the "far west," the goal alike of the traveller and the adventurer, and the El Dorado of the emigrant's misty ideas.

Leaving American House with its hall swarming like a hive of bees, I drove to the *depôt* in a hack with several fellow-passengers, Mr. Amy, who was executing a commission for me in the town, having promised to meet me there, but, he being detained, I arrived alone, and was deposited among piles of luggage, in a perfect Babel of men vociferating, "Where are you for?" "Lightning Express!" "All aboard for the Western cars," &c. Some one pounced upon my trunks, and was proceeding to weigh them, when the stage-driver stepped forward and said, "It's a lady's luggage," upon which he relinquished his intention. He also took my ticket for me, handed me to the cars, and then withdrew, wishing me a pleasant journey, his prompt civility having assisted me greatly in the chaotic confusion which attends the departure of a train in America. The cars by which I left were guaranteed to take people to Cincinnati, a distance of 1000 miles, in 40 hours, allowing time for refreshments! I was to travel by five different lines of railway, but this part of the railway system is so well arranged that I only took a ticket once, rather a curious document—a strip of paper half a yard long, with passes for five different roads upon it; thus, whenever I came upon a fresh line, the conductor tore off a piece, giving me a ticket in exchange. Tickets are not only to be procured at the stations, but at several offices in every town, in all the steamboats, and in the cars themselves. For the latter *luxury*, for such it must certainly be considered, as it enables one to step into the cars at the last moment without any preliminaries, one only pays five cents extra.

The engine tolled its heavy bell, and soon we were amid the beauties of New England; rocky hills, small lakes, rapid streams, and trees distorted into every variety of the picturesque. At the next station from Boston the Walrences joined me. We were to travel together, with our ulterior destination a settlement in Canada West, but they would not go to Cincinnati; there were lions in the street; cholera and yellow fever, they said, were raging; in short, they left me at Springfield, to find my way in a strange country as best I might; our *rendezvous* to be Chicago.

At Springfield I obtained the first seat in the car, generally the object of most undignified elbowing, and had space to admire the beauties among which we passed. For many miles we travelled through a narrow gorge, between very high precipitous hills, clothed with wood up to their summits; those still higher rising behind them, while the track ran along the very edge of a clear rushing river. The darkness which soon came on was only enlivened by the sparks from the wood fire of the engine, so numerous and continuous as to look like a display of fireworks. Just before we reached Albany a very respectable-looking man got into the car, and, as his manners were very quiet and civil, we entered into conversation about the trade and manufactures of the neighbourhood. When we got out of the cars on the east side of the river, he said he was going no farther, but, as I was alone, he would go across with me, and see me safe into the cars on the other side. He also offered to carry my reticule and umbrella, and look after my luggage. His civility so excited my suspicions of his honesty, that I did not trust my luggage or reticule out of my sight, mindful of a notice posted up at all the stations, "Beware of swindlers, pickpockets, and luggage-thieves."

We emerged from the cars upon the side of the Hudson river, in a sea of mud, where, had not my friend offered me his arm, as Americans of every class invariably do to an "unprotected female" in a crowd, I should have been borne down and crushed by the shoals of knapsack-carrying pedestrians and truck-pushing porters who swarmed down upon the dirty wharf. The transit across occupied fully ten minutes, in consequence of the numerous times the engine had to be reversed, to avoid running over the small craft which infest this stream. My volunteer escort took me through a crowd through which I could not have found my way alone, and put me into the cars which started from the side of a street in Albany, requesting the conductor, whose countenance instantly prepossessed me in his favour, to pay me every attention on the route. He remained with me until the cars started, and told me that when he saw ladies travelling alone he always made a point of assisting them. I shook hands with him at parting, feeling real regret at losing so kind and intelligent a companion. This man was a working engineer.

Some time afterwards, while travelling for two successive days and nights in an unsettled district in the west, on the second night, fairly overcome with fatigue, and unable, from the crowded state of the car, to rest my feet on the seat in front, I tried unsuccessfully to make a pillow for my head by rolling up my cloak, which attempts being perceived by a working mechanic, he accosted me thus: "Stranger, I guess you're almost used up? Maybe you'd be more comfortable if you could rest your head." Without further parley he spoke to his companion, a man in a similar grade in society; they both gave up their seats, and rolled a coat round the arm of the chair, which formed a very comfortable sofa; and these two men stood for an hour and a half, to give me the advantage of it, apparently without any idea that they were performing a deed of kindness. I met continually with these acts of hearty unostentatious good nature. I mention these in justice to the lower classes of the United States, whose rugged exteriors and uncouth vernacular render them peculiarly liable to be misunderstood.

The conductor quite verified the good opinion which I had formed of him. He turned a chair into a sofa, and lent me a buffalo robe (for, hot though the day had been, the night was intensely cold), and several times brought me a cup of tea. We were talking on the peculiarities and amount of the breakage power on the American lines as compared with ours, and the interest of the subject made him forget to signal the engine-driver to stop at a station. The conversation concluded, he looked out of the window. "Dear me," he said, "we ought to have stopped three miles back; likely there was no one to get out!"

At midnight I awoke shivering with cold, having taken nothing for twelve hours; but at two we stopped at something called by courtesy a station, and the announcement was made, "Cars stop three minutes for refreshments." I got out;

it was pitch dark; but I, with a young lady, followed a lantern into a frame-shed floored by the bare earth. Visions of Swindon and Wolverton rose before me, as I saw a long table supported on rude trestles, bearing several cups of steaming tea, while a dirty boy was opening and frizzling oysters by a wood fire on the floor. I swallowed a cup of scalding tea; some oysters were put upon my plate; "Six cents" was shouted by a nasal voice in my ear, and, while hunting for the required sum, "All aboard" warned me to be quick; and, jumping into the cars just as they were in motion, I left my untasted supper on my plate. After "Show your tickets," frequently accompanied by a shake, had roused me several times from a sound sleep, we arrived at Rochester, an important town on the Gennessee Falls, surrounded by extensive clearings, then covered with hoar frost.

Here we were told to get out, as there were twenty minutes for breakfast. But whither should we go when we had got out? We were at the junction of several streets, and five engines, with cars attached, were snorting and moving about. After we had run the gauntlet of all these, I found men ringing bells, and negroes rushing about, tumbling over each other, striking gongs, and all shouting "The cheapest house in all the world—house for all nations—a splenderiferous breakfast for 20 cents!" and the like. At length, seeing an unassuming placard, "Hot breakfast, 25 cents," I ventured in, but an infusion of mint was served instead of the China leaf; and I should be afraid to pronounce upon the antecedents of the steaks. The next place of importance we reached was Buffalo, a large thriving town on the south shore of Lake Erie. There had been an election for Congress at some neighbouring place the day before, and my *vis-à-vis*, the editor of a Buffalo paper, was arguing vociferously with a man on my right.

At length he began to talk to me very vivaciously on politics, and concluded by asking me what I thought of the late elections. Wishing to put an end to the conversation, which had become tedious, I replied that I was from England. "English! you surprise me!" he said; "you've not the *English accent* at all." "What do you think of our government?" was his next question. "Considering that you started free, and had to form your institutions in an enlightened age, that you had the estimable parts of our constitution to copy from, while its faults were before you to serve as beacons, I think your constitution ought to be nearer perfection than it is." "I think our constitution is as near perfection as anything human can be; we are the most free, enlightened, and progressive people under the sun," he answered, rather hotly; but in a few minutes resuming the conversation with his former companion, I overheard him say, "I think I shall give up politics altogether; *I don't believe we have a single public man who is not corrupt.*" "A melancholy result of a perfect constitution, and a humiliating confession for an American," I observed.

The conversations in the cars are well worth a traveller's attention. They are very frequently on politics, but often one hears stories such as the world has become familiarised with from the early pages of Barnum's Autobiography, abounding in racy anecdote, broad humour, and cunning imposition. At Erie we changed cars, and I saw numerous emigrants sitting on large blue boxes, looking disconsolately about them; the Irish physiognomy being the most predominant.

They are generally so dirty that they travel by themselves in a partially lighted van, called the Emigrants' car, for a most trifling payment. I once got into one by mistake, and was almost sickened by the smell of tobacco, spirits, dirty fustian, and old leather, which assailed my olfactory organs. Leaving Erie, beyond which the lake of the same name stretched to the distant horizon, blue and calm like a tideless sea, we entered the huge forests on the south shore, through which we passed, I suppose, for more than 100 miles. My next neighbour was a stalwart, bronzed Kentucky farmer, in a palm-leaf hat, who, strange to say, never made any demonstrations with his bowie-knife, and, having been a lumberer in these forests, pointed out all the objects of interest.

The monotonous sublimity of these primeval woods far exceeded my preconceived ideas. We were locked in among gigantic trees of all descriptions, their huge stems frequently rising without a branch for a hundred feet; then breaking into a crown of the most luxuriant foliage. There were walnut, hickory, elm, maple, beech, oak, pine, and hemlock trees, with many others which I did not know, and the only undergrowth, a tropical-looking plant, with huge leaves, and berries like bunches of purple grapes. Though it was the noon of an unclouded sun, all was dark, and still, and lonely; no birds twittered from the branches; no animals enlivened the gloomy shades; no trace of man or of his works was there, except the two iron rails on which we flew along, unfenced from the forest, and those trembling electric wires, which will only cease to speak with the extinction of man himself.

Very occasionally we would come upon a log shanty, that most picturesque of human habitations; the walls formed of large logs, with the interstices filled up with clay, and the roof of rudely sawn boards, projecting one or two feet, and kept in their places by logs placed upon them. Windows and doors there were none, but, where a door was *not*, I generally saw four or five shoeless, ragged urchins, whose light tangled hair and general aspect were sufficient to denote their nationality. Sometimes these cabins would be surrounded by a little patch of cleared land, prolific in Indian corn and pumpkins; the brilliant orange of the latter contrasting with the charred stumps among which they grew; but more frequently the lumberer supported himself solely by his axe. These dwellings are suggestive, for they are erected by the pioneers of civilization; and if the future progress of America be equal in rapidity to its past, in another fifty years the forests will have been converted into lumber and firewood—rich and populous cities will have replaced the cabins and shanties—and the children of the urchins who gazed vacantly upon the cars will have asserted their claims to a voice in the councils of the nation.

The rays of the sun never penetrate the forest, and evening was deepening the gloom of the artificial twilight, when gradually we became enveloped in a glare, redder, fiercer, than that of moonlight; and looking a-head I saw the forest on fire, and that we were rushing into the flames. "Close the windows, there's a fire a-head," said the conductor; and after obeying this *commonplace* direction, many of the passengers returned to the slumbers which had been so unseasonably disturbed. On, on we rushed—the flames encircled us round—we were enveloped in clouds of stifling smoke—crack, crash went the trees—a blazing stem fell across the line—the fender of the engine pushed it aside—the flames hissed like tongues of fire, and then, leaping like serpents, would rush up to the top of the largest tree, and it would blaze like a pineknot, There seemed no egress; but in a few minutes the raging, roaring conflagration was left behind. A forest on fire from a distance looks very much like 'Punch's' picture of a naval review; a near view is the height of sublimity.

The dangers of the cars, to my inexperience, seemed by no means over with the escape from being roasted alive. A few miles from Cleveland they rushed down a steep incline, apparently into Lake Erie; but in *reality* upon a platform supported on piles, so narrow that the edges of the cars hung over it, so that I saw nothing but water. A gale was blowing, and drove the surf upon the platform, and the spray against the windows, giving such a feeling of insecurity, that for a moment I wished myself in one of our "'coon sentry-boxes." The cars were very full after leaving Cleveland, but I contrived to sleep soundly till awakened by the intense cold which attends dawn.

It was a glorious morning. The rosy light streamed over hills covered with gigantic trees, and park-like glades watered by the fair Ohio. There were bowers of myrtle, and vineyards ready for the vintage, and the rich aromatic scent wafted from groves of blossoming magnolias told me that we were in a different clime, and had reached the sunny south. And before us, placed within a perfect amphitheatre of swelling hills, reposed a huge city, whose countless spires reflected the beams of the morning sun—the creation of yesterday—Cincinnati, the "*Queen City of the West*" I drove straight to Burnet House, almost the finest edifice in the town, and after travelling a thousand miles in forty-two hours, without either water or a hair-brush, it was the greatest possible luxury to be able to remove the accumulations of soot, dust, and cinders of two days and nights. I spent three days at Clifton, a romantic village three miles from Cincinnati, at the hospitable house of Dr. M'Ilvaine, the Bishop of Ohio; but it would be an ill return for the kindness which I there experienced to give details of my visit, or gratify curiosity by describing family life in one of the "homes of the New World."

5

CHARLES WELD, *A VACATION TOUR IN THE UNITED STATES* (LONDON: LONGMAN, BROWN, GREEN, AND LONGMANS, 1859), PP. 192–197, 245–253

At the time of my visit, Chicago had scarcely subsided from an uproar arising from a fugitive slave case. The slave belonged to a person in St. Louis, who despatched three men armed to the teeth to recover him. They waited until the inhabitants had gone to church, and, watching their opportunity, made a desperate attempt to seize the negro. Being a powerful man, he broke away, and while in the act of running was shot in the arm. The slave-catchers were arrested, and bound over in the sum of eight hundred dollars, to take their trial for the crime of assault and battery, with intent to commit murder. The excitement was intense, and further increased by an order being made to deliver the slave to his master, while the slave-hunters escaped with a nominal fine. The judges acted in conformity with the law, but the people took a very different view of the case, and, as at Boston, made a strong demonstration against slavery.

The press kept up the excitement by violent articles denouncing slavery, and particularly the Fugitive Slave Law. These called forth rejoinders from journals in favour of slavery, couched, if possible, in more scurrilous language. Here, as an example, is a letter addressed to the editor of the *Chicago Tribune*, which is a strong anti-slavery organ. The document was published in a Kentucky paper:—

"Frankfort, Kentucky,
"September 7th, 1854.

"Sir,

"The term 'Dear Sir,' is not in my vocabulary for one of your degraded stamp. Your hellish course of late, in encouraging the abduction of slaves from their masters, and your general disorganising course, will wrap the flames of the infernal regions around your cowardly craven form With tenfold fiendish heat, when, in the course of Providence, you shall take passage upon the *under-ground railroad* to his Satanic Majesty the Devil. You take great delight in obeying the mandates of the devil here on earth, in exulting over the success of a negro-stealer, in the publication of inflammatory hand-bills that smell of hell itself. But be assured that a day of rich reward is near at hand, when all the furies in maddened blackness shall fan the already intolerable flames of Tartarus into tenfold their usual heat around that body that now has enough villany attached thereto to sink it through the slight crust that is represented to divide the earth from the country where *negro abductors* go. But if in the meantime you should like to smell a little of that country before finally removing there, just cross the Mason and Dixon line, or, in other words, come to Kentucky, and we will promise you a warm reception, a good berth, and a free ticket. If your health should require it, after the summer months are over, pay our or any southern State a visit, and let it be known that you are the villanous editor of the *Chicago Tribune*, and it won't cost much to put you through on the over-ground railroad, preparatory to a final, safe, and sure ride on the under-ground railroad.

"With high appreciation for your capacity in executing the devil's designs, and your unscrupulous activity therein, I am not, nor ever will be, your obedient servant,

"LYNCH LAW."

This it must be confessed is hot writing. It does not, however, appear to have discomposed the editor of, the *Tribune*, who thus comments on the letter:—

"We will bet our hat that the writer of the above epistle is a blood (or *bloody*) relation of Mat Ward. However, we are going to Kentucky, and several other Slave States, this winter, as is our custom to do, and we will be prepared to receive our friend at Frankfort with open *arms*. We do not entertain any fears of the reception which we might meet with in Kentucky or any other southern State. Our correspondent, Lynch Law, may be, and doubtless is, a blackguard; but the generality of the people of Kentucky and of Frankfort are *gentlemen*."

It is not difficult to foresee that, with such fierce partisanship, the slave question is destined to be a source of infinite trouble and intestine warfare between the Northern and Southern States. There are a great many free blacks in Chicago, who obtain high wages in the stores and hotels. Emigrants from various European countries resort to the city in vast numbers, attracted by the flourishing accounts—not exaggerated—of plans matured, labours performed, victories achieved, and hopes in full fruition. With such prospects before him, the emigrant

>"Leaves his home with a bounding heart,
>   For the world is all before him;
>And he scarcely feels it a pain to part,
>   Such sun-bright hopes come o'er him."

The prosperity of Chicago is the more remarkable as it is not happily situated, being built almost on a level with the lake, from the waters of which the houses are only divided by piles. The drainage is very imperfect, and the odour arising from decayed matter is extremely oppressive during the summer heats. Not inappropriately was the city named Chicago, which signifies *Skunk's Hole;* the skunk being an animal bearing an unenviable notoriety for its power of discharging a foul-smelling fluid.

I was pleased to find, amidst the feverish bustle of commerce, the claims of education and literature are not overlooked. Numerous institutions for these objects exist, and others on a larger scale are in course of erection.

I spent an evening in some gardens kept by a German about two miles from the town, where the inhabitants resort for recreation. They comprise about five acres of prairie-land, which seems peculiarly well adapted to the growth of English flowers. It was very pleasant to look upon old favourites 4000 miles from home. Here I saw a sunset of wondrous glory;

> "The clouds hung in the purple skies,
> At anchor like great argosies;"

and as the sun went down among them they assumed the most brilliant colours, until all hues blended in vast caverns of fire which lighted up the West.

Fatiguing as was my journey to Chicago, that to Cincinnati, a distance of 300 miles, was much more distressing. The railway *is* or *was* execrable, and what between the terrible jolting, frequently rendering it necessary to hold on, the great heat, and the tobacco-chewing with its sickening results, I had a sorry time of it. The passengers were as rough as the road. The usual courteous prefix of *gentle* was dropped, and I was addressed as "man." These were signs that the "aristocracy of soul," as a lady described it, which reigns at Boston has not yet reached the Western States. The rude familiarity, had it not been attended by perpetual expectorations which flooded the floor of the cars, would have been amusing.

The dinner in the middle of the day was a wonderful scramble, and though fully half-an-hour was allowed for the meal, it was bolted in five minutes. There was just sufficient light to see the vines clothing the picturesque hills, as, in the evening, we drew near Cincinnati. We passed through vast suburbs composed of wooden houses; and after a long drive in a wonderful omnibus calculated to contain any number of people, I was put down at the Burnet House, one of the largest and best hotels in the States, where I slept off my fatigue, though the heat, and angry hum of baffled mosquitoes, happily outside the net, were sad enemies to sound slumber.

I purposed proceeding to Washington by a train due at Cumberland on Monday morning at eight o'clock, and was in readiness with fourteen other passengers at the proper time. An hour having passed without any sign of the train, I inquired the cause of the delay; but, as the telegraph was not in working order, no certain answer could be given. It was surmised that an accident had happened, and I was told if the train did not arrive in another hour, we should be sent on by a messenger train. Ten arrived, but no train; accordingly three cars and a baggage-waggon were prepared for our conveyance. The first car was set apart for the coloured portion of our party, consisting of three women and two menslaves. The second car was allotted to gentlemen, and the third and last to ladies. As we were favoured by the companionship of only four of the latter, no objection was made to all the gentlemen occupying seats with them. Thus, the train was very light, the only heavy carriage being the baggage-waggon, which, besides our luggage, contained a large quantity of ice packed in sawdust.

As soon as we had taken our seats, the bell rang, and we dashed off. In a few minutes the conductor made his appearance; guess'd we were very late in starting, and guess'd, again, t'would be smartish work to pull up the time. To effect this required additional speed, which I had every reason to believe could not be maintained without serious danger. The conductor, however, was a determined man; and as he evidently attached little value to his own life, it was not to be expected his passengers would be much cared for. The line, after leaving Cumberland, follows the windings of the Potomac, describing sharp curves which no English railway train could keep. Round these the engine darted with rocket-like impetuosity, the car in which we were seated swaying in a manner rendering it necessary to hold on. A more significant hint of the impending catastrophe was given by the fall of a ponderous lamp-glass on my head, with, however, happily no worse result than inflicting a rather smart blow. Presently another glass was jerked out of its socket and precipitated into the lap of a lady; the oscillations of the car meanwhile increasing in violence. Affairs now assumed a serious aspect; I felt certain we were on the eve of a smash. This was the opinion of a gentleman who had the care of two ladies; for he proceeded, with a coolness deserving a better cause, to instruct us how to place ourselves, laying great stress on the importance of sitting diagonally, in order not to receive the shock directly on the knees. We were also advised to hold the backs of the seats before us. He strengthened his advice by assuring us he was experienced in railway accidents, and added that, as there was far less danger in the middle than in the end car, it would be prudent to change our seats at the next station. During this trying time the conduct of the ladies was admirable, and when their courage was far more severely tested, they exhibited equal fortitude. For, as we expected, an accident did occur, the results of which, had we retained our seats in the last car, would have been in all probability most disastrous. In vain was the conductor urged to slacken the excessive speed. With blind, if not wilful recklessness, it was maintained; and at length, when about six miles from the station where we had changed our places, a terrific crash, the crushing noise of which rang in my ears for days, and a series of dislocatory heavings and collisions, terminating in deathlike silence and the overthrow of the car which we occupied, gave certain evidence that we had gone off the line. I have no distinct recollection how I crawled out of the car, for I was half stunned; but I remember being highly delighted when I found my limbs sound. On looking round, the spectacle was extraordinary. With the exception of about half the middle car and engine, there was scarcely a portion of the train that was not more or less broken. The wheels were whirled to great distances, and the rails for the length of many yards either wholly wrenched from the sleepers or converted into snake-heads. The poor slaves were considerably bruised; and the baggage-waggon presented a curious mixture of portmanteaus, bags, boxes, and ice. The nature of the accident was precisely as we had anticipated; the excessive speed at which we had been going, combined with defective rails, threw us off a sharp curve, on one side of which was a precipice dipping into the Potomac, and on the other a vertical face of rock, against which the cars had been thrown.

I confess, when I saw the state of things, I was extremely indignant, for, by the wilful conduct of the conductor, we had not only been placed in imminent peril of our lives, but had every prospect of being detained several hours. But when, with that social feeling engendered by misfortune, I spoke in strong terms of him to my fellow-passengers, urging that we ought to report him to the directors of the line, I found my feelings were not only unshared, but, with one exception, all rather approved than otherwise his exertions to get us on. In short, I was so entirely unsupported, that I saw the prudent course was to hold my tongue, though I determined not to let the matter drop. The exceptional case to which I allude, was a gentleman who, as soon as he had extricated himself from the ruined cars, sought the shade of a sumach-tree, and, lighting a cigar, smoked with an apparent philosophical indifference to his fate. He was an Englishman, settled for some years in Wisconsin, to which State he had gone to enjoy the sporting it affords; and as he had experienced numerous railway accidents, nearly all of which resulted from the carelessness of officials, he was not disposed to be lenient in his judgment on the present occasion. But, as he said, accidents, whether on railways or in steam-boats, are thought so little of in America, it is useless to remonstrate; certainly the behaviour of our party confirmed his words. As it was evident we should have to remain many hours at the scene of the accident, the negro who acted as water-purveyor to the train, was despatched to forage among the neighbouring farm-houses. Presently he returned with a large basket filled with hams, fowls, delicious bread, butter, and various fruit preserves. Selecting a locality shaded by a cluster of gaudy sumach-trees, and within a few feet of the clear Potomac, we set up a rude table and seats, constructed from the *disjecta membra* of the cars, and I am certain, had any one seen our impromptu pic-nic, he would not have supposed we were a set of wrecked passengers who had just escaped deadly peril. The ladies, who had exhibited a stem stoicism worthy of their country, cast aside the frigidity of manners characterising their sex at *table d'hôte réunions*, and aided greatly, by their conversation and vivacity, in causing us to forget our mishap. One went so far as to indulge in flashes of wit, and what were, doubtless, thought clever repartees. A gentleman observing, if he were a fish he would go ahead, as the river was so near, the lady in question declared, for her part, she would rather be a Jonah, if the Potomac would obligingly furnish a whale, as she would then go ahead without any trouble.

It was fortunate we had an abundance of ice to cool our water and provisions, for the sun was scorching. During our repast, which was prolonged *pour passer le temps*, the poor slaves sat apart, unheeded by all but myself. It would, indeed, have given me great satisfaction to have had it in my power to gather them within our circle; but this I knew was impossible, for there were slave owners among our party, who gave unequivocal testimony of their feelings for their black brethren. I succeeded, however, in causing our party to break up sooner than it would otherwise have done, in order that the slaves might have the remains of our repast, fortunately sufficiently ample to satisfy their wants.

The reader, who may have had practical experience of the solicitude shown to passengers by railway officials in England on the occasion of an accident, will probably be as surprised to hear, as I was to find, that no attempts were made to send us forward. A camel-engine was despatched from the nearest station to remove our cars from the line, which they effectually blocked. This it did in a very summary manner; but, when the line was clear, we had still to wait the arrival of the train from Baltimore, in cars detached from which we were to be forwarded. Under the circumstances, it was fortunate our abiding-place presented many features of great natural beauty; for the Potomac waters a lovely country.

I spent some time examining the rails over which we had passed. They were worn in many places to a mere ribbon by the crushing weight of the huge camel-engines employed to draw coal-trains. It was no longer surprising we had gone off the line; the wonder was how we had kept on so long. The conductor, indeed, admitted they did get off the rails pretty frequently; but added they rarely killed people.

At length, after a detention of five hours, we resumed our journey; and, as it was no longer possible to pull up the lost time, our speed was not excessive. The wretched state of the line kept us in a continual state of apprehension; but we fortunately reached Harper's Ferry without further accident. Here the beauties of the Potomac centre, forming a scene which Jefferson declared worth going across the Atlantic to see, as being "one of the most stupendous in nature."

The main features consist in the confluence of the Potomac and Shenandoah rivers, which pass through a gorge in the Blue Ridge Mountains, here upwards of 1200 feet high. In the distance, looking up the river, the mountains gradually blend their wooded summits, and, glancing outward, the country spreads in a soft, rich, cultivated landscape;—this is the view so highly praised by Jefferson. There was happily sufficient light to see it while the train stopped, but the rest of my journey to Relay House was performed in the dark. Had all gone well I should have reached Washington in the evening; as it was, in consequence of the accident, and being obliged to lie by at sidings to allow trains to pass, I did not get to Relay House until two hours after midnight,—of course too late for the Washington trains. With some difficulty I obtained entrance into the hotel, where I was glad to rest after a long day of more than usual fatigue and excitement. The following morning I took a train after breakfast to Washington. The country is picturesque, but not being favourable for agriculture, the curious spectacle of large tracts of land bristling with stumps meets the eye to the verge of the capital. When liberated from the cars, I fell into the hands, or arms rather, of a ravenous host of hotel touters and cabmen, whose conduct did not give me a very favourable idea of the police regulations of the United States metropolis. At length I was rescued by the agent of the hotel to which I purposed going, and, after a long drive through sandy streets, I came to a pause for some days in the Marble House.

6

WALT WHITMAN, 'TO A LOCOMOTIVE IN WINTER', IN *LEAVES OF GRASS* (LONDON: D. BOGUE, 1881), 358–359

THEE for my recitative,
Thee in the driving storm even as now, the snow, the winter-day declining,
Thee in thy panoply, thy measur'd dual throbbing and thy beat convulsive,
Thy black cylindric body, golden brass and silvery steel,
Thy ponderous side-bars, parallel and connecting rods, gyrating, shuttling at thy sides,
Thy metrical, now swelling pant and roar, now tapering in the distance,
Thy great protruding head-light fix'd in front,
Thy long, pale, floating vapor-pennants, tinged with delicate purple,
The dense and murky clouds out-belching from thy smoke-stack,
Thy knitted frame, thy springs and valves, the tremulous twinkle of thy wheels,
Thy train of cars behind, obedient, merrily following,
Through gale or calm, now swift, now slack, yet steadily careering;
Type of the modern—emblem of motion and power—pulse of the continent,
For once come serve the Muse and merge in verse, even as here I see thee,
With storm and buffeting gusts of wind and falling snow,
By day thy warning ringing bell to sound its notes,
By night thy silent signal lamps to swing.

Fierce-throated beauty!
Roll through my chant with all thy lawless music, thy swinging lamps at night,
Thy madly-whistled laughter, echoing, rumbling like an earthquake, rousing all,
Law of thyself complete, thine own track firmly holding,
(No sweetness debonair of tearful harp or glib piano thine,)
Thy trills of shrieks by rocks and hills return'd,
Launch'd o'er the prairies wide, across the lakes,
To the free skies unpent and glad and strong.

7

EMILY PFEIFFER, *FLYING LEAVES FROM EAST TO WEST* (LONDON: FIELD AND TUER, 1885), PP. 118–120

A trifle tired in the early part of the day, but both of us well upon the whole, and bearing the long jolting seemingly better than our neighbours. In the car of which we have a section, there are no less than eight children—two families, one of three, the other of four little ones, and one little girl travelling under the care of her uncle, the guard The family of four is rather a noisy and restless one; that of three, remarkably well-behaved. It comprises a boy baby, who has the aptitude of a Mark Tapley for coming out bravely under difficulties. He clearly does not derive it from his mother, unless, indeed, little vampire that he is, he has sucked it all out of her. She is a pallid blonde, with an air of indifference to things in general; and not much wonder either, for this very cheerful and eager baby had been in such haste to be born, that he had actually come into the world when the one he supplanted was only eleven months old.

We see a great deal in print about the splendour of the railway cars, and the luxurious travelling in the States. Well, the cars, that is, the Pullman cars, are certainly admirably contrived, and the workmanship of them, as seen in the ease with which the sleeping apparatus is adjusted, as perfect as workmanship can be. The commissariat also, though a little messy and unwholesome, as cooked food is apt to be in America, is as good as can well be expected under the difficult circumstances; but when luxury is talked of, let no one accustomed to the gentle amenities of life suppose that his cultivated sensibilities are going to be put to no strain. The fact that you are in a democratic country is pressed upon you from every side; no exclusiveness is here possible. The seats in the ordinary Pullman sleeping car face each other two and two, and there are means of adjusting a table between; but these sections, as they are called, are not divided off, the whole car forming but one room on wheels. It does not often happen that the company in these sleeping cars, the extra price of which makes of them practically a first class, is of the rudest; and where this is not the case, the greater circulation of air in the interior, and the larger space visible to the eye, takes something from the tedium of a long journey. The worst is, the close quarters into which you are brought with so many strange people, when at night the white jacketed negroes have turned each section into a couple of beds, one above the other, and have let down the curtains on your slumbers or meditations. Very droll it is to mark the bulging of the curtains, as the struggling bodies behind are getting in or out of their apparel As for the beds, when you once find your way to them, they are comfortable enough, wider and better than the berths at sea; but the washing apparatus, and the one little closet in which to use it, is sadly inadequate, and cleanliness for the time being can only exist as a memory, or hover before you as a blessed vision of the future. Few have the callousness to take off their clothes and go systematically through their ablutions on the inside of a bolted door at which half a dozen women and children are keeping up a devil's tattoo.

I lay in my berth the second night on our way from Chicago to Denver, resting body and mind; and looking out upon the earth that seemed as in swift flight, and upon the steadfast heaven above it, the Great Bear—the Plough, as I then preferred to think of it—nearer to the horizon by many degrees than with us, appeared to be pointing significantly to the virgin soil which had as yet never known tool or tilth of man. All for some hundreds of miles was at present wild prairie, but the iron road had invaded it, and the pioneers of progress were not far off. The horizon line of this surface, totally without incident, appeared so near, that it seemed as if one might have fallen off the world and have had nothing to hold by. The sea is ruffled by its waves, but the globe of the earth in this aspect looked smooth as a melon.

The colour and clearness, the light and glory of the heavens by day and night have been as balm to the sense, aching often for the lack of the beauty so abundantly promised.

Part 2

RIVERS OF IRON
Cultures of railway construction and management

8

HENRY L. ABBOT AND R. S. WILLIAMSON, 'NARRATIVE AND ITINERARY-PIT RIVER VALLEY', *REPORT OF LIEUT. HENRY L. ABBOT UPON EXPLORATIONS FOR A RAILROAD ROUTE FROM THE SACRAMENTO VALLEY TO THE COLUMBIA RIVER* (WASHINGTON D.C., 1857), PP. 56–75

Narrative and itinerary.—route of the main command

On May 5th, 1855, Lieut. Williamson, with the civilian assistants and myself, sailed from New York, and on May 30 arrived at San Francisco. Here lie organized the surveying party. On July 9, 1855, the command was in depot camp, near Benicia, and ready to commence field work on the following day.

The party consisted of Lieut. R. S. Williamson, Topographical Engineers, in charge of the expedition, with myself for his principal assistant; Dr. J. S. Newberry, geologist and botanist, Mr. H. C. Fillebrown, assistant engineer; Dr. E. Sterling, physician and naturalist; Mr. C. D. Anderson, computer; and Mr. John Young, draughtsman. There were also eighteen men, under the immediate supervision of Sir. Charles Coleman, the pack master.

As much of the survey was to be made in a mountainous, unexplored region, Lieut. Williamson decided to transport all the supplies by a pack train. The only vehicle was a light two-wheeled cart, designed solely to carry the instruments. These consisted of two Gambey sextants, two artificial horizons, four box chronometers, three prismatic compasses, one surveyor's chain and pins, one odometer, four Green's cistern barometers, with a case of extra unfilled tubes, four thermometers, two reconnoitring glasses, one aneroid barometer, and several smaller instruments.

July 10.—We left camp about noon. The road, at first, led over low rolling hills to the mars by edge of Suisun bay. After following this for a short distance, it passed over a nearly level country, to a small creek with slightly brackish water.

It then crossed a level plain, bordered by low hills and dotted with a few oaks, to Suisun creek, where we encamped. Much of the soil near the road to-day was rich and under cultivation.

July 11.—The road was at first slightly hilly, and bordered by a few scattered oaks. It then crossed a level plain, bare of trees, where the heat was very oppressive. We found a little lake on this plain, and the dry beds of two small streams, which were evidently tributaries in the rainy season. Towards the end of the day's march, the country again became undulating. We encamped on a small creek, near a collection of two or three houses called Vacaville.

July 12.—To-day, we travelled among the low foot hills of the Coast Range to Putos creek, where there were several fine oak, peach, and fig trees, and a vineyard. The hills could be avoided by keeping further towards the east. Lieut. Williamson made the following note upon Putos creek, in his journal: "Putos creek, at the most favorable point, requires a bridge 130 feet in length. The bed of the stream is now 20 feet below the banks, and the water less than a foot deep. In the winter and spring, the banks are nearly reached by the water. The stream, I am informed, was named after a tribe of Indians which lived upon its banks, and which were known to the Spaniards as the Putos Indians; the word 'putos', being masculine, means a lazy, worthless vagabond. Hence the creek was called Rio de los Putos. It is, however, generally called Puta creek, and sometimes Pewter creek."

The road next crossed a dry, dusty plain, several miles in width, where every breath of air felt like the blast of a furnace, so intense was the heat. We then entered a fine oak forest, which skirted the banks of Cache creek. We encamped at the lower ford of this creek, after having crossed at the upper. The following extract is from Lieut. Williamson's journal.

"This stream has, in many places, a bottom as much as a half mile wide. The width of the stream itself, at the narrowest part I saw near the upper crossing, was, I should think, about 300 yards. At the lower crossing, it was much narrower, being only about 100 yards wide, with banks 30 feet high. I am told that in times of freshet it rises so much as to overflow these banks."

July 13.—Early this morning, we reached the Sacramento river at Knight's rancho, and, finding that the most direct road to Marysville was impassable on account of mire, followed down the river to Fremont. Here we crossed by a ferry. The water was low, the river being only about 250 yards in width. At season of high water it is at least 100 yards wider, and during freshets it sometimes overflows its banks for miles. It is bordered by a dense growth of willows, sycamores and oaks. We followed up Feather river for about 8.5 miles, and encamped near Nicholas. The road to-day was level, and often led through noble forests of oak. There was little or no underbrush, and the country resembled a grand old park in appearance. Many large squirrels were seen among the trees.

July 14.—For a few miles this morning, the road continued to be bordered by the noble oak forest. The extreme shortness of their trunks gave the trees the strange appearance of having been pressed down into the ground. On leaving the forest, we travelled over a dry, dusty plain, which continued to Marysville, a fine little city, containing several brick stores and houses, and presenting a very thriving appearance. It is situated near the junction of the Yuba and Feather rivers. We encamped opposite it, on the former stream, which was turbid from the gold washing carried on near its sources. The sediment deposited by it is having a marked effect upon the navigation of Feather river.

July 15.—To-day we forded the Yuba river, and after passing through Marysville crossed Feather river by a good wooden bridge. The first stream was about 200, and the second 250 feet in width, and both were bordered by low bluffs. Lieutenant Williamson decided to make a short march to-day, as it was necessary to repair the pack saddles. We accordingly travelled only 5.8 miles, through a level, dusty country, and encamped on Feather river.

July 16.—After travelling over a very dusty, level road bordered by scattered oaks, we encamped at Hamilton. The heat was very oppressive during the day.

July 17.—The road to-day left Feather river, and struck across a dry, dusty plain, to Niel's rancho, on Butte creek. The phenomenon of mirage was very distinctly seen during the early part of the march. We crossed Butte creek and Little Butte creek, about three miles beyond it, and encamped on Chico creek. The country was flat and uninteresting. Near camp was a rancheria of Digger Indians. Their huts were partly excavated in the ground, and roofed over with sticks plastered with mud. When we visited them, at about sunset, the women were sitting on top of their houses, engaged in shelling out grain which they had gleaned from the neighboring fields. The men, nearly naked, were congregated in a large hut, gambling. A few burning sticks in the centre of the group threw a flickering light over the scene. The game was played by four men, who were seated in pairs, on opposite sides of the fire, while the background was filled up with eager spectators. Before each party was a pile of straw. One couple continually twisted up, and threw into the air, wisps of this straw, managing at the same time to conceal in it two pieces of white wood or bone. The other couple anxiously watched their movements, keeping up a monotonous, guttural cry. Whenever they thought they had detected the locality of the sticks, they clapped their hands violently, and their rivals immediately shook open the suspected wisp. If the sticks were there, the successful guessers received them, and began in their turn to throw them up; if not, the first couple continued. The excitement occasioned by this simple game was intense. The perspiration poured in streams down the naked bodies of the players, and their eyes glared in the dim fire-light like those of demons. Their voices were so hoarse as to be hardly articulate, and yet they kept on, without a moment's cessation. They might well be excited, for, as I was informed, they stake everything, even their women and children, on the result of the game.

July 18.—To-day the road lay mostly over dusty plains, destitute of timber. Dry gullies, which in the rainy season are undoubtedly the beds of streams of considerable size, were numerous. We encamped on Deer creek. During the evening quite an excitement was created by the report that a grizzly bear was in the bushes near us; but the monster proved to be only a burnt log. Grizzly bears are sometimes found in this part, of the valley.

July 19.—We travelled over a slightly undulating country to Antelope creek, where we encamped. The road crossed several places where there were sudden descents, of about twenty feet, from a plateau to a lower level; and, in distances varying from a few yards to half a mile, corresponding ascents again. These places did not resemble the beds of creeks. There was but little timber near the road during most of the day's march.

July 20.—This morning Lieut. Williamson gave me instructions to cross the Sacramento river, at lied Bluffs, with the instrument cart, and follow the ordinary route to Fort Reading; while he proceeded with the main party to examine the eastern bank. This I did, without any incident worthy of note. The country, which was slightly undulating, and occasionally timbered, differed in no important particulars from the portion of the valley traversed during the last few days by the main party. The following description of Lieut. Williamson's route to the Fort is compiled from his note book.

"After following a road over the hills, for about ten miles, this morning, we discovered that it led to a pinery among the mountains. We, therefore, turned nearly at right angles to ourformer course, and struck across the hills to Beaver creek, which we found flowing in a small canon. We then crossed a rocky plain to Liver creek, where we encamped. The hills may be avoided by keeping nearer the bank of the Sacramento.

"*July* 21.—As far as Battle creek we found the road pretty rough. At first it crossed a ridge, which might be avoided, with some rock cutting, by passing around the bluff. The rest of the road to the Fort was good, a few short, steep slopes accepted."

Fort Reading is situated on the northern bank of Cow creek, a little stream which discharges itself into the Sacramento, about a mile and a half below the post. There are dry, elevated plains northwest, and a steep bluff conducting to a higher plateau, east of the Fort. The buildings are mostly made of adobes; but some are of wood. The locality is unhealt by in the summer, on account of the prevalence of fever and ague.

We were courteously received and hospitably entertained by Major F. O. Wyse, 3d artillery, and the other officers stationed at the post. The escort here joined us. It consisted of Lieut. H. G. Gibson, 3d artillery; Lieut. George Crook, 4th infantry, commissary and quartermaster of the expedition; Lieut. J. B. Hood, 2d cavalry; and 100 men, twenty being dragoons, and the remainder artillery and infantry soldiers. Mr. J. Daniels was quartermaster's clerk, and Mr. J. B. Vinton pack master of the escort.

Various causes of delay prevented Lieut. Williamson from continuing the survey until the twenty-eighth of July. Ur. J. F. Hammond, United States army, the surgeon of the Fort, very kindly volunteered to have a series of barometric observations taken at the post, during the continuance of the field work. Lieut. Williamson accordingly left one of the barometers in his charge. His observations proved of very great value in the subsequent computation of altitudes upon the route, as is fully explained in the chapter of this report devoted to that subject.

At the recommendation of Major Heading, Lieut. Williamson employed as guide and scout an old hunter, named Bartee, but usually known as "Old Red." He proved a valuable addition to the party.

July 28.—To-day we left Fort Reading, and began our journey towards the wild region east of the western chain of the Sierra Nevada. Lieut. Crook, with the foot soldiers and the escort train, had left Fort Reading two days before our departure, and encamped at McCumber's Flat, distant 30 miles from the post. Lieut. Williamson, being detained by necessary business, sent forward his train this morning, and started about noon to follow it with his assistants, accompanied for a short distance by Dr. Hammond. We crossed Cow creek at a good ford, where the stream was about 50 feet in width, and then abruptly ascended to a level plateau, elevated about 200 feet above the Fort. We travelled 3.5 miles over this plain to the crossing of Bear creek, a branch about 30 feet in width; and then began a gradual ascent. The road soon entered a thick pine and oak forest, varied by occasional clumps of manzanita bushes. Grizzly bears are often found in this vicinity. Our train had taken a wrong road, and we were compelled, in consequence, to encamp without blankets or cooking utensils, near the small rancho of Mr. Asbury. A rather cold and uncomfortable night was spent by most of us.

July 29.—To-day we started early, and continued our course through a thick pine and fir forest, many trees of which bore long, graceful bunches of black and light colored mosses, with an occasional bough of mistletoe. We crossed two small streams, the first, Ash creek, about ten feet, and the second, Mill creek, about twenty feet in width. The water of the latter was very cold, its temperature being 47° Fahrenheit, while that of the air was 79° Fahrenheit.

At both creeks saw mills were in operation. The ascent to-day was much steeper than that of yesterday. We reached Lieutenant Crook's camp at McCumber's Flat, on Battle creek, at about 1 p.m., and our missing train arrived in the course of the afternoon. We had gained an elevation of about 3,000 feet above Fort Reading, and the clear, cool air of the mountains was delightful, when compared with the burning, sickly miasma which we had left behind. The seeds of intermittent fever, however, implanted while passing through the Sacramento valley, remained, and a large majority of the party suffered from this disease before the end of the survey.

McCumber's Flat is a small opening, thickly carpeted with grass, and surrounded by a dense pine and fir forest. Battle creek, after passing through it, disappears among the trees, and with a sullen roar struggles furiously down its rocky bed. A more pleasant camping place could hardly be desired.

July 30.—To-day, we crossed the western chain of the Sierra Nevada, by Noble's Pass. The road, which was very steep, rocky, and bordered by pine timber, followed up a branch of Battle creek. In some places it was difficult to drag even the light instrument cart up the precipitous ridges. After leaving the creek, a very steep rise conducted to a long, gently ascending slope, bare of trees, but covered with a dense growth of manzanita bushes. This slope led to the divide, which was perceptible, although by no means steep. Its elevation above the sea was 6,200 feet. A fine view was obtained from a point near the road. Lassen's Butte with its snowy crest, rose proudly above the surrounding mountains on the south. Far distant to the westward was a long line of peaks, belonging to the Coast Range, while at our feet lay the Sacramento valley. But we turned gladly from its parched plains to scan the rough country towards the east, which we were next to traverse. The course of Pit river, as it came from the dim distance, and wound out of sight among the mountains on the north, could be indistinctly traced; while dark timbered ridges, with occasional plains, filled up the rest of the picture.

The descent from the summit was at first gentle, but soon became precipitous. The Indians had recently set fire to the woods, and the smoke, mingling with the clouds of dust raised by our animals, was stifling. Near the foot of the ridge, we struck a small stream about fifteen feet in width, called Lost creek. After leaving the road and following down this creek about half a mile, we encamped with good grass and water. The forest was more open on the eastern than on the western slope of the mountains, and it was now almost entirely composed of pine. A deer had been killed on the march, and we had our first venison to-night.

July 31.—This morning, at half past five o'clock, the thermometer indicated 40° Fahrenheit, a great change in temperature from the Sacramento valley, where it had generally stood at about 65° Fahrenheit at this hour. We retraced our steps to the emigrant road, and after bidding farewell to Dr. Hammond, who returned to Fort Reading, followed it through an open and nearly level valley to the next stream, which was about twenty feet in width and called Hat creek. Both this and Lost creek are branches of Canoe creek. After crossing the stream, we left the road, and followed down the valley, without any trail. Light smoke, rising from the summits of the neighboring hills, informed us that our advance was discovered by the watchful savages, although we had seen none of them as yet. The route was good at first, although somewhat obstructed by manzanita bushes, which delayed the little cart. As we advanced, however, we had to pass several rocky ledges. The creek at length divided into two channels, enclosing a small island. This we crossed, and following the western side of the stream soon came to where it cañoned through a ledge, nearly vertical on one side, and gently sloping on the other. Crossing this with difficulty, we again struck the stream, and re-crossed it over another island to the eastern bunk. The soil became light, like ashes, and our animals sank over the fetlock at every stop. The hills soon closed in upon the creek, and we encamped with good water and grass. Lieutenant Williamson sent the guide forward to examine the route for a short distance in advance. On his return he reported it very rocky and destitute of grass. A barometer was broken to-day by the jolting of the cart.

August 1.—This morning we entered a rocky pedregal of scoriaceous trap, which taxed our patience to the utmost. It was difficult to advance with the mules, but far more so with the cart. we were forced to make long halts before a way could be found, and then to almost carry the vehicle along by hand. Once it overturned, and the shock rendered the chronometers useless for the determination of longitude for the rest of the survey. Instead of improving, the road became worse; and, at length, we turned towards the timbered hills which bounded it on the east, and travelled among them for a short distance with more ease. Before long, however, we found ourselves on the summit of a precipice of trap rock, at least one hundred feet in height, which conducted to the lava field again. The cart was let down by hand; and we toiled on, near the ledge which continued to bound the valley, until we suddenly came to a beautiful, grassy spot, intersected by numerous brooks. Here we encamped, after a most laborious march, having advanced only about 4.5 miles on our journey. A branch of the stream gushed from the face of the precipice near our camp, and, after falling about twenty or thirty feet vertically, united with another which flowed at the base of the ledge. The following note upon these springs I extract from Lieut. Williamson's journal.

"A portion of the water of the brooks gushed from a spring in the mountain side. It is highly probable that the main part comes from a canon in the hills to the northeast, but of this we have no positive proof. About a quarter of a mile below camp, all the streams, after uniting in one, disappear entirely, flowing into chasms in the scoriaceous trap. Whether it re-appears, or not, is not known. The united stream is about twenty feet wide, and belly-deep to the mules."

While examining the vicinity of camp with one of the party, I came suddenly upon an Indian, evidently reconnoitring. He was nearly naked, and armed with bow and arrows. With considerable difficulty we prevailed upon him to enter camp. After throwing him into paroxysms of delight by the sight of his ugly countenance in a small mirror, we sent him on his way rejoicing, appareled in a white shirt, and gnawing a huge piece of salt pork.

August 2.—This morning our visitor returned with about twenty of his nearly naked friends, all of whom gave us to understand that they were enduring agonies of hunger. After giving them food, we left the miserable wretches collecting the offal which remained near the cook's fire. The Pit river Indians are very treacherous and bloody in their dispositions and disgusting in their habits. They are armed with bows and arrows, which they make with great skill. The bows are sticks of soft wood, about three feet in length, backed with deer sinew. The bow string also is of sinew. The arrows are made in three parts. The head is generally of obsidian, which abounds in portions of the valley. It is carefully shaped into the usual barbed form, and lashed by deer sinew to one end of a small stick of hard wood about ten inches long. The other end of the stick is inserted into the extremity of a reed and also lashed with sinew. The reed is tipped with feathers, attached by the same kind of fastening. This weapon inflicts a dangerous injury; as the blood immediately softens the sinew, and, on attempting to extract the arrow, the reed separates from the hard wood stick, and that from the arrow head, which thus remains at the bottom of the wound. It is said that these savages sometimes poison their arrows by exposing a piece of liver to the repeated bites of a rattlesnake, and, after burying it for a short time, smearing the point with the half decomposed muss.

For about five miles to-day, the pedregal continued to be as rough as it was yesterday, and we could advance only with great difficulty. At length, however, we entered a pine forest, and soon after struck an Indian trail, which rendered travelling very much easier. It conducted us to the bank of Canoe creek, which we found flowing through a fine, grassy meadow. Again entering the forest, and coutinuing our course for a few miles further, we discovered a second fine valley, carpeted with grass and clover. Near the northern side of it flowed a tributary of Canoe creek, at least five times the size of the main stream. We encamped near the junction of these crocks, with an abundant supply of wood, water, and grass.

August 3.—Some little doubt had arisen whether the large tributary on which we were encamped was not Pit river, and Lieut. Williamson determined to leave the main party in camp to-day, and go himself, with the dragoons, to explore. He returned about noon, having followed down Canoe creek to where it discharged into Pit river. It flowed between precipitous banks, with many cascades and rapids. At its mouth it was eighty or ninety feet in width. It received no important tributary below our camp, except a branch from Lake Freaner, which flowed into it over a trap dike about fifteen feet in height.

In the afternoon, Lieut. Williamson sent one of the party to follow up the largo tributary of Canoe creek. On his return, the man reported that, about two miles above camp, the water gushed furiously from some fifteen crevices in the rocks, thus forming brooks, which united and formed the stream. He walked entirely round its sources, and returned dry shod on the bank opposite the one on which he started.

August 4.—This morning the party separated. Lieut. Williamson started with the dragoons, to explore the lower cañon of Pit river, giving me directions to advance, with the main party, to a point on the river near the mouth of Canoe creek. After leaving camp, we soon found ourselves among thick pine timber and underbrush, which greatly delayed the cart, and rendered it necessary to carry most of the instruments by hand. In some places the trail followed along the side of steep hills, and several men were constantly employed in preventing the vehicle from overturning. At length, in attempting to run over a manzanita bush in one of these places, it turned completely over; so that the mule lay on his back, struggling violently in the thick underbrush. After crossing one smaller branch, we finally succeeded in reaching a fine, grassy meadow on the bank of Pit river, about two miles above the mouth of Canoe creek. Here we encamped.

Lieut. P. H. Sheridan, 4th infantry, overtook the party to-day, with orders to relieve Lieut. Hood, who was instructed to return to the eastern States and join his regiment without delay.

The following extract from Lieut. Williamson's journal shows the result of his exploration to-day.

"We followed nearly the same trail as yesterday for about five miles, and then took a trail running east, which led to Stoneman's ridge. I went to the highest point, and obtained bearings to Mount Shasta, Lassen's Butte, and other peaks. I then ordered Bartee to follow the ridge towards the south until he found a low depression, and then to endeavor to find a good route from it to the river near

Canoe creek. This he did. I next went to the entrance of the cañon. we found it impossible to go through it on foot, on account of the precipitous Bides, which came down abruptly into the water. The north aide was black rock, inclined about 45°. The south side was infusorial earth, inclined from the horizon 60° or more. Not being able to follow the summit of the precipice, I returned down the river to camp, near the mouth of Canoe creek."

August 5.—Lieut. Hood started this morning with a small escort, on his return to Fort Reading, much to the regret of the whole party. Lieut. Williamson, with the dragoons, went to follow the liver bluff, directing me to take the train through the pass found yesterday by Bartee. The trail led over several small, rocky hills, heavily timbered with pine. After passing along the western foot of Stoneman's ridge for nearly two miles, we crossed it at a low point, and followed down a gentle slope to the river. The soil was mostly light volcanic ashes, but the trail was occasionally rocky. After riding a short distance near the stream, which was deep and sluggish, we passed the spot where Fall river, after breaking in cascades and rapids over a bluff about 30 feet in height, plunges into Pit river. About half a mile further on, we found Lieut. Williamson encamped near a small brook, a tributary of Pit river. Its water was much colder than that of the river, which had a mars by taste. Wood and grass abounded in the vicinity. Lieut. Williamson had succeeded in following the river bluff. Where the stream emerged from the mountains, and for about a mile above, he found the banks about 150 feet in height, and very precipitous. The canon was so narrow at its mouth that he could not enter it on foot.

After reaching camp, I re-filled two barometers which had been broken. During the night a mule was stolen by the Indians.

August 6.—This morning, to avoid a bend, Lieut. Williamson left the river and struck across towards the upper canon. At first, the trail passed through pine timber, but it soon entered a nearly level prairie, in some places rocky, and in others dusty. There were numerous gopher holes in it, which were dug so near the surface that our animals often broke through into them. After reaching the river again, the trail became quite rocky, and we were compelled to cross numerous sloughs, as well as the main stream twice. At length we encamped near the entrance of the upper canon. A fire soon broke out among the dry grass and bushes, which was extinguished, with difficulty, by the united exertions of the whole command. Another barometer was broken and re-filled to-day. At night the Indians stole a mule, but it was traced, found tied in one of their rancherias, and recovered by our packers.

August 7.—To-day Lieut. Williamson followed along the northern edge of the cañon, directing me to take the route among the hills with the main party. On leaving camp, we crossed the river at a shallow but very rocky ford, and immediately climbed the river bluff, which was more than 100 feet in height, and so steep that it required twenty men to pull up the instrument cart. The chief obstacle to travel to-day was a vast amount of trap rock, which covered the ground in many places. In others, the heat of the sun had baked the earth, and made it crack in a manner which rendered travelling laborious. We saw but little timber on the road; and the hills were generally low, and not very steep. In passing over the rocks, one spring and the axle of the cart were broken. I succeeded in transporting it to camp, but there found it to be irreparably injured. The body was abandoned, but the axle was mended sufficiently to hold the wheels together, in order to continue the use of the odometer.

Several Indians came into camp in the afternoon, and I saw one of them kindle a fire by rubbing two pieces of wood together. A block of cedar, about six inches square and one inch thick, perforated with a small hole, formed the lower piece. One Indian held this firmly on a horizontal rock, after having placed a little tinder under the hole. A second took a round stick, apparently of elder, about six inches long and a quarter of an inch in diameter, and, inserting one end in the hole, rolled it very rapidly between the palms of his hands. In a few moments sparks of fire fell down upon the tinder and ignited it. These savages have a fondness for smoking tobacco, which I have never seen equalled. They inhale the smoke, and, after retaining it as long as possible, force it through their nostrils in an ecstasy of pleasure. They mark their faces with black, as a sign of mourning, and with red, for ornament; but I have never seen both colors used at once. Many of them perforate the nose, and insert a straight piece of bone about an inch and a half in length.

Our camp to-night was on the river bank near the eastern entrance of the cañon, where we found an abundant supply of excellent grass. I extract the following remarks upon the canon, from Lieut. Williamson's note book.

"The river itself was shallow throughout the whole canon, and always had a space between the water and bluff wide enough for a wagon road. No falls were noticed, and I saw nearly the whole of the canon. The bluffs were from 100 to 700 or 800 feet in height, and of basaltic trap. The slope was generally of the debris from the rock, but often vertical columns of the basalt were seen. In one place I noticed veins of a red material, the color of cinnabar."

August 8.—After fording the river, which was about forty feet in width, we continued our course through a level, grassy valley, bare of trees. Several grouse, duck and curlew were shot on the march. We passed many pits about six feet deep and lightly covered with twigs and grass. The river derives its name from these pits, which are dug by the Indians to entrap game. On this account, Lieut. Williamson always spelled the name with a single t, although on most maps it is written with two. We encamped on the bank of the river, which here flowed between bluffs, from twenty to thirty feet in height, bordered by bushes. Large quantities of obsidian were found in the vicinity. The river was about thirty feet in width.

Lieut. Williamson made the following note on the day's march.

"To-day we had a level, good, but tedious ride. Opposite the middle of the valley, to the west, is an opening in the hills of considerable breadth. This looks as if the hills south of the opening were the northern slope of the range north of Fall River valley. Opposite the head of the valley the hills appear again. Near our evening camp, I went, on a ridge and found hills to the westward, not at all formidable in appearance, but which would still require work to make then, passable for a railroad."

August 9.—Lieut. Williamson directed me to remain in camp with the main party and observe for latitude, &c., to-day, while he, with Lieut. Sheridan and the dragoons, explored the road in advance. The heat was oppressive, but the bushes near the river bank afforded a thick and pleasant shade.

The following extract from Lieutenant Williamson's journal shows the result of his examination.

"We followed the Lassen trail for 2.5 miles, to where it crossed the river at the mouth of a small, dry branch. We here left the road to take the old Oregon trail, which was very distinct. It led north up the branch to the divide, and thence on, in the same direction, until we struck a spring branch in pine timber, about seven miles from the river. I went on top of a partially bald hill and had a view of the country. The hills followed to the north, probably inclining to the east. The rest of the country east of the meridian line appeared to be rolling, or slightly hilly, and covered with open pine timber. I was sorry I could not ascertain if the spring branch had a continuous bed to Pit river. Its course near its source was westerly; but there is no reason to suppose that it did not bend toward the south, and discharge into Pit river about ten miles below our camp. I feel pretty sure either that it sinks, (that is, has no continuous bed,) or that it goes to Pit river. In the latter case, the railroad should follow it up."

August 10.—To-day, we travelled over the route examined by Lieutenant Williamson yesterday, and encamped at what he termed the "spring branch." It was a little creek about ten feet in width, which flowed through a small opening bordered by pine timber. The stream was so choked up with bushes, that, in many places, it could only be reached by cutting them away. Towards the lower part of the opening, the brook spread out into a little swamp Frogs of a very peculiar species were found in the creek and swamp, in great numbers. An antelope was shot near camp.

August 11.—The party was aroused at three o'clock this morning, by Lieutenant Williamson's order; as it was very uncertain how far we might be obliged to travel before reaching water. The head of the antelope killed yesterday, had been baked by allowing it to remain all night buried among hot stones, and it furnished an excellent breakfast. We followed the wagon road through an open pine forest for about six miles, and then, finding that it inclined too much to the west, left it, and endeavored to keep, by compass, a course N. 20° W. After travelling several miles on nearly level ground through the forest, we emerged from it, and found ourselves on a rocky plain covered with sage bushes. This we crossed in about six miles, and, on reaching the summit of a line of low sandstone hills capped with trap, saw below us Wright lake. It was a fine sheet of water, about eleven miles long and four miles wide, bordered by tule. The banks were so miry that we were compelled to travel more than a mile before reaching a place where the animals could drink. We encamped in the edge of the tule, near some green willow bushes which supplied us with our only fuel, as even sage bushes had disappeared after crossing the hills.

August 12.—Our course, at first, lay along the southwestern shore of the lake, where the hills occasionally terminated very abruptly at the water's edge. The horn of a mountain sheep, weighing several pounds, was found near the trail. After crossing the low hills which border the lake, we travelled through a gently undulating region, dotted with sage bushes, for about seven miles. We then found ourselves on the edge of an abrupt descent of 200 feet, which conducted to the shores of Rhett lake. This lake was about fourteen miles long and eight miles broad. It was bordered by a wide belt of tule, the home of vast numbers of water-fowl, which rose in clouds at our approach.

On the bluff the trail joined an emigrant road, which followed down a narrow ravine to the level of the lake. This ravine was once the scene of a bloody massacre. A party of Indians lay in ambush, until an emigrant train reached the middle of the descent, and then attacked and killed nearly the whole party. Rhett lake is a secure retreat, where the savages can escape among the tule, in their light canoes, and defy a greatly superior force.

The line of hills which borders the lake on the northeastern side, is separated from the tule by a narrow strip of land, elevated but little above the water. This was covered with grass, the rich green of which presented a refreshing contrast to the sickly blue of the sage plain over which we had been travelling. The clouds of dust ceased, and we journeyed on through a much more pleasing region. After riding a few miles from the bluff, we left the road, and encamped on Lost river near where it discharges itself into the lake by several mouths. It was a deep, unfordable stream, flowing with a very sluggish current. The banks were abrupt like the sides of a canal. A few sage bushes and "bois des vachcs" supplied the only fuel.

We found, encamped near the stream, a party of men that had come from Yreka to meet and escort an expected emigrant train.

August 13.—Lieut. Williamson determined to pass around the western side of Lower Klamath lake, with Lieut. Sheridan and the dragoon detachment, to examine the route, and to ascertain whether Klamath river flowed through the lake or not. He gave me instructions to proceed with the main party to Upper Klamath lake, and, after selecting a good camping place near its southern extremity, to await his arrival. Nine of the foot soldiers were sick, and they accompanied Lieut. Williamson, to he sent, in charge of a non-commissioned officer, through the pass south of Mount Pitt to Fort Lane.

My party left camp first. We followed up the eastern bank of Lost river, through a dusty sage plain almost destitute of grass, to the Natural Bridge. The river was here about eighty feet wide and very deep; but it was spanned by two natural bridges of conglomerate sandstone from ten to fifteen feet in width, parallel to each other, and not more than two rods apart. The water flowed over both of them. The top of the most northern one inclined down stream, but it was only covered to a depth varying from six inches to two feet. The other was nearly horizontal, but the water, being unusually high, was too deep for fording. There are probably hollows under both arches, through which the river flows. Emigrants cross here with their loaded wagons. There is no ford for a considerable distance above, and none below. We passed over without difficulty, and followed a well marked Indian trail towards the north, through a level valley dotted with sage bushes and a few clumps of hunch grass. The river, which was full of short bends, was often sunk as much as thirty feet below the plain. There was apparently a good ford 4.5 miles above the Natural Bridge. The valley was about three miles wide, and bordered by high hills; those on the east being well timbered with pine, and those on the west nearly bare. The hunch grass became more abundant as we advanced, and the sage hushes fewer in number. After travelling twelve miles from the Natural Bridge, we reached a place where the river issued through a canon from the hills to the eastward; and, although the valley continued towards the north, it was entirely destitute of water. As the distance to Klamath lake was unknown, we left the trail and encamped near the mouth of the canon. The general surface of the plain was here about forty feet above the water; but it was connected by a bench, about 200 yards in width, of not more than half that height. This formed a good camping ground; being covered with fine bunch grass, while bushes and small trees for fuel were found in abundance near the edge of the stream.

August 14.—This morning some excitement was created in camp by the discovery of a huge rattlesnake coiled up under a blanket. The reptile was killed; but, as we all slept without tents on the ground, unpleasant ideas were suggested by the incident. Our course lay towards the north, through a narrow valley thinly covered with sage bushes and clumps of bunch grass.

It was bordered by timbered hills which gradually closed in upon the trail. We crossed several dry beds of streams, and also the bottom of what, in the rainy season, was undoubtedly a small lake. It was now dry, and covered with a white efflorescence. After travelling 9.6 miles we reached a low line of hills, which formed the northern boundary of the valley. Klamath river forced its way through the ridge by a narrow cañon, and, after flowing along the western side of the valley for a short distance and spreading out into a small lake, disappeared among the hills towards the west. On reaching the summit of the very low divide, composed of trap rock, we saw outspread before us Upper Klamath lake. It was a fine sheet of water, thirty miles long and twelve miles wide, bordered by timbered ridges with an occasional narrow belt of tule.

Light clouds of smoke rising from signal fires upon several of the hills satisfied us that watchful eyes were measuring our advance. We had struck a small arm of the lake, from which Klamath river issued. Following along the eastern side, we crossed a grassy meadow, and encamped at the extremity of a hilly promontory which projected into the lake. Excellent bunch grass, with bushes and small trees for fuel, abounded in the vicinity. East of the promontory, a wide field of tule prevented approach to the water; but the western shore was rocky and bold. Snakes of various kinds were very plentiful. Several large rattlesnakes were killed before we had been in camp an hour; and I counted nearly a dozen cast off skins lying within a rod of each other. Two squaws came into camp in the afternoon, with a few fish which they had caught in the lake. We gave them some presents, and they paddled rapidly away in their canoe to spread the news. The water taken from the lake had a dark color and a disagreeable taste, occasioned apparently by decayed tule.

August 15.—We remained in camp to-day, waiting for Lieut. Williamson. Several good observations were obtained for latitude and altitude.

About midnight a sudden alarm aroused camp. the cook's fire had spread, by some dead roots, to the dry grass and bushes; and a general conflagration was prevented only by the most vigorous exertions. It was at first supposed that the Indians had kindled the fire, to engage our attention while they stampeded the mules, and this idea did not tend to lessen the excitement and confusion of the scene.

August 16.—To-day was spent in taking astronomical and barometric observations, while waiting for Lieut. Williamson. A thick haze which covered the lake, entirely concealed the opposite shore. The taste of the water was so disagreeable that several vain attempts were made to discover a spring in the vicinity.

August 17.—Lieut. Williamson with his escort came into camp at noon, having made a satisfactory examination of Lower Klamath lake. A description of his route will be found in Chapter IV. Three broken down mules of the escort train were shot to-day, and every preparation was made for an early start to-morrow.

August 18.—The ridges on the eastern side of the lake, which were composed of vesicular trap, appeared to run parallel to each other in a northeast and southeast direction, and to terminate abruptly at the water's edge. A well marked Indian trail followed along the shore; but members of the party who had explored it for a short distance reported it very rocky, and impassable for "the little cart," as the odometer wheels still continued to be termed. Lieut. Williamson had observed several Indian trails diverging to the right on his last day's march; and he therefore determined to follow a southeast course, hoping to discover some good pass by which he could cross the ridges, and thus avoid the rocks and bends of the shore. After travelling about three miles in this direction through a wooded country, He thought it best to cross abruptly a steep and rocky ridge to the east. We thus reached a narrow valley, lying between two steep ranges of hills, and filled with open pine timber. There was a large Indian trail in it, which conducted us to the lake. A precipitous and rocky ridge rose abruptly from the water, leaving barely sufficient room to pass along the bank. After travelling a short distance, we reached a point where several springs gushed from the hill side, and disappeared among thick bushes surrounded by luxuriant grass. The water was clear and pure, and Lieut. Williamson at once encamped. Elder and service berries were found in abundance. A thick haze prevented astronomical observations, and concealed the western shore of the lake. Snakes, as usual in this region, were very numerous, and one of them glided suddenly among our dishes, as we were sitting down on the ground to eat.

August 19.—This morning the trail, for three or four miles, wound along the rocky side of the ridge which bordered the lake, and was, in consequence, very rough. Huge rocks, piled near the water's edge, prevented the passage of "the little cart" by that route. The hill side was sparsely covered with scattered pines, but near the lake shore springs were numerous, and the growth of bushes was often dense. Bartee, the guide, shot three bald eagles with his rifle, as we passed along the base of the crags upon which they were fearlessly resting.

In riding under the projecting limb of a tree, Mr. Daniels was knocked from his mule and quite severely injured. The country had recently been burnt over, and the want of grass compelled Lieut. Williamson unwillingly to continue the march. The trail soon diverged from the lake shore, and after passing over a dry plain entered an open pine forest. In a short time we found ourselves on the banks of Klamath river, which was flowing through a fine, grassy bottom, marked by a few clumps of willow bushes. Here we encamped. The river was about 150 feet in width, and apparently quite deep. There was a ford, however, a short distance below. Every requisite for a good camp ground was found in abundance in the vicinity.

August 20.—Mr. Daniels was much better this morning and able to ride his mule.

As had been usual of late, a dense fog obscured the view for two or three hours after starting. Our course lay up the eastern side of the beautiful valley of Klamath river. The bottom was at first open, covered with green grass, and bordered by low timbered hills. We passed several cliffs of basaltic breccia, from twenty to fifty feet in height, and occasionally ornamented with rude, Indian paintings. The current of the stream was not very rapid, and there appeared to be several fords. The trail crossed one large and fine tributary which flowed swiftly over a rocky bed. After travelling twelve miles from camp, we reached the mouth of a canon from which the river emerged. The sides were of basaltic rock and pumice-stone, and very steep. Lieut. Williamson estimated their height at 1,000 feet at the highest points. We followed the trail over the ridge on the eastern side of the river, and several times looked down into the canon. Its course appeared to be straight in the main, but small bends were numerous. The ridge was heavily timbered with pine. The forest was on fire, and an occasional heavy crash reverberating for miles, warned us to beware of falling trees. The canon was about four miles in length. A short distance beyond it northern entrance, we emerged from the forest and entered a lovely meadow, covered with clover and fine green grass. The ground was miry near the river, which was deep and sluggish, and we encamped at the edge of the timber. The meadow appeared to be an arm of Klamath marsh, and was evidently flooded at seasons of high water.

August 21.—This morning at daybreak, the fog was so dense that we could not see fifty yards in advance, but the sun soon caused it to melt away. The trail led us over a thickly timbered ridge which projected into the meadow. The soil was light pumice-stone dust, and fallen trees rendered travelling somewhat difficult. At the northeastern base of the ridge we reached the shore of Klamath marsh. This was a strip of half submerged land, about twelve miles long and seven miles broad. It was covered by clumps of tule and other aquatic plants separated by small sheets of water. Thousands of ducks, plover, and other water birds, made it their home. They were so tame that they would hardly fly at the report of a gun, but it was useless to shoot them, as the deep mud rendered it impossible to secure them afterwards. We surprised two Indians on the shore, and endeavored to make them understand that we were friendly; but they evidently distrusted our professions, and escaped as soon as possible.

Lieut. Williamson decided to follow the eastern shore of the marsh. We soon reached a collection of Indian huts built near the edge of the water. Our two friends had evidently been there before us, for the rancheria had been very recently deserted. Large quantities of food, consisting mostly of seeds of water plants and dried fish, several canoes made of hollowed logs, many baskets formed of reeds curiously woven together, and divers other valuables, were scattered around in wild confusion. The fires were burning in front of the huts, of which there were three distinct kinds. the summer lodges had vertical wails supporting lint roofs. They were composed of a framework of sticks, covered with a matting of woven tule. The winter huts were shaped like bee-hives, and made of sticks plastered with mud. We noticed only one of the third kind, which was apparently used for a council house. A hole, about four feet deep and ten feet square, had been excavated, and the earth heaped up around the sides. Large sticks planted in this mud wall supported a roof made of cross poles covered with earth. The entrance was by a flight of mud stops that conducted to the roof, from which a rude ladder led through a hole to the floor below. Each of these structures is represented in the accompanying wood cuts, together with some conical graves described below.

The dusky inmates of the rancheria had betaken themselves to their canoes, and retreated among the tule to what they considered a safe distance. They now stood, yelling like fiends and shaking their weapons at us in impotent rage. Strict orders had been given that none of their property should be injured; and we passed rapidly along the shore of the marsh, surprising a new rancheria at almost every turn. The number of these savages is very large; and nature has given them so secure a retreat, that only a greatly superior force provided with boats, could attack them to advantage. They paddled through openings among the tule, and thus accompanied us, uttering hideous howls when the labor of working their passage did not keep them quiet. We passed on the way one of their burial places. The bodies had been doubled up, and placed in a sitting posture in holes. The earth, when replaced, formed conical mounds over the heads. Near the other graves, but on a slight eminence, stood a new wall-tent, such as is used in our service. It was regularly pitched and the front tied up. On looking inside, we saw a large mound about two feet in height, the bone of which covered the whole space enclosed by the walls. A new blanket was spread over the top. Here, doubtless, was the grave of some great chief; but how the savages became possessed of the tent remains a mystery, Along the whole chain of Klamath waters we noticed, in many places, large stones laid one upon the other, forming piles from two to six feet in height. Some of the party thought that these were marks to show the trail when the ground w is covered with snow; but the vast numbers of them sometimes found within a few feet of each other, and their frequent proximity to trees which could easily have been blazed, rendered this hypothesis rather improbable.

After travelling about sixteen miles from the place where we first struck the marsh, we reached a part where it was not more than a mile wide. Seeing several mounted Indians hastily driving a number of horses across, we attempted to follow, but found the ground too miry for pack animals. As it was almost sundown,

Lieut. Williamson decided to encamp near some trees on the shore. The only water was that found stagnant on the surface of the marsh. The grass was good, but it had been eaten quite short by the Indian horses. As we had been careful to do the savages no injury, they began to doubt our hostile character, and sent in a few squaws as an experiment. As they were dismissed with presents, large numbers of men entered camp, and made great professions of friendship. We distrusted them, however, and kept a close watch upon the animals during the night.

August 22.—This morning many Indians came into camp. They were all well dressed in blankets and buckskin, and were armed with bows and arrows and a few fire-arms. Their intercourse with the Oregon settlements had taught many of them to speak the Chinook, or Jargon language, and one had a slight knowledge of English. They owned many horses, some of which were valuable animals. No offer would tempt them to sell any of the latter, although they were eager to dispose of a few miserable hacks too worthless to purchase.

The idea, which prevails in Oregon, that all Indian horses are of an inferior breed, doubtless arises from the fact that such only art brought to the settlements for sale. Near Klamath marsh we saw a few animals of a piebald color, whose graceful forms and clear, piercing eyes showed very superior blood. It may be that their genealogy extends back to the Barbary steeds introduced by the Spaniards into Mexico, and supposed to be the progenitors of the wild horses of the prairies.

Near the spot where we were encamped, the marsh was not more than a mile in width; but it extended an indefinite distance towards the east, and the Indians informed us that the journey round it was very long, and without water. They volunteered to show us a natural causeway to the other side; but it proved too miry for pack mules. Our new friends all declared that the best trail to the Des Chutes valley led round the western side of the marsh; and Lieut. Williamson finally decided to turn back and try that route. We followed almost the same trail as yesterday, and encamped near the southern point of the marsh.

A large number of Indians accompanied us, one of whom Lieut. Crook had formerly seen in Yreka. These savages were intelligent, and in every way superior to those of Pit river. By questioning them in Chinook, Lieut. Williamson, assisted by Lieut. Crook, obtained the following partial vocabulary of their language.

August 23.—This morning we started with a large retinue of savages. The trail led through open pine timber for about a mile, and then entered a fine, grassy meadow which extended towards the north to Klamath marsh. About three miles from camp we reached Klamath river, hear a sluggish stream divided into two branches by a narrow island. The water rose to the backs of the smaller mules, and Lieut. Williamson employed the Indians to transport the packs across in canoes. This the squaws, who perform all the work, did by paddling round the northern end of the island. After paying their husbands with red blankets, beads, and vermilion, which they appear to highly prize, we continues our course through the grassy meadow until we reached a clear, ice-cold stream flowing through open timber. Here we encamped. The brook rose in springs about a mile from when;

111

we struck it, according to the report of the guide, who shot three antelopes near its source in the afternoon.

Avgust 24.—This morning the Indians left us. We followed a large but crooked trail through a thick pine forest. Fallen timber of small size somewhat obstructed the way, but there were no hills. The soil was light volcanic ashes, in which the animals sank nearly to the knee if they left the beaten trail. The dust was stifling. About 13.5 miles from camp, we reached the dry bed of a stream which was fringed with willows but entirely destitute of water. About five miles further on we came to a water hole, and, as it was nearly sundown, Lieut. Williamson decided to encamp, although there was no grass. The water was good, but the hole filled slowly, and the supply was scanty. Two more holes were dug a short distance further up the ravine, but most of the animals passed the night suffering from both hunger and thirst.

August 25.—To-day we continued our march through a country similar, in all respects, to that traversed yesterday, except that, it became slightly undulating. The dense clouds of dust raised by our animals from the as by soil were suffocating. After riding about 18.7 miles from camp, we suddenly emerged from the dense forest, and found ourselves in the beautiful grassy bottom of the Des Chutes river. It was here a fine stream about thirty feet in width, and fordable although the current was rapid and the bed stony. We immediately encamped. At the water hole, this morning, two trails diverged. We followed the more easterly one; but two of the party by mistake took the other, which was equally large. It conducted them to a point further up stream and was doubtless a trail leading to the wagon road across the Cascade Range, which Lieut. Williamson subsequently examined. The supply of grass to-night was abundant, and of fine quality; the water was cold, and the position in every respect excellent for a camp. Large numbers of delicious trout, marked with red longitudinal stripes, were caught with great ease in the river.

August 26.—This morning we left the bank of the stream, and followed the trail for about seven miles through a pine forest. It passed over several low hills, upon which the soil was light and ashy. As it wound considerably towards the east, Lieut. Williamson was afraid that it might leave the river entirely, and lead to the Wallah-Wallah country. He therefore abandoned it, and turned again towards the stream, which was reached in about 1.5 miles. We crossed it at a good ford, and, to our great surprise, came upon an old nearly effaced wagon trail. This we followed with difficulty for a short distance, when it seemed to disappear in a thick growth of young trees and underbrush. After struggling forward for a short distance, we recrossed the river and again struck the wagon trail, which must have crossed to the eastern bank, near where we entered the bushes. We followed it down the river. The soil during the whole day's inarch was light and ashy. The country had been recently burned over by the Indians; and we were beginning to despair of obtaining forage for our animals, when a sudden bend revealed a portion of the river bottom thickly carpeted with luxuriant grass, Here we encamped under a few small trees. The river, which was about forty feet in width, flowed through a grassy bottom bordered by low Mulls, distant about 200 yards from the stream. The current was rapid, and the water clear and cold. Trout were abundant and easily caught.

August 27.—To-day we remained in camp, and Lieutenant Williamson made preparations to start to-morrow with Lieutenant Sheridan and the dragoon detachment, to begin the examination for a pass through the Cascade Range to the Willamette valley. The soil was so light that I found it impossible to take astronomical observations near camp. The ordinary movements of the men and animals caused a continual shaking of the ground, which disturbed the mercury of the artificial horizon, although surrounded by a trench nearly two feet in depth, it was consequently necessary, for every observation at this camp, to carry the instruments about an eighth of a mile to the bluffs above the river bottom. In the night, Lieutenant Williamson and others of our mess were taken violently sick. It was supposed by some that we had been poisoned by eating trout caught in the river; but I think that the sickness was probably occasioned by some carelessness of the cook.

August 28.—Although Lieutenant Williamson was quite unwell this morning, He started with Lieutenant Sheridan and the dragoons for the mountains. An itinerary of his trip will be found in Chapter IV. The main party remained under my charge in camp, where the customary observations were taken. Many crawfish, which when cooked were scarcely inferior to lobsters, were caught in the river.

August 29.—As the supply of grass began to fail, I moved camp about 3.3 miles down stream this morning, to a point where the river bottom spread out into a fine prairie, carpeted with an abundance of rich hunch grass. To reach this prairie, we passed through a nearly level country covered with pine forest. We encamped near some small trees on the river bank, where we found all the requisites for an excellent camping place. During the night, ice of considerable thickness formed in the water vessels, and just before sunrise the thermometer stood at 15° Fahrenheit.

August 30.—The day was spent in taking observations and computing. The glass crystal of one of the chronometers was unfortunately broken; but Mr. Coleman pounded a piece of tin until he gave it the requisite curvature, and thus supplied an admirable substitute. He had previously repaired a watch in the same manner.

August 31.—We remained in camp taking the usual observations. Early in the morning the air was quite uncomfortably cold, and the thermometer ranged below the freezing point until nearly nine o'clock. The altitude of the camp above the sea was only 4,129 feet.

September 1.—To-day we were greatly surprised by the arrival of a party of gold seekers from the Umpqua valley, who were journeying to the Coleville mines. They had crossed the Cascade Range by the wagon road south of Diamond Peak, which Lieutenant Williamson subsequently examined. After remaining a few moments with us, they continued their march. In the afternoon a corporal and two men arrived, bringing me orders from Lieutenant Williamson to join him on the second tributary of the Des Chutes river below camp.

September 2.—Our course this morning lay through a fine prairie, from half a mile to two miles in width, and bordered with pine timber. The river wound through the middle of the open space, concealed from view by a line of willows, and the trail followed its general course. The soil was mostly of a pumice-stone character, but there was an abundance of fine grass. After travelling 13.5 miles we found, by the greatly increased size of the stream, that it had received a tributary from the mountains. As the bushes were too thick to admit of riding near the water's edge, I walked back, and in about a quarter of a mile reached the junction of the two branches. The new tributary was too large to ford, and the depth and swift current of the main river threatened to give us much trouble in crossing. Beavers were very numerous in this vicinity. Continuing our march we soon reached a place where the trail crossed to the other bank; but the ford was so deep that the water rose to the backs of our largest mules. After searching in vain for a more shallow place, I decided to make rafts, rather than wet the packs and endanger the animals by driving them loaded into the swift current. The men worked hard, and at sunset all our packs and instruments had been transported to the western bank in safety, on a raft termed by lashing dry logs together. The escort were not quite so successful, and some of their property remained on the eastern bank until morning. The river was about 150 feet in width; the bottom was hard and free from boulders, and the banks were low and firm. The depth of the water and the swift current alone prevented fording.

September 3.—In examining the vicinity of camp this morning, I found the remains of an old Indian rancheria, surrounded by numerous deer and elk horns. A little above the crossing place on the western bank, several springs gushed from the rocks and united to form a stream nearly fifteen feet in width, which discharged itself into the river.

We started at about eight o'clock. The trail led near the river bank, through a pumice-stone region covered with pine timber. There were a few hills, and they gradually increased in height and steepness as we advanced. The river abounded in short bends. About five miles from camp, trap rock suddenly took the place of pumice-stone, and the stream entered the great cañon, which undoubtedly continues, without much interruption, to its mouth. The descent of the river in this canon is shown by our barometric observations to average about twenty-five feet to the mile. A bend in the trail soon brought us to the summit of a cliff above the water, and revealed a scene wild and beautiful in the extreme. The opposite bank was composed of huge masses of trap rock, piled one upon the other in wild confusion. About fifty feet below us, the river was leaping, with a low murmuring sound, from crag to crag and apparently descending one hundred and fifty feet in less than three hundred yards. The dark pines around us, and the remains of a deserted Indian rancheria, harmonized well with the scene.

After crossing several steep ridges, separated by small ravines, the trail left the river and passed over an elevated plain densely timbered with pine. A few miles further on, we descended abruptly into a narrow gorge, which conducted us to a small tributary. Here we found Lieut. Williamson in camp, and an abundant supply of good grass and water. The bottom was bordered by bluffs, about one hundred feet high, which approached each other and increased in height, both above and below camp. Immediately after our arrival it began to rain, for the first time on the survey. Some of the party, who had followed down the river beyond the point where I left it, arrived thoroughly wet, a short time before sunset. They reported their route execrable.

September 4.—This morning, after riding a few miles, we emerged from the forest, and traversed an elevated plateau, dotted with cedars and sage bushes, and marked by a few low ridges and ravines extending in a northeast and southwest direction. None of these ridges were over 300 feet in height. The air was uncommonly clear and pure. The white summits of several snowy peaks began to appear in the distance, and we pressed rapidly forward. After travelling 17.5 miles from camp, we reached Why-chus creek, near the place were Lieut. Williamson had encamped on September 1st. It was a fine stream, about 30 feet in width, flowing rapidly over rounded rocks. Its waters were slightly turbid. There was an inexhaustible supply of fine grass in the vicinity, but Lieut. Williamson decided to travel on, and encamp near the "forks of the Indian trail." We passed through an open forest for the whole distance, and encamped on a little brook which, a few miles below us, sank among the rocks. From a slight eminence above camp, the snowy peaks of the Three Sisters appeared quite near. A large meadow, which Lieut. Williamson had previously seen, and upon which he depended for grass, proved to be a cranberry swamp and utterly impassable. A sufficiency of excellent bunch grass, however, was found among the trees. Whortleberries, elder berries and service berries abounded in the vicinity.

September 5.—To-day we remained in camp, and I repared the barometer which had been broken on the recent trip among the mountains.

Lieut. Williamson instructed me to proceed to Fort Dalles to obtain provisions, and to examine the Des Chutes valley, while he continued the exploration of the mountains in the vicinity. As I had charge of a detached party during the remainder of the survey, it may be well to give a brief synopsis of the movements of each division of the command, in order to render the subsequent part of the report more intelligible. Lieut. Williamson continued his explorations among the mountains while I went to Fort Dalles. I rejoined him at Camp S, near Why-chus creek, and we again separated. He returned to the head of the Des Chutes valley; examined the pass south of the Diamond Peak; proceeded to Vancouver, and thence by the water to San Francisco. I explored the vicinity of Mount Jefferson; returned nearly to the Dalles; and then, crossing the Cascade mountains by a new pass south of Mount Hood, went to Vancouver. From that post I proceeded, by way of Fort Lane and Fort Jones, to Fort Reading, where the field work ceased.

9

'RAILWAY ENGINEERING IN THE UNITED STATES', *THE ATLANTIC MONTHLY* 2, 13 (NOV. 1858), 644–645

Among the larger and more important roads and connected systems in our country may be named the New York and Erie Railroad,—connecting the city of New York with Lake Erie at Dunkirk, (and, by the road's diverging from its western terminus, with "all places West and South," as the bills say,)—crossing the Shawangunk Mountains through the valley of the Neversink, up the Delaware, down the Susquehanna, and through the rich West of the Empire State.

The Pennsylvania Central Road: from Philadelphia through Lancaster to Harrisburg, on the Susquehanna, up the Juniata and down the western slope of the Alleghanies, through rock-cut galleries and over numberless bridges, reaching at last the bluffs where smoky Pittsburg sees the Ohio start on its noble course.

The Baltimore and Ohio Railroad: from Baltimore, in Maryland, to Wheeling and Parkersburg, on the Ohio;—crossing the lowlands to the Washington Junction, thence up the Patapseo, down the Monocacy, to the Potomac; up to Harper's Ferry, where the Potomac and the Shenandoah chafe the rocky base of the romantic little town perched high above; winding up the North Branch to Cumberland,—the terminus of the Chesapeake and Ohio Canal, and of the great national turnpike to the West, for which Wills' Creek opened so grand a gate at the narrows,—to Piedmont the foot and Altamont the summit, through Savage Valley and Crabtree Gorge, across the glades, from which the water flows east to the Chesapeake Bay and west to the Gulf of Mexico; down Saltlick Creek, and up the slopes of Cheat River and Laurel Hill, till rivers dwindle to creeks, creeks to rills, and rills lose themselves on the flanks of mountains which bar the passage of everything except the railroad; thence, through tunnels of rock and tunnels of iron, descending Tygart's Valley to the Monongahela, and thence through a varied but less rugged country to Moundsville, twelve miles below Wheeling, on the Ohio River.

These are our three great roads where engineering skill has triumphed over natural obstacles. We have another class of great lines to which the obstacles were not so much mechanical as financial,—the physical difficulties being quite secondary. Such are the trunk lines from the East to the West,—through Buffalo, Erie, and Cleveland, to Toledo and Detroit, and from Detroit to Chicago, Rock Island, Burlington, Quincy, and St Louis; from Pittsburg, Wheeling, and Parkersburg, on the Ohio, to Cleveland, Columbus, Cincinnati, Indianapolis, Louisville, and

St. Louis; and from Cleveland, through Columbus, to Cincinnati, and from Cincinnati to the Northwest.

In progress also may be noticed roads running west from St. Louis, Hannibal, and Burlington, on the Mississippi, all tending towards some point in Kansas, from which the great Pacific Road, the crowning effort of American railway-engineering, may be supposed to take its departure for California and Oregon.

The chief point of difference between the English and the American engineer is, that the former defies all opposition from river and mountain, maintains his line straight and level, fights Nature at every point, cares neither for height nor depth, rock nor torrent, builds his matchless roads through the snowy woods of Canada or over the sandy plains of Egypt with as much unconcern as among the pleasant fields of Hertford or Surrey, and spans with equal ease the Thames, the Severn, the St. Lawrence, and the Nile. The words "fail," "impossible," "can't be done," he knows not; and when all other means of finding a firm base whereon to build his bridges and viaducts fail, he puts in a foundation of golden guineas and silver dollars, which always gives success.

On the other hand, the American engineer, always respectful (though none the less determined) in the presence of natural obstacles to his progress, bows politely to the opposing mountain-range, and, bowing, passes around the base, saving, as he looks back, "You see, friend, we need have no hard feelings,—the world is large enough for thee and me." To the broad-sweeping river he gently hints, "Nearer your source you are not so big, and, as I turned out for the mountain, why should I not for the river?" till mountain and river, alike aghast at the bold pigmy, look in silent wonder at the thundering train which shoulders aside granite hills and tramples rivers beneath its feet. But if Nature corners him between rocks heavenward piled on the one hand and roaring torrents on the other, whether to pass is required a bridge or a tunnel, we find either or both designed and built in a manner which cannot be bettered. He is well aware that the directors like rather to see short columns of figures on their treasurer's books than to read records of great mechanical triumphs in their engineer's reports.

Of the whole expense of building a railroad, where the country is to any considerable degree broken, the reduction of the natural surface to the required form for the road, that is, the earthwork, or, otherwise, the excavation and embankment, amounts to from thirty to seventy per cent, of the whole cost. Here, then, is certainly an important element on which the engineer is to show his ability; let us look a little at it, even at the risk of being dry.

It is by no means necessary to reduce the natural surface of the country to a level or horizontal line; if it were so, there would be an end to all railroads, except on some of the Western prairies. This was not, however, at first known; indeed, those who were second to understand the matter denied the possibility of moving a locomotive even on a level by applying power to the wheels, because, it was said, the wheels would slip round on the smooth iron rail and the engine remain at rest. But lo! when the experiment was tried, it was found that the wheel not only had sufficient bite or adhesion upon the rail to prevent slipping and give a forward motion to the engine, but that a number of cars might be attached and also moved.

This point gained, the objectors advanced a step, but again came to a stand, and said, "If you can move a train on a level, that is all,—you can't go up hill." But trial proved that easy inclines (called grades) could be surmounted,—say, rising ten feet for each mile in length.

The objectors take another step, but again put down their heavy square-toed foot, and say, "There! ar'n't you satisfied? you can go over grades of twenty feet per mile, but no more,—so don't try." And here English engineers stop,—twenty feet being considered a pretty stiff grade. Meanwhile, the American engineers Whistler and Latrobe, the one dealing with the Berkshire mountains in Massachusetts, the other with the Alleghanies in Virginia, find that not only are grades of ten and of twenty feet admissible, but, where Nature requires it, inclines of forty, sixty, eighty, and even one hundred feet per mile,—it being only remembered, the while, that just as the steepness of the grade is augmented, the power must be increased. This discovery, when properly used, is of immense advantage; but in the hands of those who do not understand the nice relation which exists between the mechanical and the financial elements of the question, as governed by the speed and weight of trains, and by the funds at the company's disposal, is very liable to be a great injury to the prospects of a road, or even its ruin.

10

CHARLES DE LANO HINE, *LETTERS FROM AN OLD RAILWAY OFFICIAL TO HIS SON, AND DIVISION SUPERINTENDANT* (CHICAGO: THE RAILWAY AGE, 1904), PP. 1–17

A word of congratulation

March 20, 1904.

My Dear Boy:—The circular announcing your appointment as division superintendent has just been received, and it brings up a flood of thoughts of former years. I felt that you had made a mistake in leaving us to go with the new system, but it has turned out all right. I can appreciate the fact that you would rather work away from me, so as to make people believe that you can go up the official hill without having a pusher behind you.

This should be one of the proudest periods of your life. You are now in a position to do good to your company, to your fellow man, and incidentally to yourself. No matter how highly organized a road may be, the importance of the office of division superintendent is in direct proportion to the ability and earnestness of the incumbent. The position is little or big, restricted or untrammeled, just as you make it. Many a superintendent has had to double the hill of a swelled knob, and run as a last section into the next promotion terminal. You have too much of your mother's good sense ever to cause anybody else to put up signals for you on this account. Therefore do not lose your democratic manner. Keep your heart warm and regard the wider field as an opportunity to get more friends on your staff. Try to call every employe in your territory by name, as Caesar did his soldiers; for all the traffic of good-will must run in a direction toward you if you want maximum results, as they call efficiency nowadays. Good old rule 121 of the standard code says: "When in doubt take the safe course and run no risks," which, in the case of acquaintance, means if uncertain whether you know a man or not, speak to him and give him the glad hand anyway. You will have to discipline men, but that can be done without parting company with your good manners. Remember that the much-abused word "discipline" comes from the same root as the word "disciple," a pupil, a learner, a follower. It is always easier to lead men than to drive them.

When you go over the division do not try to see how many telegrams you can send, but how few. It is usually a pretty safe rule after writing a telegram on the hind end of a train to carry it by two or three stations to see if you would rather not take it back to the office yourself. The dispatchers used to tell your old dad that they couldn't have told he was out on the line as far as his messages were an indication. Another thing, do not try to plug your whistle and muffle your bell. Let everybody know you are coming. The "Old Sleuth" stunt is for criminals, not for honest employes. Be on hand so frequently that your coming is taken as a matter of course. Never hunt quail with a brass band, but bear in mind that men, unlike quail, rather like to perch on a band wagon. If you are tempted to wait behind box cars to see if the men on a night pony have gone in the hay, do not yield, but get out, see that the switches are lined up, and count the ties in front of the headlight until somebody gives her steam; just as Napoleon walked post for the sleeping sentinel. Then, if you administer a polite jacking up it will be twice as effective, even if the delay to the work that one time has continued. Remember that things are not as they should be, and it is probably your own fault if, under normal conditions, a particular movement depends upon your personal efforts. Any routine action that you take should be calculated to help many trains, or one train many times; or to help many men, not merely the trains or men in question. It is all right, in emergencies, to jump in and do the work of a conductor, of an engineman, of a switch tender, or of any other employe. The great trouble is in discriminating between an emergency and a defect which can better be remedied in some other way. The smaller the caliber of the official the more numerous the emergencies to his mind.

You should try to arrange your work so as to stay up all night at least once a week, either in the office, or better, on the road or in the yards. You will keep better in touch with the men and the things for which you, asleep or awake, are always responsible. You remember when your sister Lucy was little how we asked her why she said her prayers at night but usually omitted them in the morning. Her answer which so tickled you was, "I ask God to take care of me at night, but I can take care of myself in the daytime." It is much the same way with a railroad. From your point of view it will take pretty fair care of itself as a daylight job, but at night that proposition loses its rights. The youngest dispatcher, by virtue of being the senior representative awake, is to a certain extent general manager. The least experienced men are in the yards and roundhouses. The ever-faithful sectionmen are off the right of way. The car inspector's light and the engineman's torch are poor substitutes for the sun in locating defects. The most active brains are dulled by the darkness just before dawn. Then it is that a brief hour may sidetrack or derail the good work of many days. It is this responsibility, this struggle with nature, this helping God to work out the good in men, that makes our profession noble and develops qualities of greatness in its members.

Next time I shall try to tell you something about helping your train dispatchers.

With a father's blessing, ever your own,

D. A. D.

Letter II

Helping the train dispatchers

March 27, 1904.

My Dear Boy:—I promised in my last to say something about helping your train dispatchers. The way to help any man is first to encourage him and by showing that you appreciate his good qualities give him confidence in himself. When you come in off the road tell the dispatcher, if such be the case, "Nice meeting point you made yesterday for 15 and 16; I was there and they both kept moving almost like double track." If your division has been badly handled, the dispatcher, unaccustomed to such appreciation, will at first think this is a sarcastic prelude to having the harpoon thrown into him; but your sincerity will soon disabuse his mind of such a notion. Sarcasm in official intercourse or toward one's subordinates should never be tolerated. It is an expensive kind of extra that should never be run. When you praise a man it will add to his good feeling if some one else happens to be present. If you have to censure anyone, whether directly or through the channels, do it privately and spare the recipient all unnecessary humiliation. The official who remembers to mention good work will find his rebukes and criticisms much more effective in remedying poor work than the official whose theory and practice are to take up failures and to let successes be taken for granted.

Another way to help a man is to lead him away from the pitfalls that are peculiar to his path of work. The official who is an old dispatcher has to fight in himself the temptation to be the whole cheese. He has to learn to trust subordinates with details. Every position entails some inherent temptations. The absolute, unquestioned authority given a dispatcher in train movements breeds a temptation to be autocratic and unreasonable, to put out too many orders, to give too many instructions. Therefore, try to get your dispatchers in touch with your crews. If the former are in a skyscraper uptown, get authority to build an office for them at the terminal where most of the crews live. Personal contact is much better than long-distance communication by wire. There is enough of the latter from the very nature of the business without causing an unnecessary amount by artificial conditions.

The temptation of a legislator is to make too many laws; of a doctor to prescribe too much medicine; of an old man to give too much advice; and of a train dispatcher, once more, to put out too many orders. It used to be thought by some that the best dispatcher was the one who put out the most orders. The later and better idea is that, generally speaking, the best dispatcher puts out the fewest orders. It is always easier to give orders of any kind than it is to execute them. It is a far cry from an O. S. on a train sheet to getting a heavy drag into a sidetrack and out again. It often takes longer to stop a train and get an order signed and completed than the additional time given in the order amounts to. Even a judicious use of the beneficent nineteen order involves more or less delay. One of the lessons a dispatcher has to learn is to know when he is up against it; when he has figured badly; and when not to make a bad matter worse by vainly trying to retrieve a hopeless delay. A good dispatcher will know without being told that he has made a poor meeting point. Educate him to consider that as an error to be avoided under like conditions in the future; not as a mistake to be made worse by putting out more orders that may fail to help the stabbed train enough, and may result in having every fellow on the road delayed. If any train must be delayed, let it be one that is already late rather than one that is on time. Above all get the confidence of your dispatchers so that they will not try to cover up their own mistakes or those of others. Teach them that, in the doubtful event of its becoming necessary, the superintendent is able to do the covering up act for the whole division.

Every superintendent and higher official should remember that if the same train order is given every day there must be something radically wrong with the time table. All over this broad land, day after day, hundreds of unnecessary train orders are being sent because many time tables are constructed on the models of forty years ago. At that time, in fact as in name, there were two classes of trains, passenger and freight. To-day there are in reality at least two distinct classes of passenger trains and two classes of freights, or at least four in all. On most of the roads in the country passenger trains of whatever nature or importance are all shown in one class, the first. As a result every limited train in the inferior direction on single track has to be given right by train order over opposing local passenger trains in the superior direction. In other words, the working time table, by definition a general law, has no more practical value, as between such trains, than an advertising folder. A train order by its very nature is an exception to the general law, the time table. When the exception becomes the rule it is high time to head in or to put out a thinking flag. Some years ago your old dad after much persuasion induced his superiors to let him make four classes of trains on a pretty warm piece of single track. The result directly and indirectly was to reduce the number of train orders by twenty or twenty-five per day. Every train order given increases the possibility of mistake and disaster; the fewer the orders the safer the operation. The change was made without even an approach to a mistake or the semblance of disaster. The dispatchers being less occupied were able to give more attention to local freights, and the general efficiency of the train service was greatly increased. The wires could go down and the most important trains would keep moving. It has stood the test of years and if the old method were resumed a grievance committee would probably wait on the management.

Successful politicians and public speakers have long since learned not to disgust their hearers by trying to talk in language ridiculously simple and uncultured. For us to say that the intelligent employes of to-day cannot keep in mind four or even five classes of trains is to confuse them with the comparatively illiterate men of a bygone generation. The public school and the daily newspaper have made a part of our problem easier. We are paying higher wages than ever before, but is it not partly our own fault if we fail to get full value received?

Therefore, see if your time tables appeal to tradition or to reason; if they belong to a period when women wore hoopskirts, or to a time when women ride wheels and play golf. In brief, before you take the stylus to remove the dirt ballast from the dispatcher's eye, be sure that there are no brakebeams stuck in your own headlight.

Affectionately, your own

D. A. D.

Letter III

Handling a yard

April 3, 1904.

My Dear Boy:—You have asked me to give you some pointers on handling a yard. You will find that nearly all situations in a yard hark back to one simple rule, which is: When you get hold of a car move it as far as possible toward its final destination before you let go of it.

The training of a switchman is usually such that, if let alone, he will stick the car in the first convenient track and wait to make a delivery until he can pull every track in the yard and put with it all other cars with the same cards or marks. By this time some other fellow with a similar honesty of purpose but differently applied will come along and bury the car or block the first man in so that one engine has to stand idle. A yardmaster has to learn to keep his engines scattered and to hold each foreman responsible for the work of an engine. A good yardmaster knows instinctively where to be at a certain time to minimize the delay incident to engines bunching. The old switchman who becomes a yard-master often proves a failure because he cannot overcome his inclination to follow one engine and take a hand in the switching himself. By so doing he may perhaps increase the work accomplished by that one engine, possibly five per cent; but in the meantime the other engines, for want of comprehensive, intelligent instructions, are getting in each other's way and the efficiency of the day's service is decreased maybe twenty per cent.

Good yardmasters are even harder to discover or develop than good train dispatchers. The exposure, the irregular hours for the yardmaster's meals in even the best regulated yards make a good conductor leery about giving up a comfortable run to assume the increased responsibility of a yard. The pay of a yardmaster is little more than that of a conductor and is sometimes less. Right here is a chance for some deep administrative thought. It is so much easier to get good conductors than good yardmasters, should we not make the latter position more attractive? Some roads have done this by making it one of the positions from which to promote trainmasters, and seldom have such appointees fallen down. However, there are hardly enough promotion loaves and fishes to go around. Men get tired of living on skimmed milk on earth for the sake of promised cream in heaven. Every switch engine worked costs the company several hundred dollars per month, and the yardmaster whose good figuring can save working even one engine is more than earning his salary.

The closer you can get your yardmasters to your official family the better your administration. Pick up a yardmaster occasionally and take him to headquarters with you so that he will keep acquainted with the dispatchers. This will hold down friction and save the company's good money. A dispatcher naturally wants to get all the trains he can into a terminal, while a yardmaster is doing his level best to get trains out. With such radically different points of professional view there is a big opportunity for the superintendent and the trainmaster to do the harmonizing act, to keep pleasantly before employes the fact that all are working for the same company, that all do business with the same paymaster. Blessed are the peacemakers doesn't mean necessarily there must first be trouble. Peace carried in stock is better than that manufactured on hurry-up shop orders.

If you are looking for talent to run a yard, consider some ambitious dispatcher. Too few dispatchers have become yardmasters. The same cool head, the same quick judgment, the same executive ability are needed in both positions. The man who has successfully filled both is usually equipped to go against almost any old official job, without having to back up and take a run for the hill. The curse of modern civilization is over-specialization. The world grows better and produces stronger, better men all the while. Perhaps this is in spite of rather than on account of highly specialized organization. No industry can afford to be without the old-fashioned all around man who is good anywhere you put him.

The work of the yardmaster is more spectacular than that of the dispatcher. To come down to a congested yard among a lot of discouraged men blocked in without room to sidetrack a handcar is like sitting down to a train sheet with most of the trains tied up for orders. In either case let the right man take hold and in a few minutes the men involved will tell you who it is has assumed charge. Without realizing it and without knowing why, they redouble their efforts; things begin to move, and the incident goes down in the legends of the division to be the talk of the caboose and the roundhouse for years to come. To the man whose cool head and earnestness are bringing it all about comes the almost unconscious exhilaration that there is in leading reinforcements to the firing line. He feels with the Count of Monte Cristo, "The world is mine," I have the switches set to head it in.

Get out of your head the young brakeman's idea that yard jobs are for old women and hasbeens.

Affectionately, your own

D. A. D.

Part 3

FROM EASTERN EXCURSIONS TO TRANSCONTINENTAL TOURISM

11

ISABELLA BIRD (MRS. BISHOP), *THE ENGLISHWOMAN IN AMERICA* (LONDON: JOHN MURRAY, 1856), PP. 125–126, 133–152

But after describing the beauty of her streets, her astonishing progress, and the splendour of her shops, I must not close this chapter without stating that the Queen City bears the less elegant name of Porkopolis; that swine, lean, gaunt, and vicious-looking, riot through her streets; and that, on coming out of the most splendid stores, one stumbles over these disgusting intruders. Cincinnati is the city of pigs. As there is a railway system and a hotel system, so there is also a *pig system*, by which this place is marked out from any other. Huge quantities of these useful animals are reared after harvest in the corn-fields of Ohio, and on the beech-mast and acorns of its gigantic forests. At a particular time of year they arrive by thousands— brought in droves and steamers to the number of 500,000—to meet their doom, when it is said that the Ohio runs red with blood! There are huge slaughter-houses behind the town, something on the plan of the *abattoirs* of Paris—large wooden buildings, with numerous pens, from whence the pigs march in single file along a narrow passage, to an apartment where each, on his entrance, receives a blow with a hammer, which deprives him of consciousness, and in a short time, by means of numerous hands, and a well-managed caldron system, he is cut up ready for pickling. The day on which a pig is killed in England constitutes an era in the family history of the year, and squeals of a terrific description announce the event to the neighbourhood. There is not time or opportunity for such a process at Porkopolis, and the first notification which the inhabitants receive of the massacre is the thousand barrels of pork on the quays, ready to be conveyed to the Atlantic cities, for exportation to the European markets. At one establishment 12,000 pigs are killed, pickled, and packed every fall; and in the whole neighbourhood, as I have heard in the cars, the "hog crop" is as much a subject of discussion and speculation as the cotton crop of Alabama, the hop-picking of Kent, or the harvest in England.

Kentucky, the land, by reputation, of "red horses, bowie-knives, and gouging," is only separated from Ohio by the river Ohio; and on a day when the thermometer stood at 103° in the shade I went to the town of Covington. Marked, wide, and almost inestimable, is the difference between the free state of Ohio and the slave-state of Kentucky. They have the same soil, the same climate, and precisely the same natural advantages; yet the total absence of progress, if not the appearance of retrogression and decay, the loungers in the streets, and the peculiar appearance of the slaves, afford a centrast to the bustle on the opposite side of the river, which would strike the most unobservant. I was credibly informed that property of the same real value was worth 300 dollars in Kentucky and 3000 in Ohio! Free emigrants and workmen will not settle in Kentucky, where they would be brought into contact with compulsory slave-labour; thus the development of industry is retarded, and the difference will become more apparent every year, till possibly some great changes will be forced upon the legislature. Few English people will forget the impression made upon them by the first sight of a slave—a being created in the image of God, yet the *bonâ fide* property of his fellow-man.

A BRIGHT September sun glittered upon the spires of Cincinnati as I reluctantly bade it adieu, and set out in the early morning by the cars to join my travelling companions, meaning to make as long a *détour* as possible, or, as a "down-east" lady might say, to "make a pretty considerable circumlocution." Fortunately I had met with some friends, well acquainted with the country, who offered to take me round a much larger circle than I had contemplated; and with a feeling of excitement such as I had not before experienced, we started for the Mississippi and the western prairies *en route* to Detroit.

Bishop M'Ilvaine, anxious that a very valued friend of his in England should possess something from Ohio, had cut down a small sapling, which, when divested of its branches and otherwise trimmed, made a very formidable-looking bludgeon or cudgel, nearly four feet long. This being too lengthy for ray trunks was tied to my umbrella, and on this day in the cars excited no little curiosity, several persons eyeing it, then me, as if wondering in what relation we stood to each other. Finally they took it up, minutely examining it, and tapping it as if to see whether anything were therein concealed. It caused me much amusement, and, from its size, some annoyance, till at length, wishing to leave it in my room at a Toronto hotel while I went for a visit of a few days, the waiter brought it down to the door, asking me "if I wished to take the *cudgel?*" After this I had it shortened, and it travelled in ray trunk to New York, where it was given to a carver to be fashioned into a walking-stick; and, unless the tradesman played a Yankee trick, and substituted another, it is now, after surviving many dangers by sea and land, in the possession of the gentleman for whom it was intended.

Some amusing remarks were made upon England by some of the "Buckeyes," as the inhabitants of Ohio are called. On trying to persuade a lady to go with me to St. Louis, I observed that it was *only* five hundred miles. "Five hundred miles!" she replied; "why, you'd tumble off your paltry island into the sea before you got so far!" Another lady, who got into the cars at some distance from Cincinnati, could not understand the value which we set upon ruins. "We should chaw them up," she said, "make roads or bridges of them, unless Barnum transported them to his museum: we would never keep them on our own hook as you do." "You value them yourselves," I answered; "any one would be '*lynched*' who removed a stone of Ticonderoga." It was an unfortunate speech, for she archly replied, "Our only ruins are British fortifications, and we go to see them because they remind us that we whipped the nation which whips all the world." The Americans, however, though they may talk so, would give anything if they could appropriate a Kenilworth Castle, or a Melrose or a Tintern Abbey, with its covering of ivy, and make it sustain some episode of their history. But though they can make railways, ivy is beyond them, and the purple heather disdains the soil of the New World. A very amusing ticket was given me on the Mad River line. It bore the command, "Stick this check in your—," the blank being filled up with a little engraving of a hat; consequently I saw all the gentlemen with small pink embellishments to the covering of their heads.

We passed through a large and very beautiful portion of the State of Ohio; the soil, wherever cultivated, teeming with crops, and elsewhere with a vegetation no less beautiful than luxuriant; a mixture of small weed prairies, and forests of splendid timber. Extensive districts of Ohio are still without inhabitants, yet its energetic people have constructed within a period of five years half as many miles of railroad as the whole of Great Britain contains; they are a "*great people*," they do "*go a-head*" these Yankees. The newly cleared soil is too rich for wheat for many years; it grows Indian corn for thirty in succession, without any manure. Its present population is under three millions, and it is estimated that it would support a population of ten millions, almost entirely in agricultural pursuits. We were going a-head, and in a few hours arrived at Forest, the junction of the Clyde, Mad River, and Indiana lines.

Away with all English ideas which may be conjured up by the word *junction*—the labyrinth of iron rails, the smart policeman at the points, the handsome station, and elegant refreshment-rooms. Here was a dense forest, with merely a clearing round the rails, a small shanty for the man who cuts wood for the engine, and two sidings for the trains coming in different directions. There was not even a platform for passengers, who, to the number of two or three hundred, were standing on the clearing, resting against the stumps of trees. And yet for a few minutes every day the bustle of life pervades this lonely spot, for here meet travellers from east, west, and south; the careworn merchant from the Atlantic cities, and the hardy trapper from the western prairies. We here changed cars for those of the Indianapolis line, and, nearly at the same time with three other trains, plunged into the depths of the forest.

"You're from down east, I guess?" said a sharp nasal voice behind me.—This was a supposition first made in the Portland cars, when I was at a loss to know what distinguishing and palpable peculiarity marked me as a "down-easter." Better informed now, I replied, "I am." "Going west?"—"Yes." "Travelling alone?"—"No." "Was you raised down east?"—"No, in the Old Country." "In the little old island? well, you are kinder glad to leave it, I guess? Are you a widow?"—"No." "Are you travelling on business?"—"No." "What business do you follow?"—"None." "Well, now, what are you travelling for?"—"Health and pleasure." "Well, now, I guess you're pretty considerable rich. Coming to settle out west, I suppose?"—"No, I'm going back at the end of the fall." "Well, now, if that's not a pretty tough hickory-nut! I guess you Britishers are the queerest critturs as ever was raised!" I considered myself quite fortunate to have fallen in with such a querist, for the Americans are usually too much taken up with their own business to trouble themselves about yours, beyond such questions as, "Are you bound west, stranger?" or, "You're from down east, I guess." "Why do you take me for a *down-easter?*" I asked once. "Because you speak like one," was the reply; the frequent supposition that I was a New Englander being nearly as bad as being told that I "had not the English accent at all." I was glad to be taken for an American, as it gave me a better opportunity of seeing things as they really are. An English person going about staring and questioning, with a note-book in his hand, is considered "fair game," and consequently is "crammed" on all subjects; stories of petticoated table-legs, and fabulous horrors of the bowie-knife, being among the smallest of the absurdities swallowed.

Our party consisted of five persons besides myself, two elderly gentlemen, the niece of one of them, and a young married couple. They knew the governor of Indiana, and a candidate for the proud position of Senator, also our fellow travellers; and the conversation assumed a political character; in fact, they held a long parliament, for I think the discussion lasted for three hours. Extraordinary, and to me unintelligible names, were bandied backwards and forwards; I heard of "Silver Grays," but my companions were not discussing a breed of fowls; and of "Hard Shells," and "Soft Shells," but the merits of eggs were not the topic. "Whigs and Democrats" seemed to be analogous to our Radicals, and "Know-Nothings" to be a respectable and constitutional party. Whatever minor differences my companions had, they all seemed agreed in hating the "Nebraska men" (the advocates of an extension of slavery), who one would have thought, from the epithets applied to them, were a set of thieves and cut-throats. A gentleman whose whole life had been spent in opposition to the principles which they are bringing forward was very violent, and the pretty young lady, Mrs. Wood, equally so.

After stopping for two hours at a wayside shed, we set out again at dark for La Fayette, which we reached at nine. These Western cars are crammed to over-flowing, and, having to cross a wide stream in a ferry-boat, the crush was so terrible, that I was nearly knocked down; but as American gentlemen freely use their canes where a lady is in the case, I fared better than some of my fellow-passengers, who had their coattails torn and their toes barbarously crushed in the crowd. The steam ferry-boat had no parapet, and the weakest were pushed to the side; the centre was filled up with baggage, carts, and horses; and vessels were moored along the river, with the warps crossing each other, to which we had to bow continually to avoid decapitation. When we reached the wharf, quantities of people were waiting to go to the other side; and directly the gang-way-board was laid, there was a simultaneous rush of two opposing currents, and, the insecure board slipping, they were all precipitated into the water. Fortunately it was not deep, so they merely underwent its cooling influences, which they bore with admirable equanimity, only one making a bitter complaint, that be had spoiled his "*go-to-meetins*." The farther west we went, the more dangerous the neighbourhood became. At all the American stations there are placards warning people to beware of pickpockets; but from Indiana westward they bore the caution, "Beware of pickpockets, swindlers, and luggage-thieves." At many of the *depôts* there is a general rush for the last car, for the same reason that there is a scramble for the stern cabins in a steamer,—viz the explosive qualities of the boilers.

We travelled the whole of that night, our fellow-passengers becoming more extravagant in appearance at every station, and morning found us on the prairies. Cooper influences our youthful imaginations by telling as of the prairies—Mayne Reid makes us long to cross them; botanists tell us of their flowers, sportsmen of their buffaloes—but without seeing them few people can form a correct idea of what they are really like.

The sun rose over a monotonous plain covered with grass, rank, high, and silky-looking, blown before the breeze into long, shiny waves. The sky was blue above, and the grass a brownish green beneath; wild pigeons and turkeys flew over our heads; the horizontal line had not a single inequality; all was hot, unsuggestive, silent, and monotonous. This was the grass prairie.

A belt of low timber would bound the expanse, and on the other side of it a green sea would open before us, stretching as far as the eye could reach—stationary billows of earth, covered with short green grass, which, waving beneath the wind, completed the oceanic illusion. This was the rolling prairie.

Again a belt of timber, and a flat surface covered with flowers, brilliant even at this season of the year; though, of the most gorgeous, nothing remained but the withered stalks. The ground was enamelled with lilies, the helianthus and cineraria flourished, and the deep-green leaves and blue blossom of the lupin contrasted with the prickly stem and scarlet flower of the euphorbia. For what purpose was "the wilderness made so gay where for years no eye sees it," but to show forth his goodness who does what he will with his own? This was the weed prairie, more fitly termed "the Garden of God."

These three kinds of prairie were continually alternating with belts of timber and small lakes; but few signs of population were apparent during that long day's journey. We occasionally stopped for water at shanties on the prairies, and took in two or three men; but this vast expanse of fertile soil still must remain for many years a field for the enterprise of the European races.

Towards evening we changed cars again, and took in stores of refreshment for our night's journey, as little could be procured along the route. What strange people now crammed the cars! Traders, merchants, hunters, diggers, trappers, and adventurers from every land, most of them armed to the teeth, and not without good reason; for within the last few months, Indians, enraged at the aggressions of the white men, have taken a terrible revenge upon western travellers. Some of their rifles were of most costly workmanship, and were nursed with paternal care by their possessors. On the seat in front of me were two "prairie-men," such as are described in the 'Scalp-Hunters,' though of an inferior grade to St. Vrain. Fine specimens of men they were; tall, handsome, broad-chested, and athletic, with aquiline noses, piercing grey eyes, and brown curling hair and beards. They wore leathern jackets, slashed and embroidered, leather smallclothes, large boots with embroidered tops, silver spurs, and caps of scarlet cloth, worked with somewhat tarnished gold thread, doubtless the gifts of some fair ones enamoured of the handsome physiognomies and reckless bearing of the hunters. Dulness fled from their presence; they could tell stories, whistle melodies, and sing comic songs without weariness or cessation: fortunate were those near enough to be enlivened by their drolleries during the tedium of a night detention. Each of them wore a leathern belt—with two pistols stuck into it—gold earrings, and costly rings. Blithe, cheerful souls they were, telling racy stories of Western life, chivalrous in their manners, and free as the winds.

There were Californians dressed for the diggings, with leather pouches for the gold-dust; Mormons on their way to Utah; and restless spirits seeking for that excitement and variety which they had sought for in vain in civilized life! And conveying this motley assortment of human beings, the cars dashed along, none of their inmates heeding each other, or perhaps Him

"—— who heeds and holds them all
In his large love and boundless thought."

At eleven we came to an abrupt pause upon the prairie. After waiting quietly for some time without seeing any vestiges of a station, my friends got out to inquire the cause of the detention, when we found that a freight-train had broken down in front, and that we might be *détenus* for some time, a mark for Indian bullets! Refreshments were produced and clubbed together; the "prairie-men" told stories; the hunters looked to their rifles, and polished their already resplendent chasing; some Mexicans sang Spanish songs, a New Englander 'Yankee Doodle;' some *guessed*, others *calculated*, till at last all grew sleepy: the trappers exhausted their stories, the singers their songs, and a Mormon, who had been setting forth the peculiar advantages of his creed, the patience of his auditors—till at length sonorous sounds, emitted by numerous nasal organs, proving infectious, I fell asleep to dream confusedly of 'Yankee Doodle,' pistols, and pickpockets.

In due time I awoke; we were stopping still, and there was a light on our right "We're at Rock Island, I suppose?" I asked sleepily. A laugh from my friends and the hunters followed the question; after which they informed me in the most polite tones that we were where we had been for the last five hours, namely stationary on the prairie. The intense cold and heavy dew which accompany an American dawn made me yet more amazed at the characteristic patience with which the Americans submit to an unavoidable necessity, however disagreeable. It is true that there were complaints of cold, and heavy sighs, but no blame was imputed to any one, and the quiescence of my companions made me quite ashamed of my English impatience. In England we should have had a perfect chorus of complaints, varied by "rowing" the conductor, abuse of the company, and resolutions to write to the *Times*, or bring up the subject of railway mismanagement in the House of Commons. These people sat quietly, ate, slept, and smoked, and were thankful when the cars at last moved off to their destination.

On we flew to the West, the land of Wild Indians and buffaloes, on the narrow rims of metal with which this "great people" is girdling the earth. Evening succeeded noon, and twilight to the blaze of a summer day; the yellow sun sank cloudless behind the waves of the rolling prairie, yet still we hurried on, only stopping our headlong course to take in wood and water at some nameless stations. When the sun set, it set behind the prairie waves. I was oblivious of any changes during the night, and at rosy dawn an ocean of long green grass encircled us round. Still on—belts of timber diversify the prospect—we rush into a thick wood, and, emerging from it, arrive at Rock Island, an unfinished-looking settlement, which might bear the name of the Desert City, situated at the confluence of the Rock River and Mississippi. We stop at a little wharf, where waits a little steamer of uncouth construction; we step in, a steam-whistle breaks the silence of that dewy dawn, and at a very rapid rate we run between high wooded bluffs, down a turbid stream, whirling in rapid eddies. We steam for three miles, and land at a clearing containing the small settlement of Davenport. We had come down the Mississippi, mightiest of rivers! half a mile wide seventeen hundred miles from its mouth, and were in the *far West*. Waggons with white tilts, thick-hided oxen with heavy yokes, mettlesome steeds with high peaked saddles, picketed to stumps of trees, lashing away the flies with their tails; emigrants on blue boxes, wondering if this were the El Dorado of their dreams; arms, accoutrements, and baggage surrounded the house or shed where we were to breakfast. Most of our companions were bound for Nebraska, Oregon, and Utah, the most distant districts of which they would scarcely reach with their slow-paced animals for four months; exposed in the mean time to the attacks of the Sioux, Comanches, and Blackfeet.

There, in a long wooden shed with blackened rafters and an earthen floor, we breakfasted, at seven o'clock, on johnny-cake, squirrels, buffalo-hump, dampers, and buckwheat, tea and corn spirit, with a crowd of emigrants, hunters, and adventurers; and soon after re-embarked for Rock Island, our little steamer with difficulty stemming the mighty tide of the Father of Rivers. The machinery, such as it was, was very visible, the boiler patched in several places, and steam escaped in different directions. I asked the captain if he were not in the habit of "sitting upon the safety-valve," but he stoutly denied the charge. The vernacular of this neighbourhood was rather startling to an English ear. "Who's the alligator to hum?" asked a broad-shouldered Kentuckian of his neighbour, pointing to a frame shanty on the shore, which did not look to me like the abode of that amphibious and carnivorous creature. "Well, old alligator, what's the time o' day?" asked another man, bringing down a brawny paw, with a resounding thump, upon the Herculean shoulders of the first querist, thereby giving me the information that in the West *alligator* is a designation of the *genus homo*; in fact, that it is customary for a man to address his fellow-man as "old alligator," instead of "old fellow." At eight we left Rock Island, and, turning my unwilling steps eastward from the land of adventure and romance, we entered the cars for Chicago.

They were extremely crowded, and my friends, securing me the only comfortable seat in one of them, were obliged to go into the next, much to their indignation; but protestations were of no use. The engine-bell rang, a fearful rush followed, which resulted in the passage down the centre being filled with standing men; the conductor shouted "Go a-head," and we were off for Lake Michigan in the "Lightning Express," warranted to go sixty-seven miles an hour! I had found it necessary to study physiognomy since leaving England, and was horrified by the appearance of my next neighbour. His forehead was low, his deep-set and restless eyes significant of cunning, and I at once set him down as a swindler or pickpocket. My convictions of the truth of my inferences were so strong, that I removed my purse, in which, however, acting by advice, I never carried more than five dollars, from my pocket, leaving in it only my handkerchief and the checks for my baggage, knowing that I could not possibly keep awake the whole morning. In spite of my endeavours to the contrary, I soon sank into an oblivious state, from which I awoke to the consciousness that my companion was withdrawing his hand from my pocket. My first impulse was to make an exclamation, my second, which I carried into execution, to ascertain my loss; which I found to be the very alarming one of my baggage-checks; my whole property being thereby placed at this vagabond's disposal, for I knew perfectly well, that if I claimed my trunks, without my checks, the acute baggage-master would have set me down as a bold swindler. The keen-eyed conductor was not in the car, and, had he been there, the necessity for habitual suspicion, incidental to his position, would so far have removed his original sentiments of generosity as to make him turn a deaf ear to my request, and there was not one of my fellow-travellers whose physiognomy would have warranted me in appealing to him. So, recollecting that my checks were marked Chicago, and seeing that the thief's ticket bore the same name, I resolved to wait the chapter of accidents, or the re-appearance of my friends. I was scarcely able to decide whether this proof of the reliance to be placed upon physiognomy was not an adequate compensation for the annoyance I was experiencing, at the probability of my hoarded treasures falling into the hands of an adventurer.

During the morning we crossed some prairie-country, and stopped at several stations, patches of successful cultivation showing that there must be cultivators, though I rarely saw their habitations. The cars still continued so full that my friends could not join me, and I began to be seriously anxious about the fate of my luggage. At mid-day, spires and trees, and lofty blocks of building, rising from a grass-prairie on one side, and from the blue waters of Lake Michigan on the other, showed that we were approaching Chicago. Along beaten tracks through the grass, waggons with white tilts drawn by oxen were proceeding west, sometimes accompanied by armed horsemen.

With a whoop like an Indian war-whoop the cars ran into a shed—they stopped—the pickpocket got up—I got up too—the baggage-master came to the door: "This gentleman has the checks for my baggage," said I, pointing to the thief. Bewildered, he took them from his waistcoat-pocket, gave them to the baggage-master, and went hastily away. I had no inclination to cry "Stop thief!" and had barely time to congratulate myself on the fortunate impulse which had led me to say what I did, when my friends appeared from the next car. They were too highly amused with my recital to sympathise at all with my feelings of annoyance, and one of them, a gentleman filling a high situation in the East, laughed heartily, saying, in a thoroughly American tone, "The English ladies must be 'cute customers, if they can outwit Yankee pickpockets."

Meaning to stay all night at Chicago, we drove to the two best hotels, but, finding them full, were induced to betake ourselves to an advertising house, the name of which it is unnecessary to give, though it will never be effaced from my memory. The charge advertised was a dollar a day, and for this every comfort and advantage were promised.

The inn was a large brick building at the corner of a street, with nothing very unprepossessing in its external appearance. The wooden stairs were dirty enough, and, on ascending them to the so-called "ladies' parlour," I found a large, meanly-furnished apartment, garnished with six spittoons, which, however, to my disgust, did not prevent the floor from receiving a large quantity of to bacco-juice.

There were two rifles, a pistol, and a powder-flask on the table; two Irish emigrant women were seated on the floor (which swarmed with black beetles and ants), undressing a screaming child; a woman evidently in a fever was tossing restlessly on the sofa; two females in tarnished Bloomer habiliments were looking out of the window; and other extraordinary-looking human beings filled the room. I asked for accommodation for the night, hoping that I should find a room where I could sit quietly. A dirty chambermaid took me to a room or dormitory containing four beds. In one part of it three women were affectionately and assiduously nursing a sick child; in another, two were combing tangled black hair; upon which I declared that I must have a room to myself.

The chambermaid then took me down a long, darkish passage, and showed me a small room without a fireplace, and only lighted by a pane of glass in the door; consequently, it was nearly dark. There was a small bed with a dirty buffalo-skin upon it; I took it up, and swarms of living creatures fell out of it, and the floor was literally alive with them. The sight of such a room made me feel quite ill, and it was with the greatest reluctance that I deposited my bonnet and shawl in it.

Outside the door were some medicine-bottles and other suspicious signs of illness, and, after making some cautious inquiries, we found that there was a case of typhus fever in the house, also one of Asiatic cholera, and three of ague! My friends were extremely shocked with the aspect of affairs. I believe that they were annoyed that I should see such a specimen of an hotel in their country, and they decided, that, as I could not possibly remain there for the night, I should go on to Detroit alone, as they were detained at Chicago on business. Though I certainly felt rather out of my element in this place, I was not at all sorry for the opportunity, thus accidentally given me, of seeing something of American society in its lowest grade.

We went down to dinner, and only the fact of not having tasted food for many hours could have made me touch it in such a room. We were in a long apartment, with one table down the middle, with plates laid for one hundred people. Every seat was occupied, these seats being benches of somewhat uncouth workmanship.

The floor had recently been washed, and emitted a damp fetid odour. At one side was a large fireplace, where, in spite of the heat of the day, sundry manipulations were going on, coming under the general name of cookery. At the end of the room was a long leaden trough or sink, where three greasy scullery-boys without shoes, were perpetually engaged in washing plates, which they wiped upon their aprons. The plates, however, were not washed, only superficially rinsed. There were four brigand-looking waiters with prodigious beards and moustachios.

There was no great variety at table. There were eight boiled legs of mutton, nearly raw; six antiquated fowls, whose legs were of the consistence of guitar-strings; baked pork with "onion fixings," the meat swimming in grease; and for vegetables, yams, corn-cobs, and squash. A cup of stewed tea, sweetened with molasses, stood by each plate, and no fermented liquor of any description was consumed by the company. There were no carving-knives, so each person *hacked* the joints with his own, and some of those present carved them dexterously with bowie-knives taken out of their belts. Neither were there salt-spoons, so everybody dipped his greasy knife into the little pewter pot containing salt. Dinner began, and after satisfying my own hunger with the least objectionable dish, namely "pork with onion fixings," I had leisure to look round me.

Every quarter of the globe had contributed to swell that motley array, even China. Motives of interest or adventure had drawn them all together to this extraordinary outpost of civilisation, and soon would disperse them among lands where civilisation is unknown.

As far as I could judge, we were the only representatives of England. There were Scots, for Scots are always to be found where there is any hope of honest gain—there were Irish emigrants, speaking with a rich brogue—French traders from St. Louis—Mexicans iron Santa Fé—Californians fitting out, and Californians coming home with fortunes made—keen-eyed speculators from New England—packmen from Canada—"Prairie-men," trappers, hunters, and adventurers of all descriptions. Many of these wore bowie-knives or pistols in their belts. The costumes were very varied and picturesque. Two Bloomers in very poor green habiliments sat opposite to me, and did not appear to attract any attention, though Bloomerism is happily defunct in the States.

There had been three duels at Chicago in the morning, and one of the duellists, a swarthy, dark-browed villain, sat next but one to me. The quarrel originated in a gambling-house, and this Mexican's opponent was mortally wounded, and there he sat, with the guilt of human blood upon his hands, describing to his *vis-à-vis* the way in which he had taken aim at his adversary, and no one seemed to think anything about it. From what I heard, I fear duelling must have become very common in the West, and no wonder, from the number of lawless spirits who congregate where they can be comparatively unfettered.

The second course consisted exclusively of pumpkinpies; but when the waiters changed the plates, their way of cleaning the knives and forks was so peculiarly disgusting, that I did not attempt to eat anything. But I must remark that in this motley assembly there was nothing of coarseness, and not a word of bad language—indeed, nothing which could offend the most fastidious ears. I must in this respect bear very favourable testimony to the Americans; for, in the course of my somewhat extensive travels in the United States, and mixing as I did very frequently with the lower classes, I never heard any of that language which so frequently offends the ear in England.

I suppose that there is no country in the world where the presence of a lady is such a restraint upon manners and conversation. A female, whatever her age or rank may be, is invariably treated with deferential respect; and if this deference may occasionally trespass upon the limits of absurdity, or if the extinct chivalry of the past ages of Europe meets with a partial revival upon the shores of America, this extreme is vastly preferable to the *brusquerie*, if not incivility, which ladies, as I have heard, too often meet with in England.

The apparently temperate habits in the United States form another very pleasing feature to dwell upon. It is to be feared that there is a considerable amount of drunkenness among the English, Irish, and Germans, who form a large portion of the American population; but the temperate, tea-drinking, water-drinking habits of the native Americans are most remarkable. In fact, I only saw one intoxicated person in the States, and he was a Scotch fiddler. At the hotels, even when sitting down to dinner in a room with four hundred persons, I never on any occasion saw more than two bottles of wine on the table, and I know from experience that in many private dwelling-houses there is no fermented liquor at all. In the West, more especially at the rude hotels where I stopped, I never saw wine, beer, or spirits upon the table; and the spectacle gratified me exceedingly, of seeing fierce-looking, armed, and bearded men, drinking frequently in the day of that cup "which cheers, but not inebriates." Water is a beverage which I never enjoyed in purity and perfection before I visited America. It is provided in abundance in the cars, the hotels, the waiting-rooms, the steamers, and even the stores, in crystal jugs or stone filters, and it is always iced. This may be either the result or the cause of the temperance of the people.

12

'NEW YORK'S ELEVATED TRAIN', *FRANK LESLIE'S ILLUSTRATED NEWSPAPER* (MAY 25, 1878), P. 203

The dream of rapid transit in New York realized

Completion of the Gilbert Elevated Railroad

THE first train was ran over the entire length of the Gilbert Elevated Railroad on Monday, April 29th. It consisted of a locomotive and four passenger coaches, and made the run from Trinity Church to Fifty-eighth Street in seventeen minutes.

No 1, the present title of the new motor, is the first of twenty locomotives built after special plans by the Grant Locomotive Works for the Gilbert road, and its machinery combines all the latest improvements. The motor-car is twenty-two feet in length and eight in width, with large plate-glass windows at the sides and ends, giving ample light and ventilation. The color on the exterior is a dark olive-green, in two shades, and the interior is finished with different-colored woods. The engine and boiler are placed in the centre of the car, giving ample space for the movements of the engineer and firemen. The engine, cab and all, weighs 30,000 pounds, or about double the weight of the heaviest engines on the New York Elevated Railroad. The cars will be heated by the exhaust steam. The escape of sparks from the smoke-stack is prevented by a patent device. Each of the cars is thirty-seven feet ten inches in length, and eight feet nine inches in width. The outside is painted a light green, with panels a shade darker. The edges are ornamented with maroon color. The stripes and decorations are in dark-green and gold. The doors are placed at the ends, but it is intended to have some cars with compartments like those in English end continental railway coaches, Within the cars forty-eight passengers can be seated. In the centre, on each side of the aisle, are two seats arranged like those in the ordinary Pullman car. From this centre, side seats like those in the horse cars extend to the door. These seats will each accommodate eight persons. Crowding is prevented by little arms which rise from the cushions at intervals of nineteen inches. The upholstery is in maroon-colored morocco. The carpets are Ax-minster rugs. The ceilings have oak panels, decorated with flowers and arabesques. Vacuum brakes are used. Fourteen passenger stations are being erected on this line, at convenient distances. Five of them will have a larger frontage than the rest, covering one hundred and thirty-eight feet at Fourteenth, Twenty-third, Forty-second and Fifty-eighth Streets. Each station is a double structure, one on either side of the road, corresponding to the up and down lines. The interior of both the ladies' and gentlemen's waiting rooms are to be very tastefully furnished and finished throughout, in what is known as the Eastlake style of decoration. An ornamental ventilator springs from the ceiling in each room. The exterior of each station is to be ornamented with iron pilasters and decorated panels of the same metal. The stations can be approached on either side of the line by covered stairs of easy ascent, the sides being protected and ornamented with appropriately designed panel-work.

The work on this road was begun in March, 1876, on South Fifth Avenue, and, owing to obstructive lawsuits. but little progress was made until November last, when the Court of Appeals dissolved all the injunctions granted against Dr. Gilbert, and affirmed the constitutionality of the charter. The entire work of the road was divided Into three parts, an agreement made with a contractor for each, and favored by the unusually mild Winter, an immense force of workmen was kept busy night and day on the great enterprise, with results already appreciated by our citizens.

The work on the east-side road has not been so rapid, only a few men having been at work during the Winter. It is expected that trains will be running regularly on the Gilbert road about the 20th of May, as no reasons exist at present for any further delay, the reported sinking of a portion of the road up-town being emphatically denied by the engineers, constructors and authorities.

Any of our readers who wish to inform themselves on the various rapid transit schemes that have been brought to the attention of the public may be interested in comparing the Gilbert Elevated Railroad of to-day with the original plan of Dr. Gilbert, first published on the front page of FRANK LESLIE'S ILLUSTRATED NEWSPAPER, in the issue bearing the date of March 18th, 1871.

13

'THE EAST SIDE ELEVATED RAILWAY', *FRANK LESLIE'S ILLUSTRATED NEWSPAPER*, (SEPTEMBER 7, 1878), P. 12

The East-side

Elevated Railroad

THE line of the New York Elevated Railroad on the east-side of the city having been completed, excursion trains passed over it on August 15th, starting at Hanover Square, in front of the Cotton Exchange, and going directly to the Grand Central Depot Elevated Station. The distance from Hanover Square to Forty-second Street was made in fifteen minutes.

Through Pearl Street and Franklin Square the pioneer train was run at a moderate rate of speed, passing between the piers which are a part of the support of the approach to the Brooklyn Bridge. Beyond this point in the New Bowery the road passes over low ground, and, to make an even grade, is built at an unusual height above the pavement. Along the Bowery and Third Avenue the windows of the houses were filled with faces, and pedestrians paused to watch the train as it rattled by. Turning into Forty-second Street, the excursionists were introduced to luncheon laid out in the Station which directly adjoins the Grand Central Depot, Grand Union Hotel, and other prominent uptown buildings. The time on the return trip was thirteen minutes to Fulton Street.

The locomotives constructed by the Baldwin Locomotive Works, at Philadelphia, for the Elevated Railroad are of two patterns: the first is a four-wheeled connected locomotive, with outside horizontal cylinders and tank on the boiler for carrying the feed-water; and the second is an eight-wheeled locomotive, with outside horizontal cylinders, four wheels connected under the boiler, and a four-wheeled swing bolster truck under the tank, back of the fire-box and engineer's cab. This latter plan of engine is known as the *Forney* engine, the design having been patented by Mr. M. N. Forney, one of the editors of the *Railroad Gazette*. Both styles of engines have cylinders and driving wheels of the same size, viz., "10 × 14" cylinders, and driving wheels "38" diameter. The boilers are also of substantially the same size, so that the engines differ only in respect to the method of carrying the tank, and in the capacity of the tank—the four-wheeled engine having a tank on the boiler which has a capacity for 350 gallons of water; the eight-wheeled engine having a tank on an extension backward of the engine frames, supported by a four-wheeled truck, which has a capacity for 450 gallons of water.

In the construction of these engines especial attention has been given to their design, in order to arrive at the greatest possible strength and efficiency, as to both speed and tractive power, with the least possible weight. Steel has, therefore, been largely used in their construction. The boilers, furnaces, parallel rods, axles, wrist-pins and tires, are all of steel, and all wearing parts of the machinery are of steel, or iron case-hardened. The truck wheels in the eight-wheeled engine, instead of being the ordinary cast-iron chilled wheels, are steel-tired. The engines are all supplied with the Eames Vacuum Brake, the ejector of which is fitted with an appliance which muffles or deadens the noise of the escaping steam when the brakes are applied.

14

ISABELLA BIRD (MRS. BISHOP), *THE ENGLISHWOMAN IN AMERICA* (LONDON: JOHN MURRAY, 1856), PP. 153–158, 344–345, 439–441

The emigrants who have left our shores, more particularly the Irish, have voluntarily enacted the part formerly assigned to the slaves of the Spartans. Certain it is that their intemperance, with the evils of which the Americans are only too well acquainted, has produced a beneficial result, by causing a strong re-action in favour of temperance principles.

The national oath of the English, which has earned for them abroad a horrible *sobriquet*, and the execrations which belong to the French, Italian, and Spanish nations, are unfortunately but too well known, because they are too often heard. Indeed, I have scarcely ever travelled in England by coach or railway—I have seldom driven through a crowded street, or ridden on horseback through quiet agricultural villages—without hearing language in direct defiance of the third commandment. Profanity and drunkenness are among the crying sins of the English lower orders. Much has been said upon the subject of swearing in the United States. I can only say that, travelling in them as I have travelled in England, and mixing with people of a much lower class than I ever was thrown among in England—mixing with these people too on terms of perfect equality—I never heard an oath till after I crossed the Canadian frontier. With regard to both these things, of course I only speak of what fell under my own observation.

After dinner, being only too glad to escape from a house where pestilence was rife, we went out into Chicago. It is a wonderful place, and tells more forcibly of the astonishing energy and progress of the Americans than anything I saw. Forty years ago the whole ground on which the town stands could have been bought for six hundred dollars; now, a person would give ten thousand for the site of a single store. It is built on a level prairie, only slightly elevated above the lake surface. It lies on both sides of the Chicago river, about a mile above its entrance into Lake Michigan. By the construction of piers, a large artificial harbour has been made at the mouth of this river.

The city has sprung up rapidly, and is supplied with all the accessories of a high state of civilisation. Chicago, in everything that contributes to real use and comfort, will compare favourably with any city in the world. In 1830 it was a mere trading-post, situated in the theatre of the Black Hawk war. In 1850 its population was only 28,000 people; it has now not less than 60,000. It had not a mile of railway in 1850; now fourteen lines radiate from it, bringing to it the trade of an area of country equalling 150,000 square miles. One hundred heavy trains arrive and depart from it daily. It has a commerce commensurate with its magnitude. It employs about 70,000 tons of shipping, nearly one-half being steamers and propellers. The lumber-trade, which is chiefly carried on with Buffalo, is becoming very profitable. The exports of Chicago, to the East, of bread-stuffs for the past year, exceeded 13,000,000 bushels; and a city which, in 1840, numbered only 4000 inhabitants, is now one of the largest exporting grain-markets in the world.

Chicago is connected with the western rivers by a sloop canal—one of the most magnificent works ever undertaken. It is also connected with the Mississippi at several points by railroad. It is regularly laid out with wide airy streets, much more cleanly than those of Cincinnati. The wooden houses are fast giving place to lofty substantial structures of brick, or a stone similar in appearance to white marble, and are often six stories high. These houses, as in all business streets in the American cities, are disfigured, up to the third story, by large glaring sign-boards containing the names and occupations of their residents. The side walks are of wood, and, wherever they are made of this unsubstantial material, one frequently finds oneself stepping into a hole, or upon the end of a board which tilts up under one's feet. The houses are always let in flats, so that there are generally three stores one above another. These stores are very handsome, those of the outfitters particularly so, though the quantity of goods displayed in the streets gives them rather a barbaric appearance. The side walks are literally encumbered with bales of scarlet flannel, and every other article of an emigrant's outfit. At the outfitters' stores you can buy anything, from a cart-nail to a revolver; from a suit of oilskin to a paper of needles. The streets present an extraordinary spectacle. Everything reminds that one is standing on the very verge of western civilisation.

The roads are crowded to an inconvenient extent with carriages of curious construction, waggons, carts, and men on horseback, and the side-walks with eager foot-passengers. By the side of a carriage drawn by two or three handsome horses, a creaking waggon with a white tilt, drawn by four heavy oxen, may be seen—Mexicans and hunters dash down the crowded streets at full gallop on mettlesome steeds, with bits so powerful as to throw their horses on their haunches when they meet with any obstacle. They ride animals that look too proud to touch the earth, on high-peaked saddles, with pistols in the holsters, short stirrups, and long, cruel-looking Spanish spurs. They wear scarlet caps or palmetto hats, and high jack-boots. Knives are stuck into their belts, and light rifles are slung behind them. These picturesque beings—the bullock-waggons setting out for the Far West—the medley of different nations and costumes in the streets—make the city a spectacle of great interest.

The deep hollow roar of the locomotive, and the shrill scream from the steamboat, are heard here all day; a continuous stream of life ever bustles through the city, and, standing as it does on the very verge of western civilisation, Chicago is a vast emporium of the trade of the districts east and west of the Mississippi.

At an office in one of the streets Mr. C—took my ticket for Toronto by railway, steamer, railway, and steamer, only paying eight dollars and a half, or about thirty-four shillings, for a journey of seven hundred miles!

We returned to tea at the hotel, and found our viands and companions just the same as at dinner. It is impossible to give an idea of the "western men" to any one who has not seen one at least as a specimen. They are the men before whom the Indians melt away as grass before the scythe. They shoot them down on the smallest provocation, and speak of "head of Indian," as we do in England of head of game. Their bearing is bold, reckless, and independent in the extreme; they are as ready to fight a foe as to wait upon women and children with tender assiduity; their very appearance says to you, "Stranger, I belong to the greatest, most enlightened, and most progressive nation on earth; I may be the President or a *millionaire* next year; I don't care a straw for you or any one else."

Illinois is a State which has sprung up, as if by magic, to be one of the most fruitful in the West. It was settled by men from the New England States—men who carried with them those characteristics which have made the New Englander's career one of active enterprise, and successful progress, wherever he has been. Not many years ago the name of Illinois was nearly unknown, and on her soil the hardy settler battled with the forest-trees for space in which to sow his first crops. Her roads were merely rude and often impassable tracks through forest or prairie; now she has in operation and course of construction two thousand and seventy miles of those iron sinews of commercial progress—railroads, running like a network over the State.

At seven o'clock, with a feeling of great relief, mingled with thankfulness at having escaped untouched by the terrible pestilence which had ravaged Chicago, I left the hotel, more appropriately termed a "*caravanserai*" and my friends placed me in the "Lightning Express," warranted to go sixty-seven miles an hour.

Unless it may be St. Louis, I fancy that Chicago is more worth a visit than any other of the western cities. Even one day at it was worth a voyage across the Atlantic, and a land-journey of eighteen hundred miles.

There were a good many of the usual classes of accidents,—broken limbs and mangled frames. There was one poor little boy of twelve years old, whose arms had been torn to pieces by machinery; one of them had been amputated on the previous day, and, while the medical men displayed the stump, they remarked that the other must be taken off on the next day. The poor boy groaned with a more than childish expression of agony on his pale features, probably at the thought of the life of helplessness before him. A young Irishman had been crushed by a railway car, and one of his legs had been amputated a few hours previously. As the surgeon altered the bandages he was laughing and joking, and had been singing ever since the operation—a remarkable instance of Paddy's unfailing lightheartedness.

But, besides these ordinary accidents, there were some very characteristic of New York and of a New York election. In one ward there were several men who had been stabbed the night before, two of whom were mortally wounded. There were two men, scarcely retaining the appearance of human beings, who had been fearfully burned and injured by the explosion of an infernal machine. All trace of human features had departed; it seemed hardly credible that such blackened, distorted, and mangled frames could contain human souls. There were others who had received musket-shot wounds during the election, and numbers of broken heads, and wounds from knives. It was sad to know that so much of the suffering to be seen in that hospital was the result of furious religious animosities, and of the unrestrained lawlessness of human violence.

There was one man who had been so nearly crushed to pieces, that it seemed marvellous that the mangled frame could still retain its vitality. One leg was broken in three places, and the flesh torn off from the knee to the foot; both arms and several ribs were also broken. We went into one of the female wards, where sixteen broken legs were being successfully treated, and I could not but admire a very simple contrivance which remedies the contraction which often succeeds broken limbs, and produces permanent lameness. Two long straps of plaister were glued from above the knee to the ankle, and were then fixed to a wooden bar, with a screw and handle, so that the tension could be regulated at pleasure. The medical men, in remarking upon this, observed that in England we were very slow to adopt any American improvements in surgery or medicine.

To turn from the social to the material features of the United States: their system of internal communication deserves a brief notice, for by it their resources have been developed to a prodigious extent. The system of railways, telegraphs, and canal and river navigation presents an indication of the wealth and advancement of the United States, as wonderful as any other feature of her progress. She contains more miles of railway than all the rest of the world put together.

In a comparatively new country like America many of the items of expense which attend the construction of railways in England are avoided; the initiatory expenses are very small. In most of the States, all that is necessary is, for the company to prove that it is provided with means to carry out its scheme, when it obtains a charter from the Legislature at a very small cost. In several States, including the populous ones of New York and Ohio, no special charter is required, as a general railway law prescribes the rules to be observed by joint-stock companies. Materials, iron alone excepted, are cheap, and the right of way is usually freely granted. In the older States land would not cost more than 20*l.* an acre. Wood frequently costs nothing more than the labour of cutting it, and the very level surface of the country renders tunnels, cuttings, and embankments generally unnecessary. The average cost per mile is about 38,000 dollars, or 7600*l.*

In States where land has become exceedingly valuable, land damages form a heavy item in the construction of new lines, but in the South and West the case is reversed, and the proprietors are willing to give as much land as may be required, in return for having the resources of their localities opened up by railway communication. It is estimated that the cost of railways in the new States will not exceed 4000*l.* per mile. The termini are plain, and have been erected at a very small expense, and many of the wayside stations are only wooden sheds. Few of the lines have a double line of rails, and the bridges or viaducts are composed of logs of wood, with little ironwork and less paint, except in a few instances. Except where the lines intersect cultivated districts, fences are seldom seen, and the paucity of porters and other officials materially reduces the working expenses. The common rate of speed is from 22 to 30 miles an hour, but there are express trains which are warranted to perform 60 in a like period. The fuel is very cheap, being billets of wood. The passenger and goods traffic on nearly all the lines is enormous, and it is stated that most of them pay a dividend of from 8 to 15 per cent.

The primary design has been to connect the sea-coast with all parts of the interior, the ulterior is to unite the Atlantic and Pacific Oceans. At the present time there are about 25,000 miles of railway in operation and course of construction, and the average rate of fare is seldom more than 1*d.* per mile. Already the chief cities of the Atlantic have been connected with the vast valley of the Mississippi, and before long the regions bordering on Lake Huron and Lake Superior will be united with Mobile and New Orleans. In addition to this enormous system of railway communication, the canal and river navigation extends over 10,000 miles, and rather more than 3000 steamboats float on American waters alone.

The facilities for telegraphic communication in the States are a further evidence of the enterprise of this remarkable people. They have now 22,000 miles of telegraph in operation, and the cost of transmitting messages is less than a halfpenny a word for any distance under 200 miles. The cost of construction, including every outlay, is about 30*l.* per mile. The wires are carried along the railways, through forests, and across cities, rivers, and prairies.

15

WILLIAM H. RIDEING, 'SCENERY OF THE PACIFIC RAILWAY', *ART JOURNAL*, NEW SERIES, III (1877), PP. 105–108, 137–140

When the Mormons first settled in Utah, into which Territory we passed near Wahsatch Station, it was a part of Mexico, and it was acquired by the United States in 1848, through the Treaty of Guadalupe Hidalgo; but the Federal Government was lax, and the Mormons, who had been driven out of Illinois, appropriated it to themselves, and named it the State of Deseret. The name was changed to Utah by Congress in 1850, at which time the Territory included all of the present State of Nevada.

The area is about 54,000,000 acres, of which about 347.750 acres are under cultivation, and the value of all agricultural products in 1875 was $8,236,022. The products are principally grain and fruit, including apples, pears, peaches, plums, and grapes, in abundance; but in the valley of the Rio Virgen cotton, figs, and pomegranates, are also grown. The climate is variable, but the hottest days are followed by cool, refreshing nights. The aggregate yield of gold, silver, and lead, between 1868 and 1875, was $22,117,122. The surface of the land is elevated; the valleys are from 4,000 to 6,000 feet above the level of the sea, and the highest peak is about 13,000 feet.

Idaho and Wyoming bound Utah on the north, Wyoming and Colorado on the east, Nevada on the west, and Arizona on the south. The famous Colorado River is formed within the Territory, and its chaotic channel, hedged in with unutterable grandeur and desolation, is the key-note in which the tone of much of the scenery is struck. The population is about 125,000, including about 1,000 Indians, and the average number of persons to a family is five. There are ten railways, with a total length of 500 miles. The Union and Central Pacific roads are the longest, and cross the Territory near its northern border.

After this statistical digression, let us now return to our itinerary:

The grandest scenery of the Union Pacific Railway is crowded into the next sixty miles, and for four hours there is not a lagging moment to the tourist, whose search is for the picturesque, nor to the more scientific traveller, whose eyes are open to the marvellous geological revelations of Echo, Weber, and Ogden Cañons.

So far in the overland journey we have had no striking example of that most striking feature of the West, the cañon; and now we are to see in Echo the wall of an "open" cañon on one side and the impending cliffs of a "box" cañon on the other.

The true Western cañon is a narrow gulf in the mountains held in by cliffs, which sometimes overlap—such a formation being known as the "box;" and when the walls lean back, and are not absolutely perpendicular, the formation is classified by geographers as an "open cañon." All down the southern side of Echo the boundary is a well-rounded range of hills with enough grass upon them to hint of a superficial soil, and with a few emphatic projections of rock here and there. Another range of similar hills would make a characteristic "open cañon."

But all down the northern side there is a sheer bluff or escarpment from 500 to 700 feet in height, and of a reddish colour, which increases in warmth until it seems to glow with living heat. The contrast goes further. The opposite southern rocks are yellow, and the soil has slipped away in places, leaving a broad patch of the naked sandstone visible in the surrounding green. Occasionally a valley intersects the main cañon, and, looking through it, we can see the white tips of the Wahsatch and Uintah Mountains with the upper slopes of dark-blue or purple.

The scene has every element of impressiveness—strong, determinate colour, majestic forms, and a novel weirdness. Further, the descent into the cañon begins soon after dinner, at Evanston; the air coming from the mountains is inspiring; the afternoon light is growing mellower, and all other conditions are favourable to the highest enjoyment.

That most amusing of travellers, the Baron de Hubner, has described his impressions of this part of the overland journey as follows: "The descent to the Salt Lake is done without [?]eam, merely by the weight of the carriages, and, although the break is put upon the wheels, you go down at a frightful pace, and, of course, the speed increases with the weight of the train; and being composed of an immense number of cars and trucks, I became positively giddy before we got to the bottom. Add to this the curves, which are as sharp as they are numerous, and the fearful precipices on each side, and you will understand why most of the travellers turn pale."

There is a good deal of unconscious exaggeration in this picture, and the impressions are those of a highly-nervous person; but the real experience is sufficiently exciting as the train sweeps down and sways from side to side with increasing speed, now threatening to hurl itself against a solid cliff, then curving off like an obedient ship in answer to her helm.

Just eastward of the head of the cañon the country is undulating and breezy; farther westward it becomes more broken; the foot-hills present craggy fronts; and detached masses of rock, curiously weathered, crop out.

Nine hundred and sixty-six miles from Omaha we pause at Wahsatch Station, which is on the divide between Bear River Valley and Echo Cañon, and thence we sink lower and lower into the earth while the enclosing hills rise higher above us. Two miles from Wahsatch the train crosses a tressel-work bridge—450 feet long and 75 feet high, and immediately afterwards it crashes into the longest tunnel on the road, and through masses of reddish and purple clays.

He must be a very close observer indeed who can comprehend all of the varied beauties and curiosities that follow. The high, abrupt wall on one side, so smooth that it might have been cut by a saw, the lofty hills on the other side, and the glimpses of mountains whose snows never melt, are impressive and interesting; hut they are not the only things that make a journey through Echo Cañon memorable for a lifetime.

The stupendous rocks frequently assume the appearance of an artificial object, as at Green River and among the Bad Lands; it seems, as we round some butte of castellated form, that we are not in a region that twenty years ago was almost unknown, but in a much older country; feudal labour, and not the patient toil of the raindrops, must, we are half disposed to think, have shaped the pinnacles which taper with such fineness, and the towers that are so perfectly round. The uncommon forms are not so amazing nor so numerous as those in the Bad Lands, but they bear a close inspection, and still resemble somewhat man's handiwork.

At the head of the cañon, particularly, there is a formation called Castle Rock, which imitates an old, dismantled fortress, and near by is another formation called the Pulpit, on account of its likeness to the object of its name, and on account of a tradition that from it Brigham Young preached to the Mormons as he led them into their promised land. The railway curves around the latter, and an outstretched arm from the car might touch it. Next comes Sentinel Rock, an obelisk of conglomerate about 250 feet high, which shows the influence of "weathering," i. e., the action of the elements; and seven miles from Castle Rock is Hanging Rock, for view of which see preceding article.

From such a point of view as Hanging Rock, or the ridges above it, a much better idea of the tumultuousness of the surrounding country can be obtained than from the bed of the cañon. The earth is split by a score of transverse ravines, which extend like blue veins from the main artery and map the face of the country with shadow; isolated columns, positive and brilliant in colour, stand alone in their chromatic glory without a visible connection with the main rock from which they were originally detached; odd groups of conglomerate, much like inverted wineglasses in shape, and plainly banded with several strata of colour, sprout out like so many petrified mushrooms; and, clasping all within their basin, are the circling mountains of the Wahsatch and Uintah ranges—silvered with perpetual snow on their acute peaks, and impenetrably blue where the pines are. These two chains are among the most picturesque of all the Western mountains. They fairly bristle with peaks and lateral ridges, and they soar from the plain at a bound, so to speak, without the concealment and dwarfing effect of foot-hills.

The swift water of Weber River winds by the track through a channel overhung with bright shrubs, and the immigrant-road, upon which large cavalcades are still found travelling, crosses and recrosses the iron pathway, which from one of the neighbouring heights appears like a fine thread of silver, while the train with its locomotive and lofty Pullman-cars becomes a toy in contrast with the Titanic rocks among which it is rushing.

The cedar seems to thrive on an astonishingly poor soil, and crops out among the rocks in profusion, giving them a peculiar mottled appearance. These and a few pines strive for sustenance on the least accessible ledges, and are satisfied with never so small a hold on the rock.—A sharp curve around an immense sandstone or conglomerate butte on the right hand or northern side of the canon now changes the scene. The cañon opens into a wide valley completely surrounded by mountains; but, wherever tillage has been possible, the land has been cultivated, and a number of settlements have sprung up.

The train stops at the little town of Echo, 993 miles from Omaha, and 5,315 feet above the level of the sea, and the next station is Upper Weber Valley, whence a narrow-gauge railway turns off to Coalville, the site of an extensive deposit. The farmhouses are tidy and cheerful; the land has been fertilised by irrigation, and otherwise made the most of.

The most prejudiced opponent of the Mormons must acknowledge that they have done wonders in agriculture, and that, whatever else they may be, they are industrious, energetic, and thrifty.

Rushing through the valley, between Echo and Weber Cañons, we can now see the portals of the latter flanked on the southwest by a stupendous dome-shaped abutment of brilliant red, nearly 1,000 feet high, which is the first in a chain of similar formations extending southward, and presenting abrupt fronts all the way down. There are small alcoves between them, and they jut out obliquely, like the prows of a fleet of iron-clads. The idea of this belt of flaming red amid the verdurous surroundings, and with the grey and white mountains above it, will impress the reader as an extraordinary contrast, but it is in just such contrasts as this that the wonderful element of Western scenery consists.

In a moment more we have swept by the bluff, and the train is awaking thunderous reverberations in Weber Canon, which is deeper and wilder than Echo, including among its wonders the Devil's Gate and the Devil's Slide, a description of which will appear in the next article of this series.

WHILE the curious erosions in and near Echo Cañon, such as Witches', Castle, and Pulpit Rocks, that were mentioned in the last number of the *Art Journal*, are still in mind, we are inclined to reiterate what we have said before, of the unsatisfying enjoyment which the phenomenal in Nature affords. It is to be granted that a mere curiosity will attract the multitude, when a thing of beauty passes unnoticed; and people who could gaze on one of the empurpled peaks of the Wahsatch range, or on one of the terrific cliffs of Echo, without a touch of feeling, go into ecstasies in the contemplation of a *bizarre* rock with a supernatural likeness to something not in the least heavenly. It is noticeable how persistently the crowd of observers on the rear-platform of the car in passing through the cañons let slip the sublime and grasp what is merely odd, just as, with some audiences in the theatre, *Hamlet's* unquenchable sorrows are immediately forgotten in the humorous loquacity of the two grave-diggers. These vagaries of rock give the utmost delight to the average spectator, and it would be a pity to overlook them, as they are especially characteristic of the West; but they soon weary the better taste, and it is a still greater pity when they are allowed to monopolise the whole attention.

It is impossible, however, for the most frivolous observer to pass unawed the cliffs of Weber Cañon, between which the train is now running. They are absolutely perpendicular walls of rock; the prevailing colour is a bronze green, but green is not the sole colour. Masses of bright-red conglomerate, pale-grey limestones, bluish granites, and vari-coloured stratifications, also crop out in towers, crags, and caverns. We plunge into tunnels cut through the solid mountains; the high peaks that have hitherto been distant descend into the cañon at an angle of 80°, and loom directly above us; lateral ribs of rock project from the slopes, and some of them are of prismatic or fan-like formation. The Weber River flashes through the ravine, and breaks into a wrathy white as it leaps from ledge to ledge; even above there is no calm, and the clouds are torn into shreds, and contribute to the general tumultuousness of the scene as they drift to the east.

The geology as well as the picturesqueness of the Wahsatch range, by which we are surrounded, is interesting. The basis rocks are a series in alternating layers of quartzose, mica, and hornblendic schists. Above these rests a heavy bed of quartzites, with very regular and distinctly-marked stratifications. Above the quartzites is a bed of ashen-grey limestones, probably of the Silurian age, and a group of shales, clays, and quartzites, intervenes between this and another bed of limestone, which belongs to the Carboniferous age.

In Weber Cañon, and on the east side of the range from Ogden, there is a large group of quartzites, passing up into siliceous limestones and capped with red sandstones, and these are overcast by bluish-grey limestones containing Jurassic fossils.

In all probability, says a well-known authority, the vast area usually described as the Great American Desert, between the Wahsatch Mountains on the east and the Sierra Nevada on the west, was one great lake, in which the mountains rose as islands, and the lakes, large and small, which are scattered over the basin at the present time, are only remnants of the former inland sea. The modem deposits which cover the lowlands are mostly calcareous and arenaceous beds, and are often filled with fresh-water and land shells, indicating a very modern origin.

The range extends, with intervals in its continuity, far northward of the railway into Montana and Idaho, and many of the peaks are within the region of perpetual snow. The cañons are the result of erosion, and there are hundreds of them with vertical walls from 1,000 to 2,000 feet in height. On the left side of the track an isolated tree marks the thousandth mile west of Omaha, and near this is a notable formation called the Devil's Slide, two parallel ledges of granite, fourteen feet apart, projecting from the mountainside to a height of fifty feet—a picture of which appeared in the last article. One thousand and one miles from Omaha is Weber Quarry, from which quantities of red sandstone are obtained for building-purposes; and seven miles farther is the town of Weber, a thrifty Mormon settlement.

We soon emerge from the cañon into another fertile valley, in which the river widens and courses through several channels. The vegetation is abundant here, and there is some breathing-space between the mountains. Children offer apples, peaches, and pears, for sale in the stations; and as the writer passed through, on a warm, hazy afternoon of August, the orchards were bowed down with fruit. This pastoral element in the midst of such uncompromising sterility and wildness as the mountains suggest is a grateful relief and surprise—a relief, because the giant cliffs and buttes of the cañon are oppressive; and a surprise, because the shallowness of the soil is very apparent. When he again passed through it was late in November, and the winter had set in. The orchards were bare; the pastures were yellow and empty, and the mask of verdure being removed, it was easier to see and appreciate the difficulties with which the farmers contend. But he is not sure that the mountains did not look better under the chill grey sky of November than in the warm effulgence of the midsummer. The pines were the same, black, inflexible bars on the slopes, and the peaks and intervening ridges were edged with a steely sharpness. A light snow had fallen and spread an exquisite web over the purple rock, and in the hollows were floods of ultramarine blue.

The length of the valley is soon traversed, and in a few minutes we pass through Devil's Gate (the subject of an illustration in the last article) into Ogden Cañon, another chasm held in by walls from 1,000 to 2,500 feet in height. Ogden Cañon emerges in the Salt Lake Valley, and at about five o'clock in the afternoon we change cars at Ogden, the terminus of the Union Pacific Railway, 1,033 miles from Omaha, and 5,340 feet above the level of the sea.

Ogden is the second town of importance in Utah, and contains a population of about 6,000. It is situated on a high plateau, with mountains on every side of it, and is by far the best-looking attempt at a city that we have discovered since leaving Omaha. Not only the Union Pacific, but the Central Pacific, the Utah Central, and the Utah Northern Railways, have their termini here; and the scene in the station on the arrival of the overland train is full of life and colour. Baggage has to be rechecked; new berths must be obtained in the sleeping-cars, as the Pullman coaches go no farther, and all the annoyances which the through passenger experiences at Omaha are repeated. It is a disgraceful and inexcusable fact that though through-transportation tickets are sold at Omaha to San Francisco, neither sleeping-car tickets nor baggage-checks are issued to points beyond Ogden; but, while it is disgraceful and inexcusable, it is not by any means singular, as the Pacific Railway companies treat their passengers from one end to the other of their route with a distinguished lack of consideration.

A delay of an hour and a half occurs in making the transfers, and during this time the station-platform, as I have said, presents a very lively scene. Passengers are flitting hither and thither, promeenading, or looking after their tickets; newsboys vociferate the New York papers; eager brokers with their hands full of coin ply the travellers with offers of exchange for currency; dining-room gongs are booming furiously, and hotel-agents are earnestly soliciting custom. The moving throng is cosmopolitan in dress, manner, and language. The Ute Indian, wrapped up in resplendent blanket, and bedaubed with vermilion, rubs elbows with the sleek Chinaman in blue blouse, cloth shoes, and bamboo hat; the negro and the Spaniard, the German and the Irishman, the richly-arrayed "swell" of Paris and Vienna, and the Scandinavian peasant, mingle in the most picturesque contrasts. But what gives the scene emphasis and novelty is not the crowd itself, nor the variety of costume, but the situation—the grand, vivid hills on every side tinged with fiery light, the broken outlines of the peaks that are glowing with passionate heat, the mountain-fields of snow; the green lowlands, and above all the iridescent sky which is changing colour every moment. There are few lovelier sights than Ogden in a summer's sunset; and if, as the traveller proceeds on his westward journey, the moon should be near its full and should follow the splendours of the dying day with its chastening light, silvering the wide expanse of the lake and turning to a whiter white the low rim of alkaline shore, it will seem to him that he is leaving paradise behind.

The town spreads out from both sides of the station in broad, watered, shaded streets; the white houses are set in gardens; thrift, neatness, and industry, are embodied everywhere. What wonder that the inhabitants, like nearly all Mormons, are attenuated, weazen, and dejected-looking? To say that they are lightly-built would not be correct, for they are not built at all, but appear to be hung together by invisible wires. Every vegetable that is growing and every acre that is green has cost them untold labour, and whatever success they have attained has been wrested from the earth in a desperate struggle.

How much they have done may be seen to better advantage, however, in the capital, thirty-seven miles south of Ogden. The trains of the Utah Central Railway connect with those of the Union and Central Pacific, and the *détour* to Salt Lake City may be made in one day. The country between the latter place and Ogden is quite thickly settled, except within the first seven miles, and stoppages are made at four Mormon villages, with nothing in particular to characterise them, except the cooperative stores, with an open eye and the legend "Holiness to the Lord" painted over the doorways.

The station at Salt Lake City is fenced in with verdure, and the little cottages near the track, on the outskirts of the city—such cottages as in other cities present pictures of the meanest squalor—are rustic with the vine and trellis. The first street into which we emerge is an example of all the streets that divide the city into handsome squares or blocks; the roadway is firm and smooth; the sidewalks would be no discredit to London or Paris. Clear streams of water trickle along the curb at both sides, and feed the lines of shade-trees, not fully grown yet, that are planted with the same exactness of interval as cogs are set upon a wheel. Nothing is dilapidated; everything shows care and watchfulness; the unpleasant loafer, whom we have come to look upon as a large part of the far Western railway town, is invisible; the horse-car and omnibus conductors are impressively civil; the crowd at the station, and in the streets is a most respectable crowd.

The generosity of space is magnificent. All the streets are 132 feet wide between the fence-lines, including twenty feet of sidewalk on each side. The blocks contain about eight lots apiece, each lot measuring about one acre and a quarter, and the builders have been required to set their houses at least twenty feet back from the front fences of their lots. Fifteen or twenty years ago there was scarcely a structure of superior material to the convenient adobe; but now, when the harvest of the almost superhuman toil of pioneer days is being reaped, wood, brick, iron, granite, and stucco, are brought into use. The population of the city is about 25,000; six newspapers, (five dailies and one weekly,) are published; the theatre is a popular institution, and a freedom of speech is allowed to Gentiles which in times past would have cost them their lives.

16

W. G. MARSHALL, *THROUGH AMERICA: OR, NINE MONTHS IN THE UNITED STATES* (LONDON: S. LOW, MARSTON, SEARLE & RIVINGTON, 1881), PP. 239–241

After a run of thirty-seven miles, over ground we had already traversed, a distance which we managed to accomplish in two hours, stopping at four little stations on the way, we reached Ogden, and had to change from the cars of the Utah Central Railroad into those of the Central Pacific. Ogden, named after an old trapper who used to live in the neighbourhood, is a town of about 6000 inhabitants, is chiefly Mormon, and is the second town in point of importance in the Territory of Utah. Gentiles are fast pouring into the place, and the Mormons themselves are gradually getting "freezed out." Its streets are wide and regularly laid out, and have streams of pure water flowing at the sides, after the manner of Salt Lake City. Three times are kept here—Ogden proper, Laramie, and San Francisco times. The San Francisco time is 1 hr. 16 min. slower than Ogden, and the Ogden time is 30 min. slower than Laramie.

On reaching the station, we were received by such a clanging and banging and booming of gongs, together with such an uproarious and confused babel of voices from a number of excited individuals directly we stepped out of the train on to the platform, that it looked as if we had come to a place where everyone had taken leave of his senses. What did it all mean? In one word, it meant dinner. Yes, dinner it was, dinner and supper combined, and this is how the hour of the meal was proclaimed. There are four or five insignificant-looking little inns hard by the Ogden station, and the "runners" of these *hôtelleries*, each armed with a big gong, came forth with their satellites upon the arrival of our train, and made the most of such a windfall by intimating through the media of their gongs and their lungs how pleased they would be to see us inside their respective inns, where dinner was ready cooked and waiting for us, and how they would see us "fixed" for the meal with the smallest of amounts. Three out of the four or five came and pressed themselves on myself and my friend—they left off banging about their gongs and commenced vociferously haranguing us. As we had a couple of hours to wait before our train was due to leave for San Francisco, we began to turn a favourable ear to their vehement declarations; but so passionately did they address us, and so violently did they abuse one another, calling each other by the very choicest of American epithets in their anxiety to conclude with us a bargain which would at the same time be the most agreeable to themselves, that I thought more than once there was going to be a free fight. They called me "boss," and my friend they called "cap'n." Hitherto I had generally been known as "colonel," particularly among the negroes. I rather approved of being called by this latter appellation. "To call a man 'colonel,'" says the *Philadelphia Post*, "is to convey the idea that he is of a mild, meek, and benevolent disposition."—But to return to these hotel touts. One of them promised us each a "clean" meal for the sum of seventy-five cents; another promised us one for fifteen cents less, and offered to get, in addition, some young ladies to wait upon us. A third promised us a fifty-cent dinner, young ladies to wait, and a good bottle of wine beside—all to be included in the bargain. It is needless to observe that we closed immediately with this last-mentioned offer.

Dinner over, upon which no comment need be made, except that it was served half cold, and what was served was half cooked, we returned to the station to see about securing a section in a sleeping-car, that we might be conveyed with ease and comfort to the far-distant end of our journey. But, as might have been expected, it was too late for us now to secure any berths. We ought to have made sure of these before we left Salt Lake City. None were now to be had—all had been taken long ago. As it was, the Ogden station office for berth tickets was literally besieged with travellers, all anxious like ourselves to reach California comfortably, and everyone had to be similarly refused. So the prospect was before us of having to make the best of the situation for two nights in an ordinary car, where not only would there be no berths, nor indeed any proper accommodation for those who wished to have a comfortable sleep on the way; but no provision of lavatories, such as are in the parlour and sleeping-cars.

17

ROBERT S. MINOT, *RAILWAY TRAVEL IN EUROPE AND AMERICA* (BOSTON: A. WILLIAMS, 1882), PP. 9–12

THE START.—When the American traveller goes to the Grand Central Depot in New York, he has probably secured his ticket beforehand, as he can very rarely do in Europe; he drives to the baggage-room, where his baggage is not weighed at all, but is checked in a trice, instead of being daubed and pasted over with nasty paper labels; and he proceeds to a well-warmed, comfortable waiting-room, or more probably directly to the train, carrying himself his small baggage, and usually in ten minutes at most he is off. Had he been abroad, it would have been indispensable at a large terminal station to allow a full half-hour before the departure of the fast express train for buying tickets and registering baggage. The writer recently spent (and wasted of course) twenty-five minutes by the watch during cold weather, but under ordinary circumstances, waiting in the draughty baggage-shed, in the splendid Gare du Nord, or Northern Station, in Paris, simply to register ordinary baggage for London. There, as everywhere, it was placed in line on a truck, and had to wait for *one* machine to weigh and *one* official to register, and for a long queue of shivering, nervous, and impatient travellers to pay out odd sums, often very heavy, after an approximate verification of their "bulletins, and now and then a wordy and futile discussion with the official. As each one escaped from this trial, he marched off to the human cattle-pen, known more euphoniously as first and second class waiting-room, and rejoined his small baggage, fumbled about for a small fee to the porter who had brought it in, having previously given a larger fee to another porter who had brought in his large luggage, trundling it slowly up to the weighing machine; then he tried to compose himself. This was simply the usual trial at large stations. Our waiting-rooms (and cars too) are hot and stuffy; abroad, they are cold and stuffy.—Finally, the unpenning is announced in an outburst of official grandiloquence, and a pell-mell rush ensues, tempered only with official insolence, and obviating all the advantages and rights of first-comers. The train is amply pointed out by signs and officials, and the different classes of carriages are usually painted differently, or distinctly marked, first, second, third, and in some countries a fourth, class. As for the general appearance of the train, the locomotive is likely to strike the American eye as "an old tub."

It lacks grace and beauty, color, character, and *sex*, as a rule; in all of which features American machines excel. The cars are neat, and often elegant in build and ornamentation, especially the first-class, of course, and recently also the second. In size they resemble the long, high freight-cars used with us for hay or grain, and are divided transversely into three or four disconnected compartments, entered by a door on either side, and holding eight or ten persons each; so that a carriage contains from twenty-four to forty passengers. In style and comfort they vary, according to the fare paid. This is an admirable system, thoroughly democratic, and strangely in contrast with our *aristocratic* system; for before the days of palace cars, the poor man had almost no privilege, like the rich, of moving himself or family freely about in a nominally free country, for lack of cheap fares, and on account of false pride and social theories.

FIRST-CLASS CARRIAGES.—The first-class carriage is on a par with our best ordinary cars; but, as indeed is true of all classes, it is far lighter, length for length, than our lumbering cars, and consequently runs on good roads with a far lighter and smoother motion, although probably it "jumps" the track more easily, and in case of accident flies to pieces like a card-house. This lightness, taken in connection with the admirably adapted stuffing of the seats and the delightful head-support,—an extremely important detail quite neglected with us,—causes one to travel a whole day with as little fatigue as half a day in America; at least, such seemed to be the opinion of most travellers. Moreover, the carriages are generally upholstered with great taste and refinement. Instead of the exhausting chromatic panorama of the recent American car,—now being happily often replaced by the elegant Eastlake cars,—the eye falls on soft, sober, harmonious tints, cooling and restful to the traveller's soul. These carriages are found on all trains, and are rarely crowded; so that the traveller acquires a sort of home feeling in his compartment, and has a liberty of action and attitude impossible with us. Smoking is commonly permitted, when all the occupants are agreed to allow it; but, of course, in cold weather ventilation is nearly impossible, and there remains in the cars an ancient odor of tobacco disagreeable to sensitive nostrils. For a large party it is often exceedingly annoying to be separated in the train, as must often happen, since there is no communication after the doors are once locked, as they are nearly or quite everywhere and always, while the train is in motion. This locking is not only a vexatious attack on human dignity, but is horribly dangerous in case of accident (as recently shown at Charenton near Paris). Add to this: first, that in cold weather these carriages are almost deprived of the first of creature comforts—warmth—the only heater being a long, narrow metal box of hot water, renewed at the economical discretion of a cold-blooded and soulless corporation or government, and affording at best but a flitting, shadowy relief to the feet and legs alone; and secondly, that there are no toilet arrangements on the train; and the chief evils of the compartment system are before the reader, who may judge whether the first-class carriages on the whole surpass our common cars, or not. As for our palace cars, by day or by night, their superiority to every other railway vehicle in the world (for long journeys, at least) will scarcely be contested. They are little known in Europe, and appear to be *extremely* costly luxuries everywhere.

SECOND-CLASS CARRIAGES.—Those of an older type are wretched, rattling affairs, like our own common cars before the days of monitor tops and swell roofs; but latterly a great improvement has taken place, and now there are many specimens of this class quite as comfortable as the first, and running with a delicious smoothness, rarely known in the United States.

THIRD-CLASS CARRIAGES.—Those are often mere human cattle-cars, except that these biped cattle have the privilege of a hard wooden seat. They are as rarely heated, even in winter, as American horse-cars.

18

J. L. DOW, *THE AUSTRALIAN IN AMERICA* (MELBOURNE: THE "LEADER" OFFICE, 1884), PP. XI–XII, 19–21

This volume submits, in revised and amended form, the letters written by the author during a tour made in America during the summer of 1883 as Special Correspondent of the Melbourne *Leader*, a journal that, in its career of over a quarter of a century, has been the pioneer among Australian newspapers of this special class of reporting.

The writer landed in San Francisco early in June, and crossed the American territory, from the Pacific to the Atlantic, by way of Sacramento, the Sierra Nevada, Lake Tahoe, Virginia City, Salt Lake, Denver, Chicago, Niagara, Utica, Rutland (in Vermont,) Amherst (in Massachusetts,) and Newhaven (in Connecticut,) to New York; and thence back through Washington, Baltimore, Cincinatti, St. Louis, Kansas City, Las Vegas; Santa Fe (in New Mexico,) Yuma (in Arizona,) and Los Angeles and Fresno (in Southern California,) to San Francisco, towards the close of August, having during the trip travelled over 10,000 miles, including the frequent diversions made into the country on each side of the two main routes.

That such a trip as this can be performed in the time speaks for itself with respect to the fact that the Americans have got railway travelling up to a point approaching as nearly as possible absolute perfection. In Australia, railway travelling is something to be avoided; in America it is made so attractive that the people are induced to travel. In the one country you are cramped into a close box carriage, out of which you are only allowed to emerge and straighten your stiffened limbs at the will of the guard; in the other you have your seat by day, and sleeping berth by night in a gorgeous Pulman. The check system relieves you of all trouble with your baggage. You can get up and converse with anyone you please, from one end of the train to the other. Do you wish a smoke? Then you pass into a comfortable smoking compartment at the end of your car; thence you can go along, if you are tired of your Pulman seat, into a chair car, which is a carriage fitted with easy arm chairs and lounges, adjustable at all angles of ease, for the comfort of the passengers. At every station where the train stops you are at liberty to stroll out and look round, the tolling of the bell on the engine, and the slow movement of the train for the first half minute or so, being the signals which even stranger passengers soon learn to associate with making their way on board again. At the end of the car is the toilet room, where you wash and dress, and thence proceed along the train to the dining car, where you sit down to a repast equipped with viands and attendance, rendering a look out of the window necessary to realise that the whole affair is in a railway train, and not a first-class hotel. While at breakfast the news boy, who stays in the train and runs a general book and peanut store throughout the journey, fetches you along the newly-published paper of the particular place the train happens to be passing. This is the difference between travelling by rail in America and in Australia. In the latter case, if one travels from – say Melbourne to Sydney, you require to take a day's rest to recover. In the former, you feel as fit for business upon getting out of your sleeping-car in the morning, after covering, say, 300 miles, as if you had spent the night in your own home or in a first-class hotel. This is what enables one to get over so vast an area as the United States, and yet be fresh and fit for work all the time.

After seeing America an Australian's opinion of his own country is greatly enhanced: the Australian continent is just about equal in area to the United States, but in Australia the soil is richer, and there is more of it rich; while the only part of America that can equal the Australian climate is California. The grandest thing about America is its people. Their enterprise is extraordinary, and even a transient visitor becomes infected by it. As a people they are very bright, kind, courteous, and hospitality itself; the genuine kindness of the manner in which the Americans set themselves about obliging you, and without any fuss, even when at the expense of considerable trouble, forms a trait of their character that will long remain as one of the many pleasurable recollections of the time spent by this Australian in America.

THE *Leader* OFFICE,
    Melbourne, 1st June, 1884.

The cable street cars

A FEATURE of the San Francisco streets that is amongst the first to arrest the visitor's attention is its elaborate system of tram cars. Over a hundred streets have car roads laid down, and in some of the main thoroughfares the tracks are duplicated, triplicated and quadrupled. Some are drawn by one horse, some by a pair, and wherever you wish to go there is no delay, so frequently do they pass at all points. The conductor, by the way, has here taken the place of the fare-box system which obtains in Melbourne 'buses. The Americans have become tired of the box, and the car proprietors have found that if they wish to obtain their money they must come and collect it. There is, therefore, a driver and conductor to each car, the latter passing through at intervals, taking the fares and distributing transfer checks.

As a guard against imposition by conductors, these officials have what is called a bell punch and long strips of stiff paper numbered to two columns of twenty each. Upon collecting your fare he is obliged to punch a hole opposite a number in his slip, and in the act of punching the instrument strikes an internal bell. Thus every passenger unconsciously finds himself converted into an amateur detective, watching to see the punch hole made and the bell rung after the collection of every fare. For every full punched strip of forty fares, representing 200 cents, or 2 dols., the official has to account at night with the money. In striking contrast with the high, unwieldy, dingy coloured, steam drawn street trams of Sydney are the neat, comfortable and handily-got-into horse-drawn cars of this city.

As far, however, as the horse cars of San Francisco are in advance of the steam trams of Sydney, so in equal degree are they surpassed by the cars drawn on the running cable and stationary engine principle. At the date of my visit there were four important streets fitted with this system, and it was rapidly displacing the horse cars throughout the other parts of the town. The main thoroughfare, Market-street, had a double track nearly finished along its whole length, and several other important streets were in process of preparation.

"The perfection of street car locomotion" is my personal verdict upon this beautiful system, after a pleasant experience of rides in all directions, and the same opinion is held by all with whom I have conversed upon the question. Besides being smoother in transit than the horse cars, they are as nearly as possible absolutely without noise or vibration, and are able to successfully cope with a difficulty which the horse system fails in.

Remembering that San Francisco is level in its centre but encircled by sandy hills forming an elevated rim right round the edge of the peninsula on which the city is built, it had been found impossible before the advent of the cable plan to accommodate the people living in the streets of these portions of the city with either horse cars or cabs. The cable cars, however, glide in their smooth sailing fashion as easily up the steepest incline as they do along a dead level; and since the establishment of the cables, property in these elevated portions of the city has advanced materially in value.

This system of street railroad, which is the invention of Mr. A. S. Hallidie, of San Francisco, was first put in use by the Clay-street Railroad Co. in August, 1873, since which time it has been constantly running in the most satisfactory manner. The system consists of an endless wire rope placed in a groove below the surface of the ground between the tracks of a light railroad, and kept in position by means of sheaves upon which the rope is kept, and the motive power is obtained from a stationary engine placed at such a point of the road as is found most convenient. Upon a street having hills the engine is generally placed on the highest ground, but on a level street the usual location of the engine is midway between the two extreme points of traffic.

The rails are placed flush with the street, and present no impediment to ordinary travel. In San Francisco, indeed, it rather facilitates it, as the drays, light carts, and buggies may be seen falling in behind the car after it passes, and taking advantage of the smooth iron way to escape the rough cobble stones of the streets. The rope is grasped and released at pleasure by a gripping device which is worked by a lever, and is easily controlled by the official in charge. The cars are more smoothly started than by horses, and can be instantaneously stopped at any point of the road, even if coming down the steepest hill.

The general arrangement of the system in use by the Clay-street cable comprises an endless steel wire rope 3 inches in circumference and 11,000 feet long, lying in iron carriers supported every 39 feet on 11-inch sheaves. This rope is supported at every change of angle at the lower crossings in sheaves 4 feet in diameter, passing round a horizontal sheave 8 feet in diameter at the lower end of the line, and at the engine house around two angle sheaves each 8 feet in diameter, which lead the rope on to the grip pulleys, which latter are also 8 feet in diameter, and driven by an engine using 3700 lbs. of coal per day. A duplicate engine and boiler are kept in reserve in case of accident.

A cable outfit for one street system consists of two cars, one seating fourteen passengers and the other, which contains the lever-gripping attachment, sixteen, but on holiday time the two cars have not infrequently accommodated seventy passengers between them.

The second of the San Francisco cable roads is the California-street, on which the rope runs 17½ hours per day at a speed of six miles an hour, the cars starting every five minutes in the forenoon and every three minutes in the afternoon. This road has a gauge of 3 feet 6 inches, and a 30-lb. steel rail is used as in Clay-street, set flush with the road so as not to interfere with other traffic. The hill at the end of this street is the best portion of the city for residences, overlooking as it does the Golden Gate and bay.

After the Clay-street road had been running three years, and its superiority tested, the Sutter-street horse car company changed their system from a horse road to the running cable plan, and by the end of 1879 had re-constructed their entire road on the new system. This company has now over 3 miles of double track running on cable, the gauge of the road being 5 feet, and its greatest elevation being 167 feet above starting point. The Sutter-street company reports that their road, which was barely paying under the horse system, has increased its profits by 30 per cent. During its first cable year the passenger traffic was increased by 962,375, and the shares of the company, which were selling before the change at 24 dol., were being quoted in the stock market reports of 29th June, 1883, at 78 dol.

The third of the cables now running is the Geary-street, which operates over a level run of about 2½ miles. It has a double track, being through one of the most populous parts of the city, and since its start in 1880 has been second only in success to the California-road, which started at 90 dol. a share, and is now saleable at 130 dol., while the Sutter-street company's shares began at 37 dol., and were being quoted at the abcve date at 100 dol.

The Presidio and Ferries street cable, later constructed, and altogether very solidly built. It has nearly 2 miles of double track, and ascends at one place 5000 feel above its initial point. The engine is located on the summit of the hill. There is a curve at the intersection of two streets on this line, and the rope is deflected by means of two 8 foot horizontal pulleys. The streets descend from both directions towards the curve, and about 30 feet before reaching it the grip is opened and released from the rope, when the two cars are carried round by gravitation, after which the rope is again picked up.

With respect to cost, a summary may be made of authoritative notes collected on this point by stating that while the initial expense of laying down a cable road is considerably higher than that involved in the construction of a horse line, the permanent working expenses show a saving of over 50 per cent.

19

GEORGE EDWARD WRIGHT, 'THE CHICAGO LIMITED EXPRESS', *A VISIT TO THE STATES*, 2 VOLS. (LONDON: G.E. WRIGHT, 1887–88), PP. 362–372

The Chicago limited express

In a country as extensive as the United States, where the distances are so great and the chief cities so widely separated, the railway systems are naturally expanded to a degree hardly realized in other parts of the world. The traveller often spends a week in a railway train, and it has become a common method of making an agreeable tour for a party to charter a special railway coach or train, and live in it for days and weeks together while journeying about the country. The chief American railways leading out of New York make elaborate arrangements for long-distance travelling, and George M. Pullman is noted throughout the States, as well as in Europe, for his inventions, which secure comfort and luxury on these long American railway journeys. As the Englishman of wealth and leisure may have his yacht, so the American who is similarly blessed has his "special private car," in which he enjoys the pleasant pastime of "yachting on wheels," for he has 150,000 miles of American and Canadian railways at command, with an endless variety of scenery and attractions. These, however, are private arrangements. For the use of the general public in long-distance travelling the "Chicago Limited Express" of the Pennsylvania Railroad is regarded as the most completely-appointed passenger train that is run upon any American railway. It passes daily each way between New York and Chicago, a distance of nearly 1,000 miles, the journey being accomplished in 25 hours. The train leaves New York at 9 o'clock in the morning, and arrives at Chicago at 9 the next morning, the local time there being one hour later than New York. The service is "limited" in the sense that the train is confined to four Pullman sleeping coaches, a dining coach, where an elegant restaurant furnishes excellent meals *à la carte* for 4s., and a "composite car," the latter having a compartment for luggage and the mail bags which are carried between the terminal cities, also sleeping apartments for the train-men, and a smoking and reading room for the passengers, furnished with easy chairs, a library, writing and card tables, bath room and barber shop, the latter being an indispensable adjunct to American life. The passenger may thus relieve the monotony of the journey by getting his hair cut or indulging in that vigorous hair-cleansing process known as the shampoo for 2s. or a shave for 1s., or a bath at the rate of 40 miles an hour for 3s. He also has at hand an excellent selection of current literature and all the daily newspapers of the chief American cities in the library.

The coaches in this train are the latest productions of Pullman's Palace Car Company, and show the best skill of the American railway-car builder. To fit up the three trains conducting the daily service each way between the two leading American cities cost, without the motive power, about £60,000. The delicate and artistic decoration of the outside of these coaches shows the elaborate skill of railway-carriage ornamentation in America, and makes an apt setting for the comfort and luxury found within. The "platforms," as they are called, which make the junction between the coaches are arranged with vestibules, a recent invention of Mr. Pullman. This is done by enclosing them all around with elastic steel frames, which may be described as a sort of continuous buffer. These, extending from floor to roof, join when the coaches are coupled and are kept in place by springs which force the frames tightly together, so that the two coaches become practically one, and there is thus obtained a wonderful steadiness of motion throughout the train, with sufficient flexibility to readily move around curves. Sheets of rubber and curtains cover the lines of junction, and the interiors of the vestibules are carpeted the same as the coach, concealing any break in the continuity of floor or sides. An American railway coach always has a long aisle down the middle, with seats on either hand, and this vestibule arrangement prolongs the aisle into the next coach. The passenger moves about at will, passes from coach to coach, and when the train is standing a plate-glass door in the side of the vestibule provides exit or entrance at the stations. These Pullman coaches are furnished in the most elaborate manner, are lighted by electricity kept in storage batteries, and in honour of the "foreign relations" of America who do so much riding in them they are given foreign names, for every coach has to be named. The train upon which I rode had the four coaches named "Russia," "Spain," "Italy," and "Corinthia," and the dining coach was the "Ponce de Leon." Upon the other trains of the same service the coaches are named "England," "France," "Germany," "Ireland," "Austria," &c. Each coach is a complete hotel, with sleeping accommodations for about 30 passengers.

This train, which is arranged to make the quickest time between the metropolis of the Atlantic seaboard and the chief city of the West, secures its speed by having the fewest possible stops, the only halts made being at intervals of 100 to 130 miles, when it is necessary to change the locomotives, there being seven relays provided and five minutes' halt to make each change, during which time a small regiment of train-men examine the wheels and all the running gear, and also fill up the water-tanks and ice-boxes in the coaches, for the train carries large supplies of both, a vast amount being used by the passengers, especially in the hot American summer weather. The train leaves New York every morning and Chicago every evening, this being arranged to give the charming scenery in crossing the Alleghany Mountains each way by daylight. The nearest approach to absolute safety is secured by giving this limited train precedence over all others, and thus providing it free and unobstructed course over the line. It is literally a first-class American hotel on wheels; you eat and sleep upon the train, write and post your letters and send your telegrams; can smoke or lounge in the comfortable easy chairs provided in the forward coach; can read the newspapers and current literature; or can roam all over the train at will, which is a great comfort to the pent-up passenger on a long journey. The toilet accommodations are complete, and everything is kept in thorough cleanliness, while the coaches are carefully ventilated, and made warm in cold weather. The excellent construction of roadbed and coaches makes the movement of the train very steady. It runs at speeds from 30 to 60 miles an hour, according to the grades. It rushes steadily along, over river and mountain, through the finest scenery of the Alleghanies, past mine and mill, foundry and forge, over the farm and through the forest, and quickly into and out of village and town, where the people turn out in crowds to see the daily "whizzer" go by. It stops only to change locomotives (and then is off again in short order), and, what is of the greatest importance, it goes through "on time." As the day was changing into night the novelty was had of eating dinner on the train, with the unique and appetizing sensation of flying onward at the rate of 50 or 60 miles an hour as we sat at the flower-decorated tables. Then games and social chat among the passengers whiled away the evening, and when the time came for turning in, the nimble negro "porters" donned their snow-white jackets, pulled down the sloping upper sides of the coach, and quickly made up the sleeping berths. The passengers promenaded about, going from one end of the sinuous train to the other, a distance of 500ft., and as the curves were suddenly rounded by the swift-moving coaches they amused the onlooker by their curious gyrations in trying to keep upright. One could see back through the entire train and watch it twist about like an elongated serpent. Finally, as night came on and the "Limited" left the Ohio river valley for its long north-western journey across the rolling lands of Ohio and the prairies of Indiana and Illinois to Lake Michigan, all hands went to bed, it is hoped to enjoy the sleep of the just.

    The Pennsylvania Railroad west of Pittsburg on the route to Chicago is known as "the Fort Wayne road," or, to be more precise, the Pittsburg, Fort Wayne, and Chicago Railroad. After leaving Pittsburg, the line runs for about 26 miles northwest, down the Ohio river, amid the grand scenery of its bordering hills. It was the Ohio river and its tributaries that furnished the means of making the earliest prosperity of Pittsburg. This great river is the largest branch of the Mississippi from the eastward, and it drains a basin of over 200,000 square miles. It flows almost a thousand miles in a generally south-western course to Cairo, at the southern extremity of Illinois, where it joins the Mississippi. In its upper waters the Ohio is from 1,000 to 1,200 feet wide, according to the state of the current, the depth changing 50ft. to 60ft. between high and low water, and it flows at the hourly rate of one to three miles. It has drained a deeply carved valley in the tableland, through a thriving agricultural region, and has many prosperous cities on its banks. Our train speeds swiftly through Beaver county, at the western border of Pennsylvania, among the coal pits and forests, over an undulating surface, gradually climbing the gradient out of the Ohio valley, and leaves that river as it abruptly bends to the south-west. We then pass up the valley of the Beaver river, a considerable affluent, and after running a short distance turn westward, and in 15 miles cross the imaginary line that makes the boundary between Pennsylvania and Ohio. This is a leading State of the Mississippi valley, wealthy and powerful, a land of good agriculture and much politics, varied by mining and manufactures. In recent years Ohio was the President maker for the Union, but since the unfortunate assassination of President Garfield that honour has been transferred to New York. We enter the State in Columbiana and Mahoning counties, a continuation of the region of coals and iron so generously displayed in Pennsylvania, this being known as the Mahoning valley. The railroad runs for miles westward, still among iron and coals, over an undulating territory past the busy towns of Salem, Alliance, Canton, and Massillon, the latter being located in one of the most productive Ohio coalfields, and also having valuable quarries of white sandstone for building. We have now come into the border of the extensive region in the Mississippi valley that was first opened to civilization by the early French explorers, and this pretty town on the bank of the Tuscarawes river preserves the memory of the noted French preacher, Jean Baptiste Massillon. From the coals and iron the train then gradually moves into a rich agricultural region, and passes Mansfield, which bears the name of the great English jurist to show its worthy origin, and is the home of the leading political manager in Ohio, and its prominent candidate for President, John Sherman—one of the best known United States Senators. Its favourable location in such a fertile section naturally makes the little town of Mansfield an extensive manufacturer of agricultural machinery. As the railway goes over the rich farmland, the rolling surface gradually blends into the more level stretches of prairie, heavily timbered where not cleared for cultivation. We have gone entirely away from the region of the tributaries of the Ohio and cross into the valley of the Sandusky river, which flows northward to Lake Erie. Here is Bucyrus in a prolific natural gas region; and not far beyond the train crosses another imaginary line that makes the boundary between Ohio and Indiana and halts briefly at Fort Wayne which gives its name to the railway.

Fort Wayne is a leading town of Northern Indiana, and has probably 40,000 people. It is not only located in a wealthy farming section, but is also a centre for both railways and manufactures. Being at the highest point of the elevation diverting the waters east and west, it is known as the "Summit City." Here two smaller streams unite to form the Maumee river, which flows off to the northeast, meandering over the almost flat surface, to form the head of Lake Erie. The existence of a "summit" is thus almost imperceptible, for the land all about is a prairie, gently rolling, and without hills of any prominence. Like all of them on these broad prairies, the town is mainly built of wood. The site of Fort Wayne was visited two centuries ago by the French, who began a lucrative trade with the Indians, and prior to 1719 they had erected a trading post, and afterwards built Fort Miami. In 1760 the place fell into English hands, who also built a fort, and when it subsequently came into possession of the United States, General Anthony Wayne in 1794 erected a permanent Indian frontier fort and gave it his name. The canals and railways afterwards brought the trade that made it grow in importance. This region was the home of the Miami Indians, extending from the Maumee river westward to Lake Michigan, and southward along the valley of the Miami river to the Ohio. They were a warlike and powerful tribe, first found by the French, but afterwards, in the colonial wars, they espoused for a time the English cause, then turned again to the French and finally came back once more to English allegiance, during the American revolution. This latter course provoked almost constant hostilities between them and the colonists, then settling in large numbers beyond the Ohio river, in what at the time was designated as the "North-West Territory," out of which the States of Ohio, Indiana, and Illinois were carved. Under the skilful leadership of their renowned chief, Mishekonequah, or the "Little Turtle," they defeated repeated expeditions sent against them, some with heavy loss, but were finally beaten by Wayne in 1794. The Miamis after this overthrow declined in importance, and through the inroads of dissipation and vice had finally dwindled to barely 250 persons when they were removed to a far Western reservation 40 years ago. Some distance beyond, at Warsaw, Indiana, we cross the Tippecanoe river, a stream about 200 miles long, flowing south-west to the Wabash, and thence to the Ohio river. It is noted for the later and even greater Indian defeat on its banks in 1811, when General Harrison, afterwards President of the United States, repulsed a combined force of several tribes united under Tecumseh brother, Elskwatawa, or the "Prophet." These two chieftains were Shawnees, and they preached a crusade by which they united all the Western tribes into a concerted movement to resist the encroachments of the white man. The brother, who was a "medicine man," set up as an inspired prophet in 1805, denouncing the use of liquors and of all food and manners and customs introduced by the whites, confidently predicting that they would be ultimately driven from the land. For years these men travelled over the country stirring up the Indians. General Harrison, who was the Governor of the district, advanced against the prophet's town on the Tippecanoe, when the Indians suddenly attacked his camp, but were signally defeated. After this, the late war between England and the United States broke out, when Tecumseh espoused the Royal cause, and, appearing in Canada with a number of his warriors, the British made him a brigadier-general. He was killed in the battle of the Thames in Ontario. It is said he had a premonition of death, and laying aside sword and uniform he put on his hunting dress and fought desperately until killed. Tecumseh was the most famous Indian chief of the West.

While swiftly rolling over these broad and, in sections, densely-wooded prairies that form Northern Indiana the dawn of day came upon us, and the gathering light gradually unfolded the wealth of agriculture that makes these people so prosperous. The region of mines and coals and iron and of flaming gas torches had been left far behind, and the train had entered the purely agricultural district, spreading thousands of miles south and west of the great lakes—a district tributary chiefly to Chicago. The little towns along the railway were frequent, having grown up from the village store and cross-roads, expanded by the business of the railway and the facility and cheapness of construction of wooden houses, within brief periods from small hamlets to ambitious towns. This section not so long ago was the "West," but the quick march of events in the new country and the expansion of population have removed the "West" of to-day far beyond the Mississippi. The older States of this region have for some time put on the maturer garb of the sedate seaboard communities, and, having passed the adolescent stage, are now liberal contributors to the great tide of migration which is filling up the far Western country still 1,500 miles further beyond us. The towns the railway passes are all anxious to become great manufacturing centres, and some have already established large and prosperous mills. They have the prevalent "natural gas craze" well developed, and the tall derricks erected over the boring wells on their borders show how they are delving into the depths of the earth, with the hope that the good luck of Pittsburg and Findlay, in Ohio, and some other places may strike them, and the bonanza of cheap natural gas fuel put them on the high road to wealth. The level country is well supplied with railways, which cross and recross each other's lines in all directions, and mostly at grade, for they are almost all built upon the same level. We glide over the prairie in approaching Chicago, through a district which has been well described as having "a face but no features." It is easy railway building upon this flat surface, for it seems only necessary to dig a shallow ditch on either side of the line, throw the earth in the centre, and lay the rails upon it. Nature has made this prairie as smooth as a lake, so that scarcely any grading is necessary, and after the patches of forest give place gradually to the universal grass-covered plain that borders Lake Michigan you can see far away in every direction, as if looking over the ocean. As Chicago is approached the converging of other railways towards the same goal shows how the great lake city is the universal Mecca of American railway managers. The train crossed a score of other lines, and getting at last into a perfect maze of railroads and car-yards, it gave not only an impressive lesson of the evil of grade crossings but also convincing proof of arrival at last at the greatest railway centre in America—all the growth of the last half century.

20

LILIAN LELAND, *TRAVELING ALONE. A WOMAN'S JOURNEY AROUND THE WORLD* (NEW YORK: AMERICAN NEWS COMPANY, 1890), PP. 302–313

The United States

After seeing many other countries, I desired to know more of my own.

While I have found so much that is comfortable, charming and interesting, in other lands, the results of my observations in this one have filled me with patriotism and pride. America is new, undeniably new. It hasn't any ruined castles, but it has some of the finest scenery in the world; and our traveling accommodations are unequaled on the globe. Charles Dickens and other English writers have criticised us severely, and their criticisms were not undeserved; but America is pre-eminently a land of progress, and the improvement of even a few years is almost marvelous. In the comfort and conveniences of living as well as of traveling we now excel every other nation.

Leaving New York early in June, skirting the banks of the majestic Hudson, rushing through the valley of the Mohawk and gliding along the shore of Lake Erie, and across the plains of southern Michigan, I reach Chicago. It is a handsome city, with fine broad avenues lined with great houses of stone and iron, looming up toward the sky. A drive discloses many beautiful residences. Most artistically laid out in drives and lawns, decorated with flowers and foliage, is Chicago's beautiful park, skirted by Lake Michigan, which lies gray and glittering under the sun, stretching out beyond the reach of the eye. Altogether, Chicago is a bright and pleasant place in which to rest before proceeding westward.

Once on the train again, there is little to lure the traveler between Chicago and Denver. If you travel from choice and not from necessity, you are as glad to be on the road again as you were to rest a day, for to the born traveler there is nothing quite so satisfactory as motion. When the train moves out of the depot, or the steamer leaves her wharf, then is such a person truly happy, whether just arranging the small baggage in the seats of the sleeper, or sniffing the fresh breeze of the sea from the vessel's deck.

On, across the broad, red, muddy Mississippi River, through Iowa, where "it is so wet that a man can't live any more than a year or two without getting web footed;" across the equally red and muddy Missouri and through Nebraska, where the "grasshoppers are so thick that they stop the cars," to Colorado, and the outline of the Rocky Mountains emerges from the horizon in the distance, looking like the puckered-up edge of pie crust bounding this broad, undulating, pie-like plain.

Travelers are frequently disappointed in the appearance of the far-famed "Rockies." Seen from across the great plains their dim outlines are not imposing. Distance and perspective reduce them to mere foothills, and it is not until near and among them that you are impressed by their height and grandeur.

From Chicago to Denver was once a territory of cornstalks and barren plains. But with the advance of immigration and civilization it has become a pretty and fertile country. Where once were endless fields of unromantic cornstalks are now green banks and pretty villages. The cornstalks have gone further West to "grow up with the country." Even the plains that were once bare and desolate are now carpeted with green and bright with wild flowers, among which plump, rabbit-like little prairie dogs disport.

Denver is pretty. The city is scattered loosely about instead of being compactly built, and therefore spreads itself over a wide expanse of territory. The streets are broad, and cost but little to keep in order, as they remain hard and smooth without paving because of a peculiar quality of the soil.

Leaving Denver in the morning, three hours brings us, via the Denver and Rio Grande Railroad, into the Rocky Mountains, passing Castle Rock and Palmer Lake, and stopping at Colorado Springs, where there are many beautiful drives and several springs to visit. The roads all about are smooth and hard, and the teams at the stables very good. Manitou is within easy driving distance, although one can go there by rail.

At Manitou are iron and soda springs. It is a strictly temperance place. There is a sign on a refreshment house there which is almost as pathetic as it is honest. It reads thus: "Barley water and bad cigars." Another sign on the outside of a canvas tent where candy is sold reads: "Ice cream Parlor," which seems to describe it rather extravagantly to say the least.

The drives leading up into the narrow cañons and through Monument Park are very fine. Monument Park is a plateau with groups of large rocks and perpendicular slabs of granite of grotesque shape standing upon it. The Garden of the Gods is similar, the great chunks of granite bearing peculiar resemblances that give them names such as the "Bear and the Seal" and the "Lady of the Cañon." Most of the rock is of a deep red and yellow sandstone.

The cañons are exceedingly beautiful. Driving into them, the walls grow higher and steeper, and you seem to have reached the end of the road constantly as the walls close in before you; but, as in the Italian lakes and the Norwegian fiords, it opens up as you approach, showing another stretch of canon still narrower and still grander.

Leaving Colorado Springs, all one's anticipation is centered on the glorious scenery we are soon to pass through. For the Denver and Rio Grande possesses the great attraction of running directly through the finest part of the Colorado scenery. But it is still several hours off, and I have leisure to observe my fellow passengers.

In the opposite seat of my section sat the Pullman conductor—a gentle young Eastern fledgling, apparently consumptive, hoping for restored health from the bracing Colorado air. In the section opposite a bright, intelligent, handsome woman, who is going to visit a Mormon lady—a sixth wife—at Salt Lake. Opposite her is an extremely long, pale, crushed-strawberry haired young man, who is contemplating with much dissatisfaction the limits of the panels above him, which are to form the under crust of the niche he is destined to fill to overflowing this night. The next section contains an elderly woman and her daughter, a well-developed girl of exceedingly blonde complexion and brown eyes of most curious expression. Behind them a very disagreeable old man who had secured a whole section and was obliged to give part of it up to an old lady who happened to know him, of which piece of generosity he babbles endlessly. A woman and a boy are in the next section. Behind me an Englishman and his wife. He is of conspicuously sporting aspect—a pugilist, I should say. But, oh! where are those Englishmen who said Americans abroad were such "bad form?" Our deepest, wildest wilderness cannot produce anything so grotesquely glaring as this pair, their appearance and their dress. Behind them a little married couple of the purest American type. On the other side a woman with her boy, both seasick. Next a family of grown folks and children, one a tiny girl with laughing, dimpled face, and the sweetest blue eyes in the world. Besides the stationary people are a floating element of two women and a boy, who had insisted on traveling on the car, although there were no vacant berths to be allotted to them until midnight, and were growling about it. They came and occupied my section for awhile, and with something of an air of humor ran down the road and management, while the fledgling conductor sat and listened with an occasional gleam of comprehension in his dark consumptive eyes.

The fixed idea of sleeping car travelers seems to be that they all ought to be supplied with lower berths. As half of the berths obstinately insist on being upper, there is great dissatisfaction if the car is more than half full. These women particularly had the most rooted objection to upper berths, and an inexpugnable belief that the conductor ought to go through the car and see if there was a single unfortunate man in possession of a lower berth, and if so evict him at once for their benefit.

It has been my misfortune to meet some women who seem to think that a man has no kind of human right as against their selfish fancies. To me there is nothing lovelier than the generous courtesy extended by the stronger sex to, may I say, the finer? But if there is one sight to me more mortifying than another it is woman arrogating to herself such unselfish courtesy as a right. This was the kind of women these two were. After they had worn the berth question threadbare, they fell upon each other and quarreled and taunted and teased, with exterior good humor, howbeit, and only a gleam now and then of the real bad temper underneath.

One of these women was a type I have seen more than once. She had a handsome, placid face and an outer air of amiability that had earned for her the reputation of good nature and unselfishness. But beneath she was pure egotist, a selfish and uncharitable cynic. Sitting there next her, hour after hour, and hearing her cool, caustic replies to her friend and seeing her glance of utter ill-humor, I knew her to be a woman that I should hate with fierce, undying hatred should I be obliged to see much of her.

How confidential people grow after thirty-six hours in a Pullman car. And how one will be drawn into frank acquaintanceship after enjoying for twenty-four hours that solitude only to be found in a crowd. A young girl was just describing to me the exact kind of man she wanted to marry and the particular amount of affection she should require from him, when, as her tones grew obliviously loud with her intense interest in the subject, I glanced at the fragile young conductor and caught him twisting his face in an agonizing effort to crush a laugh that was struggling for utterance. He was looking the other way, and even after I said, "He has heard every word," and the girl was disowning every sentiment expressed as fast as she could, he made a brave effort to drive the laugh back. But it was no use; he broke down under my scrutiny, and laughed it out and confessed.

Way up in the mountains there we observed a curious formation of cones of clear sand, large and small. The small ones are supposed to have been made by ants, the larger ones by whirlwinds. The formations are precisely the same in appearance, only varying in size.

After circulating around the outskirts of the Rockies for a while, our train plunged directly in among them, and presently we entered the Grand Cañon of the Arkansas. And very grand we found it, this long, deep, winding crevice in the earth, whose walls of red and yellow sandstone stretch up perpendicularly 2,000 feet toward the sky, that is but a strip of blue above us. The train does not run very fast here, and they might run slower and still not displease the passengers. As it is, we try to look above, behind, before and below us all at once, in the vain effort to catch the complete picture. The Royal Gorge is the narrowest part of this cañon, but all of the long, sinuous cañon is so beautiful it is hard to distinguish one part of it as finer than another. As magnificent as the scenery is, there is nothing to make one nervous about it. As we look up to the top of those grim walls of stone we are much better pleased to be running smoothly along at their feet, beside the winding river, than to be standing up at the top there looking down. The road through here is one of the greatest triumphs of civil engineering in the world.

Later on we take to climbing. Around about and up the mountains we go, at the steepest of grades, now shooting into a snowshed for a little, then out again and around and about, higher and higher, looking below us at the track recently traversed and across the valley high above at the track we are expected to get around to presently; and we do, gliding around the muleshoe curve and on to the top of Marshall Pass. Looking back we see four lines of roads, sections of the spiral we have just ascended.

But the finest picture of all is to come, and many are the lamentations because we are to pass the grandest part of the road, the Black Cañon, at night. It is 11 P. M. when we enter this famous cañon. The moon is full, however, and shining brightly down into the dark chasm, lending a weird charm to the scene, touching the prominent peaks with silver light and making the deep, dark corners gloomier by contrast, while the rushing Gunnison River glitters brightly under its rays as it rolls turbulently on. The cañon is very narrow, the walls looming up grandly, sometimes shelving over the train. Our way is very winding. We cross and recross the roaring river several times, dashing from one side to the other on iron trestle bridges and around curves, with an ever changing picture of solemn grandeur about us. Great walls of granite looming above us; falls tumbling down them to the already riotous river below, and then before us rises a mighty monument of stone, a cone of solid granite pointing to the sky—the famous Curricanti Needle.

We leave the Gunnison River to go plunging down the Black Cañon, following up the Cimarron Creek which has added its waters to the Gunnison, and presently we are out of the mountains and speeding across a vast verdureless, billowy plain, hedged around with sharply cut cliffs.

Next morning we find ourselves running through the great Utah Desert, which is bounded by a range of cliffs cut sharply and ridged and guttered as if with rushing water. The sand looks baked and cracked, and is here and there swept up in ridges and hummocks and cones as if by whirlwinds. It has the appearance of having once been a sea.

We see the azure cliffs, and later, Castle Gate, as the two great sandstone pillars guarding the entrance to Price River Cañon are called, and we are in the heart of the Wahsatch Mountains. Having crossed them, we speed again across level plains, bare but for cactus, and the rest of the trip to Salt Lake is marked only by fatigue and dust.

At Salt Lake City, a young married couple and myself, strangers until then, joined forces and took an open tourist car for the beach, to bathe in the Great Salt Lake.

Of course we were on the lookout for Mormons, and eyed with suspicion any man who was accompanied by more than one woman, quite forgetful of the fact that we were two young women with one unfortunate young man between us, and therefore, by the same rule, clearly Mormons. But for the most part we saw women and children together, and a few men and young boys. Two boys behind me were telling of an acquaintance's second marriage, and how the first wife had taken it, and the progression of another courtship, and whether "she" cared anything about "him" or not. Two women and three children sat in front of me, a similar family in front of them, and again in front women and children of one family. Behind me were three women with children, and further back two seats were occupied with a large party of women and children, judging by their sociability, of two different families. There was little talk; all the light chatter and sociability that should naturally distinguish such a pleasure trip to the shore were absent. To us, who had only gone on such excursions with friends and for a social outing, there was sadness in the inertness and silence of these people.

The women were clad in calico, and their relative positions in the family scale were marked by some extra bit of finery. For instance one wore a bright new bonnet, while that of her sister wife's was shabby; another wore a faded common shawl, while the younger wife had a pretty new zephyr wrap that contrasted strangely with her coarse dress. And they were all men and women of a coarser fiber than any Caucasian people I had met outside of Utah, and apparently lower in the scale of humanity. In the women is seen the coarseness of undeveloped intelligence, of eternal drudgery, bearing the impress of writhing hearts out of which rebellion and morality had been all but crushed. Their hands were rough and hard with labor. They are not unkind to each other, these woman; there was a consideration for each other that was apparently natural and reciprocal, as of fellow sufferers under the same immutable law.

Over and over again I heard one woman say to another whose child had got mixed up with hers, "Do you want Ella with you?" And the answer being usually "yes," the child was passed over to its own mother. In this way the children were kept separate while together. Never were more pitiful sights of union and disunion, never sadder examples of crushed and broken womanhood.

I have seen poor and hard working people out for a day's pleasure in many countries; and no people perhaps enjoy their rare picnic or holiday as do the poorest and hardest worked people. But here, in Utah, was none of that boisterous and rude humor that naturally distinguishes their uncultivated ideas of pleasure. There were no heavy jokes, no clumsy chaffing, no laughter, no spontaneous conversation or pleasure in the society of one with the other; all was dead and lifeless, and overhung with the gloom of sorrow and hard work.

The whole life here is to me inconceivably sad. The families of women and children living and going about together with hearts and souls crushed and necessarily asunder; the homes with two front doors; the rows of from two to five or six, perhaps more houses together; the porches with one man and two women resting in them in the cool of the day, silent and distrait; the double house, with a woman sad and lonely on one porch, while her husband, with the other wife, is laughing and chatting on the other.

And yet, reflecting on these rows of houses, the building of each addition of which has wrung some woman's heart, I thought after all what better are we than they? This is bad enough and sad enough, and the United States certainly ought to interfere in behalf of these women as it did in behalf of those other slaves of darker skin once held and tortured in this free country.

But is Utah the only place in this great country of ours where polygamy is practiced? Is this the only spot where men maintained marriage relations with several women at one time? Is Salt Lake City the only one where women's hearts are broken? It is bad enough here, God knows, but there is a redeeming feature. There are no drunken, reckless, cast-off women, sacrificed, crushed, wholly depraved and scorned and scoffed at and despised by the fortunate few who enjoy comfort and protection, and good names. Here all names are good, and if there be any immorality, as I think, and depravity, they are all situated alike on an equal basis, and none can flout her sister women for possessing less virtue than herself.

To me it is all sad and demoralizing. The life together of many wives of one man is necessarily so. It must be the death of delicacy and of the finer emotions and sentiments. It is degrading to the women and demoralizing to the men, as any condition of master and slaves must always be, and in Utah the sex relation is reduced to that, obedience and resignation to suffering being the leading features of the religious teaching of the women.

To be sure, the situation of these women lacks that degrading monetary consideration which destroys the self-respect and reduces to the gutter our unfortunate women. In Utah every woman works hard to support herself and children and enhance her husband's means. Their symbol of the beehive is a good one, only the drones are masculine, and it is the women who work busily making honey for his kingship. Yes, I'd like to have an end put to the iniquities of Utah. I would like to have an end put to similar iniquities all over the world. "They are against the law?" Are they? Yes, but how often is the law enforced? Oh, yes, it is against the law to marry more than one woman, but a man may mislead and desert and send to death and destruction a dozen unhappy girls with impunity. The law doesn't care how many girls are ruined; all it is particular about is that a few words of legal or religious sanction shall not be said over more than one of them with the same man.

In Utah they only destroy happiness and moral perception, in our States they blight the character, and ruin the future lives as well. In Utah women have the consolation, if consolation it is, of believing that they are fulfilling the divine instruction, and while they suffer here they have hopes of a heaven hereafter. Our unfortunates not only suffer here and become outcasts, but they are doomed to eternal perdition after this life. It is a question after all which system results in the most suffering. Our social system preserves the fairest exterior, certainly, but ah, how many aching hearts are hidden beneath, and how much deeper is the degradation of our degraded. Had we not better, while we are pressing the Mormons of Utah to the wall, purge the Mormonism that exists in the "States," and which exists in the more distressing form because it is without the Mormons' religion and without their principle? I think we had.

However, we were on our way to take a bath in the Great Salt Lake, that mysterious inland sea that apparently has neither source nor outlet. Our little train ran across some sandy flats for an hour before we reached the beach, where we found bathing houses and suits. The bath fully realized our anticipations. The water was a little chilly, but so heavy with salt that one floats on the top rather too easily; it is hard work to keep under enough to swim. This makes the bathing delightful to timid people. One has not that sensation of sinking, and confidence is easy to have in a sea that insists on your remaining on the top of it. One needs to be careful not to get any water in one's eyes or mouth, for it hurts the eyes and strangles in the throat.

An hour's ride brought us back again to the hotel, where we found something to quiet the tremendous appetite the bath had awakened. In the morning we found it was a race day, and that therefore there was not a carriage to be had. We were consoled, however, when we found the Mormon Temple and Tabernacle, the Beehive and other interesting sights were within easy walking distance. Salt Lake City seems a pleasant one to live in. Even those Gentiles who are loudest in their denunciation of the Mormons speak in the highest terms of the attractiveness of their city as a place of residence. The streets are broad and bright, the climate pleasant.

The Mormon Tabernacle, a most curious oblong and squat building, is especially famous for its acoustic properties, these being so perfect a pin's fall at one end can be heard distinctly at the other extreme of the great building that holds five thousand people. We tested this to our entire satisfaction. The speaker in the pulpit can be heard perfectly in any part of the house without raising the voice above a natural conversational tone. The Tabernacle contains an organ of which they are very proud, otherwise it is a very plain and simple building. There is an allegorical picture or two painted on the walls representing the finding of the revelation by Joseph Smith, and other incidents in the history of their religious belief.

The new temple, still in process of construction, looms tall and massive beside the Tabernacle. It is not to be a hall for preaching, being divided into many chambers, where special and sacred ceremonies may be solemnized. The Endowment House is near at hand, but is closed. Rather the prettiest of the three buildings in Temple Square is the Assembly Hall, though it is not as large as the others. Its hall for preaching is cozier than the Tabernacle, and here, too, are an organ, the emblematic beehive and allegorical pictures.

From Temple Square we walk down the street, past the erstwhile residence of Brigham Young, to the great arch called the Tithing Gate, through which all produce passes and a tenth part is taken. On the top of the arch is the symbolic beehive. An eagle is standing on it and clutching it with its strong talons, which is just about what the American Eagle is up to now in sad reality. Opposite Bingham Young's we see President Taylor's residence, a fine new mansion with two front doors. The number of front doors in the houses are replete with sad suggestion to the visitor of families that live in anything but unison. And so we rove about the city, until it is time to pack up our traps and resume our journey.

Leaving Salt Lake City, we encounter the gentlemanly Pullman conductor of the Denver and Rio Grande Railroad, who kindly takes me in charge and sees us to our cars on the Central Pacific Railroad, where I am in for another long night and day. My two friends leave me in the morning, and then I fall to making new acquaintances. A bright, breezy, slangy young American starts the ball a rolling by giving me an orange. A great burly, gruff farmer seconds his motion by also giving me an orange. Another American, a "drummer," with a nose suggestive of cocktails, also gives me an orange, and still another gentleman, rather handsomer and better bred than the rest, cultivates me through the medium of a proffered orange. The drummer takes me out on the back platform, where I enjoy myself in the cool air, until I discover I am keeping the gentlemen shut in the smoking room, so delicate are they about disturbing me, when I retire. Thereafter they take turns in dropping into the seat near me for a few moments and chatting and lending me books. We were crossing barren alkali plains until near night, and I heard a great deal about the richness of this, seemingly worthless, land under irrigation.

Toward night we stopped at one little dry-goods box of a depot, about which were a few wigwams, the Indian proprietors of which came to the train and endeavored to establish themselves on a friendly footing with the passengers. The men, robed in old blue army coats and pants, with ancient black plug hats on their untidy black heads, do not suggest the dime novel brave of our childish fancy. The women look more like, with their blankets wrapped closely about them, and their pappooses strapped in approved Indian fashion on flat pieces of wood first, and then to the mother's back, where they are truly as solemn and unblinking as they have the reputation of being.

Neither men nor women had the stolid faces I had been taught to believe. Both were, on the contrary, very smiling and persuasive, not begging openly, but showing their babies and beads and volunteering information and evidently hoping to be given something in return for these courtesies. One woman did, I believe, venture a suggestion about the usefulness of ten cents. Their voices struck me as rather musical and pleasant.

There were several other ladies in the car who carried their lunch baskets, so I was the only one to go out at the dining stations, consequently I was filled with dismay when, after an early breakfast, I learned that we were not to stop for dinner until 3 P. M. (in spite of the oranges). After stopping at one place for about five minutes the slangy young man came in and shouted to another man, "That was a splendid lunch!" "Lunch!" I said with the deepest reproach, "Oh, why didn't you mention it sooner?" And then I laughed, for the sincere distress on the young man's face was too much for me. I want to say it again, and I say it boldly, the American man, be he educated or otherwise, refined or coarse, dissipated or religious, has, as a rule, the most perfectly gentlemanly manner toward women. Sometimes it would seem that the rougher and more reckless types preserve the deeper sense of respect and consideration due to ladies. Many times I have been struck by the exceeding delicacy in the courtesy of a dissolute, one might think unprincipled, man. Often I have been touched by the gentle consideration of men I had rather not come in contact with at all, much less socially.

21

LADY HOWARD, *JOURNAL OF A TOUR IN THE UNITED STATES, CANADA, AND MEXICO* (LONDON: S. LOW, MARSTON, 1897), PP. 76–80

From San José we started at 10.30 a.m. by train for Santa Cruz, a pleasant and picturesque little seaside resort on the Pacific, so blue and tempting that G. could not resist a dip. Many miles of the route thither, bordered by vast orchards of gigantic orange trees, one golden mass of fruit, led through forests of the Redwood Big Trees, far, far more beautiful and striking than even the giant "Sequoias" we were soon to see near the Yo Semite! We hurried away, at about noon, from Santa Cruz, intending to give ourselves as many hours as possible for walking back the five miles through the Redwood forests to the "Big Trees" depot, in the famous "Grove" itself.

At first we followed the road that skirts the cañon of the Santa Cruz river, through a wooded ravine. This, after a time, led down a steep descent to the river, to a ford, across it, to the opposite side—a ford impossible for us, pedestrians! So we patiently retraced our steps till we met a higher road, which we followed till it came to an end, at a small depot of the railway we had come by.

We asked whether there was no road further along that side? "No," was the answer, "but you can walk along the railway track!"

"But shan't we meet a train?" I said.

"No," he answered, "the last, till the late night one, has passed."

So, seeing no other means, we proceeded along the track. This was easy enough for a mile or two, and the views from this elevation were charming, the trees becoming more and more high and grand, with a lovely undergrowth of flowering shrubs and plants. But at last we came to where the valley widened out and the track divided into two separate lines, the more apparently-important of which stretched in a long semicircular curve, about half a mile in length, on trestles about thirty feet high, with (as is always the case in America) no side-edging, or banister, or protection of any sort or kind—merely the one line of rails supported on narrow cross-logs placed on the top of the frail-looking trestles; showing plainly, between their wide openings, the green vale thirty feet beneath, and the rushing river further on!

I tried walking along this for a few yards and then gave it up; the dizzy height and the utter sense of insecurity made it absolutely impossible; besides, the nervous feeling that, perhaps, although no "regular" train was due, a "special" might, by some possibility, suddenly come tearing along! I crept back, supported by holding the end of G.'s umbrella, till we had reached *terra firma*.

Then came the point: should we retrace our steps? or, should we follow the branch railway-track, which went straight on, and looked grass-grown and disused—and where would it take us to? and how should we cross the wide river? However, the only alternative being to retrace our steps to Santa Cruz, we decided to take our chance of this track.

For some distance we went on swimmingly till, what was my dismay to find that it passed, for a space of about fifty yards, over a deep ravine on trestles as high, and as gapingly open to the depths below, as the former!

This time, however, the transit being much shorter, and there being no other possible way of escape, except returning, I summoned all my courage, and taking tight hold of G.'s umbrella, he walking first, after superhuman efforts to conquer giddiness, to our joy we found ourselves, somehow, safe and sound on the other side.

Then joyfully we sped along, till we found ourselves just opposite the magnificent grove inclosing the "Big Trees" depot.

But, alas! there was still the wide, rushing, foaming river to be crossed! and how was it to be done? Bridge there was none, for road there was none. Impossible to ford! After looking in every direction for help and finding none, at some little distance further up the river, at last, we espied a means of transit—but, what a means! The river was wide, and there we saw, slung across at a height of about fifteen feet, fixed from high bank to bank, a narrow footway consisting of long, thin, single, narrow planks, attached to each other end by end, with a single rope, of tolerable thickness, stretched as a kind of banister, at a height of about five feet above the plank bridge, but unconnected with it, attached to two "big trees," opposite each other, on each bank of the river!

I must say I simply gasped with terror at the sight! It made one giddy even to look at it, and how would it ever be possible to even make the attempt? It seemed not only absolute madness to try, but also a physical impossibility!

However, there seemed absolutely nothing else to be done—no other possibility of getting across! The railway trestle-bridge seemed to fade into a joke in comparison with this frail and terrific foot-bridge—but we couldn't go back. So at last I said we would *try*! So we did. No sooner had G. walked on to the plank before me, I holding his hand and the rope and following close behind, than the frail single planking began to bounce violently up and down, although we crept along as slowly and carefully as possible! More dead than alive, I managed to creep dizzily along, with the help of G. and the rope, which itself swung up and down, till about halfway, when I said, "I can't go any further!" Simply, it was impossible! the great height, the deep rushing water below, the thin, narrow crazy plank, its dancing, dizzying motion. It was absolutely terrific! and by way of reassuring, G. ventured to laugh, and said he thought the plank was giving way, and would break under our weight! This really was a little too much, with merely this wretched plank between ourselves and drowning! so I sternly said, "Go on!" and we accordingly moved on, and somehow or other, I don't know how, managed to find ourselves safe on the further bank. Joy! joy! that fearful obstacle passed! Now nothing to do but to delight and revel in the marvel, the wonder, of these most extraordinary trees! The first sight of them, for the giants we had seen in the forest as we came along were mere pigmies compared with these, simply takes your breath away! It feels like an incredible dream! and this variety of the "Sequoia" (*Sequoia semper-virens*) is as beautiful as it is indescribably grand. The foliage is a glossy dark green, very like that of the yew in colour and form; the bark is a beautiful rich deep red, as also is the wood, and each tree consists of one magnificent huge central trunk, with immense and most picturesqured gnarled roots, out of which spring, all round the parent tree, ten or twelve younger smaller trees; that is, smaller as far as diameter of trunk goes, but in height these graceful and numerous off-shoots, as it were, from the roots, soar up into the sky two or three hundred feet, nearly as high as the central parent giant, which varies in diameter from fifteen to thirty feet.

No words can express the beauty, the magnificent grandeur, of this glorious grove! Every single tree in it is a giant, and a giant with its attendant family of young giants, each separate tree consisting of a group of from twelve to fifteen. One of the central parent trees that we measured had a circumference of seventy feet, and others are still larger. Hours and hours one could spend, wandering from tree to tree, or rather, from tree-group to tree-group, through endless groves! Nothing more beautiful or more wonderful could be imagined!

Too soon came the hour for departure: the train arrived towards sunset, the red-gold sun shining through those glorious groves, and we returned, in the fading light, to San José, where we spent the night at the good and comfortable Vendôme Hotel, situated in a beautiful wilderness of trees and flowers.

22

JOHN FOSTER FRASER, *AMERICA AT WORK* (LONDON: CASSELL, 1903), PP. 124–132

Railway and railway travelling

LET it be conceded that railway travelling in the United States is more luxurious than it is in Great Britain. The coaches are roomy, are built on the Pullman pattern, and you can walk from one end of the train to the other. The woodwork is polished walnut, and is ribbed with gold. The upholstery is often bright green plush. There are enough bevel-edged mirrors to make a plain woman vain and an ugly man angry.

If you pick your train you have the run of a library. You can be shaved by an attendant, and dictate your letters to a typewriter. In the smoking car you can lounge in saddle-bag chairs in the greatest comfort.

That is the kind of train an American tells you about when he is travelling in a dirty, wheezy, third- class carriage in the suburbs of London at one-eighth of the money he pays in America. A quaint kink in his mind leads him to compare what is best in America with what he finds worst in England. When, however, you describe what is worst in America with what is best in England, he complains you are not fair.

It is food for mirth to the American that we have first-, second-, and third-class carriages in England.

"Why, in God's own country we're all equal, and we have just one class," he says.

He doesn't, however, say you start by paying nearly the equivalent of third-class, and if you want to travel well and express you must pay extra, and then probably another extra.

Should you wish to travel first-class return, say from London to Aberdeen, you pay your money, get a ticket, deliver half, and stow the other half in your waistcoat pocket for coming back. If you want to travel what is practically first-class in America, say from New York to San Francisco and back again, you get a ticket a yard long, covered with rules and regulations, and it takes anything up to five minutes for the booking clerk to find it and scrawl hieroglyphics, and look something up in a book. When you arrive in San Francisco you hand your ticket over to the railway officials, and get it back again a certain number of hours before you leave.

But that ticket at two cents a mile will only take you by slow trains. If you want to travel by a fairly fast train, one that goes at forty miles an hour part of the way, and be content with twenty-five the rest, you must pay many dollars more. Indeed, there are no trains at all in America that will take you for the same price at the same speed as you can travel third-class from London to Edinburgh.

Having paid your fare and the extra money to travel express, you then go to the Pullman office, show your ticket, and pay a sovereign or more a day for a seat in the Pullman car, including sleeping accommodation. Should you want to sleep in a compartment—such as you get on an English train by paying 5s. over the first-class fare—it means the expenditure of several sovereigns.

The system is confusing and dilatory. Nowhere, outside Russia, have I found the method of selling tickets so cumbersome as in America.

If you are wise you book your baggage from your hotel through to your destination. In this matter we might copy the Americans. The railway companies give you a numbered check for each piece of baggage, and the baggage is only handed over, at the end of the journey, to the holder of the check. Thus is avoided that unseemly scramble for baggage on the platform when a terminus is reached, such as you may see a dozen times a day at King's Cross or Euston.

The American plan is expensive, but it is worth it. You tell the porter at your New York hotel you are going to Chicago. Your baggage disappears, and the porter hands you numbered checks. On nearing Chicago a representative of one of the "express companies" bawls his way through the train. You give your checks to him, telling him what hotel you are going to, and he gives you a receipt. On arriving at Chicago you jump on a street car and go to your hotel. Within a couple of hours your baggage, which you have not seen since you left it at the hotel in New York, is delivered. (Sometimes it isn't delivered for several days, but that is due to bad luck, and not to the system.) Of course you can take it to the station yourself and bring it away yourself; but it is always checked, and there is no premium on baggage-stealing such as there is under the British haphazard method.

As to speed. The American talks much about the enormous rate at which his trains travel. But striking an average they are far slower than the British. America has several really magnificent trains that maintain a speed of between fifty to sixty miles an hour. You have, however, to pay an extravagant price to journey on them.

I travelled thousands of miles by ordinary "express" trains, and the rate was about thirty-five miles an hour. Again, the trains were, as a rule, so unpunctual that I found myself removing some of the maledictions I had piled on several of our English railway systems. During the whole course of my tour only twice, when the distances were over a hundred miles, did the trains arrive in time. Twenty minutes, three-quarters of an hour, even an hour late was not unusual.

Though in the case of specially expensive trains the American railway companies beat ours in regard to speed, we beat them in ordinary general passenger traffic, and we would beat them hopelessly if there was less dilatoriness at English railway stations, and so much time were not lost examining, punching, and collecting tickets. In a phrase, travelling in England is cheaper and quicker than in America.

When I come to compare the comfort and convenience of travelling it must be admitted the American has by far the best of it. Our lauded corridor coaches are rabbit hutches alongside the American cars. Our seats are too narrow for comfort, and travelling third-class—I exclude the splendid third-class dining cars from London to the north, which no American line gives you at the price—you are huddled in a way you never are in America.

Some things exasperate the Briton when travelling trans-Atlantic fashion. In winter time the cars are uncomfortably over-heated, so that, in desperation, you would prefer the cold toes which mark an English journey, or the make-shift, unsatisfactory expedient of warming-pans. But, it must be remembered, the cars are warmed for Americans, and not for stray Britons.

And here is a point to be considered when comparing the two countries. The American is not so hardy as his British relative. He has more splash, but less stamina. Where an Englishman takes a "cold tub" in the morning the American takes a hot bath. An atmosphere which the Englishman thinks pleasant sends the American into a shiver. An American gets furious if he cannot have his room warm to stuffiness with hot-air pipes.

Therefore, one reason why the Englishman puts up, without over-much protest, with cold railway carriages in the winter months, is because he is not the chilly mortal his friend across the Atlantic generally is.

The hawkers on many American trains are a trial to patience. A lanky youth, often chewing, nasally yells the sale of newspapers, and should unfortunately his eye catch yours he pushes a halfpenny "yellow journal" in front of you and expects two-pence-halfpenny for it. You beat him off. Five minutes later he comes again selling candies. You tell him that you do not want sweetmeats. He knows better, and with dirty paws he will extract a couple of caramels and lay them on the seat. He tells you to taste, and he will come back and see what you think. Or he will put monkey-nuts (peanuts) by you without saying anything. He has eyes behind his head, for if you touch one nut he races back and is selling you five pennyworth before you can beat him off again. Within ten minutes he wants to sell you fruit. Next he comes along with a pile of paper-backed novels. If you happen to be reading you are safe. But if you are not reading he dumps a couple of novels by your side. In this way he distributes the lot throughout the cars. Then he comes back and jumps at anyone whose curiosity has led them to lift one of the novels. Out of shame a man cannot then say he will not buy.

Then the dining-car. It is switched on to trains and switched off trains, and you must eat when you can, and not when you want. I like sometimes to eat late; but frequently I had to feed at six o'clock because the car was taken off at seven. The "coloured gentlemen" who wait will wipe their perspiring foreheads with the cloth on which they wipe the plates. They insist on sugaring your tea and coffee, and eye you curiously if you prefer to do that yourself.

Probably the rudest railway officials in the world are the French. But the Americans make a good second. The American car attendant speaks with insolence, and plays the bully in a way that would lead to his dismissal in England. He is just as good as you are, and he shows it by being rude.

If you are a millionaire you may afford a "stateroom" to sleep in. But ordinarily you sleep in a made-up bed on the seats. The seat makes a lower berth, and part of the roof is let down for an upper berth. Heavy curtains are hung, so there is but a thin slice of a way down the centre of the car. Now and then your sleeping shelf is provided with an electric bulb light. Usually it is not. You disrobe as best you can in darkness behind the curtain, with an occasional backward bump into the gentleman undressing on the other side of the aisle. It is necessary to go through an acrobatic performance—the details of which cannot be revealed in print—to get your clothes off. If you are the occupant of an upper berth you do your undressing as best you can, lying down.

Ladies and gentlemen occupy the same sleeping cars. The men have often to perform their ablutions in the smoking room. Half clad you wriggle past the curtains, convulsive with folks on the inner side trying to dress; and some of the poetry slips out of life when you encounter a lady, who last night looked so sweet and captivating, sleepy-eyed, her hair in papers, and her clothing in what I think is called *en déshabillé* condition, attempting to scurry in the opposite direction.

An Englishman's first experience with an American Pullman sleeper makes him furious, unless it makes him laugh. The American sees nothing objectionable or humorous about it. He—happy mortal!—is used to it.

But when Mr. Cornelius T. Slocum launches on one of his favourite topics, the inconveniences of travelling in "them little islands of yourn," it is not difficult to retaliate.

In Philadelphia, in Chicago, in Boston, in New York, I had opportunities for inquiring into the management of several of the great lines.

I came to the conclusion that as to the handling of passenger traffic the American companies have, at present, nothing to teach the British lines. I say "at present," because, knowing something of the conservatism of English lines, I was able to appreciate the untrammelled go-ahead-ness of the American, and could see how our trans-Atlantic friends are coming along hand over fist. Unless there is a tremendous change at home, I expect that in ten years the Americans will manage their passenger service as much better than we do as they are now ahead of us in the handling of merchandise.

Take the matter of the supreme command of the lines. English lines are composed of boards of directors, titled men, often good business men, the soul of honour. Many directors know a great deal about railway management. But they have learnt it after they have become directors.

In America such a system of management would only raise a smile. The chief person on an American railroad is the president, and his position is rather more important than that of chairman of directors in England. Beneath him is the first vice-president, the second vice-president, the third vice-president, and the fourth vice-president.

Take the Pennsylvania line—the most important and best managed railroad in the world—and inquire into the history of the president and vice-presidents. You will find that they all started as cleaners, as firemen, as drivers, as clerks in the employ of the company. They have risen from post to post because they have shown their worth. The board of management is made up of men of striking character, who have gone through all grades until the highest position is reached. Ability is the only thing that counts. Some of the railway directors I met were blunt, brusque, and used language that would make English directors squirm. But they knew all about the management of their line.

I was struck with the *esprit de corps* among American railwaymen. Though I had long talks with many employees, I never heard ill-natured things said about the employers merely because they were employers. Trade unions are strong among railway workers. Rarely, however, is there friction because of the employment of non-union men. The railway companies don't care a rap whether a man belongs to a trade union or doesn't. What they care about is whether he is a good workman, sober and steady.

The "moderate drinker" finds it hard to gain employment on the Pennsylvania Railway. That company prefers teetotallers. Several companies will not employ men if they smoke cigarettes.

23

ISABELLA BIRD, *A LADY'S LIFE IN THE ROCKY MOUNTAINS* (LONDON: JOHN MURRAY, 1910), PP. 25–39

CHEYENNE, WYOMING, *September* 8.

PRECISELY at 11 P.M. the huge Pacific train, with its heavy bell tolling, thundered up to the door of the Truckee House, and on presenting my ticket at the double door of a "Silver Palace" car, the slippered steward, whispering low, conducted me to my berth—a luxurious bed three and a half feet wide, with a hair mattress on springs, fine linen sheets, and costly California blankets. The twenty-four inmates of the car were all invisible, asleep behind rich curtains. It was a true Temple of Morpheus. Profound sleep was the object to which everything was dedicated. Four silver lamps hanging from the roof, and burning low, gave a dreamy light. On each side of the centre passage, rich rep curtains, green and crimson, striped with gold, hung from silver bars running near the roof, and trailed on the soft Axminster carpet. The temperature was carefully kept at 70°. It was 29 outside. Silence and freedom from jolting were secured by double doors and windows, costly and ingenious arrangements of springs and cushions, and a speed limited to eighteen miles an hour.

As I lay down, the gallop under the dark pines, the frosty moon, the forest fires, the flaring lights and roaring din of Truckee faded as dreams fade, and eight hours later a pure, pink dawn divulged a level blasted region, with grey sage brush growing out of a soil encrusted with alkali, and bounded on either side by low glaring ridges. All through that day we travelled under a cloudless sky over solitary glaring plains, and stopped twice at solitary, glaring frame houses, where coarse, greasy meals, infested by lazy flies, were provided at a dollar per head. By evening we were running across the continent on a bee line, and I sat for an hour on the rear platform of the rear car to enjoy the wonderful beauty of the sunset and the atmosphere. Far as one could see in the crystalline air there was nothing but desert. The jagged Humboldt ranges flaming in the sunset, with snow in their clefts, though forty-five miles off, looked within an easy canter. The bright metal track, purpling like all else in the cool distance, was all that linked one with eastern or western civilisation.

The next morning, when the steward unceremoniously turned us out of our berths soon after sunrise, we were running down upon the Great Salt Lake, bounded by the white Wahsatch ranges. Along its shores, by means of irrigation, Mormon industry has compelled the ground to yield fine crops of hay and barley; and we passed several cabins, from which, even at that early hour, Mormons, each with two or three wives, were going forth to their day's work. The women were ugly, and their shapeless blue dresses hideous. At the Mormon town of Ogden we changed cars, and again traversed dusty plains, white and glaring, varied by muddy streams and rough, arid valleys, now and then narrowing into canyons. By common consent the windows were kept closed to exclude the fine white alkaline dust, which is very irritating to the nostrils. The journey became more and more wearisome as we ascended rapidly over immense plains and wastes of gravel destitute of mountain boundaries, and with only here and there a "knob" or "butte"[1] to break the monotony. The wheel marks of the trail to Utah often ran parallel with the track, and bones of oxen were bleaching in the sun, the remains of those "whose carcasses fell in the wilderness" on the long and drouthy journey. The daybreak of to-day (Sunday) found us shivering at Fort Laramie, a frontier post dismally situated at a height of 7000 feet. Another 1000 feet over gravelly levels brought us to Sherman, the highest level reached by this railroad. From this point eastward the streams fall into the Atlantic. The ascent of these apparently level plateaus is called "crossing the Rocky Mountains," but I have seen nothing of the range, except two peaks like teeth lying low on the distant horizon. It became mercilessly cold; some people thought it snowed, but I only saw rolling billows of fog. Lads passed through the cars the whole morning, selling newspapers, novels, cacti, lollypops, pop corn, pea nuts, and ivory ornaments, so that, having lost all reckoning of the days, I never knew that it was Sunday till the cars pulled up at the door of the hotel in this detestable place.

The surrounding plains are endless and verdureless. The scanty grasses were long ago turned into sun-cured hay by the fierce summer heats. There is neither tree nor bush, the sky is grey, the earth buff, the air *blae* and windy, and clouds of coarse granitic dust sweep across the prairie and smother the settlement. Cheyenne is described as "a God-forsaken, God-forgotten place." That it forgets God is written on its face. Its owes its existence to the railroad, and has diminished in population, but is a depôt for a large amount of the necessaries of life which are distributed through the scantily settled districts within distances of 300 miles by "freight waggons," each drawn by four or six horses or mules, or double that number of oxen. At times over 100 waggons, with double that number of teamsters, are in Cheyenne at once. A short time ago it was a perfect pandemonium, mainly inhabited by rowdies and desperadoes, the scum of advancing civilisation; and murders, stabbings, shootings, and pistol affrays were at times events of almost hourly occurrence in its drinking dens. But in the West, when things reach their worst, a sharp and sure remedy is provided. Those settlers who find the state of matters intolerable, organise themselves into a Vigilance Committee. "Judge Lynch," with a few feet of rope, appears on the scene, the majority crystallises round the supporters of order, warnings are issued to obnoxious people, simply bearing a scrawl of a tree with a man dangling from it, with such words as "Clear out of this by 6 A.M., or ——." A number of the worst desperadoes are tried by a yet more summary process than a drumhead court-martial, "strung up," and buried ignominiously. I have been told that 120 ruffians were disposed of in this way here in a single fortnight. Cheyenne is now as safe as Hilo, and the interval between the most desperate lawlessness and the time when United States law, with its corruption and feebleness, comes upon the scene is one of comparative security and good order. Piety is not the *forte* of Cheyenne. The roads resound with atrocious profanity, and the rowdyism of the saloons and barrooms is repressed, not extirpated.

The population, once 6000, is now about 4000, It is an ill-arranged set of frame houses and shanties; and rubbish heaps, and offal of deer and antelope, produce the foulest smells I have smelt for a long time. Some of the houses are painted a blinding white; others are unpainted; there is not a bush, or garden, or green thing; it just straggles out promiscuously on the boundless brown plains, on the extreme verge of which three toothy peaks are seen. It is utterly slovenly-looking and unornamental, abounds in slouching bar-room-looking characters, and looks a place of low, mean lives. Below the hotel windows freight cars are being perpetually shunted, but beyond the railroad tracks are nothing but the brown plains, with their lonely sights—now a solitary horseman at a travelling amble, then a party of Indians in paint and feathers, but civilised up to the point of carrying firearms, mounted on sorry ponies, the bundled-up squaws riding astride on the baggage-ponies; then a drove of ridgy-spined, long-horned cattle, which have been several months eating their way from Texas, with their escort of four or five much-spurred horsemen, in peaked hats, blue-hooded coats, and high boots, heavily armed with revolvers and repeating rifles, and riding small wiry horses. A solitary waggon, with a white tilt, drawn by eight oxen, is probably bearing an emigrant and his fortunes to Colorado. On one of the dreary spaces of the settlement six white-tilted waggons, each with twelve oxen, are standing on their way to a distant part. Everything suggests a beyond.

September 9.

I have found at the post-office here a circular letter of recommendation from ex-Governor Hunt, procured by Miss Kingsley's kindness, and another equally valuable one of "authentication" and recommendation from Mr. Bowles, of the *Springfield Republican*, whose name is a household word in all the West. Armed with these, I shall plunge boldly into Colorado. I am suffering from giddiness and nausea produced by the bad smells. A "help" here says that there have been fifty-six deaths from cholera during the last twenty days. Is common humanity lacking, I wonder, in this region of hard greed? Can it not be bought by dollars here, like every other commodity, votes included? Last night I made the acquaintance of a shadowy gentleman from Wisconsin, far gone in consumption, with a spirited wife and young baby. He had been ordered to the Plains as a last resource, but was much worse. Early this morning he crawled to my door, scarcely able to speak from debility and bleeding from the lungs, begging me to go to his wife, who, the doctor said, was ill of cholera. The child had been ill all night, and not for love or money could he get any one to do anything for them, not even to go for the medicine. The lady was blue, and in great pain from cramp, and the poor unweaned infant was roaring for the nourishment which had failed. I vainly tried to get hot water and mustard for a poultice, and though I offered a negro a dollar to go for the medicine, he looked at it superciliously, hummed a tune, and said he must wait for the Pacific train, which was not due for an hour. Equally in vain I hunted through Cheyenne for a feeding-bottle. Not a maternal heart softened to the helpless mother and starving child, and my last resource was to dip a piece of sponge in some milk and water, and try to pacify the creature. I applied Rigollot's leaves, went for the medicine, saw the popular host—a bachelor—who mentioned a girl who, after much difficulty, consented to take charge of the baby for two dollars a day and attend to the mother, and having remained till she began to amend, I took the cars for Greeley, a settlement on the Plains, which I had been recommended to make my starting-point for the mountains.

FORT COLLINS, *September 10.*

It gave me a strange sensation to embark upon the Plains. Plains, plains everywhere, plains generally level, but elsewhere rolling in long undulations, like the waves of a sea which had fallen asleep. They are covered thinly with buff grass, the withered stalks of flowers, Spanish bayonet, and a small beehive-shaped cactus. One could gallop all over them.

They are peopled with large villages of what are called prairie dogs, because they utter a short, sharp bark, but the dogs are, in reality, marmots. We passed numbers of these villages, which are composed of raised circular orifices, about eighteen inches in diameter, with sloping passages leading downwards for five or six feet Hundreds of these burrows are placed together. On nearly every rim a small furry reddish-buff beast sat on his hind legs, looking, so far as head went, much like a young seal These creatures were acting as sentinels, and sunning themselves. As we passed, each gave a warning yelp, shook its tail, and, with a ludicrous flourish of its hind legs, dived into its hole. The appearance of hundreds of these creatures, each eighteen inches long, sitting like dogs begging, with their paws down and all turned sunwards, is most grotesque. The Wish-ton-Wish has few enemies, and is a most prolific animal. From its enormous increase, and the energy and extent of its burrowing operations, one can fancy that in the course of years the prairies will be seriously injured, as it honeycombs the ground, and renders it unsafe for horses. The burrows seem usually to be shared by owls, and many of the people Insist that a rattlesnake is also an inmate, but I hope, for the sake of the harmless, cheery little prairie dog; that this unwelcome fellowship is a myth.

After running on a down grade for some time, five distinct ranges of mountains, one above another, a lurid blue against a lurid sky, upheaved themselves above the prairie sea. An American railway car, hot, stuffy, and full of chewing, spitting Yankees, was not an ideal way of approaching this range which had early impressed itself upon my imagination. Still, it was truly grand, although it was sixty miles off, and we were looking at it from a platform 5000 feet in height. As I write I am only twenty-five miles from them, and they are gradually gaining possession of me. I can look at and *feel* nothing else. At five in the afternoon frame houses and green fields began to appear, the cars drew up, and two of my fellow-passengers and I got out and carried our own luggage through the deep dust to a small, rough, Western tavern, where with difficulty we were put up for the night. This settlement is called the Greeley Temperance Colony, and was founded lately by an industrious class of emigrants from the East, all total abstainers, and holding advanced political opinions. They bought and fenced 50,000 acres of land, constructed an irrigating canal, which distributes its waters on reasonable terms, have already a population of 3000, and are the most prosperous and rising colony in Colorado, being altogether free from either laziness or crime. Their rich fields are artificially productive solely; and after seeing regions where Nature gives spontaneously, one is amazed that people should settle here to be dependent on irrigating canals, with the risk of having their crops destroyed by grasshoppers. A clause in the charter of the colony prohibits the introduction, sale, or consumption of intoxicating liquor, and I hear that the men of Greeley carry their crusade against drink even beyond their limits, and have lately sacked three houses opened for the sale of drink near their frontier, pouring the whisky upon the ground, so that people don't now like to run the risk of bringing liquor near Greeley, and the temperance influence is spreading over a very large area. As the men have no barrooms to sit in, I observed that Greeley was asleep at an hour when other places were beginning their revelries. Nature is niggardly, and living is coarse and rough, the merest necessaries of hardy life being all that can be thought of in this stage of existence.

My first experiences of Colorado travel have been rather severe. At Greeley I got a small upstairs room at first, but gave it up to a married couple with a child, and then had one downstairs no bigger than a cabin, with only a canvas partition. It was very hot, and every place was thick with black flies. The English landlady had just lost her "help," and was in a great fuss, so that I helped her to get supper ready. Its chief features were greasiness and black flies. Twenty men in working clothes fed and went out again, "nobody speaking to nobody." The landlady introduced me to a Vermont settler who lives in the "Foot Hills," who was very kind and took a great deal of trouble to get me a horse. Horses abound, but they are either large American horses, which are only used for draught, or small, active horses, called *broncos*, said to be from a Spanish word, signifying that they can never be broke. They nearly all "buck," and are described as being more "ugly" and treacherous than mules. There is only one horse in Greeley "safe for a woman to ride." I tried an Indian pony by moonlight—such a moonlight—but found he had tender feet. The kitchen was the only sitting-room, so I shortly went to bed, to be awoke very soon by crawling creatures apparently in myriads. I struck a light, and found such swarms of bugs that I gathered myself up on the wooden chairs, and dozed uneasily till sunrise. Bugs are a great pest in Colorado. They come out of the earth, infest the wooden walls, and cannot be got rid of by any amount of cleanliness. Many careful housewives take their beds to pieces every week and put carbolic acid on them.

It was a glorious, cool morning, and the great range of the Rocky Mountains looked magnificent. I tried the pony again, but found he would not do for a long journey; and as my Vermont acquaintance offered me a seat in his waggon to Fort Collins, 25 miles nearer the Mountains, I threw a few things together and came here with him. We left Greeley at 10, and arrived here at 4.30, staying an hour for food on the way. I liked the first half of the drive; but the fierce, ungoverned, blazing heat of the sun on the whitish earth for the last half, was terrible even with my white umbrella, which I have not used since I left New Zealand; it was sickening. Then the eyes have never anything green to rest upon, except in the river bottoms, where there is green hay grass. We followed mostly the course of the River Cache-a-la-Poudre, which rises in the mountains, and after supplying Greeley with irrigation, falls into the Platte, which is an affluent of the Missouri. When once beyond the scattered houses and great ring fence of the vigorous Greeley colonists, we were on the boundless prairie. Now and then horsemen passed us, and we met three waggons with white tilts. Except where the prairie dogs have honeycombed the ground, you can drive almost anywhere, and the passage of a few waggons over the same track makes a road. We forded the river, whose course is marked the whole way by a fringe of small cotton woods and aspens, and travelled hour after hour with nothing to see except some dog towns, with their quaint little sentinels; but the view in front was glorious. The Alps, from the Lombard plains, are the finest mountain panorama I ever saw, but not equal to this; for not only do five high-peaked giants, each nearly the height of Mont Blanc, lift their dazzling summits above the lower ranges, but the expanse of mountains is so vast, and the whole lie in a transparent medium of the richest blue, not haze—something peculiar to the region. The lack of foreground is a great artistic fault, and the absence of greehery is melancholy, and makes me recall sadly the entrancing detail of the Hawaiian Islands. Once only, the second time we forded the river, the cotton woods formed a foreground, and then the loveliness was heavenly. We stopped at a log house and got a rough dinner of beef and potatoes, and I was amused at the five men who shared it with us for apologising to me for being without their coats, as if coats would not be an enormity on the Plains.

It is the election day for the Territory, and men were galloping over the prairie to register their votes. The three in the waggon talked politics the whole time. They spoke openly and shamelessly of the prices given for votes; and apparently there was not a politician on either side who was not accused of degrading corruption. We saw a convoy of 5000 head of Texan cattle travelling from Southern Texas to Iowa. They had been nine months on the way! They were under the charge of twenty mounted *vacheros*, heavily armed, and a light waggon accompanied them, full of extra rifles and ammunition, not unnecessary, for the Indians are raiding in all directions, maddened by the reckless and useless slaughter of the buffalo, which is their chief subsistence. On the plains are herds of wild horses, buffalo, deer, and antelope; and in the mountains, bears, wolves, deer, elk, mountain lions, bison, and mountain sheep. You see a rifle in every waggon, as people always hope to fall in with game.

By the time we reached Fort Collins I was sick and dizzy with the heat of the sun, and not disposed to be pleased with a most unpleasing place. It was a military post, but at present consists of a few frame houses put down recently on the bare and burning plain. The settlers have "great expectations," but of what? The mountains look hardly nearer than from Greeley; one only realises their vicinity by the loss of their higher peaks. This house is freer from bugs than the one at Greeley, but full of flies. These new settlements are altogether revolting, entirely utilitarian, given up to talk of dollars as well as to making them, with coarse speech, coarse food, coarse everything, nothing wherewith to satisfy the higher cravings if they exist, nothing on which the eye can rest with pleasure. The lower floor of this inn swarms with locusts in addition to thousands of black flies. The latter cover the ground and rise buzzing from it as you walk.

I. L. B.

Note

1 The mountains which bound the "Valley of the Babbling Waters," Utah, afford striking examples of these "knobs" or "buttes."

Part 4

RAILROAD PROBLEMS AND PUBLIC HEALTH IN THE U.S.

24

SIDNEY ANDREWS, *THE SOUTH SINCE THE WAR* (BOSTON: TICKNOR AND FIELDS, 1866), PP. 11, 28–32, 107–109, 201

Manners and customs in the interior of South Carolina

ORANGEBURG C. H., September 7, 1865.

FROM Charleston to Orangeburg Court House is seventy-seven miles. Route, South Carolina Railroad. Time, seven and a half hours. Fare, five dollars. There is one train per day each way. Our train consisted of five freight-cars, the baggage-car, a box freight-car with seats for negroes, and one passenger-coach. The down train, which we met at Branchville,—where Sherman's army was to find its doom,—consisted of seven freight-cars, four of which were filled with troops on the way to Charleston and home, the baggage-car, and two passenger-coaches. Our one car was uncomfortably full when we started; but only eleven of the passengers came through.

"What sort of accommodations can I get at Orangeburg?" I asked of a friend in Charleston.

Scenes in the track of Sherman's army

COLUMBIA, September 12, 1865.

THE war was a long time in reaching South Carolina, but there was vengeance in its very breath when it did come,—wrath that blasted everything it touched, and set Desolation on high as the genius of the State. "A brave people never before made such a mistake as we did," said a little woman who sat near me in the cars while coming up from Charleston; "it mortifies me now, every day I live, to think how well the Yankees fought. We had no idea they could fight half so well." In such humiliation as hers is half the lesson of the war for South Carolina.

Columbia is in the heart of Destruction. Being outside of it, you can only get in through one of the roads built by Ruin. Being in it, you can only get out over one of the roads walled by Desolation. You go north thirty-two miles, and find the end of one railroad; southeast thirty miles, and find the end of another; south forty-five miles, and find the end of a third; southwest fifty miles, and meet a fourth; and northwest twenty-nine miles, and find the end of still another. Sherman came in here, the papers used to say, to break up the railroad system of the seaboard States of the Confederacy. He did his work so thoroughly that half a dozen years will nothing more than begin to repair the damage, even in this regard.

The railway section of the route from Charleston lies mostly either in a pine barren or a pine swamp, though after passing Branchville we came into a more open and rolling country, with occasional signs of life. Yet we could not anywhere, after we left the immediate vicinity of the city, see much indication of either work or existence. The trim and handsome railway stations of the North, the little towns strung like beads on an iron string, are things unknown here. In the whole seventy-seven miles there are but two towns that make any impression on the mind of a stranger,—Summerville and George's,—and even these are small and unimportant places. Elsewhere we stopped, as it appeared, whenever the train-men pleased,—the "station" sometimes existing only in the consciousness of the engineer and conductor.

Branchville was, however, noticeable because of the place it once occupied in Northern anxiety. There is where Sherman was to meet his fate. Have we forgotten how the Richmond papers of early February spoke? They were not at liberty to mention the preparations, etc., but they might say, etc., and the Yankee nation would have sore cause to remember Branchville, etc. Unfortunately, however, Sherman flanked Branchville, just as he had other places of thrice its importance, and it missed the coveted renown. It is nothing but a railroad junction in a pine barren, with a long, low station-house and cotton warehouse, and three or four miserable dwellings.

I found the railroad in better condition than I supposed that I should, The rails are very much worn, but the roadbed is in fair order for nearly the entire distance. The freight-cars seemed in passably good repair; but the passenger-coaches were the most wretched I ever saw,—old, filthy, and rickety. On our train was one new feature,—a colored man and his wife, whose duty it was to wait on the passengers.

I came up from Orangeburg, forty-five miles, by "stage," to wit, an old spring-covered market-wagon, drawn by three jaded horses and driven by Sam, freedman, late slave,—of the race not able to take care of themselves, yet caring, week in and week out, for the horses and interests of his employer as faithfully and intelligently as any white man could. There were six of us passengers, and we paid ten dollars each passage-money. We left Orangeburg at four, P. M.; drove eight miles; supped by the roadside; drove all night; lunched at sunrise by a muddy brook; and reached Columbia and breakfast at eleven, A. M., thankful that we had not broken down at midnight, and had met only two or three minor accidents. I am quite sure there are more pleasant ways of travelling than by "stage" in South Carolina at the present time. Thirty-two miles of the forty-five lie in such heavy and deep sand that no team can travel faster than at a moderate walk. For the other thirteen miles the road is something better, though even there it is the exception and not the rule to trot your mules. The river here was formerly spanned by an elegant and expensive bridge, but the foolish Rebels burned it; and the crossing of the Congaree is now effected in a ferry, the style and management of which would disgrace any backwoods settlement of the West.

The "Shermanizing process," as an ex-Rebel colonel jocosely called it, has been complete everywhere. To simply say that the people hate that officer is to put a fact in very mild terms. Butler is, in their estimation, an angel when compared to Sherman. They charge the latter with the entire work and waste of the war so far as their State is concerned,—even claim that Columbia was burned by his express orders. They pronounce his spirit "infernal," "atrocious," "cowardly," "devilish," and would unquestionably use stronger terms if they were to be had. I have been told by dozens of men that he could n't walk up the main street of Columbia in the daytime without being shot; and three different gentlemen, residing in different parts of the State, declare that Wade Hampton expresses a purpose to shoot him at sight whenever and wherever he meets him. Whatever else the South Carolina mothers forget, they do not seem likely in this generation to forget to teach their children to hate Sherman.

Certain bent rails are the first thing one sees to indicate the advent of his army. They are at Branchville. I looked at them with curious interest. "It passes my comprehension to tell what became of our railroads," said a travelling acquaintance; "one week we had passably good roads, on which we could reach almost any part of the State, and the next week they were all gone,—not simply broken up, but gone; some of the material was burned, I know, but miles and miles of iron have actually disappeared, gone out of existence." Branchville, as I have already said, was flanked, and the army did not take it in the line of march, but some of the boys paid it a visit.

At Orangeburg there is ample proof that the army passed that way. About one third of the town was burned. I found much dispute as to the origin of the fire; and while certain fellows of the baser sort loudly assert that it was the work of the Yankee, others of the better class express the belief that it originated with a resident who was angry at the Confederate officers. Thereabouts one finds plenty of railroad iron so bent and twisted that it can never again be used. The genius which our soldiers displayed in destroying railroads seems remarkable. How effectually they did it, when they undertook the work in earnest, no pen can make plain. "We could do something in that line, we thought," said an ex-Confederate captain, "but we were ashamed of ourselves when we saw how your men could do it."

We rode over the road where the army marched. Now and then we found solitary chimneys, but, on the whole, comparatively few houses were burned, and some of those were fired, it is believed, by persons from the Rebel army or from the neighboring locality. The fences did not escape so well, and most of the planters have had these to build during the summer. This was particularly the case near Columbia. Scarcely a tenth of that destroyed appears to have been rebuilt, and thousands of acres of land of much richness lie open as a common.

There is a great scarcity of stock of all kinds. What was left by the Rebel conscription officers was freely appropriated by Sherman's army, and the people really find considerable difficulty not less in living than in travelling. Milk, formerly an article much in use, can only be had now in limited quantities: even at the hotels we have more meals without than with it. There are more mules than horses, apparently; and the animals, whether mules or horses, are all in ill condition and give evidence of severe overwork.

I told an ex-Confederate captain, whom I talked with at the hotel, what stories I had heard about the treatment of the dead bodies, and asked him if he supposed they could be true in whole or part. "Well, you see, we had our best men all in the field, and there were a good many Alabama fellows up here, and the Major in command was a d—d villain any how, and I reckon there were some right bad things done; but our people here protested against it to General Lee and Mr. Davis, and 't was better after that." I suppose he meant after Major Gee was superseded, about last New-Year's, by General Johnson. Yet no man would dare put into print all the stories told here about the outrages on poor stark dead bodies during the months of November and December last.

The cemetery is a quiet, retired, and lonesome spot, forty rods east of the railway, seventy or eighty rods southwest of the stockade, and half a mile or so south of town. The enclosure is nearly square, and about an acre in extent. Around it is a neat, plain, high, and strong board fence, built by Stoneman's orders,—the oak posts having already done some service in the wall of the stockade. The ground slopes gently to the eastward; in the northeastern corner are two or three small oaks; in the southeastern some twenty or twenty-five small pines. The bodies were laid in thirteen long trenches. No headboards were used, no record was kept, and it is therefore impossible to tell where any particular soldier lies. There are thirteen great graves. As the heartless Rebel guards filled them, so they must forever remain.

Affairs in Western North Carolina

GREENSBORO, September 30, 1865.

THERE were three of us in the stage from Columbia to Winnsboro on the evening of the 25th,—a North Carolina planter, and an ex-Rebel colonel, beside myself. The planter was a coarse, vulgar fellow, whose whole thought seemed to be given to an effort to outwit the officers of the Freedmen's Bureau, and "git shet" of some sixty negroes on his tobacco plantation. The colonel was a man of much travel, liberal culture, and good heart,—glad the war is over, anxious to hereafter live in peace with everybody, and fearful that the negroes of the State will see very sore times before spring. We made the thirty-two miles in eight hours, at an expense of nine dollars apiece.

The trip hither from Winnsboro is made by railway, one hundred and sixty-four miles, in sixteen hours, at a cost of twelve dollars, exclusive of meals.

On that section of the road from Winnsboro to the Catawba River the rolling stock is passably good, and our train consisted of a baggage car, a negro car, a passenger car, and two freight cars. Our passengers were about a dozen negroes, twenty soldiers, three ladies, and ten citizens. Stoneman burned the long bridge over the Catawba, and it is not likely to be rebuilt before next summer.

Half a mile below the river we left our train, and were brought to this bank in a comfortable covered wagon, crossing the wide stream on an insecurely fastened pontoon bridge. It so happened that when the railroad bridge was destroyed most of the cars were below the river; and our new train consisted of an old freight car, into which negroes and baggage loaded, and a miserable second-class passenger car, with a plain wood bench on each side in place of the ordinary seats. There were neither curtains nor blinds for the windows, and the mercury stood at about ninety.

On the section of railway from Charlotte to Greensboro the rolling stock is comparatively good, many of the cars just having been thoroughly repaired and repainted. The road-bed is also in much better condition than that of any South Carolina road, though the iron is badly worn, and must soon be in great part replaced. The line runs two passenger trains per day each way, with an express freight car attached to the morning train.

Sleeping cars are apparently an unknown thing on Southern railways, and bid fair to be so for some time to come. One can't help wondering frequently how it is possible for any one to be so stupidly opposed to comfort as are large numbers of Southern persons.

Life and labor in the South Carolina low-country

CHARLESTON, October 21, 1865.

LET no man come into the Carolinas this fall or winter for a so-called pleasure-trip. Since the first week in September I have travelled over most of the stage and railway routes in the two States; and I assure you that, though I may have found some profit, I have not found very much pleasure.

The railroads are worn out, and there is not a single line in either State that should not be relaid with new iron at the earliest possible day. Half the freight cars are fit for a few months more service, but the other half and all the passenger coaches were ready months ago for condemnation; though I suppose they must be used another half-year at least, because the various companies are unable to buy new stock. The engines seem generally in rather worse order than the cars, and a careful inspection of almost any one of them is calculated to vividly impress the traveller with the uncertainty of life. That delays and accidents are numerous follows as a matter of course. It must be said, however, that the accidents do not very frequently result in loss of life or serious injury of person. The average rate of railway speed is about nine miles per hour in South Carolina, and about eleven miles per hour in North Carolina. The cost of travel is about seven and a half cents per mile; on one road it is only six cents, and on another it is about eleven cents.

25

FIGURE 2, 'THE DISCOMFORTS OF TRAVEL-WEARY PASSENGERS', *FRANK LESLIE'S ILLUSTRATED NEWSPAPER* (FEBRUARY 9, 1878), P. 389

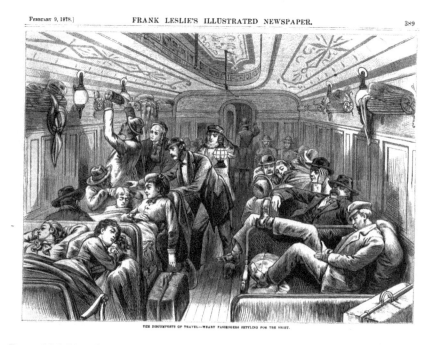

Figure 25.1 The Discomforts of Travel—Weary Passengers Settling for the Night.

26

DAVID CHRISTIE MURRAY, *THE COCKNEY COLUMBUS* (LONDON: DOWNEY & CO., 1898), PP. 9, 98–106

If it were not for the tramcars, the pavements and the elevated railway, New York would be one of the noblest cities of the world. As it is, it is overshadowed, noisy, half-obstructed, confused; a Malebolge of a place, worse than London, worse than Paris. In the course of nature it had nothing more difficult to contend with than either. Our underground railway is a stenching nuisance, to be sure, but it is only a nuisance to the people who travel by it. The elevated railway is a nuisance to the world at large, an obstruction to traffic, an obstruction to sunlight, an invasion of privacy, and away out of all whooping distance the most astonishing monument to ugliness the world can show. Now, I am informed, the New York engineers are going to burrow. Then it is to be hoped they will pull the elevated railway down, free their streets, and make their city visible.

There is no mortal thing this people can't do when once it makes up its mind. New York is awake, and is going to manage its own affairs. I got here just in time to hear the public declaration to that effect. I should like to see the city in a dozen years' time.

I have been told for years by intelligent Americans whom I have encountered in every quarter of the globe but this, all over Europe, in stray quarters of Asia, in Australia, or New Zealand, on scores upon scores of railway systems, that I had to come to this special republic to find the very perfection of railway traffic, and, indeed, of rapid transit in all its varied forms. Now all these informants of mine I take to be tarred with the same brush as myself. They have been bred to a certain system, as I have, and, like myself. They are incurably wedded to it.

Mr. Chauncey Depew, to take a very noted example, has travelled a good deal in Europe, as everybody knows, and he has lately been exalting the American railway system at the expense of the English and the Continental. From an American point of view, I have no doubt but he is quite right; but from an Englishman's point of view his laudations of his own method and his detraction of ours seem entirely unreasonable. He is not likely to change his opinion for anything I may say, and I am sure I am not likely to change my own. It is not for us a matter of national prejudice but of daily use and wont.

I have just travelled from Toronto to Chicago by the Grand Trunk Railway, and I have never in my life, in any part of the world, made a more comfortless or unsatisfactory journey. One encounters the national insolence on the French railways; the German officials are notoriously brutal; in Spain, Italy, Turkey, and other countries which, from our point of view, are only as yet partly civilized, the traveller, however cosmopolitan and complacent, occasionally feels his temper stirred by official stupidity and meddlesomeness. But taking them altogether, after a three months' experience, I will back the American railway officials against the world for a careless indifference to the comfort of the people whom they rule, and for an habitual calm, overmastering insolence of demeanour.

There is nothing in the world like the darky autocrat aboard a railway train. He takes you in charge absolutely, and domineers over you with a placidity and a trained conscious mastership, which is almost as comic as it is offensive. I remember the train de luxe between Paris and Monte Carlo, over which I have travelled, I daresay, a score of times. I recall the excellent dining accommodation; the no less excellent accommodation for sleepers; the decency, the elegance of all the appointments, the perfect table service, the civility and willingness of all officials, high and low, and I wonder that anybody who has had the opportunity of contrasting that splendid service with the slovenly American methods can approve the latter.

There is one thing which, to my mind, simply, I suppose, as a matter of education, is downright intolerable. There are no separate compartments for men and women, and last night I had to put myself to bed in the presence of three ladies, and under circumstances which were certainly embarrassing.

I found myself in the kind of berth one uses at sea, and had to dress and undress in that space at great inconvenience, abrading knees and shoulders, and bringing my head once or twice, in consequence of the uneasy rocking of the train, into pretty severe contact with the woodwork of the carriage. These gymnastics were rendered necessary by the presence of the petticoated contingent, whose members, I take it, were just as unhappy and as incommoded as myself. For the privilege of stretching myself at full length under a single blanket in that box-full of icy draughts, I paid the sum of three dollars, which, considering the accommodation afforded, and contrasting it with what one gets at home or upon the Continent, is downright extravagance and extortion.

Now, this kind of personal decency is a very delicate thing to speak about here. I have known hundreds of American gentlemen and ladies who have assured me that in this country there is a delicate sense of chivalry on the part of men toward women that is not to be found elsewhere in the world. I was prompt to believe this statement with all my heart, but I find that in the whole system of public travelling, at least, it is as little founded as it well can be. There is no consideration for women displayed by either the railway companies or the people who run the enormously profitable and astoundingly inconvenient cars. The other night, at a public meeting in New York, a gentleman of great and deserved eminence in literature, said, with what I took to be a sidelong glance in my direction, that he had known many Englishmen travelling in America who were impatient with a new country because it was not an old one, and who desired to Anglicize all things American. That may be true of whom it will, but I cannot take the accusation to myself. Yet I should dearly like to Anglicize American notions with respect to the rapid transit system of the towns.

The Americans have grown so used to English criticism that it passes by them like the idle wind which they regard not, but if I were an American I would not rest, for the honour and the credit of my own country, from denouncing that one thing. If it were my happiness to be an American woman I would raise a crusade against it. In every car which plies in the streets of every great city I have as yet visited in this country there is such an intermingling of promiscuous male and female limbs and figures as might be tolerated for an hour at a time of enormous emergency in another country, but would in no other country I have ever visited be endured as a system for a single week.

On Christmas Eve, on an elevated railway in New York, I counted in one carriage seating accommodation for fifty people. I stood myself in the bitter cold with half-a-dozen delicate and ladylike looking women on the outer platform of the car, and at Twenty-fourth street I counted the people who left the car. No fewer than fifty-two filed past me. Nobody got in at that particular station, and so the ladies and myself drifted into the car, and found one or two people still standing and every seat still occupied.

This would not be regarded by the New Yorker as at all an unusual or remarkable circumstance, but to me it seemed no less than indecent.

I take up my parable again; this American people is the most patient and long-suffering that was ever known. It allows anybody to make a profit out of it in any way. It has no resentment for intrusion upon its liberties; it allows itself to be harassed, and hurried, and driven, and bullied, and inconvenienced in a hundred ways, and makes no protest. Now and again the humorist has his joke; now and again the promiscuous indecency of this close package of men and women provokes some animal-minded creature to an outrage which is resented, and then the matter is dismissed from the public mind and forgotten.

I have in my possession an extract from the *New York Herald*, headed in big type, "Jack the Squeezer." In a second heading, in smaller, but still prominent type, I find it recorded that "Mr.——, chief bookkeeper for a savings bank, is arrested for insulting women."

"Offensive in an ' L ' train," says the third headline, while the fourth large-type heading sets forth the fact that two ladies are positive of the man's identity. In still a fifth headline I read that the person charged protests innocence, and on yet another I find him held in 300 dols. bail for trial and suspended from duty by his employer. The gentleman accused is fifty years old, bearded and eminently genteel in appearance. He is unhesitatingly picked out of a whole carload of passengers as the man who had nudged and squeezed the ladies into a state of panic and indignation during the down trip of an ' L ' road train several days before. Let me tell you the story, which I take to be moderately instructive in its way, as I find it exposed in the columns of the principal journal of America.

As the train moved slowly out of the station through the heavy fog and rain, one of the complainants, who is a lady doctor, caught a few words of an altercation which was going on between the brakesman and a passenger, who instantly elbowed his way through the crowded car and came to a halt at her side. He wore a heavy overcoat, seemed to take up a great deal more room than was actually necessary for him and appeared to enjoy the squeeze. The lady doctor gave the stranger no further thought, and was chatting unconsciously with her companion, when she found her waist embraced by the stranger's arm.

In the language of the reporter, she "grabbed the intrusive hand and threw it away from her."

Fearing a scene and thinking that the stranger's grip might have been accidental, the doctor moved away from him through the crowd and ranged up alongside two young ladies, just in time to hear one of them say,—

"It is the same man, I tell you. That creature there with the iron gray beard. If he squeezes me again as he did the other morning, I will whack him with my umbrella."

The lady was intensely excited, and her companion with difficulty quieted her. The lady doctor's companion, not knowing the reason for her friend's sudden change of position, stayed in the neighbourhood of the offender; a moment later she pushed through the crowd to her friend, the doctor, with the information,—

"Don't say a word, but that awful wretch with the beard has been grabbing me by the—the—the leg."

Three times the unknown had grabbed his victim before she could recover from the attack and beat a retreat. The indignant ladies hurried home, and one of them reported the incident to her brother. On the morrow he, accompanied by them and a detective, went to the station at which the man had originally entered the train, and there, by curious fortune, found and identified the offender at once.

Now, I do not say that this could not have happened in any other country in the world, but I do say that it is a dozen times likelier to happen in America than elsewhere, and from my own observation I am able to tell you that this kind of thing does happen with a very shocking frequency. Women here, I presume, are very much like women everywhere. They allow their own sense of shame to keep them silent, and in innumerable cases the coarse-minded brute who presumes upon his propinquity to the pretty woman and who insults her in this way is allowed to go scot free.

All this inconvenience, all this temptation to indecent assault of a minor character, is allowed by the populace of the great American cities for the profit of the shareholders in urban railways and other rolling stock.

I have not ventured to address any American lady upon this delicate topic, but I have spoken to a good many American men about it. They one and all admit the fact. Some are indignant and others take it humorously, but on the whole it seems to me to be a thing to be spoken about, and very seriously—a blot upon a high civilization.

27

WILLIAM A. PINKERTON, *TRAIN ROBBERIES, TRAIN ROBBERS, AND THE "HOLDUP" MEN* (1907), PP. 8–11, 16, 18, 20, 22, 24, 56, 58

Heretofore my addresses have been upon subjects with which most of us are familiar and, while I know there are among those present, members of this Association who have had more or less to do with the apprehension of the train robber or "hold-up" criminal, a product we have that no other country has except as our fugitives; I believe some reminiscences of these outlaws will be of interest.

As the detective agents throughout the United States of many railroad, express and stage companies and of the American Bankers' Association, and co-operating with police officials, United States marshals, sheriffs, railroads detectives and various other law enforcement authorities, for over fifty years our agency has been engaged investigating many of the robberies of railroad trains, banks and stages by this desperate robber; my father, the late Allan Pinkerton, my brother Robert and I, often in these years personally taking part in running down this now almost extinct outlaw. It is somewhat remarkable as will be noted throughout my talk, that in many instances brothers were members of individual bands, notably the Reno brothers, John, Frank, Sim and Bill; the Reitenhouse brothers; the Miles brothers, James K. and Joe, all of Indiana; the Farrington brothers, Levy and Hillary, of West Tennessee; the James brothers, Frank and Jesse; the Younger brothers, Cole, Jim, John and Bob; the Logan brothers, Harvey and Lonny; the Collins brothers, part of the Sam Bass gang, Joel, William and Albert; Bud and William Mc Daniels, part of the Jesse James gang; the Dalton brothers, Bill, Bob, Emmett and Gratton of Kansas; the Burrows brothers, Rube and Jim of Alabama; the Sontag brothers, John and George of Minnesota; the Gates brothers of California; the Jones brothers; the McCarthy brothers, Tom and Bill of Colorado; the Cook brothers, Bill and Jim of Arkansas, who were part of the Dalton gang and the Carver and Kilpatrick brothers of Texas.

The "hold-up" robber originated among bad men of the gold mining camps. Unsuccessful as a prospector, too lazy to work, and with enough bravado and criminal instinct to commit desperate crimes, he first robbed prospectors and miners en route on foot to stage stations, of their gold dust and nuggets, becoming bolder, looting stages and eventually after the railroads were built, he "held-up" railway trains and robbed express cars.

We also find them from the "dare-devils" of the Civil War, those from the Southwest who engaged in guerrilla warfare, where, as the pride of the States which sent them to the front and, because of their ambuscades, raids and lawless acts during the war, they were received as heroes when they returned to their homes. The James boys, the Youngers, the Renos, the Farringtons, the war giving them the reckless life they longed for and experience fitting them for the life of crime they inaugurated immediately after.

In the early days of the plains, the cowboy, with criminal inclination, noted for deeds of daring, began his career by cattle "rustling" and horse stealing, and then became a "hold-up" of stages and trains, committing the most of these robberies since 1875.

Also certain sensational newspapers and publishers of "yellow" covered literature, by exploiting and extoling the cowardly crimes of these outlaws and filling the youthful mind with a desire for the same sort of notoriety and adventure are responsible for many imitators of the "hold-up" robber.

The "hold-up" man operated as the footpad does to-day, concealed in ambush awaiting his victim, suddenly pouncing upon and commanding him to throw up his hands, "covering" him by thrusting a revolver in his face, then relieving him of his money and valuables. Usually the "hold-up" man to avoid identification and arrest, covers his face below the eyes with a triangular cloth or pocket handkerchief, tied back of the head, wore a soft hat well down over his eyes, although in many of the great train and bank robberies shortly after the war, no masks of any kind were worn.

The average train robbery band formerly consisted of from five to eight men, but in recent years successful robberies have been committed by from three to five men and in a few instances by a lone individual.

Usually in these train robberies, one member of the band, with red lantern or flag, at a lonely spot would signal the train to a standstill, or one or two would board the "blind end" of a baggage or express car and nearing the point selected for the robbery, would climb over the tender into the locomotive, "cover" the engineer and fireman. while others of the bandits uncoupled the express or money car and forced the engineer to carry them a mile or two distant, where the cars and safes would be forced open with dynamite. Resistance usually resulted in the death of those who interfered. Our study of the murders committed by these desperadoes shows fully 90 per cent to be assassinations, those killed generally being defenseless, or the outnumbering desperadoes by pouncing on their victims when least expected, giving them no chance for their lives.

Escapes were usually made with horses in waiting, in charge of a confederate at the place of the robbery, and often with relays of horses previously arranged, for covering five or six hundred miles, until they arrived at their homes or hiding places.

There is no crime in America so hazardous as "hold-up" robbery. Over two-thirds of those who have been engaged in these crimes, were killed while operating, or in resisting arrest, or from their wounds, lynched by posses, or as is known "died with their boots on," while nearly all others were either captured or sentenced to long terms of imprisonment or driven from the United States, becoming exiles in distant foreign climes. Those at large are constantly in fear of arrest, living secluded lives, and risking no chances of discovery by communicating with friends.

Shortly after the close of the Civil War there was an epidemic of train robberies in Indiana, especially between Indianapolis and New Albany on the Jeffersonville and Indianapolis R. R.

The State of Missouri has probably produced more train robbers than any other state in the Union and of whom the James brothers were the most desperate and vicious.

Among the Kentuckians who settled in Clay County, Mo., before the War were Doctor and Mrs. Samuels and their sons, Frank and Jesse James, sons of Mrs. Samuels' previous marriage. When the War broke out, the brothers joined the Quantrell band in their guerrilla warfare. After the War the James boys, under the leadership of Bill Anderson and operating with Cole, Jim, John and Bob Younger, Clell and John Miller, Charles Pitts, the Tompkins brothers, Jim Cummings, Dick Liddell, and other members of Quantrell's band, began prowling through West and Southwest Missouri and Eastern Kansas, looking for what spoils they could get and for years committed a series of the most despicable crimes of that period in Missouri, Kentucky and Minnesota, "holding-up" banks in the day time, robbing trains at night, murdering respectable citizens who resisted them and killing officers who attempted their arrest.

The published reports of the exploits of this band had more to do with the making of bad men in the West than anything which occurred before they began operating or since.

At the time Jesse James was killed and his brother surrendered the statement was made that neither was ever arrested or captured by officers, State or Federal, but Judge Philander Lucas of Liberty, Mo., states that during 1865–1866, about eleven o'clock one morning, the James boys, with Clell Miller, Jim Poole and George White, rode into Liberty, firing off their revolvers and acting like a lot of Indians; that they entered Meffert's saloon, had drinks, and as they left the saloon Sheriff Rickards arrested and disarmed the James boys, marched them into the Court House, arraigned them before him and that he committed them to the County jail. As a matter of fact, there were then no charges against them.

As a rule the James and Younger brothers and their associates, after each crime, would return to their home, Clay County, Mo., where they were virtually immune from arrest, either through fear of them by the respectable element or through the friendly aid they received from their admirers.

The first of their robberies we were retained to investigate was that of June 3, 1871, when the James and Younger brothers visited Corydon, Wayne County, Iowa, intending to rob the county treasurer of recently collected taxes. Jesse James entered the treasurer's office offering a one hundred dollar bill for change, but the clerk informed him of the absence of the county treasurer, who held the combination of the locked safe, but suggested that a new bank across the square, opened that day and which had one-half of its capital on deposit, might accommodate him, where upon Jesse consulted with his associates and the robbery of the new bank was agreed upon. On Jesse offering the one hundred dollar bill, the cashier opened the safe for the change, only on turning around to look into the muzzle of two revolvers. Jesse's associates who had meanwhile entered the bank, then forced the president and cashier into a back room, emptied the contents of the safe, about fifteen thousand dollars into saddle bags, relieved a new depositor, a negro preacher, who had entered, of his handful of money, then mounting their horses fled from the town, passing on their way a public meeting, in the outskirts, where a site for a new school house was being discussed, and which accounted for the county, treasurer's absence from his office, and saved his safe from being plundered.

As the bandits rode by the meeting they fired, in the air, a fusillade from their revolvers and rifles, at the same time informing the gathering of the robbery of the bank and advising that they return to town and start a new bank.

Robert Pinkerton, then a young man, with a posse traced the outlaws through the lower counties of Iowa. Then with an Iowa Sheriff, the balance of the posse having withdrawn, continued into Missouri as far as Cameron Junction, a cross road station, where the Sheriff left for additional help; but Robert Pinkerton continued following the trail to the Missouri River where the band separated, some crossing at Sibley Ferry, others at Blue Mill Ferry, all meeting afterwards at the Old Blue Mill, from which point they continued South, evidently making towards the James home in Clay County. Here, Robert Pinkerton, recognizing the folly of continuing alone withdrew.

On July 20, 1873, the James brothers committed their first train "hold-up" robbery on the Chicago, Rock Island & Pacific R. R., wrecking the train fifteen miles east of Council Bluffs, Iowa, murdered the unarmed engineer, wounded the fireman, injured passengers and robbed the express car of a large amount of money.

January 31, 1874. the James brothers aided by the Younger brothers, Clell Miller and Jim Cummings, committed their second train "hold-up" robbery, this, on the Iron Mountain Road at Gadshill, Mo., flagging the train to a standstill and "hold-up" and robbing it of $10,000. In the investigation of this robbery Joseph W. Witcher, one of our detectives from Chicago, on March 10, 1874, was overpowered, bound with ropes and put on a horse, Clell Miller and Jesse James taking him from their home in Clav County, Mo., to near Independence, Jackson County, Mo., where they assassinated him, leaving his body at the crossing of the Deerington and Independence road where the Iowa Sheriff left Robert Pinkerton three years before.

A few days later Louis Lull, a former captain of police in Chicago, but then in our employ, in company with an ex-Deputy Sheriff and a man named Daniels, met John and Jim Younger on a road near Montegaw Springs, St. Clair County, Mo., and in the effort to arrest them, Lull killed John Younger, but was himself mortally wounded, dying six weeks later. Daniels was killed and Jim Younger was seriously wounded.

The James brothers band also committed robberies on the Union Pacific R. R., at Munsey, Kas., in December, 1875, securing $55,000, also on the Missouri Pacific R. R. at Otterville, Mo., July 8, 1876, securing $17,000, and when McDaniels, one of the band being arrested with part of the booty, was killed in an attempt to escape.

In November, 1888, a United States Express messenger was "held-up" on a train near New Orleans, La., and robbed of $20,000. Investigation proved the robber to be Captain Eugene F. Bunch, alias Captain Gerald, a former newspaper editor of Gainesville, Texas.

Acting with the special officer of the Southern Express Company, and a local official, we finally located Bunch in a swamp near Franklinton, La., where, on August 21, 1892, he was killed resisting arrest.

September 30, 1891, Oliver Curtis Perry boarded a New York Central R. R. train at Albany, N. Y., sawed an opening through the rear door, crawled over the freight to the centre, covered the messenger with a revolver and stole five thousand dollars and some jewelry, after which near Utica he made his escape by cutting the air brakes, thereby bringing the train to a stop.

February 21, 1892, Perry again boarded an express train near Syracuse, N. Y., concealed himself on the roof of the express car until the train was in motion and then with a rope fastened to a hook in the roof of the car while the train was traveling fifty miles an hour, lowered himself to a window and, covering the messenger with a revolver ordered him to throw up his hands. The messenger attempted to pull the bell cord, but Perry shot him in the hand, the messenger following with several shots. Just as Perry fired his last shot, the train pulled into Lyons and he, in attempting to escape drove the fireman and engineer from a locomotive which stood on a siding, started the engine at full speed, but was followed by railroad employees on another locomotive, who subsequently overtook him and after considerable shooting caused his arrest.

On May 19, following he was sentenced to 49 years and three months in the Auburn, N. Y., State Prison, from which he escaped October 22nd, but was recaptured in less than 24 hours. Soon after showing signs of insanity he was transferred to the asylum for the criminal insane at Matteawan, from which he escaped April 10, 1895, but four weeks later was arrested by a railroad detective at Weehawken, N. J. This detective had a dispute with the Superintendent of the railroad about Perry's capture, killed him and was hanged in New Jersey for his crime.

28

JNO. C. KING AND M. D. BANNING, 'TUBERCULOSIS AMONG RAILROAD EMPLOYEES', *CALIFORNIA STATE JOURNAL OF MEDICINE* 11, 2 (FEB. 1913), PP. 70–71

Tuberculosis is ubiquitous, therefore railroad employees suffer from it. The percentage of morbidity is probably less among them than among any other large mass of employees, except those in the army and navy. They are obliged to submit to physical examination prior to employment. Life insurance actuaries claim that examination discriminates in favor of the company for a period not to exceed five years. Likewise, the examination of our men protects the company for only a limited, though uncertain, time. In the practice of my specialty I see many cases of tuberculosis among railroad men, from both eastern and western roads. As a rule, the hygienic environment of our men is above the average, particularly on this coast; partly owing to the climate, in part to the nature of the work, and largely to the fact that our company officials are quick to remedy hygienic defects. It has several times happened that superintendents and roadmasters have remodeled station and section houses in my district, at my request, and have changed plumbing and drainage.

In attempting to group the men we find that engineers and firemen are quite exempt from the disease. On the other hand, Pullman conductors furnish a large quota. Mexican peons, laboring as section hands, are frequently tubercular. Trainmen are not subject to the disease as commonly as other men of similar social grade. The same is true, I think, of shopmen. When these people succumb it is due to unhygienic housing and living rather than to shop conditions. Office men are attacked more frequently than other employees. And yet, they suffer less than occupants of average business offices, because railroad offices usually provide larger cubic area of fresh air than others. On the whole, there are few lines of employment open to workingmen where the conditions of labor involve so little menace from tuberculosis. The fact remains that a certain number of our men do have the disease. What shall we do with them?

The chief surgeons of several of our California roads have furnished me with data which I beg leave to present. Dr. E. A. Bryant, of the Pacific Electric, writes:

"Impossible to give accurate percentage, but should say that not more than one-half of one per cent. are tubercular. The policy of the company is not to accept for employment persons infected with tuberculosis. We have a rule not to admit tubercular patients to the hospital, but give them home treatment. Of course, in case of need the rule is not enforced. The company does not provide sanatorium treatment.

Dr. Huntington, of the Western Pacific, states: "As the Western Pacific Railway Company is a recent organization, we have discovered a very small percentage of our employees suffering from tuberculosis, not to exceed one-fourth of one per cent. Employees who have acquired tuberculosis while in the service of the company receive marked consideration. The company has, thus far, maintained no hospital, but has contracts with several hospitals. Tubercular subjects are permitted to remain in a hospital for a reasonable length of time. No definite limits have ever been established. The matter of the establishment of a tubercular sanatorium has never been considered."

Dr. Cochran, of the Salt Lake, reports: "We have from our own office not more than half a dozen cases per year. The policy of the company is to eliminate such cases from the service. We have no arrangement for admission to the County Hospital, for we dispose of each case as we are best able to under the circumstances individually, usually caring for them at their homes or sending them to a sanatorium, for the company does not provide for any treatment of such cases. Each case is dealt with as seems most advisable for that individual."

Dr. Morrison, of the Santa Fe, state: "We keep no special record of employees suffering from tuberculosis. The number is small, owing to the physical examination before entering the service. Under our rules, chronic diseases acquired prior to entering the service are not subject to treatment by our Hospital Association. Each case found suffering with T. B. is handled on its merits. If a man has been in the service a number of years we care for him as long as possible under conditions which seem to be required by his particular case. At our Association Hospital at Albuquerque we have a number of very fine 'tent houses' where we have sent a numbr of T. B. cases during the past four years, and have had very satisfactory results."

Dr. Ainsworth, of the Southern Pacific, records: "Of 2780 cases treated in the hospital for the fiscal year ending June 30, 1911, twenty-seven were tubercular; of 76,139 treated outside of hospital during the same period, 151 were tubercular (approximately one-fourth of one per cent.). Employees with tuberculosis are kept on the company's payroll as long as they are able to report for active duty. Tubercular employees, the same as all other employees, are entitled to one year's hospital privileges. The company has provided special facilities for the care of tubercular patients at the General Hospital in San Francisco."

It will thus be seen that while tuberculosis is uncommon, each company must face the problem. I wish to comment on two or three phases of the subject and to suggest that better opportunities for recovery be offered to those included in the title of this address than can be afforded in a general hospital.

29

'100 KILLED, 100 HURT IN TRAIN WRECK', *THE NEW YORK TIMES*, JULY 10, 1918, P. 10

Fast express and an accommodation Train in Head-On Collision Near Nashville.

MOST OF VICTIMS NEGROES

Heavy Locomotive Plows Through Coaches Carrying Men to Work—Federal Inquiry Is Ordered.

NASHVILLE, Tenn., July 9.—At least 100 persons, most of them negroes, were killed and as many more injured in a head-on collision today between two passenger trains on the Nashville, Chattanooga & St. Louis Railway at Dutchman's Bend, five miles from this city.

Most of the killed and injured were on a local train from Nashville, which carried workmen going to a nearby powder plant. The other train was an express from Memphis and the West, and, after the two engines had reared and fallen beside the track, the heavy coaches of the express plowed through the baggage car on the accommodation train and demolished two other coaches.

Many of the dead were killed almost instantly, but others were pinned beneath the wreckage and could not be removed before they succumbed. Doctors and nurses were rushed to the scene from Nashville and assisted in rescuing injured as well as caring for them. The work of clearing away the wreckage is proceeding slowly, and for that reason the exact number of dead had not been determined tonight.

As the crews of both locomotives were killed, the cause of the accident may never be established. The express train was running late, and one theory advanced was that the engineer of the accommodation train may have disregarded signals and tried to make a switch just beyond where the wreck occurred before the Memphis train arrived. There also was possibility that he may have received wrong instructions.

Three investigations have been begun—one by officials of the road, another by the State officials, and a third by the Railroad Administration. It is understood that an agent of the administration has been ordered to Nashville, and that he will undertake to fix responsibility for the collision.

Only a few women were among the killed. Most of the white persons killed were in the smoking car of the accommodation train. Train crews finally succeeded in lifting the heavy baggage car of the express train by jacks and releasing the men under it. Thirty were taken out—all but one of them dead.

Among the killed were several soldiers and sailors, including Private John P. Hussey of Ullin, Ill.; Wilson B. Harris of the Naval Reserves, whose address is not known, and a member of the Marine Corps named Alexander, whose address also could not be ascertained.

WASHINGTON, July 9.—The Railroad Administration announced tonight that George R. Loyall, assistant to the Regional Director for the South, had been ordered to Nashville to investigate the wreck near there today. Mr. Loyall is especially charged, the Administration said, with fixing individual responsibility for the wreck, if that be possible.

30

'SCORES KILLED OR MAIMED IN BRIGHTON BEACH TUNNEL WRECK', *THE NEW YORK TIMES*, NOVEMBER 2, 1918, PP. 1, 6

First Car Crashes Into Tunnel Pier and Other Cars Grind It to Splinters.

INJURED MAY REACH 100

Dispatcher, as Strike Motorman, Sends Crowded Train to Doom at 70 Miles an Hour.

TO ARREST B. R. T. OFFICIALS

Rescue Hindered by Jam of Debris in Narrow Tunnel—Hardly a Soul Escapes from First Car.

A Brighton Beach train of the Brooklyn Rapid Transit Company, made up of five wooden cars of the oldest type in use, which was speeding with a rush-hour crowd to make up lost time on its way from Park Row to Coney Island, jumped the track shortly before 7 o'clock last evening on a sharp curve approaching the tunnel at Malbone Street, in Brooklyn, and plunged into a concrete partition between the north and south bound tracks.

Nearly every man, woman, and child in the first car was killed, and most of those in the second were killed or badly injured. Rescue work in the wreckage, jammed into the narrow tunnel, was extremely difficult, and the counting of the dead proceeded slowly. At 11 o'clock eighty-five bodies had been taken from the wreckage, and the police announced that no more bodies were in the tunnel. The names of many of the injured were not obtained, but the police estimated that at least 100 had been injured.

District Attorney Lewis announced at midnight that the train was being run by a train dispatcher. This man had been pressed into service in the rush hour because of the strike of motormen, which began in the early morning. At 2 o'clock this morning, as a result of the wreck, the motormen called off the strike, leaving the adjustment of their grievances to the Public Service Commission. The District Attorney ordered all the officials of the B. R. T. who could have been responsible and members of the train crew put under arrest. He said the B. R. T. officials had withheld the name of the man who operated the train.

Mayor Hylan arrived at the Snyder Avenue Police Station shortly after midnight and consulted with District Attorney Lewis and Commissioner Enright as to what steps should be taken in ordering the arrest of the officials of the B. R. T.

Just before one o'clock this morning, the missing motorman, Anthony Lewis, who is 29 years old, was arrested at his home, 160 Thirty-third Street. Brooklyn, by Detectives McCord and Conroy, and brought to the Snyder Avenue station, where he was immediately taken into a room to be questioned by the District Attorney, Mayor Hylan and the Police Commissioner.

After Motorman ewis had been escorted to the Snyder Avenue Station and questioned, it was stated that his story indicated criminal negligence in hiring him to run the train. Mayor Hylan said:

"This man confessed that he had never run a train over that Brighton Beach line before. He also admitted that, when running around that curve, he was making a speed of thirty miles an hour."

A post on the curve warns motormen not to go faster than six miles an hour in this part of the road. When he was asked at the examination why he had taken a job for which he was unfitted, Motorman Lewis replied:

"A man has to earn a living." He said that the only experience he had had in running a motor was in switching about a year ago, but that he had been taking instruction for two days on the B. R. T. before running the train yesterday.

On the way to Flatbush the motorman said he had no intention of running away. He said he remembered nothing until he found himself at home, following the accident. He does not know how he managed to get out of the wreck, nor how he got home. He says he has an indistinct recollection of having boarded a trolley car but cannot remember what car it was. He was seated in a chair, pale as death, when the detectives reached his home. He was very nervous and seemed to be on the verge of a collapse.

After a conference with District Attorney Lewis at the Snyder Avenue Police Station, Mayor Hylan said:

"I have ordered Police Commissioner Enright to station policemen in every terminal and carbarn from which trains leave, with instructions not to permit any green motormen to take out a train. No man will be permitted to run a train unless he has had at least three months' experience."

Mayor Hylan said that he did not wish to discuss the legal and possible criminal phases of the accident until he had completed his investigation.

District Attorney Lewis, after his conference with Mayor Hylan, said:

"I have ordered Colonel Timothy S. Williams, the President of the B. R. T., and Vice President John J. Dempsey to appear at my office today and give an explanation of Lewis's running the train."

A few minutes before the accident the motorman missed a switch, according to passengers, went some distance on a wrong track and then backed up and switched again to the Brighton Beach line for Coney Island. After that the train moved at such high speed as to frighten many passengers. Some thought the motorman had lost control of the train, and others supposed he was going at unprecedented speed to make up for time he had lost. A naval officer who was a passenger said the train was making fully seventy miles an hour when it left the track.

Rams concrete partition

The first car left the rails a few feet in front of the opening of the tunnel and rammed one end of a concrete partition separating the north-bound from the south-bound tracks. It was thrown at right angles across the roadbed in front of the entrance to the tunnel. The other cars cut right through it, the second car smashing it to bits and the whole train passing over the wreckage and coming to a stop 200 feet down the tracks inside the tunnel.

Packed together as in a box without structural strength to give them any protection, the passengers in the first car were crushed and cut to pieces. Not one is believed to have escaped. After breaking through the first car the rest of the train dashed it against the partition wall and strewed wreckage and passengers along the tracks ahead, where the wheels of the cars following passed over them. Only splintered fragments of wood and broken and twisted bits of iron and steel remained of the first car.

The second and third cars, leaving the rails after their impact with the first, ran sidewise into a series of iron pillars supporting the roof of the tunnel at intervals beside the partition. The pillars cut great gashes in the sides of the cars, which were still traveling at high speed, and mowed down the passengers who were standing, striking the heads of some from their bodies.

The left sides of the second and third cars were stripped away. Scores of men, women and children were flung by the impact out of these cars against pillars and the concrete wall, where they were killed instantly or ground under the wheels after falling back upon the tracks. Some who were not flung from the car were killed inside, when they fell upon the broken iron of seats, splintered timbers and iron beams which projected through the shattered bottoms of the car. Passengers on the platforms were nearly all killed instantly. One dead man was found impaled on a broken bar of iron, which had run underneath the car, but which broke and shot up into the air like a javelin in the crash.

Firemen who took part in the rescue work said the second and third cars had fallen over so that one side formed the floor, and the passengers were heaped upon one another, some dead, some dying, some slightly injured and some unhurt, but all so tightly gripped in the wreckage and so menaced by steel and wooden splinters, that movement was impossible. Bodies were found with only slight marks of injuries, indicating death by suffocation. Small fires were reported to have started, but these, it was said, lasted only long enough to cause terror to the still conscious persons imprisoned in the wreckage.

Most of the passengers in the two rear cars escaped without serious injury, although nearly every one was cut by glass or bruised when thrown from his seat.

They were packed so tightly in these two cars that the force of the shock was broken. Women became hysterical when they learned what had happened in the front cars.

The rear cars were without light, and when passengers made their way into the tunnel, they found themselves in total darkness. Many who tried to reach the forward cars in answer to the cries of the injured found their way cut off by masses of broken wood and twisted steel which barred the entrance to the second and third cars. There was no access to either of these cars, and no means of escape for the survivors, who were pinned by broken seats or jutting timbers from the roof, sides, and floor of the car, so that they could not move. Some were pressed against dead bodies, and others jammed until they were smothered against wounded or fainting passengers.

Part 5

EXTREME ENCOUNTERS AND THE OCTOPUS

31

ROSE G. KINGSLEY, *SOUTH BY WEST; OR, WINTER IN THE ROCKY MOUNTAINS AND SPRING IN MEXICO* (LONDON: W. ISBISTER, 1874), PP. 160–162

The train from the East was delayed by a "wash" on the track; so as it was telegraphed several hours behind time, our westward train started without it, with only our three selves and two other passengers as occupants of the whole sleeping car. For eight and a half hours we ran along the northern shore of the Great Salt Lake; and woke on the 9th on the Sage Brush Desert, close to the Humboldt river, along which we kept all day. At Elko, where we stopped for breakfast, the first of the Shoshonee Indians made their appearance, idling about the station; dressed as usual in buckskin, coloured blankets, and felt hats; and at Carlin quantities of squaws, with papooses on their backs strapped up like mummies with a wicker covering to their back-board to protect their ugly little heads, crowded round the cars like hungry dogs, thankful for any scraps left from our breakfast. Nothing has ever given me an idea of more thorough degradation than the way those Indian women clawed bits of bone and skin, and either gnawed them like wild beasts, or thrust, them into their pouches, to feast on at their leisure. The mixture of races at all the stations was most striking—Indians in their blankets, and Chinese in their blue tunics, standing side by side; rivalling each other in ugliness: but with one very marked difference,— that whereas the Indians were always lounging about doing nothing, Johnny was sure to be hard at work, turning an honest, or it may be dishonest, penny.

At the Palisades Station, where the rail follows the course of the Humboldt river through a narrow cañon of strangely distorted strata, we saw immense waggon trains, which Had brought ore down from the celebrated White Pine mining district, and were now camped close to the track; the white-covered waggons drawn up side by side, and herds of mules and oxen feeding in all directions. Following down the canon for some distance, round sharp curves, we got once more on the alkali flats, and ran on all day between endless purple hills with snow-covered mountains beyond, while red willow and cottonwood grew along the river banks; a grateful relief to the wearisome glaucous green of the sage-brush; till at dusk we came to the "Sink of the Humboldt," a lake thirty miles long, into which the river— like almost all in the Salt Lake basin—flows and disappears.

During the night we climbed up 3000 feet; and by daylight on the 10th were at Summit, the top of the Sierra Nevada, 7017 feet above the sea, breakfasting by lamplight in the dining-room of the station, under sixteen feet of snow.

When we started again General P. wrapped us up in rugs and blankets, for it was bitterly cold, and we sat on the back platform of the car, running through forty miles of snow-sheds, and from time to time catching glimpses of magnificent scenery through the gaps between the sheds—snowy mountains piled up to the sky, and black pines. At Emigrant Gap we were almost out of the snow-sheds, and were running down a steep grade, with the steam shut off and every break screwed down tight. Near Blue Cañon, over the American river, we bade farewell to the snow, and looked down into the gorges, sometimes 2000 feet and more below us, as at Cape Horn, where the track is cut in the solid rock, round a precipice 3000 feet above the river, which winds among blue shadowed pine-clad hills, with silver threads of mining streams gleaming down their sides. At Dutch Flat we were in the midst of the great gold-mining district of Placer County. In some places whole hills had been entirely washed away by years of gold-washing, leaving ghastly hollows to puzzle the geologists of the future; and two or three streams, one above the other, were carried round the hill-sides under. the giant pine-trees, in iron pipes, or ditches, and flumes, like the one poor little Mliss ran over in Mr. Bret Harte's story.

32

SIR RICHARD TANGYE, *REMINISCENCES OF TRAVEL IN AUSTRALIA, AMERICA, AND EGYPT* (BIRMINGHAM: PRINTED AT THE HERALD PRESS, 1883), PP. 151–157

The Pacific Railroad is a single track, and, although a wonderful engineering work, is not by any means a substantial or confidence-inspiring line, if judged by English standards. The rails are old and worn, the bridges and viaducts very lightly constructed, and almost always of wood. I observed in several cases that the carriages were actually wider than the viaducts, many of which are open between the rails. It is hardly to be wondered at that awful accidents sometimes occur. The train in which we were travelling narrowly escaped falling into a ravine 120 feet deep. One dark night, after we had all retired to rest, we were awakened by continued whistling and ringing of bells. It was in vain that we inquired of the guards and attendants as to what was going on, for they, like their brethren all the world over, would give no information. One thing, however, they could not hide from us, for we found we were being taken across a viaduct one carriage at a time, and as we crossed we could see lights moving about at a great depth below. On arriving at Omaha, two days later, we found a full report of the occurrence in the papers. It appears that the viaduct had been discovered to be in an unsafe condition, some of its timbers having been partially burnt, and it was a matter of discussion whether we should be allowed to cross at all; it being ultimately determined, as I have said, to take one car over at a time. Ours was the last train that went over, for before daylight the whole structure had fallen with a tremendous crash. The Indians were on the war-path at the time, and it was supposed that the work of destruction was theirs. The railway here runs through some of the most magnificent scenery in the world. Sometimes its course lies through narrow valleys, or cañons, where there is just room for the railway and the river, sometimes through immense pine forests, and then again on a mere shelf cut in the face of the granite mountain, until the point called "Cape Horn" is reached. This is the turning-point between east and west, and soon afterwards the greatest elevation is attained, 8,200 feet. About sixty miles of the more exposed portion of the road is covered with sheds, to protect it from the snow. This result, however, is not attained without considerable discomfort to the passengers, as the carriages become filled with smoke and dust while passing through.

One of the passengers on our train was an old man who had not crossed the country since he went out to the far west some twenty-six years before—long before the railway had been thought of. The party with which he then travelled was so large that it had to be split into detachments for the convenience of pasturage. One night his section was attacked by Indians, who killed several of the party and drove off most of the horses and cattle. The old man had for many years been a trapper in the Indian country and had invested his hard-won earnings in horses which he was taking out west for the purpose of trade, and he was not disposed to lose them all at one fell swoop without making a bold dash for their recovery. His plan of operations was soon settled, and in the evening he set off in pursuit with half-a-dozen picked men, each with his rifle and a good store of ammunition. After some hours they came upon the scent of the Indians, and moving cautiously forward amongst the scrub, presently saw them around their fires busily engaged in dividing the spoils of the morning. The trapper being a first-rate marksman, it was agreed he should do all the firing, while the others loaded and handed up the rifles as fast as required. Every shot told, and the redskins, judging from the rapid firing that the whole party of white men were upon them, made a regular stampede, leaving horses, and cattle, and other spoil behind them. So, painfully marching on, they came at last to the Mormon settlement and on to the Salt Lake City, where they were subjected to the most cruel treatment at the hands of the "Saints." These people told the travellers it was impossible to get to California by the route they were taking, as the country was swarming with hostile Indians, and they undertook to show them a better way by which they would get there in fifteen days. Many suspected treachery, and a consultation was held, which came to no definite conclusion, except in the case of one man, who, in the heat of debate, was shot dead, It was ultimately decided to adopt the Mormon advice, and as the route did not admit of wagons, they tried to sell them to the "Saints," who, of course, would not buy, knowing they would have them for nothing before long. Many of the travellers burnt their wagons and harness rather than that the Mormons should have them, but the majority abandoned theirs, and set out without them. Instead of fifteen days the journey took thirty-nine, and only a few survived it, most of the party dying by the way, either by the hand of the Indians or from fatigue.

For about a thousand miles the railway is open to the prairie, the consequence being that frequent accidents occur through cattle straying upon the track. I counted more than twenty carcases of these unfortunates in one day, and on one occasion, while sitting on the steps of the Pullman car, I felt a sudden check, and immediately after the body of a cow flew past. The herds are looked after by men with lassoes, riding very fleet horses. American railroads being much less protected from stray animals than those in England, the locomotives are provided with an apparatus called a "cow-catcher," which consists of an iron framework projecting in front and inclined downwards as near to the rails as possible. The contrivance is successful in moving most living obstacles from the track. For instance, when a cow gets between the rails and sees the train approaching, it becomes dazed, and the iron frame striking the lower portion of the legs takes it up readily. But with a bull it is quite different: when his lordship sees his enemy approaching he puts his chin down upon his fore-feet and waits the onset with a confidence not by any means always misplaced, for in this position his head and feet form a wedge which, becoming inserted beneath the iron frame, frequently throws the engine back upon the train, causing serious accidents. When at Ogden I saw the remains of a goods train which had been wrecked in this way a week before, the engine drivers being killed, also two stow-aways, or "dead-heads," as the Yankees call them, who had secreted themselves under one of the carriages.

Waking one morning we found ourselves in a most awfully desolate country, with scarcely a sign of vegetation—a veritable dry and thirsty land, through which we travelled all day. Towards evening we came to the alkali country, and the plains looked as though they were covered with snow. This is a fearful place, where, before the construction of the railway, many poor emigrants have lain down to die. Soon after, we skirted the margin of the Great Salt Lake and entered Brigham Young's dominions, passing his first town, "Corinné." This town was founded by the Gentiles after Brigham turned them out of the Salt Lake City, but he soon drove them farther off.

We left the train at Ogden in order to pay a short visit to the Salt Lake City, which is situated thirty-six miles off, and is approached by a railway belonging to the Saints. For beauty of situation Salt Lake City is almost unrivalled. It lies in a basin more than twenty miles in diameter, and is surrounded by mountains, some of which are 12,000 feet high, and most of them covered with perpetual snow. At the time of our visit the fruit-trees were in full bloom, and, as each house is surrounded by its garden, the city occupies a large extent of ground, presenting a beautiful appearance from the United States camp, which stands on an elevation commanding the whole city, about two miles off. A portion of the old mud wall, about ten feet high, built by the Mormons to resist the attack of the Indians, still remains standing. Several of the houses are exceedingly well built, and the gardens kept in excellent order; one in particular I was much struck with, and remarked to our guide that it was the brightest and best kept place I had seen since leaving England. He told me it belonged to an Englishman who had left for his native country on the previous day. Curiously enough, when I returned home, I found this man was a brother of my butcher, and was then on a visit home. We observed two ladies sitting in the front of the house engaged in needlework, and were told that they were the two wives of the English Mormon. It was very noticeable that these ladies sat at a considerable distance apart, cordiality (unless it be of hatred) not being a characteristic of these Mormon wives in their relations with each other. At the time of our visit the "Prophet" was down south, looking out for a new location for the Saints, in view of the threatened difficulties with the Central Government. We visited the Tabernacle, and saw the preparations for the new temple, to which the deluded of all nations continue to contribute, although it is exceedingly doubtful that the building will be carried to completion. The man who showed us over the Tabernacle used to work in a London factory; but he told us with a curious twinkle in his eye that the "new job" paid him much the best. At a short distance from the city there is a sulphur spring, of considerable volume, proceeding from the side of the mountains; the temperature of the water is such that eggs can be boiled in it. We slept at Ogden that night in order to be in good time for securing places in the train going east in the morning. When the hotel bill was presented I tendered English gold in payment, having disposed of my U.S. currency. The landlord refused to take it, saying, "He would not have the—British gold." I explained to him that I had no other money, but to no purpose, so, as the train was almost due, I told him I would pay him when I came that way again, but was not sure when that would be. He quietly said, "I guess I'll take your gold," much to the amusement of the bystanders. At the station here is a printed notice cautioning travellers to "BEWARE OF BOGUS TICKET SELLERS."

33

THEODORE ROOSEVELT, 'THE ROUGH RIDERS', *SCRIBNER'S MAGAZINE* 25, 2 (FEB. 1899), PP. 136–146

The rough riders

While the officers and men were learning their duties, and learning to know one another, Colonel Wood was straining every nerve to get our equipments—an effort which was complicated by the tendency of the Ordnance Bureau to send whatever we really needed by freight instead of express. Finally, just as the last rifles, revolvers, and saddles came, we were ordered by wire at once to proceed by train to Tampa.

Instantly, all was joyful excitement. We had enjoyed San Antonio, and were glad that our regiment had been organized in the city where the Alamo commemorates the death fight of Crockett, Bowie, and their famous band of frontier heroes. All of us had worked hard, so that we had had no time to be home-sick or downcast; but we were glad to leave the hot camp, where every day the strong wind sifted the dust through everything, and to start for the gathering place of the army which was to invade Cuba. Our horses and men were getting into good shape. We were well enough equipped to warrant our starting on the campaign, and every man was filled with dread of being out of the fighting. We had a pack-train of 150 mules, so we had close on to 1,200 animals to carry

Of course, our train was split up into sections, seven, all told; Colonel Wood commanding the first three, and I the last four. The journey by rail from San Antonio to Tampa took just four days, and I doubt if anybody who was on the trip will soon forget it. To occupy my few spare moments, I was reading M. Demolins' "Supériorité des Anglo-Saxons." M. Demolins, in giving the reasons why the English-speaking peoples are superior to those of Continental Europe, lays much stress upon the way in which "militarism" deadens the power of individual initiative, the soldier being trained to complete suppression of individual will, while his faculties become atrophied in consequence of his being merely a cog in a vast and perfectly ordered machine. I can assure the excellent French publicist that American "militarism," at least of the volunteer sort, has points of difference from the militarism of Continental Europe. The battalion chief of a newly raised American regiment, when striving to get into a war which the American people have undertaken with buoyant and light-hearted indifference to detail, has positively unlimited opportunity for the display of "individual initiative," and is in no danger whatever either of suffering from unhealthy suppression of personal will, or of finding his faculties of self-help numbed by becoming a cog in a gigantic and smooth-running machine. If such a battalion chief wants to get anything or go anywhere he must do it by exercising every pound of resource, inventiveness, and audacity he possesses. The help, advice, and superintendence he gets from outside will be of the most general, not to say superficial, character. If he is a cavalry officer, he has got to hurry and push the purchase of his horses, plunging into and out of the meshes of red-tape as best he can. He will have to fight for his rifles and his tents and his clothes. He will have to keep his men healthy largely by the light that nature has given him. When he wishes to embark his regiment, he will have to fight for his railway-cars exactly as he fights for his transport when it comes to going across the sea; and on his journey his men will or will not have food, and his horses will or will not have water and hay, and the trains will or will not make connections, in exact correspondence to the energy and success of his own efforts to keep things moving straight.

It was on Sunday, May 29th, that we marched out of our hot, windy, dusty camp to take the cars for Tampa. Colonel Wood went first, with the three sections under his special care. I followed with the other four. The railway had promised us a forty-eight hours' trip, but our experience in loading was enough to show that the promise would not be made good. There were no proper facilities for getting the horses on or off the cars, or for feeding or watering them; and there was endless confusion and delay among the railway officials. I marched my four sections over in the afternoon, the first three having taken the entire day to get off. We occupied the night. As far as the regiment itself was concerned, we worked an excellent system, Wood instructing me exactly how to proceed so as to avoid confusion. Being a veteran campaigner, he had all along insisted that for such work as we had before us we must travel with the minimum possible luggage. The men had merely what they could carry on their own backs, and the officers very little more. My own roll of clothes and bedding could be put on my spare horse. The mule-train was to be used simply for food, forage, and spare ammunition. As it turned out, we were not allowed to take either it or the horses.

It was dusk when I marched my long files of dusty troopers into the station-yard. I then made all dismount, excepting the troop which I first intended to load. This was brought up to the first freight-car. Here every man unsaddled, and left his saddle, bridle, and all that he did not himself need in the car, each individual's property being corded together. A guard was left in the car. and the rest of the men took the naked horses into the pens to be fed and watered. The other troops were loaded in the same way in succession. With each section there were thus a couple of baggage-cars in which the horse-gear, the superfluous baggage, and the travel rations were carried; and I also put aboard, not only at starting, but at every other opportunity, what oats and hay I could get, so as to provide against accidents for the horses. By the time the baggage-cars were loaded the horses of the first section had eaten and drunk their fill, and we loaded them on cattle-cars. The officers of each troop saw to the loading, taking a dozen picked men to help them; for some of the wild creatures, half-broken and fresh from the ranges, were with difficulty driven up the chutes. Mean-while I superintended not merely my own men, but the railroad men; and when the delays of the latter, and their inability to understand what was necessary, grew past bearing, I took charge of the trains myself, so as to insure the horse-cars of each section being coupled with the baggage-cars of that section.

We worked until long past midnight before we got the horses and baggage aboard, and then found that for some reason the passenger-cars were delayed and would not be out for some hours. In the confusion and darkness men of the different troops had become scattered, and some had drifted off to the vile drinking-booths around the stock-yards; so I sent details to search the latter, while the trumpeters blew the assembly until the First Sergeants could account for all the men. Then the troops were arranged in order, and the men of each lay down where they were, by the tracks and in the brush, to sleep until morning.

At dawn the passenger-trains arrived. The senior Captain of each section saw to it that his own horses, troopers, and baggage were together; and one by one they started off, I taking the last in person. Captain Capron had at the very beginning shown himself to be simply invaluable, from his extraordinary energy, executive capacity, and mastery over men; and I kept his section next mine, so that we generally came together at the different yards.

The next four days were very hot and very dusty. I tried to arrange so the sections would be far enough apart to allow each ample time to unload, feed, water, and load the horses at any stopping-place before the next section could arrive. There was enough delay and failure to make connections on the part of the railroad people to keep me entirely busy, not to speak of seeing at the stopping-places that the inexperienced officers got enough hay for their horses, and that the water given to those was both ample in quantity and drinkable. It happened that we usually made our longest stops at night, and this meant that we were up all night long.

Two or three times a day I got the men buckets of hot coffee, and when we made a long enough stop they were allowed liberty under the supervision of the noncommissioned officers. Some of them abused the privilege, and started to get drunk. These were promptly handled with the necessary severity, in the interest of the others; for it was only by putting an immediate check to every form of lawlessness or disobedience among the few men who were inclined to be bad that we were enabled to give full liberty to those who would not abuse it.

Everywhere the people came out to greet us and cheer us. They brought us flowers; they brought us watermelons and other fruits, and sometimes jugs and pails of milk—all of which we greatly appreciated. We were travelling through a region where practically all the older men had served in the Confederate Army, and where the younger men had all their lives long drunk in the endless tales told by their elders, at home, and at the crossroads taverns, and in the court-house squares, about the cavalry of Forrest and Morgan and the infantry of Jackson and

Hood. The blood of the old men stirred to the distant breath of battle; the blood of the young men leaped hot with eager desire to accompany us. The older women, who remembered the dreadful misery of war—the misery that presses its iron weight most heavily on the wives and the little ones—looked sadly at us; but the young girls drove down in bevies, arrayed in their finery, to wave flags in farewell to the troopers and to beg cartridges and buttons as mementos. Everywhere we saw the Stars and Stripes, and everywhere we were told, half-laughing, by grizzled ex-Confederates that they had never dreamed in the by-gone days of bitterness to greet the old flag as they now were greeting it, and to send their sons, as now they were sending them, to fight and die under it.

It was four days later that we disembarked, in a perfect welter of confusion. Tampa lay in the pine-covered sand-flats at the end of a one-track railroad, and everything connected with both military and railroad matters was in an almost inextricable tangle. There was no one to meet us or to tell us where we were to camp, and no one to issue us food for the first twenty-four hours; while the railroad people unloaded us wherever they pleased, or rather wherever the jam of all kinds of trains rendered it possible. We had to buy the men food out of our own pockets, and to seize wagons in order to get our spare baggage taken to the camping ground which we at last found had been allotted to us.

Once on the ground, we speedily got order out of confusion. Under Wood's eye the tents were put up in long streets, the picket-line of each troop stretching down its side of each street. The officers' quarters were at the upper ends of the streets, the company kitchens and sinks at the opposite ends. The camp was strictly policed, and drill promptly begun. For thirty-six hours we let the horses rest, drilling on foot, and then began the mounted drill again. The regiments with which we were afterward to serve were camped near us, and the sandy streets of the little town were thronged with soldiers, almost all of them regulars; for there were but one or two volunteer organizations besides ourselves. The regulars wore the canonical dark blue of Uncle Sam. Our own men were clad in dusty brown blouses, trousers and leggings being of the same hue, while the broad-brimmed soft hat was of dark gray; and very workmanlike they looked as, in column of fours, each troop trotted down its company street to form by squadron or battalion, the troopers sitting steadily in the saddles as they made their half-trained horses conform to the movement of the guidons.

Over in Tampa town the huge winter hotel was gay with general-officers and their staffs, with women in pretty dresses, with newspaper correspondents by the score, with military *attachés* of foreign powers, and with onlookers of all sorts; but we spent very little time there.

We worked with the utmost industry, special attention being given by each troop-commander to skirmish-drill in the woods. Once or twice we had mounted drill of the regiment as a whole. The military *attachés* came out to look on—English, German, Russian, French, and Japanese. With the Englishman, Captain Lee, a capital fellow, we soon struck up an especially close friendship; and we saw much of him throughout the campaign. So we did of several of the newspaper correspondents—Richard Harding Davis, John Fox, Jr., Caspar Whitney, and Frederic Remington. On Sunday Chaplain Brown, of Arizona, held service, as he did almost every Sunday during the campaign.

There were but four or five days at Tampa, however. We were notified that the expedition would start for destination unknown at once, and that we were to go with it; but that our horses were to be left behind, and only eight troops of seventy men each taken. Our sorrow at leaving the horses was entirely outweighed by our joy at going; but it was very hard indeed to select the four troops that were to stay, and the men who had to be left behind from each of the troops that went. Colonel Wood took Major Brodie and myself to command the two squadrons, being allowed only two squadron commanders. The men who were left behind felt the most bitter heartburn. To the great bulk of them I think it will be a life-long sorrow. I saw more than one, both among the officers and privates, burst into tears when he found he could not go. No outsider can appreciate the bitterness of the disappointment. Of course, really, those that stayed were entitled to precisely as much honor as those that went. Each man was doing his duty, and much the hardest and most disagreeable duty was to stay. Credit should go with the performance of duty, and not with what is very often the accident of glory. All this and much more we explained, but our explanations could not alter the fact that some had to be chosen and some had to be left. One of the Captains chosen was Captain Maximilian Luna, who commanded Troop F, from New Mexico. The Captain's people had been on the banks of the Rio Grande before my forefathers came to the mouth of the Hudson or Wood's landed at Plymouth; and he made the plea that it was his right to go as a representative of his race, for he was the only man of pure Spanish blood who bore a commission in the army, and he demanded the privilege of proving that his people were precisely as loyal Americans as any others. I was glad when it was decided to take him.

It was the evening of June 7th when we suddenly received orders that the expedition was to start from Fort Tampa, nine miles distant by rail, at daybreak the following morning; and that if we were not aboard our transport by that time we could not go. We had no intention of getting left, and prepared at once for the scramble which was evidently about to take place. As the number and capacity of the transports were known, or ought to have been known, and as the number and size of the regiments to go were also known. The task of allotting each regiment or fraction of a regiment to its proper transport, and arranging that the regiments and the transports should meet in due order on the dock, ought not to have been difficult. However, no arrangements were made in advance; and we were allowed to shove and hustle for ourselves as best we could, on much the same principles that had governed our preparations hitherto.

We were ordered to be at a certain track with all our baggage at midnight, there to take a train for Port Tampa. At the appointed time we turned up, but the train did not. The men slept heavily, while Wood and I and various other officers wandered about in search of information which no one could give. We now and then came across a Brigadier-General, or even a Major-General; but nobody knew anything. Some regiments got aboard the trains and some did not, but as none of the trains started this made little difference. At three o'clock were received orders to march over to an entirely different track, and away we went. No train appeared on this track either; but at six o'clock some coal cars came by, and these we seized. By various arguments we persuaded the engineer in charge of the train to back us down the nine miles to Port Tampa, where we arrived covered with coal-dust, but with all our belongings.

The railway tracks ran out on the quay, and the transports, which had been anchored in midstream, were gradually being brought up alongside the quay and loaded. The trains were unloading wherever they happened to be, no attention whatever being paid to the possible position of the transport on which the soldiers were to go. Colonel Wood and I jumped off and started on a hunt, which soon convinced us that we had our work cut out if we were to get a transport at all. From the highest General down, nobody could tell us where to go to find out what transport *we* were to have. At last we were informed that we were to hunt up the depot quartermaster, Colonel Humphrey. We found his office, where his assistant informed us that he didn't know where the Colonel was, but believed him to be asleep upon one of the transports. This seemed odd at such a time; but so many of the methods in vogue were odd, that we were quite prepared to accept it as a fact. However, it proved not to be such; but for an hour Colonel Humphrey might just as well have been asleep, as nobody knew where he was and nobody could find him, and the quay was crammed with some ten thousand men, most of whom were working at cross purposes.

At last, however, after over an hour's industrious and rapid search through this swarming ant-heap of humanity, Wood and I, who had separated, found Colonel Humphrey at nearly the same time and were allotted a transport—the Yucutan. She was out in midstream, so wood seized a stray launch and boarded her. At the same time I happened to find out that she had previously been allotted to two other regiments—the Second Regular Infantry and the Seventy-first New York Volunteers, which latter regiment alone contained more men than could be put aboard her. Accordingly, I ran at full speed to our train; and leaving a strong guard with the baggage, I double-quicked the rest of the regiment up to the boat, just in time to board her as she came into the quay, and then to hold her against the Second Regulars and the Seventy-first, who had arrived a little too late, being a shade less ready than we were in the matter of individual initiative. There was a good deal of expostulation, but we had possession; and as the ship could not contain half of the men who had been told to go aboard her, the Seventy-first went away, as did all but four companies of the Second. These latter we took aboard. Meanwhile a General had caused our train to be unloaded at the end of the quay farthest from where the ship was; and the hungry, tired men spent most of the day in the labor of bringing down their baggage and the food and ammunition.

The officers' horses were on another boat, my own being accompanied by my colored body-servant, Marshall, the most faithful and loyal of men, himself an old soldier of the Ninth Cavalry. Marshall had been in Indian campaigns, and he christened my larger horse "Rain-in-the-Face," while the other, a pony, went by the name of "Texas."

By the time that night fell, and our transport pulled off and anchored in mid-stream, we felt we had spent thirty-six tolerably active hours. The transport was overloaded, the men being packed like sardines, not only below but upon the decks; so that at night it was only possible to walk about by continually stepping over the bodies of the sleepers.

34

FRANK NORRIS, *THE OCTOPUS: A STORY OF CALIFORNIA* (NEW YORK: DOUBLEDAY, 1907), PP. 247–262

And the black wagon went on through the darkness, unattended, ignored, solitary, carrying the dead body of Dabney, the silent old man of whom nothing was known but his name, who made no friends, whom nobody knew or spoke to, who had come from no one knew whence and who went no one knew whither.

Toward midnight of that same day, Mrs. Dyke was awakened by the sounds of groaning in the room next to hers. Magnus Derrick was not so occupied by Harran's death that he could not think of others who were in distress, and when he had heard that Mrs. Dyke and Sidney, like Hilma, had been turned out of Quien Sabe, he had thrown open Los Muertos to them.

"Though," he warned them, "it is precarious hospitality at the best."

Until late, Mrs. Dyke had sat up with Hilma, comforting her as best she could, rocking her to and fro in her arms, crying with her, trying to quiet her, for once having given way to her grief, Hilma wept with a terrible anguish and a violence that racked her from head to foot, and at last, worn out, a little child again, had sobbed herself to sleep in the older woman's arms, and as a little child, Mrs. Dyke had put her to bed and had retired herself.

Aroused a few hours later by the sounds of a distress that was physical as well as mental, Mrs. Dyke hurried into Hilma's room, carrying the lamp with her.

Mrs. Dyke needed no enlightenment. She woke Presley and besought him to telephone to Bonneville at once, summoning a doctor. That night Hilma in great pain suffered a miscarriage.

Presley did not close his eyes once during the night; he did not even remove his clothes. Long after the doctor had departed and that house of tragedy had quieted down, he still remained in his place by the open window of his little room, looking off across the leagues of growing wheat, watching the slow kindling of the dawn. Horror weighed intolerably upon him. Monstrous things, huge, terrible, whose names he knew only too well, whirled at a gallop through his imagination, or rose spectral and grisly before the eyes of his mind. Harran dead, Annixter dead, Broderson dead, Oster-man, perhaps, even at that moment dying. Why, these men had made up his world. Annixter had been his best friend, Harran, his almost daily companion; Broderson and Osterman were familiar to him as brothers. They were all his associates, his good friends, the group was his environment, belonging to his daily life. And he standing there in the dust of the road by the irrigating ditch had seen them shot. He found himself suddenly at his table, the candle burning at his elbow, his journal before him, writing swiftly, the desire for expression, the craving for outlet to the thoughts that clamoured tumultuous at his brain never more insistent, more imperious. Thus he wrote:

> Dabney dead, Hooven dead, Harran dead, Annixter dead, Broderson dead, Osterman dying, S. Behrman alive, successful; the Railroad in possession of Quien Sabe. I saw them shot. Not twelve hours since I stood there at the irrigating ditch. Ah, that terrible moment of horror and confusion! powder smoke—flashing pistol barrels—blood stains—rearing horses—men staggering to their death—Christian in a horrible posture, one rigid leg high in the air across his saddle—Broderson falling sideways into the ditch—Osterman laying himself down, his head on his arms, as if tired, tired out. These things, I have seen them. The picture of this day's work is from henceforth part of my mind, part of me. They have done it, S. Behrman and the owners of the Railroad have done it, while all the world looked on, while the people of these United States looked on. Oh, come now and try your theories upon us, us of the ranchos, us who have suffered, us who know. Oh, talk to us now of the "rights of Capital," talk to us of the Trust, talk to us of the "equilibrium between the classes." Try your ingenious ideas upon us. We know. I cannot tell whether or not your theories are excellent. I do not know if your ideas are plausible. I do not know how practical is your scheme of society. I do not know if the Railroad has a right to our lands, but I do know that Harran is dead, that Annixter is dead, that Broderson is dead, that Hooven is dead, that Osterman is dying, and that S. Behrman is alive, successful, triumphant; that he has ridden into possession of a principality over the dead bodies of five men shot down by his hired associates.
>
> I can see the outcome. The Railroad will prevail. The Trust will overpower us. Here in this corner of a great nation, here, on the edge of the continent, here, in this valley of the West, far from the great centres, isolated, remote, lost, the great iron hand crushes life from us, crushes liberty and the pursuit of happiness from us, and our little struggles, our moment's convulsion of death agony causes not one jar in the vast, clashing machinery of the nation's life; a fleck of grit in the wheels, perhaps, a grain of sand in the cogs—the momentary creak of the axle is the mother's wail of bereavement, the wife's cry of anguish—and the great wheel turns, spinning smooth again, even again, and the tiny impediment of a second, scarce noticed, is forgotten. Make the people believe that the faint tremor in their great engine is a menace to its function? What a folly to think of it. Tell them of the danger and they will laugh at you. Tell them, five years from now, the story of the fight between the League of the San Joaquin and the Railroad and it will not be believed. What! a pitched battle between

Farmer and Railroad, a battle that cost the lives of seven men? Impossible, it could not have happened. Your story is fiction—is exaggerated.

Yet it is Lexington—God help us, God enlighten us. God rouse us from our lethargy—it is Lexington; farmers with guns in their hands fighting for Liberty. Is our State of California the only one that has its ancient and hereditary foe? Are there no other Trusts between the oceans than this of the Pacific and Southwestern Railroad? Ask yourselves, you of the Middle West, ask yourselves, you of the North, ask yourselves, you of the East, ask yourselves, you of the South—ask yourselves, every citizen of every State from Maine to Mexico, from the Dakotas to the Carolinas, have you not the monster in your boundaries? If it is not a Trust of transportation, it is only another head of the same Hydra. Is not our death struggle typical? Is it not one of many, is it not symbolical of the great and terrible conflict that is going on everywhere in these United States? Ah, you people, blind, bound, tricked, betrayed, can you not see it? Can you not see how the monsters have plundered your treasures and holding them in the grip of their iron claws, dole them out to you only at the price of your blood, at the price of the lives of your wives and your little children? You give your babies to Moloch for the loaf of bread you have kneaded yourselves. You offer your starved wives to Juggernaut for the iron nail you have yourselves compounded.

He spent the night over his journal, writing down such thoughts as these or walking the floor from wall to wall, or, seized at times with unreasoning horror and blind rage, flinging himself face downward upon his bed, vowing with inarticulate cries that neither S. Behrman nor Shelgrim should ever live to consummate their triumph.

Morning came and with it the daily papers and news. Presley did not even glance at the Mercury. Bonneville published two other daily journals that professed to voice the will and reflect the temper of the people, and these he read eagerly.

Osterman was yet alive and there were chances of his recovery. The League—some three hundred of its members had gathered at Bonneville over night and were patrolling the streets and, still resolved to keep the peace, were even guarding the railroad shops and buildings. Furthermore, the Leaguers had issued manifestoes, urging all citizens to preserve law and order, yet summoning an indignation meeting to be convened that afternoon at the City Opera House.

It appeared from the newspapers that those who obstructed the marshal in the discharge of his duty could be proceeded against by the District Attorney on information or by bringing the matter before the Grand Jury. But the Grand Jury was not at that time in session, and it was known that there were no funds in the marshal's office to pay expenses for the summoning of jurors or the serving of processes. S. Behrman and Ruggles in interviews stated that the Railroad withdrew entirely from the fight; the matter now, according to them, was between the Leaguers and the United States Government; they washed their hands of the whole business. The ranchers could settle with Washington. But it seemed that Congress had recently forbidden the use of troops for civil purposes; the whole matter of the League-Railroad contest was evidently for the moment to be left in statu quo.

But to Presley's mind the most important piece of news that morning was the report of the action of the Railroad upon hearing of the battle.

Instantly Bonneville had been isolated. Not a single local train was running, not one of the through trains made any halt at the station. The mails were not moved. Further than this, by some arrangement difficult to understand, the telegraph operators at Bonneville and Guadalajara, acting under orders, refused to receive any telegrams except those emanating from railway officials. The story of the fight, the story creating the first impression, was to be told to San Francisco and the outside world by S. Behrman, Ruggles, and the local P. and S. W. agents.

An hour before breakfast, the undertakers arrived and took charge of the bodies of Harran and Annixter. Presley saw neither Hilma, Magnus, nor Mrs. Derrick. The doctor came to look after Hilma. He breakfasted with Mrs. Dyke and Presley, and from him Presley learned that Hilma would recover both from the shock of her husband's death and from her miscarriage of the previous night.

"She ought to have her mother with her," said the physician. "She does nothing but call for her or beg to be allowed to go to her. I have tried to get a wire through to Mrs. Tree, but the company will not take it, and even if I could get word to her, how could she get down here? There are no trains."

But Presley found that it was impossible for him to stay at Los Muertos that day. Gloom and the shadow of tragedy brooded heavy over the place. A great silence pervaded everything, a silence broken only by the subdued coming and going of the undertaker and his assistants. When Presley, having resolved to go into Bonneville, came out through the doorway of the house, he found the undertaker tying a long strip of crape to the bell-handle.

Presley saddled his pony and rode into town. By this time, after long hours of continued reflection upon one subject, a sombre brooding malevolence, a deep-seated desire of revenge, had grown big within his mind. The first numbness had passed off; familiarity with what had been done had blunted the edge of horror, and now the impulse of retaliation prevailed. At first, the sullen anger of defeat, the sense of outrage, had only smouldered, but the more he brooded, the fiercer flamed his rage. Sudden paroxysms of wrath gripped him by the throat; abrupt outbursts of fury injected his eyes with blood. He ground his teeth, his mouth filled with curses, his hands clenched till they grew white and bloodless. Was the Railroad to triumph then in the end? After all those months of preparation, after all those grandiloquent resolutions, after all the arrogant presumption of the League! The League! what a farce; what had it amounted to when the crisis came? Was the Trust to crush them all so easily? Was S. Behrman to swallow Los Muertos? S. Behrman! Presley saw him plainly, huge, rotund, white; saw his jowl tremulous and obese, the roll of fat over his collar sprinkled with sparse hairs, the great stomach with its brown linen vest and heavy watch chain of hollow links clinking against the buttons of imitation pearl. And this man was to crush Magnus Derrick—had already stamped the life from such men as

Harran and Annixter. This man, in the name of the Trust, was to grab Los Muertos as he had grabbed Quien Sabe, and after Los Muertos, Broder-son's ranch, then Osterman's, then others, and still others, the whole valley, the whole State.

Presley beat his forehead with his clenched fist as he rode on.

"No," he cried, "no, kill him, kill him, kill him with my hands."

The idea of it put him beside himself. Oh, to sink his fingers deep into the white, fat throat of the man, to clutch like iron into the great puffed jowl of him, to wrench out the life, to batter it out, strangle it out, to pay him back for the long years of extortion and oppression, to square accounts for bribed jurors, bought judges, corrupted legislatures, to have justice for the trick of the Ranchers' Railroad Commission, the charlatanism of the "ten per cent. cut," the ruin of Dyke, the seizure of Quien Sabe, the murder of Harran, the assassination of Annixter!

It was in such mood that he reached Caraher's. The saloon-keeper had just opened his place and was standing in his doorway, smoking his pipe. Presley dismounted and went in and the two had a long talk.

When, three hours later, Presley came out of the saloon and rode on toward Bonneville, his face was very pale, his lips shut tight, resolute, determined. His manner was that of a man whose mind is made up.

The hour for the mass meeting at the Opera House had been set for one o'clock, but long before noon the street in front of the building and, in fact, all the streets in its vicinity, were packed from side to side with a shifting, struggling, surging, and excited multitude. There were few women in the throng, but hardly a single male inhabitant of either Bonneville or Guadalajara was absent. Men had even come from Visalia and Pixley. It was no longer the crowd of curiosity seekers that had thronged around Hooven's place by the irrigating ditch; the People were no longer confused, bewildered. A full realization of just what had been done the day before was clear now in the minds of all. Business was suspended; nearly all the stores were closed. Since early morning the members of the League had put in an appearance and rode from point to point, their rifles across their saddle pommels. Then, by ten o'clock, the streets had begun to fill up, the groups on the corners grew and merged into one another; pedestrians, unable to find room on the sidewalks, took to the streets. Hourly the crowd increased till shoulders touched and elbows, till free circulation became impeded, then congested, then impossible. The crowd, a solid mass, was wedged tight from store iron tiers tore front. And from all this throng, this single unit, this living, breathing organism—the People—there rose a droning, terrible note. It was not yet the wild, fierce clamour of riot and insurrection, shrill, high pitched, but it was a beginning, the growl of the awakened brute, feeling the iron in its flank, heaving up its head with bared teeth, the throat vibrating to the long, indrawn snarl of wrath.

Thus the forenoon passed, while the people, their bulk growing hourly vaster, kept to the streets, moving slowly backward and forward, oscillating in the grooves of the thoroughfares, the steady, low-pitched growl rising continually into the hot, still air.

Then, at length, about twelve o'clock, the movement of the throng assumed definite direction. It set toward the Opera House. Presley, who had left his pony at the City livery stable, found himself caught in the current and carried slowly forward in its direction. His arms were pinioned to his sides by the press, the crush against his body was all but rib-cracking, he could hardly draw his breath. All around him rose and fell wave after wave of faces, hundreds upon hundreds, thousands upon thousands, red, lowering, sullen. All were set in one direction and slowly, slowly they advanced, crowding closer, till they almost touched one another. For reasons that were inexplicable, great, tumultuous heavings, like ground-swells of an incoming tide, surged over and through the multitude. At times, Presley, lifted from his feet, was swept back, back, back, with the crowd, till the entrance of the Opera House was half a block away; then, the returning billow beat back again and swung him along, gasping, staggering, clutching, till he was landed once more in the vortex of frantic action in front of the foyer. Here the waves were shorter, quicker, the crushing pressure on all sides of his body left him without strength to utter the cry that rose to his lips; then, suddenly the whole mass of struggling, stamping, fighting, writhing men about him seemed, as it were, to rise, to lift, multitudinous, swelling, gigantic. A mighty rush dashed Presley forward in its leap. There was a moment's whirl of confused sights, congested faces, opened mouths, bloodshot eyes, clutching hands; a moment's outburst of furious sound, shouts, cheers, oaths; a moment's jam wherein Presley veritably believed his ribs must snap like pipestems and he was carried, dazed, breathless, helpless, an atom on the crest of a storm-driven wave, up the steps of the Opera House, on into the vestibule, through the doors, and at last into the auditorium of the house itself.

There was a mad rush for places; men disdaining the aisle, stepped from one orchestra chair to another, striding over the backs of seats, leaving the print of dusty feet upon the red plush cushions. In a twinkling the house was filled from stage to topmost gallery. The aisles were packed solid, even on the edge of the stage itself men were sitting, a black fringe on either side of the footlights.

The curtain was up, disclosing a half-set scene—the flats, leaning at perilous angles—that represented some sort of terrace, the pavement, alternate squares of black and white marble, while red, white, and yellow flowers were represented as growing from urns and vases. A long, double row of chairs stretched across the scene from wing to wing, flanking a table covered with a red cloth, on which was set a pitcher of water and a speaker's gavel.

Promptly these chairs were filled up with members of the League, the audience cheering as certain well-known figures made their appearance—Garnett of the Ruby rancho, Gethings of the San Pablo, Keast of the ranch of the same name, Chattern of the Bonanza, elderly men, bearded, slow of speech, deliberate.

Garnett opened the meeting; his speech was plain, straightforward, matter-of-fact. He simply told what had happened. He announced that certain resolutions were to be drawn up. He introduced the next speaker.

This one pleaded for moderation. He was conservative. All along he had opposed the idea of armed resistance except as the very last resort. He "deplored" the terrible affair of yesterday. He begged the people to wait in patience, to attempt no more violence. He informed them that armed guards of the League were, at that moment, patrolling Los Muertos, Broderson's, and Osterman's. It was well known that the United States marshal confessed himself powerless to serve the writs. There would be no more bloodshed.

"We have had," he continued, "bloodshed enough, and I want to say right here that I am not so sure but what yesterday's terrible affair might have been avoided. A gentleman whom we all esteem, who from the first has been our recognized leader, is, at this moment, mourning the loss of a young son, killed before his eyes. God knows that I sympathize, as do we all, in the affliction of our President. I am sorry for him. My heart goes out to him in this hour of distress, but, at the same time, the position of the League must be defined. We owe it to ourselves, we owe it to the people of this county. The League armed for the very purpose of preserving the peace, not of breaking it. We believed that with six hundred armed and drilled men at our disposal, ready to muster at a moment's call, we could so overawe any attempt to expel us from our lands that such an attempt would not be made until the cases pending before the Supreme Court had been decided. If when the enemy appeared in our midst yesterday they had been met by six hundred rifles, it is not conceivable that the issue would have been forced. No fight would have ensued, and to-day we would not have to mourn the deaths of four of our fellow-citizens. A mistake has been made and we of the League must not be held responsible."

The speaker sat down amidst loud applause from the Leaguers and less pronounced demonstrations on the part of the audience.

A second Leaguer took his place, a tall, clumsy man, half-rancher, half-politician.

"I want to second what my colleague has just said," he began. "This matter of resisting the marshal when he tried to put the Railroad dummies in possession on the ranches around here was all talked over in the committee meetings of the League long ago. It never was our intention to fire a single shot. No such absolute authority as was assumed yesterday was delegated to anybody. Our esteemed President is all right, but we all know that he is a man who loves authority and who likes to go his own gait without accounting to anybody. We—the rest of us Leaguers—never were informed as to what was going on. We supposed, of course, that watch was being kept on the Railroad so as we wouldn't be taken by surprise as we were yesterday. And it seems no watch was kept at all, or if there was, it was mighty ineffective. Our idea was to forestall any movement on the part of the Railroad and then when we knew the marshal was coming down, to call a meeting of our Executive Committee and decide as to what should be done. We ought to have had time to call out the whole League. Instead of that, what happens? While we're all off chasing rabbits, the Railroad is allowed to steal a march on us and when it is too late, a handful of Leaguers is got together and a fight is precipitated and our men killed, *I'm* sorry for our President, too. No one is more so, but I want to put myself on record as believing he did a hasty and inconsiderate thing. If he had managed right, he could have had six hundred men to oppose the Railroad and there would not have been any gun fight or any killing. He *didn't* manage right and there was a killing, and I don't see as how the League ought to be held responsible. The idea of the League, the whole reason why it was organized, was to protect *all* the ranches of this valley from the Railroad, and it looks to me as if the lives of our fellow-citizens had been sacrificed, not in defending all of our ranches but just in defence of one of them—Los Muertos—the one that Mr. Derrick owns."

The speaker had no more than regained his seat when a man was seen pushing his way from the back of the stage toward Garnett. He handed the rancher a note, at the same time whispering in his ear. Garnett read the note, then came forward to the edge of the stage, holding up his hand. When the audience had fallen silent he said:

"I have just received sad news. Our friend and fellow-citizen, Mr. Osterman, died this morning between eleven and twelve o'clock."

Instantly there was a roar. Every man in the building rose to his feet, shouting, gesticulating. The roar increased, the Opera House trembled to it, the gas jets in the lighted chandeliers vibrated to it. It was a raucous howl of execration, a bellow of rage, inarticulate, deafening.

A tornado of confusion swept whirling from wall to wall and the madness of the moment seized irresistibly upon Presley. He forgot himself; he no longer was master of his emotions or his impulses. All at once he found himself upon the stage, facing the audience, flaming with excitement, his imagination on fire, his arms uplifted in fierce, wild gestures, words leaping to his mind in a torrent that could not be withheld.

"One more dead," he cried, "one more. Harran dead, Annixter dead, Broderson dead, Dabney dead, Osterman dead, Hooven dead; shot down, killed, killed in the defence of their homes, killed in the defence of their rights, killed for the sake of liberty. How long must it go on? How long must we suffer? Where is the end; what is the end? How long must the iron-hearted monster feed on our life's blood? How long must this terror of steam and steel ride upon our necks? Will you never be satisfied, will you never relent, you, our masters, you, our lords, you, our kings, you, our task-masters, you, our Pharaohs. Will you never listen to that command *'Let My people go'?* Oh, that cry ringing down the ages. Hear it, hear it. It is the voice of the Lord God speaking in His prophets. Hear it, hear it— *'Let My people go!'* Rameses heard it in his pylons at Thebes, Cæsar heard it on the Palatine, the Bourbon Louis heard it at Versailles, Charles Stuart heard it at Whitehall, the white Czar heard it in the Kremlin—*'Let My people go.'* It is the cry of the nations, the great voice of the centuries; everywhere it is raised. The voice of God is the voice of the People. The people cry out 'Let us, the People, God's people, go.' You, our masters, you, our kings, you, our tyrants, don't you hear us? Don't you hear God speaking in us? Will you never let us go? How long at length will you abuse our patience? How long will you drive us? How long will you harass us? Will nothing daunt you? Does nothing check you? Do you not know that to ignore our cry too long is to wake the Red Terror? Rameses refused to listen to it and perished miserably. Caesar refused to listen and was stabbed in the Senate House. The Bourbon Louis refused to listen and died on the guillotine; Charles Stuart refused to listen and died on the block; the white Czar refused to listen and was blown up in his own capital. Will you let it come to that? Will you drive us to it? We who boast of our land of freedom, we who live in the country of liberty?

"Go on as you have begun and it will come to that. Turn a deaf ear to that cry of 'Let My people go' too long and another cry will be raised that you cannot choose but hear, a cry that you cannot shut out. It will be the cry of the man on the street, the '*à la Bastille*' that wakes the Red Terror and unleashes Revolution. Harassed, plundered, exasperated, desperate, the people will turn at last as they have turned so many, many times before. You, our lords, you, our taskmasters, you, our kings; you have caught your Samson, you have made his strength your own. You have shorn his head; you have put out his eyes; you have set him to turn your millstones, to grind the grist for your mills; you have made him a shame and a mock. Take care, oh, as you love your lives, take care, lest some day calling upon the Lord his God he reach not out his arms for the pillars of your temples."

The audience, at first bewildered, confused by this unexpected invective, suddenly took fire at his last words. There was a roar of applause; then, more significant than mere vociferation, Presley's listeners, as he began to speak again, grew suddenly silent. His next sentences were uttered in the midst of a profound stillness.

"They own us, these task-masters of ours; they own our homes, they own our legislatures. We cannot escape from them. There is no redress. We are told we can defeat them by the ballot-box. They own the ballot-box. We are told that we must look to the courts for redress; they own the courts. We know them for what they are—ruffians in politics, ruffians in finance, ruffians in law, ruffians in trade, bribers, swindlers, and tricksters. No outrage too great to daunt them, no petty larceny too small to shame them; despoiling a government treasury of a million dollars, yet picking the pockets of a farm hand of the price of a loaf of bread.

"They swindle a nation of a hundred million and call it Financiering; they levy a blackmail and call it Commerce; they corrupt a legislature and call it Politics; they bribe a judge and call it Law; they hire blacklegs to carry out their plans and call it Organization; they prostitute the honour of a State and call it Competition.

"And this is America. We fought Lexington to free ourselves; we fought Gettysburg to free others. Yet the yoke remains; we have only shifted it to the other shoulder. We talk of liberty—oh, the farce of it, oh, the folly of it! We tell ourselves and teach our children that we have achieved liberty, that we no longer need fight for it. Why, the fight is just beginning and so long as our conception of liberty remains as it is to-day, it will continue.

"For we conceive of Liberty in the statues we raise to her as a beautiful woman, crowned, victorious, in bright armour and white robes, a light in her uplifted hand—a serene, calm, conquering goddess. Oh, the farce of it, oh, the folly of it! Liberty is not a crowned goddess, beautiful, in spotless garments, victorious, supreme. Liberty is the Man In the Street, a terrible figure, rushing through powder smoke, fouled with the mud and ordure of the gutter, bloody, rampant, brutal, yelling curses, in one hand a smoking rifle, in the other, a blazing torch.

"Freedom is *not* given free to any who ask; Liberty is not born of the gods. She is a child of the People, born in the very height and heat of battle, born from death, stained with blood, grimed with powder. And she grows to be not a goddess, but a Fury, a fearful figure, slaying friend and foe alike, raging, insatiable, merciless, the Red Terror."

Presley ceased speaking. Weak, shaking, scarcely knowing what he was about, he descended from the stage. A prolonged explosion of applause followed, the Opera House roaring to the roof, men cheering, stamping, waving their hats. But it was not intelligent applause. Instinctively, as he made his way out, Presley knew that, after all, he had not once held the hearts of his audience. He had talked as he would have written; for all his scorn of literature, he had been literary. The men who listened to him, ranchers, country people, store-keepers, attentive though they were, were not once sympathetic. Vaguely they had felt that here was something which other men—more educated—would possibly consider eloquent. They applauded vociferously but perfunctorily, in order to appear to understand.

Part 6

THE BEST IN THE WORLD
The dominion of the Canadian Pacific Railway

35

J. T. BREEZE, *THE DOMINION OF CANADA. THE GREAT INSTITUTION OF OUR COUNTRY. A POEM ON THE GRAND TRUNK RAILWAY* (MONTREAL: N.P., 1867), PP. 6–8

With attributes of various kind,
And their intrinsic energy
Causes the depths of night to flee.
Progress the motto that doth stain
The banners science lifts again,
And art with countless ensigns wave
The same on every effort brave.
The world's all new, her rugged face
Doth change with what the arts doth grace.
Science rolls back the solemn weight
That ages darkened into night.
It crush'd the genius of mankind,
Withholding light from th' world of mind.
But science with her might doth roll
This darkness from the human soul,
And raises human powers of thought
To soar where wings of angels float.
Wait, Genius, wait and gaze awhile
On error's power that did defile,
That blasted powers so pure as thine,
And crushed her light of rays divine.
Expose the principle that bound
Genius so long to the ground.
She never rose with all her power.
But had from age to age to cower.
Before the ruthless laws of wrong,
Bound her arm and chain'd her tongue.
Yea, all the powers of noble thought

Were dragg'd by chains that slavery bought.
Heaven, in favour, hath redeemed
The light that trembling genius beamed.
Her light shall reign and rule the world
'Neath banners she hath now unfurled.
Despotic power no more shall reign,
Or drag bright Genius in her train.
Wait, shall I say, to curse that power
Before which thou so long didst cower,
And then, with all thy powers awake
Thy glorious pathway to betake;
Give size and shape and form to thought
That, genius with its might hath wrought.
Science and genius, of one heart,
Shall shod their light with every art,
To scatter countless blessings free
To all the human family.
What if our fathers from above
Behold us from their thrones of love;
What if their eyes through matter pierce,
And can the scenes of life rehearse,
And see the progress earth hath made
Since their dust slumbers with the dead;—
Would they not covet to return
And let their genius with ours burn,
And pride in yet uniting free
With us to raise man's destiny?
Our country seventy years ago
How wild an aspect then did show:
Countless huts and cabins spread
Studding th' earth where lies their head;
But now fine towns and cities rise,
Pointing their spires to the skies.
Instead of rumbling wheels that rolled
Their heavy length along of old,
Genius commands some element
Of nature, go where she is sent.
And doth command from every mill
The produce of man, good or ill,
Without those weary Lours that roll'd
With waggon wheels in days of old.
Yea, time and haggard space are spanned,
Trod o'er at genius's command;
Distance brought near, and time compelled

Before her mighty power to yield.
On lightning's wing thought speeds her way,
And loaded returns in a day,
Brings mighty thoughts within her breast
From distant lands to cause us rest;
Yea, binds the human family
In every land in unity.
Man fain would imitate his God,
Would speak with kindred power abroad,
And bid all nature bow before,
And all but makes it him adore,
Constructs an iron horse of might,
Breathes in it breath of life aright,
Invests it with those attributes
That give it powers above the brutes.
In strength and swiftness would outvie
The strongest, swiftest beast of prey.
And draw behind it in its train
Loads that no power can vie again,
Stops oft to load its stomach well,
Drinks draughts to quench its thirsty spell;
It snorts with open nostrils wide,
Puffs forth its lusty breath of pride.
Hears its proud head and laughs away.
Tireless th' same road every day,
Frights both birds and beasts around.
That startle at the whistle's sound.
The genius of the forest, flies,
While art with thousand wonders rise,
And (all but) our fond fathers' dust
Rises to break the earth's deep crust
To witness what new genius reigns
In majesty on seas and plains,
That flies with such velocity,
Shaking the firmest forest tree,
Driving the ruder genius 'way
'Fore stronger light of brighter day.
The world's all new, it is ablaze;
Our fathers' eyes with wonder gaze,
Clasping their hands unitedly,
Say, Well done nineteenth century!
No more our sorrows ye shall feel,

36

CHARLES WESTLY BUSK, *NOTES OF A JOURNEY FROM TORONTO TO BRITISH COLUMBIA VIA THE NORTHERN PACIFIC RAILWAY, JUNE TO JULY 1884, BEING LETTERS TO HIS SISTER AND MOTHER* (LONDON: TAYLOR AND FRANCIS, 1884), PP. 3–6

Victoria, British Columbia,
July 9th, 1884.

My Dear Madeline, —

You will probably have received, by the time this arrives, the post-card I sent you announcing my safe arrival at this city of the Far West, as also I hope, in their due order, the cards I posted almost dany *en route*. I now propose to give you a short account of the journey and the country and scenery on the way. A good deal of the information and the Indian stories and legends are all from reliable sources, as far as I have been able to obtain such; and I trust the combination may prove instructive, geographically and historically, as well as afford amusement. As the country between Toronto, Chicago, and St. Paul is comparatively well known, and is a route constantly traversed by hundreds of people, I do not propose to enter into any details of that part of the trip, but only to confine myself to the Northern Pacific Railroad and its connection with the Oregon Railway and Navigation Company, which, as you should know from the post-cards received, is that part of the journey lying between St. Paul and the "Queen City of the West."

There was a good deal of hesitation as to how I should travel; I don't mean whether on foot, horseback, or rail, but as to the class of train to be used, for there is not only a difference in time of two days, but also a very considerable difference in the price of the ticket. A first-class ticket right through costs 128 dollars. This entitles the passenger to one seat in a first-class car, and nothing else; but it will also take him through to Portland, Oregon, in six days. In order to obtain sleeping accommodation and a through-car from St. Paul, it is necessary, in addition to this, to take a bed in a Pullman Car; this adds an expense of exactly 20 dollars, making a total of 148 dollars for fare, to which must be added 75 cents a meal for the entire journey. The choice lay, therefore, between this and the third-class, or emigrant rate, which is 71·50 dollars per ticket, right through. This entitles to a seat and bed in a through-car from St. Paul; but the journey takes, as I have said, two days longer. I finally decided to adopt this latter course; and I have had no reason to regret it—rather the contrary, for I have been able to see considerably more, and probably gather more information on account of the slowness of the travel, caused principally by the very long stops at different stations, which arc avoided by the regular express passenger-trains. In order that you may have some idea whereabouts the various places are that will be mentioned, I send you the official map of the Northern Pacific Railway; but you will find that it has been badly printed, the coloured parts are all a little to west and by south of their proper places, but you will easily rectify this; the black outline is, in the main, correct, and so you can go by that and ignore the colour altogether.

The train left the Union Station, Toronto, at 1.5 P.M. on Monday, June 23rd, and drew up in the Michigan Southern Station (or depot), in Chicago, at 7.50 the following morning, the clock being put back one hour at the Detroit river. On presentation of a through-ticket to a Canadian port, the baggage is all passed without examination. At Chicago I posted you a card. I would have preferred to leave Chicago by way of Milwaukee, but the tickets did not read that way, and so it was necessary to travel by the Rock Island and Pacific Railway, *vid* Albert Lea, to St. Paul, and this was accomplished with extreme punctuality. Up to this there is no difference, either in time or accommodation, between one and another. First-class passengers leave St. Paul again shortly after 4.0 in the afternoon, and arrive in Portland at half-past 11 in the morning of the fourth day. Emigrant passengers have to remain in St. Paul till 10 minutes to 8, and are due in Portland at a quarter past 4 in the afternoon of the sixth day. It was quite early when the train reached St. Paul; so I went to an hotel for the day, for meals and general refreshment. Of course I walked about the city a great deal, and looked down on the Mississippi river, and so on. St. Paul is the capital of the State of Minnesota, and is situated on the Mississippi river, rather over 2000 miles from its mouth, and at the head of steamboat navigation. Thirty-four years ago the city was a small out-of-the-way settlement, near St. Anthony Falls, now it has over 80,000 inhabitants. The Indian name of the locality, before there was a city, was Immigaska, which means White Rock, and was so called by them, I suppose, on account of tall white cliffs of sandstone which lie along the course of the river, and, in fact, the city is itself on the top of one of them. It seems an extraordinary place on which to have built a city, as it is quite apparent to-day that many hills have had to be levelled and thrown over into valleys to make a kind of level place; and this must have cost, and does still cost, a lot of money. The streets are lighted with gas and electricity; street-cars (*i. e.* tramways) are numerous, and so are the suburban and local trains. St. Paul is almost midway between the Atlantic and Pacific Oceans, and therefore is enabled to carry a considerable trade both east and west.

Minneapolis is another large city, about ten miles west of St. Paul, and containing about the same number of inhabitants; but I did not visit this, merely passed through in the train, and so it does not come within the scope of this letter to say anything about it, except perhaps that there seems to be every appearance of the two cities being united at no very distant date.

In order to make the journey of six days in the same car pleasant and in fact endurable, it was necessary to make preparations in advance; and in the furtherance of this a certain Captain Cook (a policeman!) was extremely useful. The emigrant sleeping-car is really a thing to be seen. It is built by the Pullman-Car Company expressly for the Northern Pacific Railway, and is arranged exactly in the same way, only there is in addition, at the rear of the car, a cooking-stove, so that with a kettle and so on, tea can be made at any time, and also, when travelling in families, dinner can he cooked comfortably from provisions the passengers bring with them; but for lone bachelors, spinsters, and the like there is every opportunity of eating to satiety at regular stations the whole way through at 50 cents a meal. The difference between these cars and the Pullman Palace Cars is the lack of upholstery; this is entirely absent, and it would not do were it otherwise. It is necessary for each passenger to provide his or her own mattress, pillow, and pair of blankets; and these you can procure for a charge, all told, of 2·50 dollars, at the Union Station at St. Paul. This is, of course, the plan I adopted; and a berth on the north or shady side of the car having been previously secured for my own personal use for the whole way, by the gallaudet Captain, and the necessary bedding arranged therein, with my instruments and so on under the seats, I was ready for the voyage, or, more strictly speaking, journey. There are upper and lower berths, exactly as in a Pullman, the upper berths being capable of being closed up when not in use, and so made as to contain the bedding of both. The lower berth is formed out of the seats, which draw together in the usual way. The cars are amply supplied with fresh water for washing and drinking purposes (this latter is "iced"), and thoroughly swept out at least twice a day. In addition to this, the passengers do not select their own seats or berths, but have them appointed; and in the doing of this the great Cook shows great discrimination and sense. The result was that I enjoyed the trip immensely, and was, on the whole, more comfortable than in a Pullman.

37

GEORGE EDWARD WRIGHT, *A CANADIAN TOUR: A REPORT OF LETTERS FROM THE SPECIAL CORRESPONDENT OF THE TIMES* (LONDON: GEORGE EDWARD WRIGHT, 1886), PP. 17–21

The province of Manitoba

WINNIPEG, MANITOBA, Sept. 1.

At 10 minutes past 15 o'clock yesterday afternoon the guard or conductor, as he is called, shouted "All aboard" on the Canadian Pacific Railway train at Port Arthur, and we resumed the western journey. The railway clocks west of Lake Superior and the time tables of this line mark the 24 hours consecutively, and the unusual circumstance causes a flutter among the passengers, and some difficulty in translating the record of watches. From midnight to midnight the hours are consecutively counted, so that what is ordinarily called 10 minutes past three in the afternoon, has become, through this novel stroke of railway enterprise, 10 minutes past 15 o'clock. The timepieces recording this have the ordinary dials, but with an inner circle of numerals marking the hours above 12. The time is also reckoned westward of Port Arthur by the Central Standard time in the American railway system, which is one hour slower than the Eastern Standard time, which controls the eastward. This, by throwing the watches one hour too fast, being added to the computations necessary under the 24-hour system, made time-keeping among the travellers quite an abstruse mathematical problem, and most of them gave it up. The railway train was started successfully, however, and moved rapidly over the level land westward past the old post at Fort William, and its town site, and then up the valley of the pretty Kaministiquia River, with its rows of comfortable looking little houses and their gardens. The cultivation here is extensive and the land good, so that the region is attractive to farmers, and much new land is being cleared. The Canadian Pacific Railway goes westward along the valley of this river and one of its affluents, following what is known as the Dawson route. This in former days was the chief portage between the head waters of the St. Lawrence and those leading into Hudson's Bay, originally used by the Indians, who carried their canoes across the intervening strip of land, and ultimately developing into a passenger route by stage and boats between the two Hudson's Bay posts of Fort William and Fort Garry. It was a roundabout way, requiring a journey of about 50 miles overland to the head waters of streams by which boat navigation could be conducted through the Rainy Lake and river to the Lake of the Woods, and then through Winnipeg River to Lake Winnipeg, whence the voyage continued southward up the Red River to Fort Garry. This was the route taken by Colonel, now Lord, Wolseley in 1870, when he made the expedition westward that suppressed the first French half-breed rebellion led by Louis Riel. Part of this route has been made the international boundary between Canada and the United States, which on its eastern portion, however, comes out upon Lake Superior at Pigeon River about 30 miles below Fort William, on what is known as the "Grand Portage."

After leaving the level and well settled region which extends for some distance back from Lake Superior, the railway route gradually ascends to the summit of the height of land separating the two great basins draining into the St. Lawrence and into Hudson's Bay. It is a country almost destitute of inhabitants and having stations only at long intervals. The summit is reached some 60 miles west of Port Arthur, and the railway goes along it for a great distance. At first the land is comparatively level, but the rough rocks of the Laurentian and Huronian ridges soon begin to show and make a wild and difficult region, timbered, and with many lakes, but hard and uninviting, almost incapable of cultivation, and consequently without habitations. When the Savanne River is crossed, which leads down towards Rainy Lake, a couple of the old boats that were used in conveying the Wolseley expedition are seen, abandoned alongside the bank, one of them having been adopted for a home by an Ojibway Indian family, who were sitting out on the shore, the squaw holding her papoose and trying to fan life into a fire to prepare something to eat. Heavy smokes from distant forest fires enveloped us, and as we moved along the lakes became more numerous, the crags larger, and the face of the country more and more broken. This univiting region continued until the Lake of the Woods was approached at Rat Portage, also part of the route taken across this section by the Indians, in which the rapids of the river leading out of the lake required a portage, and this route and river the railway crosses. There are sawmills and an extensive trade at Rat Portage, the vast extent of the interior waters leading through the mazes of these extensive lakes enabling the lumbermen to cut and float hither a large amount of logs, which are converted into timber for transportation eastward. Gradually as the train moves along, it runs out of this sterile section, and patches of good land appear, which finally become general as the road passes upon the prairie and crosses the boundary between Ontario and the Province of Manitoba. The railway goes over the Whitemouth River, where more timber is concentrated and a sawmill is at work. All along the line is bordered by piles of faggots, the settlers hauling out the firewood from their clearings to be carried to market. The signs both of habitation and cultivation become more numerous, and Whitemouth boasts an hotel not large nor pretentious, but announcing, on a sign almost as big as the shanty that held it up, the important facts that it was an "hotel," a "billiard hall," was "licensed to sell liquors," and furnished "hot meals at all hours." The timber became scant, and soon the grass prairie was all about us with the grass burning in many places, fanned by the stiff westerly gale blowing. As we moved swiftly towards Winnipeg the number of houses increased and also the evidences of cultivation, until finally the train crossed over Red River and halted at the Winnipeg station, 1,423 miles west of Montreal, and 430 miles from Port Arthur.

The land into which we have now come belongs to an entirely different system from that through which the Canadian Pacific Railway passes into the older provinces of the Dominion. The Red River of the North is an affluent of Lake Winnipeg, and brings down to it a great amount of red clay-discoloured water in times of freshet which, by tinging the lake, gave it, in the figurative Indian language, the name of "Winnipeg," or the "Lake of the Dirty Water." This Red River rises in Minnesota, and has a tortuous course for nearly 800 miles, flowing first south, then west, and finally north to the lake. Its source is 1,680 feet above the sea, and the valley in Manitoba through which it meanders has an average elevation of about 700 feet. It is the boundary between Minnesota and Dakota in the States, and divides Manitoba into two unequal parts. Flowing through a prairie, its delta at the lake is in a region of fens, marshes, and muskegs, and it has no less than six mouths. Its affluents drain an immense number of small lakes, the chief among them being the Assiniboino river, named after an Indian tribe, and coming over 400 miles from the westward. This section of country and that to the north and north-west is as remarkable a basin of lakes as that drained by the St. Lawrence. The great Lake Winnipeg has tributaries from lakes and rivers that spread over and drain a basin of some 450,000 square miles. This lake is of irregular shape, 260 miles long and from six to 60 miles wide, covering 8,500 square miles and having 930 miles of coast line. Its surface is at 628 feet elevation above the sea, and it contains many islands. For so large a lake its shallowness is remarkable, the depth nowhere exceeding 70 feet. Besides the Red River, the Barens River enters this lake from the east, the Winnipeg river from the southeast, the Saskatchewan River from the north-west, and the Dauphin River brings in from the west the waters of Lakes Winnipegosis and Manitoba. On the northern side it has no affluents, but there discharges through the Nelson River to Hudson's Bay. This river is 350 miles long and passes a series of lakes and rapids, the latter rendering navigation almost impossible, though it discharges an immense amount of water into that great inland sea. Of the affluents of Winnipeg Lake, the Winnipeg River is 165 miles long, and flows north-west from the Lake of the Woods, discharging the waters of many lakes, and having rapids in its course which descend no less than 349 feet. The Saskatchewan River comes from the Rockies, where it has two sources flowing from different directions and joining to form the stream, which is 550 miles long, and drains a basin covering 240,000 square miles. Its name is a corruption of the Cree Indian words meaning "swift current." The Winnipegosis Lake is literally the "Little Winnipeg," although it is itself quite large, being 120 miles long, 25 miles broad, and covering 2,000 square miles. It discharges through the Water-Hen River into Lake Manitoba, above which its surface is elevated 20 feet. This latter lake is about 60 miles south-west of Lake Winnipeg, is 120 miles long and 20 to 22 miles broad, and covers 1,900 square miles. It discharges into Lake Winnipeg, whose surface is about 40 feet lower. The name of Manitoba was given to it by the Indians, who attribute a supernatural origin to a peculiar agitation of a portion of its surface, and hence named it the "Supernatural Strait." It will thus be seen that the Indian names of the chief of these lakes, which are themselves great bodies of fresh water, second only to the lakes drained by the St. Lawrence, are reproduced in the province of Manitoba and its capital city of Winnipeg.

Thomas Douglas, Earl of Selkirk, bought the greater part of the region now known as Manitoba to carry out a benevolent plan of settlement, and in 1812 began the Selkirk colony on the Red River, a few miles north of the present site of Winnipeg. About the same time the Hudson's Bay Company established its frontier trading post of Fort Garry, at the confluence of the Assiniboin with the Red River. The settlement did not flourish very much in its earlier history, but after the Canadian Pacific Railway was projected and work begun at construction, the town around Fort Garry grew amazingly, and the Provincial Government was formed. The temperature and climate here have a very wide range, varying from 40deg. below zero in winter to over 100deg. above in summer, but the dryness of the atmosphere prevents the cold being severely felt. In this level prairie land, however, they can get up winds that blow with startling force. A gentle zephyr of this sort greeted our arrival that made a sudden change in temperature of 10 degrees, blew clouds of dust around the streets of Winnipeg, and was so strong that it retarded the progress of the railway trains. The province of Manitoba is a parallelogram about 250 miles long, its general surface being a level prairie of the richest land, with soils that are among the most prolific on the continent. Its eastern and western borders are hilly, and the outcrop shows in some portions near Winnipeg, but the ridges of the Laurentian formation are not seen here as they were elsewhere in our progress across Canada. The chief settlements in the province are along the Red and Assiniboin Rivers, but emigration is rapidly filling up other portions, and the craze to trade in choice town sites and good agricultural lands has been exhibited here in times past to an extent exceeding even that seen in the mushroom frontier settlements in the States. Towns and villages are consequently springing up, and the new population going in will before long give the province many places that will rival in size those of Eastern Canada. The development of transportation facilities for this prolific region is being carried on by the Canadian Pacific Railway in an extensive way, their lines radiating from Winnipeg in seven different directions. There are lines northward on both sides of the Red River towards Lake Winnipeg, north-westward to valuable stone quarries, which furnish much of the building material used for the handsome edifices of the city, southward on both sides of the Red River to the United States boundary, where they connect with

American lines leading to St. Paul and Chicago; and also westward through the Turtle River country. This extensive system involves the establishment by the railway at Winnipeg of an elaborate central terminus, and consequently the yards, stations, shops, and necessary adjuncts of traffic cover some 200 acres in the northern portion of the city, and a large business is carried on, involving the employment of probably 1,000 men. The shops alone, which are fully fitted to care for all the rolling stock on the railway division out to the Rockies with repairs and renewals, are a series of large buildings equipped with the best machinery and facilities, and having 400 hands employed.

The earlier settlement of Manitoba was by the French and Indian half-breeds, who came here to cultivate the land, it then being under the rule of the Hudson's Bay Company. The rebellion of Riel and the half-breeds against the Dominion Government, when it first took possession, was in 1869-70, being finally suppressed by Wolseley's expedition in August of the latter year. The population was then comparatively small, but since that time the stream has been moving in from all directions and of all races, the rebellion having attracted general attention to the great fertility of the lands. The chief growth has been within the last five years, and the half-breeds now are but a fraction of the inhabitants, Riel and his following having gone far away to the north-west into the valley of the Saskatchewan, beyond the lakes, where his second rebellion occurred last year. The railway has been the mainspring in bringing people here, the advancement of the various settlements along the Red River and westward having been almost marvellous since the through line was opened. The construction of the road between Port Arthur and Winnipeg, with the branch southward from Winnipeg to Pembina, was undertaken as Dominion Government public works before the Canadian Pacific Railway was chartered in 1881, the unfinished portions being afterwards completed by the company. It was from Winnipeg as a base that the building of the long route westward to the Rockies was subsequently pushed forward and recently completed. The general appearance of settlements, buildings, and population in Manitoba is in some respects similar to what is seen in the thriving frontier towns of rapid growth in the States, but there seems to be more solidity here, and a better class of people. There can nowhere be learnt, however, a more impressive lesson of the value of a railway in opening a country; and it gives every indication of such steady increase that the traffic of this region alone will before long become so vast that it will tax the energies of more than one railway to manage it. The products of the province are of the widest range. In food the people no longer need outside supplies, but grow all their own meats, vegetables, and fruits, with large quantities to spare for shipment to less-favoured neighbours. The tall elevators that stand up at frequent intervals along the railway routes tell of the wheat this rich valley produces to send to all parts of the world. Train-loads of cattle and hogs raised on these prairies are sent eastward to Canada. The dairy interest is becoming so large that several towns are extensive exporters of butter and cheese. Manufacturing establishments are springing up, and, taken altogether, this prolific province seems, after the railway journey around the rock-bound coast of Lake Superior and the sterility on the height of land between its affluents and those of the Red River, to be literally the promised land for the Canadians.

IX. – Winnipeg and its neighbourhood

WINNIPEG, MANITOBA, Sept. 2.

The flourishing city of Winnipeg, which got its present name upon incorporation as a city about 13 years ago, is built on the prairie at the confluence of the Red and Assiniboin rivers, about 50 miles above or south of Lake Winnipeg and 90 miles north of the United States boundary. The rivers flow through narrow valleys with bluff shores rising some 30ft., but otherwise the surface is entirely level. The old trading post of Fort Garry stood near their junction, in a place where the winding Assiniboin gave pretty views. A crooked path northward, taken by the ox-teams going towards Selkirk and Lake Winnipeg, gradually broadened into the main street of the city, which is now a fine avenue of 132ft. width, well-paved with wood, and having wide sidewalks bordered with very good buildings, some of which are lofty and imposing architectural structures. Along this street the city extends for two miles, and it has been built over the adjacent prairie for a long distance in both directions, the suburb of St. Boniface being across Red River, and containing the home with the cathedral and convent of Archbishop Taché, whose careful guidance has had much to do with the history of this region. The castellated "Governor's Gate" is all that remains of the walls enclosing the old Hudson Bay Fort, and two or three rather dilapidated buildings preserve the memory of the post and its fur-trading, and the subsequent theatre of Riel's first rebellion, which began with the seizure of Fort Garry and its stores. The main street is carried over part of the enclosure and crosses the river beyond on a fine bridge, while the Hudson Bay Company has erected a row of splendid stores and offices along the street in which its large business, reaching an aggregate of £200,000 annually for this place alone, is now carried on. These stores cover much surface and have connected with them a grain elevator and shipping piers on the river. Winnipeg is the centre, not only of railway traffic for this section, but of a widely extended system of inland navigation, stretching in all directions along the streams and lakes tributary to Lake Winnipeg, and by portages far up northward and westward among the Rockies, and to the Mackenzie and Peace river regions and the Arctic circle. For hundreds and thousands of miles the boats and steamers of the Hudson Bay Company and its kindred interests penetrate this maze of waterways that are a network through the interior of the continent. The company stores here are the base of operations for this vast region, supplying the peculiar classes of goods needed for the Indian trading at the interior posts, and receiving the furs that are exchanged, which are packed and shipped to England. The great warehouses are filled with the goods that this traffic deals in, but the routes taken now to reach civilization with their product are char[?]ed. The Canadian Pacific Railway brings in the blankets and supplies from England, and takes back the furs and other results of the trade. In former times the only method of ingress and egress was by way of Hudson Bay, the Nelson river, and Lake Winnipeg, the transport being long and laborious, and only available during summer and early autumn.

Around this great store-house, but with many interests having no connexion with the Hudson Bay Company, this rapidly growing city of 27,000 to 30,000 people has been gathered in a few years. The old company no longer has its almost despotic sovereignty, having sold those rights with much of its territory to the Dominion Government for £300,000. Hence the sceptre has passed into the hands of the federal, provincial, and city Governments, respectively represented by very fine buildings, two of them, the Government Post Office and the City-hall, elaborate new structures of high architectural merit, being now almost completed. The Parliament-house is another fine building, adjoining which the provincial Governor has a comfortable residence. All the leading Canadian banks have large and imposing offices in Winnipeg, and there are many stores and other buildings of impressive appearance, while the suburbs, particularly along the Assiniboin and its beautiful shores, have attractive villas where the wealthier citizens have made their residences. I was surprised to see such an elaborate and active town so far away from the sea-board, and at the rate the new building is going on and the older wooden buildings are being replaced by newer structures of white brick and stone, both plentifully produced in the neighbourhood. Winnipeg will before long become one of the most attractive Canadian cities. The busy industry, push, and nervous activity of the people are much like that shown in an American town. Everybody is busy and on the *qui vive* to make money, and fabulous fortunes have been made here on the great advance in the prices of lands. During the recent "boom" which followed the advent of the railway every inhabitant seemed to be a land speculator, and hundreds of "syndicates" were formed for dealing in town lots and new sites for settlements. I was shown a shallow lot on Main-street, barely 25ft. front and narrowing towards the rear, which was then actually sold at the enormous figure of $78,000. The inflation has passed, however, and prices, though still high, have settled to a more stable basis. There are five churches that have cost $50,000 to $100,000 a-piece, and two colleges which are amply endowed foundations, with hospitals and other public buildings. The numerous large and attractive shops show trading to be brisk, for they are filled with most varied assortments of the newest goods, and the ladies wear the latest Paris fashions. The Manitoba Club is an extensive and complete establishment, modelled after the best London standard, and furnishing a good dinner, with two joints and every variety of vegetables, for a half-crown, so cheaply can food be obtained. Such is this wonderful interior Canadian city, which has suddenly grown up, almost like a product of Aladdin's lamp, on the fertile prairie more than 2,400 miles inland from the Atlantic Ocean.

Some of the Winnipeg prices will be of interest. In the retail market, the best roasts and steaks can be bought for 6d. to 8d. per lb; boiling pieces for 2½d to 4d; and the whole carcass dressed at 3½d to 4d. Pork is 5d. per lb.; veal, 6d.; mutton, 8d. to 9d.; ham, 7½d.; breakfast bacon, 6d. to 7½d.; lard and sausage 5d.; butter,

6d. to 7½d.; and fresh eggs, 6½d. to 7½d. per dozen. Of fish the supply is large and cheap, white-fish, a most delicious fish of the trout species, retailing at 2½d. per lb.; gold eyes, a good pan fish, at a shilling a dozen; and pike and pickerel at 1¼d. to 2d. per lb. Vegetables command per bushel, from two to three shillings for potatoes, 1s. to 1s. 6d. for turnips, and 5s. for carrots. Of corn products, oats are 15d. per bushel; No. 1 hard wheat, the best product of the Red River valley, 3s.; flour, 3s. 6d. to 10s. per cwt.; oatmeal, 8s. to 9s. Of live animals, good milch cows fetch £6 to £10; working oxen are in demand at £18 to £24 per yoke; and cattle live weight are sold for 11s. to 14s. per cwt. Hay sells at 24s. per ton, and straw at 4s. to 6s. The price of milk served in Winnipeg, however, notwithstanding the wealth of good land over which the cows can pasture, is kept up to the standard ruling in the Eastern cities, 4d. to 5d. per quart. There are thousands of cattle pasturing on the prairie near the town, wire fences being placed to protect them from the various lines of railway crossing the level land in different directions, but there is not much other fencing. The lands around Winnipeg are a level prairie, treeless, excepting along the river banks. They are used mainly for grazing, not being cultivated because speculators hold them at too high figures for the farmers to buy them. The dead level land, reaching as far as the eye can see, is unbroken, save by the deep gorges washed by the water courses, though about 12 miles north of Winnipeg they have a mountain. This Stony Mountain would not perhaps be dignified by such a title in some places, but to the inhabitants of this land of monotonous level there is such gratefulness felt at the relief to the vision afforded by what the Yankees call "a little rising ground," that the people are glad to have the chance of calling it a mountain. Stony Mountain is a long ridge of rock stretching across the country at about 60ft. to 80ft. elevation, and in it are the quarries whence the cream-coloured building stone is got that is so much used in Winnipeg, while bricks are made from the white clays of this region. From the ridge, which makes quite an imposing show and becomes a very respectable mountain in contrast with the level plain, an outlook is had over the prairie and the distant valley of the Red River, where the original Selkirk settlement is in a flourishing condition, the Scotch settlers having been very prosperous.

Upon the top of the ridge is located the Manitoba Penitentiary, where 100 to 150 convicts are confined, and though it is out on the open land, without enclosing walls of any kind, and the convicts, under guard, do all the outside work, the proportion of escapes is said to be less than from any other Canadian prison. Possibly this may be because they get more wholesome food and live in considerably more comfort than is usually the lot of the frontiersman. I was told that all nationalities were represented among the convicts, the Indians and half-breeds being rather the more numerous. The renowned Cree Indian chief Big Bear and two of his tribe are confined here for their complicity in the Frog Lake massacre during the late rebellion. Big Bear is a rather sedate-looking old gentleman of about 60 years of age, in his prison garb, and devotes his time to working in the garden where vegetables are grown for the prison, and feeding some bears that are kept in a pit, and have such liking for him that he goes freely into the den with them. The lately deceased chief Poundmaker was confined here, and the Penitentiary officials denied that the imprisonment was the cause of his death. They say that all Indians have weak lungs on account of the exposure of their mode of life, and that Poundmaker, on returning to his tribe, entered into the terrible ordeal of the "thirst dance," which was ordered in honour of his release, and, after the sedentary and enervating influence of his confinement, the tortures which are a prominent part of the ceremonies were too much for him, causing the hemorrhages from which he died. Warder Bedson, of the Penitentiary, has a herd of some 60 buffaloes that wander over a surface of about six square miles near the prison, which are said to be now about the only herd of buffaloes known in this country, as the race is almost extinct.

The vast prairie southward and westward of Winnipeg is a garden spot, rich with the varied flora in July, but now having only a few of the later flowers in bloom, while the grass is beginning to show the approach of the autumn. This prairie, in Canada, is said to extend hundreds of miles to the west and northwest, its limits being only circumscribed by the mountain spurs of the Rockies. The fertile belt is much broader than it is to the southward in the States, as the mountains trend westward, broadening the region, and the sterile alkali plains and the "Bad Land" region, which cover so much of the surface on the lines of the Union Pacific and the Northern Pacific Railways, do not extend in any appreciable degree across the boundary. The climate, too, as one proceeds westward from the lakes, becomes more moderate. In the Winnipeg region the snowfall in an average season does not exceed 18in. to 20in., being much less than in Eastern Canada, while it so quickly disappears that the spring opens early. The cattle can get their own subsistence from the prairie, excepting for about four months, when the snow covers the ground with a hard crust. The horses, by pawing, however, break through this, and thus at all times can get at the grass that comes up freshly beneath. It is this great fertile plain westward from the Red River that will make the fortune of Canada, and may rule the wheat market of the world when it becomes thoroughly settled. Already the Manitoba wheat supply has a great influence upon the American wheat markets, and is increasing to enormous proportions. Although the season was dry this year, the harvest now going on is very good, the grain being as fine as any yet produced. The straw was short, and all the sustenance seemed to go into the head. As the straw has to be got rid of by burning in this fertile region, its shortness is regarded rather as an advantage by the farmer. But while the wheat yield is large, it is said that very little profit will accrue to the tillers of the soil, as they are generally in debt to the machine men. Although the farmer lives in most frugal style, in a rude little cabin that will scarcely hold his family and presents small chance for comfort, yet he must have the most improved agricultural machinery. These machines are sold on easy terms of payment by the agents who traverse the country, and show great rivalry to make sales, so that most of the farmers' earnings go to these people until the debts are paid. The Dominion Government, which is the landholder here, encourages settlement by giving away tracts to homestead settlers, the same as in the United States.

Thus, much of the land that is eligible is already taken up, while the Canadian Pacific Railway is also a large holder, its lands being in the market. The Railway Land Commissioner, Mr. M'Tavish, has an extensive office in Winnipeg, with complete surveys showing the peculiarities, soils, and other features of the lands, and says that considerable amounts are being sold at from 8s. to 16s. an acre.

To open this great prairie, as already stated, various branch lines have been constructed in different directions from Winnipeg. The most extensive of these branches stretch towards the westward, and carry out an elaborate plan, whereby the region will be traversed by parallel routes located 20 to 30 miles apart, with other branches some distance westward from Winnipeg joining them again with the main line. This process of extension is going on upon two railways to the southward of the main line, one skirting the United States boundary, while a friendly company, the Manitoba and North-Western Railway, is constructing another parallel road some distance northward of the Canadian Pacific main line. This will give the great prairie ample railway facilities for a breadth of 100 to 150 miles, with prolongation indefinitely to the westward. Some of this enterprising railway construction is in advance of much settlement, but it shows its advantages by bringing the new settlers in. One of the Canadian Pacific branches has been pushed westward 85 miles, and another, which goes along the southern part of the province just north of the international boundary, 188 miles, and both are still building indefinitely westward. I made a journey to the end of the latter road, which passes through the most fertile portions of Southern Manitoba. It is laid out upon the prairie, at first southward towards the United States boundary, and then, turning westward, on a route near the border. Its whole line, with the exception of a few miles, is laid upon the level, treeless prairie, over which the sight is only limited by the horizon. The Pembina Mountains, a series of rounded hills, covered with small timber and much brush, break the continuity of the surface for a time, and among and near them the railway crosses the Pembina River, the gradient rising at this point probably 300ft. from a lower to a higher terrace of prairie—for, strangely enough, this great flat region is at different levels. The road crosses several watercourses, all seeking outlet in the Red River, and small towns have sprung up along the line. The country nearer Winnipeg is but sparsely settled, but beyond that the settlement is more general, and the many wheat-stacks and large herds of cattle show that the farmers are quite successfully pursuing their avocation. I was surprised to see the extent to which cattle-raising is carried on, and was informed that for 50 miles beyond the end of the line the population was large and the settlement general. The soil after leaving Winnipeg was black and sticky, but in the more remote portion it has an ashen hue. The stickiness of this soil makes locomotion difficult in wet seasons; but then, as Archbishop Taché shrewdly puts it, this should be no cause for complaint, because the "stickiness makes 40 bushels to the acre." The farmers along the line having cut and stacked their wheat, awaiting the threshing, were mostly engaged in ploughing to prepare for the next crop. We went to Boissevain, the terminus of the line, 188 miles south-west of Winnipeg. This is a brand-new town of small size but great expectations. It has an hotel, a store, and two or three shops; but a considerable portion of the inhabitants were yet living in tents, not having had time to build their cabins. Beyond the town, out on the prairie, the railroad builders were at work, and said they expected to put down 20 miles more of line before stopping operations for the season. Railway building is an easy operation in this flat country if the materials are brought in, for they have to come a great distance. It consists of setting out a line of stakes, throwing up the earth from each side of the line towards the centre, and then putting down the ties and rails. After a while the road gets thoroughly ballasted and settled, when it makes a good level piece of work. Considerable trestle bridging is required, as there are many streams and lakes. It is astonishing how quickly the little villages along the lines of new railway grow up into towns, with their great elevators standing up like landmarks in this vast level plain that, it is said, has room enough and fertility enough to support 20,000,000 people.

38

W. S. CAINE, *A TRIP ROUND THE WORLD IN 1887–8* (LONDON: G. ROUTLEDGE & SONS, 1888), PP. 92–118

The Selkirks

ON Monday, September 19th, we were roused from our beds at 4 o'clock A.M., as the westward bound daily train passed through Banff at five o'clock. At the station we met with the only instance of neglect of duty on the perfectly-ordered Canadian Pacific Railway. The station-master did not condescend to leave his warm bed to see the train off, and we had to carry our luggage ourselves from the omnibus to the luggage car, and let them go on unchecked to Field, our next stopping place. It was a cold, sleety morning, and the magnificent scenery through which we passed was not seen to the best advantage, as the tops of the mountains were enveloped in snow clouds. At seven we passed a station called Silver City. Three or four years ago there was a "boom" in silver mines in the Rocky Mountains; a good deal of exploration went on, and a considerable wooden village was built. But there was no "silver," and now there is no "city." Its glory has departed, and only the empty and deserted log-houses remain to tell of its butterfly existence. Shortly after, Mount Lefroy, a commanding snowy peak 11,658 feet above sea-level, comes into view, and presently the birthplace of the noble Bow River is discerned in a small glacier wedged in between Mount Hector and Goat Mountain, both over 10,000 feet. Then the highest point of the railway is reached, 5,300 feet above the sea, at the summit lake, marshy and shallow, from which trickles a stream at each end, one of which travels 2,000 miles to the Atlantic, and the other 1,500 to the Pacific Ocean. We now bid good-bye to the beautiful Bow River, which has been our genial companion for so many pleasant days, and under the shadow of Mount Stephen, the monarch of the Rocky Mountains, said to be over 12,000 feet, and named after the president of the Canadian Pacific Railway, we enter Kicking Horse Pass. This pass received its ridiculous name from an incident connected with some obstreperous horse ridden by one of the surveyors of the line, which will stick to it for ever. A magnificent view meets the gaze. A huge valley, filled from side to side with magnificent pines and cedars, their dark green intensified by the red-brown of huge areas burnt up by forest fires, in which the enormous trunks stand up like black masts 200 feet high, and 10 or 12 feet thick, is flanked by peak and pinnacle, the Kicking Horse River meandering through the bottom like a silver ribbon. The train, with two powerful engines reversed, and every brake screwed to its tightest, slides down a gradient of 1,250 feet in less than 10 miles. The road is cut out of the sides of great cliffs, hundreds of feet above the roaring torrent, and every now and then we crawl over a trestle bridge two or three hundred feet above some gorge torn out of the mountain side by a rushing torrent. At nine o'clock we draw up at Field Station, a lonely post in the heart of the Rocky Mountains, where the Canadian Pacific Railway Company have built a comfortable little hotel, at which we decide to stay for 24 hours. It was a great comfort to know, as we came down this terrible descent, that we were travelling on rails made from good honest Cumberland Hæmatite. I have noted, with interest, but without surprise, that the word "Barrow" always appeared on the rails which the Canadian Pacific Railway have laid down in dangerous places, or where there is specially heavy wear and tear.

We found the hotel at Field one of the most comfortable and well-ordered hotels in Canada, and the manager at once claimed acquaintance with me as having "voted for me when I stood for Liverpool." Our party, consisting of four officers from the Fleet at Esquimault, Mr. F. W. Gibbs, Q.C., a most delightful and charming travelling companion, a young friend of his, my daughter, and myself, very nearly filled the little hostelry, which we had to ourselves. After an excellent breakfast, the materials for which were brought from Calgary, 130 miles away, the nearest town where a shop exists, we sallied forth to view the magnificent scenery. The landlord informed us that he had the day before set a snare for mountain goats, and invited us to go up the mountain for a mile or so, to see if any had been caught. All went except my daughter and myself, and we started off for a walk down the line, the railway being actually the only path of any kind for 30 miles each way through the dense forest which everywhere clothes the mountain sides, and which is practically impassable. About a mile from the station the valley narrowed to a very small space, with the Kicking Horse River running quietly between two gravelly banks. Here we saw a very fine bear on the other side of the river, coming in and out of the woods, seemingly hunting for something on the gravel beds. Just at that moment three or four men from Field, line inspectors, came up on a hand trolly, and we called their attention to the bear. They at once turned back to the Field Station, begging us to follow down the line keeping Mr. Bear in sight, as he showed himself every now and then out of the wood, while they fetched a miner who owned a Winchester rifle, and who was a crack shot. In about half-an-hour he arrived. We had seen the bear frequently, and pointed out the spot where we had last noticed him. The owner of the rifle at once plunged up to the middle in the icy river, waded across, and entered the wood stealthily. In a few minutes the bear trotted out on the gravel, much perturbed in his mind. Presently he seemed reassured, and began to grub in the ground with his nose. Then the hunter crept out of the bushes till he was well within range. Taking aim, he gave a shrill whistle; the startled bear threw up his head, and in a moment he was shot through the heart, and all was over. The others then rushed through the river, dragged him back through the water, and presently he was laid on the trolly in triumph. He was a fine "silver-tip" bear, about as big as a large calf, with very formidable teeth and claws. I have his skin, which I shall get dressed into a hearthrug when I reach Victoria.

On Tuesday morning, the 20th, we again took train, and journeyed as far as "Glacier House," another comfortable little hotel erected by the Canadian Pacific Railway at the foot of the great glacier which comes down from the eternal snowfields of Mount Sir Donald, the highest peak of the Selkirk Range, about 11,000 feet above the sea, named after one of the directors and first promoters of the railway, Sir Donald Smith. We reached it at noon, and after lunch started off to explore the glacier, to the foot of which a trail has been cleared. It is a fine and imposing glacier, half-a-mile wide, and seven or eight miles long, but bearing no comparison whatever with such vast ice fields as the Gomer or Aletsch glaciers in Switzerland. It was covered with fresh snow, and looked very beautiful in the bright sunlight Mount Sir Donald has never yet been climbed, and there is a legend at the hotel that the first man to reach the summit will receive a thousand dollars and a free pass over the line for his life, from the directors of the Canadian Pacific Railway. In the opinion of my friend Mr. Gibbs, Q.C., who is a member of the Alpine Club, the thousand dollars may be pocketed by the first smart Alpine Clubbist who comes along, and certainly to my comparatively inexperienced eye it did not seem impossible to an active Cumberland shepherd. It is however a superb mountain.

The scenery of the Selkirk Range is finer in all respects than the Rocky Mountains, which are devoid of glaciers, and also of any extent of snow fields. From the railway platform at Glacier House there is a view which rivals any of the notable Swiss cycloramas, and I counted at least a dozen fine peaks, all of which appeared to be at least 10,000 feet high, and whose flanks bore miles of snow fields and many picturesque, though comparatively small glaciers. The Hermit Range, so named from its fancied resemblance to a Monk of St Bernard followed by his dog, is as fine a group of snow mountains as the world can furnish.

Next morning we walked up the line to see the great snow sheds, and some of the trestle bridges which span the cataracts rushing down the sides of these magnificent mountains. One of these bridges is 176 feet high and 600 feet long, and another crossing the Canyon of Stoney Creek is 296 feet high and 450 feet long. These structures are truss bridges supported upon great timber towers, built up from the bottom of the valley far below, and Stoney Creek Bridge is the highest timber railway bridge in the world. The whole structure is of wood, cut from the forests through which the railway travels.

The snow sheds are solid buildings of crib work and piling, with very strong roofs of two courses, one of logs and another of planks, strongly backed with heavy stone work. These sheds are placed along the line wherever the devastated track of a "snow slide" or avalanche appears on the mountain side. It is impossible to describe adequately the tremendous power of these Selkirk avalanches. Enormous volumes of snow gather during the winter in some hollow high up the mountain side, and in spring rush down with a force which nothing can resist into the valley below. Everything is swept before them—trees of the largest size, boulders, soil, brushwood, are torn up and tumbled into a confused mass at the bottom of the valley. The wind caused by the avalanche is almost as resistless as the slide itself, and the trees on each side of its track for a wide area are broken into matchwood. These slides have been a great difficulty and danger to the line, and have caused stoppage of the traffic for weeks at a time, besides much loss of life. But now the trains run through the snow sheds, and their powerful roofs, inclined to the angle of the slide, enables the snow and debris to shoot harmlessly over. There are still some 3,000 men at work along the line at these various snow sheds, some of which are over half a mile long, and their many canvas encampments form picturesque incidents in the scenery through which the line passes. The Canadian Pacific Railway Company engage to feed and lodge them for four dollars a week, and right well these fellows live, with three good meat meals a day, and the finest air in the world for sauce.

During the morning we walked back up the line to Rogers Pass, the highest point reached by the railway in crossing the Selkirk Range. Here is a collection of wooden shanties, used as liquor-saloons, music and dancing-houses, and places of worse resort still, to which the more loose-living of these workmen resort. I found, however, that the bulk of them were steady, sober men, intent on saving their surplus wages, and on the look-out for favourable chances in this new country. There was a good deal of snow at Rogers Pass, which is a narrow gorge closely hemmed in by lofty snow-clad mountains.

Leaving Glacier House on Wednesday, 21st, we found attached to the train one of the handsome private travelling carriages which are used by directors and officials on the long lines which cross the American Continent, and which are travelling homes of both comfort and luxury. Shortly after starting, a coloured servant brought me a card bearing the name of Mr. Baker, the General Superintendent of the Manitoba and North-Western Railway, a line which opens up a fine agricultural district north of the Canadian Pacific Railway. Mr. Baker wished my daughter and me to ride through the beautiful scenery of the Selkirk range in his-carriage, which, being at the tail of the train, commanded a clear view, and he also asked us to dine with him afterwards. He first showed us over his car, in which he lives all the year round for nine days out of fourteen travelling up and down his line. It was a carriage somewhat longer than a North-Western first-class coach. It was divided into a dining-room, large drawing-room, kitchen, pantry, and two comfortable bedrooms, all handsomely furnished, with a small platform or terrace at each end, on one of which was kept the stores in ice-lined boxes, and the other was a sort of balcony on which to sit and view the passing scenery. An admirable dinner was served, consisting of soup, oysters, roast beef, two vegetables, pudding, and dessert, with a cup of excellent coffee. Mr. Baker was taking a holiday with some English friends. The car was shunted at any station along the line which they wished to visit, and the party were enjoying excellent opportunities for sport on the many lakes along the prairie, the resorts of a great variety of wild-fowl, as well as being able to see the whole scenery of the Rockies and the Selkirks by daylight, by hooking on to freight and ballast trains. We left them behind about ten o'clock, p.m. on an arm of the great Shuswap Lake, where they had good duck shooting next day, while Mr. Baker killed six trout over 2 lbs. each. Soon after quitting Glacier House Station, the railway descends 600 feet in two miles of actual distance. This is done by utilizing two ravines which meet at right angles, and is a triumph of engineering skill. The line runs along one side of the first gorge for about a mile, then crosses a high bridge, and comes back along the other side close to where it started, but on a much lower level; thence it runs into the opposite side 120 feet below its entrance, yet only 130 feet further down the pass; then it doubles upon itself in the main valley, crosses the river, and presently recrosses. From the top of these loops one can view six almost parallel lines of railway, each at a lower level than the others, and the whole largely composed of trestle bridges and elaborate timber cribbing. It is a wonderful sight to stand at the top and watch a train twist in and out of this succession of loops like some hissing snake. The whole forms a remarkable feat of engineering skill.

Morning found us in the Gold Range, running down the valley of the Thompson River, a tributary of the great Fraser River, into which it flowed at Lytton, a colony of gold miners. The Gold Range is not so lofty as either the Selkirks or the Rockies. There are no glaciers at all, but many of the peaks are snow-capped, and the sides of the mountains have a much greater variety of timber, giving a richness and depth of colour which is more beautiful than the dark greens of the loftier ranges. As we descend the slopes, and get into the valley of the great Fraser River, we reach the better settled parts of British Columbia, and the landscape is brightened by farmsteads, Indian villages, and Chinese camps, engaged in the three leading industries of the country—farming, salmon preserving, and mining. Every now and then a group of Indians would be seen, ingeniously hanging dried salmon on trees in such fashion that bears or other climbing animals cannot reach them. This is the country of big trees and endless forest, which must eventually become the main timber supply of the whole American Continent, as the vast and increasing population of the States consumes its own limited and rapidly decreasing lumber districts. All through British Columbia the summer is warm and rainless, and its forests are scourged by continual fires, mainly the result of careless Indians and other dwellers in tents. We saw many of these forest fires, for which, when near the line, probably sparks from Canadian Pacific Railway engines are mainly responsible. In ordinary pine woods they rage through the brushwood and undergrowth, the big trees escaping with a scorching, which does not seem greatly to injure them, except in appearance. But wherever there are big cedars the flames burn merrily, and everything is destroyed. The trunks of these trees become hollow and decayed, and when they are reached by the fire they draw like a factory chimney, and the trunk falling, with its 200 feet long in blaze, gives the fire a fresh start. It is surprising with what speed this genial climate fills up the blackened spaces with fresh vegetation, and ten or twelve years replaces the fallen giants with thriving children which an English park might feel very proud to raise in thirty years of growth.

Sometimes these fires are disagreeably hot to the passengers on board the train, as they rush through them at the rate of 25 miles an hour. On one occasion a whole train, except one carriage, was entirely destroyed. The engine driver was running through as usual, when he ran quietly off the rails into the middle of the track. The heat of the fire had expanded the rails and warped them. The passengers were all got out easily enough, as it is possible to walk from one end of an American train to the other, and no one was seriously injured except the conductor, who was badly burned in trying to get out the mails. They managed to get away the end car, a Pullman sleeping car, but the rest of the train added itself to the ashes of the forest fire.

It is, however, after all but a small percentage of these vast forests which fall under this scourge, and every station affords proof, by the quantity of logs, dressed timber, and firewood waiting despatch, that the new railway is laying the foundation for one of the biggest lumber trades in the world.

Up the valley of the Fraser, and afterwards up the Thompson, runs the only waggon road in British Columbia, from New Westminster to Cariboo, the centre of the gold-mining district, round which there are also several flourishing settlements of farmers. This road was made by the Government of British Columbia at very great cost, and the lower portion of it is now superseded, so far as through traffic is concerned, by the Canadian Pacific Railway. The traffic on this road is carried on by waggons drawn by teams of oxen, ten or twelve yoked together, and it is also used by Indians moving their camps from point to point after salmon and game of various kinds.

The Fraser River is the chief watercourse of British Columbia, rising in the far north of the Rocky Mountains, and is navigable for about 120 miles from the sea. The railway follows it for 250 miles, giving an infinite variety of beautiful scenery. Now it flows through some deep and rocky ravine, foaming and tumbling in a series of rapids and falls, then flowing in rippling stream and placid pool, forming sand bars which are being washed over for gold by the industrious heathen Chinee, and other "placer" miners, and presently broadening into a noble river, navigable by steamboats, dotted by Indian canoes salmon fishing, and bordered by variegated timber ablaze with autumn gold and copper, with every now and then a comfortable homestead farm and herds of fine cattle. At New Westminster, 15 miles from the mouth, it widens into a stream two miles across, from whence it distributes its wealth in ocean ships and steamers all over the world. I saw a vessel leave New Westminster for London with 2,200 tons of tinned salmon on board.

We got out on the morning of the 22nd, at the little roadside station of Agassiz, that we might spend 24 hours on Harrison Lake, a sheet of water 50 miles long, in the heart of the best district of British Columbia. We drove in a waggon some six miles over the very worst road I ever saw in my life, to a new hotel which has just been built on the edge of the lake, the only house upon its beautiful shores, but which we found very comfortable and scrupulously clean. The lake is surrounded by two ranges of mountains, the first densely wooded to the summit, the second bare and snowcapped. The scenery is about half way between Windermere and Como. With the exception of the rough track from the station, there is not a footpath which does not end 100 yards from the hotel in dense impenetrable forest. We spent the day on the lake, exploring its beauties, and occasionally trying for a big trout, but only catching one very small one of remarkable beauty.

The next day we went on to Vancouver, the Pacific terminus of the Canadian Pacific Railway, and brought to a close a railway journey of over 3,000 miles, which, whether for human interest or natural beauty, far exceeds any previous journey of my life.

Vancouver is the youngest town in Canada. It was commenced less than three years ago, when it was a forest of Douglas pines, cedars, and spruce, of enormous size. I measured one stump which had been sawn off about 6 feet from the ground, and it was 11 feet 8 inches across. In June last year, after it had reached a respectable infancy, Vancouver was completely burnt down, not a house escaping, so that the present "city," as the Vancouverites insist on calling it, is just fifteen months' old. It is of course still a wooden town, but several fine brick and stone buildings are already erected, and many are rapidly reaching completion. The Canadian Pacific Railway Hotel is a handsome building, almost ready for opening, which will accommodate some 200 guests. Extensive wharves and warehouses line the shore, and ocean-going steamers of 3,000 or 4,000 tons can load and discharge there. The main street is full of handsome shops, and there is a busy, hardworking population of 4,000 souls, mostly men. Vancouver will be a town of 20,000 or 30,000 population before it is ten years old.

39

JAMES FRANCIS HOGAN, *THE SISTER DOMINIONS: THROUGH CANADA TO AUSTRALIA BY THE NEW IMPERIAL HIGHWAY* (LONDON: WARD AND DOWNEY, 1896), PP. 91–96

Over the Rockies

FROM Regina to Calgary, a stretch of about 500 miles, the Canadian Pacific Railway runs through a splendid ranching country, great heaps of buffaloes' skulls and skeletons, visible at intervals from the carriage windows, telling of the success and completeness with which the great animal monarch of North America has been practically exterminated in order to make room for horses, sheep, and cattle. The ranches continue in almost unbroken succession right up to the base of the Rocky Mountains, covering the foothills, and occupying the intervening valleys. The scriptural allusion to cattle grazing on a thousand hills is at once recalled to the memory and realized with literal accuracy as the train commences its long and arduous climb to the summit of the great dividing range. At Calgary, a handsome and go-ahead town of 5000 inhabitants, called into being by the requirements of the numerous ranches for hundreds of miles around, the ascent of the Rockies may be said to begin, although their snow-clad peaks and serrated lines, stretching away as far as the eye can travel along the southern and western horizon, are by no means so close at hand as they look. The iron horse has to puff and pant for several hours yet before the Rockies are strictly and actually reached. Another engine is there in readiness to assist the train up the steepest sections of the formidable series of mountain barriers that seem to set all engineering skill and science at defiance. But here, as elsewhere, man has proved himself more than a match for the most Titanic forces of Nature. Tremendous yawning abysses have been successfully bridged, pathways for the passage of the locomotive have been hewn and blasted out of the sides of appalling precipices; long, narrow, and sinuous gorges, environed by walls that shoot up straight for hundreds, and in some places thousands, of feet, have been compelled to pay a sufficient tribute of territory to the conquering engineer; and the host of obstacles thrown in the way of his advance by rushing rivers, foaming cataracts, snow, ice, and colossal rocks have been overcome and removed by patience, perseverance, and scientific ingenuity.

The scenery throughout these 500 miles of mountain locomotion is indescribably grand and impressive—snow-clad ranges, sun-illumined glaciers, beautifully-wooded mountain-sides, awe-inspiring canons, fantastically-shaped peaks, raging torrents, and charming cascades succeeding each other in panoramic variety and interest. To enable the passengers to enjoy this glorious scenic banquet to the full, an "observation car," or carriage open on all sides, is attached to the train, and affords facilities for an unobstructed and satisfying view. The stations in this Alpine region represent either spots of special attractiveness, where hotels have been erected for the accommodation of excursionists, or mining townships that have sprung up in the vicinity of gold, silver, or coal deposits, for the Rocky Mountains constitute a rich and still largely undeveloped mineral region, as well as a theatre of unsurpassable scenic wonders and delights.

The province of the Canadian Dominion that lies between the Rocky Mountains and the Pacific may claim the credit of having practically called the great Trans-continental railway into existence, for British Columbia, before agreeing to join the Canadian Confederation, stipulated that a railway should be constructed to connect her with the Eastern Provinces, and, furthermore, that it should be commenced within two years from the date of joining the Dominion. Sir John Macdonald (the father of the Federation) persuaded the first Parliament of the Dominion to agree to these terms, although the proposal was strenuously opposed by the Liberals, who contended that the projected line had never been properly surveyed, and that the cost of its construction would tie a tremendous mill-stone of debt around the neck of the infant Dominion. Sir John, having carried a Bill to provide for the construction of the railway, dissolved the House, and appealed to the country to ratify his policy in the matter. The country endorsed his action, strengthened his hands, and solidified the growing federation. Thus the Canadian Pacific Railway was started into being—a permanent bond of union between the scattered provinces of the Dominion, as well as a monumental piece of successful engineering—in the teeth of the most formidable and terrific of natural difficulties. British Columbia did good business for itself, as well as the Dominion, in stipulating for the construction of the railway as an indispensable condition to its entering the Union. By the Rocky Mountains barrier it was practically isolated from the rest of British America, and the avenues for trade and commerce open to it in other directions were not particularly promising. The Canadian Pacific Railway has not only brought it into close and regular communication with the Eastern Provinces, but has enabled it to establish a very profitable connection with China, Japan, and Australia. The large and prosperous city of Vancouver has been created by the railway. It is the western terminus of the line, and from its capacious and picturesque harbour luxurious steamers are now regularly plying to Chinese, Japanese, and Australian ports. Walking through the streets of this extensive city, bordered with long rows of well-appointed shops and business houses, with suburbs full of charming residences, and electric railway cars racing through all the leading thoroughfares, it is very difficult to realize that a few years ago the whole site was covered with a dense forest. Victoria, at the southern extremity of Vancouver Island, is the political capital of British Columbia, and also a place of considerable trade. It is a much more compact and English-looking city than Vancouver, but the latter has a much superior commercial position, and is obviously destined to rival San Francisco, and to develop into the most important British centre on the American side of the Pacific. There is a large Chinese quarter in Victoria, and the Mongolians appear to have captured a considerable amount of the business of the place. At Vancouver I noticed a number of shops displaying announcements that Chinese were not employed on the premises, and were in no way concerned in the business, a straw significant of an effort to divert public opinion into a channel hostile to the continued employment of the "heathen Chinee." But nothing short of a prohibitory poll-tax will keep Chinamen out of British Colonies. Once they get there, the amazing adaptability of their race, the readiness with which they pick up trades, their rigidly economical mode of life, their capacity for living and sleeping in the smallest possible space, and their freedom from domestic ties and responsibilities, give them an immense and unique advantage over all other competitors in the various fields of labour and industry. In addition to Vancouver and Victoria, British Columbia possesses a third important centre in New Westminster, whose inhabitants plume themselves on the fact that the title of their city was specially selected by Her Majesty the Queen.

When I arrived in British Columbia, I found the leader of the Liberal Party in the Dominion House of Commons, the Hon. Wilfred Laurier, engaged on a political speaking tour through the principal towns of the West, a rally being deemed advisable in view of the approach of a General Election. The Liberals have not been in power in Canada since 1878, and they naturally think it is about time for their long period of banishment from the Treasury benches to come to an end. Sixteen years' exclusion from office is the penalty they have had to pay for their uncompromising adherence to the principles and policy of Free Trade. Some bye-elections they have recently won have encouraged them in the hope that the ardour of Canadian devotion to Protection—the "national policy" adopted and legalized by Sir John Macdonald and the Conservatives—is beginning to cool.

40

GEORGE EDWARD WRIGHT, *A CANADIAN TOUR: A REPORT OF LETTERS FROM THE SPECIAL CORRESPONDENT OF THE* TIMES (LONDON: GEORGE EDWARD WRIGHT, 1886), PP. 22–29

Opening a new country

BINSCARTH, MANITOBA, Sept. 3.

The fertile and attractive province of Manitoba, over which we have been going, extends westwards from Winnipeg about 188 miles by an air line to the boundary of the North-West Territory. By the winding line of the Canadian Pacific Railway the distance to this boundary is about 211 miles west from Winnipeg. The land for the whole distance is a prairie, sometimes rolling, but presenting throughout the same characteristics of rich fertile soil and the ability to support an almost limitless population. This great wheat-growing and cattle-raising prairie west of the Red River valley is the country to the development of which the best energies of Canadian statesmanship are now directed. The method of doing this in practice I have partially explained in describing the new railways that are being extended through Southern and South-Western Manitoba. But probably the best exhibition that can be given of the restless spirit of enterprise that animates the pioneers on the Canadian frontier and the capitalists, both in this country and in England, who furnish the means for carrying out the vast plans of colonization and settlement that are entertained for the now country is shown in the construction of the railway that is going through North-Western Manitoba to the wilderness beyond. We resume our journey westward from Winnipeg upon the Canadian Pacific route over the level prairie northward of the Assiniboin River. It is a monotonous, treeless expanse whereon large cattle herds are roaming, patches of the grass having been burnt over, and, after traversing 56 miles, we come to the village of Portage La Prairie, having about 2,000 inhabitants. In olden times the Indians, and afterwards the *voyageurs* of the Hudson's Bay Company, had a portage here across the prairie from the Assiniboin River about a dozen miles to Lake Manitoba, thus reaching a vast inland navigation leading far northward through the Saskatchewan River.

The country for a long distance around Portage La Prairie is a section of good farming and long settlement, the old trails through here having brought inhabitants before the railway was thought of. The threshing is going on in all directions, there are large cattle herds and every evidence of agricultural thrift. The farmers live in good buildings and have extensive shelters with straw-thatched roofs for their animals, this not being found to any extent in Southern Manitoba. The whole country seems to be under cultivation, the fields being fenced and rotation of crops practised, wheat, oats, and root crops varying with grass. The lands are quoted from £2 to £4 per acre. There is a considerable Indian village, numerous Sioux living in their wigwams at the edge of the town, the braves, however, having donned the clothing of the white man. There are also wheat elevators for the reception of the crop and storage until shipment, and a flour mill, the people having learnt the economy of making their own flour out of their own wheat. A brewery also flourishes at Portage La Prairie, which is said to have more orders for beer than it can fill, showing, as they told me, the advanced civilization of the people. From Winnipeg and the Assiniboin there is laid out the famous trail to the North-West through Portage La Prairie, that leads far away to Edmonton and Prince Albert on the Saskatchewan River, some 500 miles distant in the North-West Territory. This trail or road, at first for the Indians and afterwards for the freighters and traders, is now being superseded by the railway constructed by joint Canadian and British enterprise. It takes no small amount of energy to build a first-class railway through an almost unexplored wilderness, but knowing that this route led into a country of great fertility this road has been undertaken.

The "Manitoba and North-Western Railway" has been laid out north-westwardly from Portage La Prairie towards Prince Albert, following in general the route of the trail above mentioned, and already the construction has proceeded to the western boundary of Manitoba. This company was originally started by the late Sir Hugh Allan, of Montreal, and his family and relatives are now its chief promoters. At the close of the present season the expectation is that 180 miles will be completed, including the difficult crossing of the Assiniboin River, at the western boundary of Manitoba, and its confluent streams, and to-day 159 miles of the route are actually completed and in running order, with the grading about finished to the termination of the new line contemplated for this season. The intention is to continue building the railway at the rate of about 50 miles annually until Prince Albert is reached. The Dominion Government encourage this enterprise with a subsidy of 6,400 acres of land for each mile completed, and the company has negotiated a loan in England at the rate of $14,600 per mile (the mortgage also including all the equipment and the unsold lands) at 5 per cent. interest for five years, and afterwards at 6 per cent. The proceeds of lands sold go first to meet interest and afterwards for the redemption of the principal of the debt. The present issue of this loan is £390,000, and enough lands are already sold to pay this year's interest. To examine the method of opening the new country I went on this line out to the end of the track. The route begins at Portage La Prairie, and is laid upon the level prairie south of Lake Manitoba, following up the valley of a stream of exceeding perversity and crookedness which is an affluent of that lake and is known by the not very taking title of the White Mud River. The channel of this stream is being dredged up to the railway so that navigation may be carried on connecting the railway with the lake and its extensive system of interior waters, this improvement being a Government enterprise. The first station of importance on this new railway is named Gladstone, standing on the White Mud River some 1,400 miles from Montreal. It is a village of about 70 houses, and has a weekly newspaper, it is said of decided Tory proclivities—the *Gladstone Age*. The original name of this nearly new town was Palestine, but the popular feeling was so strongly shown against this cognomen that Gladstone was substituted. It has a fine station and refreshment room, a big water tank, and the most vigorous windmill on the line was engaged in doing the pumping when we passed along. It will probably be gratifying to Mr. Gladstone to know that one Manitoba wheatfield at his town has this year produced a crop averaging 55 bushels to the acre. The general average of this region, however, is about 25 bushels this season, though the grain is unusually heavy, weighing 62lb. to 65lb. per bushel.

    The route beyond Gladstone passes into a wooded region, and goes through the County of the Beautiful Plains. There is upon the surface of the country a most unusual formation. A broad, level, grass-covered plain stretches northward as far as the eye can see, bordered upon either hand by timber, one side being poplar and the other side chiefly oak. The rows of timber are about 2,000 feet apart, and this stretches northward, it is said, for 40 miles. It looks like a broad race-course cut out of a low forest, and was formerly a favourite resort of the buffalo. The land is poor and the soil chiefly gravel. The railway traverses this plain for about three miles and then by a bend leaves it, suddenly going into an entirely different region of rolling wooded prairie developing far to the northward into the heavily timbered ridges of the Riding Mountains, which loom up at the horizon. This is a fine country, with rich soil, and one of the best wheat-growing sections of Manitoba. The settlements are frequent, and we come to the little station of Neepawa, which in the figurative language of the Cree Indian signifies "abundance." This is a small village set on the side of a hill, crowned by the most pretentious building of all, which we are told is the Court-house. At almost all the stations there are tall grain elevators ready to receive the wheat crop of the country, each elevator bearing the name of its owner in huge letters that can be seen for at least a mile across the prairie. Ogilvie, the enterprising miller of Montreal and several other towns, has the most of these elevators thus dropped among the Manitoba wheatfields. The railway ascends heavy grades towards the more remote but higher table-lands of the North-West and approaches the Little Saskatchewan River. The town of Minnedosa was located in this region before the railway came along, the fact that the North-Western trail crossed the river ford at this place gathering two or three cabins. The railway came through in 1883, and the little settlement has expanded to a town of a thousand people, which is steadily growing. These far north-western rivers pass through the prairie in deep gorges, and it has taken skilful engineering to make this crossing. The railway builders search the country adjacent to the rivers for a long *coulée*. This is the scoured out valley of an extinct tributary stream, and by availing itself of the notch thus cut into the side of the gorge, which sometimes extends for miles away from the stream, the railway route is successfully carried over. The Little Saskatchewan River is a narrow and winding stream, subject to heavy freshets, and it brings down a vast number of logs to give occupation to the Minnedosa saw-mills. The town is set in a basin, surrounded by an amphitheatre of hills, and as the railway rises again on the other side a grand view is given over the river valley and the town below. The railway climbs up the grade to an elevation of about 1,900ft. above the sea to get upon the higher table-land beyond, the route being carved out of the hillside composed of much gravel and boulders.

There are little lakes upon this elevated prairie, and wild birds abound, for the sportsman has not yet done much in this remote region to disturb them. The shooting is very good—ducks, geese, plover, grouse, prairie chickens, snipe, and other birds being abundant. There is considerable settlement here, mainly by emigrants from Ontario province, with some Germans and Scandinavians, and the omnipresent Scotch, who are the most persistent developers of the new country. We reach Shoal Lake, where the train obligingly halts long enough for one of our companions to go out and shoot a wild duck. This is a beautiful sheet of water about six miles long, where a hotel is to be built to make the great summer resort of the far North-West. A site has been selected in a pleasant grove near the shore. This lake is elevated about 1,700ft., and the railway, which came along last year, has made near by a representative village of some 100 people, just ten months old. As no town, however small, is without its weekly newspaper in this enterprising country, I called upon the editor of the *Shoal Lake Echo*, started in May last, and found that he combined in himself the editor, compositor, and pressman, and was also the architect and builder of his newspaper office. He had a circulation of 300 copies at 6s. a year in the country round about, and was happy. This new little town and its dependent region expect to give the railway 100,000 bushels of wheat to export this season, and the managers say the whole section the railway serves will produce about 1,000,000 bushels from the very good crop just harvested. Thus we run out along this railway, and finally get upon the new track which has just been laid and is still unballasted. Moving carefully down another *coulée*, we cross the valley of Bird-tail Creek, an affluent of the Assiniboin, and beyond this go up to the top of the hill again to the station for the village of Birtle, which has 500 people living down in the valley along the creek. Here is one of the Dominion Emigration offices, and shelter sheds for the arriving settler who has no place for temporary refuge. Next there comes difficult engineering to carry the line across the Assiniboin and two or three streams that flow into it. Broad. airy. and rather startling timber trestle bridges carry it over deep valleys, and these difficulties of construction unusual in a prairie country make it a costly line to build. The engineers take the road over the Silver Creek, a deep valley, by a ponderous and lofty trestle bridge, and as they are then at an elevation of nearly 500ft. above the Assiniboin river they seek a long *coulée* to carry the line down.

It is through this, Johnson's *coulée*, that the builders are now working, and we go out over the unballasted rails that have just been laid upon the newly graded surface, the train giving a peculiarly rockaway sensation as it slowly moves out to the railway builders, and approaches what is known as the "end of the track." Here we halted for the night, sleeping in the railway coaches near Binscarth with the fresh breezes fanning us upon this remote border of north-western Manitoba, 1,538 miles west of Montreal.

Thus are railways opening up the new country, and in the morning we started out to see how they worked at constructing the new line. The long and winding embankment for the railway was cut into the hillside of the *coulée* as far as eye could see, gradually descending to the Assiniboin, which flows through a broad and deep valley worn into myriads of fissures by these abandoned stream-beds which run in every direction, while great bare round-topped hills rise high above. The brown grass and the steep and rounded formations give the scene much the appearance of a bit cut out of the Scottish Highlands. We passed Johnson's little cabin and saw him milking his cow, an Englishman who had not long ago come out to settle in the new country, and gave his name to this great *coulée*. Then, as we moved along down the ravine the various processes were seen that contribute to complete a new railway. We had come from the end of the unballasted track, and in a sheltered nook found the temporary village of part of the railway builders, who were encamped in tents like an army. There were ox-teams, wagons, and horses in large numbers, busily at work unloading ties and timber from the construction train just ahead, to carry them forward to the builders. In this veritable Arab village they said they were getting good living, as supplies were abundant and cheap, beef costing but 3½d. to 4d. per lb., butter 5d., eggs 5d. per dozen, and milk 2½d. per quart. The end of the telegraph wire was carried into one of the tents to make a temporary office, while beyond the poles were being set up and the wires stretched for a further extension of the line. Passing the construction train, which was sending a steady procession of teams forward with timber and ties, we came upon the "spiking gangs," who were fastening the newly-laid rails to the ties, and then in front of them to the "rail-layers," who were moving their carload of rails forward and carrying out rail after rail on each side to lay upon the ties, which stretched out in a long row before us. At some distance ahead, the end of the row of ties was reached where men were arranging more of them in order, from the piles which the teams deposited at the roadside. In advance of this there was only the graded line, with frequent little bridges and trestles which the carpenters were completing. Then further on were pile drivers setting the piles that were to give secure foundation for more trestles, and, finally, we came to another village of tents, where a brigade of men were building a huge trestle 800 feet long. The railway had been laid out along the *coulée* for several miles, and now at a favourable point turned to cross it by this great trestle bridge. Beyond, the engineers were adjusting the surface of the grade, which still proceeded downward towards the Assiniboin. We drove along the rough and uneven hillside road, worn into ruts by the teams, at times in danger of slipping down into the railway cuttings, and finally came out of the *coulée* to a point where there was a good view over the wide valley of the Assiniboin, furrowed with knolls and fissures, stretching far away on either hand, with the edge of the table-land high above us. It is a small and tortuous stream, chiefly employed to bring logs down to a sawmill busily at work in the valley. The foliage is just beginning to show the autumn tints, and the dying grass has turned brown from the drought that covers all the roads with dust. Far away on the other side of the river, the railway grade can be traced, climbing up the hillsides to get out of the valley again, the grading forces being at work beyond.

Such is the process of railway building on the remote borders of this new country, the graded line being laid out considerably beyond the boundary into the North-West Territory, and several hundreds of men being busily at work. This crossing of the Assiniboin, and the difficult approaches to the deeply worn bed of the river from the elevated table-lands on either side, it is said will cost £200,000 to construct, although there are no rock cuttings. We turn back and drive up to the tops of the hills, seeking the famous farm of Binscarth. On the way, lakes are passed with sedgy edges, and we stop for a little shooting. They team with wild ducks and several are bagged, also a prairie chicken or two. Everyone in this country takes his gun when he goes about, and thus varies the time with a little aport. Reaching the farm, which belongs to the Scottish Ontario and Manitoba Land Company, an elaborate establishment is found, with large herds of valuable cattle, sheep, and pigs, and about 4,000 acres under cultivation or used for cattle ranges. The wheat crop just harvested averages 40 bushels to the acre. The thorough-breds have taken frequent prizes, and, in fact, are the most valuable herd in the North-West, there being 260 of them, mostly pure Durhams. This establishment has all been made in the past four years, the company owning 30,000 acres of land and having invested in land and buildings $135,000. They have complete buildings for the farm, and are making a great impression upon the neighbouring country by their success as cattle-breeders. The colony at the farm are Ontario people and Scotch. There is to be established here next season one of Dr. Barnardo's Homes for Destitute Children, 200 boys being sent out from London to learn farm work. This enterprise is promised $1,000 bonus by the local Government and 2,000 acres of land, and it is thought will do much good by providing farm labour where it is greatly needed. All these results have been accomplished by stretching out the railway into this attractive and fertile region, where pretty much all the lands are already taken up. In fact, the frontier has been removed far beyond, by the anticipation of more railway building. The location of the route into the North-West Territory has caused settlers to flock thither, and thus when the Manitoba and North-Western Railway has been pushed to completion to its present intended terminus at Prince Albert, on the North Saskatchewan River, nearly 500 miles from Winnipeg, it is probable that the onward march of settlement may then tempt its enterprising builders still further to extend the line, until it reaches the hyperborean regions up by the Arctic circle.

XI. – entering the great North-West Territory

INDIAN HEAD, NORTH-WEST TERRITORY, Sept. 6.

In progressing westward through Manitoba and beyond there is the sharpest contrast seen between the old systems that prevailed in this country and the new methods introduced by the advent of the railway. Then the Hudson's Bay Company was the ruling power, and its stores and transportation routes and lines were almost the only means of trading, freighting, and travel. The whole region was closely kept by the traders, the settlements being sparse and the knowledge of lands and availability that escaped outside being but meagre. Few people ever attempted to pass the Chinese wall thus in effect drawn around the North-West Territory, and as a result little population ever came in, and had it not been for the change in transportation and trading methods, it would have remained thus until this day. Perhaps it was a shrewd business policy in the Hudson's Bay Company to thus jealously preserve its lucrative trading monopoly, but it was not a very good thing for opening the country. The sale of the company's sovereignty and most of its lands to the Dominion some 18 years ago prepared the way for undermining the Chinese wall, and the coming in of the new railway three years ago threw it down altogether. This made a wonderful change in the transportation and trading systems, and has caused the entire region to be overrun by prospectors and land buyers, so that settlement is becoming general, and little villages are springing up at almost all the railway stations westward from Winnipeg for a long distance. The Canadan Pacific Railway main line passes through Manitoba across the prairie west of Winnipeg towards the valley of the Assiniboin river, the surface gradually changing from a dead level to rolling land. At Brandon, a town of about 1,800 people, largely settled by English colonists, the Assiniboin is crossed. This town is the centre of a prolific wheat-growing section. The railway reaches the western limit of Manitoba at a point about 211 miles from Winnipeg and 1,634 miles west of Montreal. Near here is a little station called Fleming, named in honour of Sandford Fleming, formerly engineer of the Canadian Government railways, and always a strong advocate of these improvements, who is now director of the Canadian Pacific line.

A pleasant drive of 45 miles across country from the unfinished end of the Manitoba and North-Western Railway towards the south-west took us to the Canadian Pacific road again at the little station of Moosomin, a village of probably 300 inhabitants, a short distance beyond the Manitoba boundary. This trail between the railways crosses a level prairie generally without trees, and has to traverse the broad valley of the Assiniboin which is scoured into great ravines and fissures, between which flows, across the level floor of the depression, a narrow and crooked stream. The view from the edge of this deeply-carved valley is very fine, its timbered sides giving it a greener hue than the brown moors of the bordering prairie, parched by the summer drought. The Qu'Appelle river, which attained notoriety during the rebellion last year, flows in from its deep tributary valley some distance to the northward, while off to the south, towards Brandon, the valley appears to widen and the hills become lower. In the foreground at the top of the precipitous hill are the white and grayish buildings of the Hudson's Bay Company's post of Fort Ellice, its storehouse being down alongside the river. Here the great North-Western trail crosses the Assiniboin by a rude rope ferry, and here in former times came the company's boats from Winnipeg, some seven hundred miles by the crooked river, to land the large amount of supplies which Fort Ellice distributed to the North-West Territory. We went down into the valley, across the ferry, and climbed the hills on the opposite side to the Fort, which the changed systems introduced by the railway have reduced to the spectra of its former self, and then we went on over the miles of brown prairie among wheatfields and farmhouses and stretches of sand barrens, with an occasional shot at a covey of grouse, to Moosomin and the railway again. Fort Ellice gave the impression of a place that had become somewhat seedy, its day having gone by. A half-dozen low buildings of timber and plaster are distributed around a quadrangle with a flagstaff out on the river bank in front. The trader at the post had a small store with few customers, and the other houses and stables were rented for an inn, though the travellers are scant in number. Not very long ago this was a valuable trading post, and the scene of great bustle, when the boats came, and the wagon trains were started off, and scores of the strange Red River carts, drawn by oxen and built all of wood, without a scrap of iron in their composition, were on hand to fetch away supplies. But now all is changed. Winnipeg no longer assembles at the Fort Garry landings to see the fleets of boats depart for Fort Ellice; but, instead, the enterprising Winnipegger of to-day goes to the railway station to see the moving processions of freight cars and coaches, and hear the railway servants shout directions to the passengers. Then a week's notice could be given of the annual departure of the fleet of boats; but now, in the rapid railway development of this new country, the guard's instruction to his passengers on arrival of the train at Winnipeg is expected before long to be expanded into something like this:— "Winnipeg; ten minutes for refreshments; change cars for Vancouver, New Orleans, Montreal, Chicago, Hudson's Bay, Sitka, Pekin, and Yokohama." This will realize the moderate ambition of the Manitoban of to-day.

Having entered the North-West Territory, we resumed the Canadian Pacific railway journey towards the setting sun, through the province of Assiniboia. The line is laid across the level prairie, and here we first encountered the "mounted police," who are the standing army of the far North-West. These neat and trim cavalrymen in their scarlet uniforms and top-boots maintain order throughout the Territory, and were of great service during the late rebellion. They enforce the excise regulations, there being a prohibitory liquor law in this region, and all arriving trains are inspected to guard against the clandestine importation of spirits and beer. At present there is an agitation to have the law relaxed so as to admit beer. We are in the Indian land, and the Sioux and Crees from the numerous reserves near the railway come out to the stations to exhibit themselves and see if anything of value to them will turn up. They are a sorry lot generally, and although the Government feeds them while on the reserves, they love to wander away and put out their teepees or wigwams on the prairie, where they catch the gophers and dig up buffalo-root, and on this fare manage to subsist. Some of them I am told, especially the Sioux, have shown quite an inclination to work on the farms, being very anxious to thus earn a little money, being paid about 3s. a day. There is but little attractiveness among them however, and their numbers dwindle. It is not far from Moosomin that Lady Catheart's colony of crofters is established, and they are said to be getting on quite well. Count Esterhazy has also placed in this region large numbers of Hungarians, and expects in his comprehensive emigration movement to bring out as many as 20,000. The westward route of the Canadian Pacific railway is laid across the prairie to the southward of the deeply carved and broad *coulée* made by the Qu'Appelle river. The prairie far away to the south-west at the United States boundary rises into Wood Mountain, which is a broad ridge of 3,400ft. elevation. The lands of Qu'Appelle valley are a rich wheat-growing section, and the Hudson Bay Company has a post at Fort Qu'Appelle, with a large Indian reserve near by. This is a trading post and not a military station, and the railway passes some distance to the southward.

While journeying along over the prairie there passed us east-bound a train of freight cars laden with tea, on the through route from Japan by way of the Canadian Pacific to the Atlantic seaboard. This tea trade is an important matter for the railway, and is working a great change in the route taken to fetch teas and Japanese goods to Lower Canada and New York. I had an interesting conversation with Mr. Everett Frazar, of Frazar and Co., of Japan and China, who are the agents transporting these tea cargoes and kindred goods. One ship's cargo, numbering 20,000 packages, has already been passed over the railway in 47 days from Yokohama to Montreal and 49 days to New York. This cargo required 50 freight cars to transport, and about half of it was left in Canada for consumption, while the other half went to the United States. The trains made the distance between Vancouver and Brockville, Canada, where the tea is delivered to the United States railways, in 137 hours. A second ship, with 30,000 packages of teas and other goods, arrived at Port Moody a few days ago, and the train passing us was carrying part of her cargo, thirteen cars laden with teas. The entire consignment will occupy five or six through trains. Three other vessels, with 50,000 packages, are crossing the Pacific, the five cargoes being of an aggregate value of £400,000. A sixth cargo is now being arranged for, the intention being to start the ship from Shanghai, calling at Japanese ports. The delivery of this freight is accomplished ahead of the other transcontinental routes by moving the tea trains at a speed of about 20 miles an hour, which, added to the fact that the line across Canada is the shortest, gives the shipper much advantage. Compared with the Suez Canal route, the saving in time to Montreal and New York is 25 to 30 days, besides the advantage of avoiding transhipment at New York, which saves both expense and damage. The freightage to the railway is about £100 per car, making £25,000 or more for the whole shipment now *en route*. The distribution for the Western States is made from Winnipeg by the railways leading southward, while the Eastern consignments, as above stated, are delivered at Brockville, on the St. Lawrence, last below Lake Ontario, whence they pass to the New York Central railway system. This is the early development of a new trade route half-way around the world that may become very important.

It is on the rich soil of the Qu'Appelle Valley that the Canadian Pacific Railway passes for ten miles through the "Bell Farm," which is believed to be the largest farm of contiguous territory in the world. It covers a surface of about 100 square miles, a few sections of school lands in parts of the tract, however, not being owned by the company. In the centre of the farm is the railway station of Indian Head, so called from a curious hill on one of the Indian reserves near it on the southward. This is about 1,730 miles west of Montreal, the lands having been carefully selected before the railway was built, but in anticipation of its construction, the route having been then located. This great farm contains 53,387 acres, bought from the Canadian Government, the railway, and the Hudson's Bay Company, so that there were thus obtained all the sections in the tract. The company was incorporated in 1882, by Canadian and British shareholders, the intention being to break up and prepare for cultivation about 20,000 acres, half of which was to be summer-fallowed every year, and at the end of five years to divide the estate into small farms and sell. The original capital was £120,000, and the shareholders have paid up £60,000, while £30,000 six per cent. debentures have been issued. No dividends have yet been paid, as large expenditures have been made according to the original plan, and it was thought best to re-invest profits rather than call additional share payments. The North-West rebellion last year interfered with the farm work, as the teams were all in use for transport service to the remote region where Riel's forces were located, and this year the drought has somewhat curtailed the wheat yield, but it is estimated at about 20 bushels to the acre, the threshing being yet incomplete. There were 5,000 acres under crop this year, and next season about 10,000 acres will be cultivated. Several farms have this season been sold off to newly-arrived colonists, the terms being about 24s. per acre for unimproved land, and £3 to £3 5s. for land that has been broken and back-set and got thoroughly ready for cultivation. The president of the company says that with fair crops hereafter they expect to put aside £5,000 sinking fund annually to redeem the debentures, and pay 8 per cent. dividends, while the disposal of the lands—the larger part of the tract being held on speculation—will give a return on capital account. They have built a flour mill, and expect hereafter to grind all their wheat, thus saving freight charges and being enabled to use the refuse in feeding cattle and pigs, these in future making from their sales an important item in the annual returns. The labour question, formerly an important element, both as to cost and the difficulty of obtaining labourers, has been solved by the employment of Indians, no less than 150 Sioux having this year aided in gathering the harvest. To assist the agricultural prospects of this section it is the intention next spring to open a college in a building just erected at a cost of about £2,400, and to receive pupils, under the name of the Albany College, called after the late Duke of Albany. This will be under the personal supervision of Professor Tanner, so well known in connexion with agriculture.

I made a survey of a part of this great farm, riding over the rich black soil and seeing the threshing processes. The wheat fields, just harvested, stretched as far as eye could see from one point of observation, while in another region the ploughing had turned the black soil over in the process of summer-fallowing, so that the square miles of land to be put down in next year's wheat crop would be ready for early seeding in April. There were 200 horses, 250 cattle, and 900 hogs on the estate, and the outfit of agricultural machinery embraced 45 reapers and binders, 73 ploughs, six mowers, 40 seeders, 80 harrows, and seven complete steam outfits for thrashing. Major Bell, the manager, is one of the greatest farmers of America, of ripe experience and great ability. He tells me that in working the land, the very careful accounts kept show that it costs about 8s. per acre to originally break up and backset, while afterwards the ploughing for the crop is worth about 2s. per acre. The actual cost of producing wheat, including every expense, with interest on the cost of the land and allowance for wear and tear, is about 20s. per acre. The profit of the farm will consequently depend on the yield. They get about 3s. to 3s. 2½d. per bushel at the railway at present, while their freight charge to Montreal is 1s. 4d. per bushel. By turning the wheat into flour, for which there is a good demand in the extreme North-West, the profit is greater, and the refuse fattens the cattle and hogs, which are always in demand. His experience has shown that the proper method of treating this land is by summer-fallowing, so that a wheat crop is raised every second year. He has also divided the estate into farms of 200 acres each, finding this sub-division the best method of economical working, each small farm having its own outfit of horses and machinery, the whole being supervised by foremen, each of whom overlooks a number of these small farms. The buildings and equipment of this great farm are of the most complete character, and it is one of the institutions of Canada. The fertile soil has been found to extend to great depths in the Qu'Appelle Valley, the boring of artesian wells having brought up the same rich black loam as is on the surface from a depth of 300ft. in some places. The wheat belt does not extend a great distance further westward, however, but it is almost beyond comprehension to estimate the ultimate value as a wheat producer of this vast fertile belt in Manitoba, Assinniboia, and Dakota, which covers a surface about 500 miles long by 250 miles in width. Here is grown the famous "No. 1 hard," which yields the best flour known, and this year has such plump berries that it weighs from 62lb. to 65lb. per bushel. Such is the "fertile belt" on the future development of which Canada bases such great hopes.

XII. – the coming metropolis of the North-West

REGINA, NORTH-WEST TERRITORY, Sept. 7.

The survey we have made of the great fertile belt of Manitoba and the North-West Territory naturally directs attention to the inducements offered by the Dominion Government to settlers. The Canadian homestead policy is a more favourable one than that of the United States. In Canada the head of a family, or any male person 18 years of age, is entitled to a homestead. In the States the limit of age is

21 years. The Canadian entry may be made for any quantity not exceeding 160 acres in any land open therefor, whether within or without the railway belts, the even-numbered sections, comprising some 80 millions of acres, being held by the Government for homesteads or for sale. In the States, within the railway belts, a settler can only get 80 acres for a homestead, while the pre-emption system has been abolished. Canada, however, permits the settler to pre-empt 160 acres more Three years' residence gives the settler his Canadian land patent, while five years' residence is necessary in the States, Canada permits a second homestead entry, but this is not permitted in the States. The Canadian system also allows commutation by purchase after one year's residence. I find, after considerable observation and inquiry, that the chief settlers in this region come from Ontario and are of Scotch descent, while many Scotch also come over from the old country. There are also some English and Germans. The movement is not large, but is a steady one, each railway train bringing in families or prospectors, who drop off at one station or another and go into the interior. There is also the usual pioneer movement seen in new countries, where restless folk settle on the frontier, and, as it moves ahead, progress with it. They pride themselves on being in advance of civilization, and may in the course of a few years, by successive westward stages, start a half-dozen new settlements. It is astonishing to find these people planting themselves in all sorts of out-of-the-way places, remote from any communication, and hence it is that whenever a new railway is projected there are always settlements miles ahead that want it to come along. This new country, however, suffers from drawbacks, and all is not of roseate hue. The long drouth this year has curtailed, and in some cases entirely destroyed, the crops, many fields of wheat and oats being left uncut because they would not pay for harvesting. As one sturdy settler who had been in the bottom lands of Qu'Appelle Valley for the past four years described it, "We have more steady sunshine probably than any other place and too little rain; I am afraid the Rockies steal the rain that ought to come to us." In fact, there had been no rain to speak of in this region for nearly three months until two days ago, when copious showers began falling, and now the rich and sticky soil is almost as bad as the dust was. It clings to one's shoes and becomes so slippery that locomotion is difficult. The temperature, too, which had burnt everything up, being above 100deg. frequently during the hot spell, changed in one night with the east wind that brought the rain to 45deg., and in a few hours the foliage put on its autumn tints.

I am told that the range of temperature here from actual observation has been during the past year from 58deg. below zero in the winter to 106deg. above during the summer. This means both excessive cold and oppressive heat, and the inhabitants complain very much of their inability to keep warm in winter. The great heat and drouth of the summer, by curtailing the crops, have caused much distress among the poorer classes of farmers, many of whom will have to be helped through in some way. They generally have taken up more land than they can care for, and being unable to pay the pre-emption prices are now pleading for an extension of time. Land speculation has been carried on upon these prairies to an excessive degree, and one form of it has been the making of town sites. All along the railway lines are located magnificent town plots planned upon a scale of grandeur that includes broad avenues and public squares, and stretching over much surface. The prices of eligible corner lots are high, and the only thing wanting about them is the inhabitants. Hundreds of these embryo towns are located along the railways through Manitoba and beyond, with a few little wooden houses scattered about, and much intermediate vacancy that can be occupied at high figures that astonish the residents of the older Canadian cities. Thus are enormous fortunes made—on paper, and thus also are intending settlers of moderate means frequently frightened off.

In our steady westward journey over the prairie we have come to a tortuous little stream, meandering upon the surface towards the northwestward, called most curiously the "Pile of Bones River," or in Indian parlance the Weseana. It flows into the Qu'Apelle River about 20 miles from Regina, and near it is located this town, which is the capital of the North-West Territory. About half-way over to its mouth a trail crosses, leading far away to the northward, which was travelled by many Indians in the buffalo hunting days, who generally encamped at the crossing to kill and prepare for the winter the animals they had captured. In course of time there accumulated a great mound of buffalo bones, whitened with age, and these gave the name to the stream. The prosaic settlers who have succeeded the Indians have carried off all the bones and sold them for fertilizers down in Minnesota. This prairie, with the pretty Qu'Apelle Valley to the northward, was a favourite haunt of the buffalo, and thousands of them formerly roamed here, so that their skeletons and bones are found in many places, and quite a brisk trade is carried on at gathering and shipping them eastward for fertilizers, the bones fetching about 20s. per ton. The half-breeds who come in for supplies generally bring a cartload of bones with them and trade with the storekeepers. It was near the crossing of the Canadian and Pacific Railway over the "Pile of Bones River" that it was determined to establish the capital of the North-West Territory; and hero about four years ago the new town was located, and named in honour of Her Majesty the City of Regina, 1,779 miles west of Montreal.

Imagine a section cut out of the middle of the Atlantic Ocean, and set down a few scattered rows of wooden houses upon it, and you will have a pretty good idea of Regina as it looks upon this level prairie, stretching for miles in every direction without a tree in sight. There are probably 300 buildings in the town, which contains 1,000 people, and the most prominent object that looms up as it is approached over the prairie is the railway water tank. The city is laid out on a scale of magnificence rivalling even the usual "spread" made by frontier towns, and the consequence is that the public buildings, unable to get room in the town, are all from a half-mile to two miles away from the place. It has three hotels, named from famous American hosteleries, the "Palmer" the "Grand Pacific" and the "Windsor," but the three put together would not cover a quarter of an acre. It has one newspaper in full operation, with hopes of another. It is all located on one side of the railway, with nothing at all apparently on the other side, where the smooth prairie stretches away into indefinite space. Its railway service, too, is most curious, one passenger tram each way passing every 24 hours, both of them in the middle of the night, the west bound train passing at 15 minutes before midnight, and the east bound train at 50 minutes after midnight. This, to some extent, may restrict travel, but it cannot curtail the importance of this north-western capital, which may some day become the metropolis of Assiniboia, as it is now the home of the Governor of the North-West Territory, the meeting place of his Council, and the headquarters of his standing army—the "mounted police." The few streets of Regina are broad, and bordered with wooden side walks, the ox-carts which slowly meander through them being varied by some highly painted Indian, clad in a picturesque Hudson Bay Company's blanket, who proudly rides into town on his pony with his squaw trudging after through the sticky mud.

To the northward of Regina the beautiful Qu'Appelle Valley, now putting on the pretty autumn foliage tints, is carved out of the tableland, a depression of 250ft. to 300ft., nearly two miles broad, across the level floor of which the narrow crooked river wanders at will. A branch railway, the Regina and Long Lake road, runs out to this valley, getting down the grade through a long *coulée*, and after going about 23 miles distance, ends practically nowhere, being intended at some day to be prolonged beyond Long Lake, a sheet of water about 60 miles long and from one to four miles broad, that lays between the hills south of the river. This railway has been built within a year past, but it has little trade to boast of, as the region around Regina is but sparsely settled. The locomotive carried us out to the end of the track, and there a ranche had been established with 600 head of cattle. The drouth had been so severe, however, that but little hay was made, and as it costs £2 per ton the cattle will have to be taken west to winter. This railway carried us to a pretty spot, down on the floor of the valley, with the great scoured and rounded bluffs rising on either hand, but it was a strange sort of road. It had no stations, and the train stopped whenever any one wished to get on or off. There were no points or sidings in the entire line, and the train had to come up out of the valley backwards. Yet several ambitious towns were laid out along the line at places where not a single house was in sight, and had been named for English gentlemen who were shareholders in the company. In the rancheman's house about 500 yards from the end of the line the post office of Craven was established, the postmaster being a salaried official of the Dominion Government, receiving the stipend of 8s. a-year. Just outside of Regina and near the route of this railway, the city cemetery has been established, and contains a few graves fenced about to keep the cattle out. A passenger explained as we went by that the graveyard had not got a good start yet, the town being too young, adding "but it has hopes, mon; it has hopes." This North-Western capital, however, is best known to the world as the place of the trial and execution in November last of Louis Riel, whose grave is in St. Boniface churchyard at Winnipeg. In a little square-built brick court house, set on the edge of the town, he was tried, being brought in every day from the barracks of the mounted police, where he was imprisoned, about two miles out. At these barracks they show the wooden building which is the prison and the little cell where he was confined, and also the gaol-yard, about 30 ft. square, where the scaffold was set up on which he was hanged. Out on the prairie in a little house lives his hangman, Jack Henderson, who now hauls supplies for the post. This half-breed in his relations with Riel shows the ups and downs of life. In the first Manitoba half-breed rebellion in 1870 Henderson was imprisoned by Riel and narrowly escaped death, while in the second rebellion the tables were turned. The residence of the Governor of the North-West Territory is out on the prairie, a low-built but comfortable house on the road to the barracks, and the meeting place of the Territorial Council is also on the prairie away from the town. This strange fatality of getting all the important buildings outside the city also infects the Dominion Land office and the Bank of Montreal, neither of which are in the built up town. The mounted police, which is the constabulary of the Territory, has extensive barracks in a number of wooden buildings and stables arranged around two quadrangles, the most elaborate structure being the riding school, about 200ft. long by 75ft. broad. There are 180 men at this, the head-quarters post, and about 1,000 in the entire force, which is distributed at various posts throughout the Territory, watching against cattle and horse thieves, patrolling the border, supervising the Indian reserves, and enforcing the excise laws, which are strictly prohibitory, excepting where the Governor may give a permit allowing certain amounts of spirit or beer to be imported or used. This force, made up mostly of young Englishmen, is uniformed much like the dragoons, and their trim figures and scarlet coats, varying with the Indians, give picturesqueness to the streets of Regina. From the tower of their riding-school there is a good outlook over the prairie, showing a vast expanse of grass-covered level land without a single tree in sight, the wayward "Pile of Bones River" meandering at will across the foreground, while Regina's water-tank and clusters of little houses are seen beyond. Such is the coming metropolis of the Canadian North-West.

41

DAVID CHRISTIE MURRAY, *THE COCKNEY COLUMBUS* (LONDON: DOWNEY & CO., 1898), PP. 109, 150–156

The depôt of the Grand Trunk Railway is an emporium of din, dirt, and disorder. The streets in this quarter of the town are ankle-deep in discoloured snow. The old plague of clanging bells is maddening everywhere. I have been charged half-a-dollar for a mile ride in an omnibus. I have profoundly offended a dark-skinned aristocrat by refusing to sit at table in the height of a cross-draught, and by insisting, for the first time since I landed, on a seat of my own choice.

Things generally in this very new country are more "up-to-date" than they are with us. The cities of which I speak, the city from which I date this letter, and many others, are almost literally the children of the Canadian Pacific Railway. That great line is only eleven years old. The journey across the Continent so recently spanned provokes many strange reflections. The line threads across hundreds and hundreds of miles of prairie, level as a billiard board, and hundreds of miles of "rolling" prairie, heaving in giant billows like an arrested sea; and then traverses hundreds and hundreds of miles more along the stupendous passes of the Rocky Mountains and the Selkirks. The iron threads, as if they were veritably alive, have created and fed a ganglion here and there, and already they palpitate from end to end. That small indomitable insect, man, has done many remarkable things in his time, but he has done little, if anything, more astonishing than this same Pacific Railway. The line across the mountains is one of the engineering feats of the world, and there is probably no route on the earth's surface where the traveller may enjoy in combination so much physical comfort and such a feast of natural splendour. There are no better appointed carriages on any line, there is no better table, there is no better sleeping accommodation. The land passage across the Continent is as comfortable as the sea passage in the best appointed of modern ocean steamers in the steadiest weather, and for four days out of the six it occupies it is one long-drawn dream of splendour and delight. The beauty of the journey begins when you strike the shore of the first of the great lakes. It is like nothing so much as the waves of a tumultuous sea fixed in solidity, and quiet at its maddest moment. Every traveller has had that simile forced upon him, and no man will find another to express the scene so well; but no sea that mortal eye has gazed upon ever ran in such tremendous waves. This district passed, you come upon more level prairie, and then as night closes down you get your first glimpse of the hills. We made "The Gap"—the portal of the mountains—late at night, and had no moon, so that there was nothing for it but to turn in and wait for daylight. By morning we were two thousand feet above the sea-level, and climbing fast, and the panorama of the Rockies was about us. There are many separate magnificences in the world of mountain landscape to rival most of the views which break upon you here, but for extent and continuance you would be hard put to it to find an equal to the glory of this journey. I have never in my life experienced a fatigue of mind and spirit so crushing as that which fell upon me here. The mountain torrents with their deep voices call you to watch their swirl and leap and coil.

It is no more possible to describe the Kicking Horse River or the Frazer Cañon than it would be to shoulder one of the mountains which line their courses. The first-named is the wildest worry of waters I have ever yet beheld; the stream gnashing and howling down there in hellish chasms; tearing at its rocky confines with raging hands, leaping, twisting into hard slow coils, as if in deadly resolve to stay its course and go no further, and then streaming on again and leaping out anew with shouts of triumph and horror and despair. The Frazer River bears a broader stream, and travels a less precipitate and awful road, but there is a steadfast terrible might in it which is to the full as impressive. I saw a giant pine tree in its waters, a great stripped trunk three times the length of any tree we grow in England, whirled hither and thither like a straw in a rain-filled gutter. There is one place where a massive fragment of rock stands in the centre of the stream. It is as big as a cathedral, and the rushing waters are banked up high against it by their own impetus. There the wave rears itself, and has reared itself night and day for how many thousands of years? The great uplifted glittering coil, heaped against the rock, has never broken. It will never break for a million years to come unless some convulsion of nature shall divert the river's course, or hurl the obstacle from its base. And the base is deep, how deep only a careful mathematical calculation could tell you. Measurement by sounding, in such a torrent is out of question. But many miles further on this river runs through quiet plains, where it spreads out to a width of a mile or more, and here its volume might be estimated. The same press of waters is forced through a gorge not more, I should suppose, than three hundred feet wide in some places.

I made my return journey to Winnipeg slowly, visiting many places by the way, and seeking to familiarize myself with the spirit of the mountains, but in a very small space of time everything had changed. The forest fires had broken out, and all the vistas were obscured. A mountain side was a flat wash of deep indigo. A mile further off another mountain side was a flat wash of paler indigo; and a mile further still earth began to fade altogether and mix with the pervading impalpable formless smoke-cloud. For two or three months in the year it is vain to travel by this route if you are in search of landscape. The fires destroy millions of trees annually, and fears are sometimes expressed lest they should denude the country, but when one remembers how many hundreds of thousands of square miles of forest there are, the dread begins to grow a little visionary. These conflagrations have many beginnings. Travellers who build fires at night, and take too little pains to extinguish them, are responsible for many. The attrition of dried boughs and grasses is answerable for others. One fruitful cause is little known, and is in itself singular enough to deserve mention. Most of the trees are resinous, and the great tears they weep in the hot summer weather collect and harden, and often form in a clear globular shape which focuses the sun-rays as a burning glass would do.

42

JOHN FOSTER FRASER, *CANADA AS IT IS* (LONDON: CASSELL, 1905), PP. 153–160

The territory of Saskatchewan: far from the beaten track

IF you are racing across Canada in one of the comfortable trans-continental trains of the Canadian Pacific Railway you will stay some twenty minutes at Regina, in Assiniboia.

It is a splayed-out town that does not attract. It is uncouth and unfinished. The population, according to the census, is about two thousand, but there is not an inhabitant who won't insist it is really four thousand. It is the capital of the North-West Territories, and soon to be the capital of a new province. But if you want to pay your respects to the Lieutenant-Governor or visit the headquarters of the famous Mounted Police, or have a look at the Legislative Buildings of the North-West Government, you must drive a mile or two into the wilderness. You wonder why on earth these are not near the town. Thereby hangs a tale.

Regina in its youth, aglow with its importance as being the capital, was certain that in a few years it would have a population of a million. So it planned itself and mapped itself and staked out its boulevards for a city of a million inhabitants. The million, however, is laggard. Hence it is that the Legislative Buildings, instead of being in the centre of a busy town, are far on one side and upon the plains. Regina does not quite understand. Yet its hopes, though dim, remain.

For several weeks each year the members of the Legislative Assembly, drawn from all corners of the Territories, meet in an unassuming chamber, not unlike a stable from the outside, and settle the laws for a roll of country in which England might be dropped and not easily found again. As I stayed a couple of nights in Regina I met many of the legislators. They were varied in type, from the cultured Englishman who had come west to ranch, to the bronze-cheeked, hardfisted farmer from the wilds, to whom the pay of £100 a year was worth consideration. We gathered in the dingy room of the grimy hotel—a place that was part smoking-room, part writing-room, part reading-room, part haunt of the "shoe-shiner"—and discussed when the Dominion Government would let the Territories become a province, and have the right to run into debt. Which it has since agreed to do.

From Regina a branch line curves northwards into Saskatchewan, past Saskatoon up to Prince Albert, on the bank of the Saskatchewan River. The distance is a little over two hundred miles. Yet the train, quarter passenger, three-quarters freight, takes fourteen hours to do the journey. The average speed is seventeen miles an hour.

We had long halts at wayside stations, where towns were struggling into life. There was one town called Chamberlain. It consisted of two rude cabins and a tent.

Every embryo town was a jumble of wooden huts. There were no roads, but plenty of rutted mire. At one place we halted for twenty minutes to dine. In the darkness we halted at Saskatoon for half an hour to sup. Everything was primitive and homely. The men I sat next at table were rough but kindly mannered. It wasn't always the English language that was heard; there were plenty of men of un-English visage and un-English garb who spoke in strange tongues.

Nearly all this stretch of country was known as the desert till a land company from the States began to buy big chunks of it at a dollar or a dollar and a half an acre, boomed the region, and started to sell the land at five or six dollars an acre. Immigrants kept away from this part because immigrants had always kept away from it. As soon as it was boomed and the rush began, they tumbled over one another to get on the Prince Albert line.

The land is good—excellent. Indeed, the country, bordered on the south by the Canadian Pacific Railway line, flanked west and east by the Edmonton and Prince Albert lines, and crookedly guarded on the north by the Saskatchewan River, is among the best on the prairie. Soon the new trans-continental line, cutting right through it from Winnipeg, *via* Saskatoon, Battleford, and Edmonton, to the Pacific coast, will open up another vast wheat-growing area.

Yet busy though the Dominion is in opening up new territory, the fretworking of the land with railways is not keeping pace with the immigration. The newcomers consequently suffer. Unless they are blessed with some money—and most of those who have taken up the best positions within reach of the railway are—they must get into the back row, and that sometimes means thirty miles from a railway. Then there are the hardships, the fights with nature, the scarcity of food, the awful loneliness, men living the hermit life for months, becoming melancholy, introspective. Some die of hunger, others are to be found in the lunatic asylums. The cases are not many; they are never referred to by the paid "boomers"; but amid all the appreciation of Canada the sense of proportion should not be lost, and the sad and tragic side should not be ignored.

This was the tract to which came, three years ago, the "All-British Colony," under the guidance of the Rev. J. M. Barr. There were eighteen hundred persons with the glamour of prosperous farming in their eyes. I am not going to enter into the savage controversy which arose between the immigrants and Mr. Barr. Sufficient it is to say that they were brought out, according to them, under false pretences, that what little money they had was soon lost, and that lynching is now considered in the North-West a far too agreeable punishment for the Rev. Mr. Barr. I know nothing about Mr. Barr. But, to use mild language, it was unwise of him to launch into the wilderness a crowd of men and women who knew nothing about farming at home, and were, therefore, worse than useless in pioneer farming on the prairies. And the clerks, mechanics, and the rest, who at home didn't know a turnip field from a potato patch, for them to think that there would be no hardships, but that somehow wheat would spring up alongside them as soon as they arrived, was to proclaim themselves fools.

Mr. Barr's colony was a failure. First the Immigration Bureau had to put three or four hundred people out as farm labourers so that they might learn something about farming. Then the immigration agents had to set about placing others on homesteads. I quote from the 1904 report of Mr. Obed Smith, the Commissioner of Immigration at Winnipeg:—

"Disagreements arose between Mr. Barr and his settlers, which culminated in his leaving the colony, and the charge of the internal and personal affairs (such as stores and commercial enterprises) was taken over by the Rev. George E. Lloyd and a committee of twelve colonists, while the location of the people on their homesteads, and their subsequent assistance by way of instruction, etc., were undertaken by the Department. It was speedily discovered that a large number of people brought out by Mr. Barr were not agriculturists in any sense, and the presence of so many of these made the task of the Department's officers a most difficult one; nor, indeed, can their duties be considered ended, as the inexperienced will require assistance in one way or another until a crop is reaped from the land."

The moral of the whole business is the folly of anybody not acquainted with farming or not willing to serve a hard apprenticeship as labourers for a year or two, rushing to Canada, or being persuaded by parsons or anyone else to form a colony. Disappointment, heartache, privations are the inevitable result.

What I saw of the Doukhobors and heard from those who have intimate association with them belied the unfavourable stories which I was told in England, and which were given corroboration by what I heard in the Eastern provinces. They are of the poorest type of Russian peasantry. Their uncouth appearance, their shaggy skin coats, their lowering countenances, together with the idea that the men put the womenfolk to the plough and worked them like horses, produced a feeling of resentment among those of whiter skin who regarded themselves as more civilised.

The Doukhobors are deeply religious, but with a blind, mystic, superstitious religion which is impervious to reason. They live in daily expectation of the second advent of the Messiah. A frenzied faith that the advent is near will send them on a pilgrimage in the depth of winter seeking the Messiah. They cause much anxiety to the officials. Last year they set off on a pilgrimage, making practically no provision for feeding themselves, and turning their stock out upon the snow-swathed wilderness. Government officials, however, got the stock, sold the animals, and held the money in trust for the owners. In time the pilgrims were persuaded to return to their homes. At intervals they have renewed inclinations to search the world for the Messiah. I was at Saskatoon immediately following Lord Minto, the then Governor-General, who had arrived after a ten-days' horse ride from Edmonton by way of Battleford. I was told how the poor Doukhobors, hearing of the coming of a great man, were with difficulty restrained from greeting Lord Minto as divine.

But though their fanaticism may bring a smile to the lips of those who are more worldly, their lives are full of self-sacrifice. Most of them left Russia some five years ago for the wilds of Canada. As a religious sect they had planned the exodus from their native country for a long time. They knew hardships would be awaiting them. They regarded it as criminal to take very small children with them. So, full were they of pious restraint, that no children were born into the community for several years. Indeed, when four or five thousand of them first reached Winnipeg, there was only one baby amongst them all.

Hundreds of homesteads have now been taken up. But the Doukhobors mostly live for their community. They share in common. They own their own steam threshing outfits, and have purchased saw mills to provide lumber for their own people. I do not think, however, that the "commune" will last. Already many of the Doukhobors are beginning to lose their Russian prejudices, and are adapting themselves to Canadian ways. They have the best agricultural machinery to be obtained, and I recall meeting a banker who told me it was amazing the amount of money they were saving. The more energetic and intelligent Doukhobors are giving some signs of wavering in loyalty to the "commune." They don't see why the best workers should share and share alike with the worst. Still, the strong religious feeling which pervades the sect keeps up a sympathetic Socialism between all sections. The more adventurous borrow from the banks, and there have been no bad debts. I met a man who lent money to a Doukhobor. It was to be repaid by a certain date. At that time the weather was terrible. Yet the Doukhobor rode 150 miles to pay his debt. That is typical.

A few years back the coming of the Doukhobors to the Dominion was by no means welcomed. Now they have proved themselves good farmers, frugal, virtuous, honourable in all their dealings; and I never heard anything but praise about them from anyone entitled to express an opinion.

It is through this region the new trans-continental railway will run. Look at a map of Western Canada, find Port Simpson on the Pacific coast, which will probably be the starting point of the line, and draw a rough line to Winnipeg, being sure you pass through Edmonton, Battleford, and Saskatoon, and you will get an idea of the territory which, within a year or two, will be ripped by the plough, and help Canada tremendously to increase her yield of wheat. The very natural objection can be made that the track will be through a land where there are long and severe winters. That is true enough. But there is this—though the summer is short the summer days are long, and when wheat planted in virgin loam can be given seventeen hours of sunshine a day, with no cloudy, damp breaks, ninety days is the outside time required to raise a crop in the Territories.

Part 7

CORRIDOS AND *CALAVERAS*
Ballads of Mexican railroads

43

'THE RAILWAYS FROM VERA CRUZ TO JALAPA AND MEXICO', IN *FERGUSON'S ANECDOTICAL GUIDE TO MEXICO, WITH A MAP OF THE RAILWAYS* (PHILADELPHIA: CLAXTON, REMSEN, & HAFFELFINGER, 1876), PP. 25–38

On leaving the station of Vera Cruz, the line cuts through the fortifications of the city; crosses the boulevard Santiago; passes in sight of *La Alameda* (the Vera-Cruzian promenade); of the gazo-meter, the cemetery of *Casa Mata*, then across the laguna of Cocas, near to the spot where the Vera Cruzian defenders gave up their arms to General Scott in 1847, and then passes not far from the la-gaina of Boticario; the junction that leads to Medellin being at La Lamorana. Finally, the main line forms a sharp curve, and then runs in a straight direction to:

Tejeria, at nine and a half miles from and one hundred and six feet higher than Vera Cruz.—It was in a house of this village, to the right of the railway track, that in 1861, the Mexican general Doblado received Sir Charles Wyke and General Prim, to celebrate the treaty which had been signed at La Soledad. Not far from there, in *Casa Mata* (Mata's house), General Santa Anna proclaimed the second Mexican Republic (2d February, 1823), and near by, a bloody battle took place, previous to the taking of Tampico by General Cevallos. Between the station of Tejeria and that of Soledad there is no other village but that of *Purga*, which takes its name from the medicinal plant jalap, which grows in its vicinity. Jalapa has the same origin.

Soledad is a village of two hundred and twenty-one inhabitants, and, as the reader will remember, it gave its name to the treaty signed between Generals Doblado and Prim. Near by, is the longest bridge of the whole line, erected on the same spot where stood the old highway bridge. It is supported by pillars, under four of which runs a river. Its waters are shallow in winter, but torrential in the rainy season.

Cameron station comes next, (thirteen and one-quarter miles from Soledad).—The only interesting part of the village are the ruins of a house burnt in April, 1864, by the Mexican army, and in which several French chiefs and officials lost their lives. Eight miles further on, and forty-seven and one-quarter miles from Vera Cruz, is *Paso del Macho*, which was a central point for the railway employés during the construction of the line, *i. e.*, from 1865 to 1870; it contains one thousand four hundred inhabitants. Its altitude is one thousand five hundred and sixty feet.

After having left behind him, not without a certain satisfaction, the movable mounds of sand of the coast, continually destroyed and reformed elsewhere by the northers, the traveller has witnessed a gradual change in the aspect of the country, and he looks forward whence comes a softer breeze, and breathes freely its aromatical odors. At the height of Soledad, beds of chalk are to be found alternatively superposed with similar sands and gravels to those of the coast, and on the other side of Paso del Macho, towards Cordova, conglomerations of white calcareous soil predominate; whereas, near to the latter city, vapors are frequent.

At three miles from the station of Paso del Macho, the train runs over the bridge of San Alejo, three hundred and eighteen feet long and thirty-six feet above a ravine. It is entirely built of cast and wrought irons. The vegetation below is so high and thick, that the bridge seems as if it also sprung from out of the earth; for, we are here in the presence of the wonders of nature and the progress of science. From this bridge, under which rushes the river San Alejo, one can witness, at the same time, all the treasures of a tropical climate and the works of man.

Thenceforth, on each side of the line, sugar-cane and coffee plantations succeed to virgin forests, lighted up by innumerable fireflies, and in the midst of which one's eye is attracted from the creepers entangled amongst the shrubs at one's feet, to the numerous parasites which invade the trees above one's head. The scene is animated by a variety of birds of brilliant plumage, flying from branch to branch, and the echo repeats their joyful songs.

The parasites merit the special attention of tourists, as well as of botanists and horticulturists; they are of the orchid and bromelia Specie and of an infinite variety, from the thick drooping green leaf and multicolored flowers, to the upright red bromelia. The most complete collection of them that exists, is at the *Jardin des Plantes* de San Francisco, calle de San Juan de Latran at Mexico. The former director, Mr. Tonel, and his successor, Mr. J. B. Van Gool, have also made a specialty of the culture of agaves and cactuses, from the common maguey, that produces the pulque, to its most recent novelties. An hour spent in this garden is not lost.

At a mile and a half from the bridge of San Alejo stands Mount Chiquihuite, through the basis of which runs a tunnel of two hundred feet long.

Chiquihuite bridge.—Then, to his left, the traveller may admire a deep and picturesque precipice, down which, from rock to rock, falls in pulverized spray the silvery stream of a murmuring cascade, over which is thrown the bridge of Chiquihuite, two hundred and twenty feet long.

The richness and variety of the scenery is such, that the tourist does not perceive that he leaves the road rapidly behind him, and that he is now going up a mountain, then down a slope, as can be seen by the difference of the levels; for, on arriving at the station of *Atoyac*, the height is only one thousand five hundred and thirteen feet, *i. e.*, forty-seven feet lower than at the previous stations. Atoyac is situated at fifty-three and one-half miles from Vera Cruz, and at the extremity of the iron bridge of the same name, (three hundred and thirty feet long), that crosses over the river also called Atoyac, the mouth of which is at Vera Cruz From this river and Mount Chiquihuite the soil is of a calcareous nature and contains a kind of lithographic stone. There are no traces of fossils, which denotes that it is of the tertiary formation. Then follow the bridges of San José, Rio Seco, and another of smaller importance.

After Soledad begins the ascent of the mountains around which the railway takes a serpentine course with its iron girdle. Up to Atoyac the ascent was *very feeble*, the distance from the coast being fifty-three miles, and the altitude only one thousand five hundred and thirteen feet; but, from there, it became so steep that it required the Fairlie engine, which takes up a rise of four per cent, a burden of one hundred tons nett of cargo, at the rate of twenty-five miles an hour. Between Atoyac and *Cordova*, at sixty-five and three-quarters miles from Vera Cruz and two thousand seven hundred and thirteen feet above it, the train runs through a rich and splendid country which yields all the products of a tropical climate, and especially the *frijol*, a small, dark brown bean, which has a peculiarly rich flavor. It is the Mexican national vegetable and is also esteemed by foreigners. It is largely exported to Havana and the neighboring islands.

Cordova is a town of nine thousand five hundred inhabitants, situated in a small valley.—Its origin goes as far back as 1618. In 1609, an attempt at establishing the town was made; but a revolt of the slaves, under Yanga, was an impediment. The project was to build a station to protect carriers on their way from Vera Cruz to the interior. When Viceroy Diego Fernandez de Cordova, Marquis of Guadalcazar, came into power he took up the matter again, and on the 18th April, 1618, he gave authorization to thirty colonists of Huatusco to establish the station. The spot chosen was a small hill, then known as Guilango or Huitango, and situated, as the tourist will remark, in a most eligible situation. The highway travellers and the neighbors who gathered around soon gave importance to the rising village. The first occupants lived on the product of the wild fruit-trees; the banana was their bread; the banana and nopal gave them fruit; maguey furnished them with *pulque*, and its fibre served to weave their garments. Then they cultivated oranges and other fruits which they sold at Orizaba and Vera Cruz, and finally they grew sugar-cane and built factories. In 1757, there were already thirty-two sugar-mills, and in 1759, as many as twenty-two *haciendas* (farms), all situated around the town, and which, according to M. Segura, produced one thousand three hundred tons of sugar a year. Then sprung up distilleries of *aguadiente* (alcohol). In 1863, the number of haciendas was thirty-one, and the *rancheros* twenty-four (smaller farms). Foreign plants were also cultivated, for we find that tobacco was grown at Cordova as early as 1756. The coffee tree and the Manilla *mango*, (a fruit), were imported into this region by the Spaniard, Juan Antonio Gomez. In 1825, there were already seventy-five thousand feet of coffee, and one year later the number was five hundred and twenty-three thousand four hundred and fifty. Quina has also been introduced to the environs of Cordova. This thriving centre was in full prosperity, and was rapidly increasing in riches and civilization, when Hidalgo raised his cry of independence. Its position, which had been so favorable to its development, was the cause of its ruin. Alternatively occcupied by the royalists and the independents, by the sanguinary Hevia and the wild Iturbide, it was finally choosen for the *rendezvous* of the chiefs of the two parties, to sign the treaty by which Spain recognized the Independence of the Mexicans.

Since 1812, the date of the first emancipation of slaves on the Mexican territory, the natives, who are naturally indolent and indifferent, partly abandoned the fields and factories; it was then that immigration was so much wanted; but as it did not come in sufficient quantities, Cordova, once so opulent, is now forsaken; the land is overrun with weeds, and the mills are in ruins!. . . . . . .

The city itself is two miles from the railway station, with which it communicates by a tramway at every train. There are no monuments worthy of notice, but it is placed in a charming and advantageous situation, being surrounded by mountains, and near to Rio Seco (Dry river), the waters of which have an average temperature of 68° Fahrenheit. As it is only at a moderate altitude, and not far from the sea, it enjoys, at the same time, the daily tropical heat and the evening sea breeze. The vomito negro is seldom engendered there, so that all these advantages attract to Cordova each year, a great number of Vera Cruzians. Five miles further on the line, is the station of *Fortin*, which received its name from a fort or tower, now in ruins. The soil of the mountains around Orizaba and Fortin is of a grey black calcareous kind; it also extends as far as the cofre of Perote, and is of the cretacean formation.

On leaving Fortin, the traveller needs to give a hasty glance at the immense horizon which extends to the base of the Peak of Orizaba; for, shortly afterwards, the railway track turns sharply to the right, and the train slides over a bridge under which rushes a torrent at the depth of ninety-two feet, embedded between the declivities of the mountains, covered with virgin and evergreen vegetation; and after having thrown a rapid look to the right, on the mountains above, let the tourist cast an eye of admiration at the sight below his feet to the left. There, is the barranca of Metlac (Metlac Ravine), in all its horror and splendor. . . . The spectator's attention will be drawn so rapidly from one marvel to another, that it is only when he is under the first of the five tunnels which succeed one another at a short distance, that he reflects on the daring of an enterprise such as the ascent by steam of the *Cumbres*.

Before coming to the ravine of Metlac itself, there are two small bridges of little importance; therefore, let the traveller direct all his attention towards the main viaduct, and look ahead so as to enjoy the view of it, as it forms a curve of 325 feet radius over the river. He will see also the serpent-like train, the head of which, the Fair lie engine, moves along easily, although the ascent up the hill is 3%.

El puente de Metlac (Metlac Bridge), measures 350 feet in length, and is built of cast and wrought iron. It came from the works of Crumleie (England). It rests on eight pillars, also of iron, which are borne on basis of masonry. So as to prevent the train from running off the track at the curve, the rails are of pure steel; and at every seven feet distance is an iron brace to keep the rails in their places; besides, there is a third one called *guard rail*. The barranca of Metlac begins at the foot of the Peak of Orizaba, it being formed by the waters which filtrate from its heights. After many windings, it first disappears near Mount *Cacalote*, and finally at the base of Mount Chiquihuite. Its narrowest part measures 900 feet, and its greatest depth is 375 feet. Its borders may be compared, for their steepness, to those of Niagara, near the Falls.

At three miles from the barranca is Mount *Sumidero*, into the interior of which the river Sonso disappears momentarily, but reappears further on. A short while afterwards, the valley of Orizaba is in sight. It presents to the eye the appearance of an immense luxurious garden, in the middle of which, the town detaches itself with its flat roofed and white houses and haciendas, intersected now and then with domes and steeples, looking like thimbles and needles compared to the Peak, which stands 17,375 feet above the level of the sea; and the everlasting snowy head of which pierces the first range of clouds, and glitters above them, enlightened by the rays of the rising sun; for, at the hour the train reaches Orizaba, when there is not a norther on the coast, the fiery orb has power enough to gradually dissolve the vapors of the night, and unveil, to the eyes of the amazed admirer a uniform, blue sky.

Orizaba is at eighty-two miles from Vera Cruz, and in the State of the same name. Its population averages 12,500 inhabitants. Its original Astec name was *Ahauializapan* (Joy in the water), which passed through the following modifications before it became Orizaba: *Aulicava, Ullizava, Olizava*. At first, it was a village founded by the *Techichimeca* tribe, and was conquered by Montezuma I., in 1457; but it was only elevated to the dignity of a town in 1774. Three rivers run near the city, viz: the *Ojo de Ingenio*, containing alcaline, slightly sulphureous: the *Rio Blanco*, also impregnated with alcaline and large quantities of carbonate of lime; and the *Rio de Orizava*, a little salt in dry weather, but full of vegetable *detritus*. During the rainy season, its water creates dysentry, fevers, &c. There is a large spinning and tissue mill, as well as a paper factory, and three flour mills. Argileous, calcareous, and flint stones are to be found in quantities all around the city. Its climate is rather humid, though healthy; the easterly wind being the predominating one. The plateau on which it stands is 4,027 feet higher than the level of the sea, and the average temperature is 72° Fahrenheit.

It was the first city to which the conquerors made haste, with the hopes of finding the accumulated riches of which the natives gave such a glowing account. In 1521, the Astec chiefs, *Cuatlochtlan* and *Hoatechco*, plotted the murder of the Spaniards left at Orizaba by Hernand Cortes; but Gonzalo de Sandoval arrived in time to save them without shedding blood. The first church was built by the monks of San Francisco themselves, with the help of the Indians; it was situated on the spot where stands actually the church *del Calvario* (of the Calvary). During the fight for the Mexican independence, Orizaba was besieged several times by Morelos. In 1862, the French armies took up their quarter-general within its walls; and the unhappy emperor Maximilian often made it his residence. In the environs, there are several water falls:—the *Barrio Nuevo, Rincon*

Grande, Puente Santa Anna and *Tuspango*, the rivers of which give hydraulic power to the mills.

In the direction of the western part of the city is Mount *Borrego*, known in the annals of the French invasion, as the point where the Mexican army, 5,000 strong, was routed by 100 zouaves in the middle of the night. Orizaba contains twelve churches; but their architecture is like that of all the churches erected by the Spaniards, and they only vary inside by the variety of their adorned altars, paintings, and relics, more or less authentic. Hotels: *de las Diligencias*, $2 a day, including room, board, service, and light—*de San Pedro*, $1, for the same items; *de Las Cuatro Naciones*, and *del Ferrocarril*. The rolling stock of the Railway company is built and repaired at Orizaba—After passing the small station of *Encinal* the next one we then look forward to is that of *Maltrata*, at 94½ miles from Vera Cruz and 5,550 feet above it. Although it only contains 2,000 inhabitants, this borough has more importance than that of Ingenio, which is as fully inhabited. The tourist will be able to compare them, for the train passes through the lattei at 4½ miles from Orizaba. Up to Ingenio the scenery and vegetation continue the same as from Paso del Macho: luxuriant plains, mounts and valleys; odoriferous plants and savourous fruits; bright feathered and cheerful birds; but at a few miles from there the aspect gradually changes and you see the natives by your side wrap themselves up in their *zarapes* and *rebozos*, make a rapid sign of the cross, and murmur the dreaded name of *El Infernillo* (the little hell); for such is the name of a deep precipice between two mountains. All traces of vegetation has disappeared, not a tree, nay, not even a shrub, to be seen, and still less any living being. A scanty stream disappears from rock to rock into its depths and murmurs in a hollow tone, as though it protested against its fate which condemns it to fall in scattered spray into the dark abyss; for the light of the sun never penetrates into its recesses. The passage of the train detaches small stones from the barren rock around; they roll into the Infernillo, and the echo alone would tell us, after we are gone by, that they had reached the sombre bottom, were not the noise drowned by the rattling of the train.

The traveller, like the Dant and Telemachus, son of Ulyssus, when they came from the dark dominion of Pluto, after having sought, the one for his beloved Laura, the other for his father, breathes with ease and satisfaction on leaving behind him the desolate Infernillo, where the traces of so many eruptions are seen at every step; for he now comes to life again as he penetrates into the valley of *La Joya* (the Jewel) and it well merits its name as "the little hell" is worthy of its title. *Maltrata* is placed in the middle of that sweet little valley. Nothing is more refreshing to the sight, nor more satisfactory to the mind, than to contemplate the view now before us, and the passage of the Infernillo appears to us as a horrible nightmare!

On the right side of the cars stands a mountain covered with moss and grass, spotted with bright wild flowers and crowned with a forest of secular trees. To the left, the valley extends itself to the horizon, similar to an evergreen carpet, through which runs, like a riband, a silvery rivulet on a golden bed of sand. Whilst the spectator is admiring the beauties, of which our feeble pen can only give a slight idea, the train arrives at the station. There, as at all the other depots of La Tierra Caliente, the natives bore you with the parasitical orchids, bananas, pineapples, oranges, etc., but as a compensation, under an open shed, one may indulge in a cup of coffee, grown in the neighborhood; and if it be not good, it is because it is not well roasted nor properly steeped. Still what a difference when we compare Mexican coffee to that of Moka, Massaoua, Suez, Cairo, Alexandria, etc. As in many other cases, the French invasion has changed the Mexican *desayuno* (breakfast). Only ten years ago, when the diligence stopped at a *Fonda* (inn), the only beverage offered to you was chocolate; now, it cannot be obtained at any price. But let not the tourist, who is come to see and not to eat delicacies, lament over their deficiency; but let him lift his eyes towards the mountain up which he is about to ascend. The railway track is only visible now and then as it winds round the steep declivities, amidst the vapors of the clouds which bathe the crest of the Cumbres. Now and then the opening of a tunnel appears like a black spot. But before the locomotive attains that height, it will have to run over 13 miles of rail, now placed on artificial plateaus, supported by masonry, then plunged into the bowels of the mountain, and then again, suspended on an iron-bridge of more than 300 feet long and thrown over ravines and precipices.

But the engine cannot accomplish its journey without taking in water at *La Tangue* (the tank), near to the station of *La Bota*, (the Boot); a small station in the mountain at three miles from Maltrata. The name of "La Bota" was given to the station on account of a spot in the mountain which assumes the shape of Victor Emanuel's kingdom. *La Toma del agua* (water-giver), is a source that gives water to the tank of La Bota; it was struck upon by the laborers whilst cutting through the rocky mountain, and it was, as M'Quin calls it, in his witty and picturesque Irish language, "as valuable to the railway company as if it were a gold mine." If we refer to the Jewish tradition, it was thus that Moses brought forth *from a rock*, the water that quenched the parching thirst of the people of Israel. But there must be some error as to the site; for Moses' fountain, now shown to tourists, is in the middle of the desert and there is *no rock*. If this really is the spot, the only admissible theory is that he caused an artesian well to be sunk, the source being surrounded at a distance by lofty mountains.

More surprises are still in store even for the most insatiable tourist. When he sees the natives mutter something between their lips, he may be sure that he is not far from the Winner Bridge, at three miles from Boca del Monte; it measures 96 feet in length, but very narrow, and was called after an engineer who lived near by. It is fully 3,600 feet above the valley which we have left 80 minutes before. It is supported by four iron spider-web looking columns, resting on piles of masonry. From this bridge and at several other parts of the circular ascent, when there are no clouds below, one can enjoy the view of the valley of Maltrata, which presents the appearance of a draught board, with its fields of uniform square and varied colors, its flat top buildings, representing the draughts and its steeple imitating the queen; but all so small that they look like a bouquet of lilies in a garden. Soon after, the road passes through the mountain, and when it comes out of the tunnel, it runs for half a mile in a cut, 200 feet long, at the end of which the tourist comes in sight of the station of:

Boca del Monte.—Here the traveller, at the sight of a copious *déjeuner à la fourchette*, forgets his recent emotions and the coolness of those lofty regions to satisfy a craving hunger, and he does not find the price of seventy-five cents too dear.

Before now, he has acknowledged *in petto* that our advice to provide an overcoat to protect him from the dampness of the condensing clouds and the fresh breeze of the mountains was wise, for Boca del Monte stands at an altitude of 7,922 feet above Vera Cruz, from which there is a distance of 107¼ miles; the same garment will henceforth be useful against the dust, which is very compact in dry weather. As the remainder of the track to Mexico does not present any serious ascent, the Fairlie engine is here replaced by an ordinary one.

San Andres Chalchicomula (126 miles from Vera Cruz).—This village is about four miles from the railway station, but there is a diligence which meets every train; the municipality of the village is studying the project of constructing a tramway. San Andres is situated at the foot of the Peak of Orizaba, which partly belongs to M. Rosains, of San Andres, who extracts ice from its summit and to whom applications must be made to make its ascent. The population of San Andres Clialchicomula averages 4,000. It is cited in the history of Mexico under the name of *Xalchicomulco*. A powder explosion that took place on the 6th March, 1862, killed 1,025 Mexican soldiers and 14 officers, and wounded 205 others, all were buried on the spot. It was there also, and on the 23d March, 1862, that Manuel Robles Pezuela was shot for having joined the army of the intervention.

La Rinconada, at 139 miles from the coast—is known in the history of modem Mexico, because Juan N. Rosains made, in 1811, his declaration in favor of Independence in the hacienda of Rinconada, which can be seen from the cars. The said chief was executed ultimately at Puebla, under Anastasio Bustamente. There is also a service of diligence for San Andres. On leaving San Andres, the reader has to his left a chain of mountains, known as the Sierra de Chiconquita, at 30 miles behind which in a straight line lies Puebla; at 44 miles further on stands Popocatepetl, and at a right angle towards the north, at 18 miles distant, is *Ixtacihuatl* (the woman in white). The altitude here is only 7,732, therefore we have been coming down the hill from Boca del Monte; but henceforth we shall alternatively ascend and descend until we reach Mexico. Eleven and one-fourth miles more and we come to the station of:

San Marcos at 113 miles from Mexico,—and near to Nopalacan, a small village situated at the junction of the highway that leads from Puebla to Jalapa, *via* Perote, as well as of the conceded line of railway from Vera Cruz to Puebla, *via* Jalapa and Perote . . . . Between this station and the next the traveller has a full view of Mount Malinche (*Malitzin*), the name of which was given to Cortes by the Astecs. Several legends are attached to the name and mountain. According to one of them the ghost of the royal daughter of a king, named Malitzin, haunts the lake of Chapultepec . . . at daybreak; she also makes her appearance at a source near to the convent of *Atzcapozalco* (oh, happy monks)! But the legend does not say if she attends the two places at the same time. The other legend is still more marvelous and tragic:

A long time ago, (all old tales begin so,) the mountains of *Malinche, Popocatepetl* and *Ixtacihuatl*, were no more nor less than animated monsters, having the use of their limbs and tongues, of which they made an immoderate use, as we shall see hereafter. *Ixtacihuatl*, (the white lady), was the wife of Popocatepetl, and a very unhappy one too. Her husband was always smoking, thence his name, and Ix-tacihautl, who was very nervous, could not bear the smell of sulphur, which is quite natural, for we know ladies who cannot even support the smell of tobacco, much less of sulphur. The unlucky spouse, in her sorrow, threw an eye of despair on the brilliant and elegant Maiinche, the star of America, for she was smitten by his brightness. He was born on a rich soil and was of noble extraction, and she hoped that for love of her, he would deposit at her feet the treasures of his fairy land, thus charming the loneliness of her barren regions. The star was not insensible to the unhappy fate of the White Lady, and he pitied her from the bottom of his heart. Now, from pity to love there is but one step, at least, so say people who have experience in the matter. Ixtaciliuatl was happy while listening to the sweet harmony of the zephyr which caressed her cheeks, and which was impregnated with the odoriferous perfumes of the rich vegetation of her lover's land; and they would pass days after days (read ages after ages), exchanging under the blue sky of the tropics the sweet word "love." But lo! one day, the old smoker surprised them in the midst of their ecstasy; and as he did not quite approve of the nature of their conversation, he slew both his consort and her paramour, *car les maris ne font pas toujours rire*. But pursued by remorse and his unextinguished passion for the departed wife, he regretted that he had not limited his vengeance to the Egyptian custom, imported into Anuhuac, and which consisted in cutting off the noses of unfaithful wives; but it was now too late, and in his despair he gave up his soul to the Gods, who changed the mortal remains of the three monsters into mountains, so that they might serve, then and forever, as an example to unfaithful wives. It appears, that from that day to this, there is not one in the country from whence the White Lady can be seen. From that day also the pygmies of Anuhuac rejoiced in contemplating, wrapped in their white winding sheets, the gigantic *Gog* and *Magog*, whose simple murmurs did no longer shake mounds and vales!

By the time the reader has admired Malinche and wandered in the supernatural world, the train arrives at

Iluamantla, 102¼ miles from Mexico.—Its name is mentioned in the history of the Independence, together with that of Sesma, one of its heroes; and also in the war against the American invaders. The name of President Juarez has been added to its original one, for it has been recently called Huamantla Juarez.

Geologists will find there fine specimens of marble, which has a great resemblance to the soap stone of California; but more so to the Algerian onyx.

On the line between Huamantla and the next station there are several iron bridges thrown over the torrents and waterfalls, produced by the drainings of Malinche. (The Astees pretend that they are the tears shed by the daughter of Malinche!)

Apizaco, at eighty-six and one-half miles from Mexico.—This is the junction of the branch line to Puebla, and from that fact the village took birth. There is a good restaurant, where an excellent meal is served for seventy-five cents at the arrivals of the up and down trains; English, French, German and Spanish spoken. The altitude here is 7,910 feet; but at the hacienda of Acocotla, which we passed on the road, we were as high as 8,310 feet, the culminant point of the line.

Guadalupe (hacienda), is at a distance of seventy-seven miles from the capital.

Soltepec, seven and one-half miles further on, and 8,224 feet above the level of the sea.—Hence the track goes down a gentle slope to the capital.

Apam, at fifty-seven and one-half miles from Mexico.—This borough is the central point for the sale of pimienta, especially of the *quesadilla* and *chalupa* kinds, which are the basis of all Mexican cooking. In the plains of Apam there are many haciendas, amongst which is that of San Diego Notario, where the Mexican General, Porfirio Diaz, gained a victory over Leonardo Marquez, in April, 1867, during the conflict between Maximilian and Juarez.

Irolo, at forty-seven and three-quarters miles from Mexico—is the central market for the sale of *pulque*, the stations of Soltepec, Apam, Ometusco and La Palma being the most important deposits. This beverage is extracted from the plant called *maguey* (aloes), which the traveller has seen so many of since the train left Boca del Monte, and which cover the plains to the gates of the capital, and even the whole valley. This plant is the manna of the natives. It gives them fruit, liquid, paper, yarn and needles. When the plant arrives at maturity (ten years old), it measures as many as eighty-five feet in circumference. An incision is made at the foot of it, generally in the centre; the heart is cut out to form a reservoir, into which the juice of the leaves collects. This juice is aspired by the breath into a long dried pumpkin, called *Acocotl*, (water throat) and then emptied into a sheep's skin. In this state it is called *Tlachique* (mild pulque). It is taken to the hacienda, poured on a cow's hide, stretched on a frame, the hair being inside, and left there to ferment; after which, it is put again into sheep's skins and shipped. The pulque of temperate regions is far superior to that of the hot climates. This process was first put into use by a maiden, the handsome Xochitl, who was married to Tepalcaltzin, a Tolteca king on the 26th April, 1045. Pulque is the national drink, as wine is that of the east and south of France, and cider of its western region. The natives cut a leaf of each plant into the shape of a cross, so that it may live long and yield much.

Ometusco, at forty-two miles from the capital, is the station where travellers alight to take the diligences to the mining county of Hidalgo *via* Pachuca, Tulancingo, etc.

La Palma comes next, but is of little importance.

Otumba lies at thirty-four and one-fourth miles from Mexico; it is a small town of 4,584 inhabitants. In 1520, a handful of the conquerors, seconded by the

Tlascala Republicans, faced the Mexican army in the mountains which surround the city. For seven days they fought in sight of the pyramids of Teotihuacan; but the temerity and valor of the former triumphed over the patriotism and fanaticism of the latter; 278 years later (1798), at the feet of other pyramids, which served as models to those of Teotihuacan, another celebrated invader addressed his soldiers thus: *"Du haut de ces pyramides quarante sicles vous contemplent!"*

San Juan Teotihuacan, at twenty-seven and one-fourth miles from the capital, *i. e.*, at one and a half hour's ride by the train, is the station where visitors take the diligence to visit the pyramids of Teotihuacan. . . .

Tepexpan, at twenty and one-fourth miles from Mexico, is the last station but one before reaching the capital. At each train there is in attendance a conveyance for Texcoco, a city situated on the eastern side of the lake of the same name, and on the western borders of which stands Mexico City itself. After having followed the borders of the above lake for several miles, the traveller perceives *Guadalupe Hidalgo* on the other side of the track, *i. e.*, to his right. As this town, by its historical facts and religious importance, merits a special visit, we have classed it in the chapter of "Villages." . . .

Arrival.—Now, let the traveller strap up his rug and rehearse the words he has learned, by that time the train will be in the station. Those who have taken through tickets will be met at the station by the agency's correspondent, and everything will be provided for them, conveyance and apartments; but those *qui ne sont pas aussi favorisés*, must take a carriage, for the cars which meet the train stop on the grand square. After having been jolted about on the uneven pavement of the city they will arrive at the hotel, which they have chosen out of our list. . . . The fare of the carriage, for any drive, is two reales or twenty-five cents and double that amount for one hour or part of an hour. It is customary to give the driver a gratification, but not obligatory. . . .

In Mexico, although there are restaurants under the same roof as the hotels, they do not belong to the same proprietors; therefore, if travellers have not made preliminary arrangements, on taking their tickets, they will need to make terms with each one.

There is a service of horse cars from the depot to the Plaza Mayor and *vice versa*. It leaves the square at 5:00 P. M. to meet the train from Vera Cruz, and at 4:30 A. M. to take the passengers for the five o'clock train for Vera Cruz.

Passengers' baggage for conveyance in the passenger trains is received and booked in Buenavista station every day, from 9:00 A. M. to 12:00 M., and from 2:00 to 4 P. M. The luggage office is also open, as well as the ticket office, one hour before the departure of the trains. The Express Mexicano, Calle de Escalerina, takes charge of travellers and luggage for the station and abroad.

44

'THE CORRIDO OF THE ELECTRIC TRAINS', IN 'CORRIDOS FROM THE PORFIRIATO (THE EARLY 1900S)' IN NORA E. JAFFARY, EDWARD W. OSOWSKI AND SUSIE S. PORTER (EDS.), *MEXICAN HISTORY: A PRIMARY SOURCE READER* (WESTVIEW PRESS: 2010), PP. 288–291. TRANSLATION BY THE EDITORS FROM ORIGINAL PUBLICATION IN HIGINIO VAZQUEZ SANTA ANNA, CANCIONES, CANTARES Y CORRIDOS MEXICANOS (MEXICO: SEGUNDO TOMO, LEÓN SÁNCHEZ, 1925–1931), PP. 244–245, 247–249

"The *Corrido* of the Electric Trains"

Oh, how beautiful, how blessed
it is to ride the electric train
and sit there so happy,
so free!

Oh! How beautiful, how swift
one travels so dauntless
on this classy train
without fears or anxiety.

'THE CORRIDO OF THE ELECTRIC TRAINS'

The bell so sonorous,
is heard with jubilation,
and it always arrives so swiftly
anywhere it goes.

It is a magnificent invention
that can be seen today in Mexico,
[and] that so surprises
everyone in the Capital.

It seems diabolic,
but it is only scientific,
and the shining, admirable
result of progress.

And the city is full of delight.
Enthusiasm is widespread.
Because the new era
and the height of enlightenment have been commemorated.

The close of the century arrived,
fastened with a golden brooch,
sure that with [the] next one
there will be many more good things to come.

Now, all so content,
together we sing frenetically.
Long live the electric train!
Long live enlightenment!

The great battalion thirteen,
and so, so many people—
all were festooned
and all the songs were played.

The fifteenth of January
of the year nineteen hundred
the new event took place
during the afternoon.

There were speeches and toasts
and a sumptuous banquet,
pleasure reigning everywhere
and order of the most enduring.

—It's as if something from the Devil
—Well, now you see Don Simón,

that the train goes on its own
has no compare.

Among the townspeople
and even those from the highest ranks
talk of the train is heard,
with fright and with surprise.

—What foreign devils!
says a nasally old lady,
Such inventions of the wicked
to earn their daily bread!

—For there is no doubt,
says another of ninety,
it's the devil himself,
believe me you, Doña Petrona.

—They say they are electric,
but this is just a pretense
to conceal
there is something of Satan about.

—God save us, Casildita,
from riding in one of those cars,
surely they would take one
straight to Hell.

—I don't even want to see them.
The priests can excommunicate us,
Aunt Bruna,
I am off to confession.

—Well, of course, it is the devil
who pulls those train cars along, by damn!
These days, Doña Charo,
everything is electric.

—Didja' see the electric light,
the telegraph, an' phonograph,
and a thousand other things,
that frighten almost everyone.

—Any old thing, comadre [dear lady],
of these things in which the devil may abound,
they say they are electric,
just so as not to scare us.

—But that is not the case, no, no, no,
and they try to fool us,
so that soon we are turned over
to Mister Don Satan.

—And there have already been two deaths
out by Chapultepec;
the trains ground them up
before they even knew it.

—Am I wrong? Well, just tell me,
if this isn't something from hell.
Oh, caramba! In my time,
would this sort of thing [have] been done!

And in this sort of way
the old ladies talk today,
frightened by the occurrence
of the modern streetcars. . . .

There is no risk of being run over
because they can be stopped,
on the spot,
more quickly than mules.

Cordial greetings to our current president,
who with intelligence knows how
to unite peace with progress.

45

JOHN STEALEY III (ED.), *PORTE CRAYON'S MEXICO: DAVID HUNTER STROTHER'S DIARIES IN THE EARLY PORFIRIAN ERA, 1879–1885* (KENT, OHIO: THE KENT STATE UNIVERSITY PRESS, 2006), PP. 741–743, 745–746

[Monday, 7 April 1884]

... All the stores in the City closed on account of the Stamp tax the first act of a rebellion. Went to the Central R.R. office & bought tickets to El Paso—Parker says he cant sell through to Denver. Saw Eckhart who says he will secure me the best state room near the end as most convenient. Coming out met Genl Wilson, Dana Col Cannon—Higgins & others. They are just returned from Morelia & saw Church there. Camacho came up & I on request presented Genl Wilson to him. W. has letters for him. Called at the Legation on my return & saw Harry Morgan, the Minister being out. At noon sent our trunks and beds to the R.R. Station who delivered them to the care of the Baggage Master. Wife & I then took cars for Judge Morgans—She visiting the family and I the Legation I explained to the Minister my plan of leaving the Cemetery under charge of Walters he being subordinate to the Minister in Case of doubt. The Judge requested me to call on his sister Mrs Genl. Drum at Washington—& I took leave going to the house for wife & there we took leave of the family Thence through a drizzle to visit Mrs Tyng & I went to the house opposite to take leave of Gorsuch & Frisbie. F. confirmed Admiral Cooper's statement of the official visit to the President in which it was understood that it was the private secretarys neglect & that the President was much mortified at the delay nevertheless the Admiral declined the second dinner offered by the Governor of Vera Cruz[1]—Coming out met wife & an increasing rain which induced me to take a carriage & drive home. soon after another basket of provisions & wine arrived from Mrs Morgan, rather overstocking us so that we left some of an beef & ham cans at home in Mexico. Pinto has observed the packing going on & has been clinging to us uneasily as if she anticipated desertion. Her flowery days are ended & she suspects it. Engaged Hack 209 to call for us to morrow morning at 5 o clock. I took up my fountain pen presented by Lieutenant

Very and find it convenient & easily handled—At night Judge Hall called to take leave & said Pitkins was certainly to succeed Morgan as Minister within a month. As H. is a "Gobe Mouche" I dont set much store in what he says. Clark[e] & Aikins called later.

[Tuesday, 8 April 1884]

Retired Early & slept profoundly until roused by Wife at 3^{30} A.M—at 4^{30} the Hack came—We dressed took Coffee & departed at 5 followed by Pinto's wailing back she being locked in with her pups. We reached the Station at 5^{30} some half an hour or more too early—Met the Genl Wilson & Dana who had slept in their travelling Car—Ms Higgins Genl Wilson & the Cannons called over & took leave, saying they would be in Denver before we left there. At 6 the Gate opened & we boarded our Car already occupied by the 3 Austins—10 Arabs—Machedo and a Mexican with an American wife—Nineteen persons in all. Saw a daughter of Gomez Farias at the Gate & divers other acquaintances taking leave of friends—At 6^{30} precisely the train started & our journey commenced[.] The morning delightful & our car in all respects satisfactory. The fields showed corn sprouting—Corn several weeks advanced—fresh green peas & wheat in head. The trees in lines like Lombardy Poplars in form but with willow leaves—Passed El Tajo at 8 & Tala at 20/9 —All of us complained a little of sea sickness—At 10 we lunched on crackers, Cold tea potted ham Hard boiled eggs & Claret which sat well. I have never started on an important trip so smoothly & with so little emotion of any Kind, either of hope or regret. At 10^{30} the human fly "La Mosca" Amy Austin got up & revealed herself. She was the girl that figured at Orrin's Circus in some very hazardous & astonishing feats on the wire & Trapeze—walking on a plank Ceiling twenty feet in the air she was English artless & childlike dirty grammarless & rather attractive looking. Austin her brother played the Banjo & his wife who skated & trapezed was very pretty—petite & of Jewish type—She dressed handsomely & wore diamonds of some value besides some very rich silver & gold Jewelry—She spent most of her time sitting on the platform with a stout Rail Roader from Guadalaxara Otherwise her manners were quiet & respectable—This party had three parrots which were a source of Great Amusement to us & others & Amy had a love of a poodle of the Puebla breed, infinitely small & cute looking. The Arabs were picturesque looking fellows, very respectable in their manners & readers of the Koran. Their Sheik was a handsome dignified fellow with a wife who was a Paris Milliner The party generally spoke Arabic & more English than any other Foreign tongue. At some of the stoppages met my Louisiana friends Cummings and Capehart who are en route for Queretero—At 1^{30} P.M. the cars stopped for dinner at San Juan del Rio. The town rising amidst its groves & greenfields looked very pleasant. Here a Sharp looking woman the wife of a Quiet Mexican of our Company informed us she was an American and none of these Circus people or Arabs. About two o clock the Wood pile on the Tender was discovered to be on fire and many unavailing attempts were made to extinguish it with buckets of Water. Finally the burning portion of the wood was thrown off & the train went on to replenish at the next wood pile. Queretero & its environs looked familiar to us as we passed. The day since breakfast had been intensely hot & we suffered with the suffocating heat & dust. At Salamanca we saw a beautifully located town & a very well dressed and comely Indian population—our armed Rural Guard who stood on our platform with his pistol & carbine called our attention to these people as his fellow Citizens & Kindred. Here John bought a good pair of buckskin gauntlets for a dollars [*sic*]. We reached Silao at 7 P.M. where the train supped—The country from San Juan del Rio to this place is open plain & generally well cultivated—I met Col. Brown here and a number of other acquaintances & also got a glass of lemonade[.] There is a fine American Eating house here & the last on the route. We had had a hot uncomfortable day & here closed it by going to bed.

[Wednesday, 9 April 1884]

Rose at 6 AM—profoundly refreshed—the road running smoothly all night—The moon shone & we had glimpses of Lagos which seemed covered with snow—The day agreeably cooler than yesterday. We passed through vast plains covered with Dragon trees in the night & at dawn saw a lake in the distance & cultivated plains without tree or shrub of any Kind—a desolate adobe village on the banks of a half dry stream all mud color—The just before sunrise we entered the City of Zacatecas. It was located partly in a hollow & straggling up a wide ravine with numerous mining pits and sheds, aqueducts & tramways straggling across the vale, then another portion of the town spread out on a higher bench all overlooked by a cliff crested mountain—As we stopped saw groups of miners around and a buzzard like priest followed by half a score of black veiled women enter a tramway car. These cars were drawn by 5 mules each and the houses were dark or dirt coloured with a fair number of church towers & domes—There was no greenery and no growth upon the hills except dwarf dragon trees & cactus. The soil of a red brown but the picture was arid & desolate as the sun rose. Passed the ridge at Zacatecas & entered again on the plain country more or less cultivated but always naked of trees or shrubs. Stopped at Caleva where we changed engine & attachments. The Company is digging a well here to supply the Engines with water. Wife had heated me a cup of coffee at 6 A.M. but John & I took breakfast with a Chinaman who had an eating tent here. Our breakfast was very savoury & the Celestial a tall good looking fellow of his race. On the train the Arabs offered me a drink of aguardiente which I tasted & found beneficial & we all feel better than we did yesterday. We have made in the first 24 hours 738 Kilometers, about $\frac{2}{5}$ths of our journey—A fat frowsey American selling old newspapers got on the platform & talked Coarsely but sensibly—They raise corn here with very little result in proportion to the labour & surface cultivated, all for the lack of water—a few cattle wandered in the field nibbling the slender corn stalks and the unploughed plains seemed to produce nothing but cactus & very little grass. Ahead saw a lake & dried up slashes in the center of which was an establishment of Seven tall stone stacks whitewashed which looked like a semicircle of immense Sibley tents. They stood amidst trees on the bank of the lake & were evidently a hacienda of some sort—for around wandered sheep, goats, horses & cattle. At 9³⁰ stopped opposite Fresnillo 5 miles distant & bought good oranges at 25cts per dozen—They also made Tortillas by the road side. The soil apparently good 12 to 20 inches deep & moist producing naturally wild sage & dwarf Mimosa—Passing Fresnillo crossed a broad mountain slope densely covered with Dragon tree & nopal like a green forest then in into another plain with a town or large Hacienda to the left and two pyramidal rock peaks appearing over the ridges in front. The Stations here were built of boards and cross ties. The Hacienda to our left was Calafasa—At Cañitas stopped a long while in an immense area covered with mesquite & dwarf Mimosa—There was here a corral of horses donkeys, sheep & goats—very little population visible the country being unavailable for lack of water and things growing still worse as we go north. The ladies & the Arabs having found a broom swept our our Car which was an improvement Mrs S. & John have made acquaintance with our Neighbors of the Circus & Skating rink—The elder ladies examining Madame Austin s Jewelry & John playing cards with "La Mosca." The air has been pleasant to day we are all well but the train seems to have made but little progress—about sunset we came in sight & passed a group of flat topped Mountains like Depot Sheds & houses, the most artificial natural objects I ever saw but of Gigantic proportions and with a touch of sublimity with their beauty—The moon rose fair & pleasant & we retired at 9 o clock.

[Thursday, to April 1884]

Bumping, backing & filling all night without making much progress apparently & arose at 6 A.M. with the train standing at Lerdo Station the sun just peeping over the hills at the hour named—The locality was bare & dusty ribbed with R.R. tracks and several trains lying quiescent around us—Wife got us a cup of Coffee I moistened my face & wiped it with a towel & walked to the Station house about 200 yards distant where I saw a group of persons collected. Here I found a man with fresh bread & bought a reals worth with some dickering about change as he refused to take Mexican Coppers and offered in change Chihuahua cuartillos of Copper about the size of the Mexican tlaco, which I in turn refused they being worth in Mexico only 1½ cents instead of 3 their value here—I finally found a Silver real & got my bread. There was a Canvas tent near with a bush addition with a sign "French Restaurant & Fonda" John & I however met Ma-chedo coming from there who reported the coffee disgusting and the whole feed a swindle—Machedo who is without supplies has to depend on what he can get hap-hazard which is very little in this region there being no eating houses established between Silao and Chihuahua—we seem to have made little headway yesterday not more than 100 Kilos & no one seems to Know how & when we are to get on—We are however well provisioned—the company rather entertaining the surroundings picturesque & we can let them take their time. The neighbouring ridges are sharp peaked & serrated resembling the Rocky mountains—to our right is the great Bolson de Majuini from which we are separated by a picturesque peak and chain of Mountains—Bought some fruit & a pie—At 7 A.M. we hooked to a fast train

& started running rapidly & with a delightful temperature After a long stretch of desolation entered an improved Country on the banks of a river & stopped at a dining place at 1^{30}. We dined luxuriously in our Bunk on Cold turkey—pie—cheese & Claret—leaving the open country we wound through a narrow gorge entering another valley hemmed in with picturesque hills and at 7 RM reached the Chihuahua Station The city was dimly visible half a mile distant so we took tea in our Bunk[.] The Arabs started some circus Jollity in which I assisted & was repeatedly applauded—After our slight of hand tricks Austin got out his Banjo and soothed us with Music—and then we started, the moon rose & we slipped quietly & pleasantly to bed as if we were on a ship in Mid Ocean.

[Friday, 11 April 1884]

Arose at 5^{20} took Coffee & an Orange & sniffed a fresh breeze which savours of the north—We were passing through a miserable looking Country—Dark levels convered with dead ragged growth—black hills stoney jagged & desolate—no population nor animals—reach Paso del Norte about 7 A.M. There is a handsome American Station house on the Mexican side and a town that looks like a collection of Brick yards—relieved by some trees & irrigated Gardens & vineyards. The Rio Grande is about the size of Cacapon River in dry Seasons, but it was muddy & thick as Chocolate—The crossing was provisional the Bridge not being yet finished—On the American Side the town of El Paso was alive with progress with handsome Modern Stores & buildings & crude like a lusty youthful Giant . . . .

Note

1 Minister Morgan reported the *contretemps* involving Admiral Cooper to the secretary of state. The admiral did refuse the proffered dinner in Vera Cruz on the ground that he had to sail the next morning. Despatch No. 774, P. H. Morgan to Frederick T. Frelinghuysen, Secretary of State, 24 Mar. 1884, Despatches from United States Ministers to Mexico, 1823–1906, M97, roll 77, General Records of Department of State, RG 59, NACP

46
FIG. 3. *SHOOTING ON A TROLLEY*, FIG. 4. *GRAN CALAVERA ELÉCTRICA*, FIG. 5. *COLLISION OF AN ELECTRIC STREETCAR WITH A HEARSE*, FROM JOSÉ GUADALUPE POSADA'S MEXICAN PRINTS, ROBERTO BERDECIO AND STANLEY APPLEBAUM (EDS.), *POSADA'S POPULAR MEXICAN PRINTS* (NEW YORK: DOVER PUBLICATIONS, 1972)

Figure 46.1 Entire broadside (an issue of Vanegas Arroyo's "Street Gazette" series) about a shooting on a trolley (see Fig. 84 and commentary on it, and commentary on Fig. 62).

Figure 46.2 "Gran calavera eléctrica" (Big trolley calavera). Broadside; z; 1907. A cemetery.

Figure 46.3 "Choque de un eléctrico con un carro fúnebre" (Collision between a trolley and a hearse); z.

47

JOHN L. STODDARD, *LECTURES*, 10 VOLS. (BOSTON: BALCH, 1899), VOL. VII: MEXICO, PP. 89–90, 93–94, 97–98, 101–102, 105

In a few hours we had reached the edge of the great Mexican plateau, and, with some trepidation, began the wonderful journey toward Vera Cruz. I rightly call it wonderful, for the railway by which it is accomplished is one of the most remarkable specimens of engineering skill and courage that the world can show. Most of the descent of eight thousand feet is made in about twenty miles. The steepness of the track can, therefore, be imagined. Railroad grades seldom exceed a fall of one foot in a hundred; but here there is at times an incline of four feet in a hundred. Standing on the rear platform, we experienced the sensation of *sliding* down the mountains, and it seemed wonderful that the heavy train did not rush downward to destruction. What kept it from so doing was a monstrous double engine, used, not only to pull its heavy burdens up the mountains, but also to restrain them in the descent. When necessity requires it, one-half of the engine works in a direction opposite to that in which the train is moving, in order to retard the almost overwhelming force of gravitation. It is a serious undertaking; for any undue impetus on the edge of these stupendous cliffs would mean swift death to every one on board. Few accidents, however, have occurred; no doubt because they are so constantly anticipated. It is where men are heedless from a sense of perfect safety that real danger lies; not in the iron bridge watched carefully from hour to hour, but in the little culvert or the loosened rail.

I was astonished to perceive that though a brakeman stood on every car there were no air-brakes on our train. "We could not keep them," was the explanation. "As fast as we put them on, the natives, who are inveterate thieves, cut them off and carried them away. In fact, until we riveted the spikes that hold down the rails, they stole them also; and rubber pads on the steps of Pullman cars invariably suffered the same fate." I noticed that steel ties were used instead of wooden ones, and that the sides of the cars were made of corrugated iron; since it is claimed that wood will not endure the sudden changes, daily, from the intense heat of the tropics to the cooler table-land.

The scenery on this route is magnificent. At times we saw a broad expanse of cultivated fields three thousand feet below us, the whitewashed buildings on their surface resembling dice upon a checker-board. The trees looked so diminutive, that they recalled the tiny playthings of our childhood called "Swiss Villages." At one point, the descent was so precipitous, that the Indians, who had been selling fruit and flowers at a station half up the mountain, ran down the rocks and reached another halting-place before our train arrived, and were ready to renew their traffic. A characteristic feature of this railway journey was the variety of life and merchandise discernible at every station. No sooner would we halt than scores of dark-hued men and women swarmed about the cars, crying their wares in harsh, discordant tones which sounded like a chorus of creaking signs on a windy night. The number of these Indian traders, the miscellaneous objects which they sold, and above all the amount of necessary bargaining, in broken English and Spanish spoken on the installment plan, were both novel and amusing. Every part of Mexico seems to have a special article to tempt the tourist. In one place oranges are sold, the next produces baskets of all shapes and sizes; at Irapuato strawberries are offered every day, the whole year round; another place is famous for its handsome canes; another still, for opals or for onyx. Everywhere we heard the cry of "Pulque! Pulque!" and had that nauseating mixture offered us by hands that looked more uninviting than the drink itself,—all mute, inglorious witnesses of the scarcity of soap.

At length we reached our destination for the night, the little town of Orizaba. It was the edge of evening when we strolled through its streets. The temperature was as high as that of New York in July. The air was heavy with the odors of luxuriant vegetation. Occasionally a tufted palm outlined its graceful form against the sky; yet, even then, we were not really in the Hot Lands. Compared with Vera Cruz and its adjoining territory Orizaba is cold; and the inhabitants of the coast actually come to this elevation for relief from heat, and to escape yellow fever which is here unknown. Perpetual summer reigns along this Mexican terrace; not hot enough to make existence unendurable, yet with an air sufficiently relaxing to cause ambition to appear a farce, exertion an absurdity, and any special interest in life beyond a cup of coffee, the aroma of a fine cigar, the music of a mandolin, and the smile of a fair señora, not worth the trouble that it costs. Yes, if there be a district in the world especially adapted to a life of *dolce far niente*, it is the natural terrace on which lie the little towns of Cordova and Orizaba, filled with the fragrance of magnificently timbered forests, and situated equidistant from a plain of almost equatorial heat and the cool shadows of Chapultepec.

On the Vera Cruz railway we traveled no further toward the coast than Orizaba, because the health officials had informed us that if our car descended to the Hot Lands, we should be quarantined on our return. Moreover, although this route is best adapted for a view of Mexico's temperate zone, in order to really see the tropics, another grand descent is preferable, along the recently completed railroad down the mountains to Tampico. Accordingly, we made our way to a different point on the edge of the Mexican plateau, prepared this time to take a plunge into the real Tierras Calientes.

It was seven o'clock in the morning when we left our car, and, on the brink of the great table-land, seated ourselves on vehicles, which, though much larger than our ordinary hand cars, nevertheless resembled them. Two benches crossed each, one in the front the other in the rear, and in the space between was a heavy brake, upon the strength of which the safety of our lives depended; for we were now, by the force of gravity alone, to slide down from the temperate to the torrid zone, upon a curving track, in places steeper than the road to Vera Cruz. Of course, we might have taken a regular train upon this route, but from no ordinary conveyance could we have viewed and photographed the scenery to such advantage as from these open cars. The difference was as great as that between riding in a covered barouche and in an open wagon. There was no danger of a collision, for we had seen the telegraphic order sent to hold the up-train at the base of the mountain till we should arrive. "Had the instructions been received and understood?" "Click, click, click," came the reassuring answer. It was all right; the track was clear, and it belonged to us. Vamanos! The ride that followed was incomparably the most exciting of my life. Now we went dashing through a tunnel which had a temperature as cooling as a shower-bath, or whirling round a precipice upon a shelf of rock, beneath which was a gorge two thousand feet in depth; a moment later, we would slide in a straight line along the glittering grooves with a momentum that would have been frightful, but for the steady hand maintained upon the brake. Even when thus controlled, it seemed at times as if the car were actually alive and leaping forward on the rails like a thoroughbred on the race-track; for we were making a descent of seven thousand feet in fifteen miles, including the windings of the track. I must confess that there were moments when I felt a little nervous, and once, when we had attained a speed that made a gentleman from Chicago turn pale and raise his eyes toward heaven, as if considering what his chances were of going there, I called a halt and took some photographs. The railroad winds about the mountains in tremendous loops, like a gigantic serpent. Compared with many feats of engineering here, the famous Pennsylvania Horseshoe Bend sinks into insignificance. The scenery was glorious. The mountains, glistening to their summits with luxuriant vegetation, appeared to be covered with soft, velvet mantles. At times we heard that rare and most delightful sound in Mexico,—the music of a waterfall.

"What is that?" I presently inquired, turning my field-glass toward a mountain summit far above us, "can a farm be located at such a height?"

"Yes," said our guide, "it is a corn plantation, and a good one too."

"But how can it be cultivated?"

"Well," said the man, with a twinkle in his eye, "no one can really climb there to work it; but the owner plants it from a distance by firing the seed from a shot-gun; and, when the corn ripens in the fall, he harvests the crop with rifle. You see the bullets cut the stalks, and, naturally, the ears of corn at once fall down the perpendicular cliffs!"

48

MEXICO'S GREAT ISTHMUS ROUTE: A SOUVENIR OF THE VISIT OF PRESIDENT PORFIRIO DÍAZ TO TEHUANTEPEC TO INSPECT THE ISTHMUS RAILWAY AND THE PORT WORKS AT COATZACOALCOS AND SALINA CRUZ (N.P, 1905), PP. 1–5

AS Mexico's Isthmus Route is about to become a dominant factor in the transcontinental and interoceanic traffic of America, some account of the Tehuantepec Railway and the terminal ports of Coatzacoalcos and Salina Cruz, which together constitute that route, will be found of interest to every class of readers. Such an account is rendered the more timely by the fact that Gen. Porfirio Diaz, the illustrious Mexican President, who has taken so constant and enlightened an interest in the completion of the Tehuantepec route, has just made a trip of inspection to the Isthmus, during which he examined carefully every phase of the enterprise and had the satisfaction of seeing how efficiently it is being handled by the famous English contracting firm of S. Pearson & Son, Ltd., who have, in the face of great difficulties, met and vanquished with admirable pluck and energy, practically rebuilt the railway; are transforming the terminal ports, and finally are the partners of the Mexican Government, which owns the line, for the exploitation of the route for a term of years.

Owing to the magnitude of the subject and the limitations of space, the description must be rather eclectic than exhaustive.

Brief geographical and physical description of the Isthmus of Tehuantepec

The Isthmus of Tehuantepec is situated in the southern portion of Mexico in the States of Vera Cruz and Oaxaca. It lies between 16° and 18° n. lat. and 94° and 95° long. w. of Greenwich. The distance from ocean to ocean in a beeline is 125 miles. One noted topographical feature of the Isthmian territory is its comparatively level character. The rise from the Atlantic or Gulf side is very gradual and culminates in the Chivela Pass at a height of only 730 feet, whence the descent to the Pacific is comparatively abrupt. The sudden depression in the Sierra Madre at the Isthmus from heights of over 3,000 feet in Chiapas and Oaxaca is an instance of the manner in which Nature often cooperates with the designs of man.

The latitude and inconsiderable elevation of the Isthmus of Tehuantepec might seem to argue an extremely hot climate in that region, but in reality the winds that constantly blow from ocean to ocean, either from north to south or from south to north, mitigate the tropic heat and produce a mild and agreeable temperature.

In point of salubrity there can be no comparison between Tehuantepec and Panama, the superiority of the Mexican Isthmus being incontestable.

Signor Gaetano Moro, the able Italian who was at the head of the scientific commission that surveyed the Isthmus of Tehuantepec in the years 1812–43. under the Garay concession. makes the following note-worthy statement in his report, which was published in English at London in 1844: "During the long sojourn of the commission in the Isthmus they had often to undergo hard and severe toils, and were frequently exposed to the most trying inclemencies of the weather, and yet neither themselves nor their numerous attendants experienced any illness indicative of an unhealthy climate."

It is related that a colony of Europeans was once established on the Isthmus and by an unaccountable want of foresight the colonists were left without provisions for such time as had to elapse before they could raise their own crops, and although everything seemed calculated to favor the development of an epidemic, no disease appeared among them, and those who died perished more from want than any other cause.

Finally, the French traveler, M. Michel Chevalier, speaks of "the healthfulness of the country at some distance from the sea," adding that it is well known that the Isthmus was once densely populated, and that he saw no reason why it could not be so again.

All the towns and villages of the Isthmus have their centenarians, and the indigenous population are among the most active, vigorous and intelligent Indians of the Republic.

In comparing the merits of the rival transcontinental routes, the salubrity of Tehuantepec is an important factor in its favor.

The natural products and resources of the Isthmus are numerous and varied. The soil and climate are adapted to the growth of corn, coffee, cacao, tobacco, rice and sugar-cane. The forests abound in game, and the rivers, lagoons and oceans in fish. Interspersed among the woodlands are park-like tracts of good grazing land for cattle. The dense forests yield not only a variety of useful timber, which in Spanish times was sent to Habana for shipbuilding purposes (hence the name El Corte given to the upper reaches of the Coatzacoalcos River), but also cabinet-woods, dye-woods and woods producing precious gums, resins and balsams. Medicinal plants, spices (particularly vanilla), oranges and other tropical fruits, indigo, cotton and other fibers are also among the products of the vegetable kingdom. Orchids, rare ferns and exquisite flowering plants abound in the forests.

Domestic birds, particularly the turkey, thrive to a marked degree at certain points on the Isthmus. The bees which fill the woods, where there are so many flowers, yield a fine quality of honey and wax. The dye known as cochineal has, from time immemorial, come from the Tehuantepec region.

Various spots on the Isthmus have been successfully bored for oil and this promises to become an industry of great importance. Alabaster and gypsum occur in different points. The lagoons in the southern portion of the Isthmus contain immense salt deposits.

There are several thermal springs for which curative properties are claimed.

The Isthmus is well watered. The most extensive river is the Coatzacoalcos, which flows into the Gulf of Mexico near the town of the same name. This river, from its confluence with the Malatengo to the sea, measures 258 kilometers. Near its mouth it is over 2,000 feet wide, and is a noble stream.

Nearly all the other rivers of the Isthmus are tributaries of the Coatzacoalcos. The exceptions, of course, are the Tehuantepec River, which empties into the Pacific, and the rivers which flow into the lagoons on the Pacific Coast.

Such is the famous Isthmus of Tehuantepec, where much foreign capital 'is being invested in various lines, but particularly in tropical plantations, which, considering the marvelous fertility of the soil, ought, with competent and careful management, to yield good returns.

Advantages of Tehuantepec route

The advantages offered by Mexico's Isthmus for interoceanic communication are of various kinds.

In the first place, we may consider the advantages arising from geographical situation. In this respect it may be laid down that, other things being the same, that Isthmus can claim the preference which is nearest to what has been called the axial line of the world's trade, which is a line drawn from Hong-Kong, in China, to Yokohama, in Japan; thence across the Pacific to San Francisco; thence across the United States to New York, and finally across the Atlantic to Liverpool.

The opening-up of a trade route across the Isthmus of Tehuantepec will be of special benefit to the Middle West of the United States, and particularly to the Mississippi Valley. Admiral Shufeldt, U. S. N., who reported, some thirty-five years ago, on the feasibility of an inter-oceanic canal at Tehuantepec, stated that such a canal would be a natural prolongation of the Mississippi River to the Pacific Ocean, and that it would bring New Orleans 1,400 nautical miles nearer to San Francisco than a canal via Darien. The distance from the mouth of the Mississippi to the northern terminal of the Tehuantepec Railway is 810 miles, and the total distance by rail and water from Chicago to the Pacific Ocean by way of the Mexican Isthmus is only 1,875 miles.

The average saving in distance by the Tehuantepec route over Panama to all points on the Atlantic Coast of the United States and Europe is about 1,250 miles. The ordinary freight steamer makes about ten miles an hour, or, say, 250 miles a day, requiring five days longer via Panama, assuming the time of crossing the two isthmuses to be the same. It will take a steamer about one day to pass through the Panama Canal, and the freight about two days to pass over Tehuantepec from ship to ship, leaving still four days to the advantage of Tehuantepec. The extra cost of the four days to a steamer, say $2,000, plus the canal tolls, would make a 5,000-ton cargo cost about $10,000 via Panama. No doubt the cost by Tehuantepec would be no greater, and there would still be the saving in time of four days, which, to quick freight, is of great importance in this age of rapid transportation.

49

JOHNSON SHERRICK. *LETTERS OF TRAVEL* (N.P., 1905), PP. 191–198

Scenes in old Mexico

BEFORE we left the City of Mexico, we paid a visit to the "floating gardens." These are queer places about seven miles from the city. During the winter, which is their dry season, large flat-bottom boats, filled with fertile earth or soil, are floated on the water of a wide canal. By the seeping of the water through small crevices of the boat the earth is kept moist. In this· ground they plant garden vegetables, which produce in abundance. The products find a ready market in the city. The ground for many miles around is very level and now they have many small canals or ditches through this vast fertile and level plain, forming hundreds of small islands. These islands are, on an average, about thirty feet wide. They receive moisture from the little canals that surround them, which makes them wonderfully fertile. In company with Mr. and Mrs. Rockwell, of Kansas, we took a flat-bottom boat at the edge of the city on the main canal which leads out to these famous gardens. The sun was shining brightly, as it shines there every day. A gaudy canvas spread over the bow in a very primitive style afforded shade for us as we proceeded on our way down this strange and interesting canal. Our "captain" propelled his own craft with a pole, which he ran down to the bottom of this wide, but shallow canal, and pushed the boat as he walked the deck. His uncovered feet, bare, black legs, and unassuming, smiling face, made us feel as if we were on some of the islands of the South seas. On the shores we could see various sights, evidently like the scenes of the orient, as we slowly glided on our way. On the shore, sitting in the hottest sun and upon the ground, were many dark and black-haired women, with bare head and arms, washing garments. Young and old, and some with their babies strapped upon their backs, where they were sitting and rubbing their clothes to make them clean. The soap they use grows in the ground as turnips do in the north, and their washboards are dark, flat stones, lying on the ground near the water's edge. Here they sit in the broiling tropical sun, half clad, dipping and rubbing the soiled clothing, and spreading them upon the sand and grass to dry.

On the path along the shore were caravans of donkeys and mules loaded down with bales of straw, green and peculiar looking grasses and other products of the soil, staggering under their great loads in the dusty pathway, on their way to the city. We also passed large flatboats laden to the edge, with curious vegetables from the gardens below, on their way to market. Presently we saw a very low stone bridge ahead of us across the canal. We wondered if we would have to get off our boat and walk below to another, but our captain soon informed us by peculiar motions, while he jabbered something (which, of course, was more than Greek to us) that we should lie down on the bottom of the boat. We obeyed orders, of course, and he untied some rope and let the canvas top down over us when we passed under the bridge, which was not more than three feet above the water. In an hour we were at the gardens, where we took a smaller boat and two other black-skinned natives pushed us over the small waterways that run in and among the many island gardens. Before we proceeded far we stopped by a little cottage built of sticks and thatched with cane, I presume the home of our boatman, who gathered from the poppies and other flowers that grew in great profusion around this humble abode, two most beautiful bouquets and presented them to the ladies. A little "tip," a smile, and we were off, moving among the many little islands where every product of the tropical gardens was green and growing and the borders of each little island were lined with flowers of every hue. The birds from bush to branch were chirping their favorite songs; the natives were splashing the water from the ditches over the ground, and it seemed to me a fairy land where all was peace and plenty. It was so unlike the mountain and desert lands of this country which we had seen before, and where want and misery seemed to prevail that the contrast surprised me. Leaving the gardens we passed through a village of cottages and the place reminded me of the Java villages I saw at the Chicago World's Fair. The village school ma'am had around her quite a lot of little native girls and boys, clad in their primitive style and studying their lessons aloud. Half the native people of this country go about everywhere in their bare feet, many of them with bare legs. Some of them wear sandals, while others who are of the first class, dress as we do. Schools are being carried on now all over the country, compulsory education is the law, and improvements among these people are very marked of late. Capital from England, Germany, France and the United States is being largely invested here. The government is considered stable and all the prospects of this country are good. Pulque (Pulka) is the national drink for these people, and is to Mexico what beer is to Germany. It is drawn from the maguey plant (which much resembles the century plant often seen in the United States). Many acres of land are used for the cultivation of this plant and thousands of barrels of the juice are sold to the people in the many drinking places, much like beer and other liquors are sold at home. This drink will intoxicate if too freely imbibed.

We left the City of Mexico a few days ago over the Mexican railroad for a trip to Vera Cruz, which lies down on the great Gulf of Mexico. We did not make this trip to see the city of Vera Cruz so much as we did to see and go over the picturesque scenery through which the road runs; and truly it is a grand and fascinating trip. We left Mexico City at 7 o'clock in the morning. The first three hours we rode through almost endless maguey fields. Then until 2 p. m., through sand and dusty desert lands, after which the train began the descent of nearly ten thousand feet to the city of Vera Cruz. First in and among the lofty mountain peaks, through tunnels winding around yawning precipices, apparently scaling the mountain side, 'round and 'round the cliffs, the train, with its trusty and faithful engine, descends cautiously and carefully downward, and we see thousands of feet below. Nearly everyone is standing and looking through the car windows. Not a word of mirth is spoken, the scene is too terrible. The shadow of danger pervades the air and a conscious look of fear glances from one countenance to another. Far below we see a line and a tiny toy train of cars apparently moving but almost imperceptible. "What is that?" exclaims one. "That is this railroad, with a freight train ahead of us in the valley we are going to." "It can't be possible," says another. "But it is," said an officer, and in due time we found it so. It seems almost impossible that engineering skill could possibly carve a roadbed from these mountain sides. A descent of a mile straight down is made by running ten miles without getting one mile nearer Vera Cruz. A sigh of relief seemed to come over all of us in the car when the valley was safely reached. We remained over night at Orizaba, a quaint old town of 15,000 people, eighty-two miles west of the gulf and four thousand feet above the sea level, just at the head of the region where the tropical lands begin. All day, before we came down in this fertile valley we could see, as we supposed, near by, from our car windows, the snow that lies on the top of three or four mountains, yet they were from sixty to one hundred miles away.

At that place we took a conveyance and were driven through byways and over fields to visit the large sugar plantations, banana fields and coffee orchards. They are interesting fields, new and novel to us and a great pleasure to visit. The sugar is made from juice of the cane, which grows here the whole year, and also makes good feed for cattle and mules. Bananas grow on small trees which are cultivated like corn, and planted in rows about eight feet apart. The tree resembles a palm growth and will bear fruit for several years. Coffee grows on bright green bushes in a red pod or berry, which is opened by hand, the kernel (which is the coffee) taken out, dried, and prepared for market. The next morning we left Orizaba and proceeded to Cordoba, which is the center of the coffee district, in the state of Vera Cruz, and about twenty miles from Orizaba. The railroad runs between these two towns through a section of tropical fruit and flower growing lands, which is the most beautiful landscape and fascinating country I ever beheld. Standing on the platform of the rear car I saw the changing beauty of varied scenes which words can never picture. On both sides of the road were the mountains in the close distance, varied and grand. The soft, mild, morning breezes that came down the valley played with the leaves of the shrubbery that fills this magnificent valley, and kissed the yellow cheeks of the ripe oranges that hang in profusion among the green leaves of the trees on which they grow. The green hedge fence that lines the railroad for miles was covered and dotted with various colors of most beautiful flowers. The banana trees with their yellow bark, purple blossoms and clustering fruit, mellowed down the acres of green with spots of gold-like hues.

The coffee trees, planted in long rows, sparkled with bright red berries that hung like Indian beads amid the green leaves of its parent tree. Indeed we were sorry to leave these garden lands, but our train sped away and soon we were again on desert plains on our way to the sea, and the beautiful valley we left behind us seemed but the swift flying pleasure of a fairy dream. We did not stay long at Vera Cruz. The weather was hot there and the stench from the sewers on the streets caused us to come up to this place which is a very good place to spend a few days. The weather is cool and damp here. The town has a population of about fourteen thousand, and lies four thousand feet above the sea level. It rains nearly every day, but for some reason in nature the clouds will not rise high enough to cross the mountain and rain on the table land of Mexico, hence it does not rain at all in winter time in the city of Mexico.

All the tropical fruits grow here in abundance and the soil produces much, consequently the people here get along well; they are much better dressed, and beggars, misery and want are not seen like in the dried up districts we see so often in Mexico. In the cemetery on the hill stands a monument upon which is inscribed, "To the memory of the fallen victims of the American invasion." We go from here to Pueblo, thence back to the City of Mexico, after which we will proceed northward towards California. The Grand hotel here is the finest and best kept that we have found in all Mexico.

Halapa, Mexico, March 18th, 1896.

50

JOHN KENNETH TURNER, *BARBAROUS MEXICO* (CHICAGO: C. H. KERR, 1910), PP. 49–69

Over the exile road

Yaquis traveling to Yucatan, after arriving at the port of Guaymas, Sonora, embark on a government war vessel for the port of San Bias. After a journey of four or five days they are disembarked and are driven by foot over some of the roughest mountains in Mexico, from San Bias to Tepic and from Tepic to San Marcos. As the crow flies the distance is little more than one hundred miles; as the road winds it is twice as far, and requires from fifteen to twenty days to travel. "Bull pens," or concentration camps, are provided all along the route, and stops are made at the principal cities. All families are broken up on the way, the chief points at which this is done being Guaymas, San Marcos, Guadalajara and Mexico City. From San Marcos the unfortunates are carried by train over the Mexican Central Railway to Mexico City and from Mexico City over the International Railway to Veracruz. Here they are bundled into one of the freight steamers of the "National" company, and in from two to five days are disembarked at Progreso and turned over to the waiting consignees.

On the road to Yucatan the companion of my journeys, L. Gutierrez DeLara, and I, saw gangs of Yaqui exiles, saw them in the "bull pen" in the midst of the army barracks in Mexico City; finally we joined a party of them at Veracruz and traveled with them on ship from Veracruz to Progreso.

There were 104 of them shoved into the unclean hole astern of the freight steamer *Sinaloa,* on which we embarked. We thought it might be difficult to obtain the opportunity to visit this unclean hole, but, luckily, we were mistaken. The guard bent readily to friendly words, and before the ship was well under way my companion and I were seated on boxes in the hold with a group of exiles gathered about us, some of them, tobacco-famished, pulling furiously at the cigarettes which we had passed among them, others silently munching the bananas, apples and oranges which we had brought.

There were two old men past fifty, one of them small, active, sharp-featured, talkative, dressed in American overalls, jumper, shoes and slouch hat, with the face and manner of a man bred to civilization; the other, tall, silent, impassive, wrapped to the chin in a gay colored blanket, the one comfort he had snatched from his few belongings as the soldiers were leading him away. There was a magnificent specimen of an athlete under thirty, with a wizened baby girl of two held in the crook of one arm, an aggressive-faced woman of forty against whom was closely pressed a girl of ten shivering and shaking in the grasp of a malarial attack, two overgrown boys who squatted together in the background and grinned half foolishly at our questions, bedraggled women, nearly half of them with babies, and an astonishingly large number of little chubby-faced, bare-legged boys and girls who played uncomprehendingly about the floor or stared at us from a distance out of their big solemn black eyes.

"Revolutionists?" I asked of the man in overalls and jumper.

"No; workingmen."

"Yaquis?"

"Yes, one Yaqui," pointing to his friend in the blanket. "The rest are Pimas and Opatas."

"Then why are you here?"

"Ah, we are all Yaquis to General Torres. It makes no difference to him. You are dark. You dress in my clothes and you will be a Yaqui—to him. He makes no investigation, asks no questions—only takes you."

"Where are you from?" I asked of the old man.

"Most of us are from Ures. They took us in the night and carried us away without allowing us to make up bundles of our belongings."

"I am from Horcasitas," spoke up the young athlete with the babe on his arm. "I was plowing in the field when they came, and they did not give me time to unhitch my oxen."

"Where is the mother of your baby?" I inquired curiously of the young father.

"Dead in San Marcos," he replied, closing his teeth tight. "That three weeks' tramp over the mountains killed her. They have allowed me to keep the little one—so far."

"Did any of you make resistance when the soldiers came to take you?" I asked.

"No," answered the old man from Ures. "We went quietly; we did not try to run away." Then with a smile: "The officers found more trouble in looking after their men, their privates, to prevent them from running away, from deserting, than they did with us."

"We were one hundred and fifty-three at the start, we of Ures," went on the old man. "Farm laborers, all of us. We worked for small farmers, poor men, men with not more than half a dozen families each in their employ. One day a government agent visited the neighborhood and ordered the bosses to give an account of all their laborers. The bosses obeyed, but they did not know what it meant until a few days later, when the soldiers came. Then they knew, and they saw ruin coming to them as well as to us. They begged the officers, saying: 'This is my peon. He is a good man. He has been with me for twenty years. I need him for the harvest.'"

"It is true," broke in the woman with the aguestricken child. "We were with Carlos Romo for twenty-two years. The night we were taken we were seven; now we are two."

"And we were with Eugenio Morales for sixteen years," spoke another woman.

"Yes," went on the spokesman, "our bosses followed us, begging, but it was no use. Some of them followed us all the way to Hermosillo. There was Manuel Gandara, and Jose Juan Lopez, and Franco Tallez, and Eugenio Morales and the Romo brothers, Jose and Carlos. You will find them there now and they will tell you that what we say is true. They followed us, but it was no use. They had to go back and call vainly at our empty houses for laborers. We were stolen—and they were robbed!

"They died on the way like starving cattle," went on the old man from Ures. "When one fell ill he never got well again. One woman was deathly sick at the start. She begged to be left behind, but they wouldn't leave her. She was the first to fall—it happened on the train between Hermosillo and Guaymas.

"But the cruelest part of the trail was between San Bias and San Marcos. Those women with babies! It was awful! They dropped down in the dust again and again. Two never got up again, and we buried them ourselves there beside the road."

"There were burros in San Blas," interrupted a woman, "and mules and horses. Oh, why didn't they let us ride? But our men were good. When the little legs of the *ninos* were weary our men carried them on their backs. And when the three women who were far gone in pregnancy could walk no more our men made stretchers of twigs and carried them, taking turns. Yes, our men were good, but now they are gone. We do not see them any more!"

"The soldiers had to tear me away from my husband," said another, "and when I cried out they only laughed. The next night a soldier came and tried to take hold of me, but I pulled off my shoes and beat him with them. Yes, the soldiers bothered the women often, especially that week we starved in Mexico City, but always the women fought them back."

"I have a sister in Yucatan," said a young woman under twenty. "Two years ago they carried her away. As soon as we arrive I shall try to find her. We will keep each other company, now that they have taken my husband from me. Tell me, is it so terribly hot in Yucatan as they say it is? I do not like hot weather, yet if they will only let me live with my sister I will not mind."

"To whom do all these bright little tads, these *muchachos,* all of the same size, belong?" I inquired.

"Quien sabe?" answered an old woman. "Their parents are gone, just as are our babes. They take our children from us and give us the children of strangers. And when we begin to love the new ones, they take them away, too. Do you see that woman huddled over there with her face in her hands? They took her four little boys at Guadalajara and left her nothing. Myself? Yes, they took my husband. For more than thirty years we had never been parted for a single night. But that made no difference; he is gone. Yet perhaps I am lucky; I still have my daughter. Do you think, though, that we may meet our husbands again in Yucatan?"

As we breasted the Veracruz lighthouse, the shoulder of a Norther heaved itself against the side of the vessel, the ocean streamed in at the lower portholes and the quarters of the unhappy exiles were flooded with water. They fled for the deck, but here were met by flying sheets of rain, which drove them back again. Between the flooded hold and the flooded poop the exiles spent the night, and when, early the next morning, as we drove into the Coatzacoalcos river, I strolled aft again, I saw them lying about the deck, all of them drenched and shivering, some of them writhing in the throes of acute seasickness.

We steamed thirty miles up the Coatzacoalcos river, then anchored to the shore and spent a day loading jungle bulls for the tough beef market of New Orleans. Two hundred ordinary cattle may be coaxed through a hole in the side of a ship in the space of two hours, but these bulls were as wild as wolves, and each had to be half butchered before he would consent to walk in the straight and narrow way. Once inside, and ranged along the two sides of the vessel, they fought, trampled each other, bawled as loud as steam whistles, and in a number of instances broke their head ropes and smashed through the flimsy railing which had been erected to prevent them from over-running other portions of the lower deck. In a bare space at the stern of the vessel, surrounded on three sides by plunging, bawling bulls, were the quarters of the "Yaquis." It was stay there and run the risk of being trampled, or choose the unsheltered deck. For the remaining four days of the journey, one of which we spent waiting for the Norther to pass, the "Yaquis" chose the deck.

At last we arrived at Progreso. As we entered the train for Merida we saw our friends being herded into the second class coaches. They left us at the little station of San Ignacio, on their way to a plantation belonging to Governor Olegario Molina, and we saw them no more.

In Yucatan I soon learned what becomes of the Yaqui exiles. They are sent to the henequen plantations as slaves, slaves on almost exactly the same basis as are the 100,000 Mayas whom I found on the plantations. They are held as chattels, they are bought and sold, they receive no wages, but are fed on beans, *tortillas* and putrid fish. They are beaten, sometimes beaten to death. They are worked from dawn until night in the hot sun beside the Mayas. The men are locked up at night. The women are required to marry Chinamen or Mayas. They are hunted when they run away, and are brought back by the police if they reach a settlement. Families, broken up in Sonora or on the way, are never permitted to reunite. After they once pass into the hands of the planter the government cares no more for them, takes no more account of them. The government has received its money, and the fate of the Yaquis is in the hands of the planter.

I saw many Yaquis in Yucatan. I talked with them. I saw them beaten. One of the first things that I saw on a Yucatan plantation was the beating of a Yaqui. His name was Rosanta Bajeca.

The act, though not intentionally so, perhaps, was theatrically staged. It was at 3:45 o'clock in the morning, just after roll-call of the slaves. The slave gang was drawn up in front of the plantation store, the fitful rays of the lanterns sputtering high on the store front playing uncertainly over their dusky faces and dirty white forms. There were seven hundred of them. Now and then a brighter lantern beam shot all the way to the towering tropical trees, which, standing shoulder to shoulder, walled in the grass-grown *patio*. Under the hanging lanterns and facing the ragged band stood the *administrador,* or general manager, the *mayordomo primero, or* superintendent, and the lesser bosses, the *mayordomos secundos,* the *majacol* and the *capataces.*

"Rosanta Bajeca!"

The name, squeaked out by the voice of the *administrador,* brought from the crowd a young Yaqui, mediumsized, sinewy-bodied, clean-featured, with well-formed head erect on square shoulders, bony jaw fixed, dark, deep set eyes darting rapidly from one side to another of the circle which surrounded him, like a tiger forced out of the jungle and into the midst of the huntsmen.

"Off with your shirt!" rasped the *administrador,* and at the words superintendent and foremen ringed closer about him. One reached for the garment, but the Yaqui fended the hand, then with the quickness of a cat, dodged a cane which swished at his bare head from the opposite direction. For one instant—no more—with the hate of his eyes he held the circle at bay, then with a movement of consent he waved them back, and with a single jerk drew the shirt over his head and bared his muscular bronze body, scarred and discolored from previous beatings, for the whip. Submissive but dignified he stood there, for all the world like a captive Indian chief of a hundred years ago, contemptuously awaiting the torture of his enemies.

Listlessly the waiting slaves looked on. A regiment of toil, they stood half a dozen deep, with soiled calico trousers reaching half way to the ankles or rolled to the knees, shirts of the same material with many gaping mouths showing the bare bronze skin beneath, bare legs, bare feet, battered grass hats held deferentially in the hands—a tatterdemalion lot, shaking the sleep from their eyes, blinking at the flickering lanterns. Three races there were, the sharp-visaged, lofty-browed Maya, aborigine of Yucatan, the tall, arrow-backed Chinaman and the swarthy, broad-fisted Yaqui from Sonora.

At a third command of the *administrador* there stepped from the host of waiting slaves a giant Chinese. Crouching, he grasped the wrists of the silent Yaqui. The next moment he was standing straight with the Yaqui on his back in the manner of a tired child being carried by one of its elders.

Not one of that throng who did not know what was coming, yet not until a *capataz* reached for a bucket hanging high on the store front did there come a tension of nerves among those seven hundred men. The whipper extraordinary, known as a *majocol,* a deep-chested, hairy brute, bent over the bucket and soused his hands deep into the water within. Withdrawing them, he held high for inspection four dripping ropes, each three feet long. The thick writhing things in the dim lamplight seemed like four bloated snakes, and at sight of them the tired backs of the ragged seven hundred straightened with a jerk and an involuntary gasp rippled over the assemblage. Laggard slumber, though unsated, dropped from their eyes. At last all were awake, wide awake.

The ropes were of native henequen braided tight and thick and heavy for the particular purpose in hand. Water-soaked, to give them more weight and cutting power, they were admirably fitted for the work of "cleaning up," the term whereby corporal punishment is known on the plantations of Yucatan.

The hairy *majocol* selected one of the four, tossed back the remaining three, the pail was carried away and the giant Chinaman squared off with the naked body of the victim to the gaze of his fellow bondsmen. The drama was an old one to them, so old that their eyes must have ached many times at the sight, yet for them it could never lose its fascination. Each knew that his own time was coming, if it had not already come, and not one possessed the physical power to turn his back upon the spectacle.

Deliberately the *majocol* measured his distance, then as deliberately raised his arm high and brought it swiftly down again; the bloated snake swished through the air and fell with a spat across the glistening bronze shoulders of the Yaqui!

The *administrador,* a small, nervous man of many gestures, nodded his approval and glanced at his watch, the *mayordomo,* big, stolid, grinned slowly, the half dozen *capataces* leaned forward a little more obliquely in their eagerness, the regiment of slaves swayed bodily as by some invisible force, and a second gasp, painful and sharp like the bursting air from a severed windpipe, escaped them.

Every eye was riveted tight upon that scene in the uncertain dimness of the early morning—the giant Chinaman, bending slightly forward now, the naked body upon his shoulders, the long, uneven, livid welt that marked the visit of the wet rope, the deliberate, the agonizingly deliberate *majocol* the *administrador,* watch in hand, nodding endorsement, the grinning *mayordomo,* the absorbed *capataces.*

All held their breath for the second blow. I held my breath with the rest, held it for ages, until I thought the rope would never fall. Not until I saw the finger signal of the *administrador* did I know that the blows were delivered by the watch and not until it was all over did I know that, in order to multiply the torture, six seconds were allowed to intervene between each stroke.

The second blow fell, and the third, and the fourth. I counted the blows as they fell, ages apart. At the fourth the strong brown skin broke and little pin-heads of crimson pushed themselves out, burst, and started downward in thin tricklets. At the sixth the glistening back lost its rigidity and fell to quivering like a jellyfish. At the ninth a low whine somewhere in the depths of that Yaqui, found its devious way outward and into the open. Oh, that whine! I hear it now, a hard, hard whine, as if indurated to diamond hardness by drilling its way to the air through a soul of adamant.

At last the spats ceased—there were fifteen—the *administrador,* with a final nod, put away his watch, the giant Chinaman released his grip on the brown wrists and the Yaqui tumbled in a limp heap to the ground. He lay there for a moment, his face in his arms, his quivering, bleeding flesh to the sky, then a foreman stepped forward and put a foot roughly against his hip.

The Yaqui lifted his head, disclosing to the light a pair of glazed eyes and a face twisted with pain. A moment later he rose to his feet and staggered forward to join his fellow bondsmen. In that moment the spell of breathless silence on the seven hundred snapped, the ranks moved in agitation and there rose a hum of low speech from every section of the crowd. The special "cleaning up" of the morning was over. Five minutes later the day's work on the farm had begun.

Naturally I made inquiries about Rosanta Bajeca to find out what crime he had committed to merit fifteen lashes of the wet rope. I ascertained that he had been only a month in Yucatan, and but three days before had been put in the field with a harvesting gang to cut and trim the great leaves of the henequen plant. Two thousand a day was the regular stint for each slave, and Bajeca had been given three days in which to acquire the dexterity necessary to harvest the required number of leaves. He had failed. Hence the flogging. There had been no other fault.

"It's a wonder," I remarked to a *capataz*, "that this Yaqui did not tear himself from the back of the Chinaman. It's a wonder he did not fight He seems like a brave man; he has the look of a fighter."

The *capataz* chuckled.

"One month ago he was a fighter," was the reply, "but a Yaqui learns many things in a month in Yucatan. Still, there was a time when we thought this dog would never learn. Now and then they come to us that way; they never learn; they're never worth the money that's paid for them."

"Tell me about this one," I urged.

"He fought; that's all. The day he came he was put to work loading bundles of leaves onto the elevator which leads to the cleaning machine. The *mayordomo*—yes, the *mayordomo primero*—happened along and punched the fellow in the stomach with his cane. A half minute later a dozen of us were struggling to pull that Yaqui wolf away from the throat of the *mayordomo*. We starved him for a day and then dragged him out for a cleaning up. But he fought with his fingers and with his teeth until a *capataz* laid him out with the blunt edge of a machete. After that he tasted the rope daily for a while, but every day for no less than a week the fool fought crazily on until he kissed the earth under the weight of a club. But our *majocol* never faltered. That *majocol* is a genius. He conquered the wolf. He wielded the rope until the stubborn one surrendered, until that same Yaqui came crawling, whimpering, on hands and knees and licked with his naked tongue the hand of the man who had beaten him!"

During my travels in Yucatan I was repeatedly struck with the extremely human character of the people whom the Mexican government calls Yaquis. The Yaquis are Indians, they are not white, yet when one converses with them in a language mutually understood one is struck with the likenesses of the mental processes of White and Brown. I was early convinced that the Yaqui and I were more alike in mind than in color. I became convinced, too, that the family attachments of the Yaqui mean quite as much to the Yaqui as the family attachments of the American mean to the American. Conjugal fidelity is the cardinal virtue of the Yaqui home and it seems to be so not because of any tribal superstition of past times or because of any teachings of priests, but because of a constitutional tenderness sweetened more and more with the passing of the years, for *the one* with whom he had shared the meat and the shelter and the labor of life, the joys and sorrows of existence.

Over and over again I saw this exemplified on the exile road and in Yucatan. The Yaqui woman feels as keenly the brutal snatching away of her babe as would the cultivated American woman. The heart-strings of the Yaqui wife are no more proof against a violent and unwished-for separation from her husband than would be the heart-strings of the refined mistress of a beautiful American home.

The Mexican government forbids divorce and remarriage within its domain, but for the henequen planters of Yucatan all things are possible. To a Yaqui woman a native of Asia is no less repugnant than he is to an American woman, yet one of the first barbarities the henequen planter imposes upon the Yaqui slave woman, freshly robbed of the lawful husband of her bosom, is to compel her to marry a Chinaman and live with him!

"We do that," explained one of the planters to me, "in order to make the Chinamen better satisfied and less inclined to run away. And besides we know that every new babe born on the place will some day be *worth anywhere from* $500 *to* $1,000 *cash!*"

The cultivated white woman, you say, would die of the shame and the horror of such conditions. But so does the brown woman of Sonora. No less a personage than Don Enrique Camara Zavala, president of the "Camara de Agricola de Yucatan," and a millionaire planter himself, told me:

"If the Yaquis last out the first year they generally get along all right and make good workers, but the trouble is, *at least two-thirds of them die off in the first twelve months!*"

On the ranch of one of the most famous henequen kings we found about two hundred Yaquis. One-third of these were men, who were quartered with a large body of Mayas and Chinamen. Entirely apart from these, and housed in a row of new one-room huts, each set in a tiny patch of uncultivated land, we discovered the Yaqui women and children.

We found them squatting around on their bare floors or nursing an open-air fire and a kettle just outside the back door. We found no men among them, Yaquis or Chinamen, for they had arrived only one month before—all of them—from Sonora.

In one house we found as many as fourteen inmates. There was a woman past fifty with the strength of an Indian chief in her face and with words which went to the mark like an arrow to a target. There was a comfortable, home-like woman with a broad, pock-marked face, pleasant words and eyes which kindled with friendliness despite her troubles. There were two woman who watched their fire and listened only. There was a girl of fifteen, a bride of four months, but now alone, a wonderfully comely girl with big eyes and soft mouth, who sat with her back against the wall and smiled and smiled—until she cried. There was a sick woman who lay on the floor and groaned feebly but never looked up, and there were eight children.

"Last week we were fifteen," said the home-like woman, "but one has already gone. They never get well." She reached over and gently stroked the hair of the sister who lay on the floor.

"Were you all married?" I asked.

"All," nodded the old woman with the face of a chief.

"And where are they now?"

"Quien sabe?" And she searched our eyes deep for the motive of our questions.

"I am a Papago," reassured De Lara. "We are friends."

"You are not working," I remarked. "What are you doing?"

"Starving," said the old woman.

"We get that once a week—for all of us," explained the home-like one, nodding at three small chunks of raw beef—less than a five-cent stew in the United States—which had just been brought from the plantation store.

"Besides that we get only corn and black beans and not half enough of either of them."

"We are like hogs; we are fed on corn," put in the old woman. "In Sonora we made our *tortillas* of wheat" "How long will they starve you?" I asked.

"Until we marry Chinamen," flashed the old woman, unexpectedly.

"Yes," confirmed the home-like one. "Twice they have brought the Chinamen before us, lined them up, and said: 'Choose a man.' Twice."

"And why didn't you choose?"

This question several of the women answered in chorus. In words and wry faces they expressed their abhorrence of the Chinamen, and with tremulous earnestness assured us that they had not yet forgotten their own husbands.

"I begged them," said the old woman, "to let me off. I told them I was too old, that it was no use, that I was a woman no longer, but they said I must choose, too. They will not let me off; they say I will have to choose with the rest."

"Twice they have lined us up," reiterated the homelike one, "and said we must choose. But we wouldn't choose. One woman chose, but when she saw the rest hang back she pushed the man away from her. They threatened us with the rope, but still we hung back. They will give us but one more chance, they say. Then if we do not choose, they will choose for us. And if we do not consent we will be put in the field and worked and whipped like the men."

"And get twelve *centavos* a day (six cents American) to live on," said the old woman. "Twelve *centavos* a day with food at the store twice as dear as in Sonora!"

"Next Sunday morning they will make us choose," repeated the home-like woman. "And if we don't choose—"

"Last Sunday they beat that sister there," said the old woman. "She swore she'd never choose, and they beat her just like they beat the men. Come, Refugio, show them your back."

But the woman at the fire shrank away and hung her head in mortification.

"No, no," she protested, then after a moment she muttered: "When the Yaqui men are beaten they die of shame, but the women can stand to be beaten; they cannot die."

"It's true," nodded the old woman, "the men die of shame sometimes—and sometimes they die of their own will."

When we turned the talk to Sonora and to the long journey the voices of the women began to falter. They were from Pilares de Teras, where are situated the mines of Colonel Garcia. The soldiers had come in the daytime while the people were in the field picking the ripe corn from the stalks. They had been taken from their harvest labor and compelled to walk all the way to Her-mosillo, a three weeks' tramp.

The Yaqui love for the one who suckled them is strong, and several of the younger women recounted the details of the parting from the mother. Then we spoke of their husbands again, but they held their tears until I asked the question: "How would you like to go back with me to your homes in Sonora?"

That opened the flood-gates. The tears started first down the plump cheeks of the cheery, home-like woman, then the others broke in, one at a time, and at last the listening children on the floor were blubbering dolefully with their elders. Weeping, the unhappy exiles lost their last modicum of reserve. They begged us please to take them back to Sonora or to find their husbands for them. The old woman implored us to get word to her boss, Leonardo Aguirre, and would not be content until I had penned his name in my note-book. The bashful woman at the fire, aching for some comforting, hopeful words, parted her dress at the top and gave us a glimpse of the red marks of the lash upon her back.

I looked into the face of my companion; the tears were trickling down his cheeks. As for me, I did not cry. I am ashamed now that I did not cry!

Such is the life of the Yaqui nation in its last chapter. When I looked upon those miserable creatures there I said: "There can be nothing worse than this." But when I saw Valle Nacional I said: "This is worse than Yucatan."

The contract slaves of Valle Nacional

Valle Nacional is undoubtedly the worst slave hole in Mexico. Probably it is the worst in the world. When I visited Valle Nacional I expected to find it milder than Yucatan. I found it more pitiless.

In Yucatan the Maya slaves die off faster than they are born and two-thirds of the Yaqui slaves are killed during the first year after their importation into the country. In Valle Nacional all of the slaves, all but a very few—perhaps five per cent—pass back to earth within a space of seven or eight months.

This statement is almost unbelievable. I would not have believed it; possibly not even after I had seen the whole process of working them and beating them and starving them to death, were it not the fact that the masters themselves told me that it was true. And there are fifteen thousand of these Valle Nacional slaves—fifteen thousand new ones every year!

"By the sixth or seventh month they begin to die off like flies at the first winter frost, and after that they're not worth keeping. The cheapest thing to do is to let them die; there are plenty more where they came from."

Word for word, this is a statement made to me by Antonio Pla, general manager of one-third the tobacco lands in Valle Nacional.

"I have been here for more than five years and every month I see hundreds and sometimes thousands of men, women and children start over the road to the valley, but I never see them come back. Of every hundred who go over the road not more than one ever sees this town again." This assertion was made to me by a station agent of the Veracruz al Pacifico railroad.

"There are no survivors of Valle Nacional—no real ones," a government engineer who has charge of the improvement of certain harbors told me. "Now and then one gets out of the valley and gets beyond El Hule. He staggers and begs his way along the weary road toward Cordoba, but he never gets back where he came from. Those people come out of the valley walking corpses, they travel on a little way and then they fall."

This man's work has carried him much into Valle Nacional and he knows more of the country, probably, than does any Mexican not directly interested in the slave trade.

"They die; they all die. The bosses never let them go until they're dying."

Thus declared one of the police officers of the town of Valle Nacional, which is situated in the center of the valley and is supported by it.

And everywhere over and over again I was told the same thing. Even Manuel Lagunas, *presidente* (mayor) of Valle Nacional, protector of the planters and a slave owner himself, said it. Miguel Vidal, secretary of the municipality, said it. The bosses themselves said it. The Indian dwellers of the mountain sides said it. The slaves said it. And when I had seen, as well as heard, I was convinced that it was the truth.

The slaves of Valle Nacional are not Indians, as are the slaves of Yucatan. They are Mexicans. Some are skilled artizans. Others are artists. The majority of them are common laborers. As a whole, except for their rags, their bruises, their squalor and their despair, they are a very fair representation of the Mexican people. They are not criminals. Not more than ten per cent were even charged with any crime. The rest of them are peaceful, law-abiding citizens. Yet not one came to the valley of his own free will, not one would not leave the valley on an instant's notice if he or she could get away.

Do not entertain the idea that Mexican slavery is confined to Yucatan and Valle Nacional. Conditions similar to those of Valle Nacional are the rule in many sections of Diaz-land, and especially in the states south of the capital. I cite Valle Nacional because it is most notorious as a region of slaves, and because, as I have already suggested, it presents just a little bit the worst example of chattel slavery that I know of.

The secret of the extreme conditions of Valle Nacional is mainly geographical. Valle Nacional is a deep gorge from two to five miles wide and twenty miles long tucked away among almost impassable mountains in the extreme northwestern corner of the state of Oaxaca. Its mouth is fifty miles up the Papaloapan river from El Hule, the nearest railroad station, yet it is through El Hule that every human being passes in going to or coming from the valley. There is no other practical route in, no other one out. The magnificent tropical mountains which wall in the valley are covered with an impenetrable jungle made still more impassable by jaguars, pumas and gigantic snakes. Moreover, there is no wagon road to Valle Nacional; only a river and a bridle path—a bridle path which carries one now through the jungle, now along precipitous cliffs where the rider must dismount and crawl, leading his horse behind him, now across the deep, swirling current of the river. It takes a strong swimmer to cross this river at high water, yet a pedestrian must swim it more than once in order to get out of Valle Nacional.

51

ROBERT WELLES RITCHIE, 'THE PASSING OF A DICTATOR', *HARPER'S MAGAZINE* 124 (1911–1912), PP. 782–789

The passing of a dictator

FOLK were sitting about the tables in the patio of the Hotel de Jardine, sipping their afternoon coffee and turning the pages of the latest extras, ink-smeared with hectic headlines. Two children pushed a tin train of cars over one of the graveled paths beneath the patio oaks. Waiters drowsed by the kitchen corner, and the porter at the high doors giving on to the street had his head on his breast.

Then the Voice came. A murmur, far removed, muffled and indefinite—a murmur hardly to be distinguished above the plashing of the fountain; a minute and the timbre of it had strengthened and deepened; another minute and a crackling syncopation broke the monotony of sound. From afar the Voice spoke stronger and in a strange, animal note. Folk dropped their papers and started, heads cocked, to catch the meaning of the unwonted sound. Waiters moved away from the kitchen door out into the patio so that they could hear better. The two children piloted their train safely into the station by the goldfish pond, then sat with questioning eyes on the elders about them. Nearer and louder, louder, louder, sounded the Voice.

A nurse stepped out on the balcony above the patio and screamed as she ran down the stairs to the children. She gathered them into her arms and stumbled blindly back up the stairs, along the balcony, and into one of the suites opening thereon. Her scream, the agitation of her flying skirts, awoke the porter at the gate. For just an instant he sat still, his face puckered in puzzlement, then he jumped to the two high wooden gates giving on to the street, and slammed them shut. He slipped an oak beam through the hasps and double-braced the doors by other beams upended against the cobbles of the court-yard. The maître d'hôtel had rushed out of his little glass office meanwhile, and was calling excitedly to the waiters; they sped through passageways, and their disappearances were followed by the banging of wooden shutters over windows, the slamming of doors, the frantic trundling of barricades into place. And then high over the clatter and the pounding the Voice snarled—a vicious, bestial snarl that was ear-filling and terrible.

The Voice was of the mob. On an afternoon in late May of 1911 Mexico City was rising against its master. Out of the kennels of mean streets, whose meanness marble palaces and flowering gardens screen, the *canaille* of the capital had come pouring, had whirled into mob coalescence, and now were baying and coursing the streets to seek the life of that master. Don Porfirio, the once beloved—Don Porfirio Diaz, dictator and builder of Mexico for more than thirty years—was the master.

All rules of psychology fall before the manifestations of the Latin-American temperament; so an attempt at analysis of the events of one hour in that May afternoon would be as bewildering to the Anglo-Saxon mind as the deciphering of Norse runes to a sign-painter. At four o'clock the capital of the republic was a city in order (though the north was in rebellion), President Diaz was supreme in his seat, and his hand was heavy over a populace still cowed through memory of the weight of that hand. At five o'clock Mexico City was in rebellion, savoring of the Terror, its streets were choked with the mob; and Diaz, the feared, was a fugitive from his people, besieged in his own house, with no barrier between himself and death but four slender lines of soldiery. One hour had served to pull down the whole fabric of a dictator's building. In one hour the people of the capital, who had cheered themselves hoarse just a year before when the head of the nation rode through the streets in the triumph of the Centennial, were whirled away in a blood-lust that drove them in solid masses of thousands against the barriers of the Calle Cadenas, where their President lay sick in his bed. Custom of years, instilled always through fear, and latterly, also, through an hysterical sort of affection for the strength of a strong man, had been dropped like a garment, and the mob, seeing its master falter, was ready to pull him down.

Porfirio Diaz in his age had been lulled out of his eternal vigilance by the flattery of sycophants, who cut his power from under him even while they glorified him with the tinsel and band-music of the Centennial celebration. The revolution of Madero, petty at first, grew to grave proportions. Too late the master of Mexico found that the strength that had stayed him for thirty-two years had gone. Five thousand revolutionaries had pressed to within two days' march of his capital, his army was unavailing, his one-time advisers had fled the city. He had announced in his extremity that before the end of May he would resign the Presidency. As the end of May approached, through some devious semiofficial channel, information had been carried to the press that on the 24th Diaz would send his message of resignation to the Chamber of Deputies.

An orderly crowd of several thousand cluttered the streets leading to the marble Chamber that afternoon, waiting word from within the bronze gates that the dictator had abdicated. As the thousands waited, a few enthusiasts, still loyal to the weakening cause of the old warrior, wormed their way through the crowd, distributing dodgers, which urged that the Chamber of Deputies would seal the fate of Mexico if it accepted the resignation of Diaz. The temper of the crowd was not in sympathy with the call of the pamphlets; the distributors were hustled and their sheets trampled; an angry, muttering undertone sounded through the babble of voices. Then, a few minutes after four o'clock, just as the keeper of the Chamber doors swung open the bronze gates, one of the journalists from the press gallery, glorying in the opportunity to pose before the crowd, jumped out of the door, leaped to the top of the steps, and held up his hand for silence.

"A trick! A trick!" he exclaimed. "Diaz has not resigned. The old fox has fooled us again!"

That instant order disappeared and the flux of anarchy began.

There is something devilish in a mob's birth. Out of ten thousand conflicting spurs of action comes, in the snapping of a finger, a sinister unity of purpose, which knows not the individual brain that conceived it, nor the logic of its action. Ten thousand clods, jumbled in confusion, are instantly turned into a single straight furrow. Looking from a window of the Chamber of Deputies that afternoon, one saw the waving arms of the journalist messenger conjure a sprouting stubble of brandished arms over the field of hats up and down the Calle de Factor. For a minute there was a confused weaving of conflicting currents over all the crowd. Faces were seen to be disfigured by an infectious paroxysm of madness, Men stooped and clawed at the cobbles under their feet at the primal dictates of mob madness. Other men went racing from the fringes of the crowd into the side streets, eager to carry the flame to new tinder. Then came unity. Two barefooted women of the slums, their nakedness only half concealed by ragged coffee-sacks, and their Indian faces alight with savagery, held between them aloft on two sticks a piece of white bunting, upon which a lithograph likeness of Francisco Madero had been pasted. Slowly the two women began to pace through the swirling tides of humanity, rhythmically waving back and forth their banner of sedition. Men crowded for places behind them. Now the nascent procession was of three ranks, now of five, now it filled the street from curb to curb. The two women walked ahead and alone, screaming and singing in an intoxication of the mob call; behind them, the mob. The mob found voice, and it was a bestial, unhuman voice.

Quick as ever the thousands in front of the Chamber of Deputies found a singleness of purpose, recruits came by other thousands. Bricklayers clambered down from their scaffolds, carrying with them heavy staves and scantlings. Teamsters left their wagons in the middle of the streets, but brought their goods and whips. Even the beggars jumped from their nestling-places before the cathedrals and kept pace on bandaged feet. Catching the roar of the mob, storekeepers worked feverishly to pull down iron shutters before their plate windows, to barricade doors with heavy staves. Cocheros, knowing the vicious temper of the mob, whipped up their nags and skittered around corners in advance of the vanguard. Before the first of the marching thousands had turned into the broad Cinco de Mayo, lined with clubs and fashionable restaurants, the avenue was like a street in a besieged city. Yet still recruits came, smaller bodies of the riotous merged themselves with the greater band, and the course of the march was toward the Calle Cadenas, where in his bed lay the President who would not resign.

The early darkness of spring settled just as the parading thousands began to close in on the Calle Cadenas. Upon both flanks of the short street, where stood the marble house of the President, the assault was made. The first of the rabble to arrive found that a double line of the mounted gendarmes of the Federal District blocked entrance into the street at both ends; the uniformed cavalrymen sat their horses, knee to knee, with carbine-butts resting on their hips. The vanguard of the slow-moving procession pushed against the horses' breasts, recoiled, and was hurled by pressure from behind once more upon the double line of soldiers. There were shouts of individuals trampled, the flickering movement of men dodging hoofs, the quick snaffling of mounts made to close holes in the dike of resistance, and then the mob came to a halt. Just those double lines of armed horsemen at either end of a dark alleyway between walls—within the guarded space the marble house where Diaz lay—and stretching far at either end of the blocked thoroughfare the solid masses of humanity, inflexible, unreasoning, and mad with the lust for killing.

Then, finding itself temporarily checked, the mob bayed at the guarded President. Out of the roaring bass of the multitude treble shrieks were distinguishable. "Death to the tyrant!" "Death—death to Diaz!" Other voices taunted with vivas for Francisco Madero, vivas for the revolution. The jackals of the city, confident of security in the anonymity of the mob, bravely baited and insulted the old lion of Puebla, whose absolutism had been an ever-present terror for longer than a generation.

Minute by minute the temper of the mob grew more dangerous. When, after it had been held in check for half an hour or more, a troop of the Ninth Cavalry swung down through the Avenida San Juan Lateran and began to cleave a passage through the press to reinforce the gendarmes at the Calle Cadenas, a savage snarl of rage swept from block to block. A pistol-shot cracked over the solid pavement of heads, then another and another. Once more a concerted rush was made upon the guards, and they would have been swept back had not the troopers of the Ninth speared their way to the crumbling line of defense, and with flat sabers and gun-butts blunted the crest of the oncoming wave before its strength was irresistible. Porfirio Diaz, in the darkened house, heard the terrible mouthing of his people baffled.

Then the mob, cheated in its initial purpose, began to divert its energies into channels dictated only by sheer spur of lawlessness. In segments of tens of hundreds it split up and down its length, side streets became choked with slow-moving masses, and flying squadrons of roughs sped ahead of each band to do pillage wherever the menace of the advancing roar should drive shopkeepers to hasty refuge. Staves and beams nailed across store windows were wrenched off to serve as weapons. Where brick piles offered ammunition, there the gangs paused, and when they moved on again the piles had vanished. Occasionally came the tinkling of shattered glass, and at the crash the pack yelped and screamed. One band of several hundred marched to the office of *El Impartial*, the government's organ. A volley of stones smashed every window facing the street: the crowd hooted. One of the black spaces representing a window spit a thin pencil of fire, and a peon in the mob clawed wildly at his neck for an instant and dropped. Then frenzy. Barrels and kindling from a building under construction near by were piled against the high doors giving to the court-yard. Gasoline plundered from a garage was spilled upon the tinder, and the match struck. When a company of *Bomberos* came with its engine to the call of the flame's light, the engine was tipped over and the mob jeered.

But suddenly the far circle of the flame clipped sparks from steel, rising and falling. Down from the end of the street rode a squadron of gendarmes; sabers chopped on scattering heads viciously. The mob dissolved.

The city slipped closer to the Terror with the passing of the night hours. The failure of Diaz to send in his message had been the inciting cause of the rioting, but the mob that had seized upon that pretext for its inception, finding itself unopposed in the main, now asserted its will through promptings of insolence and the instinct for destruction. Street after street, upon which darkness had settled with the stoning of the arc lights, echoed with the clamor of marching thousands. The "Viva Madero!" came more and more insistently, and with the throaty hoarseness of a battle-cry. Wherever a company of the mounted gendarmes tried with careful patience to turn the head of a crowd away from one of the public buildings, it was met with jeers and was dared to draw guns and shoot. No strong hand of command was behind the gendarmerie; the mob knew that the strong hand of old was now palsied, and that there was none to give the accustomed merciless orders to slay.

It was ten o'clock, and the Plaza Zocalo, which lies before the great Cathedral of Mexico, was black with thousands. From every converging avenue more marching bands came to choke the plaza spaces. A single line of cavalry was drawn up before the façade of the new National Palace, opposite the Cathedral front. The horsemen sat immovable, by their presence denying the crowd only the right to rush the palace building. But that single denial was a defiance in the eyes of license. As the pack grew denser it moved closer upon the cavalry line. Insults and taunts failed to bring even a quiver to the arms that held rifles, butts down, on saddle-pommels. Tension grew, minute by minute. Of a sudden came the sharp crash of splintered glass, and the clatter of stones against the marble front of the Palace; half of the hundred windows on the plaza side were broken. The vicious roar of the crowd drowned an order that the commander of the cavalry troop gave, but rifles came down to bear on the black masses, and the quick recoiling of the mob's front sent a backward wave through the press. Yet those behind, who could not see the sudden menace, yelled again and sent another shower of stones against the white facade.

Then came the stab and bark of shots all down the line of the cavalry. One standing on the Cathedral steps at the mob's back saw the sudden, fiery lightning spurt forth, saw the great block of humanity waver, split in a dozen lines of cleavage like a plate of glass punctured, and then disintegrate. No longer the roar of insolent mastery; instead, shrill individual cries of terror and shrieks of pain sounded over the pounding of thousands of feet. The cavalry charged—a single, rigid line, moving like the cutting blade of a reaper. In five minutes the Plaza Zocalo was emptied. Only ten or a dozen sprawling blots on the pavements showed where the dead lay.

The city awoke to dread next morning. Still lawless bands paraded the streets. More men were shot—in front of the office of the Minister for Foreign Affairs and at the foot of the statue of Carlos IV. Up and down, past the flowering Alameda and in the Cinco de Mayo, tireless cohorts of the riff-raff from the slums made ceaseless pilgrimages behind improvised drum corps of oil-can beaters. Still Porfirio Diaz was President, and three hundred soldiers guarded his house.

At two o'clock in the afternoon, senators and deputies met in the Chamber of Deputies. All of the approaches to the Chamber were blocked by detachments of infantry and cavalry, which had been hurried into the city from the battleground of Morelos overnight. Back of the hedge of steel ten thousand rioters massed themselves in a circle about the meeting-place of the law-makers. The marble Chamber was practically under siege. Each senator and deputy as he came through the lanes of soldiery was admitted to the Chamber through a little postern gate, and crossed bayonets barred his passage until his identity was established. Within the shadowed congress-hall men walked on tiptoe and spoke in whispers; the heavy silence was punctuated by the rattle of gun-butts on the cobbles outside, and occasionally the dull diapason of the voice of the populace sounded, muffled by the walls. The speaker of the deputies ascended the rostrum and rapped with his gavel; the tapping of the little mallet was as startling as a pistol-shot. "Señores, a message from the President of the Republic," the speaker announced. The clerk stood in his place and began to read:

"Señores,—The Mexican people, who generously have covered me with honors, who proclaimed me as their leader during the international war, who patriotically assisted me in all works undertaken to develop industry and commerce of the Republic, establish its credit, gain for it the respect of the world and an honorable position in the concert of the nations: that same people has revolted in armed military bands, stating that my presence in the exercise of the supreme executive power was the cause of this insurrection.—"

A sick man in his bed, and with the roar of sedition in his ears, had reviewed the years of his building in his hurt pride.—

"I do not know of any facts imputable to me which could have caused this social phenomenon; but permitting, though not admitting, that I may be unwittingly culpable, such a possibility makes me the least able to reason out and decide my own culpability."

Therefore, the message continued, the President of the Republic had decided that to prevent the spilling of more blood he would lay his resignation before the representatives of the people. And in these final words Porfirio Diaz claimed the justice of a dispassionate judgment upon his dictatorship:

"I hope, Señores, that when the passions which are inherent to all revolutions have calmed, a more conscientious and justified study will bring to the national mind a correct acknowledgment, which will allow me to die carrying engraved in my soul a just impression of the estimation of my life, which throughout I have devoted and will devote to my countrymen."

There was silence then. Some shadow of the power that had been seemed to press upon the consciences of the people's delegates. A deputy moved the acceptance of the President's resignation, and the vote was polled. There were only two to dissent from the will of the majority—old men who had fought with Diaz against Maximilian, and had seen his triumph at Puebla. There was silence in the great hall even when the speaker announced that Porfirio Diaz was no longer President of Mexico. Suddenly a deputy jumped to his feet, and with a dramatic lifting of his hand he shouted: "President Porfirio Diaz is dead! Long live Citizen Porfirio Diaz!" Just at that instant a deep-throated shout sounded from the streets, where the news had carried, and the spell in the Chamber was broken. Delegates stood in their places and cheered madly; they embraced one another in quick Latin impulsiveness, eddied down the aisles to the street doors, singing the national anthem. Only two old men remained seated, heads bowed and tears dropping upon their beards; they were the two dissenters who remembered the glory of Puebla and the might of Puebla's victor.

Where blood had stained the pavements of the city twelve hours before, delirious throngs now danced. The thousands marched again, but it was not to destroy. The vivas did not rasp with the menace of anarchy, but were roared in an abandon of joy. Even at four o'clock the next morning, the morning of the 27th, the streets had not been deserted by the roisterers, but if any of them saw three closed automobiles without lamps speeding through the darkened streets in the direction of the San Lazaro station they paid no heed. The automobiles drew up within the station yard, and gates were closed. Out of one of them stepped an old man, whose neck was swathed in shawls and who leaned heavily on the arm of an officer in the Mexican army as he walked to a train in waiting. The American conductor saluted the old man before he took his arm to help him up the steps into the Pullman. Then four sleepy children, a nurse with a week-old infant in her arms, three heavily veiled women, and several men who carried sword-cases under their arms, were piloted to the train. An engine with three baggage-cars behind it, each filled with soldiers of the machine-gun detachments of the Eleventh Infantry, moved out of the yards first; behind it came the train of the refugees, and in the rear another short train, carrying a battalion of the Zapadores. So in the dark the deposed master of Mexico began his flight from his capital to the sea.

The fate that directs the destinies of the average Mexican peon seems always to move with a certain perverse malignancy. Does he want political liberty or only an extra drink of aguardiente, he dies getting it. His fate leads him blindfolded, ever on the edge of a chasm, where one misstep will blot him out. So it was nothing but their presiding evil genius which dictated that daily for a week before the abdication of Diaz a band of two-hundred-odd revoltosos in the state of Puebla had made it a practice to stop the train out of Mexico City running over the narrow-gauge line to Vera Cruz. In theory they stopped it to see that no soldiers of Diaz should be sent out to reinforce the feeble garrisons on the Gulf coast, but probably the perfect joy in doing a simple, lawless act was the sole inspiring cause of their vigilance. They did not rob, did not molest the few passengers who dared a railroad journey during those troublous days; the petty excitement of stopping the train, firing a few shots in the air, and voicing a few vivas for the revolution was their sole reward.

No word of the coming of Diaz's train had been sent along the railroad line. The American manager of the railroad in Mexico City feared to trust local telegraphers with train orders, so the light engine running as pilot and the three short trains behind it sped down the slopes of the high plateau toward the sea unheralded and without a schedule. Before the sun was high the band of rebels camped near the railroad track in a barren *maguey* desert near the town of Oriental heard an engine whistle and saw smoke lifting beyond the spur of the nearest bald knob. They mounted and ranged themselves on both sides of the track; one rode toward the advancing engine with the customary red flag. The pilot engine swung around a curve, the American engineer at the throttle saw the red flag, saw the double line of armed horsemen stretched along the track ahead, then shut off his steam, and, with his fireman, went and lay down behind the parapets of the tender. Behind was the first guard train. It slowed down to a halt just as the careless rebels cantered up to demand the opening of the baggage - car doors. But the doors opened unbidden, and from the space within each the slender barrel of a machine-gun protruded. There was no parley; simply the infliction of death by level sprays of bullets.

Before the riderless horses had plunged a hundred yards into the thicket of the maguey plants, Diaz's car had stopped behind the guard train. The ex-President commanded the women and children in the Pullman to lie flat between the seats, as the conductor afterward told the story in Vera Cruz, and then with his son, Col. Porfirio Diaz, the General stepped down and walked along the track to where his soldiers were kneeling by the side of the baggage—cars ahead, answering the shots that came from the clumps of the bayonet plants. He stood at command with his back to the door, where the machine - guns crackled. Under cover of the machine-guns' fire he ordered the infantry battalion of the Zapadores regiment to advance into the thicket and complete the work that the first hail of lead had begun. The soldiers heard the voice of their old commander, went into the thicket, and killed. The brush was over in half an hour. Diaz went on his way to the sea, while buzzards wheeled down from far heights to settle among the spikes of the desert plants.

On the sand-dunes back of the city of Vera Cruz, where unsightly gas-tanks are clustered and the railroad tracks criss-cross the filled ground, Gen. Victor Huerta, Governor of Vera Cruz, picked temporary lodgings for Diaz and his family against the sailing of the German steamer Ypiranga for Santandar. Because the old, weather - beaten house stood alone on the sands and could be surrounded on all sides by troops, it was the only safe refuge for the fleeing dictator. From the rickety gallery Diaz could look out over the blue bay to the ancient gold-and-white fortress of Santiago at the harbor mouth; past that fortress, and through the shark-infested waters of the bay, he, a revolutionary and a fugitive from a government he was attempting to overthrow, had swum to safety from the side of an American steamer thirty-seven years before. Against the walls of that fortress other revolutionaries had stood with bandaged eyes in more recent time, and his had been the word—the word of the dictator—that had loosed the volleys against them.

Diaz's last day in Mexico began with a tragedy. Two hours after midnight on May 31st one of the soldiers of the Eleventh Regiment on outpost guard near the beach caught sight of a dodging shadow that skittered in and out among the freight-cars on the railroad spur. The soldier waited until the shadow ran boldly out on the sands, and then he challenged. The shout was unheeded. The guard fired, and the shadow dropped to the beach. It was only a prisoner escaping from Santiago; a poor wight of the army, who had been in the dungeons for murder of a comrade, and who on that night had won his way through the bay, only to plump into the guard of a fugitive President. General Huerta narrated the incident of the killing of the convict to Diaz in the morning. The old warrior heard the story through, and then shook his head with a gesture of compassion. "Poor devil," he said; "but the end of his flight is more happy than mine."

At ten o'clock Diaz expressed the wish to say farewell to the remnant of his army, and orders were given for mustering the battalions of the guards that had come down from the capital with the ex-President's train, and of the sailors from the gunboats *Zaragoza* and *San Juan de Ulloa*, who had reinforced the infantrymen in the protection of the bleak house on the dunes. In the hot sunshine the soldiers of the Eleventh and the Zapadores were drawn up in double rank before the lower gallery of the house, the sailors flanked them, and directly in front of the steps the machine-guns that had dealt death in the maguey desert two days before were trundled to position, their slender, shining barrels pointing down toward the gold and red roofs of the city. The soldiers stood at rest; those of the Eleventh were all Oaxaca Indians, natives of Diaz's own state, and believers in him as in the power of the saints. They stood there in their wrinkled olive uniforms and heavy, thonged sandals, eyes strangely alight as if with a religious exaltation. A sign from Heaven—a miracle worked by the saints to show that Don Porfirio would still triumph over his enemies, as of old! That was the cry in the eyes of those Indians; discipline caused mouths to pucker with restraint of words that would be voiced. On the gallery a hundred officers of the Palace Guard, who had hurried away from Mexico City to bid their old commander godspeed even at the risk of punishment, had ranged themselves in two lines. Minutes passed and the waiting burdened the nerves of the loyal ones.

Then Don Porfirio stepped out from the dark doorway into the morning radiance, and he stood, bareheaded, before them. The sun searched every lineament of the bronzed face, but found no line of weakness and no stamp of age save its dignity. Steady eyes, strong mouth, heavy jaw of the fighter and broad forehead of the thinker: all the mien of that old Porfirio Diaz, conqueror and inflexible ruler, was there—magnetic, dynamic, compelling. He began to speak, and his voice was at first powerful and unshaken; there was a surprising note of virility in it. He said that this was to be the last time that ever he would address his soldiers—his soldiers, much beloved. For that day his exile from Mexico would begin; he was going to Europe, never to return to his home land unless some danger from foreign source should threaten.

"I give you my word of honor," the strong voice continued, "that if ever sudden danger from without threatens my country I will return, and under that flag for which I have fought much, I with you at my back, will learn again to conquer." A sudden choking blotted Diaz's speech, and his eyes showed tears.

"And now, my soldiers—last of the army of Porfirio Diaz—I say farewell. You have guarded me to the ultimate moment—you have been loyal. My soldiers, blessing—take the blessing of your old commander! More—more I cannot—say!"

He stopped, and a sibilant intaking of the breath passed down the line of brown faces where stood the Oaxaca Indians. Then, one by one, the officers of the troops sheathed their swords, advanced to the steps, and there embraced their old commander-in-chief. Their grief was frank; tears fell upon Diaz's hands as he said farewell to each. The last officer had returned to his position, and still Diaz stood, his eyes passing in slow review the faces of his soldiers. Abruptly one of them near the steps dropped his gun, and before interference could check him he had thrown himself on the steps at Diaz's feet. With his head on the old warrior's boots he called hysterically in a speech not Spanish, and caressed the knees of his master. Diaz looked down at the soldier for an instant, patted his black head, and then spoke a low word of command. The Indian stepped quickly back to the ranks, picked up his rifle, and brought it untremblingly to the salute.

A few hours later the fallen dictator, with his family, passed in a hedge of his soldiers' bayonets through the streets of Vera Cruz to the steamer. Vera Cruz was kind at the last. Its women filled the refugee's cabin with flowers, and its men crowded the pier end, and with roaring vivas sped Porfirio Diaz to his exile.

52

JOHN REED, *INSURGENT MEXICO* (NEW YORK: D. APPLETON, 1914), PP. 175–187, 191–204

"On to torreon!"

At Yermo there is nothing but leagues and leagues of sandy desert, sparsely covered with scrubby mesquite and dwarf cactus, stretching away on the west to jagged, tawny mountains, and on the east to a quivering skyline of plain. A battered water-tank, with too little dirty alkali water, a demolished railway station shot to pieces by Orozco's cannon two years before, and a switch track compose the town. There is no water to speak of for forty miles. There is no grass for animals. For three months in the spring bitter, parching winds drive the yellow dust across it.

Along the single track in the middle of the desert lay ten enormous trains, pillars of fire by night and of black smoke by day, stretching back northward farther than the eye could reach. Around them, in the chaparral, camped nine thousand men without shelter, each man's horse tied to the mesquite beside him, where hung his one serape and red strips of drying meat. From fifty cars horses and mules were being unloaded. Covered with sweat and dust, a ragged trooper plunged into a cattle-car among the flying hoofs, swung himself upon a horse's back, and jabbed his spurs deep in, with a yell. Then came a terrific drumming of frightened animals, and suddenly a horse shot violently from the open door, usually backward, and the car belched flying masses of horses and mules. Picking themselves up, they fled in terror, snorting through wide nostrils at the smell of the open. Then the wide, watchful circle of troopers turned *vaqueros* lifted the great coils of their lassoes through the choking dust, and the running animals swirled round and round upon one another in a panic. Officers, orderlies, generals with their staffs, soldiers with halters, hunting for their mounts, galloped and ran past in inextricable confusion. Bucking mules were being harnessed to the caissons. Troopers who had arrived on the last trains wandered about looking for their brigades. Way ahead some men were shooting at a rabbit. From the tops of the box-cars and the flat-cars, where they were camped by hundreds, the *soldaderas* and their half-naked swarms of children looked down, screaming shrill advice and asking everybody in general if they had happened to see Juan Moñeros, or Jesus Hernandez, or whatever the name of their man happened to be.... One man trailing a rifle wandered along shouting that he had had nothing to eat for two days and he couldn't find his woman who made his *tortillas* for him, and he opined that she had deserted him to go with some ——— of another brigade.... The women on the roofs of the cars said, *"Valgame Dios!"* and shrugged their shoulders; then they dropped him down some three-days-old *tortillas,* and asked him, for the love he bore Our Lady of Guadelupe, to lend them a cigarette. A clamorous, dirty throng stormed the engine of our train, screaming for water. When the engineer stood them off with a revolver, telling them there was plenty of water in the water-train, they broke away and aimlessly scattered, while a fresh throng took their places. Around the twelve immense tank-cars, a fighting mass of men and animals struggled for a place at the little faucets ceaselessly pouring. Above the place a mighty cloud of dust, seven miles long and a mile wide, towered up into the still, hot air, and, with the black smoke of the engines, struck wonder and terror into the Federal outposts fifty miles away on the mountains back of Mapimi.

When Villa left Chihuahua for Torreon, he closed the telegraph wires to the north, stopped train service to Juarez, and forbade on pain of death that anyone should carry or send news of his departure to the United States. His object was to take the Federals by surprise, and it worked beautifully. No one, not even Villa's staff, knew when he would leave Chihuahua; the army had delayed there so long that we all believed it would delay another two weeks. And then Saturday morning we woke to find the telegraph and railway cut, and three huge trains, carrying the Brigada Gonzalez-Ortega, already gone. The Zaragosa left the next day, and Villa's own troops the following morning. Moving with the swiftness that always characterizes him, Villa had his entire army concentrated at Yermo the day afterward, without the Federals knowing that he had left Chihuahua.

There was a mob around the portable field telegraph that had been rigged up in the ruined station. Inside, the instrument was clicking. Soldiers and officers indiscriminately choked up the windows and the door, and every once in a while the operator would shout something in Spanish and a perfect roar of laughter would go up. It seemed that the telegraph had accidentally tapped a wire that had not been destroyed by the Federals—a wire that connected with the Federal military wire from Mapimi to Torreon.

"Listen!" cried the operator. "Colonel Argumedo in command of the *cabecillos colorados* in Mapimi is telegraphing to General Velasco in Torreon. He says that he sees smoke and a big dust cloud to the north, and thinks that some rebel troops are moving south from Escalon!"

Night came, with a cloudy sky and a rising wind that began to lift the dust. Along the miles and miles of trains, the fires of the *soldaderas* flared from the tops of the freight-cars. Out into the desert so far that finally they were mere pinpoints of flame stretched the innumerable camp-fires of the army, half obscured by the thick, billowing dust. The storm completely concealed us from Federal watchers. "Even God," remarked Major Leyva, "even God is on the side of Francisco Villa!" We sat at dinner in our converted box-car, with young, great-limbed, expressionless General Maximo Garcia and his brother, the even huger red-faced Benito Garcia, and little Major Manuel Acosta, with the beautiful manners of his race. Garcia had long been holding the advance at Escalon. He and his brothers—one of whom, José Garcia, the idol of the army, had been killed in battle—but a short four years ago were wealthy *hacendados*, owners of immense tracts of land. They had come out with Madero.... I remember that he brought us a jug of whisky, and refused to discuss the Revolution, declaring that he was fighting for better whisky! As I write this comes a report that he is dead from a bullet wound received in the battle of Sacramento....

Out in the dust storm, on a flat-car immediately ahead of ours, some soldiers lay around their fire with their heads in their women's laps, singing "The Cockroach," which tells in hundreds of satirical verses what the Constitutionalists would do when they captured Juarez and Chihuahua from Mercado and Orozco.

Above the wind one was aware of the immense sullen murmur of the host, and occasionally some sentry challenged in a falsetto howl: "*Quien vive?*" And the answer: "*Chiapas!*" "*Que gente?*" "*Chao!*" ... Through the night sounded the eerie whistle of the ten locomotives at intervals as they signaled back and forth to one another.

The army at Yermo

AT dawn next morning General Torribio Ortega came to the car for breakfast—a lean, dark Mexican, who is called "The Honorable" and "The Most Brave" by the soldiers. He is by far the most simple-hearted and disinterested soldier in Mexico.

He never kills his prisoners. He has refused to take a cent from the Revolution beyond his meager salary. Villa respects and trusts him perhaps beyond all his Generals. Ortega was a poor man, a cowboy. He sat there, with his elbows on the table, forgetting his breakfast, his big eyes flashing, smiling his gentle, crooked smile, and told us why he was fighting.

"I am not an educated man," he said. "But I know that to fight is the last thing for any people. Only when things get too bad to stand, eh? And, if we are going to kill our brothers, something fine must come out of it, eh? You in the United States do not know what we have seen, we Mexicans! We have looked on at the robbing of our people, the simple, poor people, for thirty-five years, eh? We have seen the *rurales* and the soldiers of Porfirio Diaz shoot down our brothers and our fathers, and justice denied to them. We have seen our little fields taken away from us, and all of us sold into slavery, eh? We have longed for our homes and for schools to teach us, and they have laughed at us. All we have ever wanted was to be let alone to live and to work and make our country great, and we are tired—tired and sick of being cheated...."

Outside in the dust, that whirled along under a sky of driving clouds, long lines of soldiers on horseback stood in the obscurity, while their officers passed along in front, peering closely at cartridge-belts and rifles.

"Geronimo," said a Captain to one trooper, "go back to the ammunition train and fill up the gaps in your *cartouchera*. You fool, you've been wasting your cartridges shooting coyotes!"

Across the desert westward toward the distant mountains rode strings of cavalry, the first to the front. About a thousand went, in ten different lines, diverging like wheel spokes; the jingle of their spurs ringing, their red-white-and-green flags floating straight out, crossed bandoliers gleaming dully, rifles flopping across their saddles, heavy, high sombreros and many-colored blankets. Behind each company plodded ten or twelve women on foot, carrying cooking utensils on their heads and backs, and perhaps a pack mule loaded with sacks of corn. And as they passed the cars they shouted back to their friends on the trains.

"*Poco tiempo California!*" cried one.

"Oh! there's a *colorado* for you!" yelled another. "I'll bet you were with Salazar in Orozco's Revolution. Nobody ever said *'Poco tiempo California'* except Salazar when he was drunk!"

The other man looked sheepish. "Well, maybe I was," he admitted. "But wait till I get a shot at my old *compañeros*. I'll show you whether I'm a Maderista or not!"

A little Indian in the rear cried: "I know how much of a Maderista you are, Luisito. At the first taking of Torreon, Villa gave you the choice of turning your coat or getting a *cabronasso* or *balasso* through the head!" And, joshing and singing, they jogged southwest, became small, and finally faded into the dust.

Villa himself stood leaning against a car, hands in his pockets. He wore an old slouch hat, a dirty shirt without a collar, and a badly frayed and shiny brown suit. All over the dusty plain in front of him men and horses had sprung up like magic. There was an immense confusion of saddling and bridling—a cracked blowing of tin bugles. The Brigada Zaragosa was getting ready to leave camp—a flanking column of two thousand men who were to ride southeast and attack Tlahualilo and Sacramento. Villa, it seemed, had just arrived at Yermo. He had stopped off Monday night at Camargo to attend the wedding of a *compadre*. His face was drawn into lines of fatigue.

"*Carramba!*" he was saying with a grin; "we started dancing Monday evening, danced all night, all the next day, and last night, too! What a *baile!* And what *muchachas!* The girls of Camargo and Santa Rosalia are the most beautiful in Mexico! I am worn out—*rendido!* It was harder work than twenty battles. . . ."

Then he listened to the report of some staff officer who dashed up on horseback, gave a concise order without hesitating, and the officer rode off. He told Señor Calzado, General Manager of the Railroad, in what order the trains should proceed south. He indicated to Señor Uro, the Quartermaster-general, what supplies should be distributed from the troop trains. To Señor Munoz, Director of the Telegraph, he gave the name of a Federal captain surrounded by Urbina's men a week before and killed with all his men in the hills near La Cadena, and ordered him to tap the Federal wire and send a message to General Velasco in Torreon purporting to be a report from this Captain from Conejos, and asking for orders . . . . He seemed to know and order everything.

We had lunch with General Eugenio Aguirre Benavides, the quiet, cross-eyed little commander of the Zaragosa Brigade, a member of one of the cultivated Mexican families that gathered around Madero in the first Revolution; with Raul

Madero, brother of the murdered President, second in command of the Brigade, who is a graduate of an American University, and looks like a Wall Street bond salesman; with Colonel Guerra, who went through Cornell, and Major Leyva, Ortega's nephew, a historic full-back on the Notre Dame football team. . . .

In a great circle, ready for action, the artillery was parked, with caissons open and mules corralled in the center. Colonel Servin, commander of the guns, sat perched high up on an immense bay horse, a ridiculous tiny figure, not more than five feet tall. He was waving his hand and shouting a greeting across to General Angeles, Carranza's Secretary of War—a tall, gaunt man, bareheaded, in a brown sweater, with a war map of Mexico hanging from his shoulder; who straddled a small burro. In the thick dust-clouds, sweating men labored. The five American artillery men had squatted down in the lee of a cannon, smoking. They hailed me with a shout:

"Say, bo! What in hell did we ever get into this mess for? Nothing to eat since last night—work twelve hours—say, take our pictures, will you?"

There passed by with a friendly nod the little Cockney soldier that had served with Kitchener, and then the Canadian Captain Treston, bawling for his interpreter, so that he could give his men some orders about the machine guns; and Captain Marinelli, the fat Italian soldier of fortune, pouring an interminable and unintelligible mixture of French, Spanish and Italian into the ear of a bored Mexican officer. Fierro rode by, cruelly roweling his horse with the bloody mouth—Fierro, the handsome, cruel and insolent—The Butcher they called him, because he killed defenseless prisoners with his revolver, and shot down his own men without provocation.

Late in the afternoon the Brigada Zaragosa rode away southeast over the desert, and another night came down.

The wind rose steadily in the darkness, growing colder and colder. Looking up at the sky, which had been ablaze with polished stars, I saw that all was dark with cloud. Through the roaring whirls of dust a thousand thin lines of sparks from the fires streamed southward. The coaling of the engines' fire boxes made sudden glares along the miles of trains. At first we thought we heard the sound of big guns in the distance. But all at once, unexpectedly, the sky split dazzlingly open from horizon to horizon, thunder fell like a blow, and the rain came level and thick as a flood. For a moment the human hum of the army was silenced. All the fires disappeared at once. And then came a vast shout of anger and laughter and discomfiture from the soldiers out on the plain, and the most amazing wail of misery from the women that I have ever heard. The two sounds only lasted a minute. The men wrapped themselves in their serapes and sank down in the shelter of the chaparral; and the hundreds of women and children exposed to the cold and the rain on the flat-cars and the tops of the box-cars silently and with Indian stoicism settled down to wait for dawn. In General Maclovio Herrera's car ahead was drunken laughter and singing to a guitar. . . .

Daybreak came with a sound of all the bugles in the world blowing; and looking out of the car door I saw the desert for miles boiling with armed men saddling and mounting. A hot sun popped over the western mountains, burning in a clear sky. For a moment the ground poured up billowing steam, and then there was dust again, and a thirsty land. There might never have been rain. A hundred breakfast fires smoked from the car-tops, and the women stood turning their dresses slowly in the sun, chattering and joking. Hundreds of little naked babies danced around, while their mothers lifted up their little clothes to the heat. A thousand joyous troopers shouted to each other that the advance was beginning; away off to the left some regiment had given away to joy, and was shooting into the air. Six more long trains had come in during the night, and all the engines were whistling signals. I went forward to get on the first train out, and as I passed the car of Trinidad Rodriguez, a harsh, feminine voice cried: "Hey, kid! Come in and get some breakfast." Leaning out of the door were Beatrice and Carmen, two noted Juarez women that had been brought to the front by the Rodriguez brothers. I went in and sat down at the table with about twelve men, several of them doctors in the hospital train, one French artillery captain, and an assortment of Mexican officers and privates. It was an ordinary freight box-car like all the private cars, with windows cut in the walls, partitions built to shut out the Chinese cook in the kitchen, and bunks arranged across sides and end. Breakfast consisted of heaping platters of red meat with *chile,* bowls of *frijoles,* stacks of cold flour *tortillas,* and six bottles of Monopole Champagne. Carmen's complexion was bad, and she was a little stupid from the gastronomic combination, but Beatrice's white, colorless face and red hair cut Buster Brown fashion fairly radiated a sort of malicious glee. She was a Mexican, but talked Tenderloin English without an accent. Jumping up from the table, she danced around it, pulling the men's hair. "Hello, you damned Gringo," she laughed at me. "What are you doing here? You're going to get a bullet in you if you don't get careful!"

A morose young Mexican, already a little drunk, snapped at her furiously in Spanish: "Don't you talk to him! Do you understand? I'll tell Trinidad how you asked the Gringo in to breakfast, and he'll have you shot!"

Beatrice threw back her head and roared. "Did you hear what he said? He thinks he owns me, because he once stayed with me in Juarez! . . . My God!" she went on. "How funny it seems to travel on the railroad and not have to buy a ticket!"

"Look here, Beatrice," I asked her; "we may not have such an easy time of it down there. What will you do if we get licked?"

"Who, me?" she cried. "Why, I guess it won't take me long to get friends in the Federal array. I'm a good mixer!"

"What is she saying? What do you say?" asked the others in Spanish.

With the most perfect insolence Beatrice translated for them. And in the midst of the uproar that followed I left. . . .

First blood

THE water train pulled out first. I rode on the cow-catcher of the engine, which was already occupied by the permanent home of two women and five children. They had built a little fire of mesquite twigs on the narrow iron platform, and were baking *tortillas* there; over their heads, against the windy roar of the boiler, fluttered a little line of wash. . . .

It was a brilliant day, hot sunshine alternating with big white clouds. In two thick columns, one on each side of the train, the army was already moving south. As far as the eye could reach, a mighty double cloud of dust floated over them; and little straggling groups of mounted men jogged along, with every now and then a big Mexican flag.

On the cannon-car

THE first car of the repair train was a steel-encased flat-car, upon which was mounted the famous Constitutionalist cannon "El Niño," with an open caisson full of shells behind it. Behind that was an armored car full of soldiers, then a car of steel rails, and four loaded with railroad ties. The engine came next, the engineer and fireman hung with cartridge-belts, their rifles handy. Then followed two or three box-cars full of soldiers and their women. It was a dangerous business. A large force of Federals were known to be in Mapimi, and the country swarmed with their outposts. Our army was already far ahead, except for five hundred men who guarded the trains at Conejos. If the enemy could capture or wreck the repair train the army would be cut off without water, food or ammunition. In the darkness we moved out. I sat upon the breech of "El Niño," chatting with Captain Diaz, the commander of the gun, as he oiled the breech lock of his beloved cannon and curled his vertical mustachios. In the armored recess behind the gun, where the Captain slept, I heard a curious, subdued rustling noise.

"What's that?"

"Eh?" cried he nervously. "Oh, nothing, nothing!"

Just then there emerged a young Indian girl with a bottle in her hand. She couldn't have been more than seventeen, very lovely. The Captain shot a glance at me, and suddenly whirled around.

"What are you doing here?" he cried furiously to her. "Why are you coming out here?"

"I thought you said you wanted a drink," she began.

I perceived that I was one too many, and excused myself. They hardly noticed me. But as I was climbing over the back of the car I couldn't help stopping and listening. They had gone back to the recess, and she was weeping.

"Didn't I tell you," stormed the Captain, "not to show yourself when there are strangers here? I will not have every man in Mexico looking at you. . . ."

I stood on the roof of the rocking steel car as we nosed slowly along. Lying on their bellies on the extreme front platform, two men with lanterns examined each foot of the track for wires that might mean mines planted under us. Beneath my feet the soldiers and their women were having dinner around fires built on the floor. Smoke and laughter poured out of the loopholes. . . . There were other fires aft, brown-faced, ragged people squatting at them, on the car-tops. Overhead the sky blazed stars, without a cloud. It was cold. After an hour of riding we came to a piece of broken track. The train stopped with a jar, the engine whistled, and a score of torches and lanterns jerked past. Men came running. The flares clustered bobbing together as the foremen examined the damage. A fire sprang up in the brush, and then another. Soldiers of the train guard straggled by, dragging their rifles, and formed impenetrable walls around the fires. Iron tools clanged, and the "Wai-hoy!" of men shoving rails off the flat-car. A Chinese dragon of workmen passed with a rail on their shoulders, then others with ties. Four hundred men swarmed upon the broken spot, working with extraordinary energy and good humor, until the shouts of gangs setting rails and ties, and the rattle of sledges on spikes, made a continuous roar. It was an old destruction, probably a year old, made when these same Constitutionalists were retreating north in the face of Mercado's Federal army, and we had it all fixed in an hour. Then on again. Sometimes it was a bridge burned out, sometimes a hundred yards of track twisted into grape vines by a chain and a backing engine. We advanced slowly. At one big bridge that it would take two hours to prepare, I built by myself a little fire in order to get warm. Calzado came past, and hailed me. "We've got a hand-car up ahead," he said, "and we're going along down and see the dead men. Want to come?"

"What dead men?"

"Why, this morning an outpost of eighty *rurales* was sent scouting north from Bermejillo. We heard about it over the wire and informed Benavides on the left. He sent a troop to take them in the rear, and drove them north in a running fight for fifteen miles until they smashed up against our main body and not one got out alive. They're scattered along the whole way just where they fell."

In a moment we were speeding south on the handcar. At our right hand and our left rode two silent, shadowy figures on horseback—cavalry guards, with rifles ready under their arms. Soon the flares and fires of the train were left behind, and we were enveloped and smothered in the vast silence of the desert.

"Yes," said Calzado, "the *rurales* are brave. They are *muy hombres*. *Rurales* are the best fighters Diaz and Huerta ever had. They never desert to the Revolution. They always remain loyal to the established government. Because they are police."

It was bitter cold. None of us talked much.

"We go ahead of the train at night," said the soldier at my left, "so that if there are any dynamite bombs underneath——"

"We could discover them and dig them out and put water in them, *carramba*!" said another sarcastically. The rest laughed. I began to think of that, and it made me shiver. The dead silence of the desert seemed an expectant hush. One couldn't see ten feet from the track.

"*Oiga*!" shouted one of the horsemen. "It was just here that one lay." The brakes ground and we tumbled off and down the steep embankment, our lanterns jerking ahead. Something lay huddled around the foot of a telegraph pole—something infinitely small and shabby, like a pile of old clothes. The *rurale* was upon his back, twisted sideways from his hips. He had been stripped of everything of value by the thrifty rebels—shoes, hat, underclothing. They had left him his ragged jacket with the tarnished silver braid, because there were seven bullet holes in it; and his trousers, soaked with blood. He had evidently been much bigger when alive—the dead shrink so. A wild red beard made the pallor of his face grotesque, until you noticed that under it and the dirt, and the long lines of sweat of his terrible fight and hard riding, his mouth was gently and serenely open as if he slept. His brains had been blown out.

"*Carrai!*" said one guard. "There was a shot for the dirty goat! Right through the head!"

The others laughed. "Why, you don't think they shot him there in the fight, do you, *pendeco*?" cried his companion. "No, they *always* go around and make sure afterward——"

"Hurry up! I've found the other," shouted a voice off in the darkness.

We could reconstruct this man's last struggle. He had dropped off his horse, wounded—for there was blood on the ground—into a little dry arroyo. We could even see where his horse had stood while he pumped shells into his Mauser with feverish hands, and blazed away, first to the rear, where the pursuers came running with Indian yells, and then at the hundreds and hundreds of bloodthirsty horsemen pouring down from the north, with the Demon Pancho Villa at their head. He must have fought a long time, perhaps until they ringed him round with living flame—for we found hundreds of empty cartridges. And then, when the last shot was spent, he made a dash eastward, hit at every step; hid for a moment under the little railroad bridge, and ran out upon the open desert, where he fell. There were twenty bullet holes in him. They had stripped him of all save his underclothes. He lay sprawled in an attitude of desperate action, muscles tense, one fist clenched and spread across the dust as if he were dealing a blow; the fiercest exultant grin on his face. Strong, savage, until one looked closer and saw the subtle touch of weakness that death stamps on life—the delicate expression of idiocy over it all. They had shot him through the head three times—how exasperated they must have been!

Crawling south through the cold night once more. . . . A few miles and then a bridge dynamited, or a strip of track wrecked. The stop, the dancing torches, the great bonfires leaping up from the desert, and the four hundred wild men pouring furiously out and falling upon their work. . . . Villa had given orders to hurry. . . .

About two o'clock in the morning I came upon two *soldaderas* squatting around a fire, and asked them if they could give me *tortillas* and coffee. One was an old, gray-haired Indian woman with a perpetual grin, the other a slight girl not more than twenty years old, who was nursing a four-months baby at her breast. They were perched at the extreme tip of a flat-car, their fire built upon a pile of sand, as the train jolted and swayed along. Around them, backed against them, feet sticking out between them, was a great, inconglomerate mass of sleeping, snoring humans. The rest of the train was by this time dark; this was the only patch of light and warmth in the night. As I munched my *tortilla* and the old woman lifted a burning coal in her fingers to light her corn-husk cigarette, wondering where her

Pablo's brigade was this night; and the girl nursed her child, crooning to it, her blue-enameled earrings twinkling,—we talked.

"Ah! it is a life for us *viejas*," said the girl. "*Adio*, but we follow our men out in the campaign, and then do not know from hour to hour whether they live or die. I remember well when Filadelfo called to me one morning in the little morning before it was light—we lived in Pachuca—and said: 'Come! we are going out to fight because the good Pancho Madero has been murdered this day!' We had only been loving each other eight months, too, and the first baby was not born.... We had all believed that peace was in Mexico for good. Filadelfo saddled the burro, and we rode out through the streets just as light was coming, and into the fields where the farmers were not yet at work. And I said: 'Why must I come?' And he answered: 'Shall I starve, then? Who shall make my *tortillas* for me but my woman?' It took us three months to get north, and I was sick and the baby was born in a desert just like this place, and died there because we could not get water. That was when Villa was going north after he had taken Torreon."

The old woman broke in: "Yes, and all that is true. When we go so far and suffer so much for our men, we are cruelly treated by the stupid animals of Generals. I am from San Luis Potosi, and my man was in the artillery of the Federacion when Mercado came north. All the way to Chihuahua we traveled, the old fool of a Mercado grumbling about transporting the *viejas*. And then he ordered his army to go north and attack Villa in Juarez, and he forbade the women to go. Is that the way you are going to do, *desgraciado*? I said to myself. And when he evacuated Chihuahua and ran away with my man to Ojinaga, I just stayed right in Chihuahua and got a man in the Maderista army when it came in. A nice handsome young fellow, too,—much better than Juan. I'm not a woman to stand being put upon."

"How much are the *tortillas* and coffee?" I asked. They looked at each other, startled. Evidently they had thought me one of the penniless soldiers crowded on the train.

"What you would like," said the young woman faintly. I gave them a peso.

The old woman exploded in a torrent of prayer. "God, his sainted Mother, the Blessed Niño and Our Lady of Guadelupe have sent this stranger to us tonight! Here we had not a centavo to buy coffee and flour with...."

I suddenly noticed that the light of our fire had paled, and looked up in amazement to find it was dawn. Just then a man came running along the train from up front, shouting something unintelligible, while laughter and shouts burst out in his wake. The sleepers raised their curious heads and wanted to know what was the matter. In a moment our inanimate car was alive. The man passed, still yelling something about "*padre*," his face exultant with some tremendous joke.

"What is it?" I asked.

"Oh!" cried the old woman. "His woman on the car ahead has just had a baby!"

Just in front of us lay Bermejillo, its pink and blue and white plastered adobe houses as delicate and ethereal as a village of porcelain. To the east, across a still, dustless desert, a little file of sharp-cut horsemen, with a red-white-and-green flag over them, were riding into town....

At the gates of Gomez

WE had taken Bermejillo the afternoon before,—the army breaking into a furious gallop five kilometers north of the town and pouring through it at top speed, driving the unprepared garrison in a rout southward,—a running fight that lasted five miles, as far as the Hacienda of Santa Clara,—and killing a hundred and six *colorados*. Within a few hours afterward Urbina came in sight above Mapimi, and the eight hundred *colorados* there, informed of the astonishing news that the entire Constitutionalist army was flanking them on their right, evacuated the place, and fled hotly to Torreon. All over the country the astounded Federals were falling back in a panic upon the city.

Late in the afternoon a dumpy little train came down the narrow-gauge track from the direction of Mapimi, and from it proceeded the loud strains of a string orchestra of ten pieces playing "*Recuerdos* of Durango,"—to which I had so often *baile*'d with the Tropa. The roofs, doors and windows were packed with Mexicans, singing and beating time with their heels, as they fired their rifles in a sort of salute upon entering the town. At the station this curious equipage drew up, and from it proceeded—who but Patricio, General Urbina's fighting stage-driver at whose side I had so often ridden and danced! He threw his arms around me, yelling: "Juanito! Here is Juanito, *mi General!*" In a minute we were asking and answering each other a million questions. Did I have the photographs I took of him? Was I going to the battle of Torreon? Did he know where Don Petronilo was? And Pablo Seañes? And Raphaelito? And right in the midst of it somebody shouted "Viva Urbina!" and the old General himself stood at the top of the steps,—the lion-hearted hero of Durango. He was lame, and leaned upon two soldiers. He held a rifle in his hand,—an old, discarded Springfield, with the sights filed down,—and wore a double cartridge-belt around his waist. For a moment he remained there, absolutely expressionless, his small, hard eyes boring into me. I thought he did not recognize me, when all at once his harsh, sudden voice shot out: "That's not the camera you had! Where's the other one?"

I was about to reply when he interrupted: "I know. You left it behind you in La Cadena. Did you run very fast?"

"Yes, *mi General*."

"And you've come down to Torreon to run again?" "When I began to run from La Cadena," I remarked, nettled, "Don Petronilo and the troops were already a mile away."

He didn't answer, but came haltingly down the steps of the car, while a roar of laughter went up from the soldiers. Coming up to me he put a hand over my shoulder and gave me a little tap on the back. "I'm glad to see you, *compañero*," he said. . . .

Across the desert the wounded had begun to straggle in from the battle of Tlahualilo to the hospital train, which lay far up near the front of the line of trains. On the flat barren plain, as far as I could see, there were only three living things in sight: a limping, hatless man, with his head tied up in a bloody cloth; another staggering beside his staggering horse; and a mule mounted by two bandaged figures far behind them. And in the still hot night we could hear from our car groans and screams. . . .

Late Sunday morning we were again on "El Niño" at the head of the repair train, moving slowly down the track abreast of the army. "El Chavalito," another cannon mounted on a flat-car, was coupled behind, then came two armored cars, and the work-cars. This time there were no women. The army wore a different air, winding along in two immense serpents each side of us—there was little laughter or shouting. We were close now, only eighteen miles from Gomez Palacio, and no one knew what the Federals planned to do. It seemed incredible that they would let us get so close without making one stand. Immediately south of Bermejillo we entered a new land. To the desert succeeded fields bordered with irrigation ditches, along which grew immense green alamos, towering pillars of freshness after the baked desolation we had just passed through. Here were cotton-fields, the white tufts unpicked and rotting on their stalks; corn-fields with sparse green blades just showing. Along the big ditches flowed swift, deep water in the shade. Birds sang, and the barren western mountains marched steadily nearer as we went south. It was summer—hot, moist summer, such as we have at home. A deserted cotton-gin lay on our left, hundreds of white bales tumbled in the sun, and dazzling heaps of cotton-seed left just as the workmen had piled it months before. . . .

At Santa Clara the massed columns of the army halted and began to defile to left and right, thin lines of troops jogging out under the checkered sun and shade of the great trees, until six thousand men were spread in one long single front, to the right over fields and through ditches, beyond the last cultivated field, across the desert to the very base of the mountains; to the left over the roll of the flat world. The bugles blared faintly and near, and the army moved forward in a mighty line across the whole country. Above them lifted a five-mile-wide golden dust-glory. Flags flapped. In the center, level with them, came the cannon-car, and beside that Villa rode with his staff. At the little villages along the way the big-hatted, white-bloused *pacificos* stood in silent wonder, watching this strange host pass. An old man drove his goats homeward. The foaming wave of troopers broke upon him, yelling with pure mischief, and all the goats ran in different directions. A mile of army shouted with laughter,—the dust rolled up from their thousand hoofs, and they passed. At the village of Brittingham the great line halted, while Villa and his staff galloped up to the peons watching from their little mound.

"*Oyez!*" said Villa. "Have any troops passed through here lately?"

"*Si, señor!*" answered several men at once. "Some of Don Carlo Argumedo's *gente* went by yesterday pretty fast."

"Hum," Villa meditated. "Have you seen that bandit Pancho Villa around here?"

"No, señor!" they chorused.

"Well, he's the fellow I'm looking for. If I catch that *diablo* it will go hard with him!"

"We wish you all success!' cried the *pacificos*, politely.

"You never saw him, did you?"

"No, God forbid!" they said fervently.

"Well!" grinned Villa. "In the future when people ask if you know him you will have to admit the shameful fact! I am Pancho Villa!" And with that he spurred away, and all the army followed. . . .

Chapter VI

The compañeros reappear

SUCH had been the surprise of the Federals, and they had fled in such a hurry, that for many miles the railroad was intact. But toward afternoon we began to find little bridges burned and still smoking, and telegraph poles cut down with an axe—badly and hastily done bits of destruction that were easily repaired. But the army had got far ahead, and by nightfall, about eight miles from Gomez Palacio, we reached the place where eight solid miles of torn-up track began. There was no food on our train. We had only a blanket apiece; and it was cold. In the flare of torches and fires, the repair gang fell upon their work. Shouts and hammering steel, and the thud of falling ties. . . .

Part 8

SUGAR, COFFEE, AND BANANAS
Railroads in Cuba, Central America, and British Jamaica

53

DAVID TURNBULL, *TRAVELS IN THE WEST: CUBA, WITH NOTICES OF PORTO RICO, AND THE SLAVE TRADE* (LONDON: LONGMAN, ORME, GREEN, AND LONGMANS, 1840), PP. 194–197

The expense of travelling on the railroad is of course greater than it would be in Europe or America. To suit all classes of customers, however, they have established no less than four different rates. Passengers in the first class coaches, when going the whole distance, pay as nearly as possible at the rate of sixpence sterling a mile, in the second class four-pence, in the third class three-pence, and in the fourth class two-pence; and these rates are proportionally increased for shorter distances, when passengers are taken up or set down at the intermediate stages. The tariff of freight seems also high, although from the enormous expense of bringing produce from the interior to a convenient place of shipment, and carrying back the necessary supplies for the estates, there can be no doubt that if the company were to exact as much as the planters along the line would find it for their interest to pay, the existing rates might safely be doubled, or, perhaps, increased even threefold. An idea of this may be formed from the following specimens:—For a box of sugar, which usually weighs from three to four hundred weight, the charge for the whole forty-five miles is a dollar and a quarter or five shillings sterling; for a bag of coffee, weighing usually from 175 to 200 lbs., two shillings; for a barrel of flour, three shillings; and for most other articles in nearly the same proportion.

As no similar work exists within the tropics, the deep cutting in some portions of the line, and especially the tunnel within a few miles of the Havana, deserve a much closer geological investigation than I had leisure or opportunity to bestow upon them. As yet, the tunnel is only large enough for a single train of carriages, being 14 feet wide, by 16 feet high, and 325 in length; but the deep open excavations at its southern extremity are still more fruitful of interesting discoveries in the detail of volcanic formations, than the interior of the tunnel itself.

The gross produce of the railway, for the first month after it was opened, up to the terminus at Guines, amounted to $36,000, of which $24,000 arose from the conveyance of passengers, $10,000 from the freight of produce, and $2000 for the transit of goods going inland from the Havana; and during that period, the leading article of sugar, from which the projectors anticipated the greatest returns, had not come into operation, as the canes were not yet ripe, and the process of grinding had scarcely been begun.

As a commercial speculation, the probabilities of its success are subject to several deductions to which it would scarcely be exposed in any other country. If, for instance, any serious accident were to occur through the habitual negligence of the unpaid slave attendants, the natural timidity of the Creole population might possibly deter them from exposing their persons to the real or supposed danger of the new mode of conveyance, however advantageous it might be in point of cheapness and rapidity. For a long time to come they will, probably, be dependent on foreign engineers for working the locomotive engines and repairing the machinery; and it has often been remarked that, although public undertakings are begun with zeal and spirit in these tropical regions, they are seldom prosecuted with corresponding energy or perseverance, after they have lost the charm of novelty. It remains to be seen how far this principle will affect the future profits of those who embark their capital in similar speculations.

Several branches from the railroad have been proposed for the purpose of connecting it with the southern coast of the island, one in particular by San Antonio de los Baños, and the other terminating in the neighbourhood of Batabano. As it has been found, however, that the agricultural produce of these districts must necessarily be brought to some point or other of the present line without extension, it has been thought more advisable, that the southern branch should terminate near the town of Guanimar, which would bring in the produce of the rich and highly cultivated southeastern districts, extending from San Marcos to La Guira.

In the year 1838 another company was formed for the construction of a railway between Cardenas and Soledad de Bemba, divided into 500 dollar shares, of which nearly 600 were taken almost immediately, either by proprietors along the line, or by merchants interested in the trade of Matanzas. On looking over the prospectus prepared by the distinguished secretary, Don Domingo del Monte, I find an instance of Spanish delicacy worthy of note as a national characteristic. Two engineers, both Spaniards, having presented themselves as candidates for the superintendence of the work, the meeting of proprietors finding them so nearly equal in point of qualification, felt it impossible, from motives of delicacy, to decide between them, and therefore resolved on allowing the selection to be determined by lot, content with the assurance that in either case the enterprise would be the first of the kind that had been undertaken by a Spanish engineer throughout the whole extent of the monarchy.

54

W. T. BRIGHAM, 'AN UNCOMMERCIAL REPUBLIC', *SCRIBNER'S MAGAZINE* 1 (JAN.–JUNE 1887), PP. 711–716

General Barrios did all in his power, and with the money raised among his people commenced the "Ferrocarril del Norte" (Northern Railroad). Here again the old habits weighed against the Guatemalans. They had not, like the northern nations, grown up in railroading, and they were cheated on every side in the unaccustomed work. A few miles were built on the thirty-six-inch gauge system, when the contractors failed, and the death of Barrios put a temporary stop to the *empresa*.

A good illustration of the lack of capital among the people is shown in the method of raising the capital stock of this railroad. The par value of a share was $40, payable in quarterly instalments of $1 each, the whole payment thus extending over ten years, an arrangement intended to make the undertaking popular and engage the interest of even the poorer Indios. The man who subscribed for twenty shares was looked upon as a wealthy and most public-spirited citizen. Now, it was not possible to open subscription offices all over the republic, so subscriptions were made payable in adhesive stamps, which could be purchased as postage stamps were, and whenever forty of these special stamps were attached to the *accion* it was a fully paid share and entitled to dividends (if earned by the railroads), or could be turned over to pay for public lands at its par value.

In the absence of commerce, there is but little travelling, and the stranger finds great difficulty in obtaining information about roads, even from the *jefes* of the departments through which the roads pass. It is, of course, not peculiar to Guatemala to find ignorance of local geography and complete inability to judge of distances, but the Guatemalans have a happy way of indicating the condition of a road in the expressions, "a big league," "a little league," and on rivers they usually reckon distances by *vueltas* or bends. While the North American must have express trains and considers every way-station an attack on his comfort, his neighbor in Central America hires men enough to carry his luggage—and each man can carry from five to six arrobas (an arroba is twenty-five pounds)—and mounting his horse or mule, plods leisurely along up hill and down dale, his bearers generally keeping up with him. There is very little wear and tear in such a journey, one is never in a hurry, and it is hurry that exhausts one, not reasonable work.

For myself, it was a restful kind of travel. My saddle-bags contained the needful clothes, my blanket was rolled behind the saddle, my rubber poncho with map and note-book in front. One man carried a coffee-pot and a supply of coffee and sugar, my hammock, and a photographic outfit; another, a supply of photo-plates, my son's hammock, and various articles gathered on the way. We rode along chatting and enjoying everything, even the rain that ran into our boots, and when we wished to make a photograph, a whistle brought our *mozo* to our side, and in less than fifteen minutes the camera was unpacked (and everything must be rainproof), two exposures made, and we were again in the saddle. Much more convenient than an express train! Then, where no one travels, a journey is an exploration.

When the road branches, and this is not very common in Guatemala, our map and compass stood us in stead, for guide posts are unknown, and there are no intelligent police to tell one the right way. Getting into a railway train and being fired, as it were, at the mark of our destination is a very helpless, lazy way of going from place to place. The phrenologist's "bump of locality" would be in danger of atrophy, and would be of no more use than the eyes of a cave-fish, if one always trusted to others to deliver him by the right road to the right place. A correct map is of course a sufficient guide, but Guatemala has never been surveyed and has no correct map. Two so-called maps, one made in Germany (the best for names), the other in France, and both by government aid, are only sketches, and while mountain-ranges and rivers seem drawn at haphazard, the principal towns are frequently twenty miles from the position on the map. The maps that the Indios made for Cortez as he pushed his way through unknown forests were probably as correct as these showy maps of Guatemala. Commerce has not yet required the survey, and in the meantime a traveller of reasonable intelligence can estimate the distances from town to town by the time his steady-going steed consumes, and the mountainous nature of the country permits many a bird's-eye view; then, the features of the land are so varied and distinct that, once seen, they are not easily forgotten.

It is sad to think that when commerce opens this country its charm will be lost. Years ago I crossed the Nevadas in the overland stages; and, as the six or eight horses rattled over the long grades, it was quite possible to put one's self *en rapport* with the country—every gulch, every cañon, every sink, every divide, had an individuality; even the dust of each valley seemed distinct, and the whole way was a panorama sharply drawn and vividly colored. Now commerce has removed these slow coaches; and the traveller of the present day is whirled through miles of snow-sheds, and scarcely less dismal tunnels, losing thus some of the finest scenery on the whole line, and one day of his journey becomes much like another. So will it be in Guatemala; a single day will take one from Livingston to the capital, where now five days must be spent on horseback and in canoe, and all will take the shorter and cheaper way, although they lose every bit of the national flavor. We earnestly advise all genuine travellers to see Guatemala before the projected railroads are built. Arcadia cannot always remain Arcadia, and the new life infused into the republic by the late President Barrios will be felt yet more widely.

Even now the inland people of Guatemala want to get out; the fever of business has infected them from the North, and they have already planned far beyond their means. It is interesting, however, to see how this Eden is to be modernized, civilized, and spoiled. I have been over the routes in Guatemala most likely to be laid with rail, and found no difficulties that would be considered formidable in the way of engineers—the greatest, perhaps, being the ravages of the comajen, an insect that rapidly destroys dead timber, as ties, piles, trestles, etc.

First in importance may be placed a line from Livingston to Coban, perhaps one hundred and twenty miles, which would open the fine coffee-region of Alta Verapaz, and so encourage the extension of plantations, or *cafetals*, that crops would sometimes come to our markets (now all goes to England). This road would pass through the mahogany and pine-forests north of the Lago de Izabal, and would be comparatively easy to construct, and sure to pay its way from the first train. To-day all the coffee of this region is taken by ox-carts to Pansos, and shipped to Livingston by river steam-boats at a very heavy freight; but in a few years the traveller will miss the picturesque camps of the ox-drivers by the road-side at night, for he, and the coffee, and other freight, will pass rapidly through the fine scenery in railway-carriages.

From Coban the line will some day extend to the Mexican system, and then the luxurious dweller in the North will have his winter home, his tropical villa on the shores of the Rio Dulce. Second in importance I place the Ferrocarril del Norte, already mentioned as commenced, on the line from Puerto Barrios to the capital, a distance of about two hundred and twenty-five miles. The route through the valley of the Motagua is already surveyed, and most of it graded; thence it extends to Zacapa, Chiquimula, and Jutiapa, a dry route, easy of construction; from the last place a branch might descend sixty miles among the volcanoes to San Salvador, and the main line continue over a broken mountain-chain to Escuintla, where it would join the road now in operation between Guatemala City and San José.

The third road needed will extend from Ocós, the new port on the border of Soconusco, to Escuintla, which promises to become the railroad-centre of the Pacific coast; and this shore-line would gather in the finest *cacao* known, now not exported because so costly, and, besides this, much sugar. From the highlands between Escuintla and Antigua one can see this entire route extending, over level or gently rolling ground, among little plantations that might be enlarged a hundredfold, over streams easily bridged with iron, and through forests that would furnish an abundance of timber. A road from the capital due north through the sugar-region of San Geronimo, Salamá to Coban, would complete the interior net-work. Among other advantages in constructing the Coban line first, would be the exploitation of the coal-deposits in the limestone-ranges of Alta Verapaz, thus furnishing fuel for the whole system.

So much for the internal circulation of Guatemala as hoped for in the future, when the *caminos de herradura* (bridle-paths), now the general ways of communication in Central America, have given place to the *ferrocarril*. Let us glance at the connections with her neighbors. The people of British Honduras are about to build a road from Belize to Peten, about one hundred and fifty miles, opening a vast timber-region and extensive logwood-ranges, as well as fine fruit-land. At present the traveller goes by *pitpan* up the Belize River to Garbutt's Falls, on the boundary of Guatemala, and thence by bridle-path to the lake, a journey of two weeks. Every winter the Indios come down to Belize, bringing their few native products and manufactures; among the latter, huge mahogany bowls or platters, even five feet in diameter, which serve the Hondureñans for wash-tubs. It is no common thing for a white man to make this journey now, for the forests about Peten are deserted and the roads in the wet season execrable. The mail for Peten usually goes by way of Coban, and is carried by a *mozo* on foot, not always a safe way, for once, no mail arriving for weeks, a search was made, and the remains of the unfortunate carrier were found in his hammock, high between two trees. Snake or insect poison had been his bane.

British Honduras cannot be called a progressive colony. She concentrates herself on Belize and other shore-towns, and has left the interior unexplored, and has not even a *camino de herradura* to connect these various shore-towns. Stann Creek, a large Carib settlement, Monkey River, Allpines and Punta Gorda, are quite as isolated as Livingston, and only the fruit trade with New Orleans keeps them alive. The distance between Belize and Livingston by water is one hundred and twenty-five miles, by land fifteen miles farther, with several rivers of depth to bridge.

Spanish Honduras is far behind her more northern namesake in some respects, but she exports more fruit, and had it not been for the fiasco of the Interoceanic Railway, over which many an English or French investor still feels sore, she might have had the first rail communication between the Atlantic and the Pacific. Now the wretched toy road, thirty-five miles long, between Puerto Cortez and San Pedro Sula is all she has to show for a debt of $27,000,000. It is but fair to say that plans are matured for a line to carry out this original way to the capital Tegucigalpa, and thence to the Gulf of Fonseca, on the Pacific coast. A more practicable line is partly surveyed from Trujillo to Puerto Barrios, and this would take all the fruit from the Hondureñan coast to Livingston, where the facilities for shipping are far greater than at the ancient port of Trujillo. Coco-nuts, plantains, bananas and limes seem here in their native soil, and the line of New Orleans steamers that contracts for the fruit of this region does a most profitable business.

With such schemes even partly developed the Republic of Guatemala cannot long enjoy her present hermit-like life; greater riches than Cortez and Alvarado dreamed of will attract new invaders, and at no very distant day our Uncommercial Republic will be like any other republic, busy, prosperous, and—commonplace.

55

NEVIN O. WINTER, *GUATEMALA AND HER PEOPLE OF TO-DAY* (BOSTON: L. C. PAGE AND COMPANY, 1909), PP. 24–29

We left Retalhuleu the following morning before daylight for the ride to Guatemala City. The distance is about one hundred and fifty miles, but it was a fourteen hour journey according to the schedule, which is a fair illustration of the speed of railroad travel in this country. The train was a mixed one made up of freight and first and second class passenger coaches, the latter being continually crowded with Indians. After a soldier had taken the names and destination of all the passengers the train was allowed to proceed.

The mail coach on this train consisted of a small corner in one car and was in charge of one clerk. This fellow got off at a station for some purpose but lingered a little too long, and the train had started when he reached it. He was afraid to jump on the train in motion and followed us as far as we could see him, waving his hands wildly and racing in the hot sun. The conductor was obdurate and would not stop for him, so the last half day's run was made without a mail clerk and I do not know what the people did for their mail. As a rule, however, that is not very heavy. The conductor dismissed the matter by saying that "he had no business to leave the train."

Through this part of the republic the cochineal used to be cultivated extensively. The cochineal is a little insect which clings to the leaves of the *nopal*, a species of the cactus. The insects on the leaves give it a very peculiar "warty" appearance. Just before the rainy season begins the leaves of the *nopal* are cut off and hung in a dry place. Then they are scraped, the insects being killed by being baked in a hot oven which gives them a brownish colour and makes a scarlet or crimson dye; or, they are put into boiling water, when they become black and furnish a blue or purple dye. When prepared for market they are worth several dollars per pound, as it is slow and tedious work to separate the insects from the cactus. It is estimated that there are seventy thousand insects to the pound. When you consider that more than a million tons of the cochineal dye were exported in a single year at one time, a slight idea may be gained of the magnitude of the industry before the cheaper chemical dyes destroyed the market for the cochineal. At present the insect is cultivated only for local use, as the natives prefer it to colour their gayly-hued cotton and woollen fabrics. It can be said of it that the colour will stand almost any amount of rain and sunshine and the tints are as beautiful and pure as one could desire.

The greater part of the land along the line of this railway is cultivated after a fashion, but only in a careless and desultory way. None of the towns are very large and the villages poor but fairly numerous. At Escuintla the passengers were obliged to change to the Central Railroad and take the train which had come up from the coast on its way to the capital.

After leaving Escuintla the road skirts around the base of Agua and begins to climb up the mountain range. In the next thirteen miles the road ascends more than twenty-five hundred feet, which takes it into another zone. The track crosses numerous large and deep gorges. The tangled, tropical forests have disappeared and coffee and cane plantations become numerous. The smooth slopes of Agua and Fuego are rich in cultivation. At nearly every station women appear with all kinds of fruits for sale, as well as eggs, cakes, *dulces* (candies), etc. Never did I eat more delicious pineapples than those secured right here. They were great, luscious, toothsome fruits. Oranges cannot compare with the cultivated and developed fruit of California, but bananas were fine and much better than the fruit generally sold at our own fruit stands.

Lake Amatitlan is passed and a pretty little body of water it is nestling in the hollow of the hills. There are many boiling springs near its shores, which show how near it is to the unsettled forces of nature. The washwomen take advantage of this water heated by nature, as it saves them trouble and fuel and is always ready for use. The villages become more numerous as the city is approached, and factory buildings and the white walls of the *haciendas* which dot the landscape here and there make a pleasing contrast. Some lava beds are passed showing that nature has created disturbances in the past quite freely. At last the final ridge is passed, and there, nestling in the valley, is the City of Guatemala. Its situation is some what similar to the valley of Mexico, though it is not nearly so large; neither are the surrounding barriers of the mountains so high; nor are the lakes present, which gave the City of Mexico the name of the New-World Venice.

A couple of years ago it was impossible to travel by rail all the way from Guatemala City to the Gulf coast, and it was necessary to leave the city on the back of that sadly-wise, much-neglected creature—the mule, for there was no carriage road. This method of travel entails hardships, but I believe that it has its compensations. Byron says:

> "Though sluggards deem it but a foolish chase,
> And marvel men should quit their easy chair,
> The toilsome way, and long, long league to trace,
> Oh, there is sweetness in the mountain air,
> And life, that bloated ease can never hope to share."

Two other Americans, residents of the country, were going and invited me to join them. The liveries wanted three hundred dollars each from us for three saddle mules, a cargo mule and *mozo* (servant). An old Indian in the country furnished the same for sixty-five dollars each—just about five dollars in gold—which was cheap enough for a four days' journey to the railroad and back.

56

HENRY R. BLANEY, *THE GOLDEN CARIBBEAN: A WINTER VISIT TO THE REPUBLICS OF COLOMBIA, SPANISH HONDURAS, BELIZE, AND THE SPANISH MAIN VIA BOSTON AND NEW ORLEANS* (BOSTON: LEE AND SHEPARD, 1900), PP. 73–85

El Salvador

AT the head of the "Old Line" of the Costa Rica railroad, which has been built for 20 years, one leaves the railroad station at Guápiles and approaches the hacienda of El Salvador (property of the United Fruit Company), through a beautiful avenue of royal palms and cocoanut trees, enriched with the scarlet leaves of crotons, and shaded by orange and lemon trees. From the piazza of the house an uninterrupted view of broad pastures opens out toward the north, the distant hills lost in purple mist. The United Fruit Company employ a first-class butter-maker at this pen, as it would be called in Jamaica. The writer noticed the enormous quantity of manure going to waste. Of course the land is exceedingly rich, needing no manure to give good results; but there are many uses that this rich fertilizer can be put to. A practical market gardener would see unlimited profit and opportunity in Costa Rican markets for high-class vegetables, the gardens being enriched with refuse bananas rejected at the track benches and added to by the manure of the stables. Lettuce, beets, melons, radishes, cucumbers, etc., would grow luxuriantly here. The most of these vegetables, with few exceptions, at present are of an inferior quality in local markets.

El Salvador is a plantation of 3000 acres (1800 manzanas), with 100 manzanas given over to the cultivation of bananas by 26 laborers and ploughmen. The plantation holds 3000 head of cattle, in three divisions.

The semi-annual stock taking, or rather the counting, sorting, and inspection of the bulls, cows, steers, calves, and horse kind of the farm, had just commenced at El Salvador upon the arrival of the writer. Under the superintendence of Mr. Thomas Kissock, the manager, the three different herds, each in turn, were driven through various gates, by three expert Costa Rican cow-boys toward the principal pen, the bulls bellowing and the cows lowing in defence of their young sucking calves. The cowboys dashed recklessly, but with fine precision, about the broad fields, calling, cursing, and expostulating with backward cow or stubborn heifer. The horses the cowboys rode were under splendid training and discipline, inclining here and there with marvellous swiftness and sure-footedness over the broken ground, fording brooks in a burst of spray, and spattering the mud in every direction, the cowboys giving their peculiar cry of "Váca, váca"; and with much waving of hats, hot expostulations, and deep guttural exclamations the bewildered herds were soon driven on, one by one, past the vigilant eye of the manager; sick or diseased animals—few in number, by the bye—were cut out from the crowd, thrown by a twist of the neck to the ground, and an examination of the ills that cow flesh is heir to occupying but a few moments in each case. About six fine saddle-horses are in constant use, and, as is usual with all Costa Rican horses, are guided by the reins pressed against the neck; they change their easy running gait to the gallop, the trot, and the lope as required. A commissary house near the railroad station, well stocked and ably managed, forms one of the many sources of revenue of the plantation. Here the Jamaican laborer buys his machete, boots, lanterns, saddles, cotton goods, groceries, liquid goods, etc., at reasonable prices, principally paid for by the men in checks on their monthly account.

A large bath-house, through which dashes a cool and agreeable stream of water, is one of the many comforts of the hacienda El Salvador.

La Emilia

The plantation of La Emilia, now the property of the United Fruit Company, was formerly owned by Mr. Minor C. Keith for 14 years; it is within one and a half miles from El Salvador, and has about the same number of acres. Manager Kissock finishes most of his fat cattle and breeding stock here. Over these broad acres, with good horses, we went, fording two streams; flocks of screaming green parrots cross our path, huge guava trees draped with Spanish moss and hanging vines grace the landscape. We find a pleasant situation for the house of the manager, who sometimes resides here, and has a liking for rare orchids, which flower on the veranda. The Turialba volcano is in sight from the house, and the prevailing winds are mostly from the southeast; the rain in the afternoon comes from the mountains, in the morning from the eastward.

The Banana River Plantation

The United Fruit Company

A branch railroad runs about 14 miles through the cocoanut trees and banana plants, and as the train skirts the beach the roar of the breakers pounding on the yellow sand fills one's ears. There are about 50,000 cocoanut trees along this shore. Just beyond Westfalia station commences the Banana River Plantation: there are at least 1200 acres of bananas, and between the rows there are many cacao trees (chocolate), the land being peculiarly suitable for cacao. The railroad is shortly to be extended through the property; at present there is about 12 miles of a 3 ft. 6 in. gauge track running close to the sea, about halfway it branches inland and extends toward the distant range of Talamanca, which rises to the south. There is good hunting in the season: deer, alligators, monkeys, and ducks, and farther back, near the mountains, jaguars or spotted tigers, also the puma (American lion) and panthers can be shot; there is occasionally a fine skin that can be purchased at some of the stores on the line. The tigers are shot by the Indians on the Banana River about 15 miles from the terminal of the railroad, and they bring the skins to the shopkeepers who sell supplies. The Costa Rica government allows one shotgun or rifle to each traveller entering Costa Rica, but the rifle must be a sporting rifle, and not a Mauser. The ride on the railroad is a very interesting one; from the car platform as the train proceeds numerous chances can be had to practise with revolvers on hawks, alligators, and monkeys. The country that the railroad passes through is about the wildest on the coast and gives the traveller the best idea of tropical nature in its most retiring moods.

Zent farm and plantations

From the junction of the railroad at La Junta, a branch line extends for eight miles to the Zent Plantations of the United Fruit Company, consisting of:—

Chiripo	1000 manzanas.
Boston	1200 manzanas.
Sterling	250 manzanas.
Victoria	500 manzanas.
Zent	1000 manzanas.

Zent is very valuable and extensive property; there are 700 to 800 men employed in the cultivation of the finest banana lands that are owned by the United Fruit Company. Zent has the reputation of being very unhealthy, but in only isolated instances did the writer note any signs of malarial sickness; this is now being counteracted by changes in the situation of the homes of the employees.

The plantations are 50 feet above the sea, and certainly those farms on the banks of the river could not be in a more beautiful and healthy situation. There is now under construction 20 miles of railroad called the Limon extension, destined to open the plantations and make them more in direct touch with the steamers. The railroad has two engines and many cars to assist the rapid transit of the fruit. Mr. William. H. Kyes, the manager, considers that ploughing is a waste of time here, the ground being so rich, and cleaning and cutting away the stumps is all that is necessary for good results; the managers of the plantations on the "Old Line" are of a different mind, however.

The 50 horse kind on the plantation are not eating their heads off by any means in the stables. Toward the west the Turialba volcano looms up, forming a purple shadow at evening; the plantations resting at the base of the range of mountains which extend to thè sea.

Colombiana

The United Fruit Company

This plantation, consisting of 1000 acres, is situated on the old line of railroad about halfway to Guápiles.

Under the efficient management of Mr. Arthur, the banana cultivation is carried to its highest point; thorough cultivation between rows by eight teams of mules with ploughs render the fruit taken from this plantation hard to equal. One meets old-fashioned Southern hospitality here upon visiting this beautiful and interesting spot; plantation life is seen in all its charm. Mr. Arthur has two fine turkey-cocks, great pets of the family, who are trained to cheer for Admiral Schley and General Wheeler. Mr. Arthur calls the turkeys to him and says, "Now, boys, cheer for Schley." "Gobble, gobble, gobble," call the turkeys. "Now for General Wheeler." "Gobble, gobble, gobble," repeat the prize birds, and they strut about in conscious knowledge of their beauty and intelligence.

The hacienda of Mrs. Arnold is situated on a commanding eminence 350 feet above Port Limon and about one mile from the market-place. The farm contains about 1000 manzanas: 250 manzanas in bananas, 100 manzanas in cacao (chocolate), the balance consisting of primeval woods and undeveloped land. A few hundred feet from the house is an elevation looking out over Limon and the distant sea. Here is an ideal situation for a first-class hotel. The air is pure and fresh, the grounds and gardens already prepared at the expense of thousands of dollars. Every variety of croton, beautiful specimens of cocoanuts, cacao, rubber trees, cactus, oranges, and limes—surely here is a fine investment for Northern capitalists. A first-class hotel, similar to the Titchfield House, Port Antonio, Jamaica, would undoubtedly succeed here. The cacao, or chocolate, tree flourishes on this plantation under the very best of conditions, the color of the pod when ripe being a brilliant orange-yellow; heaps of cacao in the pod may be seen in the season lying by the road, ready to be transported to the house. The plantation, in addition, has some 7000 young cocoanut trees. The cacao (chocolate) harvest gives two crops a year, and in the one month of November the plantation clears 40 cwt. of cacao. The beans are in a compact form, 36 to 40 to the pod, and surrounded by a white and acid-tasting jelly which makes the far-famed cacao butter. The crop of cacao from Mrs. Arnold's plantation is sent exclusively to England. The cacao takes six years to mature, but bears at three years old. The average crop is quoted at two pounds per tree. Costa Rica cacao cannot be purchased under 40 cents gold per pound, being of such excellent quality.

A most enjoyable and novel horseback ride can be taken through this property, which extends from two to four miles along the edge of the sea. As one rides through several miles of bananas and cacao, gradually the bananas are left behind and you enter the primeval tropical forest, dense, gloomy, shot with bars of vivid sunlight; occasionally the bark of a distant baboon or the shriek of an angry parrot is the only sound which breaks the silence of nature. The enormous trees towering to the sky, covered with vines and orchids, shut out the sun, and this part of the ride will be thoroughly appreciated, as the trees act as an enormous umbrella.

An hour's ride brings the party to the edge of the sea, where a small but safe harbor has been planned, the entrance and harbor being masked by a small island which forms an excellent breakwater. A beautiful sandy beach half a mile long should be mentioned, as it constitutes a valuable addition to the property; and a practicable road from Port Limon to this harbor would go far toward developing this gem of Costa Rica.

The Las Mesas Coffee Estates, Ld.

The Las Mesas Coffee Plantation is situated about 3600 feet above the sea, and is a flag station on the Costa Rica railroad. There are about 250 manzanas in coffee, and some 50 manzanas in sugar for the manufacture of dulce. The company have a grand situation south of Turialba, 250 feet above the railroad.

The works for preparing the coffee for shipment is within 100 yards of the railroad; below these buildings can be seen other broad vistas of coffee belonging to the company, which, by the way, is a close corporation of a limited number of stockholders, principally Canadian capitalists.

From the station of the railroad a winding road passes up the cliff, which is 250 feet high, connecting the hacienda and northern half of the estate with the southern half. Coffee is seen here in different stages of growth—from the little tender shoot just budding from the ground, to grand masses of the trees 12 to 14 feet high, and from a few days old to four years of age. The lower portion of the estate below the drying patios is in the shape of an oval, acres in extent, and surrounded by the great purple ridges of the mountains, marking the course of the Reventazon River.

All the processes of preparing the coffee for the market can be seen here to perfection with the most modern machinery, consisting of pulpers and dryers, and washing tanks for separating the berries from the husk; all arranged with the idea for economizing labor, the berry not being touched by the hand after it has been stripped from the tree until it is bagged ready for the American market. A visit to this interesting property, via San José, will well repay the visitor to Costa Rica.

Plantation life

Many of the plantations are widely separated from the centre of law and order, lost in the dense forests of the hot belt, and far from fresh supplies of food. Naturally, there is little central authority; it is usually vested in the "mandador," or manager of the property, who is sometimes a local judge of the district.

The Jamaican negro seldom gives any trouble; he is usually respectful and reasonable if rightly managed. There are, of course, exceptions; usually these are men who have a little smattering of law, and stand strictly on their rights (as they conceive them) as British subjects, and bluster at any opening given them.

At the hacienda, the managers of the different divisions of the plantation meet at meals and dine together in company, the food consisting of canned goods, hot bread, fresh milk, yams, eggs, plantains, and occasionally venison, the conversation at table consisting of jokes at one another's expense, the victim bearing it with commendable patience, and retorting with fluency. The rooms in which the men sleep, on the second floor (usually with a chum), are comfortable, clean, and homelike. The veranda on the ground floor is large and spacious, littered with saddles, riding leggins, boots, and spurs, or packages of goods.

In the evening, when there may be ladies present, the musical genius brings out his guitar and keeps his audience enthralled for hours. Spanish songs, negro ragtime, latest operas, soar out into the tropical night and cause the crowd of humble retainers in the yard to chuckle in sympathy and delight. Early every morning, by 6 a.m. at least, each overseer departs on his little high-spirited horse to make his rounds, looking up the different gangs of workmen, directing their work, and taking stock of the plantation on the hoof. To accompany any one of the managers on their inspection tour is an experience in itself. They are tireless and exact in the fulfilment of their duties, and receive with complacency any praises from the Northern visitor as to the fine condition of their division.

57

HENRY R. BLANEY, *THE GOLDEN CARIBBEAN: A WINTER VISIT TO THE REPUBLICS OF COLOMBIA, SPANISH HONDURAS, BELIZE, AND THE SPANISH MAIN VIA BOSTON AND NEW ORLEANS* (BOSTON: LEE AND SHEPARD, 1900), PP. 87–93

The Republic of Honduras

HONDURAS was discovered by Columbus during his fourth voyage, about ten years after his first expedition. The locality first seen by him was the island of Guanaja, the most easterly of the group now called the Bay Islands, where he arrived on the 30th of July, 1502. He reached the mainland on the 14th of August, at a point which he named Punta de Caxinas, a cape stretching out into the sea and forming what was afterward known as the bay of Truxillo. Honduras is next heard of when Gil Gonzales Dávila, while on a voyage from Sto. Domingo to Nicaragua in 1524, steering too far to the westward, reached the coast near the bay now called Puerto Cortez.

The principal ports of Honduras on the Atlantic side are Puerto Cortez, Omoa, Coiba, Truxillo. The beautiful and spacious harbor of Puerto Cortez was discovered in 1524. Cortes, in writing to the king of Spain, gave Puerto Cortez high praise. The bay is somewhat in the shape of a horseshoe, with great depth of water close to the shore.

At Puerto Cortez the sea breeze is constant and refreshing. There is very little to cause one to stay more than a week here, though the traveler will be well cared for at Hotel Lefèbvre. The principal street of Puerto Cortez is a disgrace to the town, consisting of the railroad track only; the railroad is certainly handy and convenient, for it is constantly in the way.

There was an amusing smuggling case at the Custom House last year,—a dozen revolvers, several thousand cartridges for them, and some thousand of rifle cartridges were smuggled in kegs of nails; a keg broke in the handling at the Custom House (the cartridges and revolvers being in a central compartment with nails at both ends), and thus were discovered; the party to whom they were consigned (a respected citizen of San Pedro Sula) disclaimed all knowledge of them, and the ammunition was seized by the government.

The authorities of Puerto Cortez have a very laughable method of challenging at the guardhouse, in the evening, visitors and inhabitants when passing from one end of the town to the other. The passer-by is halted peremptorily at the cuartel, and made to give an account of himself; this system of police is very hurtful to the reputation of the town, and cannot be too greatly condemned.

One of the most interesting things to study in Puerto Cortez is the exiled Louisiana Lottery Company, which has its headquarters here under the name of the Honduras Lottery Company. On the left-hand side of the railroad, and facing it, is the beautiful house owned by this company. Should the visitor desire a change from the hotel in the town, he will do well to seek a room here, as the manager's wife will willingly take him in as a paying guest. For further information regarding the status and statistics of this remarkable organization, I would refer the inquiring mind to the article in *Harper's Weekly* of August 3, 1895.

The well-known firm of Messrs. Geo. D. Emery, Boston, Massachusetts (Chelsea), imports into Boston from Puerto Cortez 3000 logs of mahogany a month.

The United Fruit Company have regular sailings of their steamers from New Orleans for this port, sailing every Thursday at 9 a.m., and from Mobile trimonthly. The exportation of bananas from Puerto Cortez is at the present time very large, the steamers of the United Fruit Company carrying large cargoes, about 125,000 bunches a month. In 1891, the banana trade was only in its infancy, and not more than 320,000 bunches a year were exported from this port, the statistics of the manager of the railroad at that date being very interesting, as showing the difficulties of the planters at that time, now happily nearly overcome. From September to December, each year, the excessive rains on the railroad are liable to cause a decrease of shipments; the rains sometimes entirely shut off the upper and most productive part of the road, and during this time many thousands of bunches are lost to the planters.

To the estimates of shipments made by the railroad to Puerto Cortez will have to be added at least 25 percent for fruit lost to the fruit growers, caused by the breaking down of trains, making it impossible to receive fruit for shipment, as the fruit would be too old; and from 8 to 10 per cent to be added for fruit arriving in Puerto Cortez in bad or bruised condition, and thrown away, no account of which is taken by the railroad.

There is a very large amount of vacant land along the line of the road, which would all be planted in bananas if the railroad was kept in any kind of condition.

The Lillian iron mine, at El Pariso, 26 miles on the railroad from Puerto Cortez (the property is about four miles square), is managed by Senor A. C. de Leon. It is now being developed, and is a very valuable property.

The Inter-oceanic Railroad, from Puerto Cortez to San Pedro Sula, is 38 miles in length, fare $3.00 Honduras money. At the present time (1900) the railroad is in a very inferior condition. The cars are uncomfortable and dirty. There is a hope that the railroad will shortly be acquired by Northern capitalists, who will give the railroad needed attention.

San Pedro Sula has a population of about 3000 inhabitants, and is situated on the plain of Sula, surrounded by hills, the tops covered by the low clouds. There is a fine Catholic church and a Protestant meeting-house. The Rio de Las Piedras flows through the plain. There are three main streets running the entire length of the town. The air and climate of San Pedro is very good, and a pleasant change from Puerto Cortez, being at least ten degrees cooler.

The principal hotel is very poor, but will serve to stay at for at least a day or two. To reach Tegucigalpa, the capital of Honduras, from San Pedro Sula, mules may be hired at the hotel for the journey of about 250 miles, a journey of a week. The cost of hiring a mule is $15 to $20 gold per week, with like amount for servant and mule; cargo mules carry 200 pounds, and the charge for them is $12 gold for the journey. Cost of provisions $1 per day, for servant and mule extra; plenty of small change, and a cloth hammock is recommended, and one should take his own saddle, as those for hire are not comfortable. . . . This road (one can hardly call it a road) is a bad one in the dry season; in the wet season it is impassable. The road from Tegucigalpa to the Pacific Ocean is about 75 miles and much easier, connecting by steamer on the Pacific with Panama and San Francisco.

Tegucigalpa (City of the Silver Hills) is the largest and finest city of the republic of Honduras. By the census of 1887 it contained 12,587 inhabitants. The exact date of its founding is not known, but it existed as a native settlement before the Spanish conquest. The city is situated in a valley 3200 feet above the sea, on the eastern bank of the Choluteca River, or Rio Grande; the river at this point is about 200 feet wide. The streets are narrow, the houses are built of adobe, whitewashed, and painted in brilliant colors. The central point of the city is the central park. In the centre is a bronze equestrian statue of Morazan, the hero of Central American independence. On the east side of the plaza is the principal church. It is, with the exception of the cathedral at Comayagua, the largest and handsomest church in Honduras. It was built in 1782. The church is of the Moorish style, all pure white; it has a clock and bells; there are no seats. It has two towers and an imposing facade, the roof terminating in a dome over the altar. The principal altar is of carved wood richly gilded. On the walls are some ancient paintings. The water supply of the city is very good, brought from the Rio Jutiapa, a distance of 12 miles.

58

EDGAR M. BACON AND EUGENE MURRAY-AARON, *THE NEW JAMAICA* (NEW YORK AND KINGSTON: A. W. GARDENER, 1890), PP. 73–82

Along the railway

We are accustomed to railways that rush four-in-hand along northern river banks, or burrow shrieking into the mountain sides, or span cañons, or traverse the almost limitless plains where the sage and the chaparral flourish. We climb sierras that way now, cross valleys and watercourses, explore wildernesses, and there seems nothing strange or unnatural in seeing the brightest sky stained by the locomotive smoke rings, or hearing the deepest solitude disturbed by its strident voice.

But here is a railway that pursues the even tenor of its way between groves of mangoes, cactus hedges, logwood copses and banana walks; steals into vistas framed by great silk cotton trees and winds by the edge of streams over which the cocoanuts lean and beside which the pineapples grow. It mounts foot by foot to the higher island levels, around the heads of glens where the strange trees stand deep in ferns, and crowned with bright blossoms and gay moss streamers.

There is nothing in the world that indicates progress in industrial matters more than a successful railway. Every puff of an engine that is drawing its share of a steady output of produce, talks in a language that is intelligible to the dullest man. In the catechism of mechanics the question, "What is the chief end of a railway?" should be answered thus: "The chief end of a railway is to develop the country through which it passes; to make land valuable; increase commerce, and contrive, by such honest means, to afford a dividend."

At the Kingston station one is struck with the unique character of the place and the people; especially the latter. The cars drawn up to the platform, are built upon the same pattern as those of any English railway. They are divided into transverse apartments, which are entered from the side, having no connection with each other. The guards here are polite colored men, in a military-looking uniform. In place of the various phases of British or American life, we find a heterogeneous assortment of humanity with greater contrasts of color, character, creed and costume.

The Creole of position with his visiting cousin from Europe, or the American continent, takes his place in a first-class carriage. There is apt to be a pretty girl or two in his party, but they are for the most part, too demure to notice the stranger who is trying to use his eyes to the best advantage. There are colored people, black people, white people; there are faces that show Castilian origin, others of a Caledonian cast, many that are browned by more than exposure to a tropic sun.

Here is the bare-armed, braceletted, long-haired, coolie woman, with her babe partly wrapped in the gaudy shawl that is thrown half around the mother's head, half over her shoulder. Her wealth is apparent to all eyes, for she carries it where all may see, displayed upon wrists, forehead, breast, ankles; in fact anywhere that there is a chance to place a hoop or a bangle. Then there are others: soldiers, dressed in white and red uniforms; negro market women, bundle topped; newsboys and porters. These all speak a various language, in which they have a Babel proficiency. It pretends to be English; it sounds as though "Jabberwocky" had found a local habitation.

We do not believe there is a case on record where the stranger has been able at once to understand the English of the Jamaican of the lower class.

The train-shed into which the station building proper opens is about three hundred feet long, and wide enough to admit several trains abreast. Beyond this structure are the shops, engine houses, etc.

After passing the purlieus of the city, among the first scenes to attract attention are the extensive stock yards of Cumberland Pen, one of the large properties of the island, where great herds of horses and cattle are bred and grazed. Cumberland Pen embraces a good race-course, and its turf events are always looked forward to with considerable interest, by both Creoles and aliens.

The grazing pastures as seen from the railway, present a clean, well-trimmed appearance. As high as a cow can reach the leaves of the mangoes are close cropped as though by a machine. One could sight along the under sides of them as along the level of a ceiling. Beneath, the grass is as smoothly trimmed. Cows, and indeed all hoof-kind, are great conservers of park and lawn. At another place, where the road crosses some little stream or canal, a widening pool by the wayside is literally full of horses, playing or standing shoulder deep, enjoying that advantage gained over the flies. So we pass from point to point of interest, here stopping at some way station and anon skirting a sugar plantation beyond whose levels of corn green cane the picturesque buildings, mills and aqueducts cluster, and along whose borders the rows of bamboos stand sentinel.

There is something which strikes one with surprise in every phase of Jamaican industry, and this element is not wanting here. As the water comes from the aqueduct, it is distributed in channels or trenches, and we have seen a number of women sitting by the side of one of these little canals, throwing the water with their hands upon the cane rows. At one point, a very fine aqueduct, built of stone and supported on numberless arches, crosses the railway. It is picturesquely draped with moss vines and ferns. The water it conducts is drawn from the Rio Cobre, the beautiful river that waters the plain of St. Catherine.

Half way between Kingston and Spanish Town we get glimpses of the harbor head and the distant Healthshire Hills; or, as the old books call them, "Hellshire Hills."

One is continually struck with the indications of natural richness and fertility of the country, and the little advantage that is taken of these means of wealth by the inhabitants. It is probably true that the country is underpopulated. It is certainly a fact that every mile of it calls loudly for more intelligent methods of labor, and more earnest purpose in utilizing the natural resources. On the lower end of the line, the estates and fruit cultivations are made more valuable by the Rio Cobre canal, a public work accomplished several years ago, which has added thousands of pounds in value to the lands through which its irrigating stream passes. But beyond this there seems to be very little done to add to those natural gifts of soil and climate which we have more than once dwelt upon. From the very beginning to the conclusion of planting and gathering, the Jamaican cultivator rests in the knowledge that it would be a difficult matter to starve him out. One potent reason for this apparent apathy is a real want of capital. The man who clears his woodland with machete and fire, may be alive to the value of stump pulling machinery yet find it beyond his means. But many of the smaller cultivators are perfectly content to work according to old methods. Their oranges, they say, are the best in the world; why seek by grafting or budding, to improve them? Acres run to waste, and their owners wonder that foreigners doubt that they are making the most of their opportunities. Well, perhaps they are right. Why should they not rest, since nature is so willing to assume all the responsibility of crops and harvests?

Among the various products which the Jamaica Railway has made marketable one of the most valuable is logwood. At many of the stations we see great piles of the sticks, or of crooked roots, ready for shipment. Car after car passes us, loaded with this same wealth. The logwood grows wild, thousands of acres of it cover the hill-slopes. All of this might be handled, transported, marketed, to greater advantage if right machinery were introduced. We have spoken of stump pullers, such as are used in the United States for similar work. As the custom now is to ship not only the trunks but the roots of the logwood, the gain of grubbing in a more systematic, nineteenth century way would be enormous. Or, supposing the root to be out of the ground, proper appliances for crushing it would reduce its bulk, and practically increase the carrying capacity of every car engaged in shipping it by just so much. Or, better still, by the investment of capital in a properly arranged plant for extracting the dye from the logwood *before* it is shipped, the industry would without question receive an enormous impetus. What we wish to point out is that here is an almost unworked field for the investor, whose predilection for agriculture, fruit growing or manufacture could be indulged in the security which a well-equipped, firmly-established railroad affords.

After passing Spanish Town and May Pen, with its fine iron bridge and View of the dry bed of a river that has found a subterranean channel, we soon strike a perceptible up grade and gradually rise to higher levels, and towards Porus, the present terminus of one section of the road.

There are now two main sections, the junction being at Spanish Town. At the end of one is Porus, at the other Ewarton. Both of these towns are in the county of Middlesex, the first in the parish of Manchester and the other in St. Catherine.

Beyond Porus it is proposed to extend the line, and in fact, the addition is now being built through the delightful hill country north of Mandeville, past Shooters' Mountain, and toward the region of Cornwall County, known as the Cockpit country, from its deep sink holes and wild, cavernous character. The lines run by Balaclava, and across the Black River. Here some of the most difficult engineering work of the road is being accomplished. Through Vauxhall and Ipswich the road will extend to the Great River, and along that stream to the neighborhood of the Lethe estate and thence to Montego Bay, thus opening up one of the pleasantest as well as one of the richest parts of the island.

The other section, that which now terminates at Ewarton, will branch from Bog Walk, cross the mountains east of St. Thomas-in-the-vale, and follow the course of the famed Rio d'Oro, where the Spaniards were supposed to have had the secret of the Indian gold mine; a tradition not unlikely to be well founded, as the region gives fair indication of gold. From the Rio d'Oro, the railway will run through the lower part of St. Mary's to the Flint River, continue to follow that stream to its junction with the Wag Water, and following that, reach the coast at Annotto Bay, going thence eastward up the coast to Port Antonio. The projection of a third line to cross Trelawney and St. James, is also spoken of.

It was in the year 1843 that the Jamaica Railway Company was incorporated. The line was opened for traffic in November of that year. It was at first only operated as far as "The Angels," near Spanish Town, a distance of fourteen miles from Kingston, at a cost of £222,250. It had but one track. From then to 1867 work was virtually at a standstill. Then an extension from Spanish Town to old Harbour Market was carried through at a cost of £60,000, being opened to the public in July, 1869.

Since 1867 the history of the road may not be uninteresting, showing as it does the gradual reception of a new idea, the final appreciation of business energy, and the success which attends intelligent management.

After the opening of the extension the business of the company increased gradually, till in 1875, its revenue reached the sum of £24,200, again of £13,478 in six years. In '77, Sir Anthony Musgrave, as stated in a previous chapter, interested himself in the affairs of the railway, entered into negotiations with the company and effected the purchase of the road by the government. At this time the capital represented was £267,250.

Part 9

RAILROADS AS THE AMAZON IN TROPICAL BRAZIL

59

FRANZ KELLER, *THE AMAZON AND MADEIRA RIVERS. SKETCHES AND DESCRIPTION FROM THE NOTEBOOK OF AN EXPLORER* (PHILADELPHIA: J. B. LIPPINCOTT, 1875), PP. 140, 157–158

Usually the traveller sees so little of these dangerous neighbours, the Aráras and Parentintins, that he might be tempted to take the fearful tales of the caoutchouc gatherers for mere inventions of their awe-stricken fancy; but a few light pirogues of the former, which drifted down a lateral affluent, and the total absence of any settlement on the domain of the latter, disposed us to think otherwise. Moreover, the black corner-posts of a burnt cottage near Crato (marked as a town on the geographical maps, but in reality but one house and a few sheds), told their own tale of a whole family having been murdered and roasted there a few years ago by the Parentintins. As in such cases nothing at all is done by the Brazilian Government, whose principle (very different from the fire-and-sword policy of the Portuguese) it is to spare the natives as much as possible, the few unprotected settlers must make room if they would not incur the danger of sharing the fate of their neighbours. The only mode of evading the difficulty thus created, of uniting humanity towards the natives with a sound protection of the settlers, so necessary for the future prosperity of the country, is to found Indian colonies—Aldeamentos or Missions—among the Indians themselves. But this gigantic work, as is well known, has been undertaken successfully only by the Jesuits, and even by them under particularly favourable conditions.

To many it may appear that such mixed races bear in themselves the germs of destruction, nature generally having a tendency to return to the pure types; but closer observation of the present (so-called) white population of the northern provinces of Pernambuco, Ceará, Parahyba do Norte, Maranhao, and Para, will clearly show that so much of the Indian element has survived there that more than one-third, or a fourth part, of the whole population must be ascribed to it. Even if it be more and more diminished by increasing immigration, and should it at last be discernible only by an experienced eye, yet there it is, and it has been the means of profit to the thinly-peopled country; and surely no one will assert that the black-haired, dark-eyed mestizoes of these countries are less fit to live and work under the glowing rays of the tropical sun than the fair sons of the North.

However, I am still far from joining in the unwarrantable lamentations of novel-writers over the impending extinction of a mythical red race, far superior to the white in heroic virtues and noble qualities of heart. Such a red race exists only in their imaginations. The indolent, sensual, and sometimes treacherous race of real life will and must give way to the growing exigencies of over-peopled Europe. The titles of possession enjoyed by the autochthon, important as they may be in his own narrow and childish judgment, are abolished in the Court of Appeal which takes cognisance of the wider needs of the world. And to ultra-sentimentalists of the novelist type I should like to put this query: "Is not the prosperity of the family of some hardworking settler, trying with the sweat of his brow to create a new home for his children and his grand-children, of more importance than the comforts of a set of savages, with which that prosperity might possibly interfere?" Moreover, by way of justifying this complete extrusion of an unwilling race, a really higher civilisation, in the form of agriculture and regular industry, should replace the hitherto prevalent system of wild robbery; the hidden treasures of the country should be explored for the benefit of mankind at large, and the last traces of that narrow Spanish-Portuguese system of destruction, which took only its own ego and the immediate span of time into consideration, must for ever disappear. In the United States, we may well wait patiently for the completion of this process, which draws to a close with the inflexible rigidity of a law of nature. There the waves of immigration already touch the foot of the Rocky Mountains. There the wigwam is destroyed to make room for the railway station or the streets of nascent cities, and Indian savagery and modem culture, unable to exist side by side, must daily come to bloody conflicts. But in the South American States, in Brazil especially, which owns provinces, with a population of only 40,000, larger than Germany, all hands, be their number never so small, should be turned to account, particularly as the bulk of European emigration is not likely to turn in that direction for the present. The association of the Brazilian Indians with useful communities in aldeamcntos, on a larger scale, is also favoured by the consideration that their character, on the whole more gentle and peaceable than that of the North American Indians, does not offer insuperable obstacles to earnest and persevering attempts. What the speculating spirit of the Jesuits conceived and brought about, should we despair of achieving through the agency of a Government animated by higher views?

60

NEVILLE B. CRAIG, *RECOLLECTIONS OF AN ILL-FATED EXPEDITION TO THE HEADWATERS OF THE MADEIRA RIVER* (PHILADELPHIA: J. B. LIPPINCOTT, 1907), PP. 367–369, 380–383

On his return trip from La Concepcion to San Antonio, with Bruce and his men, the chief engineer stopped at San Carlos and, from that place, walked several miles inland to Byers's camp in order to warn him, as well as the others, of the impending danger from Parentintins. Reaching the camp about sunset, he presented Byers with a quart bottle of French brandy, probably intended as a nerve tonic to strengthen that gentleman for the prospective tales of savage atrocity about to be inflicted upon him. Not wishing to alarm the men, Mr. d'Invilliers deemed it wise to wait until they left camp in the morning, before mentioning the object of his visit to Byers.

To those who never knew "Joe" Byers as, behind his back, he was affectionately called by his men, it may be necessary to explain that his whole mind and heart were concentrated upon his work. There was no possibility of conversing with him long on any other subject than railroads. It was railroad morning, noon and night, railroad on Sunday as well as during the week, railroad at table and railroad in his dreams by night. Though kindhearted, he had a supreme contempt for those who permitted any obstacle, difficulty or danger to interfere with the accomplishment of the one object he deemed worth living for, the construction of railroads. Naturally no human being could long endure the strain of working with such unceasing energy and such unvarying fixedness of purpose, unless something occurred to relieve the high nervous tension he was under. This necessary relaxation "Joe" Byers endeavored to obtain in a liquid form, but only on rare occasions and after long continued arduous labor. The effect of his potations was only noticeable on account of an unwonted hilarity of manner and, however much the keenness of his intellect might be impaired regarding other matters, on the subject of railroads and railroad work, his mind was at all times perfectly clear.

Unfortunately Mr. d'Invilliers and his brandy arrived when Byers had long been leading a life of forced abstinence from intoxicating liquors, and, when, next morning, the time came for the chief engineer to deliver his warning and depart, Byers was in such a jovial mood that no subject, not strictly pertaining to railroad work, made any impression upon him. With face as long and serious as that of a funeral director, the chief engineer gave all the details of the plundering of Bruce's camp and the murder of King by the Parentintins, at the same time mentioning the precautions Byers should adopt to protect his men. Then he waited to see what effect his words had produced, but a respectfully quizzical look from his auditor was the only indication of intelligence. A second time he went over the whole story and his reasons for apprehending an attack by the Parentintins on Byers's camp, but with the same result.

Finally, thinking Byers's lack of appreciation might be due to want of familiarity with Parentintin history, he gave him all the facts in regard to the tribe, which he had obtained from Keller's report, frequently repeating the word Parentintin. Then Byers's face began to assume a weary expression, and, as Mr. d'Invilliers paused for reply, he said in tones of peevish and fretful remonstrance "Don—I don't care a d——n for your *pair of two tin canteens*."

A few weeks later, while Byers was moving camp and his party was divided between the old camp and the new, the savages sacked the former and carried off in the night, while the men were asleep, such articles as they fancied. Among them I recall the spade used in setting posts, the target belonging to the level rod and some of the highly polished brass attachments of the transit and level. Fortunately the midnight visitation was not attended by loss of life, but the men were nevertheless badly frightened in the morning. It was afterwards noticed that none of the bodies of men killed by the savages were subsequently mutilated. It is, therefore, probable that both Keller and ourselves were wrong in attributing such depredations, as occurred, to the Parentintins. They were probably committed by the Acanga Pirangas (Red Heads), who were supposed to live on the Jamary River south and east of San Antonio and were in the habit of covering their heads with some red pigment.

Disintegration and collapse

LANDING at San Antonio, October 11, 1878, we found that the primitive structure, formerly used as headquarters by the engineers, had been abandoned. The new office building had been completed some time before and was then occupied by engineers, contractors and clerks.

Though entirely destitute of ornamental features, it was substantially constructed, admirably adapted to the climate, conspicuous on account of its location and far superior to any similar structure on the rivers above Para. Offices, equipped with every essential convenience for drafting and clerical work occupied the entire first floor. The second story was divided into comfortable sleeping apartments, some of them furnished with American beds and all opening on spacious verandas, where the occupants could assemble for social intercourse, obtain an excellent view of river and town, recline in their hammocks and exchange stories of toil and suffering in camp and on the line.

The six months' term of service, to which all employees were bound by contract, had expired on the 19th of August, and, as men could not be expected to continue indefinitely in a service, which brought no reward, present or prospective, save privation, sickness and death, it was not surprising that an exodus had begun at that date, but to their credit it can be said that only a very small and insignificant minority of the whole number, who returned to the States, abandoned the enterprise until they were physically unfit to remain.

Few had sufficient money due them to pay for their return passage and the contractors were under no obligation whatever to send their men home until they had served two years. Departing employees were supplied with orders on Philadelphia and Pará for the amounts due them, but, as a general rule, payment was refused when these orders were presented and, not until years afterwards, were many of them even partially paid. The regular steamers usually required cash in payment of passage and the great majority of homeward bound passengers were compelled to accept cheap transportation and inadequate food, which the contractors obtained for them on returning lighters and schooners as far as Pará.

Some, unable to afford even the luxury of semistarvation and two weeks of broiling sun on board the lighters, resorted to canoes and rafts. To the present time no one knows how many of them ever reached the seaboard alive, but many, who succeeded, found the situation at Pará even more intolerable than at San Antonio.

The engineer corps, originally consisting of 54 men, but subsequently increased to 57, when we returned on October 11th, could only muster 26 and some of these were unfit for duty. It was obvious that, after deducting the number required for office work and construction, the remaining force would hardly be sufficient to form one field party. Mr. Collins had therefore, made a contract with Joseph Byers and C. H. Patterson to establish the final location of the railway, as far as the Caldeirão do Inferno, at a cost of $500 per mile.

During our absence the colony at San Antonio had passed through the most unhealthy season of the year and 35 men whom we left on the 9th of July, alive and enjoying as good health as any of ourselves, three months later were lying in the "banana patch," as the graveyard was commonly called. Of these deaths 17 had occurred in the month of August alone, but the number of cases of sickness seems to have reached a maximum in July when the official report of T. M. Fetterman, the druggist, showed an average of 100 prescriptions a day and from 30 to 50 dispensary patients. On the same authority it can be stated that as high as 300 persons were at one time under treatment at their places of residence or in the hospital. Of course, that does not tell the whole story nor give any idea of how many were dosing themselves with quinine without a doctor's prescription.

No record of events is now known to exist, which would make it possible to present a complete account of what occurred at San Antonio while we were absent, but some extracts from private letters and other papers, submitted to the writer, will enable the reader to catch an occasional glimpse of the situation then and afterwards.

On July 12th Commander Selfridge of the *Enterprise*, with one of his officers, visited San Antonio, and turning to his published report, we find the following: "San Antonio is notoriously unhealthy.... I have never in my life seen a more unhappy and unhealthy body of men than the workmen on the railroad.... Hardly a single one had escaped attacks of fever and the pale cadaverous looks of nearly all of them were truly pitiable."

61

FRANK VINCENT, *AROUND AND ABOUT SOUTH AMERICA: TWENTY MONTHS OF QUEST AND QUERY* (NEW YORK: D. APPLETON AND CO., 1890), PP. 249–250, 260–261, 265–266, 303

Maua is twelve miles from Rio, and is simply a landing-place for the steamer, with the buildings of the railway service. A train of four cars awaited us. The cars were fitted with transverse benches made of straw, a side door admitting to each bench. The locomotives used are made in Philadelphia, the cars are of English make. The steamer passengers filled the train. They appeared to be mostly business men, though there were also some ladies and children. We were quickly whisked eleven miles across a forest-clad plain, to the foot of the mountains, where our train was divided into two, run on the Riggenbach system. The road appears to mount directly upward through a sort of valley in the ridge, with very little turning, and with no specially steep slopes. The speed is greater than that upon any similar road I know of; it is at least double that of the Corcovado Railway. One high iron bridge is crossed, but no great engineering obstacles present themselves. As we ascend, we occasionally obtain magnificent views of the plain behind us, and of fine rocky peaks and cliffs before us. Not, however, until we near the summit of the pass—called Raiz do Serra (Root of the Ridge)—does the wonderful splendor of the prospect become apparent. Then one can look down upon the brown track of the road, by which we have just mounted, as it runs through the dense green forests. We distinctly see the station at the foot of the ridge, and then the road crossing the plain to the bay; and, carrying our eyes out over this, we notice first Governor's Island, and then far beyond we detect the Sugar-Loaf, Corcovado, Gavea, and Tijuca. Rio can be recognized only on a particularly clear day. As we continue, the atmosphere becomes pure and cool. Before the rack-road was built, it was customary to ascend the ridge by a capital macadamized road—a wonderful piece of engineering—of which you frequently catch glimpses in the ascent. A light coach, with powerful brakes and six mules, was used. At the summit of the serra—the cog-rail section is four miles long—the divided train is reunited, and a Philadelphia locomotive takes us quickly over the remaining two miles to the station of Petropolis and the end of our journey.

Our whole time from Rio was but two hours. At the station a great crowd had collected, a few to receive expected friends, but most merely to gratify an idle curiosity. Touters for half a dozen hotels race up and down the platform, and omnibus and hack drivers shout at you over the low paling. One hears a different language on every side. It is like some famous Swiss resort. And this comparison is strengthened when you enter an omnibus and are driven up long avenues of shops and cottages, with small walled-in rivers flowing through the streets and wooded hills, and rocky peaks towering upward on every side.

San Paulo lies upon a great plain, with low hills upon the entire horizon. It is a city of about fifty thousand inhabitants. The houses are of one story. There is a pretty public garden, with a tall tower from which a wide survey of the neighboring country may be had. Tramways reach the suburbs, where are many charming country-houses, at one of which—that of Mr. Squire Sampson, a retired American railway contractor—we were royally entertained for several days. San Paulo may be said to be the headquarters of the coffee interest, and from here run four lines of railway to the great coffee districts of the interior. Brazil, I may remind the reader, yields more than half the coffee consumed in the world, and the United States takes more than half the quantity exported. There are two and sometimes three coffee harvests in a year.

From Campinas we made an excursion, in one day, to several of the neighboring coffee estates. The country roads were very bad, and I did not wonder that "buckboard" wagons were the favorite vehicles. Immediately upon leaving the city, the straight rows of the coffee-trees are everywhere seen extending along the bases of the lower hills. In fact, it is the same all the way along the railway, from Rio to San Paulo, and on to Campinas. Almost the only other cultivated products that attract attention are maize and mandioc, which are all consumed in the country. Perhaps the chief dependence of the people is upon mandioc. This is a shrub, with large roots, which, after being scraped to a pulp and pressed, are baked on hot iron or earthenware plates. The mandioc, when washed and dried, furnishes the tapioca of commerce. There is, of course, a similarity about the manor-houses of all the great fazendas. Most of them are placed high up on the side of beautiful valleys, with magnificent outlooks, and all have splendid fruit-orchards and flower-gardens, in which you see growing, side by side, the choice representatives of two zones. The houses are of enormous size, and are approached by massive flights of steps.

From San Paulo we took the English railway to Santos, its seaport, about forty miles distant, whence we intended to return to Rio by sea. The railway runs through an uninteresting expanse of country, until it reaches the summit of the coast range of mountains—the Serra do Mar—down which runs a cable road, a distance of five miles in four "inclined planes." A train coming up balances that on which you descend. The height of the ridge is about twenty-five hundred feet. The wire cables used are an inch and a half in diameter. There are powerful engines located at the top of each incline. The steepest incline is ten per cent. This road has been open some twenty-odd years. Its original cost was very great, running, as it does, upon the steep flanks of valleys where much stone-work was required.

Owing to the peculiar topography of this section of country, enormous floods of rain fall during a single brief storm. In order to draw off these dangerous inundations, frequent sluices are built beneath the road-bed, and massive conduits almost continuously follow its surface. Destructive land-slides occasionally occur, notwithstanding precaution has been taken against them. The views from the summit of the Serra do Mar are superb. You look into a great valley full of bright-green trees, and away to peak after peak in the distance toward the sea.

Reaching the plain, a short run took us to Santos, a town of about twenty thousand people, built at the foot of some green hills and adjoining a short but deep river, which permits large steamers to approach its wharves, or at least anchor near by. Santos is probably the second seaport of the empire in the value and importance of its exports. It is **a** hot, dirty, damp, unwholesome place, but there is a large healthy suburb, about four miles distant, toward the sea, at the south, and reached by a tramway.

At one point in the Boa Vista Mountains a terrific torrent, swollen by the recent great rains, had swept away a bridge and a long stretch of the railroad. Here we had to leave oar train and walk down to an improvised bridge, spanning an enormous gully, through which the stream still raged over large bowlders of loosely strewed rocks. Crossing, we found another train awaiting us upon the opposite bank, and on we went again, this time with a very compact and powerful French locomotive. That part of the range near There sopolis, specifically styled the Organ Mountains, characterized by needle-like spires, now stood grandly forth. And we had not gone many miles farther before the peak of Tijuca, behind the city of Rio, was dimly marked against the heavens. Next I saw my old friend the Corcovado, and then the massy Sugar-Loaf, whose changeless serenity, compared with the transiency of individual human lives, reminded me of Turgeneff's remarkable prose-poem on mountains. We arrived at Nictheroy, seven hours from Canto Gallo. Nictheroy is a large flat town, with tramways extending in every direction, and a handsome public garden. At the northern extremity are a large arsenal and good ship-building docks. To Rio we took a ferry-boat, much like those plying in New York Harbor, though without provision for horses and carriages. It takes about half an hour to cross the bay. Once more I drink in the wonderful and beautiful panorama. From a few not very widely separated points you get a score of distinct Rios. These are views of which I am sure I never could tire. It is fairy-land. Especially alluring is the entrance to the harbor, through which you can look far out to sea. But the spell is broken as I land and take the tram to the English hotel.

62

NEVIN O. WINTER, *BRAZIL AND HER PEOPLE OF TO-DAY* (BOSTON: L. C. PAGE AND COMPANY, 1910), PP. 91–95, 127–133, 254–256

Minas geraes and mining

THERE is another route to Bello Horizonte, the capital of the state of Minas Geraes, but I chose the one through Petropolis, because I was to have the pleasure of the company of the American Embassador. Petropolis was the one time capital of the state of Rio de Janeiro. There are other cities in the state of Bio besides Petropolis. Among these are Therezopolis, which occupies a magnificent site on a commanding hill that gives a fine view of the surrounding country, and Nova Friburgo, the oldest immigrant settlement in Brazil. This city was established almost a century ago by a number of Swiss colonists, and is reached by another railway of almost an equal ascent with the route to Petropolis, heretofore described. This little colony has grown into a prosperous settlement and preserves many of the characteristics of the race which founded it.

Boarding the semi-weekly express train at Petropolis, which is here termed "*grande velocidade*" we were soon winding around the hills and through the narrow passes threaded by the river. Occasionally little primitive villages and a few unimportant adobe towns picturesquely grouped along the banks of the stream were passed. The scenery is beautiful as pass after pass unfolds itself on the journey down to lower altitudes. One is impressed by the extent of mountainous territory which is encountered by the traveller all over the republic, with the exception of the country traversed by the mighty Amazon and its tributaries. It is a constant surprise to see the vast amount of soil in Brazil that is actually without development. Mile after mile of this land, which is within a comparatively short distance of the capital, had the appearance of never having been occupied by settlers, or ever having been disturbed by agriculturists. Although broken it could well be adapted to the raising of stock, at least for sheep and goats, for these animals would find sustenance. It seemed to me that cattle could be raised profitably also, since it would not be necessary to feed them, as pasture will grow all the year round.

The few natives who did live in the little mud-brick huts, with thatch roofs, that cling to the side of the hills eked out a very poor existence, if one judged by the appearance of everything around their homes. A few chickens and pigs with plenty of dogs, perhaps a mule and a cow, constituted the only stock that one could see. A little patch of corn, a banana stalk or two, and perhaps a patch of mandioca root, seemed to be the only attempt at agriculture of the improvident negro or poor whites who dwell on these beautiful hills. The houses contain only the very crudest of furniture with rude beds and the very simplest of culinary outfit. Nature is perhaps too bountiful, and man depends upon that bounty rather than his own exertions.

The mandioca is a small shrub with a tuberous root that grows in nearly every part of Brazil. It grows to the enormous size of fifteen and twenty pounds, and somewhat resembles an enormous radish or sugar beet. In its natural state it contains a very poisonous juice which must be eliminated before the real substance can be used for food. It is first pressed and then washed, and the water must be thrown away for it is poisonous. The root is then ground into a meal which is very rich in starch. One large root will sometimes produce as much as two gallons of this prepared meal. After being crushed the meal is at once roasted, or otherwise it will turn sour and be spoiled. Tapioca is one of the products of this tropical tuber. The utilization of this root was first discovered by the Indians, who found a method of getting rid of the poisonous qualities. To-day, the mandioca, or farina, flour is one of the principal articles of food in Brazil, not only among the poorer classes but also with the well-to-do. Many of the articles served on the hotel tables are thickened with the mandioca meal. This, with rice and beans, furnishes the almost exclusive food of the poor. On the railway trains one will see that this meal comprises one of the chief articles of the lunches which have been brought by one's fellow passengers.

It is perhaps wrong to think only of the practical in the midst of scenes of natural beauty, but as our train whirled along with its *grande velocidade*, past rapids which could be converted into incalculable power for the manufacturing so essential in the world, I could not refrain from thinking what fine power was here going to waste. A little of it is utilized in generating electricity for the cities of Nictheroy and Petropolis, and there are a few cotton mills run by the water power of this stream. Not one unit of the available power is utilized, however, although in this land of expensive fuel there is a great call for electric power and current. At last the Parahyba River, a still finer stream of water, is reached and the railroad follows up this stream. At Entre Rios (which means "between the rivers") a change is made from the Leopoldina Railway to the Central, which is a government line. After a couple of hours the train reaches Juiz de Fora, which is the largest town in the state of Minas Geraes.

From Campinas the journey was continued over the Mogyana Railroad, a narrow gauge track. The line passes through coffee plantations for some distance, and then into uncultivated lands, where the only industry is the raising of stock. A part of the land traversed is abandoned agricultural land, and part of it has never been under cultivation. The cattle seen on these farms are only of fair quality, for not much care has been taken in breeding the animals up to a high standard. With many bends and graceful curves the road follows a stream, cuts across valleys and around hills. There is no part of the ten hours' journey when hills of fair size are not a prominent feature in the foreground. A number of towns are passed, and a few very narrow gauged railroads run off to plantations, which cannot be seen from the railroads. The soil is almost the colour of dried blood, and this red dirt filters in through the windows in great clouds. This blood-red dust colours everything it touches with a reddish hue. The clothing is soon tinted with it, and even the children's complexions show the effects, for Brazilian children, like their cousins all over the world, like to play in the dirt. But this red soil is good coffee land, and coffee plantations are seen crowning the summits of the hills. At last the train reaches Riberão Preto, near which are situated the best and largest coffee plantations, not only in Brazil but the world. The town is comparatively modern, for this district is newer than Campinas, and it has been growing in importance year after year in the past two decades. It is now a city of ten or fifteen thousand people.

At the station were waiting carriages from the hospitable "Monte Alegre" *fazenda*, the residence of Colonel Francisco Schmidt, who is known as the "coffee king." This man came to Brazil as a poor emigrant boy a half century ago, and hoed coffee trees for other *fazenderos*, and on lands which he now owns. Seated on the broad veranda of "Monte Alegre," one could see avenues of coffee trees stretching out over the hills, and good coffee lands are always hilly, until they were lost in the horizon. Although it was not possible to see, yet one knew that they continued in the same unbroken rows down the other slope. I rode in a carriage with the Colonel for hours through a continuous succession of coffee trees, during the three days that I was his guest, with no end in sight. When you consider that there are from two hundred and fifty to three hundred trees to each acre, you will readily realize that the number of trees soon runs into the thousands, then into the tens of thousands, and finally into the millions. So do not be surprised when I tell you that this coffee king has already growing upon his various *fazendas* the almost incredible number of eight million coffee trees. I did not see all of them, but I saw so many that numbers lost their meaning, and I could only think in millions.

Twenty-three million pounds of coffee were marketed by this man in one year. This is enough to give every man, woman and child in the United States and Canada a cup of coffee for breakfast for one week. He has twenty railroad stations on his thirty-two different *fazendas*. He has twenty machines run by water or steam power for cleaning coffee, and acres upon acres of drying yards, all of which are scenes of activity in the harvesting season. Nearly a thousand horses are employed in the work of the plantations, besides more than that number of mules and oxen. There is also a fully-equipped sugar mill, which turns out thousands of pounds of refined sugar each year. In fact, the Colonel told me, as we were seated at the great dining table, that would seat forty persons, and which was spread with the good things of life: "Everything on the table, except the flour used in making the bread, was raised on this plantation."

The Colonel reminded me of the feudal lords of old, for the eight thousand people who live on his plantations not only depend on him for labour, but look up to him and tip their hats respectfully whenever they see him. The work of taking care of the coffee trees is all let out to families at so much a thousand trees per year, and a family will take care of five thousand trees. The price paid is from $25.00 to $30.00 per thousand per year for hoeing and cleaning the fields, and they are paid in addition to this for picking the coffee at established rates. Furthermore, they are permitted to plant corn and beans in between the coffee rows which gives them an extra profit. Day labourers are paid at the rate of $.90 to $1.00 for each day's work.

Everything about this plantation is conducted in a systematic manner, and in that is the secret of Colonel Schmidt's success. The thirty-two farms are all connected with his home by telephone, for which more than eighty miles of telephone wire have been strung. Everything, including plumbing supplies, is kept in systematic order and the owner himself knows where each article may be found. Machinery when not in use is carefully stored under shelter to protect it from rust. A half dozen blacksmiths, as many woodworkers, harnessworkers, shoemakers, etc., are kept on the plantation, and even a private tailor is employed at the house. A dozen or more general stores are operated for supplying the wants of the employees. With this and much more detail this great plantation is run on modern business Methods, with as perfect a system of bookkeeping as the average business man employs. From these books can be told at a glance the exact cost of each plantation for each year, its production and the net profit to the owner. And, above all, the Colonel is a charming host, and finds time to make it interesting for those, like myself, who visit him where he is king.

The "Dumont" *fazenda* adjoins the one just described, and it is the second largest plantation in Brazil, and perhaps in the world. It was formerly owned by the family of Santos Dumont, the aeronaut, but is now under the control of an English company. They own a private railroad with more than forty miles of track, which runs to Riberão Preto. The track is only twenty-six inches wide, and the cars are rather narrow with room for only one person on each side of the aisle. A special train, with the best car the road possesses, drawn by a Baldwin engine, was sent for us and we were taken over the coffee plantation, which possesses nearly five million trees. It was also very interesting to travel over the thousands of acres owned by them, in and through the rows of coffee trees which almost brushed up against the car in places, in this comfortable, if diminutive coach, and see the methods of culture and care of the coffee, which is slightly different than that pursued on the other. It was also interesting to find an up-to-date American in charge of the vast interests of this English company, and to know that one of our own nationality is making good in the coffee-raising industry as well as in other lines. This company markets all its own coffee through an auxiliary company in England in packages under its own labels. The "Dumont" *fazenda* is also conducting an experiment in rubber culture, and now has forty thousand trees growing, some of which are almost ready to tap. If rubber continues to advance, as it has in the past year, this part of their plantation may prove more profitable than the growing of coffee.

One must go a thousand miles up the Amazon, and then six hundred and sixty miles up the Madeira River to Santo Antonio de Rio Madeira, where this line begins, and which is in the very heart of South America. Above the rapids there are several hundred more miles of navigable waters, upon which a service of steamers is maintained. There are few people in that section of the country, and it may never be popular with immigrants. The line is being constructed in pursuance of an agreement with the Republic of Bolivia when the Acre (pronounced Ack'-ray) territory was ceded by that government to Brazil. The rich eastern slope and fertile plains of Bolivia are practically bottled up. Its products, including a large rubber and cacao production, either had to be transported over the Andes, or around a couple of hundred miles of rapids and cataracts on the Madeira River, to the part of the stream where navigation is uninterrupted. From there they were carried down on steamers to Manaos, or Pará, and then to the markets of the world by ocean-going vessels. This line will be about two hundred miles in length, and will open up one of the richest sections of Bolivia, a part of Peru, which also borders on the Acre territory, and the rich territory itself, which produces a large amount of rubber and cacao, and much of which has never been exploited at all. Many native Indians inhabit this section, and their little rafts and row boats navigate all the streams. In these the Indian rubber gatherers visit the different sections, tap the trees, and bring the rubber to the establishments of the various companies engaged in the rubber trade, which may be found in many places.

The first sod for this railway was turned in 1871, but this auspicious beginning soon ended in disaster. Again, in 1878, a second attempt was made, and work was prosecuted faithfully for a year. A survey was cut through the almost impenetrable forest, and four miles of track were completed. At that time, however, sanitation was not understood as well as now, and the great mortality stopped the work, as it did in Panama. This time a sensible beginning was made by first looking after the health conditions, and practically the same methods are employed as are followed by the United States on the Isthmus. Sanitary buildings were erected with provision made against infection from mosquito bites, and a fully equipped hospital was built and furnished. By these means the health of the twenty-five hundred employees has been looked after in a thoroughly scientific way. At the present writing about fifty miles of track have been completed, and a dozen engines are already at work. Forces of workmen are engaged in cutting down the forest, grading, laying track and rails, and all the other processes incidental to building a railroad. Nature has not changed one iota, for malarial fever is still malarial fever, the rainfall is as great as ever, and vegetation is just as luxuriant; but science has taught man how to conquer nature, and it will not be many years until locomotives will be hauling freight and passengers around these falls in a few hours, where formerly it required weeks. Americans may take a pardonable interest in this project, for it is American energy and American equipment that is doing the work.

Part 10

CONQUERING *AMÉRICA DEL SUR*

Railroad cultures in the River Plate, Chile, and Caribbean South America

63

CENTRAL ARGENTINE RAILWAY COMPANY, *LETTERS CONCERNING THE COUNTRY OF THE ARGENTINE REPUBLIC (SOUTH AMERICA), BEING SUITABLE FOR EMIGRANTS AND CAPITALISTS TO SETTLE IN* (LONDON: WATERLOW AND SONS, 1869), PP. 1–16, 32–33

The Argentine Republic

(THE FIELD, *April* 10*th*, 1869.)

BUENOS AYRES SHEEP FARMING, &c.

SIR,—Having just arrived from Buenos Ayres, a few lines upon the affairs in that part of the world may be interesting to your numerous readers.

The letter that I sent over to THE FIELD while I was staying there, I am happy to say, was read and approved of by some of the English settlers; but there was one fault to be found with it, and that was that I did not say sufficient to deter young men from going there, spending their little cash capitals, and coming to absolute want.

There is very little chance of a young man bettering his prospects in sheep farming. Sheep farming has had its day. It is possible it may revive, but I cannot advise a young man to go there and stop till it does, for he may go to another part of the world and make his money in the meantime.

It is my opinion the River Plate is not the country for Englishmen to go to; not one out of ten like it after they arrive. Their brother Englishmen look upon a "greenhorn" as an inferior being; consequently they would leave it as soon as possible for some other part, or come home again; but unfortunately their pockets get empty and very often their stomachs. I do not mean to say there is any fear of starvation, especially in the camp (country in general), because of meat being so plentiful; but in town, where the emigrant knows no one, it is very often the case that he feels the pinchings of hunger. In the camp, although there is not always work to be found, at any house where he calls he can get plenty of meat and matè, if a native's—if an English one, meat, biscuit, and tea.

Of all the countries in the world, there is none to beat the River Plate for easy living; that is to say, for a man to get plenty to eat and drink by doing so little work; but he must not look for any comforts.

The English farm labourer will find it very difficult to get anything to do, for there are so many French and Italians who will do the work with less pay, and live on meat and mate, that estancieros (those having two or three leagues of land of their own) prefer employing these to an Englishman; and I am sorry to say, some English estancieros employ these before one of their own countrymen.

For managing cattle it is impossible to do without a Gaucho, for he is so brought up to it that he can do the work of three English. In fact, I think the cattle can tell the difference between a Gaucho and an Englishman, for as soon as the Gaucho rides round the cattle and begins to make a noise, at the same time twirling the lasso round his head, they all make for the rodeo (a place where they are all collected every morning), and this saves a great deal of trouble. If one should be lost, the Gaucho is not long in finding it again; he can see the missing animal almost before anyone else can see the herd that it is in.

Just before I left the country, the owner of the place where I was staying sold his land, and had only one flock of sheep to sell; but such was the low price they were fetching, that he could only get the offer of 11 dollars (22d.) each for them. He made the bargain, and the man went to fetch them away, but while staying there, the sheep being then in the corral ready for counting, he altered his mind and would not have them. This flock a few years ago had some of Mr. Hannah's rams put in, which cost the owner from £10 to £15 each.

The news from England, stating the low price of River Plate wool, and a reduction in the price of tallow, made a further reduction in the price of fat sheep. The latest price quoted in the "Buenos Ayres Standard" was from 25 dollars to 28 dollars each.

Sheep farmers are finding out that they must do something else besides keeping sheep and cattle if they want to make money. A little attention is being paid now to the plough. I have seen some ploughing done a few miles from Buenos Ayres, with the small American plough; it was badly done. One of the large harrows used on our farms would have turned the ground up almost as well.

The steam cultivator is used up the River Plate, but I have not heard with what success.

I think, to be successful in growing good corn, deep ploughing will suit the land best, as it will eradicate, all roots of thistles, carretilla, &c.

As soon as an emigrant lands, the first difficulty he would have to encounter is the language; and this is about the worst, for he cannot make known his wants, and is quite at a loss what to do or where to go. He is also very much disappointed at finding the difference between the Buenos Ayres and North American dollar. Before going to the River Plate he is told that a man can earn from 26 to 30 dollars a day; this to him is a great sum, because he is under the impression that the dollar is worth 4s. 2d. He may naturally think he is going to pick up gold in the streets. But how much disappointment and disgust would be saved if he were told that the Buenos Ayres dollar is worth only 2d.! As for employment, the common labourer on the railway can only get 26 dollars a day, equal to one American dollar, 4s. 2d. After paying for board and lodging, he will not have much of this left for himself. If he can keep from drink, it will be better for him; but unfortunately the temptation is so great that he cannot stand up against it.

There is no place that I know of for an English emigrant to go to as soon as he arrives, unless it is at his own expense. At the end of the mole or pier there is a notice in Spanish, informing fresh arrivals that they can find a home in Calle Corrientes; but is of very little use to the English, for they pass by without taking the least notice of it, because they cannot read it.

Before leaving Buenos Ayres I visited the Saladeros—places were cattle are killed, for the purpose of making charqui or dried beef. The way it is done may not be generally known, therefore, I will give an explanation as well as I can. The cattle that are to be killed are driven into a large corral, capable of holding from 700 to 800 head; outside this, adjoining, a smaller one is made that will hold 40 or 50: an opening is made in the larger for the purpose of driving the cattle into the smaller as they are wanted; a cross-bar is then dropped to keep them in. In the smaller, and opposite the entrance, another opening is made, about a yard and a half wide; from this a tramway is laid to the end of a long plied, on which runs a truck that fits into this opening, and level with the bottom of the corral. Across this opening a large beam is thrown to about the height of the animal's head; on this beam a wheel is fixed horizontally, through which a rope is passed, one end being fastened to two horses outside, the other made into a lasso. The Capataz, or head man, then throws the lasso and catches an animal; the order is then given to the men on horseback to go on, and it is drawn up to this wheel and on th truck. While in this position the Capataz, standing on the beam, stabs it behind the horns, cutting the vertebrae in two; it falls as if dead. I really thought it was dead, for it was taken away by two men to where one was wanted to be skinned, without any signs of life until five or ten minutes afterwards, when the man who was going to skin it let the blood out; it then gave several kicks with its hind legs.

The skinning and cutting up are done upon the ground. It is astonishing to see how quickly it is done; they are not so particular as our butchers; if a large piece of beef should be cut off with the skin, it is all the same. After the cutting up, others are employed to separate the meat from the bones, to the thickness of about an inch, and as wide as possible. This is then thrown into a heap and salted, afterwards hung upon poles in the sun to dry. I need not assure my readers that the meat is not very tempting.

The weather this last summer has been one of extraordinary dampness; rain has fallen more or less every two or three days; the roads in some places are impassable; and bullock carts are a long time taking the wool into town. Such a summer has not been known by the oldest inhabitant.

In consequence of the great moisture, there is a great number of mosquitoes. About Ranchos they are very troublesome, but up the River Plate, almost as bad as a plague.

Crime, both in town and camp, is on the increase; a man's life is not safe, especially if he is known to have a little money with him. The last murder was committed on the beach. A man who had been paying his master's bills was in the act of returning to the boat to go home, about five o'clock in the evening, when many people are taking their evening walks. He had not got many yards from the last house, and was crossing to the pier, when a black man went behind him and gave him two stabs, killing him almost instantly. The murderer was taken, and handed over to the authorities; but it is the opinion of many that he will be kept in prison about a year, and then sent adrift again to kill some one else. This is only one instance out of many.

The "Buenos Ayres Standard" remarked lately that "if the Government could not stop it, Lynch law must come into force."

If other papers would copy this letter, they would greatly benefit many of their own countrymen, for I found many in Buenos Ayres who could get nothing to do.

For my part, if I cannot find anything to do here, it will not be the River Plate that will see me again, unless things should take a different turn: my attention will be drawn to a British colony.

If any gentleman wishes to know more about Buenos Ayres, I will gladly give him all the information that lies in my power, but letters must be accompanied with two stamps for reply.

C. J. Jessop.

424, Old Kent Road, March 15.

(The Field, *April 17th*, 1869.)

The River Plate

Sir—Having noticed in your last issue a letter from Mr. Jessop on the subject of sheep farming in Buenos Ayres—apparently written to deter his fellow countrymen from emigrating to that part of the world, and with that object painting their prospects in the darkest possible colours—I wish, as one who has had a long and varied experience of the camps of the Argentine Confederation, which leads me to a conclusion opposite to that at which Mr. Jessop has arrived, to give your readers the opportunity of hearing what is to be said on the other side, and of forming an impartial opinion upon the subject.

Judging from Mr. Jessop's letter, I should infer that his personal knowledge is confined to the province of Buenos Ayres, which is as likely to give an adequate idea of agricultural prospects throughout the Confederation as a knowledge of market gardening in Surrey or Middlesex would impart that of general farming throughout the United Kingdom. However that may be, I cannot at all agree with him, except in so far—that for the present prospects of sheep farming (for wool growing) are no better in the River Plate than they are in our own colonies. Still, I do not consider that emigration should be discouraged; but I am of opinion that anybody going out there with the object of farming should direct his attention to cattle breeding and cereal cultivation, in both of which I believe great things are to be done, especially if (in regard to the first) means are devised, as they probably will be, for sending meat to the home market. In this case, Australia can never ultimately compete with the River Plate, on account of its much greater distance, higher rates of freight, &c. In regard to the second, I hear by the last mail that my manager is selling wheat at a very remunerative price. With a virgin soil of unexampled richness, of boundless extent, at a nominal price, no other expense than that of turning up the ground to sow the grain, and a magnificent climate, there is really no limit to what may be done in this direction. As Australia cannot in the long run compete with the River Plate in the exportation of meat to Europe, when fairly established, so Chili and the countries on the West Coast of South America will be precluded from competition in that of grain by the greater propinquity of the Argentine Confederation to the great European markets.

For both of these objects the province of Buenos Ayres is, as I can state from considerable experience of the Confederation, by no means so well adapted as the frontier provinces of Cordoba and Santa Fé, in which, owing to the absence of the carratilla and thistle mentioned by Mr. Jessop, the pasture is better suited to the rearing of cattle and the soil better for agricultural purposes. It is only within the last five years or so that Englishmen have bought land in these provinces with the object of settling; and hitherto, from the absorption of the military resources of the country in the Paraguayan war, they have had unprecedented difficulties to contend with in the inroads of the aboriginal Indians. These are now checked, as I have heard on most reliable authority by the newly elected and enlightened president of the republic, Senor Sarmiento, who has sent to the frontiers the various regiments returning from the war, so as to secure the safety of the country. In addition to this, the last mail brings full reports of a most interesting visit paid by the governor of Cordoba to some English estancias (or farms) in that province. He inspected and highly approved of some agricultural implements used by the farmers, such as the steam plough, Abyssinian wells, threshing machines, reaping ditto, drills, &c., and he expressed a warm interest in the success of the English, and has promised his best aid in furtherance of it. These provinces have, notwithstanding the obstacles above described, made steady progress, one of the principal marks of which is the Great Central Argentine Railway, between the capital towns of Rosario and Cordoba. The line which connects them is nearly finished, and affords an easy mode of transport for the produce of the interior provinces of the Confederation to the river Parana, and so on to the sea. It has been opened to the public for a considerable portion of its distance, and will be available through its whole length at the end of the present year.

Mr. Jessop says that the English in the River Plate are to a man discontented, and desire to leave the country. Well, they may have been so under the heavy discouragements to which they have lately been exposed, especially such of them as may have gone out with little or no capital, which is as necessary here (in a smaller degree) as it is in Australia or anywhere else. This discontent is, however, mainly attributable to the undoubted failure of sheep farming to profit, which has hitherto been the chief attraction to the country, and which has shared the universal depression. It is quite recently, within the last two years, that attention has been given to agriculture. "There is a silver lining to every cloud," and my honest conviction is, that instead of abandoning enterprise in these countries, no better time can be found than the present for advantageously investing in land for the purpose of settling. The price of and has not yet recovered the recent depression, and the probability is, that owing to the cessation of the war, and the more efficient administration now inaugurated, it will shortly be greatly enhanced.

I must not conclude without remarking on Mr. Jessop's opinion that the language of the country is an obstacle to the English emigrant. That Spanish is the language is a fact; but it is also a fact, that of all the European languages it is the most easy of acquirement. I have myself known men of no educational acquirements attain a sufficient knowledge of it for conversational purposes in two or three months; while it has the undoubted advantage—coupled with the fact that the country is not under European or English rule—of preventing that influx of settlers who would be otherwise tempted by the fine climate and magnificent soil to overrun the country, and thus place the purchase of land beyond the means of those who have not got abundant capital.

In all new countries there are difficulties and obstacles to surmount or be yielded to, as the temperament of those who have to encounter them may incline them. But I have enough faith in my countrymen to believe that those who are worth anything will surmount them, and I think Mr. Jessop is doing them a very questionable service in seeking to close, especially at such a time, one healthy outlet for the honest and redundant industry of England.

SANTA FECINO.

SIR,—Mr. Jessop has favoured your readers with his opinion respecting the River Plate as a place for emigrants to settle in. Having just returned from thence, suffer me also to express my views upon the same subject; and first let me mention what portion of that country I have visited during the last two years. I have travelled 250 miles north of Monte Video, in the Banda Oriental; 60 miles north of Buenos Ayres; 150 miles south of the same, and 500 miles to the north-west; and over the whole of this, with the exception of a few swampy places, and that upon which timber is growing, I did not see an acre of land which does not in my opinion offer every inducement for emigrants to settle upon.

Let me now mention what I have done there myself since May last. I broke up with Benthall's cultivator 150 acres of land, 40 of which I sowed with wheat, 60 with flax, and 50 with maize. The wheat crop failed, and from three causes; first, I sowed the wrong seed, next, I sowed it two months too late, and lastly, wheat should not have been sown at all, as it does not thrive there the first season. My maize when I left was not ready for harvest, so I cannot tell you the yield of it; all the natives, however, said that it looked splendid. My flax crop turned out exceedingly well, and yielded an average of 20 bushels of seed and two tons of straw per acre. For the seed I have been offered 15s. per bushel, and for the straw £4.10s. per ton, in all, £24 per acre. The cost of growing, harvesting, and seeding a crop of flax need never exceed £4 per acre: *and as land can be purchased within easy distance of a railway station at* 10s. *per acre, to be paid for by five yearly instalments of* 2s. *each, what can a man wish for more?*

During my stay I visited a Swiss colony of about 5,000 persons in Entre Rios. They have only been there two years and a half, and last season they sent 12,000 sacks of wheat to Buenos Ayres for sale. The yield, they told me, was 80 sacks for every sack sown. In addition to this, they grew maize, flax (for the seed only), and potatoes; and one man informed me that he grew three crops of flax in one year. A more thriving-looking place I have seldom seen. In another part of the country, a gentleman has inclosed a mile square of camp, and ploughed it up for wheat. When I was there he was harvesting his crop, and, as near as I could judge, he had from seven to eight sacks per acre, worth about 26s. per sack. First-class wheat was quoted in Buenos Ayres, when I left, at 40s. to 42s. per sack.

The best land I have seen lies along the line of the Great Central Argentine Railway, leading from Rosario to Cordova. Here there are millions of acres of a slightly undulating character, and with a soil from 6ft. to 10ft. in depth, with not a tree or bit of scrub to impede the plough, and all of it lying idle for want of hands to till it. With oxen and horses at 50s. each, what better opening could a man have? Touching the labourer, the ordinary rate of wages is not so high where I have been as Mr. Jessop mentions. I have, however, a letter in my pocket from a gentleman out there, offering to provide 500 acres of land to be increased hereafter to 5,000, together with houses, food, horses, oxen, seed, implements, &c., for any labourers who may be sent out to him; and so soon as the cost of the food consumed by them is paid for, he is willing to share the profits with them, one-half going to the master, the other to be divided amongst the men. With such an arrangement as this, each labourer ought to earn at least £100 per annum—no bad return for his services, to my thinking, and this, in my opinion, may be made, with proper management, to develop a system of emigration which shall be self-supporting, as no labourer should object, if these profits are realised by him, to set apart a portion of his earnings for the purpose of bringing out more people, the money to be repaid by them in a similar maner.

I could give you much more information upon this subject, but fear to trespass too much upon your time and space. I will therefore only add that if any of your readers would like to meet me, when I am in London, to discuss these matters, and will write me a line to say so, I shall be happy to appoint an early day for the purpose, and will give them notice of the same, either by letter, or advertisement in the "Times" newspaper.

Caine, Wilts, April 14.   T. L. HENLY.

(THE FIELD, *April 24th*, 1869.)

The River Plate

SIR,—Having had my attention called to a letter in your issue of April 10, on Buenos Ayres as a field for English emigrants, in justice to that much-maligned country I hope you will allow me space to reply to it.

I, too, like your correspondent, have just returned from the River Plate, having been engaged there for five years in farming; but, unlike him, I go back again convinced that there is no country in the world that affords more inducements to all classes of industrious emigrants. This difference of opinion among people about a country which they profess to know, suggests at once that there is wilful misrepresentation somewhere; and he is sure to get the credit of it who reports well of the country, for he is supposed to have some personal interest in inducing people to go there. Even at the risk of incurring this suspicion, I venture to differ in opinion from your correspondent. It is the old story over again of a divided report among the spies who went to search out the land—"a land that floweth with milk and honey; but there we saw the giants, the sons of Anak." The question is not as to the richness of the land, but are the giants to be overcome? Your correspondent admits that "of all the countries in the world there is none to beat the River Plate for easy living—that is to say, for a man to get plenty to eat and drink by doing so little work;" and then he goes on to enumerate the giants. There are hardships to be endured; there are French and Italian labourers, and English estancieros who like to employ them; there are Gauchos who look after cattle better than Englishmen; sheep at 22d. a head; people who speak a gibberish that John Bull doesn't understand; dollars that are only worth 2d,; mosquitoes that are "as bad as a plague;" and murderers as numerous, who are ready to lake the life of any man who is known to have a little money about him. Therefore Mr. Jessop concludes "the River Plate is not the country for Englishmen to go to." Looking a little more closely at these gigantic evils, we shall find them after all to be only such difficulties as are to be met, and must be overcome, in any new country.

First, regarding the hardships, your correspondent says "the emigrant must not look for any comforts," and if he calls at an English house he will only get meat, biscuit, and tea. Admitting for a moment the truth of this statement, are our young men so delicately nurtured that they cannot subsist on such fare for a year or two until they can start an establishment on their own account, and live more luxuriously? And are there not thousands of our poor people who would be glad of an abundant supply of these despised victuals? A friend told me he was once seated at the table of a Scotch estanciero, and at his side was a "gentle shepherd" recently arrived, who, as he sipped his champagne, languidly remarked to him, "I rather like sheep farming;" and the story, while it proves that tea is not the only beverage in the country, shows also the ideas of some of the practical young farmers that come to the River Plate. It is quite true that many lazy people content themselves with very poor living, but it is equally true that a very little trouble will provide the table with garden and farm produce of every kind.

Secondly, about the French and Italians who cut out the English labourers, I have only to say that the latter are invariably of two classes: runaway sailors, and young men who have never been accustomed to work, commonly knows as "loafers"—a kind of people who are as little in demand in the British Colonies as at the River Plate. Farm labourers have as yet not gone to the River Plate on their own account; but those who are taken there by employers invariably improve their position. It is a fact that the Gauchos look after cattle better than Englishmen, but that can be no disadvantage to the English farmer who has to employ them.

As for the language, the Spanish is perhaps the easiest of all European idioms. Your correspondent says, the first difficulty the emigrant will have to encounter is the language, "and that is about the worst;" and in saying so he loses his case. If the language is the greatest difficulty to be encountered, the others cannot be very large.

As for the paper dollar, it is a pity for all parties that it is not worth 4s. 2d.; but this, I confess, is one of those inevitable evils of life which emigrants as well as other people must bear.

The plague of mosquitoes of which your correspondent complains I may pass over, as any man who would be deterred from emigrating by such a trifle had better stay at home.

The statement that a man's life is not safe, especially when he has a few dollars in his pocket, is equally absurd, and I have no doubt your correspondent derives his ideas about the prevalence of crime from the columns of the "Buenos Ayres Standard," the editors of which paper invariably make the most of a "good murder" Their intention in writing so strongly on the subject of crime is to arouse the sleeping authorities; but, unfortunately, it often serves to terrify new comers. I have travelled in the most populous as well as the most remote parts of the country, and have never been molested. And here let me state that the remark about the necessity for Lynch law, which your correspondent quotes from the "Standard, was made on the occasion of the murder of an Englishman, which afterwards was found to have been provoked by a crime too abominable to describe, and the verdict of every right-thinking Englishman in the River Plate was "served him right."

It would occupy too much of your space to describe the prospects of farming in the River Plate, and I refrain from doing so, more especially as I intend to write fully on the subject id one of our newspapers.[1] I would say, however, to labourers, only go out under contract of employment; and to capitalists, turn your attention to agriculture, and not to sheep. And let everyone who is interested in the subject make full enquiries for himself, and not trust implicitly to the representations of any disappointed settler who may return to this country.

Broom Park, Lanark, April 19. THOMAS PURDIE

SIR,—I have read with interest the letters of Mr. Jessop, "Santa Fecino," and Mr. T. L. Henley, in the two last numbers of THE FIELD; and, as all information regarding the River Plate is anxiously looked for in THE FIELD, I think it only fair to intending emigrants to give them both sides of the story.

Having only just returned from there, after many year's sojourn, I leave many interests behind, and I may say have left all my friends; but, for all that, I consider it one of the worst possible places for an English emigrant. Already too much harm has been done by the English paper there—the "Buenos Ayres Standard"—writing in its "Reviews for Europe" high-flown and ridiculous accounts of the place, while in its papers for circulation in the country just the reverse is pictured. How many fine young fellows have I known, thus deluded, take to drinking and other vices, and become a disgrace to their own countrymen in Buenos Ayres, sink down to become "Puesteros," and lead a life of misery and degradation, as bad as our own convicts in Australia! And mark, this is no exaggeration—far from it. Through my business as a saladerista (and owning several sheep farms), or owner of an establishment where animals are killed for their hides and tallow, while the meat is salted and dried for the slave markets of Brazil and Cuba, I have travelled over the country far and near, and can say that the colonies in the Banda Oriental (the oldest-settled, mind, in South America) are not flourishing, but in a state of bankruptcy; and this applies to the French as well as the Swiss. Under a settled and firm Government, they might be different, and things might prosper; but in the continued state of inquietude that exists, through revolution and the total disregard of life, law, and justice, an Englishman, unable to speak a word of the language, stands a very poor chance of doing well. This applies to the Argentine Confederation as well as the Banda Oriental, and I am sure I shall be borne out by all settlers (not recent) that an English colony is much to be preferred.

With respect to the province of Santa Fé, where, on the railway from Rosario to Cordoba, at and about Frayle Muerto, a number of young Englishmen are settled, having bought land at from £100 to £200 to the square league, what has resulted? Why—and not so very long since, either—three poor Englishmen were killed in their house (the houses are obliged to be built fortress-like) by Indians, and all the cattle in the neighbourhood were driven off, the owners only escaping with their lives by hard riding, until not a soul was left in Frayle Muerto or for leagues around. This is another feature, apart from internal revolutions, when your horses are articles of war, yourself left alone, perhaps (servants having fled), subject to insults, and in danger of losing your life if the best of your provisions are not placed before the rabble Gauchos soldiery. I could mention cases where English women have been violated and carried off into captivity; in only the last inroad made, some forty-five to fifty persons were taken.

Of what use is cheap land, even if you do understand the language? The cartage and freight to market costs as much almost as it is worth. It is true, meat is cheap, mutton being pretty good, although beef will never prove an article of export for the European markets, being so inferior; every other article is very dear, and clothing exorbitantly so. I contend, then, with all deference to your correspondents (not one of whom I know or have ever seen), that it is not a good place for an English emigrant.

Have I said enough to caution your readers? Have we not examples in those before us? The Welsh colony of 150 persons in the South, unable to keep themselves, would have been starved to death but for us in Buenos Ayres, their fellow-countrymen, supporting them, with the aid of Government, for over two years. Then again the colony of Californian emigrants in Santa Fé, who are men accustomed to a hard life in America, buying land at £50 the league, the very finest in the province—they did not succeed. And as in Frayle Muerto, all those who were able—excepting, of course, the actual owners of land—have left.

Above all, I would say, beware of land on halves of profit—the improving of land not your own. Should they want land, let them get it of their own. The Monte Videan Government will give small farms of fifty to sixty acres to all settlers in Rosario Colony who build themselves a sod or mud house, on condition of their paying cost of transfer—1 dol., equal to 4s. 2d.—for making out the title deeds.

I am trespassing too much on your valuable space; but if you can spare me room, I will send you further letters, and only trust that other newspapers will copy the few observations I have made, and so deter, if only one of our surplus population, from leaving for any part of the River Plate.

AN OLD SCOTCHMAN.

(THE FIELD, *May* 1*st*, 1869.)

The River Plate

SIR,—I have just returned from a fortnights run into Germany, and on looking over the back numbers of THE FIELD, have come across Mr. Jessop's letter in your issue of the 10th, and also the two letters in reply on the 17th inst. I cannot allow this matter to pass over without having an indignant say on the subject, if you will kindly allow me to occupy your space for a few lines.

I take it that Mr. Jessop is one of those unfortunate individuals, without money or money's worth in the shape of ability and perseverance; and that he is also without friends, or the knack of making them in the foreign country that he may elect to favour with his temporary sojourn—one who expects to find the poor benighted natives awaiting his arrival with open arms, each striving to be first to throw gold into his lap. I also agree with your correspondent "Santa Fecino" in supposing that Mr. Jessop was only a very short time in the country, and did not extend his researches beyond the immediate neighbourhood of Buenos Ayres. During a residence of twelve years in the River Plate, I have met with a good many such men, who would be far better at home, but whose desultory and slight experiences, when published in such an influential journal as THE FIELD, are calculated to do an infinite degree of harm, even when contradicted by those who, like "Santa Fecino," can speak with some authority on the topic.

It is quite true that sheep farmers who have bought when prices were high have had hard times of it during the last three or four years, on account of the fall in the value of stock, following as a natural consequence that of wool. This, like every other raw material, has had its periods of inflation and depression; but it is not to be supposed that this article alone will not recover its former value, and, as sheep have never been so cheap as now, I hold that this very fact makes the present the most favourable time for investing in them. The establishment of gracerias (boiling-down places) has already checked their downward tendency, and opened up a new and unlimited market for superabundant stock. A great change is coming over sheep farming, and a man owning a capital of £400 or £500, and investing at present prices, is certain (if steady) to realise a fortune in a few years.

Unfortunately, however, it is too true that numbers of young Englishmen have lately invaded the River Plate, without friends or introductions or dollars, and who are too proud or too lazy to turn their hands to serious labour, but who, with pipes in their mouths and hands in their pockets, are contented to loaf away their days in the house of any estanciero sufficiently hospitable to give them board and lodging gratis. Men such as these do no good either to themselves or their entertainers, whose hospitality they generally abuse, and eventually they return home and write to the papers as martyrs, warning others not to be taken in as themselves have been. I am afraid that I must class Mr. Jessop among the number I have just described.

As "Santa Fecino" and Mr. Henly have given you some information respecting cereals, permit me to mention a few facts *in re* sheep farming.

Fact No. 1. In April, 1864, two neighbours of mine in the Monte Videan camps dissolved partnership, dividing 8,000 sheep. The one took his half stock away; the other remained on, and purchased the estancia on credit for a sum of 10,000 dols. (these dollars were worth 4s. each, so that he paid about £2,000 for the land). In three years' time this gentleman, from sales of sheep and wool, not only paid off the debt owing on the camp, but before coming home in May, 1867, sold 8,000 sheep at about 6s. each, and brought the money to England, having let his estancia to a good tenant at a fair rental.

Fact No. 2. A friend of mine went out in January last year, and purchased 3,000 sheep, renting land. He has now 4,500 head, and funds at his agent's in Montevideo to carry him over next shearing.

Fact No. 3. A few years ago a man of the name of Richards had the management of two flocks, and as remuneration received one-third of the increase. He had not a penny capital, but by care and thrift is now one of the richest English estancieros and owner of a fine camp.

I could multiply these facts almost without end, but fear to encroach too much on your space.

In conclusion, allow me to caution your readers not to be influenced too much by such flimsy reasoning as Mr. Jessop uses, that, because he has not succeeded in making his fortune, therefore the River Plate is no country for Englishmen to go to. Let them, before arriving at this conclusion, seek surer information from some old hand, whose experience and advice will be of value. The River Plate offers, without doubt, the very best field for emigration to those young men who are steady in their habits, and have a little capital to commence with—far more so than any of our English colonies; but to those who have neither money, application, nor friends abroad, I would say, "Stop at home; you are not likely to succeed in the River Plate, or elsewhere."

A. P.

South Norwood, April 24.

SIR,—Your correspondent, "An Old Scotchman," condemns the River Plate because he has seen many people who have not succeeded there. I should say, however, as the owner of a saladero, together with several sheep farms, he must have done pretty well there himself, for I can hardly fancy a person possessed of means sufficient to purchase all these at the onset going to the River Plate at all. What I ground my hopes of success upon is this: given land at 2s. per acre, within ten miles of a railway station, and a perfectly level road leading thereto; given any number of mares for cultivating the same at a cost of £1 each, together with meat at less than 1d. per lb., farina (a very good substitute for flour) at 1d. per lb., and yerba (a capital substitute for tea) 2d. per lb., for the emigrant and his men to live upon until such time as he can provide himself with better fare; given also an average price, say, of 25s. per sack for his wheat, which at present is brought into the country from Chili and the United States, subject (in addition to the enormous cost of carriage) to an import duty of 15 per cent.—and I would ask any farmer at home, if he had the same chance, what would he expect to make of his land? Would he, with a virgin soil of almost unexampled fertility, and averaging from six to ten feet in thickness, consider ten sacks of wheat to the acre an extraordinary crop? Have we not heard of nearly double that quantity being grown sometimes in this country? I am quite willing to admit that some of the settlers have purchased land too far in the interior, and consequently are debarred at present from turning the same to good account. I also allow that the Indians have from time to time committed some of the ravages spoken of by "An Old Scotchman," and I therefore think it advisable that the settlers should keep well together. At the same time, I am sure your correspondent will allow that half a dozen Englishmen well armed would defy any number of Indians almost, and that the latter, finding no horses or cattle worth speaking of to drive away, would very likely never trouble them at all. I look at it that in the battle of life we must all risk something; the soldier, the sailor, the engine driver, and the miner, all risk their lives to a certain extent, and so must those who go to the River Plate for a livelihood. If a man is afraid to do so, he had better stay at home. As for "young men who take to drinking and other vices, and so disgrace their countrymen in Buenos Ayres," all I can say is this, that if any country can be found where such persons will not carry on those disgraceful practices, by all means let them go there, as they do much more harm than good at the River Plate. I still think that country, on the whole, the best place to settle in; and as a proof of this I may mention that I have taken a farm of 1,500 acres near Frayle Muerto, 1,000 acres of which have been already ploughed up nearly two years, upon which I intend sowing wheat, flax, and maize this season. Should my life be spared so long (of which, so far as Indians are concerned, I have very little fear), I will let you know the result before nine months are over.

Caine, April 28.   T. L. HENLY.

---

3. Are the soil and climate favourable to agriculture on a large scale? Where are the best lands situated, and what is their value? Can foreigners purchase and hold landed property, and get good and secure titles? Are there register offices?—In answer to the first question, I will refer to the opinion of a gentleman who has already written some valuable letters to THE FIELD under the *nom de plume* of "Holderness." He examined most carefully the lands of the River Plate from Santa Fé as far south as Patagonia, and afterwards explored the prairies of the Western States of America. He purchased a large estate in the province of Santa Fé. He writes to me saying that he considers the region of the River Plate, as a field for agriculture, equal in every respect to the Western Prairies, and superior in climate. It is really difficult to say where the best lands lie where all is more or less a virgin soil of excellent quality. I think we might affirm that the best are those in the provinces whose climate offers fewer vicissitudes in the temperature and the weather—Buenos Ayres, Santa Fé, and Entre Rios. The price of land varies of course, and where the population is so sparse it must vary a great deal; while in the vicinity of the large coast towns it may be worth from £2 to £5 the acre; land equally as good near the frontiers may be had for 2s. and even less. In Santa Fé the lands within a radius of five leagues around Rosario are worth from 17s. 6d. to 20s.; fifteen leagues off they are to be had for from 5s. to 8s. Everything depends, not on the quality of the soil, but the quality of the grass, and the situation in reference to centres of population. The lands adjoining the Great Southern Railway in Buenos Ayres advanced in price fivefold from the simple fact of the railway passing through them. In a like manner the Central Argentine Railway has enhanced the price of lands adjacent to it. At the same time, fine lands in the northern part of the province of Santa Fé, in Indian territory, can be bought for 6d. the acre. Foreigners enjoy all kinds of civil immunities on a par with the natives, except voting and holding political offices. There are offices in every town, where any transaction in transfer of landed property is registered, with this difference between the system there and here: there the original deed remains archived, and a copy only is given to the parties interested. Titles can be examined in these offices.

4. *What kind of lands are those in possession of the Central Argentine Railway Company? Are they pastoral or agricultural? Are they now available to the emigrant?*—These lands are situated between the 31st and 33rd degrees of south latitude, and commence twelve miles from Rosario, ending twelve miles from Cordoba. The upper portion is partially wooded, but the lower portion is pampa or prairie land. There is only a small portion of it "soft grass" pasture—that is, grass fit for the finer class of sheep. The coarse grass will have to be eaten down by cattle, or ploughed up to make it what the sheep farmers call refined land. But for agricultural purposes there is no finer land in the Republic; and the zone in which the tract lies is the most temperate in the region of the River Plate. I understand that a scheme for the colonisation of these lands, about a million of acres, is now under the consideration of the Board of Directors.

Note

1 See further communication from Mr. Purdie on page 24.

64

JOHN FOSTER FRASER, *THE AMAZING ARGENTINA. A NEW LAND OF ENTERPRISE* (LONDON: CASSELL, 1910), PP. 134–138

The story of the railways

I THINK I have made it clear that, accepting Argentina as an amazingly fertile country, it is the railways that have chiefly been instrumental in making it one of the most prosperous lands, with a big part to play in providing food for the world. Today 95 per cent. of its stock and produce is carried over some part of the 20,000 miles of line representing nearly £200,000,000 of British capital.

I remember riding in a coach attached to a freight train across some hundreds of miles of sand and sage bush, an impossible region from an agriculturist's point of view.

"This is an unprofitable stretch," I remarked to the railway official who was my companion.

"Not at all," was the reply; "you see, we have a full load, and we get paid mileage, whether we run through good or bad land."

That is one of the causes of railway profits in Argentina: the enormous distances freight often has to be carried.

It was not my lot to travel over all the railway systems in the Argentine, but I travelled over the most important of them, and from first to last I was enthusiastic. The rolling stock is excellent; the permanent way is better than over similar country elsewhere, and as for the comfort of the passengers it is certainly unsurpassed. Frankly, I often felt like rubbing my eyes in order to make sure I was "roughing it" in Southern America.

Nowhere, out of Russia, have I seen the coaches so admirably adapted for small or large parties. You can have a section of a coach self-contained, dining-room, bedrooms and bathroom, suitable for families; and meals can be supplied from the buffet. If you travel over a certain distance you cannot miss having a buffet car; the law insists. Also the law insists on dormitory coaches on the all-night journeys. They are more commodious, because on most of the lines the gauge is wider than in England. There is none of the uncomfortable sleeping behind curtains, with, maybe, a stranger in the bunk overhead, and then having to wash in the smoking-room, which the long-suffering men of the United States put up with under the notion they possess the most luxurious travelling in the world. When you come to "special cars," a thing we know nothing about in England except for royalty, the United States comes first, but I would say Argentina is a close second.

Nothing could be jollier—when a sand storm is not on the wing—than travelling with pleasant friends in a reserved coach. It is like a flat. There is a sitting-room, and on a chill evening the fire burns brightly in an open grate. On a hot afternoon you have your easy chairs out on the platform at the rear and, with legs cocked up on the rail, you can smoke your cigar. You press a button, and when the attendant has brought you an iced cocktail you agree that "roughing it" in Argentina is a delightful experience. If your car is properly equipped with a good kitchen and a good cook, and there is a decent "cellar"—hospitality is one of the legitimate boasts of the people—you fare as well as you would do in a first-class hotel. Were it not that I might be thought a sybarite, I could write like a chef about the menus I experienced and enjoyed in my long excursions throughout the land.

"This is a nice chicken," I said to my host one night. "Yes, we have a chicken run under the car," he answered. I laughed, for I imagined the innocent stranger was having his leg pulled; but the next morning personal inspection assured me there was a "run," in the shape of a long galvanised screened box beneath the car.

It was pleasant to have a bedroom four times the size of a crib on an English "sleeper," to have a writing-table with electric light, and a bathroom adjoining. But the chief joy of a special car was that there was no changing to catch trains. Instructions were given that we would stop at a certain place at nine o'clock in the morning. The car was detached and shunted into a siding. We lived on the car and slept on it. Orders were given that we were to be picked up by the 8.15 local train in the morning, taken down a branch line forty miles, attached to the express which would be coming along at seven o'clock, and were to be released somewhere else at 10.15 and put into a siding. I lived this sort of life for nearly a month. It was the best possible way of seeing the country.

Sometimes we travelled from point to point during the night; sometimes we camped, as it were, at a little wayside station, with the silence of the plains around us except when a great goods train went roaring by. We kept up the joke about "roughing it." After a dinner party, when the coffee and liqueurs were on the table, and the sitting-room was pouring billows of cigar smoke from the wide-open windows, we leaned back in our big chairs and hoped that other poor devils who were "roughing it" in the wilds were having no worse a time than we were.

Of course, the passenger traffic—except around Buenos Aires—is a secondary consideration compared with agricultural produce. It is estimated that the area of land suitable for agriculture but not yet cultivated is 290,000,000 acres, really all beyond the zone of railway influence. At a greater distance than fifteen miles from a railway station the cartage of the produce becomes so expensive and difficult that the profit disappears. Information supplied me by the Argentine Agricultural Society shows that the average cost of cartage is 0.70d. per mile per cwt. Therefore, whoever has his farm farther than fifteen miles from a station has to pay 10d. per cwt. for cartage. Lands lying within the agricultural zone, but distant more than fifteen miles from a railway station, lose enormously in value, as they cannot be utilised except for live stock. To find a means of facilitating and cheapening the transport of cereals would be to double the production and value of the lands. The Agricultural Society thinks the solution may lie in the construction of cheap auxiliary lines of the simplest kind, which, laid down parallel to the principal lines at a distance of nineteen to twenty-two miles, or at right angles to them, would hand over to cultivation considerable. zones of valuable fertile lands, and concentrate the produce in the loading stations at a fair cost to the farmers.

The question is well asked, if the 20,000 miles of rails are only sufficient to permit the cultivation of 70,000,000 acres, how many will be necessary when nearly 300,000,000 more acres are being worked? At present about 1,000 miles of fresh railroad are being laid down each year. £20,000,000 a year is being put into new railroad construction. Yet thirty years ago (1884) the total amount invested in Argentine railways—now running into hundreds of millions—was only £18,600,000. In 1885 all the railways in the Republic transported cargo amounting to a little over 3,000,000 tons. In 1905 it was over 12,500,000 tons. In 1918 it was moving toward 40,000,000 tons.

65

CARLOS MARÍA DE PENA, *THE ORIENTAL REPUBLIC OF URUGUAY AT THE WORLD'S COLUMBIAN EXHIBITION, CHICAGO, 1893* (MONTEVIDEO: N.P., 1893), PP. 24, 36–38

13th. *Rio Negro Colony*. This colony is situated in the tenth district of the department of Tacuarembo, between the Rio Negro and the rivulets Cardozo and Cacique grande. It has a superficies of 38,216 square cuadras, (28,198 hectares, 8,602 metres), out of which 1,249 square cuadras, (921 hectares, 6,133 metres) form the district of the village called "Teniente General M. Tajes"; the remaining part is divided into 361 *chacras* or farms.

The area of each *chacra* varies from 29½ to 88½ hectares.

A third part of the *chacras* are already occupied, and although the colony is of a quite recent foundation the results obtained by the settlers cannot be hoped to be better The colony possesses already six dairies. It is sure to become, very soon, one of the most important agricultural settlements, on account of its good situation, which permits the easy exporting of its products by the railway, not only to the interior of the Republic but also to the very frontier of Brazil.

The land is very good for plowing, on account, also, of its situation and of the many rivers that run through it, and is quite fit for the sowing: of wheat and maize, and also for the culture of tobacco and the grape vine.

The village "Maximo Tajes" that belongs to the same colony has a railway station, a fruit market, a public square, a post-office, a police-office, and very soon they are going to build a church and a school.

14th. *Antonio Crespo Colony*. It was founded in 1891 in the sixth district of the department of Tacuarembo, in the place called "Aldea," a league and a half distant from San Fructuoso.

15th. *Stajano Colony*. In the department of Durazno and at a short distance of the so-called town, the capital of the department, was recently founded a new colony, called "Stajano Colony." It has an area of 7,378 hectares and between 300 and 400 inhabitants; all along the river Yi it possesses many thick woods. The railway station is only one kilometre distant from the town.

During these last two years, in all the rural districts devoted to cattle feeding, they have everywhere begun preserving part of the land for the culture of cereals, potatoes, etc. . . . forages and trees fit for cutting and burning. Thus the production of the land has been increased still, and also the rural activity, preparing a total transformation in the cattle feeding and general rural industry of the country.

Means of communication and conveyance

All the towns and villages of Uruguay littoral communicate with the capital by the regular service of beautiful steamers between Montevideo and Salto, stopping in all the ports of the Uruguay and Argentine Republic littoral.

Other steamers start from Montevideo for Paraguay and Matto-Grosso (Brazil.)

The lines of transatlantic steamers establish constant communications between the Republic and European and American ports.

By land, a great many places in the Republic are put in communication by the railways and by the telegraph, established also between Montevideo and Europe, Brazil, the Pacific and Argentine Republic.

Where the railways are not yet established, there is a good and regular service of stage-coaches.

Railways

There are already seven railway lines in the Republic, the service of which is quite regular and comprehends an extension of 1,567 kilometres.

Some other lines are in way of formation, and for some others the necessary preliminary studies have begun, comprising a new extension of 1,231 kilometres.

The railways already established are:

1st. *The Central Uruguay Railway*. It starts from Montevideo, runs through the whole territory of the Republic, till it reaches the capital of the Department of Rivera, on the very frontier of Brazil, in front of "Santa Ana do Livramento," that is to say, with an extension of 575 kilometres. Besides this, it has also another line of 32 kilometres from "25 de Agosto" to "San Jose."

2d. *The Northeast Uruguay Railway*, between Montevideo and Minas, with an extension of 122 kilometres.

3d. *The "East Extension" Railway*, between Toledo Station, which belongs to the Northeast Uruguay Railway and Nico Perez, with an extension of 206 kilometres.

4th. *The North Railway*, between Montevideo and Santa Lucia, where are established the municipal slaughter houses. This railway furnishes with meat all the Montevideo markets and has an extension of 23 kilometres.

5th. *The Northwest Uruguay Railway*, from Salto to the River Cuareim, through the Department of Artigas, with an extension of 178 kilometres. In "Paso del Correo," where this line stops, begins the Brazilian Uruguayana Line.

6th. *The Midland Uruguay Railway* joins with the Central Railway in "Paso de los Toros" and with the Northwest Railway in the town of Salto and has its principal station in Paysandu, with an extension of 317 kilometres.

7th. *The North Uruguay Railway* between Isla Cabellos, which belongs to the Northwest Line and San Eugenio in front of San Juan Bautista (Brazil). It runs through the Department of Artigas and has an extension of 114 kilometres.

River steamers

There exist many important navigation companies with beautiful and comfortable steamers for the service of the River Plate, Uruguay and Parana.

Among these companies the English company *Platense* must be mentioned. With its twenty steamers it represents an important capital. It possesses its own docks and wharfs in this republic and in the Argentine Republic. The principal steamers of the *Platense* are called: *Venus, Eolo, Apolo, Minerva, Olimpo, Saturno, Cosmos and Helios*, the finest of all, recently constructed. All these steamers have electric light on board. They all go to Buenos Ayres and stop in Martin Garcia, Nueva Palmira, Mercedes, Fray Bentos, Gualeguaychu, Concepcion del Uruguay, Paysandu, Villa Colon, Guaviyu, Concordin, Salto and vice versa.

The steamers of the other companies have more or less the same itinerary.

The movement of goods and passengers is important and has always given good benefits to all the companies.

The journey between Montevideo and Buenos Ayres is of a few hours. The steamers start form Montevideo at 6 p. m. and get to Buenos Ayres, generally, at 4 next morning. The very same day, at 10 a. m. they start again for the ports of the Uruguay; getting to Salto the next day.

Stage coaches

In all the departments where railways are not yet established there is a regular service of stage coaches putting the various railway lines in communication and making easier the conveyance of goods and passengers.

Tramways

In Montevideo there are nine tramway lines: 1st Union and Maronas Tramway; 2nd Paso del Molino and Cerro Tramway; 3rd Eastern Tramway; 4th Buceo and Union Tramway; 5th. North Tramway; 6th Oriental Tramway; 7th Reducto Tramway; 8th Montevideo Tramway; 9th Central Tramway. In nearly all the streets of Montevideo there is a tramway line and with such a shortening of the distances life and activity are a great deal increased.

In the centre of the town the tramway ticket costs 4 cents, and from one extremity of the line to the other it costs 10 cents.

During the year 1891 all these tramways made 916,798 journeys, which represent 9,285,940 kilometres, they conveyed 18,000,000 passengers. They possess 507 coaches and 3,622 horses. The number of men employed by the tramway companies is 1029. They have 14 stations.

In the town of Paysandu there is also a tramway line.

66

W. H. KOEBEL, *PARAGUAY* (LONDON: T. F. UNWIN, 1917), PP. 231–239

Traffic and development

IT was in 1913 that occurred one of the most important events in the history of Paraguay. It is true that this was in no way connected with politics, presidents, or constitutions. All that actually occurred, in fact, was the establishment of the steam ferry across the Alto Paraná River, by means of which communication was opened up between the Paraguay Central Railway and the Argentine North Eastern Railway. But the link was actually of the most momentous order; for it was the last in the lengthy chain by which the inland State of Paraguay for the first time in its history was given a direct road to the sea independent of the watery highway offered by its great river.

By means of this steam ferry, which bodily transports the trains between Posadas on the Argentine shore and Encarnación on the opposite Paraguayan bank, Asuncion is now in direct railway communication not only with Buenos Aires, but with the Uruguayan capital of Montevideo in addition. The true importance of this achievement has been considerably obscured by the shadow of contemporary events. From the point of worldwide acknowledgment it was certainly unfortunate that the fruit of all the years of work and preparation should have come to maturity just at a period when the countries of the Rio de la Plata—suffering from the European complications hatched in the Balkans—were undergoing a financial crisis. This in itself was sufficient to depress the spirits of the most resolute share-holders; but when in the following year the great European War broke out, scarcely a ray of light seemed to be left on the horizon.

It was inevitable, of course, that this gigantic catastrophe should lead to an unprecedented situation in Paraguay. Thus, instead of the "bumper" freights and financial profit which in ordinary circumstances could scarcely have failed to attend the enterprise, a far less satisfactory situation had to be faced. This has been admirably explained in the Paraguay Central Railway's report for the year ending on the 30th of June, 1915:—

"The situation of Paraguay has been entirely abnormal: the economic life of the country passed through a period of rapid changes. Much of the business effected during the past year has been incidental to this abnormal condition; that is to say, is perhaps due less to a healthy increase in the output of produce, where increase has occurred, than to efforts to adjust changing values to the new conditions.

"For example, produce has in some cases been exported in satisfaction of debts abroad, whereas in normal times money payments would have been made. In some cases the depreciation of the currency enabled exporters to purchase native products at unusually favourable prices, but the rise in freights, etc., and the congestion of ocean traffic soon tended to make these profits illusory. The depreciation of the currency enabled the timber companies to save on wages and to sell in Argentina, where a stock of Paraguayan timber has accumulated. On the other hand, the same cause affected the internal cattle trade adversely, and the depreciation of the paper money has, perhaps more than anything else, contributed to the impoverishment of the people."

It is clear enough that a situation such as this could not fail to result in a fall in traffic receipts. But, although the vastly increased commerce that had been anticipated with so much reason has not yet materialized, there is no question whatever but that its advent is merely postponed, and that when once the normal situation has been re-established in South America and throughout the world, the benefits of this most important railway communication must be experienced to the full. In the meantime some of the results of the traffic workings of recent years will be found in the Appendix.

It has practically become an axiom now among the railway experts of South America that a railway line makes its own traffic. This has proved the case even where the lines have been flung out into a desert and unpopulated country. As it happens, the region through which this new line passes, both to the north and south of the Alto Paraná River, is neither desert nor unpopulated. It is, in fact, that very garden of South America in which the Jesuits of old raised their varied and very abundant crops. All that has been required to invest these districts with their former smiling fertility has been the touch of a railway line, and a few whiffs of smoke from an engine! But for this matter-of-fact magic the neighbourhood has cried out in vain until now—and even now, as has been explained, the magic touch cannot become operative until the return of normal conditions.

The journey by rail from the Atlantic coast to Asuncion is a sufficiently remarkable one, and affords a notable instance of the triumph of the engineer over natural obstacles. Should the traveller start from Buenos Aires he will soon discover that, in the ramifications of the railway route, the stream of the Alto Paraná is not the only one which separates him from Asuncion. Less than three hours' run, as a matter of fact, brings him to the bank of the mighty main river itself, the Paraná proper. Here, at the port of Zárate waits the giant steam ferry-boat that receives the long train in three divisions on its deck, and that sets out on her voyage along the waters of the river. To those who choose to remain within the railway carriages the sensations of this completely, noiseless progress, void, moreover, of any vibration, is sufficiently strange.

A far more interesting plan, however, is to alight from the railway carriage and to mount to the spacious upper deck, whence the ramifications of the various channels of the river can be observed. After four hours or so of this passage of the still waters, the square bow of the ferry fits itself into the groove prepared for it at Ibicuy on the Entre-Rios shore. After this the train rumbles off on to the land lines, forms itself again into a single row of carriages, and makes its way to the north through the Argentine province of Entre-Rios.

At the important railway centre of Concordia the waters of another great South American river, the Uruguay, come in sight. At this point, by ferrying across the stream—but on this occasion independently of the railway carriages—and entering the train at the Uruguayan city of Salto on the opposite bank, direct communication is available with Montevideo, the Uruguayan capital that reposes on the northern bank of the great estuary, just where the Atlantic Ocean ends and the river begins.

From this point onwards the interest of the journey waxes with an almost bewildering rapidity. By the time that the junction of Monte Caseros has been reached, the wealth of verdure and blossom that comes pressing forward to the line at intervals has notably increased. Here and there is caught a glimpse of the upper waters of the Uruguay River—clear and sparkling reaches, these, that differ completely from the broad yellow flood nearer the mouth.

As the train enters the northernmost Argentine province of Misiones—the northernmost, that is to say, so far as these eastern territories are concerned—the enchanting slopes, valleys, and patches of woodland make it perfectly clear that the garden of South America chosen of old by the Jesuits has been entered. The soil has become a rich red—a tint that in its way suggests the Devon earth. This ruddy shade is characteristic of these regions that still largely await development, of the coffee lands of Brazil, and of a great part of Paraguay itself.

It is undoubtedly fertile to a degree, this warm, bright earth of these favoured neighbourhoods. It possesses, moreover, various peculiarities of its own. In periods of drought its dust clouds are formidable, and in times of heavy rain the mud into which it resolves itself is not only unusually deep, but at the same time most extraordinarily tenacious. He who takes an involuntary roll in the mud of Paraguay and of these neighbouring districts must make up his mind to bear the ruddy stains on his clothes for a very long time to come; for it is no more to be banished by a casual application of the ordinary brush than is a host of swamp mosquitoes to be discouraged by such inefficient opponents as a pair of human hands. But, so far as the Paraguayan soil is concerned, it is easy to put up with such minor inconveniences in view of its most generous services as a producing agent.

Advancing steadily northwards over the new line, once again the waters of a great stream come in sight. Embowered in a more luxuriant screen of verdure than those other waters to the south, the beautiful Alto Paraná River endeavours to bar with its stream the way into Paraguay. It now entirely lacks that success it enjoyed in the past. The railway companies have seen to that, and the steam ferry which awaits the train lies against the bank in massive proof of their triumph.

The great vessel which takes the train upon its deck at this port of Posadas is modelled on exactly the same lines as the one which plied between the southern ports of Zárate and Ibìcuy, and sets out upon the waters with a similar conviction of tremendous power, which, for some reason or other, seems far more apparent here than it does in the ordinary steam vessel. In one respect, however, this second passage is more momentous than was the first. It is an international one, and its conclusion lands the traveller in the Paraguayan port of Villa Encarnación.

From this point ten hours or so of railway travel take the passenger to the end of his journey. But there will be much to see before he arrives at the town of Asuncion. It is true that, on the whole, the landscape closely resembles the smiling country of Misiones; but with every northward mile the subtropical exuberance becomes more manifest. The lapacho-trees grow taller, and the spreading clusters of their pink blossom still more abundant. The forest patches that alternate with the rolling open country become denser, while the clearings in the woodland are more closely populated with a dancing flight of gorgeous butterflies, and carpeted with an added profusion of brilliant flowers.

The speech of the populace is now Guaraní—a proof that we have really and truly left the cosmopolitan ethics of the south far behind. We are, in fact, among the landscape, people, and fruits of Paraguay. Since these are described in other places, we may leave them for the present, and turn to some of the practical considerations of the railway.

The disadvantageous circumstances which prevailed when the junction with the Argentine railways was effected have already been referred to. These have naturally affected the time-tables of the international trains. In the first place it had been intended to run three international trains each way in the week; but the present crisis has caused the number of these to be reduced to one each week.

As I have already endeavoured to point out, it would be absurd to estimate the prospects of the railway from this. The mere possibility of reaching Asuncion in fifty hours from Buenos Aires must in normal times offer an outlook sufficiently tempting to be resisted by very few who have the means to afford the trip, whether they be commercial folk or tourists. But before dealing with these latter the larger political and industrial situation, as influenced by the railway, must be considered.

The tendency of lines such as this to reduce disturbed populations to a condition of ordered and occupied tranquillity has already been referred to. That this influence will be exerted in Paraguay before long is, humanly speaking, as inevitable as that the country through which the line passes must receive an industrial impetus such as it has never before experienced. As it is, both the cattle and the orange traffic from Paraguay are showing signs of considerable development. But the future of the railway is bound up with the future of the Republic—it is a platitude, this—and no rapid progress can be looked for until a normal situation has come about again in the world.

The next important feature of the railway development in Paraguay will be the connection by rail of the inland Republic with Brazil: this line will run from Asuncion to the east, tending very slightly to the north. The railway will enter Brazil in the close neighbourhood of the famous Falls of Iguazú, where it will be linked up with the Brazilian systems connecting with Rio de Janeiro, São Paulo, Santos, and all the principal ports and cities of the centre and south. By this means, indeed, an alternate railway connection with the Uruguayan capital of Montevideo will be offered.

The first sections of the line, starting from Asuncion, have already been completed. The topographical difficulties of the further sections, where the line enters the mountainous country, are naturally very much greater than those of the first, and the progress here cannot be expected to proceed with the same rapidity. When this work, however, has been completed the strategical situation of the inland Republic, instead of being disadvantageous, will have much to commend it. Asuncion, in fact, will form one point of a great railroad triangle, the other two points being respectively Buenos Aires and Rio de Janeiro. This will mark the completion of the main railway ramifications of the international system of Argentina, Paraguay, Uruguay, and Brazil.

Another railroad which in course of time must prove of great interest has been begun, running southward from Paraguarí station on the Central Paraguay railway. It is possible that this may be eventually carried to the south as far as the Paraná River.

67

MRS. GEORGE B. MERWIN, *THREE YEARS IN CHILI* (NEW YORK: FOLLETT, FOSTER, 1863), PP. 1–9, 121–123

We left New York on the 20th of July, and on the 28th of August entered the harbor of Valparaiso.

The voyage to Aspinwall was eventless, but full of interest and delight for us, to whom this seafaring experience was an entire novelty. On the 27th of July, we saw Cuba; and on the 28th we beheld the mountains of Jamaica, clothed from sea to summit with the perpetual verdure of sugar-fields and cocoa-groves. The day was warm and bright, and we ran two hours along the coast, before putting into the bay of Port Royal—our vision feasted now with the glories of the land, and now with the beauty of the sparkling and joyous sea.

As you enter the bay, you see Port Royal on the right, crouching with low huts upon the level sands amid sheltering cocoa-nut trees; and at the head of the bay, Kingston, lying beneath a mountain that rises abruptly from the water, covered with dark masses of vegetation, and looking at first glance like a great thunder-cloud fallen heavily athwart the sight.

Here we stopped for coals, and before we made fast to the dock of the decaying city, the water about the steamer swarmed with unwonted life and activity: innumerable young negroes clove the waves with their arms, and the air with their shouts, noisily besieging the passengers for money: "One dime, massa!" "One dime, missus!" When a coin was thrown to them, they dived through the transparent water and brought it up with unerring certainty, splashing, sputtering, blowing the brine from their faces, and greedily vociferating for more.

A plank walk was laid from the deck of the steamer to the coal-yard, and about one hundred negresses, scantily attired in ragged dresses that left bare the arms and neck and fell only to the knees, began the work of coaling. Each had a tub holding about a bushel, which she filled, and balanced on her head with one hand while she marched up the steep plank, keeping time to a chanted refrain. At the coal-hole the tubs were emptied without being removed from the head by a sudden jerk of the neck and twist of the body; and the women passed off at the other end of the ship, in endless succession.

The hand of decay lies heavily upon Kingston. The narrow streets are filled with loose sand; the pavements are broken, and the houses almost universally dilapidated. Nevertheless, there were some handsome stores, where we found the merchants very polite, after we had struggled through the crowds of negro boys who met us at every door and gate-way, with vociferous invitations to enter. In the street, we saw not more than one white man to a hundred black ones, and the bitterest antipathy seemed to exist between the two races.

Disembarking at Aspinwall, on the 31st, with the usual scenes of bustle and confusion, we took the Panama Railroad for Barbacoa, twenty-three miles distant, and plunged suddenly into the heart of tropic scene. For a few miles from Aspinwall, the road passes through a swamp on crib-work of logs, filled in with stone and earth, with the water on either hand thickly matted with aquatic plants. Traversing this swamp, we entered a great forest, magnificent with gigantic trees, all clambered with pendant, blossomy vines, and gorgeous with flowers of every hue. It was now the middle of the rainy season, when, in this tropical land, a few weeks suffice to clothe in vivid verdure everything left undisturbed. In one place near the road, stood on old pile-driver, garlanded with luxuriant creepers; and in another, a dismantled locomotive was dimly discernible in a mass of green. Again, in harsh and ghastly contrast with this exuberant vegetable life, the end of a coffin protruded from a fallen bank, grimly wreathed with verdure.

After three hours' travel, we arrived at Barbacoa, and quitting the cars, left behind us the civilization of the North and found ourselves not only in a tropical climate, amidst tropical scenery, but tropical mud, discomfort, and squalor.

Barbacoa stands on the bank of the Chagres River—a few bamboo huts, with a hotel distinguished by weather-boarding from the rest. We stopped at this hostelry for refreshments—taking our way from the cars to the house, over a path of what seemed grass, but was really the delicate and beautiful sensitive-plant, that shrank fearfully from the feet falling upon its tender leaves.

The place was full of Californians returning to the States, who gave us terrible accounts of the roads before us—for we were to take boats to Cruces, and thence struggle on with mules to Panama, *by mud*.

The railroad between Aspinwall and Panama has long been completed, and the perils and perplexities of the old-fashioned passage of the Isthmus are historical, rather than actual. I do not think, however, that their becoming

"Portions and parcels of the dreadful past,"

has invested them with any tender hues of romance. They remain in my mind to this day a harsh reality of mud, deprivation, and affliction. I recount them with the sole consolation that for me they are past forever, and that no one hereafter will encounter them. Only, dear reader, as you are whirled along by steam over a passage memorable with direful struggles, bestow a sigh upon the hardships of pre-railroad travelers!

At the inn of Barbacoa we remained two hours, provisioning and bargaining for boats. When at last our arrangements were completed, we made our way through the town, and clambered down the steep muddy banks of the river to the water's edge, where we found about two hundred others, trying to embark, and mingling their tumult with the cries of the boatmen, who were shrieking loud demands of "*Hombre, acquí*" on every hand. With great ado, a score of us succeeded in seating ourselves in a boat twenty feet in length—roofed, and with canvas at the sides, to be let down in case of rain. Our baggage was carried in the same boat, and served for seats; and then we had a captain, or steersman, and six boatmen, who propelled our craft keel-boat fashion, by setting poles against the river bottom, and walking from the bow to the stern of the boat, on a narrow plank at either side. The greater part of the boats on the river were of this sort—some being distinguished by a red flag fluttering at the stem. The scene was rather pretty as a number of them pushed from the shore, into the middle of the river, with their gay bannerols waving, and freighted with men, women and children in various costumes.

Our boatmen were great brawny fellows (naked but for a hat, and a piece of cloth girt about the loins), who accompanied every impulse of their poles with a deep sonorous grunt. We had not gone far, when we discovered that two of them were drunk; and presently one of them tumbled into the river. The current ran very rapidly, and we feared that the tipsy *hombre* was lost, when he came to the surface, and swimming after the boat, clambered in, only to make a second involuntary plunge, which sobered him.

On the banks of the river, which rose to a height of from four to twenty feet, we saw occasional patches of corn, and now and then a few cattle, and bamboo huts; but, for the most part, the view was shut off by impenetrable growths of trees, and interlacing vines and shrubs, through which a man could scarcely have hewn his way with an axe.

The afternoon was one of intense enjoyment to me; my eyes never wearied of the novel and ever-changing landscape, and the rich and beautiful forms of vegetation. At half-past five we rounded to in front of Gorgona, a town then consisting of about forty bamboo huts, with a plaza and a populace enlivened by a mimic bull-fight. Here our captain declared that his men must have something to eat, and the gentlemen of our party going in search of food, returned with a dozen slices of ham and ten hard-boiled eggs—the only provisions to be had in all Gorgona. After an hour's delay we pushed off, and ascending the stream to the upper part of the town, our boatmen again ran the boat ashore, sprang out, struck a pole in the ground, made the boat fast, and, before we had time to think, plunged into the bashes and disappeared. It was now growing dark; no other boat was in sight; none of us could speak the language of the country; and all the tales of robbery and murder that we had ever heard, occurred to us, and some, at least, felt very uncomfortable. A party of the gentlemen went ashore to the Alcalde, to learn, if possible, the reason of our detention, and were told that it was unlawful for any boat to navigate the river during the night. I was afterward told that a few months previous, a boat striking a snag was wrecked, and the passengers were drowned.

The *hombres* were promptly arrested, tried, and shot for murder. On the following day, we ourselves found that it would have been impossible to proceed in a dark night, for the river was full of snags and sand-bars.

All the boats that had left Barbacoa with us, had been made fast along the shore at Gorgona, and discovering that we were not entirely alone, we set about rendering ourselves as comfortable as possible. A boat load of passengers, with the mails, tied up alongside, and the mail agent offered our gentlemen beds on the letter-bags, and left us more room. From the other boat, we borrowed a candle and three matches, to be used in case of necessity. The night was very dark; a steady rain began to fall, and we crouched down upon our baggage, very hungry, weary, and miserable creatures. After a while the children became uneasy, and we all suffered agonizing suspense while the attempt was made to light the candle. Two of the matches proved dead failures; but the third was a success. This excitement subsided, and I slept until roused by a crackling noise under my feet. On examination I found that I was trampling on my bonnet, which had dropped from my head. The comfortless night at last wore away, and at daylight our boatmen returned and put our boat in motion. At nine o'clock we reached Cruces, where the noisy scenes of the embarkation were repeated. Three men siezed the three small children of our party, with the announcement of "Me picaninny Panama," and following their guidance, we ascended a slippery bank, and made our way between two rows of huts, through a street ankle-deep in mud and filth, swarming with pigs, poultry, donkeys, and children, to the St. Charles Hotel, where our martyrdom was consummated with a breakfast, which was the very abomination of indigestion.

On the 14th of August, we went by rail a little distance into the country, to dine with a friend who has a contract for building some of the railroad bridges. We found our friend living in a shanty near a gorge in the coast range of mountains, where the grade is very steep, and where five bridges are required within one mile. A large number of *peones* were at work here, each of whom the contractor paid five reales a day, and furnished with a sufficiency of bread and beans. They had a brush shanty in which to sleep at night; a stone oven to bake their bread, and a large iron kettle to cook their beans. The bread was leavened with yeast; pieces of the dough were weighed, made into loaves, and covered with a dirty poncho, and then placed in the sun to rise. At noon, old nail kegs, filled with cooked beans, were placed on the ground; three or four laborers squatted around each keg, and with a piece of bread in one hand, and in the other a stick flattened at the end, or mussel-shell, with which to scoop up the beans, they ate their dinner. When their hunger was satisfied, they threw themselves on the ground, and drew their hats over their eyes for a few moments' *siesta* The dress of these *peones* consisted of a wide pair of cotton drawers, a shirt, and a conical straw hat. The poncho is worn mornings and evenings, and when the weather is cool. At night, it is used for bed covering.

The railroad bridges are very expensive structures. The lumber for their construction is all Norway pine; and the iron girders are brought from England. The piers and abutments are built of very fine granite (resembling the famous Quincy stone), which is found in great abundance near by.

On the *diez y ocho* of this year, I attended grand mass in the church of La Matriz. The building was decorated with flags; and inside, the two rows of pillars were adorned with gay ribbons, and the altar flamed with lighted candles. A soldier stood on guard at each door to prevent the ingress of the lower classes. The church was soon filled with ladies, wearing superb black silks, vails, diamonds and white gloves, who knelt on mats, spreading their flounced skirts to the utmost extent. We arrived at ten o'clock in the morning; at eleven, the *Intendente*, with the officers of the army and navy, and the foreign consuls, escorted by military and a band of music, entered the church, and threaded their way through the kneeling groups to the chairs which had been placed for them. The religious ceremonies were similar to those at Santiago, but less imposing. The bishop of Valparaiso officiated. The attendance of military and naval officers at these observances is enforced by the loss of a month's salary for every failure to be present. I was extremely amused by the performances of one of these near me. He was dressed in full uniform and watched the ceremonies very narrowly, lest he should not make his genuflections at the proper time. At his feet was a lady whose skirts covered a vast area, and every time the officer knelt, he planted the end of his sword firmly upon her dress, which she attempted to extricate—so that their time was occupied in the ineffectual struggle. The Danish Consul, whose gorgeous uniform had evidently been made for him when he was a much thinner man, told me that, after kneeling fourteen times, he gave up in despair and exhaustion, and remained quietly seated during the rest of the service.

68

FRANCIS E. CLARK, *THE CONTINENT OF OPPORTUNITY*, SECOND ED. (NEW YORK: YOUNG PEOPLE'S MISSIONARY MOVEMENT OF THE UNITED STATES AND CANADA, 1907), PP. 181–189

The famous journey across the Andes

THERE is as yet but one practicable route across South America, and that is in about south latitude 35°, where the continent narrows to a width of some 900 miles, and where it is divided between the two rival powers of Chile and Argentina.

Of course there are other passes, if one wishes to risk the dangers and hardships of a journey of many weeks on mule-back, over the difficult mountain trails, and down the interminable miasmatic stretches of the Amazon or the La Plata to the sea, but, speaking in general terms, the only way for the ordinary traveller to cross South America is to journey down the dreary desert of the west coast by steamer for three thousand miles from Panama, until he reaches Valparaiso, and then by rail and coach, or on the back of the patient mule, cross from the Pacific over the rocky backbone of the continent to Buenos Ayres on the Atlantic coast.

Even this route is difficult and hazardous enough to satisfy any one whose bump of adventure is not abnormally developed.

The first hundred, and fifty miles of the journey from Valparaiso presents no difficulties and little excitement. A comfortable Chilean train, built on the American plan and drawn by a German engine, hurries one away from the dilapidation and ruin of earthquake-shaken Valparaiso, over the foot-hills of the Andes, and through the dusty valleys of Chile, where (in March) it has not rained for at least seven months.

One can make himself comfortable in a Pullman drawing room car if his inclination is for luxury, and eat his dinner in a well-equipped dining car. The heat and dust and other discomforts of travel are farther relieved by clusters of delicious Muscatel and Black Hamburg grapes (or varieties very much like them), by baskets of fine purple figs, and good looking, but poor tasting, peaches, pears and apples, which can be bought for a few cents at almost any station. This (March) is the fall of the year, it must be remembered, and all kinds of fruits are in their glory.

At Llai Liai (which, being interpreted, means Windy Windy) is the junction for Santiago, where passengers from the beautiful capital of Chile join our train which keeps on, headed for the high mountains, until it reaches Los Andes, where we must stop for the night.

If the traveller has tears let him prepare to shed them now, for his serious troubles begin at this point. In the first place, he is bundled out of the train here in the dead of night, and must find a carriage of some sort, more or less dilapidated, which will rattle his bones over the stones of Los Andes at a tremendous pace for about a mile, until he reaches a very poor inn with a very big name,—the "Grand Hotel Central."

Here he will be shown a not over-clean bed in a dirty room, perhaps occupied (the room, not the bed) by three or four other fellow beings. But he is so dead tired that he would be thankful for a rug on the floor. At midnight he turns in, and at 3:30 A. M. the landlord sticks his head through a hole in the curtain which divides his sleeping apartment from the family bedroom, and tells him that it is time to get up, as the coach goes to the train in half an hour.

The traveller rubs open his sleepy eyes which he feels have only just closed, dresses hastily, drinks a cup of execrable coffee and eats a crust of hard bread cut from the loaf the day before, pays eight dollars in Chilean money for this accommodation, and is again rattled over the stones, through the black darkness that comes before dawn, to the railway station. Here he finds a comfortable little narrow gauge train of the rack and pinion mountain road awaiting him, and while it is yet pitch dark the train moves off up the mountains to Juncal, the present terminus of the railway on the Chilean side of the Andes.

An hour after the train starts the stars fade out, and the early dawn breaks over the eastern hills. First they grow gray and cold, the gray turns to steel-blue, the blue to a rosy pink, and, at last, the highest peaks are lit by the earliest rays of the sun, and another glorious day has begun in the high Andes. Indeed, all the days are glorious in this region at this time of year. Never is there a rain-storm, almost never a cloud in the sky.

Few countries have such a delicious climate as Chile. It is seldom too hot and rarely too cold. The Antarctic current cools the air along the shore, and the mountain breezes temper the air in the interior. Nothing could be more charming than this railway ride. On the Chilean side of the lower mountains, there is a little vegetation in spite of the long rainless season, and around the poor little mud huts, which one sometimes sees, climb creepers and flowering vines, as though nature was doing her best to cover up their squalor.

Everywhere the mountains grow from grand to grander. Great white peaks that seem to leap 20,000 feet into the air, occasionally burst upon the view. In one place the train rushes through a narrow gorge over a shelf cut out of the solid mountainside, with a brawling stream a thousand feet below. This is called "The Soldier's Leap," because of the impossible tradition that a soldier of the Republic, when hard pressed, once took this broad jump. As he probably was not endowed with wings, the story is hard to believe, but the name is a good one, and the tradition adds spice to the journey.

We are sorry when Juncal is reached, and we should be sorrier still if we knew what was ahead of us. Before the train fairly comes to a stop, there is a grand rush, helter-skelter, "catch as catch can," for the coaches which are drawn up in line, waiting for the eighty passengers who are to cross the mountains. The theory is that the first coach that gets its load will be the first to start, and so will avoid some of the dust of the other twenty that will race on behind.

This theory, like some others, does not always work in practice, and the first are often last, and the last first, in getting started, according to the will and word of the conductor, who accompanies the whole party. The theory however has the advantage of making everybody hurry, and, in a surprisingly short space of time, crack goes the whip of the driver, and the four horses, driven abreast, start off at a breakneck pace over one of the roughest of roads, swinging down a steep incline at the rate of twelve miles an hour, and then up an equally steep pitch at fall gallop, until our breathless horses, thoroughly winded, stop to rest as do all the train of four times twenty panting horses, making a long line halting on the mountainside.

Before we go any farther, I ought to describe one of these mountain coaches. Let not my readers conjure up pictures of swinging Concord coaches, balanced on great leather springs, or even of Swiss diligences with their comfortable and comparatively roomy seats. The Andean "coach" is peculiar to the country, and, let us hope it will never be copied, but will quietly disappear when the railway tunnels the mountains and renders it obsolete. It is a very small cramped affair, holding four people when crowded. The seats run sideways, and the top and sides are covered with white canvas like a butcher's wagon. The canvas is buttoned down tight except at the back, to keep out the intolerable dust. The springs are very inadequate, if indeed there are any at all, and one feels to the centre of his being every bump and stone and water-bar in the long six hours' journey.

There are two rival companies that convey passengers, but the coaches are equally bad; in fact they seem to be just alike except that those of one line are painted black, and the other yellow. These companies are deadly rivals, however, and their drivers frequently indulge in races in the most inopportune places, as we found to our cost; for our driver being outdistanced by his rival, attempted to take a short cut over a little rise of ground, which was never meant for a coach. The coach tipped, the horses floundered among the rocks, and we saved ourselves from a serious smash-up by all jumping out and righting the coach, and walking up the hill until it got into the road once more. Another coach in our procession tipped entirely over, but no one was hurt, and fatal accidents, I am told, are remarkably rare, considering the fact that three times a week nearly a hundred people take this journey.

By interminable zigzags the coach road mounts the mountain. Starting at about 5,000 feet above the sea, it climbs more than 7,000 feet in some fifteen miles to the summit of the pass, 12,796 feet above the sea. The top of Mt. Blanc is but a little higher than this pass, and Mt. Washington and Mt. Jefferson would dwindle into foothills as seen from this gigantic Andean range.

Many of the views are sublime and such as can be seen nowhere else in the world. Rough, rugged, barren in the extreme in the higher ranges, Nature has done her best here to pile Ossa on Pelion, and to enable man to mount on them to the stars. In early April we found the pass warm at midday, and almost entirely free from snow, though sometimes it is absolutely closed to travel after the middle of April, and even in February tunnels occasionally have to be dug through snow banks, and mules have to be substituted for the coaches. The pass is usually open, however, for travellers from November until the end of April, and sometimes into May, but is closed during the winter months of June, July, August and September.

As we approach the top on the Chilean side, the zigzags grow more numerous and arduous, until, in looking back, one can count as many as twenty curves over which he has come. The scenery, at the same time, becomes bolder, grander, more sublime. Mountain peaks, twice ten thousand feet high, tower about us, and we are overwhelmed by their overpowering vastness and sterility. Nowhere, except in Montenegro and the Canadian Rockies, have I seen such massive natural monuments, and the latter are relieved by vegetation up to the tree line. There seems to be no tree line in the Andes.

On the top of the pass is one of the most remarkable statues in the world; an heroic figure of the Christ, upholding a cross. On the base of the pedestal are the emblematic figures of Chile and Argentina clasping hands as a symbol of their settlement of the boundary dispute, which at one time seriously threatened war; a war happily averted by arbitration, which assigned the summit of the Andes as the boundary between the nations.

Under the pedestal is the inscription

> *"He is Our Peace*
> *Who Hath Made Both One."*

The magnificence of the surrounding scenery, the isolated loftiness of the natural pedestal and the character, the appropriateness, and the beauty of the statue itself all combine to make "The Christ of the Andes" perhaps the most impressive monument in the world.

Immediately after passing the monument we are on Argentine soil, and then commences a descent of some 2,000 feet to the town of Las Cuevas. In some respects this is the most hair-raising part of the journey. The descent is very rapid, the zigzags very numerous, the curves very sharp. The driver whips up his horses, who also scent the oats in the distant town which we can see almost from the top. At breakneck speed we dash along. There is no wall and no stone posts, as on the Swiss roads, to guard the side, and every side is either a precipitous mountain or a fathomless precipice. Around every curve the coach slews with only two or three wheels on the ground, and the precipice only four inches from the outside wheel, but a special Providence protects the travellers, and we reach Las Cuevas safe and sound, to be sure, but covered with such a coating of fine yellow dust that our own mothers would hardly know us.

The rest of the journey to Buenos Ayres is comparatively easy. A narrow gauge rack and pinion road takes us to Mendoza, some four hours away. Grand Andean scenery charms us on every side, with Mount Aconcagua (23,393 feet), the highest mountain in the western hemisphere, occasionally visible, while other mountains scarcely less mighty, loom on every side.

At Mendoza, which is among the foot-hills of the Argentine Andes, we change again to a broad gauge road, where comfortable sleeping cars wait to carry us to Buenos Ayres, 650 miles away, a journey that takes some twenty-three hours.

Except for one range of hills, the whole distance is over an absolutely flat plain, but a plain of marvellous fertility, covered with innumerable flocks and herds, and producing bumper crops of corn and wheat. A vast world's granary six hundred miles wide and hundreds of miles from north to south, are the prairies of Argentina.

But this article has to do with the mountain journey, and, before it is ended, I may well answer the question which has already been often put to me, whether it is practicable and worth while for the average traveller to take it. It certainly is, if the said average traveller is willing to put up with a few discomforts. It depends largely upon one's previous point of view.

Was it Mark Twain who said to the unskillful barber who asked him if the razor was easy: "It depends upon what you call it; if you call it shaving it is pretty hard,—if you call it skinning it isn't so bad." So if you are thinking of a pleasure journey, a charming ride over the Andes such as you would have in Switzerland or the Pyrenees, it is pretty hard; if you call it getting across the Andes over a new, rough, undeveloped desert country, it isn't so bad. If you can stand dirt, heat and cold; if you do not wince too much at the abuse of horses and mules; if you can endure considerable extortion without grumbling; if you can see your trunks and other baggage pitched about and thrown over by the worst baggage smashers in the world; if you do not wholly lose your equanimity when your trunks are opened on the road and the contents stolen, as mine were; if you can "eat your peck of dirt" in a few hours instead of a lifetime, and enjoy the dirt; if your nerves are strong enough to stand a ten mile gallop on the edge of a precipice; if you want to see the most magnificent scenery in the world; if you enjoy a spice of adventure; if you would have memories and mental pictures that will remain fresh and vivid for a lifetime; if you would see the most magnificent works of God and some of the most daring engineering feats of man; you will take this journey when you have the opportunity, and be thankful all your life that you have done so.

At any rate, this route is far shorter than the alternative route through the straits of Magellan, taking only two days instead of ten, and it costs only half as much.

In five years (or more likely ten) the tunnel through the Andes will be completed, and the whole journey will be made by rail. Then the route will be robbed of all its terrors—and more than half of its joys.

69

JOHNSON SHERRICK, *AROUND THE WORLD AND SOUTH AMERICA* (CANTON, OHIO: THE REPOSITORY PRESS, 1912), PP. 235–243

Santiago de Chile, March 10th, 1910.

THIS city is the capital of Chile, and is the largest place on the Pacific coast, except San Francisco, in North America.

It was on the morning of March the 4th that we, with a number of other passengers, of the S. S. "Bleucher," took a special train at Buenos Aires and proceeded to travel by rail over the plains of northern Argentine. I was glad to change, for a while, to land travel, but we did not have the dustless air to breathe that is so delightful on the sea. Rains are not infrequent on those level lands; but in late summer it is like August time in Ohio, and we encountered on part of the way, between the Atlantic ocean and the mountains, a very penetrating dust.

For nearly a thousand miles, our train speeded over a curveless railroad and as level as the sea. I viewed with great interest the countless numbers of sheep, cattle and horses that were grazing on the pastures. As far as one could see, on either side of the road, the lands were covered with live stock.

At places, ostriches in great numbers could also be seen on the green sward of an apparently endless plain. Their long strides, juking heads and crooked necks made a queer sight among the animals. These giant, vain and ugly birds were strutting around as if they were the lords of all the fowl creation—seemingly proud of the fact that the feathers they shed are eagerly sought for in the markets of the world. As to their real value, only a fashionable lady can answer.

I saw large fields of corn (maize), but not such corn as we grow in the United States. It is planted thickly at the time the ground is plowed, after which it receives no further cultivation. It grows wild, so to speak, on those fertile lands. Of course, the small per cent that is cultivated, produce large ears which they husk and use as grain. Usually, before it is ripe, the stock is turned in to fatten on the green corn. Being closely planted and not cultivated the stalks are tender and the ears are small.

The people who own those lands are the few; they secured them in early days, and they are the millionaires of this fast-growing country now. Nearly all the meat that supplies the markets of western Europe is produced so cheaply in the Republic of Argentine that I know of no place that can compete. It is a great source of wealth for that country, and the people who are the owners of those vast plains have princely incomes.

That country is also a great wheat country; no-where on earth does that grain thrive better than on the soil of Argentine. The harvest was over, the threshing was mostly done, and all we could see as we passed through was the stacks of straw and stubble fields. Ships are being loaded now; some are already on the high seas carrying the new wheat to the hungry hordes of the old world. For hundreds of miles, the lands are dotted with stacks of hay; not a barn did I see. The weather is so mild, that even in winter time the stock is not in need of shelter.

I never will be able to realize the magnitude of those vast plains, or conceive the numberless domestic animals that are born, raised and murdered in South America—to appease the carnivorous appetites of us human beings, or to satiate that cannibal-like desire of human nature, for one animal to feed upon the flesh of another.

In the morning of the second day, the sun rose beautifully. The air was void of dust, and delightfully cool. The horses, seemingly wild, were scampering on the plain. The cattle were resting on the green sward and quietly chewing their cuds. As we approached nearer the mountain regions, more trees hove in sight attracting the birds and adorning the landscape. The enjoyment of that morning journey, amid those scenes of a pure rural life, I never can forget. It was about the middle of the forenoon, when we came in sight of Mendoza, a beautiful little city in the midst of miles and miles of vineyards, all ladened with the most delicious grapes. At luncheon, a great quantity of that fruit was on our dining-tables, fresh from the vines; and, I must say, that I never ate of more delicious grapes in my life. The truth of this assertion is attested by the fact that when our party had finished their luncheon, every grape had disappeared.

Mendoza lies near the foot hills of the giant Andes mountain range. It is the place where we leave our special train and take little narrow gauge cars on the mountain-climbing railroad.

It was about the middle of the day, when the two little engines proceeded to climb the eastern side of that terrible mountain range. For several hours our "iron horses" puffed along the way, as they proceeded upward by the side of a dashing mountain river, that flows downward, and roars through a winding way. We passed through tunnels, over high bridges, crossed dangerous chasms and along terraces which hang like shelves on the sides of the mountains. The trip is very interesting and our journey entertaining; but O! what a contrast; the day before we were gliding over the level plains, amid the green fields on fertile lands; the day after, our train was slowly passing between the rugged mountain peaks and over barren rocks.

Late in the day, our little train reached the end of its road, about three hours late of the schedule time. There we saw, near by, the top of Aconcagua, the highest mountain in the western hemisphere, nearly 24,000 feet above the level of the sea and white with that mantle of snow that never melts. All around us were many other peaks covered with snow, some had glaciers and large fields of ice hanging on their sides. Blasts of cold winds blew down through the pass, and we shivered as we stood in the sunshine, although we were warmly clad.

The summit of the pass was two thousand feet above us, and over it we must go ere the sun-light leaves us, for the road down on the Chilean side is very dangerous after dark. Some of us on wagons, drawn by four sure-footed horses, and others on mules, we made all possible haste to reach the top. Over a zigzag path, steep and risky, we hurried on and upward. Just as the rolling old earth was turning away from the sun, we reached the highest point on our way, the top of the pass, and the boundary line between Argentine and Chile, where stands the noted monument on which the figure of Christ proclaims peace to the two Republics forever. It was placed there by mutual consent to mark the boundary line over which their contention for a long time caused much trouble and war. It is very appropriate, indeed, that the Prince of Peace should represent the good feeling that now exists between these two kindred nations. The fact that Argentine and Chile are both Christian nations; the statue of Christ standing between them in the attitude of counseling peace and good will, keeps intact a sentiment of great worth to all the people concerned.

The chilly winds and approaching night, made us all feel that we should not tarry long at this historic place. Down another steep and dangerous zigzag way, the faithful horses went at a lively gait and soon brought us to the station of another narrow gauge railroad, on the Chilean side of the mountain range, where a train of four little cars had been waiting for several hours to convey our belated party to Los Andes, which town lies 9,000 feet lower at the base of the mountains. It was 10 o'clock at night, when our little train arrived there. We were hungry and tired, and very much in need of rest. Being three hours late our dinner was delayed at the Los Andes hotel until nearly 11 o'clock that night. No provision was made for us to remain for the night; but a special train was provided, on the wide-gauge state railroad, with fine large coaches, (built in the United States,) to convey our party here, where we arrived at three o'clock on Sunday morning, five hours later than the scheduled time. The Grand and other good hotels were prepared to receive the North American travelers, who were expected to arrive early in the evening, so none of our party had any trouble to secure excellent accommodations. After a strenuous day in the mountains, and most of the night in weary travel, I was glad to share in the comforts of this good hotel.

The mountains of South America are more lofty, but not so rocky as those in North America. Some of our party experienced much difficulty, as we were coming over the pass a few days ago, in getting sufficient oxygen, in the rarified air. to enable them to breath easily; in fact, two persons fainted and several were quite ill on account of the altitude. Any person with a weak heart should never attempt to cross there. Before another year passes, a tunnel will be completed through the mountain, 2,000 feet below that pass, which will enable travelers to cross the continent, from ocean to ocean, on a steam railway without changing cars.

A little incident occurred, while we were crossing the Andes, personal to myself, which surprised me greatly. As we were proceeding with the aid of horses and their native Indian drivers, high up among the mountain peaks, a stranger—looking very much like our noted scout, "Buffalo Bill"—stepped up to me and said, "Why, Johnson Sherrick; what are you doing here in this God-forsaken place?" With a keen eye he looked at me, waiting my reply. I was slow to speak. "Are you not Johnson Sherrick?" said he. "That is my name," said I; "but I really don't know you." "Can't you remember that young man McMillan that sold you folks powder in Canton years ago?" I could not remember him; but, nevertheless, I asked him how long he lived in South America and what he was doing here. He told me that he had charge of that caravan and was engaged in taking people over the mountains beyond the reach of railroads.

I do not know that his right name is McMillan, but I do know that he withheld from me all such information of his friends and relatives in the States of North America that might lead to the discovery of his whereabouts. Perhaps he, like many others, who have found a refuge in South America, feels that his presence at home is not congenial just now. And it may be that he prefers just such a life as he finds there among those lonely and rugged mountains.

I was pleased to learn that, in this beautiful city of Santiago de Chile, there resides a fellow countryman, who was born and reared as near our home as the city of Massillon, Ohio. Taking a carriage, I drove through the city for miles ere I succeeded in finding his home, which is more like the home of a Spaniard than the dwelling of an American. I was admitted by his daughter, who took me through a hall into an open court, where I found, amid the flowers and shrubbery, a little fountain of water playing in the sunshine. The young girl could not speak in English, but pointed to a door that stood open on the court, through which I entered and found my American friend, Mr. John Shertzer, resting on his couch. When I told him that I lived in Canton, Ohio, he was very pleased. He said, "Only one person have I seen from my boyhood home, since I left there forty years ago." I did not talk long with him before I realized that his, was an eventful life.

After the railroad was completed, I was employed by the Peruvian government to survey the Nitrate Mines. This valuable product is found native in enormous quantities in the rainless districts on the borders of Chile, whence the world's supply is obtained. Its chief uses are as a fertilizer and for the production of nitric acid and saltpeter.

The Peruvians disputed the Chilian line and considered a part of those very valuable mines as lying in their country. The Peruvians were driven off the mines by the Chilians, and we, (myself and my assistant engineer,) were captured. We were afterwards released, and told that if we were ever found again trespassing on their mines for the Peruvians, we would be executed.

70

ADOLFO DE CLAIRMONT, *GUIDE TO MODERN PERU: ITS GREAT ADVANTAGES AND VAST OPPORTUNITIES* (TOLEDO, OHIO: BARKDULL, 1907), PP. 50–60

A guide to Peru

Tumbes is a small town of 2200 inhabitants, on the Tumbes River, and situated on the boundary line between Peru and Ecuador. It has in the neighborhood some extensive petroleum deposits, which are now being rapidly developed. At Zorritos, close by, an important refinery has been successfully worked for many years past.

It was near to Tumbes that Pizarro first landed, at a spot known as Comendador Creek, 25 miles south. Tumbes was then a flourishing town, and the ruins of a once famous temple are still to be seen in the vicinity.

PAITA (population about 3500) is 120 miles south of Tumbles, and in point of commerce is the third largest port of Peru. It possesses a hotel, a theater, churches, etc; and there is a railway to Piura, the capitol of the department some 60 miles (by rail) inland.

PIURA is the most important town in the north and is the centre of the cotton-growing industry of Peru. It has some 10,000 inhabitants, a branch of the bank of Callao, Chamber of Commerce, and other public buildings, and possesses a very dry and salubrious climate; on this latter account it is much visited by persons suffering from rheumatism and similar ailments, the method of cure resorted to there having proved very beneficial. There are several very extensive cotton estates traversed by the railway, which, to those interested in cotton culture would well repay a visit. Trains run daily.

There is also an extension of the line from Piura to Catacaos, 6 miles distant, and one of the most important centers of the straw hat industry.

To the north of Paita and 55 miles distant is the small port of Talara, remarkable for the extensive petroleum deposits in this vicinity. Several large and important refineries and pumping stations have during the last few years been established in the immediate neighborhood, and it is believed that the industry is capable of very great development. Special tank steamers are already employed distributing the oil along the coast.

PIMENTEL is 152 miles south of Payta. It has a railway serving the inland towns of Chiclayo and Lambayeque, ten and nine miles distant respectively. There is considerable rivalry existing between Pimentel and Eten (the next port), and the railways from both towns running through the same districts.

ETEN. This port is situated 9 miles south of Pimentel and 155 miles (direct) from Paita. It has a fine iron pier 2,000 feet long, the railway running out to the pierhead; but the roadstead is exposed, and has a very heavy surf. The valley inside of Eten is well populated and richly fertile, producing sugar, rice, tobacco, etc., in considerable quantities. There is a railway (broad Gauge) from Eten to PATAPO (30 miles), passing most of the principal towns and estates.

The village of Eten, three miles from the port, is one of the principal centres of the straw industry. The hats (Panama straw), cigar cases, etc. made here are much esteemed for their fineness of texture and excellent workmanship, and command very high prices.

The towns of CHICLAYA (population 11,325), 12 miles from Eten, LAMBAYEQUE (population 6,250) capital of the province and 29 miles distant and FERRENAFE, 29 miles from Eten, are important commercial centers; in the vicinity are the estates of Cayalti, Patapo, Pucula, Almendral, Tuman and Pomalca, which produce together some 8,000 tons of sugar and 2,000 tons of rice annually, the total productions of rice for the Department being about 10,000 tons per year.

Near to Pucala are the ruins of a notable Inca fortress.

PACASMAYO is 34 miles south of Eten; population 2,000. There is a fair commercial movement considering the size of the town. The port is good and possesses a fine pier, 1,000 yards long. The chief exports are sugar, rice and cattle, products of the fertile regions in the vicinity.

There is a railway from Pacasmayo connecting the port with the principal towns of the interior.

CAJAMARCA, the capital of the department of that name, built at the foot of Mount Cumbe (16,000 feet), with a population of 15,000. Cajamarca figures largely in the history of the Conquest, and it was here that Atahualpa was captured by Pizzarro and held prisoner.

SAN PEDRO de LLOC, a small town of some 5,000 inhabitants. A tramway unites the town with the railway station, a mile and a quarter distant.

CHEPEN, a population about 5,000; a centre of commerce with the interior. Near here is the extensive sugar estate of Lurifico.

GUADULUPE, population 4,000. An agricultural fair of considerable importance is held here annually, at the commencement of December. The town is also surrounded by several estates of importance.

SALAVERRY, 66 miles from Pacasmayo and 256 miles from Callao, is an active commercial seaport, with a population of about 1500. The principal exports are sugar, rice and alcohol, from the neighboring valleys of Chicama and Chimu; also moderate quantities of metals.

It is connected by rail with the town of Trujillo, as well as with various other places of importance in the interior.

TRUJILLO, the capital of the department, is one of the most important commercial places of the North. It is a well built city, with a population of 10,000; is a Bishop's See, and possesses a branch of the bank of Callao, Chamber of Commerce, Cathedral and several other buildings of note.

This was one of the first towns founded by Pizarro; and the visitor will therefore find much to interest him from a historical point of view. Some two miles distant are the ruins of an ancient city called Chan Chan, founded by the Chimu tribe of Indians, and which gives evidence of an advanced state of civilization in its inhabitants. There are also, nearby, the remains of an Indian Temple to the sun.

The towns of note inland are: CHICAMA, CHOCOPE and ASCOPE, the latter being the terminus of the railway, and carrying on a fair trade with the interior. All of these towns are, however, chiefly devoted to agriculture, and in the vicinity there are some extensive sugar estates.

SALAVERRY to CALLAO. The minor ports from Salaverry to Callao are served by the Pacific Steam Navigation Company's Coast Line, running fortnightly between Callao and Pimentel.

The principal of these ports are:

CHIMBOTE, a small town 61 miles to the south of Salaverry, situated in an extensive and well-sheltered bay, considered by many the finest on the coast. Inland of the town is a very fertile valley enclosing various extensive sugar estates.

These are passed by the railway which at present runs from Chimbote to Suchiman only, but which it is the intention to carry on to the southern extremity of the valley of Huaylas.

There are in the interior various silver mines of importance being worked.

SAMANCO and CASMA are small seaport towns, shipping metals from the mining districts in the interior, and also small quantities of sugar.

HUARMEY, 43 miles south of Casma. The Ticapampa Mining Co. have extensive silver producing establishments inland from this port.

SUPE and HUACHO, 90 and 70 miles from Callao respectively, export sugar and cotton from some fairly important estates in the vicinity, as well as metals from the interior. Inside of Huacho is a very fertile valley, from which Lima and Callao draw large supplies of agricultural produce and fruit.

At all of the above ports there is a land telegraph line communicating with Callao and Lima.

CALLAO, the principal port of Peru, has a good harbor, a very fine dock and breakwater.

At La Punta, about two miles to the south of Callao, there are several good hotels and excellent bathing. This place being at the extremity of the neck of land separating Callao Bay from Chorrillos Bay, and exposed to the sea breezes from the south and north, enjoys a bracing and healthy climate, and is much esteemed by invalids on this account. There is a railroad between La Punta and Callao. The hotel rates are modern, from $2 to $3 per day.

LIMA, the capital is about eight miles inland from Callao, and is connected therewith by two railways, that of the English Railway Co. and the Ferro-Carril Central del Peru.

Lima is the second largest city of the South Pacific, and possesses many fine squares and churches, a prettily arranged park, a public library and other buildings, which merit a visit. The city is built on the banks of the river Rimac, some 500 feet above the sea level, and possesses a very equable and agreeable climate. It has a population according to the last census

The city is covered by a very complete system of tramways, and the principal streets are lighted by electricity. Hotels are numerous and good, and the tariffs moderate.

In the vicinity of Lima, and connected there with by direct lines of rail are the seaside resorts of Ancon, Magdalena, Miraflores, Barranco and Chorrillos, much frequented during the summer by the people of Lima and Callao.

CERRO de PASCO, 12,000 inhabitants, one of the richest mining districts in the country. It is situated at an altitude of 16,500 feet, and about 100 miles north of Oroya. A line of rail connecting this town with Oroya is shortly to be built.

TARNA, a thriving commercial town some 15 miles to the east of Oroya. It has a population of about 9,000 and is well spoken of on account of its dry and temperate climate.

JAUJA, at an altitude of 11,150 feet, is the chief resort of consumptives and persons suffering from bronchial affections, its climate being peculiarly beneficial in such cases. Apart from its high standing as a health resort, Jauja is not a town of much importance, though under the Inca rule it was a flourishing and populous city. The population of the town and its suburbs is said to be 21,000. It is situated about 30 miles to the south of Tarna and 50 miles south to Oroya.

There are also the towns of CONCEPCION and HUANCAYO to the south and CHANCHAMAYO to the east of Tarna, and distant about two day's mule ride; and HUANUCO a similar distance to the north of Cerro de Pasco.

CERRO AZUL, 72 miles south of Callao, is a surf port, dependent upon Callao Custom House. It exports fair quantities of sugar from the adjacent valley of Canete. The chief town of the district CANETE, is about five miles inland.

TAMBO de MORA is a minor port, 105 miles south of Callao and 14 miles north of Pisco; chiefly occupied in the export of wine, cotton, sugar and agricultural produce, from the rich valley of Chincha, the estimated produce of which is 224,000 gallons of aguardiente (brandy), 12,500 gallons wine, 1,200 barrels rum and 15,000 quintals of cotton per year. The town of CHINCHA is situated six miles from the port of Tambo de Mora.

PISCO, 116 miles south of Callao, serves as the outlet for a rich and fertile valley covering an extensive area. Though chiefly devoted to the culture of the vine and cotton, for which its climate is particularly suitable, it exports in large quantaties all kinds of agricultural produce. The town of Pisco contains about 4,000 inhabitants; it possesses a tramway, and a fine pier 600 yards long; also a railway to Inca, the capitol of the department, 46 miles distant.

ICA has a population of 10,000, devoted to wine and cotton production and commerce with the interior. It is a neatly built and well situated town; and in the immediate vicinity are several small medicinal lakes, highly recommended for diseases of the skin and stomach, and for rheumatism. The province of Ica is said to produce 700,000 gallons wine, 90,000 gallons spirits and 40,000 quintals cotton annually.

The principal towns in the interior are:

HUANCAVELICA, population 9,000, 120 miles from Ica. Close to this town is the famous quicksilver mine of Santa Barbara.

AYACUCHO, population 10,000, 182 miles from Inca. Remarkable filigree work, and other specimens of the silversmith's art are produced here.

CASTROVIREYNA, some 100 miles from Ica, a mining district of considerable note.

Ica is the highway to all these places.

Ten miles out from Pisco are the CHINCH A ISLANDS, once famous for their guano deposits, from which Peru obtained an immense revenue.

LOMAS, 152 miles from Pisco and 201 miles from Mollendo.

Both of these places are but of minor importance, the staple productions of the surrounding country being cattle, which are shipped along the coast in large quantities, minerals wool and cotton. There are various silver and copper mines being worked in the interior.

MOLLENDO, the second port of the Republic, is a town of 5,000 inhabitants. It possesses two hotels, and is of considerable importance commercially; as, being the port for Arequipa, Cuzco etc., as well as for the interior towns of BOLIVIA, it ships large quantities of alpaca and sheep's wool, skins, coca leaves, bark, silver, tin and copper ores, to the value of about 400,000 annually. It is the western terminus of the railway to Santa Rosa (Cuzco), Puno and La Paz (Bolivia.)

AREQUIPA, the capital of the department, is a city of about 35,000 inhabitants, built at the foot of the extinct volcano Misti (18,650 feet high), and at an altitude of 7,550 feet above the sea level. It is an important commercial city, and not with out interest to the visitor; is well built, (the houses being constructed generally of blocks of lava has a cathedral, a bank, chamber of commerce, theatre, and some good hotels, as well as a club. There are several thermal baths in the immediate neighborhood, and on account of its altitude the town enjoys a pleasant and healthy climate.

Between Arequipa and Puno various silver mines are being profitably worked on a large scale.

From Arequipa the line extends to Puno, a neatly built city of some 6,600 inhabitants, on the shores of Lake Titicaca. Puno is at present the eastern terminus of the railway into Bolivia, though the line is about to be continued to La Paz direct.

The remarkable Lake Titicaca lies across the boundary line between Peru and Bolivia; it is situated at an altitude of 12,500 feet above the sea level, and has an area of over 5,000 square miles. Two fairly commodious steamers ply on the lake regularly in connection with the arrival of the trains at Puno, and convey passengers across to Chililaya (Bolivia), a distance of 90 miles. From Chililaya there is a coach service to La Paz, seven hours distant.

LA PAZ is now the capital of Bolivia, and almost all the commerce with the interior is carried on through that town. It contains some 26,000 inhabitants, and being situated at a considerable altitude enjoys an agreeable climate, though the surrounding country is barren and poor. There are five fairly good hotels in La Paz.

SUCRE, the former capital, is some some 70 miles to the south, and is a fairly extensive city, with a population of about 40,000. Near to Sucre is the town of POTOSI, renowned for its rich silver mines. These mines are said to be inexhaustible and it is calculated that, since they were first systematically worked in 1545, they have produced metal to the value of many hundreds of millions sterling.

I think it right in the interests of humanity, and especially on behalf of the numerous persons in this country who suffer so terribly from consumption, to draw attention to the great benefit such sufferers would derive if they would undertake the journey to Bolivia. The air in the regions of 'La Paz' Sucre and Oruro is so highly rarefied and dry that it kills the bacilli, the length of time required depending upon the stage the disease has attained; patients in the first or second stage would be completely cured after a short sojourn, but those in the third stage would probably have to remain a few years. No doctors or medicine are required, the air being all that is necessary, although an almost complete abstinence from alcoholic drinks is essential. If persons in the earlier stage of the complaint would go without delay, they would after a few months be able to return completely restored to health. Numerous persons suffering from consumption are annually sent to Italy, etc., where a cure is generally hopeless, whereas, if they would only undertake the longer journey to Bolivia, they would in most cases regain their health."

CUZCO. The city of CUZCO is supposed to have been founded by Manco Capac, the first Inca, in 1043, and it was taken by Pizarro in 1543. The population is about 18,500. Visitors to this interesting locality will find much to attract their attention, as, being, the ancient capital of the Incas, it still possesses many remarkable relics of their empire, particularly the great Temple of the Sun, which furnished such prodigious wealth to the Spanish invaders, the palaces of Manco Capac and his successors, the Inca canal, etc. The ruins of the famous Inca fortress of Saxihuaman attract visitors from all parts of the world. The more modern constructions of note are the cathedral, one of the finest and most remarkable buildings of the kind in the country, the university, museum, cloth factory, and several other buildings. The city is situated at an altitude of 11,000 feet above the sea level.

Cusco exports large quantities of cocoa, chocolate, coffee, vanilla, cocoa, indigo, sarsaparilla, quinine, and other medicinal barks and herbs, all of which are abundantly produced in the neighborhood. Considerable quantities of gold are also yearly exported from the Carabaya district in the vicinity; and the engineers have been sent out from Europe to survey this with a view to a systematic exploitation of its hidden wealth.

Fifteen miles from Cuzco is the valley of Urubamba, the summer resort of the people of Cuzco, 9,000 feet above the sea level. The celebrated ruins of Ollanta and Tamo, ancient fortifications of the Incas, are situated in this valley.

The regular through steamers call at Mollendo, northbound, every Sunday and Wednesday; going south, calls are made every Tuesday and Saturday. There is a telegraph cable station there, and land lines communicate with Arequipa, Cuzco and La Paz.

ILO is a minor port about half way between Mollendo and Arica. Its chief trade is the export of wines, spirits and olives, for which the surrounding districts have a high reputation.

OPPORTUNITIES FOR EMIGRANTS. In the Highlands of Peru, there are immense opportunities for raising cattle, which is now being done in a very small and poor manner.

71

MARIE ROBINSON WRIGHT, *THE OLD AND THE NEW PERU* (PHILADELPHIA: G. BARRIE & SONS, 1908), PP. 367–374, 377–386

The Oroya railway, the highest in the world

THE central mining region of the sierra is connected with the chief national seaport by the Central Railway, or, as it is popularly called, the Oroya Route, one of the most important lines of Peru and the most remarkable in the world, not only because of the altitude attained at its highest point, sixteen thousand feet above sea level, but as a colossal feat of engineering unequalled in railway construction. No other railway route compares with that of Oroya as an example of daring enterprise in the face of tremendous obstacles; and it stands a great monument to the awakened spirit of progress which began to be shown as soon as militarism declined in Peru, and which has become especially evident in the moral and material development of that country within the past decade.

The building of the Oroya railway was begun in 1870, under the direction of a North American engineer, Mr. Henry Meiggs, with whom the contract for its construction was signed by the Peruvian government. Within six years, the line was opened up to traffic as far as Chicla, ninety miles from Callao, at an altitude of thirteen thousand feet, and was graded and placed under construction from that point to Ticlio, near the summit of Mount Meiggs, where the Galera tunnel pierces the peak at an altitude of sixteen thousand feet, the highest place along the line. In 1877, Mr. Meiggs died, and the work was suspended, having already cost nearly five million pounds sterling. The war with Chile followed, bringing a train of evils in its wake, and the government found it impossible to continue the construction until 1891, when the line was taken over by the Peruvian Corporation and completed to Oroya, being opened in 1893. A branch line had been built by Mr. Meiggs from Lima to Ancón soon after beginning his work, and to this have since been added the Morococha branch, from Ticlio to Morococha, and the Cerro de Pasco line, the property of the Cerro de Pasco Mining Company, from Oroya to the great mining centre. The Oroya Route has recently been extended to Huancayo, and is under construction to Ayacucho. It will be continued to Abancay and Cuzco, to unite with the line connecting Cuzco with Puno, which is to be extended to the Desaguadero River on the boundary between Peru and Bolivia, where it will join the Guaqui and La Paz railway, to form part of the great Pan-American system. From Cerro de Pasco northward, the trunk line has been built as far as Goillarisquisga, and is under construction from that point to Huánuco, to join other links in the chain which, when completed, will extend, in Peru, from the border of Ecuador to Lake Titicaca.

From Callao to Oroya, the distance is less than a hundred and fifty miles, but along this short route the railway passes through every variety of scenery and climate, from the sandy level of a tropical coast to the frozen peaks of the lofty *puna*, far above the limit of vegetation. Between these extremes lie the flourishing sugar plantations and maize fields of the coast; orchards of chirimoyas, paltas, peaches, apricots, granadillas, oranges, lemons, etc., that grow on the lower slopes of the sierra; all the flowers, ferns, and mountain shrubs that flourish in rocky glens and shady ravines under nature's most favorable conditions, up to a height of ten thousand feet; and, above this limit, the bare, bleak aspect of the *puna*, where mining establishments mark the locality of rich veins of precious metal, and the circle of the horizon is everywhere limited by snowclad summits. Along the valley of the Rimac River, from the sea to its source, the Oroya railway climbs the sierra with innumerable curves and yet without a single decline throughout its length until the highest altitude is passed in the Galera tunnel, and the descent begins on the slope of the inter-Andean valley. More than twenty bridges cross the river along the course of the railway; the mountain side is tunnelled in many places, and in others the line hangs over precipices projecting so far out that a stone dropped from the car as it curves along the brink falls on the opposite bank of the river below.

The journey from Lima to Oroya may be made in a day, the train leaving the station of Desamparados at eight o'clock in the morning and arriving at Oroya at five in the evening. It affords an opportunity to see one of the scenic wonders of the world, and is an experience never to be forgotten. As the train leaves the Lima station, a short distance from the Balta bridge and within full view of the broad bed of the Rimac, the retreating city offers only a partial glimpse of its gleaming church towers and the avenues of shade trees that adorn its suburbs. The picturesque Cerro of San Cristobal, with a cross illuminating its summit, stands out in clear relief against the sky and may be seen until the train passes behind the Andean foothills on its way to Santa Clara. Although this point is more than a thousand feet above sea level, it differs little in aspect from the country around Lima. Wherever the waters of the Rimac have been brought into service to fertilize the gardens and plantations of the valley, exuberant vegetation exists, and abundant harvests smile under the blue skies; it is only beyond this strip of green that the sandy plain and gray, barren hillsides are to be seen. That the Incas had all the coast region under cultivation is indicated by the existence of their ruined cities in the very midst of the desert and their *andenes* along hillsides that, to-day, are counted of little value for agricultural purposes. At Santa Clara, a short walk from the station takes one to the ruins of an Incaic town, which, to judge from what remains, must have been a very populous settlement centuries ago. Its appearance to-day is one of utter dreariness, and it is difficult to imagine what charm such a site could have offered for the location of a city.

For fifteen miles beyond Santa Clara, the railway train climbs upward until the town of Chosica is reached, the scenery increasing in beauty as the valley narrows between the hills of the sierra and the foliage of the mountain side grows fresher and of more gorgeous hues. Chosica is one of the most popular health resorts of Peru, and has a delightful climate all the year round. Situated in the midst of mountains at an altitude of three thousand feet, it possesses many advantages as a sanitarium for invalids, and is a pleasant place of residence for those who like a restful and quiet retreat. The sky is blue during most of the year, and the pure atmosphere is exhilarating to tired nerves and overwrought spirits. Here one may enjoy life in its simplicity, as Chosica has not taken on the fashionable airs and expensive luxuries of the modern spa, though supplying its greatest benefits. Aside from its attractiveness as a health resort and a picturesque mountain city, Chosica is important as the first distributing point for the electricity which supplies light and power to the cities of Lima and Callao and their suburbs.

From Chosica to Matucana, the scenery is ever-varying and always magnificent. The train climbs five thousand feet within a distance of thirty miles, crossing the chasm of the river many times and plunging through tunnels that succeed one another with remarkable frequency. Purguay and Corona are the first bridges of importance along the line. Soon after leaving them behind, the train sweeps around the magnificent curve of San Bartolomé, passing through its famous orchards and gardens, and bringing into view all the glories of mountain foliage that adorn the sierra at this altitude. Purple and white heliotrope, convolvulus, clematis, the maguey plant, and the cactus are seen in profusion. Birds of bright plumage and butterflies of variegated wings give life to a scene which is impressively silent, save for the hard breathing of the locomotive as it plods sturdily around the curves. Though the valley broadens at San Bartolomé, it is soon enclosed again between gigantic walls of mountains; and, a few miles further on, the Verrugas bridge, the longest and highest of the Oroya Route, spans the space between opposite walls of granite that rise from the river bed to tower among the clouds. This bridge is five hundred and seventy-five feet long and two hundred and twenty-five feet above the river, which looks like a ribbon of silver as it sparkles at the bottom of the ravine. After crossing Verrugas bridge, the train disappears for a moment in the tunnel of Cuesta Blanca, emerging in the midst of the grandest scenery imaginable as it pushes on through Surco and across the Challapa bridge to Matucana, where a welcome half-hour's stop is made. Matucana is, like Chosica, a favorite health resort, and the pines and eucalyptus trees of the neighborhood give added healthfulness to its pure mountain air. Few people suffer from the rarity of the atmosphere at this altitude, though it is well to spend a night here, if one can spare two days for the trip to Oroya, the rapid ascent from sea level to sixteen thousand feet above being a severe trial to the respiration. *Soroche*, as the mountain sickness is called, does not attack everyone, nor is there any certainty as to its visitation; many people have made repeated trips without feeling any inconvenience, and have been surprised by an attack when they thought themselves immune, while others never reach the high altitudes without suffering from *soroche*. The degree of this most uncomfortable experience varies according to one's constitution. With some it is confined to a strenuous effort "to get one's breath," while, with others, the sensation is that of having the head slowly squeezed in a vice, or inflated by some process that threatens to burst it like an over-filled balloon. None of the phases of *soroche* are agreeable, but, happily, the disturbance disappears as soon as a lower altitude is reached.

As the railway follows the valley of the Rimac toward its source, the river gorge becomes ever narrower, the enclosing mountains higher, and the scenery more wildly grand and rugged. The railway train follows the tortuous line of the gorge, zigzagging along the precipice, visible only for a few seconds from any point along the route. After leaving Matucana, the course is taken through the very heart of the sierra, the train crossing first the bridge of the Negra quebrada, then the great links of Tambo de Viso and Champichaca in quick succession, these wonderful structures spanning the chasm at short intervals of three or four miles. From the car window, the passenger looks down into the depths below and up to the towering peaks, and feels much as if travelling in mid-air. At Tamboraque, which is situated nearly ten thousand feet above the sea, the scene changes, and the region of the higher sierra comes into view, with its mining towns and snow mountains. San Mateo quebrada, in the depths of which lies the picturesque town of the same name, is hardly passed before the train crosses, a mile away, one of the most remarkable bridges of the whole line, the Infernillo. It stretches across a narrow ravine between two walls of rocks, both of which are tunnelled so as to provide a passage for the railway. As the train flashes out on the bridge from invisible depths on one side and disappears as mysteriously on the other, the effect is singularly weird. From this point to Galera tunnel the ascent is very steep and winding, the train climbing five thousand feet in twenty-five miles, crossing several bridges and passing through a number of tunnels.

All along the Oroya Route, from San Mateo to its terminus in the sierra, are scattered mining towns of growing importance. Rio Blanco, five miles from San Mateo, has important smelting works, and Chicla, four miles away, a thousand feet higher up the Cordillera, lies in the heart of a rich mineral district. It occupies a picturesque location, especially as seen from the car window after the train has made the immense loop necessary to carry it across the valley and up the opposite slope on its way to Casapalca and Ticlio. From this eminence a magnificent view of the valley appears, with Chicla nestling below and snow-clad mountains looming in the distance.

Casapalca is a typical mining town of the sierra, with its smelters spread over the bare, brown hillside, its great chimneys and its smoke. It is situated at an altitude of thirteen thousand feet, and has a cold climate all the year round, invigorating and healthful. From Casapalca to Ticlio the distance is about ten miles, and the region of perpetual snow appears as the train pulls up the last few leagues toward the Galera tunnel. The summit of Mount Meiggs, which is seventeen thousand five hundred and seventy-five feet high, is nearly always wrapped in snow, though the tunnel entrance is below the perpetual snow line.

Of the sixty tunnels along the Oroya Route, that of Galera is the longest, measuring nearly four thousand feet in length. It is in the middle of this tunnel that the highest point along the line is reached. From this tunnel eastward, the train descends toward Oroya, passing through the mining town of Yauli and skirting the bank of the inter-Andean River Mantaro, a branch of the Perene, which, later, joins the Ucayali on its way to the main waters of the Amazon. When the train stops at Oroya, sunset is already approaching, and the colors of the retiring monarch of day are to be seen reflected on the surrounding peaks and glowing in the western sky. From the window of the little hotel where lodging is found for the night, one looks on a humble though interesting scene of pastoral simplicity. Llamas graze wherever the coarse puna grass is found, and an occasional vicuna may be seen. The altitude of Oroya is little more than twelve thousand feet, and a greater descent is made from Oroya to Jauja and Huancayo, the latter being only about ten thousand feet above sea level. From Oroya to Cerro de Pasco, the railway makes an ascent of nearly two thousand feet.

A trip over the southern route—new railways and public roads

IN no country have greater obstacles been overcome in the construction of railways and public roads than in Peru, the physical features of which present the most varied peculiarities. The millions that were spent in building the Oroya railway alone would have sufficed to cover many times its mileage on a level plain; and nearly all the railways of the country present evidences of difficult engineering and expensive construction. The lines at present in operation cover about fifteen hundred miles, while those projected and under construction will more than double that mileage. Most of these railways are the property of the state, the Peruvian Corporation having the use and management of them until 1956. Several important lines belong to Peruvian or foreign enterprises, or to private concerns; and in the extension of existing railways, these enterprises play an important part. The branch from Oroya to Cerro de Pasco was built by North American capital; and new lines are being constructed by other foreign companies. The railways which in 1890 were turned over to the Peruvian Corporation for a term of years in cancellation of the foreign debt of Peru, included, in addition to the Central, or Oroya Route, the Southern railway, and the shorter lines from Paita to Piura, sixty miles; from Pacasmayo to Guadalupe and Yonan, the same distance; from Salaverry to Trujillo and Ascope, fifty miles; from Chimbote to Suchiman, thirty miles; and from Pisco to Iea, fifty miles. Some of these lines have since been extended, the Southern railway having been completed to Cuzco in the present year.

The Southern railway covers a distance of two hundred and eighty-five miles, from the seaport of Mollendo to Juliaca, where it divides, the main line going from Juliaca to Cuzco, two hundred miles to the north, and a short branch extending south for twenty-five miles to the port of Puno, on Lake Titicaca. The first section of this railway was built in 1870, from Mollendo to Arequipa, across the arid sandhills of the coast. A journey over this part of the road has little to offer in variety of scenery, yet there is a peculiar fascination about its drifting crescents that seem to move with rhythmical undulation like the waves of the sea. Barren and dull as the prospect appears, it is not without interest, because so unlike anything one sees elsewhere. Along the first part of the route, a glimpse of green fields brightens the view as the train skirts the valley of Tambo before entering the Pampas of Cachendo and Islay, where not a blade of grass is to be seen. But the most of the route lies across the Pampas until, within a few miles of Arequipa, the sierra comes into view, and the fertile valley of Vitor is passed, with its plantations of maize and its flourishing orchards. From this point, a new railway is being built to the valleys of Siguas, Majes, and Camaná, in southwestern Arequipa. As the train speeds through Uchumayo, Tiabaya, and Tingo, the dreariness of the desert is forgotten in the smiling gardens of the *campiña*, and when a curve of the road shows Arequipa's white towers against a background of green, with the snow-crowned Misti just behind, the traveller is ready to believe all that enthusiasm relates in praise of its charm.

Mollendo, the seaport terminus of the Southern railway, is one of the most important cities of the southern coast. As it lies within the arid region, its water supply comes from the sierra eighty-five miles distant, through an aqueduct made of iron pipes, from which half a million gallons of water are discharged daily. This is said to be the longest iron aqueduct in the world. The port of Mollendo is visited by all ships trading on the west coast, and is the chief outlet for an extensive region in Peru and northwestern Bolivia. In order to improve the port, a breakwater is now being constructed along a reef of partially submerged rocks, extending about six hundred feet to the northeast of Ponce Island, which forms the harbor. This breakwater will protect the bay from the heavy surf which formerly dashed over the rocks, and will thus facilitate the working of the launches in loading and unloading merchandise from the ships, besides increasing the discharging capacity of the port. The breakwater consists of a sea wall of concrete on the inner side of the reef, with heavy concrete blocks weighing many tons, placed irregularly to seaward to break the force of the surf. A new landing-place of iron and concrete is also to be constructed.

The railway from Mollendo to Arequipa reaches its highest altitude at its destination, Arequipa being situated eight hundred feet above sea level. From Arequipa to Puno the ascent is much greater, reaching fifteen thousand feet at Crucero Alto, about midway along the route. The first train from Arequipa to Puno arrived at the shore of Lake Titicaca on the 1st of January, 1874. The cost of this railway was four and a half million pounds sterling. Along its route are several bridges, and a tunnel four hundred feet long pierces the mountain about thirty miles east of Arequipa. As the train begins its ascent from Arequipa to Juliaca, the city remains in view for several miles, and the white crest of the Misti flashes in sight several times before it is hidden finally behind the higher peaks of the sierra. After crossing the Chili River, over a massive bridge sixteen hundred feet long and seventy feet above the stream, the train makes a rapid run to Yura, fifteen miles distant, where the most noted mineral springs of Peru are situated, a singularly picturesque resort.

From Yura, the ascent soon brings one to the region of the *puna,* and here very little vegetation is to be seen. Pampa de Arrieros is as bleak and barren as a plateau at an altitude of thirteen thousand feet always is; and the train speeds along for thirty miles with little change of scene until it crosses the Sumbay bridge and climbs up to Vincocaya and Crucero Alto. From Pampa de Arrieros, a magnificent view of the snow mountain Coropuna is presented, this lofty peak towering nearly twenty-three thousand feet above the level of the sea. The volcano Ubinas comes into view a few leagues beyond Vincocaya, just before the station of Lagunillas is reached. Lagunillas, or "Little Lagoons" is so called from the lakes of Cachipascana and Saracocha, which lie on the boundary line between the Departments of Arequipa and Puno, at an altitude of thirteen thousand six hundred feet, more than a thousand feet higher than Lake Titicaca. There are few signs of human activity at the smaller railway stations of the *puna,* only a few cloaked figures appearing on the platform as the train stops; but at the junction of Juliaca the scene is one of animation, and many enterprising venders congregate outside the car windows to sell their wares. The Indian women, in their short skirts and *mantos,* or shawls, and their flat, stiff-brimmed hats, present a curious spectacle to the foreign traveller. Their dress is very sombre, in contrast to the bright colors worn by the Indians of the lower sierra. In Puno, one sees both the Aymará and the Quichua Indians, these two races meeting on the shores of Lake Titicaca. The Aymarás are better sailors than their cousins of the lower valleys, and the native boats, or balsas, that ply the lake are usually owned by Aymará traders. The balsas are made of the reeds of totora which are found on the banks of the lake, and are so lashed together as to make the skiff water-tight and not easily capsized.

A few months after the opening of the railway from Moliendo to Puno, two screw steamers, the *Yavary* and the *Yapura,* were launched for service on the lake, having been brought out from England in pieces, which were carried up to Puno with great difficulty and put together in the company's factory on the lake shore. New steamers have since been added; the *Inca* and *Coya,* recently launched, have a capacity of five hundred tons, are lighted by electricity, and provide accommodations for a hundred passengers. The voyage from Puno across to Guaqui, the Bolivian port, is made in a day.

From Juliaca to Cuzco, the journey is one of constant and varied interest. Nature presents many aspects in snow peaks and sloping valleys, and on the plateau are to be seen herds of llamas and alpacas. At the railway stations, groups of Indians offer for sale curiously-shaped objects in pottery, and the brilliantly colored blankets of this region. The jars, water-bottles, and ornaments which they make are often highly glazed and wrought in unique fashion. Horses, bearing cavaliers of the time of Charles V., in full armor, are favorite ornaments, though there are also water-carriers and peddlers with packs on their backs, and market women of wonderful dimensions. Most of these articles are made to be useful as well as ornamental, serving as water-bottles, toothpick-holders, match safes, etc. As works of art these efforts are among the crudest, but they are made by the most primitive process and represent much patience and industry. At Pucará, these venders throng the station platform, Juliaca being more noted for its blanket weavers. The Indians are very industrious, and whatever load they may be carrying is never allowed to interfere with their spinning, which goes on all the time, the bundles being strapped on their backs so as to leave their arms free.

From Tirapata, the headquarters of the Inca Mining Company and an important town of the plateau, the railway crosses a bridge and makes a slight ascent to Ayaviri and Santa Rosa, and a steeper climb to La Raya, which is the highest point between Juliaca and Cuzco. La Raya marks the boundary between the Departments of Puno and Cuzco, and is also the summit of the watershed which divides the Amazon system from that of Lake Titicaca. It is situated at an altitude of fourteen thousand one hundred and fifty feet above sea level. From La Raya, the train descends rapidly to Aguas Calientes (hot springs), Marangani, and Sicuani, two thousand five hundred feet lower, in the valley of the Vilcanota River. Before the completion of the railway to Cuzco, a diligence carried passengers from Sicuani to the ancient Inca capital, and, although the modern method of travel is to be preferred for many reasons, there was something charming in the drive along the old coach road that cannot be enjoyed by the traveller who is being whirled over the route at railway speed.

Formerly, the train arrived at Sicuani in the evening and passengers spent the night in one of the quaintest and most interesting towns of Peru, before taking the diligence to continue their journey to Cuzco. The market place of Sicuani is a glow of color when the Indians fill it with their wares. In the early morning they may be seen coming down the mountain into the town, the men wearing a dress introduced by the Spaniards during the time of the viceroyalty, with knee trousers and a coat of the period of Louis XIV., the women gorgeous in their *almillas*, or chemises of bright red or yellow; their *chamarras*, jackets of bright blue or green velvet; their *chumpes*, many-colored scarfs wound around their waists; and their flat, broad-brimmed hats made of cloth, lined with red and covered with silver braid. They scurry along the mountain road in high glee, their llamas in the lead with heads erect and long straight ears adorned with tassels of red, yellow and green woollen yarn. All the dignity of the procession is borne in the stately carriage of the llamas, whose leisurely movements are never disturbed by anything but fright.

Since the railway has been opened to Cuzco, there is no longer any necessity to break the journey between Sicuani and that city, as was done in the days of the diligence, when a stop was made at Cusipata, "the happy place," after a wonderful ride along the valley of the Vilcanota, crossing the Checcacupe River and revelling in scenes full of historical interest and romantic charm. The second day's ride used to take one from Cusipata to Cuzco, past the ruins of Viracocha's famous temple, and close to the lake of Urcos, where, tradition says, the chain of Huascar was buried when the Inca's subjects learned that the Spaniards were coming to Cuzco. This wonderful chain of gold, which is said to have been long enough to enclose the plaza of Cuzco three times and so heavy that each link weighed a hundred pounds, has been the object of many expeditions to Urcos. Near this spot, Almagro and Pizarro fought one of their bitterest battles, and in the neighborhood tradition locates many victories of the Incas' armies in earlier times.

The rope bridges formerly swung across the river have in many cases been replaced by bridges of stone, though a few of the older construction remain and are still strong and serviceable. Ruins of the ancient aqueducts are to be seen, as well as the Incaic *andenes* of the mountain side. The road passes through deep gulches mantled with green and under the shadow of sheer palisades towering a hundred feet above. Rippling streams pour their silvery tide into the river that winds its broadening course along the valley, and pepper trees, eucalyptus, furze bushes six feet high, and prickly cactus, grow in profusion along the roadside. The present railway follows closely the old diligence road. From Urcos, a branch line has been surveyed to the port of Tahuantinsuyo, on the Madre de Dios River, and another line is projected to connect the city of Cuzco with Santa Ana, the capital of the province of Convencion, in the same department. The immense importance of the railway to Santa Ana lies in the facilities it will afford for traffic in the region of the Montaña that is richest in coca and other valuable products. The law authorizing the construction of this line, prepared by Dr. Benjamin de La Torre, was passed by Congress in October, 1907, and the work is to be completed in three years more.

Not only have the Central and Southern railways been extended and supplemented with branch lines within the past four years, but nearly all the existing railways of the republic have been brought to form links in the general system which the government has planned for the facilitation of traffic throughout the whole country. From the trunk line,—which, when completed, will extend from the border of Ecuador in the northwest to that of Bolivia in the southeast,—branches are being built to the head of navigation on all the great waterways of the upper Amazon. These lines will open up the vast region of the Montaña to the ports of the Pacific, and will multiply the available resources of the country a hundredfold. Products of the interior which have been cut off from the consumers of the coast by the great wall of the Andes, will be exchanged for goods brought to the Pacific ports; and months will be saved in the transportation of articles required for household use in the Amazon valleys. It will no longer be the custom for deputies from Iquitos to travel to Lima by way of Europe and Panamá, as at present, rather than across their own country, because the foreign trip takes less time. One of Southern railway, with the port of Tahuantinsuyo on the Madre de Dios; another is being built from Oroya to the Ucayali River, passing through Tarma and along the present road to the Pichis and Perené Rivers. It is to be completed in 1913. A third line is entirely new, to be constructed from the port of Paita to Puerto Limon on the Marañon River, with a branch to Puerto Yurimaguas on the Huallaga.

All the railways projected and under construction to connect the Pacific seaports of Peru with the Amazon tributaries are of political as well as commercial importance, as they will serve to unite in closer bonds the people of the coast, the sierra and the Montaña, hitherto so remote from one another as to have few interests in common, except such as tradition and sentiment have preserved.

The port of Paita offers many advantages as the Pacific terminus of a railway to the Amazon waterways. From Paita to Puerto Limon the distance is only four hundred miles, and from Puerto Limon to Pará it is nearly three thousand miles. At present, most of the commerce of the Montaña is carried down to Pará over the Amazon and its tributaries, and many of the river routes are even longer than that from Puerto Limon. It is estimated that the railways between the Pacific coast and the Amazon will not only provide much more rapid transportation, but also a more economical service.

The railways of the coast have been extended during the past four years both longitudinally and in the direction of the sierra. From the port of Tumbes a line was recently completed to La Palizada and the landing-place of the port was improved by the construction of a steel pier eight hundred feet in length. The Pacasmayo and Yonan railway has been extended to Chilete and Cajamarca, to afford an outlet for the cereals and other products grown in those sections of the sierra. From Chimbote to Huaraz and Recuay one of the most important of the coast railways has been built. A line is projected to run direct from Cerro de Pasco to the coast, with its seaport terminus at Huacho, the concession for its construction having been given to a North American capitalist. An important new railway connects the port of Ilo with the city of Moquegua; it was completed during the last months of President Pardo's administration. Along the shore of the Pacific, a railway has recently been completed from Lima to Huacho on the north, and another is under construction from the capital to Pisco in the south.

Not only has railway construction received a great impetus under the energetic and progressive government of the past few years, but the public roads of the country have been extended and improved, new bridges have been built, new wharves constructed in several ports, and greater attention paid to commercial facilities than ever before.

72

EDWARD WHYMPER, *TRAVELS AMONGST THE GREAT ANDES OF THE EQUATOR* (NEW YORK: C. SCRIBNER'S SONS, 1892), PP. 385–391

ALTHOUGH our work amongst the Great Andes of the Equator was completed upon arrival at Chuquipoquio, a Public Duty still remained to be performed. It had been concluded from the tameness of my attitude on the 17th of January [see p. 89] that travellers could be defrauded with impunity, and be kept prisoners without fear of consequences. In the Public interest, it was desirable to correct this idea. The road-measuring was a slow operation, and when the people attached to the Tambo, out of curiosity came to inspect us, they afforded a convenient opportunity for a discourse to them upon the iniquity of their ways; and I emphasized my remarks in a manner which I trust left such an abiding *impression* as will render it less likely in the future that an Englishman will be robbed in this neighbourhood.

We departed from Riobamba on the 8th of July, intending to take what is termed the Railway Route to Guayaquil; and, mounting the slopes that enclose the basin on the south, arrived at dusk at the village of Nanti (10,669 feet). The next place being a good distance away, we stopped at the highest house or hut, which was occupied by some half-Indians. In the night there were wailings and lamentations, and Campaña came to ask if I would *sell a candle*, as the mother was dying, and there was not a light of any sort to be found in the whole village!

Next morning, five and a half hours of hard going brought us to the village of Guamote, and here we struck the southern continuation of the Moreno (or Quito) Road. At this part, and until we diverged from it in the afternoon of July 10, it was mostly in excellent condition,—a fine, broad highway, more than sufficient for the wants of a thickly-populated district, though passing over bleak, uncultivated moorland (*paramo*), which it would be too complimentary to term a howling wilderness. From Guamote to the end of this day's journey, we neither met nor passed either man or beast, and the natural repulsiveness of the surroundings was heightened by skulls and skeletons lying on each side of the road, of unburied men who had perished in one of the revolutionary combats. At 5 p.m. we came to a large (apparently deserted) Hacienda, called Galti, and a little farther south halted for the night at a hut (11,772 feet) about three hundred feet above the road.

On the 10th, we travelled without seeing a house or person until we caught sight of the village of Alausi on the other side of a deep valley, and then stopped perplexed, not knowing how to get to it, or where to go. A casual man, who turned up at the right moment, said that by breaking away to the west we could make a short cut to the Bridge of Chimbo (the terminus of the Bail way). We followed his advice, and, after many windings through a wild, wooded country, found ourselves at dusk at the commencement of the descent towards the Pacific; plunged down the forest-covered slopes, and at 7 p.m. were brought—to a stand by darkness when about 9000 feet above the sea. Not a soul had been seen since the casual man. All of us went to bed supperless, as the food was nearly exhausted. Off again soon after sunrise, we descended 4400 feet without a break, and then came to a diminutive Hacienda, called Cayandeli, where a solitary man in possession declared there was nothing to eat.

During the last two days, the route had skirted the eastern of the Range of Chimborazo. The slopes which we had now to descend were at its extreme southern end. Since leaving Riobamba, views had been confined either to the immediate surroundings or to a few miles away, and Chimborazo and its allies were invisible. The same, too, was the case with the country on the east. We passed Sangai without seeing it, or any of the mountains in its vicinity. On entering the forest, the range of vision became even more circumscribed by the tortuous bends of the ever-winding track. Sometimes it was ill-marked, overgrown and readily lost. We went astray, and at night on the 11th were still in the jungle, and retired to rest, supperless, on the top of the packing-cases.

The Bridge was a wooden structure, spanning the River just before it turned abruptly to the west. The Railway was hidden away in jungle, and had to be *discovered*. There was no station or train; nor house or hut; nor person or means of procuring information. The right bank of the river formed the Terminus. The line ran up to the edge of the stream, without stops to prevent the train running into the water, and looked as if it had been cut in half by the torrent. The only indication of civilization was a contractor's shed, mounted on wheels. Campaña went down the rails in search of life, and learnt that a train *might* arrive to-day, *or perhaps* it would come *mañana*. We waited in hungry expectation (paying off the arrieros in the meanwhile), and about twelve o'clock *the* train hove in sight, bringing three persons and nothing more.

Shortly before leaving Quito, General Veintemilla spontaneously favoured me with a letter to the Railway authorities, directing them to afford every attention, assistance, etcetera. This letter was shewn to the persons in charge of the train, and they were informed that we were famished, and ready to purchase any food that could be spared. The President's letter bore fruit. The Conductor brought out two small pine-apples, and presented them with many polite phrases,—the pine-apples were mine; he himself and all that he had was mine, and so forth. I tried to *buy*, but he would not hear of it; and, as there was no time to waste, the pine-apples were cut up forthwith into five portions—the donor consuming a share.

The train ran as far as the first station smoothly, and there the engine went off the track. While affairs were being rectified, I sent into the village, and having acquired the materials for a good, square meal, entertained the Conductor as my guest. "Now," thought I, "that pine-apple account is balanced."

At Yaguachi, after again expressing my obligations, I was about to leave, when the Conductor put his hand on my shoulder and stopped me. "The fares!" General Veintemilla's letter was comprehensive, and might have covered anything from special trains downwards, and I remarked that it seemed to imply free transit. "No," was the reply, made with admirable readiness, "it embraces everything *except* that." "How much?" "Three pesos and a half apiece." I paid the amount like a lamb, and was going off, when the Conductor again stopped me. "There is the baggage." "How much?" I paid his charge, but there still seemed to be something on his mind. "Is there anything else?" "Yes, Señor; *your Excellency has forgotten to pay for the pine-apples!*"

We wont by steam-launch from Yaguachi to Guayaquil and there separated,— Campaña returning to Quito *via* Bodegas, and the Carrels going by steamer to Panama. During the next fortnight, I lived principally in the hotel called *The Ninth of October*; where, although in a certain sense solitary, I was never without company. The wonderful exuberance of life chased away drowsiness, and, when sleep came, one's very dreams were tropical. Droves of mice galloped about at night, and swarms of minute ants pervaded everything. The harsh gnawings of voracious rats were subdued by the softer music of the tender mosquito. These, the indigenous inhabitants, were supplemented by a large floating population; and, in all, I collected fifty species of vermin in a single room. A few selections are given in the accompanying plate from 'my bedfellows at Guayaquil.'

73

MARIE ROBINSON WRIGHT, *BOLIVIA: THE CENTRAL HIGHWAY OF SOUTH AMERICA* (PHILADELPHIA: G. BARRIE & SONS, 1907), PP. 203–218

A new era for Bolivia—important public works—railways—telegraph lines

COVERING an area of about seven hundred thousand square miles, and presenting a variety of geographic and geologic conditions unsurpassed by any other country of the globe, the problem of transportation, upon the satisfactory solution of which so much depends in the promotion of national progress in any country, has been one of paramount importance in Bolivian politics ever since the organization of the republic. Large sums have been paid by the government for the improvement of roads, the building of bridges, and the maintenance of communication between the principal cities, but the country's finances have always been taxed to the limit by efforts which proved more or less inadequate to the task, with the result that although the budget continually shows large amounts spent in roadways and bridges, the problem of transportation in Bolivia is only now, for the first time, giving promise of a satisfactory solution. There are, nevertheless, evidences of excellent road building on all the principal highways, especially those connecting the departmental capitals, and in some instances, as along the route from Sucre to Potosí, and in the environs of Cochabamba, massive stone parapets and bridges are seen, which compare favorably with the best examples of work done by expert engineers in this branch of construction in any part of the world. But nearly all the highroads pass through the cañons of the Cordilleras in some part of their course, and during the rainy season, from November to March, a flood frequently rushes down these *quebradas* with such destructive force that every vestige of road building is swept away in a day. For this reason, wagon roads are abandoned during the wet months and all travel in the interior is done on muleback, usually by a route more precipitous than the coach road, but safer because it passes chiefly along the higher ledges, with only an occasional descent into the bed of the cañon. As stated elsewhere, the only railways now in operation are the lines connecting La Paz with Guaqui, on Lake Titicaca, and Oruro with the seaport of Antofagasta, though surveys have been made and the work of construction has commenced on a new railway system, which will completely change industrial and commercial conditions in Bolivia.

The history of railroad building in Bolivia dates from the year 1887, when the government issued a decree calling for proposals for the construction of railways throughout the republic. The following year a proposal was received from the mining company Huanchaca de Bolivia to build a railroad from the Chilean frontier to the city of Oruro, passing by the mining establishment of Huanchaca. The national Congress approved the proposal, with slight modifications, in a decree issued on November 29, 1888. The rights acquired by the company were transferred the next year to the Antofagasta and Bolivia Railway Company, Limited, an English corporation, which now operates the line. This company has a guarantee from the government of six per cent per annum for twenty years on the capital invested in the construction of the line, which guarantee became effective on the delivery of the railway at Oruro on May 15, 1892, amounting to forty-five thousand pounds sterling, though this is only nominal so far as the Bolivian government is concerned, the revenues derived from the line more than covering the guarantee. The railway is five hundred and fifty-five miles long, from Antofagasta to Oruro, and ascends from about twenty feet above sea level at Antofagasta to more than twelve thousand feet, crossing the high plateau from Uyuni to Oruro with little variation from its greatest altitude. It is the longest single line track in the world of such a narrow gauge, only two feet six inches wide, throughout its entire length. The Huanchaca company owns and operates for its exclusive benefit a branch road from Uyuni to Pulacayo and Huanchaca, the centre of its mining industry, nine miles distant. The Bolivian section of the Antofagasta and Oruro railway is under the direction of Mr. Hugh Warren, a railroad manager of large experience and mature judgment. He has his headquarters at Oruro, the present Bolivian terminus of the road. The line will soon be extended to La Paz. Passenger trains leave Oruro every day for Challapata and Uyuni, and three times a week for Antofasgasta. They run at an average speed of twenty-five miles an hour, the entire trip having frequently been made, on a special through train, in twenty-three hours. The roadbed is excellent, and the maximum gradient does not exceed two and ninety-eight one hundredths per cent. The locomotives are of American manufacture, from the Baldwin, the Rodgers, and the Stevenson locomotive works. The passenger cars are modern, well built and extremely comfortable. The scenery along this road is magnificent, and some of the bridges which cross the great ravines are counted among the highest in the world. The construction work of this road was done under the direction of an English engineer of eminent talent, Mr. Josiah Harding, who built one of the greatest incline railways of the world at Junín, Chile, and who is now engaged in studying the route of the proposed Arica and La Paz railway. From Uyuni to La Paz, the traveller seems to be always within close distance of the snow-covered summits of the Andes, which rise above the horizon of the high plain like great white temples overtopping the clouds. As seen from the car window, the mining towns of Poopo and Machacamarca, and others which lie along the route, present a very picturesque appearance. But the beautiful scenery of this road hardly surpasses that of the railway from La Paz to Guaqui, on Lake Titicaca, which has in view the majestic Illimani and Sorata and a whole range of lesser peaks clothed in perpetual snow.

The Guaqui and La Paz railroad was the first constructed by the Bolivian government out of public funds. Its successful inauguration was due to the initiative of ex-President General José Manuel Pando, who, in 1900, authorized an expert Bolivian engineer, Señor Mariano Bustamente y Barreda, to make the necessary studies and plans. When these were finished, they were approved by Congress; and a law was passed in the same year, authorizing the construction of the road and appointing a board of directors to supervise its management. In order to meet the expenses of building, it was provided that all revenues from the alcohol monopoly and from rubber taxes in the department of La Paz should be set aside for three years for this purpose. The line was completed and opened to traffic on October 25, 1903. Its total length is fifty-nine miles, from the port of Guaqui to the Altos, or, more correctly, to El Alto de La Paz, the road ascending from twelve thousand five hundred feet at Guaqui to fourteen thousand feet at Viacha and descending not more than two hundred and fifty feet to El Alto station. The gauge is three and one-third feet wide, and throughout the entire distance the tracks cross what appears to be almost a level plateau, with Lake Titicaca behind and the wonderful white mountain peaks in front glistening in the sun. The total cost of the line, including interest during its construction, amounted to one hundred and seventy thousand nine hundred and eighty-one pounds sterling. On May 31, 1904, a contract was signed by the government with the Peruvian Corporation, Limited, which owns and operates the Southern Railway of Peru from the port of Mollendo to Lake Titicaca, as well as the lake steamers that cross from the Peruvian border to the Bolivian port of Guaqui, the terms of the treaty giving to the Peruvian Corporation control and administration of the railway under a seven years' lease, thereby affording it a through system of transportation from Mollendo to La Paz. The corporation loaned the government fifty thousand pounds sterling at six per cent interest, for the purpose of constructing an electric car line to connect El Alto de La Paz with the city, and in addition to this sum the government recognizes a previous indebtedness of about twenty thousand pounds sterling, all of which will be charged against an amortization fund of forty per cent to be reserved from the revenues of the railway, the corporation retaining sixty per cent of the railway revenues for operating expenses during the term of its lease. If at the end of seven years the total obligation has not been covered by this amortization fund, the government agrees to extend the lease or pay the balance.

The history of this railway during the three years that it has been in operation is one of continued and increasing prosperity. It has been a paying investment from the first, never having yielded less than seven per cent dividends since its inauguration. Statistics furnished by the acting director of public works of Bolivia, Mr. Pierce Hope, under whose management the road was finally completed, show that the receipts for the month of January, 1906, were sixty-four thousand two hundred and eighty bolivianos. The increase in the freight receipts of 1905 was fifty per cent over the year previous. The electric line from El Alto terminal down the incline, or La Bajada, to the city station of Challapampa was completed and opened to traffic on December 1, 1905. It is five miles long, and has the same gauge as the main line from Guaqui, with a grade of six per cent. The locomotives used on the railway and the electric cars for the incline were purchased in the United States. The revenue from traffic over this part of the line for the month of January, 1906, was fourteen thousand four hundred and eighty bolivianos. The trip from Guaqui to the city takes about two hours, and will no doubt be a feature of one of the famous tourist routes of the world some day. Not only does it offer the grandest scenery on the picturesque road from Mollendo to La Paz, one of the most beautiful routes in the world, but it possesses especial interest in the wonderful ruins of Tiahuanaco, which are situated at about an hour's ride from Lake Titicaca. It affords also the novel experience of travelling by rail and steamer above the clouds and of enjoying a trolley ride down La Bajada to one of the most interesting and foreign-looking cities in America, La Paz, standing radiant in the sunlight just below the highest peaks of the Andes.

But though the railways from Antofagasta to Oruro and from Mollendo to La Paz take the tourist through wonderful and varied scenes, a more rapid route is being built in the new railway from Arica to La Paz, which will bring the metropolis of the Altaplanicie within fourteen hours of the coast, instead of three days, the time now required by the most rapid route. Chile has already begun the construction of the Arica and La Paz line in accordance with the recent treaty between the two countries. It will pass through the rich copper region of Corocoro, thus facilitating the shipment of the valuable ores of this district, and will connect with the Guaqui and La Paz road at Viacha. Either Corocoro or Viacha will be the junction of a line which is proposed to connect La Paz with Oruro, in conformity with the arrangements made by the government for the construction of a general railway system. A decree passed by the national Congress on November 13, 1905, shows that the government has determined to carry into immediate effect extensive plans for railway expansion, some of which have been under consideration from time to time during previous administrations, but have never until now been practically developed to the degree necessary for their successful consummation. The decree referred to declares: that the executive is authorized to contract for and execute with all possible simultaneity the construction of the following railways: from Viacha or Corocoro to Oruro, from Oruro to Cochabamba, from Uyuni to Potosí, from Potosí to Tupiza, and the first section of one hundred miles of the line from La Paz to Puerto Pando, at the head of navigation on the Beni branch of the Madeira River, employing for the purpose the funds derived from the indemnity paid by Brazil and the guarantees stipulated in the treaty of peace celebrated with Chile. The executive is equally authorized to carry out any financial operations that may be deemed indispensable, in the event that the funds above named are not sufficient for the construction of the railways indicated, but without compromising more than the said railways in the responsibility of such operations. As soon as the railways above determined are constructed, the following lines will be built: from Oruro to Potosí, from Cochabamba to Chimoré at the headwaters of the Mamoré branch of the Madeira, from Macha or from Potosí to Sucre, and the second section of the railway from La Paz to Puerto Pando. For the construction of the railway from La Paz to Puerto Pando the funds derived from the increased tax on coca will also be employed, as the object of this road is to serve the interests of the coca producing region.

For the construction of the proposed new railways the Bolivian government has already completed negotiations with the well-known firm of New York capitalists, Messrs. Speyer and Company, whereby, in conformity with the decree of Congress, a general system of railways will be built, to connect the principal Bolivian cities with one another, with the chief river ports of the Amazon and the Paraguay, and with such railways of neighboring republics as have a direct seaport terminus. By this practical method the country will be opened up to industrial and commercial development, which could never be hoped for under existing circumstances, as the obstacles to communication presented by the mountainous character of western Bolivia and the unsettled conditions of eastern Bolivia are apparently insurmountable by any other means than the establishment of railway connection. The importance of this enterprise on the part of the government can hardly be estimated. It means practically the launching of Bolivia into the full tide of modern progress, with no turning back to the old ways of muleback travel and other seventeenth-century systems of transportation. When the interior becomes more accessible through a regularly established schedule of trains, which will bring the chief cities within a few hours of one another and within a reasonable distance from the seacoast, the rapid evolution of industrial activity will no doubt see the building up of many large fortunes in the rich mining districts, on the vast cattle plains, and in the farming communities, to say nothing of the inexhaustible possibilities of the rubber country. Foreigners are not slow to appreciate this fact. As soon as it became known that Bolivia intended to spend millions of pounds sterling in the construction of railways, not only railway, mining, and rubber syndicates began to seek larger investments than formerly, but new enterprises, involving the development of cattle raising and other neglected industries, turned in this direction, and the outlook is already growing brighter than it has ever been before in the history of the country.

For more than a year active preliminary work has been in progress throughout the entire route of the proposed system, at first under the direction of an American engineer, Mr. W. L. Sisson, and then under his successor, Mr. W. L. Gibson, who is the present directing engineer of the enterprise. Señor Jorge E. Zalles, as secretary of the Commission of Studies, has made himself master of every detail connected with the work. Surveys have been completed between Viacha and Oruro, one hundred and thirty-eight miles; Oruro and Cochabamba, one hundred and thirty miles; Uyuni and Potosí, one hundred and twenty miles; Potosí and Tupiza, one hundred and fifty miles; Oruro and Potosí, one hundred and ninety-five miles. By an examination of the map it will be seen that, in the extensive system proposed, railway communication will be established, through Bolivian territory, between the Atlantic and Pacific seaboards, and, by means of the great Amazon and La Plata river systems, with the whole vast region of eastern South America. Argentina has been authorized to extend her Central Northern Railway as far as Tupiza; and as soon as Bolivia completes her lines from Tupiza to Potosí, from Potosí to Oruro, from Oruro to Viacha, and from Viacha to Arica, there will be established a trunk line across the continent which will bring the Pacific port of Arica within five days' distance of Buenos Aires. By extending north to Santa Cruz the branch line now under construction from the Argentine Northern Central Railway to the Bolivian border at Yacuiba, and by building another line to Santa Cruz from the Paraguay River at Puerto Suarez, opposite the Brazilian port of Corumbá, over a route which has already been reconnoitred and approved, both lines to be joined and pushed on further to a river port of the Beni, an easy outlet will be gained for the whole of eastern Bolivia, and the flourishing capital of the department of Santa Cruz will quickly develop into the Chicago of what may some day be one of the richest agricultural and cattle-raising countries in the world. Eastern Bolivia presents no such difficult problems of railway construction as the western part of the republic, and the lines projected through this region can be completed at much less cost. When the various South American continental lines are joined to cross Bolivian territory, this country, which has been most difficult of access up to the present time, will become the great central highway for South American traffic, increasing in commercial importance as its own trade with other nations is developed with greater facility.

The formal inauguration of the new railway system took place in Oruro on July 4, 1906, when the supreme government went in a body to Oruro to initiate the work of construction from that point. It was an occasion of general rejoicing, all patriotic Bolivians recognizing the important significance of the ceremony, which was brilliant and imposing. The programme of the day was worthy of so memorable an occasion, being distinguished by impressive solemnity. The ceremonies began with the celebration of the *Te Deum* in the cathedral at nine o'clock. His Grace Archbishop Pifferi officiated, assisted by high dignitaries of the church. The president of the republic, accompanied by his ministers of state and the foreign diplomatic corps, attended the service, at which were present important government authorities from every city of Bolivia. The learned archbishop of La Plata, in pronouncing a benediction upon the great work, alluded in gracious terms to "the coöperation of the generous inhabitants of North America" in the new enterprise, and paid a high tribute to the progressive spirit manifested by President Montes and his ministers, to whom its successful inauguration was due, praying that the earthly blessings to be derived from its material benefits "may serve as a motive and stimulus to elevate the thoughts to the incomparable, unlimited, and eternal riches of the Kingdom of Heaven." After the benediction, President Montes received at the hands of Señor Francisco Lopez Chavez, the Bolivian representative of the construction company, a handsome silver shovel, which was presented to his excellency with an appropriate address. In a firm voice, which thrilled the vast audience by its magnetic eloquence, President Montes made the address of inauguration, which was characterized throughout by sentiments of practical patriotism, expressed in such sentences as: "The greatness and strength of nations is not proved by declaiming ideals and aspirations which they have neither the knowledge nor the energy to realize, but by the degree of effective force which is exercised in a practical way in the civilization and exaltation of mankind." In closing, his excellency applied to the present act the famous prophecy of Pedro Domingo Murillo, with a slight variation: "The initial step made to-day toward the resurrection of Bolivia shall never be detained." The Act of Inauguration was signed with a gold pen, presented to the president by Dr. Isaac Aranibar, ex-prefect of Cochabamba, in the name of "La Patria." The president turned the first shovelful of earth with the significant words: *Que el arma del caudillaje sea reemplazada con el arma del trabajo*—"May the arms of war be replaced by the arms of labor." At the official banquet which closed the programme of the day, the American minister, Hon. Wm. B. Sorsby, in an eloquent response to a toast in honor of his country's anniversary, referred to "the singularly appropriate coincidence that Bolivia should solemnize the inauguration of her industrial independence on the same day as that which commemorates the political and industrial independence of the first American republic." It was, indeed, peculiarly fitting that a date which is celebrated the world over as the anniversary of the first Declaration of Independence in the New World should have been chosen to commemorate an event which sets the seal of commercial freedom upon a country that has struggled for nearly a century against the oppression of limited trade facilities. The Fourth of July will henceforth signify to the Bolivian patriot the inauguration of a new era in the life of his country, an era not less glorious in its history than that which was established in the land of his North American cousin on July 4, 1776. For political independence can do little toward bringing about national greatness without its practical counterpart, commercial independence; and national liberty finds its highest development in the friendly intercourse of countries bound together by ties of mutual interest. It commemorates the victory of a patriotic people determined to reap the full reward of national independence; and it marks the last struggle against conditions that belong to centuries gone by, and which have been forever overcome by the spirit of modern enterprise.

Until the new railway system is completed and put in operation, Bolivia will continue to depend upon the present means of transportation, which, with the exception of the two railways previously mentioned, is altogether by wagons, muleback, or river navigation. The Cordillera Real, or Royal range, of the Andes has always proved an effective barrier to easy communication between the Bolivian plateau and the great eastern plains, with their wealth of natural production awaiting development, and the few mountain passes through which wagon roads and bridle paths have been opened represent herculean efforts to overcome natural conditions with limited resources at command. Public highways are either national or municipal property, the former being built and maintained by the government from appropriations granted by Congress, while the latter are made and controlled by the municipalities. The national highroads connect the principal cities and mining centres of the republic. With the exception of the main roads, which unite the department capitals, and are used for passenger as well as freight service, these highways chiefly abound in the higher sections of the Andean range, where the valuable mining properties are located, and they are nearly all narrow, precipitous, winding paths, which have been built up by Indian labor and are maintained at great cost. Along these trails the most valuable freight is taken on the backs of mules, donkeys, and llamas, without danger even to the most costly and delicate ware, so careful are the Indians of their charge. Exquisite French mirrors, rare bric-à-brac, and the finest crystal and porcelains for the palatial administration houses, are carried across a country which is everywhere broken by ravines, and over a pathway often covered by an avalanche of rocks from the mountain sides after a heavy rain, yet a long month's journey will be concluded without the record of a single breakage, so marvellous is the Indian's skill in this humble task. The government provides *postas*, or sheltered places, at intervals of from eight to fifteen leagues, where travellers may rest and purchase forage for their animals. The *posta* is in charge of a government employé, who is paid a reasonable salary to take care of the place, to keep forage on hand for sale, and animals for hire, as well as to provide bed and meals at a fair price, and a *postillón* if required as guide. No charge is made for the use of this shelter. It is the custom of well-to-do travellers in this country to carry their own beds and provisions, except on the coach roads. Mules can be hired from *posta* to *posta* at twenty centavos, about nine cents in gold, for each mule per league, and ten centavos per league for the *postillón* who accompanies them. The house in which shelter is provided is usually a low solid structure of adobe, built around a courtyard, or *patio*, and having from five to ten or more rooms, each with a door opening on the courtyard and banks of adobe built out from the wall, to serve as beds. It has no windows. Along the coach roads the houses of the *postas* are more like hotels, and the traveller may journey without carrying either food or provisions, as both are furnished at the various stopping places. The coach roads are open to traffic only during the winter months, as in the rainy season it is impossible to keep them repaired without even greater expense than it costs to build a railroad, and with more uncertain results. The most important coach roads are: from La Paz to Oruro, one hundred and sixty-five miles; from La Paz to Corocoro, seventy miles; from La Paz north to Achacachi, sixty-six miles; from Oruro to Cochabamba, one hundred and forty miles; from Challapata, on the Antofagasta Railway, to Sucre, two hundred miles; from Sucre to Potosí, one hundred miles; and from Uyuni to Potosí, one hundred and ten miles. There are excellent bridle paths, or, as they are called, *caminos de herradura*, from Cochabamba to Sucre, three hundred miles; from Potosí to Tarija two hundred and forty miles, to Tupiza one hundred and eighty miles, and to Challapata one hundred and twenty miles; from Cochabamba to Santa Cruz, three hundred and eighty miles; and from La Paz to the various towns of the Yungas. As the statements vary regarding distances, according to the humor and endurance of the traveller, and the exact measurement has only been made in a few instances, it is impossible to do more than give an approximately correct idea of the locality of the more important cities as regards their distance from one another.

Travel in eastern and northeastern Bolivia is best undertaken at the season of the year when the waterways are navigable, as nearly all routes connecting with the towns of the Beni and Santa Cruz necessitate navigation through a great part of the distance. On the western plateau the traveller arranges his journey for the winter months, to avoid the rainy season, but in eastern Bolivia the summer months are most desirable for the trip because then the rivers are high, and navigation is an easy problem, whereas in winter the delays are sometimes very tedious on account of there being little or no water in the upper streams of the great river systems. All the branches of the Amazon River are navigable, some of them, as the Acre, Purús, Madre de Dios, Beni, Mamoré, and Guaporé, admitting steam launches and other vessels of from five to six feet draft. In the southeast, the Paraguay and the Pilcomayo Rivers are navigable for vessels of two hundred tons. Lake Titicaca and Lake Poopo, on the Altaplanicie, are both navigable. Lake Titicaca carries steamers of heavy tonnage, but Lake Poopo, and the Desaguadero River, which connects it with Lake Titicaca, are navigable only for lighter vessels. The Desaguadero River, which is one hundred and eighty miles long, is navigable for steamers of five hundred tons over part of its length, and carries good-sized vessels from Lake Titicaca to Lake Poopo. Communication is better established, both by land and water, in this part of Bolivia than in any other section.

Closely connected with the various systems of transportation are the telegraph lines of the country, which constitute an important feature of intercommunication by serving as the means of determining the condition of roads in various sections, thus making it possible to keep them in repair and to promote the interests of traffic generally. The director-general of telegraphs, Senor Don Carlos Torrico, has made a careful study of the telegraph system, and several reforms have been inaugurated under his administration. Señor Torrico has served his government in many important capacities, having been Prefect of Potosí prior to accepting his present office. Under his able direction the telegraph system has not only been improved, but important new lines have been put in operation with perfect satisfaction. The system now covers an extent of three thousand miles, of which eight hundred miles are under private ownership, and the annual receipts have increased from eighty-three thousand bolivianos in 1904 to one hundred thousand bolivianos in 190Ç, with an equal average, about one hundred and fifty thousand each, of despatches sent and received from the various offices of the republic. These offices are established in all the chief cities and along the principal highways, a long-distance telephone system operating in connection with the telegraph; so that more remote towns have communication with the main line. An appropriation has been asked of Congress for the sum of one hundred and forty-four thousand bolivianos, with which to reorganize and repair the entire system and to place it on a more efficient basis. The international telegraph service has been recently improved by the extension of a line from Uyuni to Ollagüe, in Chile, and by the reconstruction of the existing line between Tupiza and La Quiaca, in Argentina.

Communication with Peru is established by a telegraph line through Guaqui, controlled by the Peruvian Corporation. Connection with Europe is made by way of Argentina, and with the Pacific and North American ports through Guaqui or by Ollagüe and Antofagasta.

A new era has dawned for Bolivia. It comes in answer to the abounding faith and unfailing confidence of Bolivians in the possibilities of their country and in their persistent determination and indefatigable efforts to overcome all obstacles in its development. To the world at large, ignorant of the real conditions which have combined to militate against progress and prosperity in this country of unlimited natural wealth, the retarded growth in industrial and commercial importance which statistics seem to prove can hardly be fairly considered. It is necessary to gain accurate knowledge by a visit to the country and a study from actual observation, as well as from information to be secured only in the country itself.

Bolivia is not so far away, either from Europe or North America, as many people imagine. A very pleasant trip may be arranged to Bolivia, starting from European ports or from New York, on one of the commodious steamers of the Royal Mail Steam Packet Company or the Hamburg-American Line, and direct from New York by a steamer of the Panamá Railroad Steamship Company, all of which make the trip in six days to Colon. The rapid increase in the earnings of these lines to the Isthmus of Panamá shows the growth of interest in this part of the world, and a tendency of travel to turn elsewhere than to Europe and Japan, as formerly, especially in the case of tourist trade. According to the latest report which the board of directors of the Panamá Railroad Company made to the Isthmian Commission,—the United States government now being sole owner of the capital stock of the company,—this route is rapidly becoming an important ocean highway between North and South America, destined to increase the social as well as political relations between countries hitherto more widely separated than those of any other continents. The balmy climate of the southern waters makes a trip from New York to Panamá an additional pleasure, and every year marks an increase of travel over this popular route.

After a six days' trip, including many charming features, the traveller may spend a few days in Colón and Panamá, enjoying their tropical scenes and the atmosphere of industrial activity which has become so marked since the inauguration of the canal construction, or he may proceed at once southward on one of the steamers of the Pacific Steam Navigation Company, or of the South American Steamship Company, both of which lines have comfortable and well-appointed steamers, from Panamá to Guayaquil, Callao, Mollendo, Arica, Iquique, Antofagasta, Coquimbo, Valparaiso, and other South American ports. The Pacific Steam Navigation Company has its head offices in London, with its chief South American office in Valparaiso, under the direction of Mr. J. W. Pearson, who has made the company's line to Panamá as commodious and desirable a means of travel as an ocean voyage can be under the most favorable conditions. Even nervous passengers find little to disturb the pleasure of a trip from Panamá to the South American ports as far as Valparaiso, for the sea is nearly always as smooth as glass and the weather superb. From four to five days are required to make the voyage from Panamá to Guayaquil, and the same time is taken from Guayaquil to Callao, the port of Lima, Peru, as many stops are made along the route, though direct, fast steamers could easily make the trip from Panamá to Callao in four or five days. From Callao to Mollendo requires from three to four days, according to the delays in intermediate ports. To the traveller making his first trip along this route it is particularly interesting to watch the loading and unloading of fruits and other products of this tropical region. Everything is brought out to the steamer in *lanchas*, or lighters, and sometimes the harbor swarms with purveyors of merchandise. Disembarking at Mollendo to go to Bolivia by what constitutes the shortest route, at least until the Arica and La Paz Railway is completed, the traveller is conveyed by train over the Peruvian Southern Railway to Arequipa, a charming old city situated at the base of the famous volcano Misti, where the University of Harvard has a meteorological observatory. Everyone spends a day or two in Arequipa before proceeding to Puno, the terminus of the road, on the Peruvian border of Lake Titicaca. The director of the company, Mr. George Clarke, has spared no effort to improve the railway facilities of this line and to provide every possible comfort for those who take the trip. People having cardiac troubles may suffer a disagreeable experience for a short time while crossing the greatest altitude, nearly fifteen thousand feet above sea level. But the recompense is great, the scenery being imposing in grandeur. From Puno a steamer transfers passengers to Guaqui on the Bolivian side of Lake Titicaca, and the trip, whether made at night or in the daytime is, under favorable circumstances, the most charming experience imaginable. The new steamers, appropriately named the *Inca* and *Coya* are of five hundred or more tons, the older ships, of which the *Yavary* is one of the best, being much smaller. Sometimes the lake is rough, and no sea is more irritating to those who suffer from *mal de mer* than this beautiful lake when the surface loses its mirror-like calm. The rough seas of the English Channel, the Bay of Biscay, and the Caribbean do not disturb one's comfort half so much as the staccato movement of this mysterious body of water, which seems to be unsettled as often from subterranean as from atmospheric causes. If the steamer makes a day trip the passengers land at Guaqui at about nine o'clock in the evening, and if a night trip, a little later than that hour in the morning. The remainder of the journey, as elsewhere described, takes one to the city of La Paz, from which various interesting journeys may be made to the other cities.

If preferred, the traveller wishing to visit Bolivia need not go ashore at Mollendo, but, continuing down the Pacific coast as far as Antofagasta, may take a train from that port to Oruro, finishing the journey to La Paz by diligence, or may choose one of the numerous routes by diligence or muleback leading from Oruro, Challapata, and Uyuni, the principal stations of the railway, to the interior cities of Cochabamba, Sucre, and Potosí. A delightful trip, which includes visits to all the South American countries, may be made by the Pacific Steam Navigation Company's line from Liverpool, which has a fortnightly service between Liverpool and Valparaiso, with connecting steamers from Valparaiso up the west coast to Panamá. All these steamers are elegantly fitted up for the passenger service, and carry a band of musicians for the entertainment of those on board. They are large twin-screw steamers, four of the transatlantic line being of ten thousand five hundred tons, while those of the Pacific coast service are of six thousand tons. The steamers from Liverpool call at Brazilian, Uruguayan, and Argentine ports on their way to Valparaiso. At least a dozen different steamship lines connect Europe and North America with South American ports, the Royal Mail Steam Packet Company and the Hamburg-American Line having handsomely appointed ships to Brazil and Argentina; while the Lamport and Holt steamers from New York to Brazil and Argentina are commodious, and the service provided on board is constantly improving in character. All these lines permit of the passengers making connections at Buenos Aires to continue the trip to Bolivia, either by railway over the Argentine Northern Central to Tupiza, and thence to Potosí on muleback, a novel treat in these days of universal rapid transit, or from Buenos Aires across the Andes, also by railway, to Valparaiso and thence to Antofagasta and Oruro; it is possible to take an all sea route, by the Pacific Steam Navigation Company's line from Buenos Aires through the Straits of Magellan as far as Antofagasta, or Mollendo. By whatever itinerary, the journey is worth while, and aside from the novel features it presents, it is sure to prove more restful than the average summer outing to popular European resorts. As a means of escaping the vigorous northern winters it is as desirable as for a relief from the excessive heat of the summers, the South American winter corresponding to our summer, which makes the trip a particularly pleasant change, especially in Bolivia where the winters are comparatively mild. The best seasons in which to visit Bolivia are spring and autumn, when the weather is modified from the extremes of either winter cold or summer heat.

74

SANTIAGO PÉREZ TRIANA, *DOWN THE ORINOCO IN A CANOE* (NEW YORK: CROWELL, 1902), PP. 240–248

The Apure is 695 miles long, of which 564 are navigable. The Apure in its turn receives numerous tributaries, some of which are navigable for short distances.

The Arauca, the Meta and the Guaviare, are also navigable.

The Casiquiare Canal unites the upper Orinoco with the Rio Negro branch of the Amazon. It is about 300 miles long, with an average depth of 30 feet, and has a strong current in the direction of the Negro. The list of affluents of the Orinoco and of its tributaries would be a very long one, and would serve no useful purpose here.

Evidently the Orinoco and the Orinoco system, with their innumerable ramifications in all directions, form a basis for the easy exploitation of the vast sources of natural wealth which exist in the immense territory through which their waters flow.

That territory lies within the borders of the Republics of Colombia and Venezuela. Up to the present neither nation has seriously attempted to utilize the valuable elements so bountifully offered by Nature. In the matter of navigation, ocean-going steamers sail frequently as far as Ciudad Bolivar. From this latter point river steamers ply once or twice a month up the Orinoco, turning into the Apure as far as San Fernando de Apure, and during the tonga-bean harvest follow the course of the main river generally as far as the Caura, where the harvesters established their central camps a good many years ago. An effort was made to establish navigation on the Orinoco and its affluents above the rapids, and also to run small steamers in the navigable part between the Atures and Maipures rapids; but the French company, which held a charter practically placing the whole region at its disposal, failed of its object, after spending a considerable amount of money. During our journey, in several places we could see, rotting in the sun, the remnants of broken-down steamers, which appeared uncanny objects in those surroundings. The rapids, acting as a barrier, have deterred traders and explorers. The upper part of the Orinoco is the most abundant in natural wealth. As I have had occasion to note in these pages, india-rubber, *piazaba*, tonga bean, resinous and medicinal plants, are found in practically unlimited quantities along the shores of all the rivers above the rapids, and the small proportion which is gathered is generally shipped through the Rio Negro by way of the Amazon, as traders prefer that long and tedious journey to the difficulties of the Orinoco Rapids.

Yet to give life to the Orinoco, to establish a stream of natural products down its waters, and to facilitate the opening of the forests and mountains beyond the rapids, it would not be necessary to carry out work of a very stupendous nature, beyond the resources of the peoples and the nations most interested in the work. A cursory glance at the elements of the problem reveals the possibility of carrying out a plan, the general outlines of which might be the following:

A line of steamers should be established plying at least twice a month between Ciudad Bolivar and the highest accessible point for navigation below the Atures Rapids.

The old road along the rapids, which extended from that highest point of navigation to beyond Maipures where the river is again free and open, should be reconstructed. A railway could be built along either shore, the ground being mostly level and hard. It would not be necessary to undertake great engineering works, and the road-bed itself would require neither deep cuttings nor terracing, nor expensive culverts and works of drainage, and the few bridges required, being of short span, would not run into high figures.

Steam navigation should also be established beyond the rapids on the rivers forming the upper basin. This could be done at first by means of small steam-launches such as are used in the affluents of the Amazon River, but the service should be carried out faithfully and periodically, even though at first freight and passengers were lacking. People in Spanish America are generally very sceptical as to these enterprises, but once a feeling of confidence was created, explorers would flock both from Colombia and from Venezuela, as they would know that they would have an outlet for whatever products they might gather.

The Indians on the Vichada, and even those on the Meta, would supply abundant labour, and the exports of natural products would soon furnish all the freight that might be desired to make the whole arrangement of steamers above and below the rapids, and the railway along the same, a paying concern.

A line of steamers should also follow the course of the Meta River as far as La Cruz, a port situated about ninety miles from Bogotá, thus tapping the import and export trade of the most thickly-populated region of Colombia, the inhabitants of which in the three provinces of Santander, Boyacá, and Cundinamarca, are over 1,500,000 in number.

Supposing four steamers to be needed for navigation on the lower river and on the Meta, to be bought at Ciudad Bolivar at a cost of £10,000 each, £40,000 would be required under this head. Taking the length of the railway at 60 kilometres, including the bridges, at a cost of £2,000 per kilometre, £120,000 would be required for the railway; and supposing that ten small steam-launches of twenty to thirty tons burden were started for the rivers on the upper basin, £20,000 would be required—in all, £180,000 for the whole undertaking.

The preceding figures are not imaginative, and might, perhaps, be reduced in actual practice. If it has been possible to raise the capital required for the construction of a railway of upwards of 200 kilometres in length along the shores of the Congo, where climate, distance, and natives combine to establish far more serious obstacles than exist on the Orinoco, should it not be possible to find the capital for the establishment of modern means of transportation in a region which offers far brighter and surer prospects than the Congo? Let it be remembered that from Colombia and from Venezuela civilized white, coloured and Indian labour could be found in abundance, and that Europeans engaged in the undertaking, and provided with steamers, could in two days, if on the Meta, reach the high and healthy plateaus of Bogotá and find themselves in a civilized community where they would lack none of the luxuries or comforts of their own land; and that in the Lower Orinoco they would have Ciudad Bolivar, to which the same remarks, barring the advantage of climate, may be applied. The two Governments of Colombia and Venezuela, equally interested in the development of the Orinoco basin, might unite their efforts and guarantee in a form satisfactory to European capitalists the paltry yearly amount required to pay the service of interest and sinking fund on the £180,000. Taking the interest at 6, with a sinking fund of 1 per cent., £12,600 yearly would be required—that is to say, £6,300 for each Government. I know that at the present moment such a task would be well-nigh impossible, but I also know that if a sincere effort were made, notwithstanding the universal feeling of distrust, it would be possible to create securities specially applicable to this purpose, which would satisfy the most exacting capitalist.

In the midst of the daily turmoil and agitation and sanguinary struggle which constitutes the life of those democracies, these problems, urgent and vital as they are, pass unheeded; and the more the pity, for in their solution lies the basis of a permanent peace. Prosperity begets abhorrence of internal revolutions. The development of Mexico is a case in point, from which Colombia and Venezuela might take heed. Woe to them if they do not! The world begins to sicken at the very mention of the constant strife which converts into a positive hell those regions where Nature has shown herself prodigal beyond measure in all her gifts. Not only the valley of the Orinoco, with its boundless prairies, its dense forests, and its innumerable affluents, but the uplands of the Andine regions and the plains extending in Venezuela towards the North Atlantic or Caribbean Sea, and in Colombia to the Pacific Ocean, are coveted by nations where humanity is overcrowded by races which would fain establish colonies in those regions. The development of humanity cannot be stayed; the human wave, even as the stream of water contained by a dyke, will sooner or later break through the walls that imprison it and flood the surrounding country. It were well for men animated by real patriotism in Colombia and in Venezuela to ponder over these possibilities, so that the two nations might themselves open the flood-gates for immigration without delay, so that the new-comers would prove a fresh source of strength and power, helping to build up on the basis of the now existing nations free and mighty commonwealths, rather than as conquerors, who (whether they come from the North as wolves in sheep's clothing under cover of the Monroe doctrine, or from across the ocean, driven by necessity stronger than all political conventionality) would come as masters.

Now is our accepted time. The moments are counted during which the danger may be averted and the inevitable turned to account; but, alas! feuds and errors deep-rooted in medieval soil, luxuriant in this our twentieth century, darken the minds of men, influence their judgment, turn away their activity from the real aims that would lead their nations to greatness, and force them into barbarous struggles which the world regards with amazement and brands as crimes against mankind.

75

HENRY R. BLANEY, *THE GOLDEN CARIBBEAN: A WINTER VISIT TO THE REPUBLICS OF COLOMBIA, SPANISH HONDURAS, BELIZE, AND THE SPANISH MAIN VIA BOSTON AND NEW ORLEANS* (BOSTON: LEE AND SHEPARD, 1900), PP. 4–12

Upon leaving Kingston, Jamaica, the steamer heads south, crossing the Caribbean Sea, the cool northeast trade winds pouring across the decks in an ever increasing deluge, the intense blue of this protected sea sparkling and seething under a tropical sun. The farther one goes south upon the Caribbean the more tender becomes the lovely sunset sky; effects of color are noticed which one never sees elsewhere; the vessel heels to the breeze and cleaves with a regular motion the broad expanse of sea. The thermometer marks an easy 80°, and we lounge about in a dreamy ecstasy, getting acclimated with rapidity. After two days, a part of the Andean mountain system raise their majestic heads above the horizon, and the long pier at Sabanilla comes into sight, as the picturesque shore of South America lies before us. The Andean plateau, the main axis of the continent, extends along the entire western coast; it supports parallel ranges, which constitute the Andean system. The high peaks of one of these parallel ranges can be seen at sunrise from Sabanilla, the tops covered with snow; but one has to look for them before sunrise, as the mountains disappear under the direct rays of the sun.

Travellers land at the Great Pier (four thousand feet long), at the station Puerto Colombia, in Sabanilla Bay. The steamer stops here usually thirty-six hours or more, giving the tourist or business man time to take the Barran quilla Railway and visit the interesting town of Barranquilla, eighteen miles from the sea. The time taken in reaching the town by the railroad is one hour and fifteen minutes; fare, $4.05 (first class) Colombian currency; the money exchange usually standing at about $5.00 paper for $1.00 gold. Return tickets (good for two days), $4.80 paper. Only hand-bags will be allowed to pass with first-class passengers at time of disembarking.

Barranquilla covers a large area of territory, and has a population of forty thousand. It is a very healthful town, the thermometer ranging from 85° to 95°

normally; the lowest mark noticed was about 72°. The water supply is from the Magdalena River, and when filtered is excellent, and newcomers can drink it with safety. There are several good hotels in Barranquilla; prices range from $4.00, paper, to $6.00 per day.

Barranquilla has three Catholic churches and a Protestant chapel under the Presbyterian Board of Missions. The steamship lines whose steamers touch at Sabanilla are the United Fruit Company, Royal Mail, French Line, Hamburg Line, Atlas Line, and others. Sabanilla is left behind during the night; we proceed to Cartagena through pitchy darkness and a gloom of thunder-storm; the steamer plunges forward into a sable curtain, as lightning flashes vividly and torrents of tropical rain are driven across the deck by the northeast trades. The *Boca Chica* at sunrise! The narrow and deep entrance of the harbor of Cartagena is very interesting and absorbing in its characteristic charm and novelty, for the steamer makes a complete circle on its course from Sabanilla before it reaches the wharf. To the left, one sees a low-lying, green, white-edged shore, sparsely settled; and in a retired cove, cut off from all contact with humanity, a leper settlement of about twenty houses lies forgotten beneath the palms, and lines the white winding thread of beach with its wretched hovels. Ahead rises the hill of *La Popa* with its white-walled convent on the extreme end, forming a landmark seen for miles at sea, and covered with a luxuriant tropical vegetation.

The city of Cartagena, reflected in the clear waters of the harbor, is seen (from the deck of the teamer as it reaches the wharf) spread out along the shore, a city full of color, with its red tiled roofs and multi-tinted balconies glowing in the beams of the rising sun.

CARTAGENA is more Spanish than Spain itself. The quaint and rich architecture of the earliest period is here held in suspension, as a fly in amber. Whole streets blaze in tropical colors of blue, pink, and yellow; rare and curious balconies clog the sky line as one passes from square to square, the carving rather of a rough and cumbrous order, rarely, if ever, delicate.

Certain streets, however, remind one of Malaga, others of Algiers or Tunis. The old city sleeps under a moist and torrid climate, slowly decaying, the energy of its citizens being expended in seeking the nearest refreshment saloon, and excitedly discussing the latest news of the money exchange. The experienced traveller, in sympathy with tropical conditions, lands in Cartagena eager for the renewal of old associations and sensations acquired in other countries about the equator, and they rush upon him with a vengeance. Every sensation is accentuated and enlarged abnormally; the street cries are tropically Spanish, negro, and Indian; razorback pigs squeal on every corner; though the streets are badly paved, yet there are no bad smells, the copious rains that wash the streets at regular intervals are antiseptic, and the city is healthful for a foreigner of any nation. The citizens are civil and courteous, English being spoken on every hand, and the American and Englishman is welcomed with open arms, especially if the rate of exchange is advancing!

From the wharf of the Cartagena Terminal and Improvement Company Ld. (where the steamer lands the traveller) it is only a short ride of five minutes by rail to the city, the Cartagena-Magdalena Railway continuing for sixty-five miles to Calamar on the Magdalena River, both railway and terminal wharf being under the same Boston ownership and efficient management. An easy entrance to the country, through the custom-house, assisted by courteous employees, a mad ride through the multi-colored streets to the American Hotel, and then quiet and rest in the cool and spacious rooms and corridors, which the Spaniard, inured to tropical conditions, knows how to rear so well. The weather conditions to an unacclimatized Northerner are rather trying at first, though the humid heat is steady and regular—something that one can count on from day to day; then the evenings are delicious, and the early morning a revelation for freshness.

The northeast trade winds blow regularly every day from ten o'clock until midnight, tempering the heat and making Cartagena a paradise for invalids. One of the most interesting and enjoyable jaunts out of Cartagena is the railroad journey of about four hours on the Cartagena-Magdalena Railway. The cars are comfortable, and the conductors, who speak English, arrange everything for the comfort of the passengers. The train glides smoothly along through the suburbs of Cartagena, mounting rapidly toward the higher hills surrounding the city; from these terraces, several hundred feet above the sea level, occasional glimpses are seen of Cartagena, glistening in the sun, the yellow walls of the fortifications lying mellow against the deep blue sea. The vegetation along the track, wet with dew, sparkles in the early morning sunlight. At Santa Isabel (the first station on the road) broad savannas, affording fine grazing fields for sleek cattle, spread out and melt into blue haze in the distance.

The railroad company own a large plantation here, and maintain fine water rights, which serve to supply Cartagena with water; huge iron tanks, mounted on railway trucks, transport the water on the railway daily to the city. Calamar (the terminal of the railway on the Magdalena River) is a small town with very wide streets, the houses of one story and built of adobe. Travellers will find a small hotel in Calamar, managed by a Frenchman, where breakfast may be obtained. There is time enough after breakfast to walk about the town and inspect the Magdalena River, also the handsome steamers, of the Compania Fluvial de Cartagena, before taking the return train to Cartagena. The hotel gives a fair Spanish breakfast, and as an extra a good bottle of French claret. The brown flood of the noble Magdalena River rushes by Calamar to the sea, spreading out to over half a mile in width opposite the wharf. The banks are low, resembling the shores of the Mississippi River below New Orleans. On the return trip to the "Most noble and most loyal city," one notices at Turbaco how cool and fresh the air becomes. Turbaco is quite a health resort for the inhabitants of Cartagena; many business men own summer houses, and arrange to have their families live there during a portion of the year.

A carriage ride to *La Popa*, or a walk along the enormous walls (which surround Cartagena) in the cool of the evening, will give one a good idea of the city. Sea bathing is very enjoyable on the northern shore below the city wall, where a bathhouse, or shed, has been erected for the protection of bathers. It is perfectly safe to bathe here, and one should make it a point to visit the beach once a day to keep down the temperature of the body.

There is something about Cartagena which causes one to depart reluctantly; for after you have been at the hotel for a few days an acquaintance is made with the other guests, who keep you informed as to the news and local gossip of the town. In two rows of rocking-chairs, facing each other in the wide entrance door leading to the patio, the guests of the hotel and their visiting friends sit by the hour in the evening, smoking and chatting, and one studies them with interest. There is the slim and dapper book-keeper of a local German commission house, who speaks English, Spanish, German, Russian, and Dutch; a travelling man who engages in the risky business of selling dynamite throughout Colombia, and who rejoices in the unique name of Apple; a department manager of a certain railroad occasionally puts in his appearance and attempts to sell broken-down boilers at high prices to exasperated chums; the dynamite salesman declaims with fervor about backwoods travel to an admiring audience; little black boys of the town dodge about the door of the hotel and beg for coin, and, when ignored, claim an easy-looking bachelor as "Papa," amid quizzing remarks from friends of the victim.

They are interesting men to meet,—these fun-loving and genial members of the local foreign colony,—and in after years we will recall with enjoyment the many pleasant moments passed in their society.

76

HAMILTON MERCER WRIGHT, *A TRAVELER IN NORTHERN COLOMBIA* (WASHINGTON, D. C.: GOVERNMENT PRINTING OFFICE, 1918), PP. 6, 8, 10, 12, 14

A traveler in northern Colombia

As cities go in the Western Hemisphere, Cartagena is ancient. It was founded by Don Pedro de Heredia, in 1533, 243 years before the United States of America signed its Declaration of Independence. Philip II, history records, commanded that the city be made impregnable to assault and vast sums were expended upon its fortifications. Soon it became a repository of the treasure collected throughout the Andes and Central America to await shipment to Spain in proud galleons convoyed thither by heavily armed frigates. It was a lure to freebooters. In 1585 Cartagena was sacked by Sir Francis Drake who, under threat of firing the city, extorted a heavy ransom. It resisted an assault by combined British land and sea forces in 1741. It was captured, however, by the Spanish, during the War of Independence in 1815. But it was retaken by the patriots in 1821.

To-day Cartagena is, emphatically, a city of the present. Trading schooners, steam launches, and long, narrow craft with picturesque lateen sails, crowd the magnificent yacht harbor outside the city walls. Just beyond the fine escarpment rising from the water the beautiful plaza or prado, a park and boulevard combined, ornamented by many commanding sculptures, is at all times crowded by vehicles and motor cars. The market place next to the prado and separated from the city by the yacht harbor is a hive of industry. Through the mighty arched gates of the walled city, and across the prado, run crowded automobile busses to the newer suburbs near the base of La Popa. A contrast between ancient and modern is given by the steel freight cars lying on tracks close to the massive walls built more than three centuries ago.

The scenes inside the city walls abound in interest for the lover of the beautiful and quaint. Cartagena has no rival in its architecture, to my mind, among any of the old Spanish cities I have known in Latin-America or the Orient. It has splendid examples of the ecclesiastical architecture of the Spanish renaissance, tinged with the picturesque Mooresque blendings that bespeak the influence of the Crescent in Spanish architecture. The close block grouping of the buildings gives the city the appearance of singular massiveness and solidarity. The imposing cathedral and monastery, the fine churches, the densely shaded parks with their statues and tropical shrubbery, the streets with their overhanging balustrades, and the shops displaying the finest wares of North American, European, and local manufacture are worth a visit of many days. Nor must one forget the university, for Cartagena has long been recognized as a seat of learning. Indeed, the city is held to rank as an educational center second only to Bogotá, the capital. It is not out of place to observe here that Columbia has long been celebrated for her academies, universities, and scientific schools, as well as for her literary achievements, the writings of her novelists, poets, historians, naturalists, and travelers.

Cartagena itself rises almost from the water with the curling waves of the Caribbean Sea upon one side and the inner harbor upon the other, the harbor and ocean almost meeting at the railroad embankment that extends from the pier. The depot of the modem railway which runs to Calamar, about 60 miles distant upon the Magdalena River, is just outside the three arched gateways that give entrance to the city. In the old days bells were rung each night at 8.30 o'clock to summon the inhabitants within the walls and the gates were closed at 9. Although the gates are never closed now, Cartagena still keeps up the quaint custom, a modern factory whistle replacing the bells of old. Through the gates are said to have passed billions of wealth representing the treasure mined for centuries up and down the Andes. Colombia alone has produced more than $700,000,000 in gold since the coming of the Spanish, the production now ranging between five and six million dollars annually.

The Magdalena River is the great artery of Colombian commerce. It is a majestic stream suggesting the Mississippi. Fine steel river boats, electrically lighted, run up and down the river between Bar-ranquilla and La Dorado, 600 miles up, connecting with Cartagena at Calamar. At La Dorado passengers take the train around the rapids to Beltran, thence by train to Girardot, an important coffee district, whence the train is finally boarded for the capital, Bogota, 8,300 feet above sea level. The trip on the Magdalena River is one of the famed journeys of the world. There are two large competing fleets of river steamers and a number of smaller craft running out of Barranquilla, which is at the delta of the Magdalena River and about 10 or 12 miles from the Caribbean Sea.

The delta abounds in strange sights. The giant river, which has a shallow bar across its mouth, prohibiting the entrance of large steamers, separates into innumerable channels seeking exit to the sea. I once took the picturesque 75-mile delta trip between Cienega on the Santa Marta Railway and Barranquilla, traveling through the inlets that seem like narrow canals and are bordered on either side by dense forests or by occasional clearings where woodcutters are engaged chopping cordwood for the distant city factories. The delta channels serve as feeders for Barranquilla traffic. Through them are transported the products of the land. Modern steel dredgers keep the principal channels cleared for travel. Much of the country that is not periodically inundated or densely forested is rich in agriculture.

Fish are abundant both along the seacost and in the inland streams and estuaries. At Santa Marta the fishermen catch very fine sea mullet, bass, and other large edible fish. Fishing is a very considerable industry. In the inland lakes and estuaries, in addition to the fishermen with their nets, baited drop lines, and fish traps, great flocks of loons and pelicans are to be seen busied with similar intent. This is not surprising, for in flora, fauna, and mineral wealth Colombia is a land of plenty. It is destined to become one of the most productive countries of the Western Hemisphere. Glance at a map of Colombia and you will see why this is so. The giant Andes, which inclose on three sides a great broken table-land in the southern and south-central part of the Republic around Bogota, separate into three distinct mountain chains as they come north—the western, central, and eastern Cordilleras. The western Cordilleras, following the Pacific coast, continue on into Central America. The eastern Cordilleras, terminating in the lofty, snow-clad Santa Marta Mountains, run north almost to the Caribbean Sea, sending great flanks and ridges out into the waters. Between the central and eastern Cordilleras lies the great valley of the Magdalena River, one of the richest valleys in South America. Between the central and western Cordilleras lies the valley of the navigable Cauca River, flowing into the Magdalena about 200 miles above its mouth, and descending from an elevated plain 5,000 feet above sea level about the busy, modern city of Medellin.

Colombia thus possesses every climatic range from the subtropical, through the successive stages of the Temperate Zone to that of the lofty region of glaciers and eternal snow. For the artist, the lover of color, of majestic mountain masses, appalling gorges, roaring torrents, primeval forests of luxuriant tropical growths, flowering vines and delicate orchids, Colombia is a paradise. Moreover, the climate of northern Colombia, which is warmer than that of the southern highlands, has a peculiar charm both upon the seacoast which is cooled by the sea breezes and in the foothills which are cooled by the proximity to the mountains and also by the monsoon. The monsoon, as I have known it, is a wind that comes up about 3 o'clock each afternoon, subsiding, for a time, at sundown, and is felt in greatest intensity between 9 and midnight. And Colombia has plant life as varied as its climatic zones. There is perhaps no country in the world which has a greater diversity of fauna and of birds and insects.

The vast valleys in themselves constitute empires in area. The huge Magdalena Valley produces the finest cotton, corn, and sugar cane. The fertile uplands are no less productive of other crops, and wheat will some day become an important staple. There is, too, a tremendous future for Colombia in cattle raising. It exists not only in the lowlands and foothills of the Cordilleras, but in the high llanos or pasture lands. On the eastern slopes of the Cordillera Oriente following the tributaries of the Orinoco River eastward, there are more than 250,000 square miles of fertile grassy pasture and plains in eastern Colombia and western Venezuela capable of pasturing more than 100,000,000 head of stock. This is affirmed to be one of the largest areas of fertile, open, unoccupied land in the world. While in Colombia I heard that a railroad would be built out from Bogota to reach the southern part of this country. In the foothills and lowlands of the Cordillera Oriente I have seen as fine cattle as I have ever seen anywhere in the world. A cattleman from the western plains of the United States, whom I met in Colombia, told me that, in his judgment, no country in the world has such almost illimitable areas of vacant pasture adapted to the raising of vigorous stock. A wealthy Colombian gentleman who has gone extensively into stock raising said that it did not cost him over $1.75 per head, American currency, to raise his grazing steers up to the butchering point. The Government of Colombia encourages responsible livestock men. A bill has been introduced into both branches of the Colombian Legislature favoring the establishment of meat packing and refrigerating plants.

The climatic conditions that produce luxuriant grasses give glorious foliage. In the lowlands everywhere were beautiful morning-glories in bloom and other flowers of infinite variety and hue, cloaking the country in a riot of lovely color—blue, yellow, white, red, and golden—acacia trees, too, burst into bloom, presenting at a short distance the effect of a single great mass of color. In the world there are not more beautiful ornamental flowers, palms, trees, and shrubs than are grown in Colombia. Grass flowers, too, are abundant. Small star-shaped flowers they are of red and blue, everywhere adorning the foothills. And I recall lovely groves of blossoming trees, much like peach trees, near the coast, with a profusion of pink blooms of fragrant scent. Japan itself in blossom time, with all its gorgeous cherry orchards blooming, does not surpass Colombia in the blossoming season in early winter and for many months thereafter. Indeed, a number of plants bloom throughout the year. Moreover, the flowers are fragrant, for Colombia is not a land where the blossoms have no scent and the birds no song.

Of birds there are many, brilliantly colored, audacious, familiar, busy songsters by the thousands. Particularly do I recall a saucy brown and white Chupa Huevo, egg robber, that came under my observation during some pleasant days at Rio Frio, near the foot of the Santa Marta Mountains.

The little whistler was never disturbed by my presence, for the song bird in Colombia does not know the small boy with the gun. Another brilliant whistler is a yellow and black oriole which can easily be taught to carry a tune and is very popular in captivity. When I first heard one of these birds I thought it was some clever boy whistling. Canaries, linnets, humming birds, long-tailed blackbirds, and pigeons are abundant. Of the latter the most plentiful is the small brown plump partridge-shaped pigeon that is found in great droves on the country highways and will flutter ahead of the traveler only when he comes very near.

Rabbits, conies, partridges, and other game familiar to sportsmen in more northern latitudes are to be found in the foothills. The tapir is found in the thick woods and brush, through which it beats deep trails. The animal has been shot by coffee ranchers at an elevation of 5,000 feet above sea level and is said to range up as high as 8,000 or 9,000 feet above sea level, crossing the loftiest of the lesser ridges.

I met an American gentleman who, while hunting some 20 years ago in the Santa Marta Mountains, came upon wild coffee, with the result that he established a thriving coffee plantation upon which he now lives. Originally he had gone down to install electric lighting plants at Santa Marta and Barranquilla. Most of the coffee, Colombia's greatest agricultural crop, is raised in the far interior and reaches the coast via the Magdalena River.

But let us return to civilization, to Barranquilla, the most important seaport of Colombia. The city has a population of between 55,000 and 60,000 persons and is reached by the 17-mile railroad line from the deep-sea wharf at Puerto Colombia upon the Atlantic. It is the chief point of transshipment for freight, coffee, gold, hides, Panama hats, platinum, rubber, tobacco, and all the varied products that come down the Magdalena River and are sent by rail for export via Puerto Colombia. In a single year Colombia has exported as much as $16,600,000 worth of coffee to the United States. Total gold exports run normally over $6,000,000 (American currency); platinum over $600,000; Panama hats close to $1,000,000; hides over $2,900,000, and this represents but a part of the cattle slaughtered, as Colombia consumes much leather in the manufacture of harness, saddles, shoes and for other purposes.

Barranquilla itself is located three-fourths of a mile from the Magdalena River, but steamers and steel and wood freight carriers come directly to town through several deep channels leading from the river. The main channel skirts one side of the city past mill and factory, by the picturesque evercrowded market place, past still more manufactories, returning to the river by another course. Barranquilla is one of the fastest-growing cities on the Caribbean Sea. It is a solid, substantial, even beautifully built community, of which the finest architectural feature is the broad central plaza and very ornate modern cathedral.

77

FASSENDEN N. OTIS, *ILLUSTRATED HISTORY OF THE PANAMA RAILROAD* (NEW YORK: HARPER & BROTHERS, 1862), PP. 46, 49, 72, 75–82, 85–86, 89–92, 95–98, 103–104, 110, 115–116, 121, 127

Health of the Isthmus

It may interest the general reader to know that more than 196,000 passengers have been transported over the road during the five years ending in December, 1859, and it is not known that a single case of sickness has occurred during or in consequence of the transit since the entire opening of the road in 1855. The diseases contracted by persons in transit previous to that time were of a purely malarious character, and identical with the intermittent (fever and ague) and bilious fevers of the Western States, always found resulting from great exposure and fatigue, so often unavoidable while the transit was performed upon mules and in open boats, occupying from two to five days, the traveler frequently obliged to live upon the vilest food, and sleep upon the wet ground or in the but little less comfortless huts of the natives; the comfortable railway carriage, and the passage from ocean to ocean reduced to *three hours*, having fully demonstrated a *perfect* immunity to the traveler from all those varieties of sickness long popularly recognized under the head of *Panama Fever*. The sanitary condition not only of Aspinwall, but of the country along the entire line of the road, has also been improved by the filling in and draining of the swamp and low land to such a degree that the congestive forms of fever among the laborers and residents which, during the earlier days of the road, were the chief causes of mortality, are now rarely met with, and the whole line of the transit will, in point of healthiness, compare favorably with many of the equally recent settlements in the Western States.

Safety to property

The amount of specie conveyed over the road from 1855 to 1860 was over three hundred millions of dollars, *without the loss of a single dollar;* and during the same period there were sent over the road nearly 100,000 bags of mail matter (the greater part of which consisted of mails between the Atlantic States and California), not one of which was lost. And of the many thousands of tons of freight which have been transported over the Panama Railroad since it was first opened, the losses by damage and otherwise do not exceed five thousand dollars.

The early history and present condition of the road, at least so much of it as has been thought would prove interesting and serviceable to the general reader, has been presented. The sources of its present business have been shown, and some idea of its probable increase from these; but a large and important field within the legitimate scope of the enterprise demands a little attention from its bearings on the future business of the road. A glance at the geographical situation of the Isthmus of Panama, in its relation with Australia, China, Japan, and the Sandwich Islands, will discover the capacity of the transit to shorten the distances from those countries to the markets of the United States by so many thousands of miles as must make it an eventual necessity for the trade, at least a large portion of it, to seek this, the only direct route between the Atlantic and Pacific Oceans.

Traveler's guide

As the traveler enters the harbor of Navy Bay he can not fail to observe the beauty of the scene spread out before him. On the right and in front of the harbor, which sweeps around a semicircle of some three miles in extent, the primeval forest of the tropics, with its dense vinous undergrowth and its towering cocoa and palm trees, meets his view; on the left, from the iron light-house on the extreme seaward point, the brightly-painted Americo-Spanish town of Aspinwall extends, its long covered wharves filled with the shipping of many nations. A verandaed street skirts the shore, and a dense equatorial forest rising up behind is relieved by the faint and misty mountain range, which forms the *back-bone* of the Isthmus, and connects the great *Cordillera* of the northern and southern continents—the Rocky Mountains and the Andes. This harbor (said to have been discovered by Columbus during his third voyage, and by him named "Navy Bay") is three miles in length by two in breadth, with an average depth of seven fathoms, affording good anchorage ground in every part. Since the establishment of the Panama Railroad it has been a rendezvous for the United States Atlantic squadron, and one or more frigates of the first class may usually be seen at anchor; also a United States storeship, which has its permanent station here.

The city of Aspinwall, which has grown up from the necessity of its position as the Atlantic terminus of the railroad, while answering its purpose as a receiving and transhipping depôt, has but little, architecturally, to recommend it to notice, the dwellings, some two hundred in number, being of wood, and built in a style midway between the New England house and the verandaed structures usual in the tropics. They are built on land leased from the Company by private individuals.

The voyager coming to Aspinwall by the United States mail steam-ships will be landed at the end of an immense wharf belonging to the Company, and will find it worth his while to take a walk about the town ere making the transit of the Isthmus. First, it may not be amiss to notice the wharf itself, which extends from the shore out upon a coral reef, nearly a thousand feet, to where a depth of water exists sufficient to float the largest ships. It is forty feet in breadth, and covered by a lofty metallic roof; the piles upon which it stands are coppered to protect them from the *teredo,* a boring worm which infests these waters, and rapidly destroys every kind of timber unless thus protected. At the upper end of the wharf a grove of cocoanut-trees shoots up through the flooring, and at any and every season of the year the cocoanut, in the bud, the blossom, and full grown, may here be seen. Several large iron tanks are situated at the head of the wharf, each of a capacity of several thousand gallons. The whole island of Manzanilla, upon which Aspinwall is situated, a mile in length by three quarters in width, being a low coral foundation, has no springs of water, and that obtained by digging is so brackish that rain-water is used instead; these tanks, filled by the rains which prevail for more than half the year, before the establishment of the great reservoir, furnished the supply of water for the shipping during the dry season. At the head of the wharf you reach the quadruple track of the railway. Proceeding toward its Atlantic terminus, you pass, on your left, the line of stores, shops, and hotels which were visible from the entrance of the harbor. The shops, perhaps half a dozen in number, usually display a very respectable assortment of goods, principally ready-made clothing, fancy articles, and groceries. Among them are several quite extensive importing houses of French, English, and American merchandise, and Havana cigars for the South American market and the shipping visiting the port.

 The hotels, of which there are, great and small, at least a dozen, have, for this country, very fair accommodation for all classes of travelers, at from one to four dollars per day; but little business, however, is done among them except on the arrival of the passenger steamers of the California line. In 1852, when these hotels were erected, travelers were often detained here for several days, when the landlords drove a brisk trade; but now the ship-loads of passengers are seldom detained here more than two or three hours, and, although a brisk business is done for the time, the publican finds his opportunity too brief to realize much profit.

 At the end of the row stands the Panama Railroad Company's office, a respectable fire-proof two-story brick building, into the upper windows of which the wires of the Isthmus Telegraph converge. The poles, or, more properly, the pillars, which serve to support the wires of this telegraph line, from their symmetry, strength, and novel construction, are worthy of particular notice. They are apparently of *hewn stone.* Some two years since, after much trouble and expense had resulted in consequence of the rapid decay of the wooden poles formerly used, Colonel Totten conceived the idea of moulding a support of concrete. A small straight stick of the necessary height was placed upright, and surrounded by a jointed wooden mould, fifteen inches in diameter at the base, tapering to about eight inches at the top, and sunk into the earth sufficiently for firm support; this was filled with *concrete,* and allowed to stand for several days. When the mould was removed, it was found firm and strong, and apparently every way adapted to the purpose. This fact once settled, the entire line was supplied with these quasi stone columns, but little exceeding the unsightly wooden poles in expense, and perfectly weather and insect proof. It is now nearly two years since their establishment, and they bid fair, extraordinary occurrences excepted, to last for a century.

Farther along the track, on your right, you pass the main railroad wharf, at which any day in the year several vessels, sail or steam, may be seen actively discharging cargoes for shipment across the road. A couple of hundred yards brings you to a massive stone structure three hundred feet long by eighty wide, through whose broad-arched entrances a triple track is laid. This is the freight depôt of the Panama Railroad Company, and the following description by a recent visitor will give the traveler an idea of its usual internal appearance:

"Bales of quina bark from the interior were piled many tiers deep, and reached to the iron triangular-braced roof of the edifice. Ceroons of indigo and cochineal from San Salvador and Guatemala; coffee from Costa Rica, and cacao from Ecuador; sarsaparilla from Nicaragua, and ivory-nuts from Porto Bello; copper ore from Bolivia.; silver bars from Chili; boxes of hard dollars from Mexico, and gold ore from California; hides from the whole range of the North and South Pacific coast; hundreds of bushels of glistening pearl-oyster shells from the fisheries of Panama lay heaped along the floor, flanked by no end of North American beef, pork, flour, bread, and cheese, for the provisioning of the Pacific coast, and English and French goods for the same markets; while in a train of cattle-cars that stood on one of the tracks were huddled about a hundred meek-looking lamas from Peru, on their way to the island of Cuba, among whose mountains they are used for beasts of burden as well as for their wool."

Its situation is on the direct line of the road, its seaward side opening by great doors out upon the waters of the bay, so as to allow vessels of light tonnage to discharge cargo directly into the depôt, while for the heavier a covered wharf extends from the centre into six fathom water. On emerging from the farther extremity of the freight-house, a hundred paces brings you to the *Mingillo*, or native market-place. A few lusty half-naked negroes, descended from the African slaves of the old Spanish dominion (who form a large proportion of the littoral population of the Isthmus) are generally seen supplying their customers with fish, cassava, bananas, plantains, and many other fruits and vegetables of the country, from out the bongoes which lay alongside the wharf, or, grouped on the shore over smoking kettles of *sancoche*, ladling out this favorite compound to their native patrons. Large quantities of the vegetable ivory-nut are also brought here by the natives for barter and sale. Sometimes a few aboriginal Indians from the region of San Bias (some sixty miles down the coast) may be seen here. Rather under the medium stature, they are broad-shouldered and muscular, with the straight black hair and high cheek-bones of the North American tribes. They have a peculiar interest from the fact that they belong to a tribe never subjugated by the *Conquistadores*, but who have maintained an unwavering hostility to the Spaniard since the first discovery of the country, and have cherished such a jealousy of their independence that, to the present day, no white man has been permitted to land upon their shores. Their usual dress consists of a simple fold of cloth tied about the loins, though they are not unfrequently seen clad after the manner of the Spanish natives, in a loose shirt and loose cotton or hempen trowsers. Though apparently apathetic and uncommunicative, there is a considerable degree of intelligence in their expression, and a conscious independence in their bearing, that gives one a fair idea of the races which Columbus and his followers found here in the days of old. They have recently allowed one or two small trading schooners twice or thrice a year to anchor near their shores and traffic with them, receiving calicoes, beads, and other ornaments, machetas, etc., in exchange for tortoise-shell, ivory-nuts, and gold dust; but every attempt to explore their country has been uniformly resisted. Their chief weapon is the bow and arrow (the arrow armed with fishbones), in the use of which they are said to be very skillful, and to be in the habit of using it effectively not only upon land, but in their waters; with barbed palm-wood arrows some four feet in length, they have the reputation of being able to transfix large fish at a distance of two or three feet beneath the surface.

Along the opposite side of the railway from the *Mingillo* lies a broad lagoon covering a couple of acres, and connected with the waters of the harbor by a narrow opening under the road. This lagoon is crossed at about the centre by a recently-made street, and will soon be still farther reduced in extent by others. A line of low tenements, principally occupied by the native population, a few stores, and a large hotel, the Aspinwall House, bound its opposite shore, beyond which a dense swamp-forest shuts off the view. Proceeding a little farther, you pass "Johnson's Ice-house," or, rather, if you have an eye to creature comfort, you will not pass it, for it is a depôt for ice and such things for the inner man as may be preserved in it of northern product. Five ships a year come consigned to this establishment from the Boston Ice Company, and Johnson, "the Ice-man of the Isthmus," is decidedly a man whose acquaintance is worth cultivating in this climate. Turning now to the left, toward the sea-beach, which forms a semicircle around this end of the island, the driving surf of centuries has washed up along its whole extent a wide barrier of shells and coral. Upon this you will first observe the hospitals of the Railroad Company, a couple of large, airy buildings, surrounded by generous tiers of piazzas, about which a general air of tidiness and comfort prevails. Although built for the exclusive use of the Company, strangers requiring medical aid are permitted to avail themselves of their advantages. A little to the left is a long wooden building, which contains the lecture-room, library, and club-room of the employes of the Company. A well-selected library of several hundred volumes, and the standard periodicals and journals, may be seen here; there are also materials for a snug game of billiards, backgammon, or chess. Three or four neat little cottages come next along the line of the beach, the residences of the principal officers of the Company, with little garden-plats in the rear, and an occasional cocoa-tree throwing pleasant shadows over them. A little farther on is a fine corrugated iron dwelling, the residence of the Royal Mail Steam Packet Company's agent; next to this is seen the general domestic rendezvous of the Railroad

Company's officials (usually known as the "Mess-house"), imbedded in a grove of cocoa and banana trees. Within fifty yards of the rolling surf, the sea-breeze ever playing through its surrounding foliage, it would be difficult to find a more desirable tropical residence.

Still farther on to the right are the buildings of the terminus, car repositories, etc., and machine-shops, whose tall chimneys send up steady columns of smoke, while the ring of many hammers breaks cheerily upon the ear. Along the beach a nicely-graded road has been constructed, which extends the entire circumference of the island, and for more than two thirds of its course it passes along or through the dense and luxuriant tropical forest with which nearly one half the island is still covered. The "Paseo Coral," as this beautiful walk or drive is called, was built by the citizens of Aspinwall, every facility and aid being rendered by the Railroad Company; and morning and evening, especially on Sundays and holidays, it is a favorite resort of the inhabitants of all classes, a few on horseback or in light wagons, but the great majority on foot Any lover of the beautiful in nature will find it worth his while to make a tour of this "Paseo;" on one side charming glimpses of the ocean and of the "Archipelago" (which cuts off the island of Manzanilla from the main land) meet the eye at every turn, and at almost any point the conchologist may step out upon the coral reef and find sea-shells, fans, and coral to an indefinite extent; on the other, a great variety of tropical vegetation invites the lover of botany to cull from its varied and luxuriant growth; here and there narrow paths lead from it to little native plantations of banana, papaya, and yam, imbedded in which the native hut, with its severely simple furnishing, may be seen, and will convey to the traveler an idea of the habits and character of the native inhabitant of this country. The land in and about Aspinwall, though highly productive, has not yet been brought under proper cultivation to any extent, though several promising plantations have been recently established by foreign residents; fowls, yams, and tropical fruits are, however, found in plenty, and native beef is abundant; the harbor also abounds in excellent fish, and the neighboring islands afford an unlimited supply of the finest green turtle, the usual market-price of which is five cents per pound. Aspinwall, though belonging to New Granada, has a separate civic government, the control of which is possessed chiefly by residents from the United States, most of whom are connected with the Panama Railroad Company.

Eminent scientific men from the United States, England, and Germany have already spent considerable time and labor in explorations here, but the results of their researches have not as yet been given to the public. As, however, few travelers over the road have any opportunity other than that afforded by the rapid railway transit to examine the objects of interest on its course, a brief account of the more prominent and readily recognized will perhaps be deemed sufficient for the general reader.

In making the journey over the railroad to the Pacific terminus, starting at the depôt at Aspinwall, a third of a mile brings you to that part of the island shore where the railway leaves it, and crosses over the frith to the swamps of the main land. At this point, which is crossed by an artificial isthmus (built originally of piles and crib-work, but since replaced by solid stone and earth), the channel is about two hundred yards in width, broadening rapidly to the eastward into a miniature archipelago, with a dozen little islands overgrown with mangrove bushes, and lying upon its glassy surface like emeralds upon a mirror. To the westward it again expands into a wide, placid basin, only separated by a narrow belt of foliage from the waters of the bay. The shores on every hand are skirted with a dense growth of mangrove bushes, which droop deep into the water, while directly in front, through the vista opened by the railway, an apparently interminable forest meets the eye. These waters abound in the beautiful varieties of fish known among the natives as "flores del mar," or "the flowers of the sea:" in shape and size they resemble the sun-fish of our Northern lakes, and are remarkable for their varied and brilliant colors.

The mangrove bushes are not unlike the banyan-tree in the manner of their growth. Their branches, shooting downward, frequently enter the soil, take root, and, interlacing again and again, form a barrier requiring a stout hatchet or machete to overcome. Many of the branches which dip into the water are loaded with a variety of the Crustaceæ, almost, if not quite, identical with our Northern oysters, varying in size from a dime to a dollar: several pounds often depend from a single bough. Submerged by every tide, they are well nourished and exceedingly palatable, and, although so small, well worth the trouble of opening. English snipe, plover, teal, heron, and pelican are abundant about here at certain seasons.

About a mile farther on, to the left of a spur of high land, through which the railway passes by a deep long cut, is seen the tall forest of Mount Hope, upon which is located the general cemetery of Aspinwall. A pleasant winding path through the thick undergrowth soon brings you upon the spot. Dense foliage surrounds it on every side. This place was selected for a burial-ground shortly after the commencement of the road, and many victims to the hardships of the work and the virulence of the climate were then buried here; but those days of trial have passed, and the long grass waving over their graves tells of the years since then. A few are recent, and marked by simple monuments; among them will be noticed several of the officers of the United States Home Squadron. The lamented Strain (whose suffering and heroism as the leader of the ill-fated Darien expedition are still fresh in the memory of his countrymen) lies buried here. The surrounding woods, especially toward evening and in the early morning, are vocal with the notes of numerous birds. The sweet and sonorous whistle of the *turpiale* and the cooing of the turtle-dove mingle with the harsh cries of the parrot tribe and the still harsher note of the toucan. Frequent opportunities occur of procuring these different varieties of birds from the natives, as they are more or less numerous along the entire line of the road, and become domesticated with little trouble. The turpiale, which is about the size of a robin, with deep black and bright yellow plumage, is quite equal to the magpie in intelligence and cunning, and is one of the finest whistlers known. The toucan, a dark scarlet-breasted bird, about the size of a pigeon, with a heavy serrated bill six or seven inches in length, is one of the ornithological curiosities of this region; picking up its food on the point of its huge beak, by a sudden jerk it tosses it up half a yard, and as it falls catches it deep in its throat; it also makes extraordinary motions over the water when attempting to drink. The habits of the toucan in this respect were noticed by the early Spanish-American priests, who, averring that this bird, in drinking, made the sign of the cross over the water, called it "Dios te de" (God gives it thee). Considerable land in the vicinity of Mount Hope has been cleared, and cultivated with success and profit. Proceeding along the track beyond Mount Hope, you begin to bring more fully into view the wondrous wealth of the Isthmian forest. For a space of fifty feet on either side of the solid track embankment the original growth has been swept away and replaced by a rich display of aquatic plants, through whose broad shining leaves myriads of callas and long, slim-petaled pondlilies struggle out to fill the air with their delicious perfume. This low and recent vegetation is walled in by a primeval growth of a variety and luxuriance that almost defies description. Palm-trees, slender and tall, from under whose crowns hang long scarlet and yellow tassels; palms, low and huge, with trunks scarce lifted above the slimy ooze, sending out graceful pinnate leaves half a dozen yards in length; great cedro and espabe trees, towering up like giants for a hundred feet, then sending out strong arms that almost clasp each other across the clearing, their trunks covered with thick vines and parasites. These and many other varieties are so closely set and interwoven together that the eye fails to penetrate into the depths of the forest. The great number and variety of parasitic growths can not fail to attract constant attention. Almost every tree and shrub supports more or less of these treacherous leeches, in form and size ranging from the simple tuft of grass to the enormous growths whose branches equal in magnitude those of the largest trees, and frequently exceed those of the poor victim from which their strength is drawn. Some are seen which had originally taken root upon the trunks of large and thrifty trees, which, under their exhausting demands and vice-like embrace, have died and rotted out, leaving the well-conditioned leech, though a mere shell, upright, and so like the original tree that, except for occasional apertures which discloses the hollowness within, their villainy might at a little distance escape detection. Many bear beautiful and fragrant flowers. A curious and exceedingly common variety springs from seeds deposited in the ordure of birds upon the highest trees, sending long fibrous tendrils, without a single branching twig, down to the earth, when it again takes root, and increases in size until it frequently at tains a diameter of five or six inches. Often trees, so decayed that otherwise they must have feilen, are by these supports retained in their upright position for many years. The smaller ones, combining pliability with great strength, are much used as cordage by the natives. Trailing vines and blossoming creepers are on every side in great profusion and luxuriance, enwrapping the trees and hanging in variegated festoons from the branches. As you proceed, every moment new, and, if possible, richer varieties of vegetation pass in quick review, until you are almost lost in wonder and admiration. At about three miles from the terminus a bend is cut off in the small sluggish stream, called the Mindee, whose waters are half concealed by the overhanging verdure; along its banks the tall and graceful bamboo, that giant of the grasses, adds a new beauty to the scene. The waters of the Mindee, which empties into Navy Bay about a mile and a half from Aspinwall, abound with alligators, often of great size, which afford plenty of exciting sport to parties from the city, who make occasional incursions upon them, and to the natives, who value them greatly for their oil, which is used for medication, and their teeth, which are worn as potent charms. Not unfrequently these ugly beasts crawl out into the pools along the railway track, where they may be seen basking in the sun, scarcely deigning to lift their unwieldy heads as the train thunders by.

Passing the seventh mile-post, you emerge from the swamp, and come to the Gatun Station, located upon the eastern bank of the Eio Chagres, which is at this point about fifty yards in width, and here makes a great bend, opening beautiful vistas through the dense forests up and down its course. This bank of the river is formed by a ridge of low hills, across the foot of which the railway runs. A few yards from the road, on the high ground to the left, are the buildings of the station. A large, two-story framed building, about forty feet in length by thirty in breadth, surrounded by piazzas and balustrades, is the residence of the local superintendent and the foreign workmen employed on this section. Suitable out-buildings are situated in the rear, and a little garden in front, where the roses and peonies, the pinks and pansies of our northern clime, challenge comparison with the orchids, fuchsias, and passiflores of the tropics; and there are radishes, cucumbers, and lettuce contrasting curiously with the native products of the place. With a few unimportant exceptions, this establishment is similar to that of all the stations, which are situated about four miles distant from each other along the entire length of the road. The duty of the local superintendent is not only to keep the track along his section in perfect repair, but to give his personal attention to all matters which can in any way impede the safety or dispatch of the regular trains; and to this ample service, in a great measure, is due the immunity from accident which has characterized the running of the Panama Railroad from its first establishment to the present day. On the opposite shore of the river stands the ancient native town of *Gatun*, which is composed of forty or fifty huts of cane and palm, and situated on the edge of a broad savanna that extends back to a range of hills a mile or two distant. This place is worthy of mention as a point where, in the days by-gone, the bongo-loads of California travelers used to stop for refreshment on their way up the river; where "eggs were then sold four for a dollar, and the rent for a hammock was two dollars a night."

From Gatun the course of the road lies along the base of an irregular line of high lands that rise up from the eastern side of the valley of the Rio Chagres, and a few hundred yards brings you to the Rio Gatun, a tributary of the Chagres, which is crossed by an iron truss-girder bridge of ninety-seven feet span. The dense swamp-growth looms up on either side like a wall, while rising out of it, close on the left, are two fine conical peaks, called "Lion" and "Tiger" hills, which attract attention by the regularity of their outlines and the dense and gorgeous forests with which they are covered. These hills received their titles from the immense numbers of howling monkeys which inhabited this district previous to and during the construction of the road, and whose frequent roaring made the night hideous, and were often mistaken by the uninitiated for the formidable animals which their cries closely resembled. These, as well as several smaller varieties, still abound in the neighborhood, and their howlings at nightfall are frequently heard, but the progress of improvement has driven them from the immediate vicinity of the road.

Passing the Lion Hill Station, which has a fine cultivated clearing on the high ground behind it, the vegetation becomes less dense, and more decidedly aquatic in its character; large patches of cane-brake, huge tree-ferns, low palms in great variety, and scrubby mangroves, rise out of the dark pools in the swamps by the road-side. Along this section is found that rare variety of the Orchid family, the *Peristera elata*, known as the "Espiritu Santo." Its blossom, of alabaster whiteness, approaches the tulip in form, and gives forth a powerful perfume not unlike that of the magnolia; but it is neither for its beauty of shape, its purity of color, nor its fragrance that it is chiefly esteemed. Resting within the cup of the flower, so marvelously formed that no human skill, be it never so cunning, could excel the resemblance, lies the prone image of *a dove*. Its exquisitely moulded pinions hang lifeless from its sides, the head bends gently forward, the tiny bill, tipped with a delicate carmine, almost touches its snow-white breast, while the expression of the entire image (and it requires no stretch of the imagination to *see* the expression) seems the very incarnation of meekness and ethereal innocence. No one who has seen it can wonder that the early Spanish Catholic, ever on the alert for some phenomenon upon which to fasten the idea of a miraculous origin, should have bowed down before this matchless flower, and named it "Flor del Espiritu Santo," or "the Flower of the Holy Ghost," nor that the still more superstitious Indian should have accepted the imposing title, and ever after have gazed upon it with awe and devotional reverence, ascribing a peculiar sanctity even to the ground upon which it blossoms, and to the very air which it ladens with its delicious fragrance. It is found most frequently in low and marshy grounds, springing from decayed logs and crevices in the rocks. Some of the most vigorous plants attain a height of six or seven feet; the leaf-stalks are jointed, and throw out broad lanceolate leaves by pairs; the flower-stalks spring from the bulb, and are wholly destitute of leaves, often bearing a cluster of not less than a dozen or fifteen flowers. It is an annual, blooming in July, August, and September, and has in several instances been successfully cultivated in the conservatories of foreign lands. In former times bulbs of the plant could rarely be obtained, and then only with much labor and difficulty; but since their localities have become familiar to the less reverential Anglo-Saxon, great numbers have been gathered and distributed throughout different parts of the world, though their habits and necessities have been so little appreciated that efforts to bring them to flower usually prove ineffectual; if, however, they are procured in May or June, *after the flower-stalk has started*, when sufficient appropriate nutriment resides in the bulb to develop the perfect flowers, they can be safely transplanted, and will flower under the ordinary treatment adapted to the bulbous plants of colder climates. The bulbs, dried or growing, may be procured either at Aspinwall or Panama at from two to five dollars per dozen.

The next station is called "Ahorca Lagarto," "to hang the lizard," deriving its name from a landing-place on the Chagres near by; this, again, named from having, years back, been pitched upon as an encampment by a body of government troops, who suspended from a tree their banner, on which was a lizard, the insignia of the Order of Santiago. The land around this station, though low and level, is covered with a noble forest-growth, among which is found the huge cedro-tree, from which the native hollows out his canoe, sometimes of fifteen or twenty tons burthen; its broad, plane-shaped roots extend out on every side like buttresses, and its trunk towers up, without a branch, for a hundred feet, supporting a canopy of foliage often fifty yards in diameter.

Leaving behind this city of verdure, a chain of high and densely-wooded hills on the left is brought into view, and, winding along its base, another station, called "Bujio Soldado," or "Buyo Soldado" (*"the Soldier's Home"*), is passed. Here opens, on the right, a fine view up the Rio Chagres. A mile farther on is an excellent quarry of freestone along-side the track, from which large quantities of building and ballasting material have been quarried by the Company. A little farther on, upon the edge of the steep river bank, is the site of a cottage, notable as having been the favorite residence of the late J. L. Stephens, the celebrated author and traveler, who spent much of his later life in developing this great railway enterprise; but little now remains except its ruins, and the stately palm that long ago threw its shadow over his once beautiful garden. From this point beautiful views up and down the river are visible, while across, the high opposing bank stretches back in a broad plateau, covered with low foliage, from among which occasional tall trees shoot up, until it meets a range of distant hills. Continuing your course, with an occasional view of the river, which winds like a great serpent along this tortuous valley, you soon come to the native town of "Bueno Vistita" ("beautiful little view"). This is a collection of thirty or forty rude palm huts, skirting the track, and occupied by the families of native laborers along the road.

Leaving Frijoli, fine fields of Indian-corn may be seen here and there nestled under the hills; dense groves of palms and superb displays of convolvuli are also found along this section for a couple of miles, when you approach the lofty banks of the Chagres at Barbacoas, and cross the river by a huge wrought-iron bridge six hundred and twenty-five feet in length, eighteen in breadth, and standing forty feet above the surface of the water, and said to be one of the longest and finest iron bridges in the world.

The cultivation of the lands at this point is said to date back for more than two centuries, and to have been worked originally by the Jesuits. At about half a mile from the bridge the San Pablo Station is passed, and a little farther on a fine quarry of recent volcanic rock; from thence, through occasional cleared and cultivated lands, you pass to the station at Mamei and the native town of Gorgona, noted in the earlier days of Chagres River travel as a place where the wet and jaded traveler was accustomed to worry out the night on a raw hide, exposed to the insects and the rain, and in the morning, if he was fortunate, regale himself on jerked beef and plantains. The road now, leaving the course of the river, passes on through deep clay banks and rocky cuts, presenting little novelty beyond the magnitude of the labor expended upon them in establishing the railway, until, sweeping around a hill, the beautiful meadow-lands of Matachin open to the view. Here, rising in their stateliness, the classic sheaves of the royal palm shed an air of Eastern beauty over the landscape. A native village dots the foreground; on the left the waters of the Chagres, broadened at this point by the Rio Obispo (its greatest tributary), is seen through the ceiba groves that skirt its banks, while on the right and in front the scene is bounded by a group of conical hills covered with short grass and studded with palms. The completion of the Panama Railroad in 1855 was here celebrated with great ceremony and rejoicing, and the corner-stone of a monument to its originators and constructors was erected upon the crest of the highest and most beautiful of these hills. The railway has several side branches at Matachin, and is the usual point of meeting for the trains from either terminus. As there is usually a little delay on such occasions, the natives take advantage of it to traffic with the passengers. Almost every hut displays something for sale: cakes, "dulces," or native candy, and the various fruits of the region. Here the oranges are unusually fine. There is also a saloon, kept by a native, where very good English beer, French claret, crackers and cheese, etc., may be obtained.

From the station at Obispo the grade is ascending, with a maximum of sixty feet to the mile. Continuing to rise for about three miles, you pass the "Empire Station," and reach the "Summit," or highest elevation of the railway above the mean level of the Atlantic and Pacific Oceans. Here is a little native settlement called "Culebra" ("the Snake"), noted as having been the terminus of the road in 1854. Then, passengers arriving at this place by the cars from the Atlantic shore were compelled to mount upon mules, and flounder on through heavy sloughs and rapid streams, along the borders of deep ravines and over precipitous mountains, exposed to drenching rains in the wet season, and a broiling sun in the dry, not unfrequently attacked and plundered by banditti, with which the road was then infested, until, after a whole day's labor and peril, they arrived at Panama, only twelve miles distant "Culebra" at that time was a thrifty place, boasting of two or three hotels, imported ready-made from the United States, into which often more than a thousand men, women, and children were promiscuously stowed for a night There were also twenty or thirty native huts, about twelve feet square, each of which was considered of ample dimensions to house a dozen wayworn travelers, only too thankful to find a spot of dry ground upon which to spread their blankets; but its glory has departed, and scarce a vestige remains to tell of its former estate. From Culebra the road passes through a deep clay cutting from twenty to forty feet in depth, and nearly a third of a mile in length. At this point commences the Pacific slope of the road, with a descending grade of sixty feet to the mile.

Crossing by bridges of iron the San Pedro Miguel and the Caimitillo (narrow tide-water tributaries of the Rio Grande), the Rio Grande Station is passed. From thence, through alternate swamp and cultivated savanna, the muddy bed of the Rio Cardenas is crossed; when, leaving the Rio Grande to the eastward, a fine stretch of undulating country around the base of Mount Ancon is brought into view, enlivened by native huts and cultivated fields. About a mile farther on may be seen the long metallic roofs of the railroad buildings of the Pacific terminus peeping out from a grove of cocoa-trees, and a little beyond them, and to the right, the Cathedral towers, the high-tiled roofs and dilapidated fortifications of the city of Panama, while through the intervening foliage occasional glimpses of the "ever peaceful ocean" assure the traveler that the transit of the Isthmus is nearly accomplished, and a few minutes more brings him safely into the spacious passenger depôt of the Railroad Company at Panama.